Climate Change, Technology Transfer and Intellectual Property:
Options for Action at the UNFCCC

Dalindyebo Shabalala

Cover design by: Karin Marleen Dijkstra ©2014
© Dalindyebo Shabalala 2014

CLIMATE CHANGE, TECHNOLOGY TRANSFER AND INTELLECTUAL PROPERTY
Options for Action at the UNFCCC

DISSERTATION

to obtain the degree of Doctor at
Maastricht University,
on the authority of the Rector Magnificus, Prof.dr. L.L.G Soete
in accordance with the decision of the Board of Deans,
to be defended in public
on Wednesday 15 October 2014, at 16.00 hours

by

Dalindyebo Bafana Shabalala

Supervisor:
Prof. mr. Anselm Kamperman Sanders PhD (Lond)

Assessment Committee:
Prof. mr. dr. Gerard-Rene de Groot (Chairman);
Prof. Carlos Correa, University of Buenos Aires;
Prof. dr. Michael Faure;

Acknowledgements

For inspiration and for starting me on this journey, I thank all my colleagues at the Center for International Environmental Law (CIEL), but especially, Marcos Orellana, Nathalie Bernasconi-Osterwalder and Dan Magraw.

and for everything, to my wife Karin - all I am is from you.

TABLE OF CONTENTS

CHAPTER 1-A MALTHUSIAN MOMENT AT LAST?..1
   I. INTRODUCTION..1
   II. DEFINING TERMS AND FRAMEWORK 8
      II.1 Defining the term "barrier" in the intellectual property and climate change context.........9
      II.2 Defining technology transfer...17
      II. 3 Defining Climate Technologies..24
   III. THE APPROACH OF THIS THESIS 24
   IV. THE AUDIENCE 30

CHAPTER 2-THE SCOPE, TIMING AND GEOGRAPHICAL TARGETS FOR TECHNOLOGY TRANSFER OF CLIMATE TECHNOLOGIES..31
   I. INTRODUCTION..31
   II. THE TIMING TARGET..33
      II.1 Mitigation...33
      II.2 Adaptation..35
   III. THE SCOPE OF TECHNOLOGIES 39
      III.1 Mitigation..39
      III.2 Adaptation...50
   IV. THE GEOGRAPHIC TARGET 59
      IV.1 Mitigation..59
      IV.2 Adaptation...70
   V. CHAPTER CONCLUSION 73
      V.1. Timescale..74
      V.2. Scope of technologies...75
      V.3. Geographical Scope...75

CHAPTER 3-EVALUATING THE EXISTING EVIDENCE IN INTELLECTUAL PROPERTY AND CLIMATE CHANGE...82
   I. INTRODUCTION..82
   II. VECTORS FOR TECHNOLOGY TRANSFER 84
   III. THE EPO/UNEP/ICTSD STUDY...89
      III.1 Scope, Timing and Geography...89
      III.2 Findings and analysis...90
      III.3 Conclusions to draw from the study 93
   IV. THE COPENHAGEN ECONOMICS/IPR COMPANY STUDY 94
      IV.1 Scope, Timing, Geography..94
      IV.2 Findings and Analysis..95
      IV.3 What conclusions may be drawn..96
   V. DECHEZLEPRÊTRE ET. AL. STUDY..97
      V.1 Scope, Timing, Geography...98
      V. 2 Findings and analysis..99
      V.3 What conclusions may be drawn...99

VI. JOHN BARTON ICTSD STUDY 100
VI.1 Scope, Timing, and Geography 100
VI.2 Findings and analysis 100
VI.3 What conclusions can be drawn? 101
VII. THE CHATHAM HOUSE STUDY 102
VII.1 Scope, Timing and Geography 102
VII.2 Findings and analysis 103
VII.3 What can be concluded? 105
VIII. HASCIC ET AL OECD STUDY (2010) 105
VIII.1 Scope, Timing and Geography 106
VIII.2 Findings and Analysis 106
VIII.3 What can be concluded? 108
IX. RESULTS FROM TNAs, NAMAs AND NATIONAL COMMUNICATIONS 108
X. COMPARATIVE ANALYSIS AND CONCLUSIONS 110
X.1 Scope of technologies 110
X.2 Ownership and distribution of patenting 113
X.3. Licensing 114
X.4 Conclusion 114
XI. LESSONS FROM OTHER MEAs AND SUCCESSFUL CASES OF TECHNOLOGY TRANSFER 115
XII. THREE TRENDS THAT IMPLICATE THE INTELLECTUAL PROPERTY STRUCTURE OF CLIMATE TECHNOLOGY MARKETS 118
XII.1 Increases in Patenting of Climate Technologies 118
XII.2 Increases in Public sector Financing of Climate technologies 121
XII.3 The Role of Emerging Economies 126
XIII. CONCLUSION 147

CHAPTER 4-EVALUATING THE IMPLEMENTATION MECHANISMS FOR TECHNOLOGY TRANSFER IN THE UNFCCC 150

I. INTRODUCTION 150
II. BACKGROUND: THE MULTILATERAL FRAMEWORK ON TECHNOLOGY TRANSFER 152
II.1. Evolution of the Multilateral Framework on Technology Transfer 153
II.2. Technology Transfer in Multilateral Environmental Agreements 155
III. THE LEGAL FRAMEWORK FOR TECHNOLOGY TRANSFER IN THE UNFCCC 158
III.1. The Legal Basis for Technology Transfer Obligations in the Climate Change Regime 158
IV. IMPLEMENTING STRUCTURES FOR TECHNOLOGY TRANSFER WITHIN THE UNFCCC 161
IV.1 The Expert Group on Technology Transfer 162
IV.2 The Clean Development Mechanism 167
IV.3 The Global Environment Facility (GEF) 186
IV.4. Non-UNFCCC Multilateral and Bilateral delivery under Article 4.1(c), 4.3 and 4.5, National Communications and the Role of Nationally Appropriate Mitigation Actions (NAMAs) and National Adaptation Plans of Action (NAPAs) 189
IV.5 Conclusions 203
V. DEVELOPMENT OF THE NEW TECHNOLOGY TRANSFER FRAMEWORK AND THE ROLE OF INTELLECTUAL PROPERTY IN THE NEGOTIATIONS AT THE UNFCCC 203

VI. Conclusion..211

CHAPTER 5-IDENTIFYING THE RANGE OF INTELLECTUAL PROPERTY INTERVENTIONS.............213

I. Introduction...213
II. Intellectual property beyond the border 214
III. Market failures in international technology transfer and technology transfer interventions..216
IV. The Role of Intellectual Property protection in the Vectors for International Technology Transfer...218
V. Technology transfer interventions by newly industrializing countries: A historical survey.....225
VI. Constructing a list of the types of technology transfer interventions....................235
VII. Conclusion 241

CHAPTER 6-INTERPRETING TRIPS AND THE LIMITS ON UNILATERAL ACTION 243

I. Introduction...243
II. Meeting the Standard of Necessity in the WTO and TRIPS 245
    II.1. The Necessity test in the broader WTO jurisprudence..246
    II.2. The necessity test in the TRIPS Agreement 253
III. The Availability of IP Measures to Address Technology Transfer for Climate Change 259
    III.1. Exceptions to Rights...259
    III.2. Compulsory licenses 277
    III.3. Compulsory licenses and other action to address anti-competitive practices...........287
    III.4. Working Requirements...290
    III.5. Patent exclusions and special treatment for climate technologies.....................293
    III.6. Parallel importation..296
    III.7. Setting Specific standards for patentability including disclosure 297
    III.8. Limiting the number of allowable claims in a patent, potentially down to 1. 299
IV. Conclusion 300

CHAPTER 7-THE ROLE OF OTHER MULTILATERAL REGIMES 304

I. Introduction...304
II. The UNFCCC and its legal relationship to the TRIPS Agreement and other fora........304
III. the WTO and its relationship to other fora 307
IV. Human Rights and technology transfer for climate change 313
    IV.1. Are there Obligations in Human Rights Law that Relate to Technology Transfer?....314
    IV.2. What are the Possible Avenues for Adopting a Rights-Based Approach to the Arguments for Technology Transfer for Climate Change?...328
    IV.3. The relationship between Human Rights, Intellectual Property and Climate Change 331
V. Conclusion 333

CHAPTER 8-SYSTEMIC INTEGRATION AND ACTION ON NORM-SETTING AT THE WTO AND THE UNFCCC..334

I. Introduction...334
II. Describing the Boundaries of Conflicts & Inter-Regime Tensions........................335

III. The Principle of Systemic Integration **338**
IV. Systemic Integration applied to Technology Transfer at the UNFCCC **339**
    IV.1. Objectives and Methodologies 340
    IV.2. Competencies 346

CHAPTER 9-PROPOSALS FOR ACTION AT THE UNFCCC 350

I. Introduction **350**
II. Drivers and Principles for Framing UNFCCC Action – Uncertainty and Peaking Dates **354**
III. An illustrative Portfolio of Proposals for action at the UNFCCC **360**
    III.1. Market access, Encouraging FDI and Licensing 361
    III.2. Reducing barriers to transactions 371
    III.3 Enabling Joint Research & Development, Demonstration and Deployment 377
    III.4. Increasing the effectiveness of existing UNFCCC mechanisms 384
    III.5 Increasing the effectiveness of existing flexibilities available under TRIPS 386
IV. Chapter Conclusion **390**

CHAPTER 10-SUMMARY 393

BIBLIOGRAPHY

List of Abbreviations

BATs	-	Best available technologies
CBD	-	Convention on Biological Diversity
CDM	-	Clean Development Mechanism
CO2	-	Carbon Dioxide
CTC&N	-	Climate Technology Centre & Network
DNA	-	Designated national Authority
DOE	-	Designated Operational Entity
EPO	-	European Patent Office
EST	-	Environmentally Sound Technologies
EU	-	European Union
FDI	-	Foreign Direct Investment
GEF	-	Global Environmental Facility
GHG	-	Greenhouse gases
IEA	-	International Energy Agency
IGCC	-	Integrated gasification combined cycle combustion
IPRs	-	Intellectual property rights
LDC	-	Least Developed Country
MEA	-	Multilateral Environmental Agreement
MRV	-	Measurable, Reportable and Verifiable
NAMA	-	Nationally Appropriate Mitigation Action
NAPA	-	National Adaptation Plan of Action
NIEO	-	New International Economic Order
OECD	-	Organization for Economic Cooperation and Development
PHEV	-	Plug-in Hybrids and electric vehicles
R&D	-	Research and Development
SME	-	Small and Medium-sized Enterprises
TEC	-	Technology Executive Committee
TIA	-	Technology Implementing Agreement
TNA	-	Technology Needs Assessments
TRIMs	-	Agreement on Trade Related Investment Measures
TRIPS	-	Agreement on Trade-related Aspects of Intellectual Property
SIDS	-	Small Island Developing States
SC/USC	-	Super-critical and ultra-supercritical coal
UNCED	-	United Nations Conference on Environment and Development
UNCTAD	-	United National Conference on Trade and Development
UNEP	-	United Nations Environment Programme
UNFCCC	-	United Nations Framework Convention on Climate Change
VCLT	-	Vienna Convention on the Law of Treaties
WGTTT	-	Working Group on Trade and Transfer of Technology

WTO - World Trade Organisation

Chapter 1
A Malthusian Moment at Last?

I. INTRODUCTION

In 1798, Thomas Malthus saw an ever rising population and falling agricultural production as people moved to the cities. He examined the causes for these changes and concluded that the United Kingdom was on the verge of a demographic catastrophe. It seemed inevitable that there would be mass starvation or at least a permanent state of abject poverty for the vast majority of its population.[1] Malthus argued that increases in agricultural productivity could not keep pace with population growth. The availability of land, the loss of farmworkers and the reduction of soil quality placed an absolute limit to growth on agricultural productivity.[2] While he placed no limits on the capacity of the earth to continue increasing agricultural production, he argued that population growth would always outpace such production. He saw little option but to seek limit population growth, but saw no (at the time) morally acceptable means of doing so, except to limit welfare transfers to the urban poor.

The fact that 19th century Europe did not see mass starvation and instead had massive increases in agricultural production has been seen as a rebuke to Malthus' thesis.[3] The key gap in Malthus' approach was his inability to predict the role that technology would play in increasing agricultural productivity during the industrial revolution. He did not fully foresee the effects of the mechanization of farm production[4], nor the role that colonialism and the expansion of trade would play in

---

[1] Malthus, T. R. *An essay on the principle of population*, (London: J. Johnson, in St. Paul's Churchyard, 1798.)
[2] Ch. II, Malthus, T. R.
[3] Although as Johnson notes, there were sporadic famines in Ireland and some other western European countries, there was no permanent stagnation in living standards. See p2, Johnson, D. Gale, "Population, Food and Knowledge" 90 The American Economic Review 1 (2000).
[4] See p2, Johnson, D. Gale, "Population, Food and Knowledge" 90 The American Economic Review 1 (2000).

providing new sources and venues for agricultural production.[5] It was a mix of policy and the ingenuity of invention driven by necessity that provided an escape from the demographic trap that was a consequence of Malthus' thesis. Technology saved the early industrial revolution from the limits imposed by land availability, and the transition to fossil fuels. The resultant new chemical industry created newer, cheaper products, better food preservation and a whole host of benefits that increased survivability.

The heirs of Malthus can be found in the twin 20th century movements to address environmental degradation and population growth.[6] Largely originating in the developed global north, advocates of global limits on population growth saw, in the newly independent developing country states, a demographic time bomb. Here you had rapidly developing countries, all of whom were seeking to increase their production and consumption of goods to the same or greater rate than those of developed countries. This was combined with increased access to welfare transfers, to medical treatments for diseases, and to reductions in maternal and child mortality. Much like Malthus, those who feared a population bomb argued that the planet could not produce sufficient goods to support such a global population, if it continued to grow at the rates foreseen. The World Scientists' Warning to Humanity, issued in 1992 stated:

> The earth is finite. Its ability to absorb wastes and destructive effluent is finite. Its ability to provide food and energy is finite. Its ability to provide for growing numbers of people is finite. And we are fast approaching many of the earth's limits. Current economic practices which damage the environment, in both developed and underdeveloped nations, cannot be continued without the risk that vital global systems will be damaged beyond repair. Pressures resulting from unrestrained population growth put demands on the natural world that can overwhelm any efforts to achieve a sustainable future. If we are to halt the destruction of our environment, we must accept limits to that growth.[7]

They saw limits on the capacity for agricultural and other goods to increase at a sufficient rate that would keep pace with consumption growth. Unlike Malthus, who advocated a reduction in welfare transfers,[8] the new Malthusians sought active government policies to discourage population growth in the face of the absolute limits on the capacity of the planet to produce enough resources to support a global

---

[5] Although, as a matter of principle, Malthus saw such expansionism as the inevitable result of shortages of food brought on by population increases. See Ch. III.6, Malthus, T. R. *An essay on the principle of population*, (London: J. Johnson, in St. Paul's Churchyard, 1798.)
[6] Union of Concerned Scientists, "World Scientists Warning to Humanity" Union of Concerned Scientists, (1992) Available at: http://www.ucsusa.org/about/1992-world-scientists.html (last visited August 15, 2014)
[7] Union of Concerned Scientists, "World Scientists Warning to Humanity"
[8] Ch. V, Malthus, T. R. *An essay on the principle of population*, (London: J. Johnson, in St. Paul's Church-yard, 1798.)

population that consumed at the level of the comfortable middle classes in the global north. Recent data has limited the power of population advocates as it has shown that, once a significant level of GDP is reached, population growth appears to stabilize or reduce.[9] This has been most marked in those countries with low immigration and high per capita incomes, such as in Europe and Japan.[10] This has been driven by two things: the first is a social phenomenon that Malthus took little account of; that the driver for large families among poor people was not the easy availability of food but the necessity to have many children to ensure that a sufficient number survived to adulthood to provide for their parents in their old age.[11] Reductions in child mortality due to medicines created a situation where this was no longer necessary. However, large families remained the norm in many countries due to the second issue: the inability of poor people to access the means of controlling their own fertility.[12] The new fertility technologies such as the IUD and especially the contraceptive pill have been transformative in making it possible for those families assured of being able to ensure their children's survival to have fewer children per family.[13] Again, technology provided an escape.

The core concept that has been adopted by advocates of limiting population growth from the environmental movement is that of carrying capacity i.e. the ability of an ecosystem to sustainably support the network of production, consumption and waste of its constituent elements in the long term. Using this concept, some have argued that we may have already overshot the carrying capacity of the earth and have begun to consume the resources that would be necessary to sustain future populations.[14] In particular the argument is that it is unsustainable for everybody to consume at the level of the average European or American consumer without creating some form of planetary disaster.[15] The argument for carrying capacity goes beyond just the issue of consumption. Because the processes of production and consumption have network effects and feed back into the ecosystem, the carrying capacity of a system is also defined by its ability to absorb and recycle waste. Overpopulation or more specifically, levels of consumption that have the same effect, can therefore result in degradation of the ecosystem. Such degradation can lead to disease and starvation events that reduce population to a level that will allow the ecosystem to recover. The new element that

---

[9] WRI "Population Growth: Stabilization" in *World Resources 1998-1999: Environmental Change and Human Health – 1998: A Guide to the Global Environment,* A joint publication of the World Resources Institute (WRI), the United Nations Environment Programme (UNEP), the United Nations Development Programme (UNDP) and the World Bank (New York and Oxford: Oxford University Press, 1998).
[10] Id.
[11] Id.
[12] Id.
[13] Id.
[14] Daily, G and P Erlich "Population, Sustainability and Earth's Carrying Capacity" 42 BioScience, 761 (1992); Millennium Ecosystem Assessment *Ecosystems and Human Well-being* (Washington DC: Synthesis. Island Press, 2005).
[15] See Arrow, K et al. "Are We Consuming Too Much?" 18(3) Journal of Economic Perspectives 147 (2004)

environmentalists have brought to the table is the argument that even at relatively stable populations, some levels and kinds of production, consumption and waste may be irreversible, creating permanent changes in the nature of the ecosystem itself. This results not in population crashes but in ecosystem crashes in which the evolutionary and adaptive niches of the creatures and plants that make up the ecosystem are destroyed.[16] In such a situation, the ecosystem changes irreversibly to become unsuited or hostile to the species that formerly inhabited it.[17] With the prospect of irreversible climate change we may be encountering the very real possibility of an ecosystem crash for much of humanity, a true Malthusian moment.

The Earth continues to experience record-breaking temperatures caused by increased atmospheric concentrations of carbon dioxide (CO_2) and other greenhouse gases (GHGs).[18] The impacts of this unprecedented warming include: increased floods and drought; rising sea levels; the spread of deadly diseases such as malaria and dengue fever, and; increasing numbers of violent storms and weather-related catastrophes.[19] Climate change presents a challenge to almost all areas of human economic activity because of our reliance on greenhouse gas emitting fossil fuels and fossil fuel products, the key driver of global modernization in the 20th century.[20] Addressing climate change therefore appears to require that we give up the prospect of modernization and presages unprecedented changes and limits in our patterns of production and consumption.

However, it may be that, just as in that post-industrial period when Europe made the transition from whale oil to fossil fuels and transformed agricultural production, technology may yet save us, or at least buy us time in which to consider our options. Policymakers and citizens[21] cling to the possibility that climate change can largely be addressed through the rapid dissemination of existing technologies, such as energy efficient light bulbs, windmills, solar panels, and the development of new ones such as carbon capture and storage, smart grids, and artificial meat. We may not have to give up our comfortable lifestyles in the US and Europe, or the promise of lifting millions out of poverty, in China and India and the rest of the developing world.

---

[16] See Millennium Ecosystem Assessment *Ecosystems and Human Well-being* (Washington DC: Synthesis. Island Press, 2005)
[17] See p18, UNEP, *Towards a Green Economy: Pathways to Sustainable Development and Poverty Eradication*, (Nairobi: UNEP, 2011).
[18] See p30, IPCC, *Climate Change 2007: Synthesis Report. Contribution of Working Groups I, II and III to the Fourth Assessment Report of the Intergovernmental Panel on Climate Change* [Core Writing Team, Pachauri, R.K and Reisinger, A. (eds.)] (Geneva: IPCC, 2007).
[19] See p48, Id.
[20] See Stern, D and C Cleveland, "Energy and Economic Growth" Rensselaer Working Papers in Economics 0410, March 2004. Available at: http://ideas.repec.org/p/rpi/rpiwpe/0410.html (last visited August 15, 2014)
[21] See e.g. Leonhardt, D "There's Still Hope for the Planet" New York Times, July 21, 2012; p193, Stern, N. et al. *The Economics of Climate Change: The Stern Review* (Cambridge: Cambridge University Press, 2007).

For that hope to become reality requires a massive effort in the near term to ensure distribution of existing technologies, and a significant effort in the longer term to invest in R&D and distribution of new innovations. That effort has to be global and can only be accomplished by unprecedented levels of global cooperation. In terms of global cooperation, the global community has already accomplished a significant amount. 194 countries, including the US, are parties to the United Nations Framework Convention on Climate Change (UNFCCC)[22] signed in 1992. 192 countries, not including the US, are party to the Kyoto Protocol to the UNFCCC.[23] The world has agreed to unprecedented levels of cooperation to develop and disseminate technologies to mitigate and adapt to climate change.[24]

The UNFCCC and the Kyoto Protocol were built on a fundamental political bargain directly involving technology transfer and cooperation. On one side, during the first commitment period of the Kyoto Protocol, developed[25] countries would take primary responsibility for emissions reductions.[26] They would move toward low-carbon or carbon-free economies, while transferring technology to enable developing countries to make progress on carbon efficiency.[27] Thus, carbon leakage, i.e., the shifting of polluting carbon-inefficient industries from developed to developing[28] countries, would be avoided, through direct transfers[29] and other measures such as emissions trading.[30] In addition, developed countries would provide financial and technical assistance to developing countries to build capacities to adapt to the negative impacts of climate change.[31] On the other side, the success of the first phase, including the transfer of technologies to enable clean development, would then enable developing countries to take on emissions reduction obligations. Since 1992, there has been significant growth in

---

[22] United Nations Framework Convention on Climate Change (UNFCCC), New York, 9 May 1992, *in force* 21 March 1994, 1771 *United Nations Treaty Series* 107
[23] Kyoto Protocol to the United Nations Framework Convention on Climate Change (Kyoto Protocol), Kyoto, 10 December 1997, *in force* 16 February 2005, 2303 *United Nations Treaty Series* (2004) 148.
[24] Article 4, United Nations Framework Convention on Climate Change (UNFCCC), New York, 9 May 1992, *in force* 21 March 1994, 1771 *United Nations Treaty Series* 107
[25] This term will be used interchangeably with the term "Annex 1" to refer to those countries listed in Annex 1 to the UNFCCC, which has significant overlap with membership of the Organization for Economic Cooperation and Development (OECD). This usage is what is common within the context of UNFCCC discussions and is common usage in many other international venues. Where more specificity is required this thesis will refer specifically to UNFCCC Annexes, Kyoto Protocol Annexes, or to the specific grouping in the regime being discussed.
[26] Article 4 UNFCCC, and Annex I, Kyoto Protocol
[27] Article 4.3 UNFCCC
[28] This term will be used interchangeably with the term "non-Annex 1" to refer to those countries NOT listed in Annex 1 to the UNFCCC. This has considerable overlap with the G77plusChina grouping within the United Nations General Assembly (as well as other international venues). Where more specificity is required this thesis will refer specifically to UNFCCC and Kyoto Protocol Annexes, or to the specific grouping in the regime being discussed.
[29] Article 4.3 and 4.5 UNFCCC
[30] Article 10 – 12, Kyoto Protocol
[31] Article 4.5 UNFCCC

the deployment of renewable energy technology worldwide.[32] There have been great increases in R&D budgets.[33] The world appears to be moving in the right direction.

The problem is that the growth in renewable energy in R&D budgets remains, as it has historically, largely confined to developed countries (and, more recently, China).[34] The vast majority of developing countries appear to have been left out of the boom. Developed countries, it is argued, have largely failed to provide effective transfer of environmentally sound, climate-related technologies as they are legally obligated to do under Article 4 of the UNFCCC.[35] The response of developing countries has been two-fold: a refusal to take on any GHG emissions reduction obligations until progress has been made on provision of financial resources and technology, based on Article 4.7 of the UNFCCC;[36] and a demand that international rules on intellectual property be relaxed, so that they would be free to copy and adapt climate technologies without waiting for financial support or permission from developed countries.[37]

Why did developing countries raise the issue of intellectual property (IP)? One of the great successes of recent international economic law for developed countries was the establishment of an agreement that all countries comply with a common, minimum set of high intellectual property standards. The Agreement on Trade-related Aspects of Intellectual Property (hereinafter "TRIPS Agreement")[38] was signed as part of the Agreement establishing the World Trade Organisation (WTO)[39] and made these

---

[32] See p11, IEA "Clean Energy Progress Report: IEA input to the Clean Energy Ministerial" IEA/OECD, June 2011.
[33] See p30, 36, 39, 54, Id.
[34] See p54, Id.
[35] See e.g. Khor, M. "Climate Change, Technology and Intellectual Property Rights: Context and Recent Negotiations" Research Paper 45, South Centre, April 2012.
[36] Article 4.7 UNFCCC states: "The extent to which developing country Parties will effectively implement their commitments under the Convention will depend on the effective implementation by developed country Parties of their commitments under the Convention related to financial resources and transfer of technology and will take fully into account that economic and social development and poverty eradication are the first and overriding priorities of the developing country Parties." This was reflected in the Bali Roadmap, the outcome of the 13th Conference of the Parties and the 3rd Meeting of the Parties in December 2007. Para. 1(b), "Bali Roadmap" Decision 1/CP13 in UNFCCC "Report of the Conference of the Parties on its thirteenth session, held in Bali from 3 to 15 December 2007, Addendum Part Two. Action taken by the Conference of the Parties at its thirteenth session." FCCC/CP/2007/6/Add.1, 14 March 2008.
[37] UNFCCC "Negotiating Text" FCCC /AWGLCA/2010/14, 13 August 2010 ; p34, UNFCCC "In-session draft texts and notes by the facilitators prepared at the twelfth session of the Ad Hoc Working Group on Long-term Cooperative Action under the Convention" FCCC/AWGLCA/2010/INF.1, 29 October 2010.
[38] Agreement of Trade-related Aspects of Intellectual property (TRIPS Agreement), Annex 1C to the Marrakesh Agreement establishing the World Trade Organization (WTO Agreement), Marrakesh, 15 April 1994, *in force* 1 January 1995, 1867 United Nations Treaty Series (1995) 4.
[39] Marrakesh Agreement establishing the World Trade Organization (WTO Agreement), Marrakesh, 15 April 1994, *in force* 1 January 1995, 1867 United Nations Treaty Series (1995) 4.

standards subject to the dispute settlement system of the WTO.[40] That dispute settlement system created an unprecedented ability to enforce the rules on intellectual property. Developing countries argue that the TRIPS Agreement unduly restricts their ability to take measures to encourage and enable technology transfer.[41]

What is not clear and has made an appropriate response difficult for the international institutions involved is whether this is true as a matter of fact. Does the TRIPS Agreement actually proscribe action by developing countries to address IP-related constraints on technology transfer? If so, in what ways? What can, and should the UNFCCC do to respond if there are problems?

The question that I aim to address in this thesis is a ***contingent*** one. I do not seek to answer the *empirical* question of whether or not the actual distribution of intellectual property rights, as they are today, pose a barrier to technology transfer at the global level. While this is a crucial and important question, I argue that it is not the most relevant one. Precisely because the functioning of patent protection is the prerogative of national industrial policy, the questions regarding the necessity to act to address the role of intellectual property in technology transfer and climate change will arise at the national level. This is why I focus on the capacity to act, which is a necessary condition for answering the question of whether, in a specific national circumstance, where a country finds it is necessary to act, they able to do so. This is not to say that global patterns of existing IP protection are not important context, but the key to the question of whether there is necessity to act on intellectual property lies in case by case and sector by sector analyses at the national level. The scale and speed of the need to act is determined by each country's obligations on reduction of greenhouse gas (GHG) emissions and its vulnerability to climate change, within the broader context of the global set of obligations. Thus, while all countries must act to address climate change, each country, within the limits imposed by the global need, will have to determine which sectors, which technologies and which actors are to be addressed to ensure that they can mitigate and adapt to climate change. What has to be determined then is, firstly, what actions, if any, can countries take to address such problems should they arise; and secondly, what actions can and should the UNFCCC take to facilitate such action?

My hypothesis is that if we properly take into account several factors: the timing of climate mitigation peaking dates and adaptation impacts; the scope of technologies to be addressed; and the scale of money and investment required: that developing countries really only have regulatory and market structuring responses

---

[40] Understanding on Rules and Procedures Governing the Settlement of Disputes (DSU), Annex 2 to the Marrakesh Agreement establishing the World Trade Organization (WTO Agreement), Marrakesh, 15 April 1994, *in force* 1 January 1995, 1867 United Nations Treaty Series (1995) 4.
[41] See p6, South Centre "Submission by the South Centre to the Technology Executive Committee (TEC) on ways to Promote Enabling Environments and Address Barriers to Technology Development and Transfer and the Role of the TEC" South Centre, 2012.

available to them to effectively address the climate challenge. Thus, as one of a set of market creation and regulating mechanisms, developing countries will have to address intellectual property in structuring their technology markets. I will examine whether, as it stands, the TRIPS Agreement provides sufficient flexibility to enable countries to structure their climate technology[42] markets to ensure maximum diffusion.

Thus for the purposes of this thesis, the key question with respect to intellectual property and climate change is whether, in a situation where the behaviour of specific intellectual property holders bars, or unduly limits, the adoption, adaptation and replication of a specific climate technology in a specific domestic sector do UNFCCC member states have the tools necessary to address such behaviour or are these blocked, or hindered to an undue extent by the TRIPS Agreement? If so, can and should the UNFCCC take action to enable the use of such tools or provide other ways to enable such action?

The question of whether intellectual property poses a barrier is a necessary precursor to the question of what kinds of actions the UNFCCC should take. Where the TRIPS Agreement can be seen to be a significant barrier to the use of such tools, then the UNFCCC may need to take action directed at the norms and standards on international intellectual property. Where intellectual property is not seen to be a barrier, are there nevertheless actions that the UNFCCC can take to ensure diffusion of IP protected technologies at the rate and scope required to meet the climate challenge?

II. Defining Terms and Framework

The aim of this thesis is to construct a proper basis for analysis, with clear operational definitions for what constitutes technology transfer, what constitutes a barrier, and what constitutes necessity to act to address those barriers. In this way it aims to go beyond the simplistic framing that focuses on the static question of specific examples of IP protected technologies not being transferred and focuses instead on targets for action: for timing; for scope; and for geography. The question of what actions the UNFCCC should take on intellectual property has been much discussed in the UNFCCC negotiations (see chapter 4), and in the literature (see Chapter 3 for more). I contend (in Chapter 3) that a significant problem for all prior research in this area is a failure to provide a proper basis for analysis and therefore the mechanisms and proposals for addressing the problem have been inappropriate and lacking in scale. This analytical framework, the answer it provides from the analysis of the TRIPS Agreement, and the implications that this has for what actions the UNFCCC can and should take are the major contribution of this thesis to the state of the art. To do so I focus closely on the terms being used: "barrier"; "necessity"; and "technology transfer".

---

[42] This general term will be used to refer to both technologies for mitigation and for adaptation.

II.1 Defining the term "barrier" in the intellectual property and climate change context

The definition of what is a barrier is therefore crucial to this thesis. I do not ask whether the existing framework poses an absolute barrier to the flow of technologies. While a useful and interesting exercise it is essentially static and does not focus on the question of capacity to act. The important issue in defining a barrier is understanding the nature of the object being described as a barrier. Here there is a crucial distinction that needs to be made with respect to intellectual property subject matter i.e. between technological products and technological knowledge.

At the core of the issue of technology transfer is the role of patents. Patents can be a positive force, providing incentives for the production and dissemination of new knowledge and facilitating licensing which allows the exchange of knowledge to occur securely and predictably. They are a key business tool, allowing entrepreneurs to use them as collateral for investors as they raise money, to show investors a future business model based on exclusive use (or out-licensing) of the patent. In established enterprises patents can be a way of insuring against the risk of moving into a new market sector, or a way of blocking or limiting market entry by competitors into an established sector. Finally, patent owners can engage in actual production of the technology themselves, which many do. All of these are legitimate exercises of the rights conferred by a patent. While patents provide the strongest possibility for such business strategies, some of the same frameworks can be applied to other forms of intellectual property. It is simply that patents provide the strongest possibility of exclusion and precisely because they are aimed at technical fields, implicate a significant share of business undertakings either as a tool of ownership or as a determinant of the freedom to operate.

Enterprises that engage in licensing can follow several strategies including[43]:

- Licensing without production; this may allow for non-exclusive as well as exclusive licensing; generally the plan is either to charge a significant amount for a single license and receive royalties from an ongoing concern or license multiple times to many actors to maximize returns;

- Licensing to companies to carry out proof of concept, demonstration and possible commercialization; again, the rightholder tends not be the one with the capacity to do so or to enter into production;

---

[43] Drawn from p6, Lee, B et al. "Who owns our Low Carbon Future: Intellectual Property and Energy Technologies" Chatham House, September 2009.

- Strategic licensing to suppliers and non-competitors to enable production and supply chain management upstream and downstream of the main activity of production by the rightholder; this is largely vertical to subsidiaries, parent companies and other tightly integrated partners such as in joint ventures;

- Licensing to competitors; this can be used to parcel out markets, so that the license is restricted to a product type or a geographical area in which the rightholder has no interest and can use the license to commit the licensee to not entering the market in which it operates itself.

While all of these are rational actions by firms, from a public policy and global welfare perspective some of these behaviours, in the aggregate, may not be optimal for technology innovation and diffusion to address climate change. Where interests converge, companies may also engage in cross-licensing or standardization exercises to better enable production for all of them related to core or common technologies that they all need to participate in the market. One iteration of this is the patent pool in which firms 'pool' their patents to license them jointly to non-members but to also allow the members free or low cost access to each other's technologies. Where the pool contains complementary technologies, this can be a vehicle for increasing market efficiency but where the patents cover similar areas and functionalities, significant problems of monopoly power arise. [44]

The patent system has several built-in safety valves to ensure that appropriate patents are given (requiring patent applications to meet basic criteria such as novelty, inventive step, industrial applicability) and that others can test and learn from the invention (providing research exceptions and requiring disclosure), encouraging follow-on innovation, and preventing wasteful duplication of efforts. However, patents may sometimes have negative effects. For example, patents may (but not always) create a type of monopoly control through the exclusive rights they confer on the owners of patented technology or knowledge. The existence or use of a patent may reduce competition, maintaining high prices for a product above marginal cost of production as the patent owner has no incentive to lower the price of the technology, make it more competitive or allow others to reproduce or use it.[45]

Patents are well-suited to encouraging innovations, encouraging initial disclosure of knowledge but, other than licensing, are not specifically directed at increasing diffusion of technologies. In some circumstances, the exclusive rightholder has an interest in limiting diffusion of the knowledge so that they can be the sole

---

[44] See den Uijl, S et al. "Managing Intellectual Property Using Patent Pools: Lessons from Three Generations of Pools in the Optical Disc Industry" 55 California Management Review 31 (2013).
[45] Boldrin, M and Levine, D "The Case Against Patents", 27 The Journal of Economic Perspectives, 3 (2013)

producer of a product for which they can charge a high per unit price. This ability to focus on the high-priced niche market is intrinsic to the patent grant, for products. However, diffusion requires broader production and where demand is high, a producer who can provide all products at a price accessible by all relevant consumers.

Intellectual property is a trade-off between present (static efficiency) anti-competitive costs and the generation of future technologies (dynamic efficiency). Governments are constantly assessing the appropriate balance between static and dynamic efficiency and use several tools to shift the balance in one direction or another depending on specific policy goals and needs at a particular time. The tools that they use to do so include: compulsory licensing, working requirements, patent exceptions, patent exclusions and the broad application of competition law to restructure markets in technological knowledge and technological products.

In the context of IP interventions to address technology transfer there is a key distinction which is sometimes hidden in the broader rhetoric and debate around the appropriateness and purpose of actions taken by developing countries. It is crucial for the purposes of discussing technology transfer to distinguish between the price of a ***product*** embodying knowledge/technology and the price of the knowledge/technology itself. Generally, as a function of normal pricing, the price paid for goods will include the price paid by the producer/seller for the access to the knowledge/technology. The concerns and goals will be very different depending on whether the primary concern is access to the products embodying the knowledge/technology or the knowledge/technology itself.

Where the issue is access to goods there are two levels of concern. The first is ensuring the normal flow of goods by making certain that prices of products are not set so high that it is too expensive for the relevant economic actors to afford. The second level, which applies to climate change the most, is ensuring that prices of products are not set so high that they make it too uneconomical to adopt climate technologies. A model of the access to goods discussion can be found in the access to medicines debate that took place at the WTO, leading up to the adoption of the Doha Declaration on the TRIPS Agreement and Public Health in 2003.[46] In the face of public health crises, countries and individuals have had limited funds and an inability to purchase all the drugs necessary to meet the needs of their populations. The results have been avoidable deaths and increased costs to society of chronic and untreated diseases. However, as

---

[46] See Declaration on the TRIPS Agreement and Public Health, adopted on 14 November 2001 by the Fourth WTO Ministerial Conference, Doha, Qatar (WT/MIN(01)/DEC/2). See also Abbott, F M "Innovation and Technology Transfer to Address Climate Change: Lessons from the Global Debate on Intellectual Property and Public Health", ICTSD's Programme on IPRs and Sustainable Development, Issue Paper No. 24, International Centre for Trade and Sustainable Development, Geneva, Switzerland, 2009.

Abbott points out, there are crucial differences with respect to climate change.[47] For example, in the field of renewable energy, there may be range of technological solutions to the same problem available, unlike in pharmaceuticals where a particular drug tends to lay claim to a whole treatment pathway.[48] In contrast, electricity, or more broadly energy, is a fungible commodity which can be produced by multiple kinds of technologies and 'sold' in multiple market paths.[49] In addition, the pharmaceutical industry largely maintains control of its innovations rather than out-licensing as is the case in many other industries.[50] Finally, for many products related to renewable energies, the IP premium may be a small part of the overall cost, although the empirical data on this is scarce. This may be due to simply higher costs of capital involved in generating the hardware, but also to more distributed and more frequent licensing due to competition between technology holders, keeping the premium lower. In both cases, the importance of maintaining a competitive number of producers in the market is crucial for keeping product prices low.

Where the issue is access to the knowledge there are multiple concerns, primarily related to those situations where there is a need to change production processes themselves. In such cases, where access to technologies is required to change the nature of a production process, some of the most difficult problems to overcome are refusals to license, the high cost of licensing, and patent owners maintaining a monopoly on the knowledge so as to prevent competition. The final element is particularly undesirable as without it, countries or firms can produce competing products, thus more efficiently achieving widespread dissemination of the knowledge and products. The knowledge about the technology may then be used to adapt it to local market conditions. For a full transition to a low carbon economy, the best available existing technologies need to be incorporated into production and consumption processes in developing countries. Achieving low carbon economies in developing countries cannot be achieved through sale of products alone into developing country markets. Such an approach would result in the complete absence of developing country firms and 100% market share of the domestic economy by developed country firms. The only way in which low carbon economies can reasonably be achieved is by transforming firms in developing countries rather than pushing them out of business. However, as noted, where the concern is to get products into the hands of consumers and relevant actors as quickly as possible, decreasing any barriers to imports of any kind (including lowering of tariff barriers and allowing parallel importing) then becomes a

---

[47] See p3, Abbott, F M "Innovation and Technology Transfer to Address Climate Change: Lessons from the Global Debate on Intellectual Property and Public Health", ICTSD's Programme on IPRs and Sustainable Development, Issue Paper No. 24, International Centre for Trade and Sustainable Development, Geneva, Switzerland, 2009.
[48] See p10, Id.
[49] Id.
[50] Id.

crucial part of policy, and concerns about protecting local firms may need to move to the background.

All these concerns prompt responses from governments to address supply problems. Actions taken to reduce monopolies and force sharing of knowledge, or to enforce lowering of prices of goods, may affect incentives to produce future technologies. The extent and effect of that lowering are in dispute but it is clear that at least some firms will act as if they believe this to be the case. In addition, the patent is a market-based mechanism. Intervention I would argue, then, need only occur when there is a market failure – based on the principle that intervention is justified either:

- where there is insufficient distribution of products embodying a technology in the national market to meet demand at a price that is affordable. This justification may be even stronger in a situation of emergency, threats to survival, the environment, health, human rights and other fundamental needs that economic policies such as intellectual property are designed to achieve;

- where there is insufficient distribution of knowledge to enable a critical number of producers in the market to adopt climate technologies and ensure their participation in the market in the face of regulatory or market requirements to lower carbon emissions. This implies of course that there are national regulatory standards aimed at climate mitigation and adaptation.

In that sense, the market conditions described are the ones that define the **"necessity"** for a government to act. As Arrow argues, there are significant situations where government intervention may be necessary to either create markets (in the case of the intellectual property grant) but also to address gaps and failures where the market is unlikely to generate certain kinds of public goods or enable certain public welfare outcomes because of the aggregate of individual firm decisions.[51] That concept of necessity has to underpin any analysis of whether the TRIPS Agreement poses a barrier to developing country action in such cases. This requires us to focus on the ways in which the concept of necessity is treated within the TRIPS Agreement and the broader corpus of WTO law, to determine the extent to which it limits the conditions under which 'necessity' is said to exist to a narrower set of market conditions than those above. This is why in Chapter 6, I carry out an in depth examination of the treatment of "necessity" as a trigger for action. In addition, then we would also examine not just whether such conditions were considered to trigger the necessity to act, but also whether the permissible actions allow countries to take the scope of action, within the right time frame, in the appropriate territory to address the market condition. This is

---

[51] Arrow, K "Economic Welfare and the Allocation of Resources for Invention' in *The Rate and Direction of Economic Activity Economic and Social Factors* (Princeton: Princeton University Press, 1962).

what, properly understood, would constitute a barrier to action, within this thesis, and constitutes the basis for analysis in Chapter 6 of whether TRIPS poses a barrier.

Clearly there are interventions beyond the intellectual property sphere that could be carried out, and I do not intend to argue that intellectual property may be the only or primary barrier. However, it is one of a complex set of interactions that, on the whole, present issues for developing countries, and many of them have a basic problem at their core: cost of action.

Most interventions on IP are aimed at the supply-side; how to ensure that there are enough products or technologies on offer in the market. A significant part of the technology transfer picture is the demand-side; the creation or expansion of markets for products and technologies. On the demand-side countries can take action to increase or expand markets, such as[52]:

- Establishing performance standards either on technologies or at sector level for energy efficiency or other climate goals;
- Leveraging government procurement of climate technologies;
- Establishing Feed-in tariffs for clean and renewable energy;
- Removing fossil fuel subsidies, for production and consumption;
- Establishing, credible and predictable legal frameworks for technology related transactions, including enforcement of intellectual property rights;
- Increasing competition in large monopoly or quasi-monopoly markets, especially in energy and infrastructure-related sectors;
- Increasing market transparencies;
- Reducing tariffs and taxes on crucial inputs to small and medium enterprises in supplier relationships with foreign firms in the low carbon sectors;[53]

In terms of actions to create market demand for renewable energy for example, many developing countries have already taken significant unilateral action to put policies in place, (by 2010 over 45, including all emerging economies) including renewable energy targets.[54] Others have made explicit pledges for GHG reductions by 2020 within the UNFCCC framework (e.g. Brazil, India, China, Mexico, and South Africa).[55] To a significant extent, developing countries have signalled to markets that

---

[52] See also Chapter 23, p6, Stern, N. et al. *The Economics of Climate Change: The Stern Review* (Cambridge: Cambridge University Press, 2007).
[53] p33, Maskus, K E "Encouraging International Technology Transfer" ICTSD Issue Paper No. 7, May 2004.
[54] See p226, UNEP, *Towards a Green Economy: Pathways to Sustainable Development and Poverty Eradication*, (Nairobi: UNEP, 2011). Available at: www.unep.org/greeneconomy, (last visited August 15, 2014)
[55] See Fekete, H. et al "Emerging economies – potentials, pledges and fair shares of greenhouse gas reduction" ENVIRONMENTAL RESEARCH OF THE GERMAN FEDERAL MINISTRY OF THE ENVIRONMENT, NATURE CONSERVATION AND NUCLEAR SAFETY Project-no. (FKZ) 3711 41 120, (Umweltbundesamt,

they seek to take action and seek funding and investment to do so, even where the full range of policy interventions has yet to be implemented.

Developing countries can also take actions to better enable capacity for absorption, imitation and adaptation of technology by:
- Increasing education (both in relevant research based universities and in firms);[56]
- Reducing brain drain by ensuring opportunities for employment and entrepreneurship for trained scientists, technologists and engineers;
- Increasing subsidies and preferential tax treatment for research and development activities in firms and in universities, linked to ensuring commercialization of research;
- Establishing networks of research institutions in specific key sectors and directly funding research and development of technologies;
- Establishing durable physical and soft infrastructure for transport and exchange of goods and information; in particular low cost access and connection to global information networks is a crucial issue especially for small and medium enterprises.

More generally, there are governance issues endemic to some countries that are a hindrance to the functioning of markets as a whole requiring that countries ensure:

- stable, predictable and transparent governance structures for commercial activity;
- stable macroeconomic policy.

However, to the extent that such problems exist and actions are taken, the cost of action falls on national budgets and is sometimes passed directly on to consumers and taxpayers.[57] In the context of the UNFCCC and the framework for burden-sharing[58], (which this thesis adopts) where such actions are undertaken by developing countries, the costs should be financed by developed countries as part of their

---

Bonn, April 2013). Available at: http://www.umweltbundesamt.de/publikationen/emerging-economies-potentials-pledges-fair-shares (last visited August 15, 2014)
[56] p34, Maskus, K E "Encouraging International Technology Transfer" See also p70, Maskus, K "The Role of Intellectual Property Rights in Encouraging Foreign Direct Investment and Technology Transfer" in Maskus, K & C Fink (eds.) *Intellectual Property and Development: Lessons from Recent Economic Research* (Washington D.C.: World Bank, 2005).
[57] See p369, Stern, N et al. *The Economics of Climate Change: The Stern Review* (Cambridge: Cambridge University Press, 2007).
[58] Article 4.7 of the UNFCCC states: The extent to which developing country Parties will effectively implement their commitments under the Convention will depend on the effective implementation by developed country Parties of their commitments under the Convention related to financial resources and transfer of technology and will take fully into account that economic and social development and poverty eradication are the first and overriding priorities of the developing country Parties.

UNFCCC obligations. Which brings us to one of the primary issues that drives this thesis: it is in the **absence** of such financial support that developing countries have sought to push for greater flexibility to address intellectual property issues that may arise.

To a significant extent, the necessity for a developing country to take action to address intellectual property would be alleviated by developed countries providing full financial support for developing country actions addressing climate change mitigation and adaptation, including local adoption, adaptation and reproductive capacity. This is clearly true for those actions meant at ensuring access to goods, but also true for those actions related at addressing the cost of licensing. Where developed countries provide all the funds necessary to pay the costs of licensing for technologies, much of the necessity to act is absent. It is the failure to do so by developed countries that has prompted developing countries to argue for the necessity to intervene in intellectual property markets in a way that imposes no costs on them but on developed country actors. In Chapter 4, I discuss the existing mechanisms, the ways in which they are linked to financial support and why they have been and may continue to be unsatisfactory mechanisms for addressing technology transfer.

However, there are limitations to what pure financial support can accomplish especially when the primary need is for adoption, adaptation and replication of the knowledge/technology. In those circumstances, it is likely that firms in developing countries may run into broader problems such as refusals to license, restrictive licensing terms (grant-back conditions, geographic and export restrictions; non-compete clauses), non-availability of trade secrets and know-how. While there may be a market price to get around these restrictions, there are significant circumstances in which that market price may be prohibitively high and creates such an opportunity cost that it may make other actions or the commercial viability of the venture or the firms involved questionable. In addition, there may be structural limitations to licensing, such as the tendency for licensees to prefer exclusive licenses that limit the diffusion of technologies to one or two firms rather than all relevant actors in the market.

Where foreign firms engage in foreign direct investment and joint ventures, host countries may still see a need to encourage spillovers into their domestic markets, beyond subsidiaries, joint ventures or single supplier or purchaser firms. Countries may seek to exercise interventions that address these issues as well.

This discussion above identifies crucial elements to defining a barrier: are there market conditions that create a necessity to act at the national level? If so, does the TRIPS Agreement address the full scope of that necessity as a trigger for action? Finally, does the TRIPS Agreement limit the kinds of action that would address the full scope of that necessity in terms of timing, scope of technologies, and geographical scope?

The nature of the climate challenge is precisely one that requires a dynamic understanding of what constitutes a barrier. The operational definition that this thesis

will be working with defines an intellectual property barrier as one that prevents countries from:
1. *Appropriately defining necessity as:*
   a. *Affordability - ensuring that prices of products and/or know-how are not set so high that it is too expensive for all the relevant economic actors to afford.*
   b. *Adoptability - ensuring that prices of products and/or know-how are not set so high that they make it commercially unviable for all relevant actors to adopt climate technologies.*
   c. *Adaptability – ensuring sufficient distribution of knowledge (information, skills, know-how) to enable a critical number of existing producers/service providers in the market to adopt, adapt and replicate climate technologies and ensure their participation in the market.*
2. *Taking actions that:*
   a. *address the full scope of technologies required by them to meet the climate change mitigation and adaptation needs;*
   b. *at the rate and level of diffusion appropriate to achieving those mitigation and adaptation needs;*
   c. *in the developing countries and regions that most effectively meet the climate change need.*

In this I take the market barriers approach defined by the OECD and the IEA: that a market barrier is one that "slows the rate at which the market for a technology expands".[59] It focuses not on an absolute bar, but in the market effect and the dynamic rate at which technology diffusion should occur.

II.2 Defining technology transfer

In order to avoid confusion it is also necessary to establish an operationally appropriate definition of the term "technology transfer".[60] The first thing to note is that we are not addressing technology transfer in the domestic sense, which is the movement of research from the development phase into deployment and commercialization. Here I mean international technology transfer, as in the flow of technological goods and knowledge across borders. We can consider that transfer happens when technology is first transferred from one country to another and is then adopted by public entities or private firms, being built into either their means of producing goods and services, or

---

[59] See p19, IEA "Creating Markets for Technologies" (Paris: OECD/IEA, 2003)
[60] This discussion on definitions is drawn from an earlier version discussed in Shabalala, D et al. "Climate Change, Technology Transfer and Human Rights" CIEL/ICHRP (Working Paper 2010). Available at: http://www.ichrp.org/files/papers/181/138_technology_transfer_UNFCCC.pdf (last visited August 15, 2014)

built into the products and services themselves. Despite there being broad agreement as to the positive impact technology transfer can have, there is no universally recognized or legally enforceable definition as to what technology transfer is or what form it must take.

Within the realm of trade agreements, the closest definition was the United Nations Conference on Trade and Development (UNCTAD) Draft International Code of Conduct on the Transfer of Technology which defined it as "the transfer of systematic knowledge for the manufacture of a product, for the application of a process or for the rendering of a service and does not extend to the transactions involving the mere sale or mere lease of goods."[61] The definition is followed by a statement that transfer of technology transactions are arrangements between parties involving transfer of technology (as defined), particularly in: the assignment of industrial property, the provision of know-how and technical expertise, the provision of technological knowledge to install and operate equipment and the provision of the contents of technical cooperation arrangements. The full definition also includes:[62]

> (a) The assignment, sale and licensing of all forms of industrial property, except for trademarks, service marks and trade names when they are not part of transfer of technology transactions;
> (b) The provision of know-how and technical expertise in the form of feasibility studies, plans, diagrams, models, instructions, guides, formulae, basic or detailed engineering designs, specifications and equipment for training, services involving technical advisory and managerial personnel, and personnel training;
> (c) The provision of technological knowledge necessary for the installation, operation and functioning of plant and equipment, and turnkey projects;
> (d) The provision of technological knowledge necessary to acquire, install and use machinery, equipment, intermediate goods and/or raw materials which have been acquired by purchase, lease or other means;
> (e) The provision of technological contents of industrial and technical cooperation arrangements.

The draft code was never adopted. The definition, however, was not one of the major bracketed elements of the draft and was not a significant factor in the failure

---

[61] Article 1.2, UNCTAD Draft International Code of Conduct on the Transfer of Technology. See p262 UNCTAD "Compendium of International Arrangements on Transfer of Technology: Selected Instruments - Relevant Provisions in Selected International Arrangements Pertaining to Transfer of Technology" UNCTAD/ITE/IPC/Misc.5, UNCTAD 2001. Available at: http://www.unctad.org/en/docs//psiteipcm5.en.pdf
[62] Article 1.3, UNCTAD Draft International Code of Conduct on the Transfer of Technology in UNCTAD, See p263 Id.

to adopt the code.[63] The definition of technology transfer that it generated remains one of the first and most influential iterations at a multinational level of what technology transfer means.

Even though technology transfer is stated as an objective of the TRIPS Agreement,[64] and Article 66.2 requires developed country members to put in place incentives to encourage their enterprises to carry out technology transfer to LDCs, there is no definition of technology transfer in the TRIPS Agreement. Therefore it was hardly a surprise when developed country members submitted reports to the WTO's TRIPS Council on their compliance with this obligation[65] that there was not a shared understanding of the concept of transfer of technology.[66]

In the WTO Working Group on Trade and Transfer of Technology[67] (WGTTT), work on defining technology transfer has not progressed: developing countries concerned that too broad a definition would encompass inappropriate activities, and developed countries concerned that too narrow a definition would not address enabling environments in developing countries and broader capacity building activities that were being funded by bilateral and multilateral development assistance.[68] While the WGTTT has largely devolved into a discussion group, it has nevertheless produced some useful documents on taxonomies and categories of measures for consideration by WTO members.[69] The 2002 background note provided by the secretariat usefully identifies 4 stages of technology transfer:[70]

1) Cross border transfer or acquisition
2) Learning – acquiring know-how and know-why
3) Adaptation – fitting the technology to local conditions
4) Diffusion – the spread of the technology within a country

---

[63] See p26, Gehl Sampath, P and P Roffe, "Unpacking the International Technology Transfer Debate: Fifty Years and Beyond" ICTSD Programme on Innovation, Technology and Intellectual Property Working Paper; International Centre for Trade and Sustainable Development, (2012).
[64] Article 7, TRIPS Agreement
[65] On 19 February 2003, the Council for TRIPS adopted a decision establishing arrangements for the submission by developed country Members of annual reports on their implementation of Article 66.2 and their annual review by the Council for TRIPS. (See "Implementation of article 66.2 of the TRIPS Agreement - Decision of the Council for TRIPS of 19 February 2003" - IP/C/28)
[66] Minutes of Meeting of Council for Trade-Related Aspects of Intellectual Property Rights - IP/C/M/55 – 21 December 2007, par 175 (Brazil) and par 183 (Switzerland)
[67] Established after the Doha WTO Ministerial as part of the Doha Development Round, para. 37, Ministerial Declaration, Ministerial Conference, Fourth Session Doha, 9 - 14 November 2001, WT/MIN(01)/DEC/1, 20 November 2001.
[68] Report of The Working Group on Trade and Transfer Of Technology to the General Council, WT/WGTTT/5, 14 July 2003.
[69] See e.g. A Taxonomy on Country Experiences on International Technology Transfers: Note by the Secretariat, WT/WGTTT/W/3, 11 November 2002.
[70] See p2, Id.

For a successful technology transfer to have occurred, all four of these stages must be enabled. For the purposes of climate change especially, diffusion into the rest of the economy is paramount. Combined with an understanding of the channels of technology transfer, the target of technology transfer and the content of technology transfer, it may be possible to have a sufficiently operationalized definition of technology transfer for the purposes of this thesis.

I also draw from the definitions of technology transfer that are found in the environmental arena, especially multilateral environmental agreements (MEAs) as we are specifically concerned with technology transfer as understood in the UNFCCC. The clearest and most well-articulated provisions can be found in Chapter 34 of Agenda 21 of the 1992 Rio Declaration on Environment and Development.[71] The final text that was adopted by the parties discussed the transfer of environmentally sound technology, and, in Article 34.18, outlines activities that government can take to engage in technology transfer including:

> (a) Formulation of policies and programmes for the effective transfer of environmentally sound technologies that are publicly owned or in the public domain;
> (b) Creation of favourable conditions to encourage the private and public sectors to innovate, market and use environmentally sound technologies;
> (c) Examination by Governments and, where appropriate, by relevant organizations of existing policies, including subsidies and tax policies, and regulations to determine whether they encourage or impede the access to, transfer of and introduction of environmentally sound technologies;
> (d) Addressing, in a framework which fully integrates environment and development, barriers to the transfer of privately owned environmentally sound technologies and adoption of appropriate general measures to reduce such barriers while creating specific incentives, fiscal or otherwise, for the transfer of such technologies;
> (e) In the case of privately owned technologies, the adoption of the following measures, in particular for developing countries:
>
>> i. Creation and enhancement by developed countries, as well as other countries which might be in a position to do so, of appropriate incentives, fiscal or otherwise, to stimulate the transfer of environmentally sound technology by companies, in particular to developing countries, as integral to sustainable development;

---

[71] Agenda 21 of the Rio Declaration on Environment and Development adopted at United Nations Conference on Environment and Development (UNCED), Rio de Janeiro, 3-14 June 1992. Available at: http://sustainabledevelopment.un.org/index.php?page=view&nr=23&type=400&menu=35 (last visited August 15, 2014)

ii. Enhancement of the access to and transfer of patent protected environmentally sound technologies, in particular to developing countries;

iii. Purchase of patents and licences on commercial terms for their transfer to developing countries on non-commercial terms as part of development cooperation for sustainable development, taking into account the need to protect intellectual property rights;

iv. In compliance with and under the specific circumstances recognized by the relevant international conventions adhered to by States, the undertaking of measures to prevent the abuse of intellectual property rights, including rules with respect to their acquisition through compulsory licensing, with the provision of equitable and adequate compensation;

v. Provision of financial resources to acquire environmentally sound technologies in order to enable in particular developing countries to implement measures to promote sustainable development that would entail a special or abnormal burden to them;

vi. Development of mechanisms for the access to and transfer of environmentally sound technologies, in particular to developing countries, while taking into account development in the process of negotiating an international code of conduct on transfer of technology, as decided by UNCTAD at its eighth session, held at Cartagena de Indias, Colombia, in February 1992.

(f) Improvement of the capacity to develop and manage environmentally sound technologies

This definition in Agenda 21 has been a guide for the kinds of activities expected from developed countries in multilateral environmental agreements (MEAs) when they bargain to provide technology transfer in exchange for developing country participation. When developing countries point to lack of delivery of technology transfer they point to the failure to take the kinds of actions agreed to in Agenda 21.

In the area of climate change specifically, the International Panel on Climate Change (IPCC) has also suggested a definition in a study on methodological issues in technology transfer.[72] However, that definition has not yet been adopted by the Conference of the Parties nor the UNFCCC Secretariat and the Expert Group on Transfer of Technology.[73] The IPCC defined technology transfer as:

---

[72] Metz et al., "Methodological and Technological Issues in Technology Transfer", A Special Report of the Intergovernmental Panel on Climate Change, July 2000. Available at: http://www.ipcc.ch/ipccreports/sres/tectran/index.htm (last visited August 15, 2014).

[73] See Chapter 2 for an outline of the architecture of the bodies responsible for technology transfer in the UNFCCC.

a broad set of processes covering the flows of know-how, experience and equipment for mitigating and adapting to climate change amongst different stakeholders such as governments, private sector entities, financial institutions, NGOs and research/education institutions. [...] The broad and inclusive term "transfer" encompasses diffusion of technologies and technology co-operation across and within countries. It covers technology transfer processes between developed countries, developing countries and countries with economies in transition, amongst developed countries, amongst developing countries and amongst countries with economies in transition. It comprises the process of learning to understand, utilise and replicate the technology, including the capacity to choose and adapt to local conditions and integrate it with indigenous technologies.[74]

This is a less than useful approach as it fails to draw on Agenda 21 and fails to address the specific meaning of the term as used in Article 4 of the UNFCCC outlining technology transfer obligations of developed countries. By being overly inclusive and insufficiently specific the IPCC provided little guidance. The Expert Group on Technology Transfer (EGTT) working within the mandate provided by the Marrakech Accords[75] did not define technology transfer but worked within a framework that addressed:

- Technology needs & needs assessments
- Technology information
- Enabling environments
- Capacity building
- Mechanisms for technology transfer

The compromise reached in the Marrakech Accords means that intellectual property is not directly mentioned but may be addressed through the enabling environments theme of work which focuses on regulatory actions taken by governments. The enabling environments framing however, creates a clear emphasis on technology importing country measures, rather than on technology exporting country actions

Building on the UNCTAD Draft Code of Conduct and on Chapter 34 of Agenda 21, I propose the following understanding of what constitutes technology transfer defining a package: four modes of technology transfer, the balance of which can be varied according to the specific needs of the country. All must take place to ensure

---

[74] Metz et al.
[75] UNFCCC "Development and Transfer of technologies" Decision 4/CP.7 in "Report Of The Conference Of the Parties on its Seventh Session, held At Marrakesh from 29 October to 10 November 2001: Addendum - Part Two: Action Taken By The Conference Of The Parties" FCCC/CP/2001/13/Add.1, 21 January 2002.

successful technology transfer, diffusion and uptake. The modes of technology transfer are:

- **Transfer of Physical Capital and Goods ((outside of the firm or wholly owned subsidiary)** including, but not limited to: specialized equipment; goods embodying or incorporating the relevant technology or idea. This largely entails financing for purchase of such goods.
- **Transfer of Skills and Know How (outside of the firm or wholly owned subsidiary)** including, but not limited to: licensing or assistance with the purchase of proprietary knowledge, provision of technical and manual skills training; scientific and academic training; training and technical advice and assistance, necessary to maintain, operate, adapt and reproduce a viable system or technology. This would include scientific and educational exchanges, workshops, field education, funding, training and capacity building all along the research chain: - research, development, demonstration, deployment, and commercialization. This is largely aimed at ensuring learning – acquisition and application of know how leading to an understanding of the principles of why the technology works and building the capacity to adapt and replicate it.
- **Transfer of Information and Data ((outside of the firm or wholly owned subsidiary)**, including but not limited to: manuals; designs; blueprints; operating instructions; scientific and technical publications and reports. This would include greater access to scientific and technical information, patent office publications and data. This is embodied in the formal documents and detail of patent information, licenses, as well as information to learn how to operate, adapt and replicate the technology. This is meant to provide a durable basis for building on and being able to adapt the technology.
- **Transfer of ability to adapt and improve the technology** including, but not limited to: no limitations on production and export under licenses for domestic use or export to other developing countries; no restrictions on improvement and ownership of improvement of the technology; establishment of R&D facilities in the country in which the project is placed; creation of joint R&D project or projects.

The proposed definition incorporates the vector and the content of technology transfer. It takes into account that there are conditions to be met in developing countries but does not require those to be in place before technology transfer activities can take place. While proprietary knowledge is part of the kinds of content transferred, it forms part of a broader package of measures. Most importantly it ensures that technology transfer is something that goes beyond basic hardware sales and servicing, and aims at actual transformation of know-how and skills related to production. Implicit in this is that such transfer entails spillovers beyond the boundary of the firm to other actors. I also include in here the idea that it is not sufficient to simply allow a wholly-owned subsidiary to exercise the technology where this does not result in learning beyond the boundaries of the firm. This is an instrumental choice based on what the actual goal meant to be achieved is. The shorthand that I will be using in this thesis to refer to this framework will be a definition of technology transfer that asks whether it enables *"localization of technology, leading to adoption, adaptation and replication."*

II. 3 Defining Climate Technologies

Finally, there is a need to discuss exactly what a climate technology is. While the scope of technologies will be covered in Chapter 2, it is important here to note that there are really two categories of technologies that are discussed. The first is climate mitigation technologies and the other is climate adaptation technologies. Under those two categories lie a whole host of potential sub-categories. There is also some disagreement as to whether some technologies may be properly considered to be climate technologies e.g. nuclear energy, if they do not also comply with the definition of an environmentally sound technology from Article 34.1 of Agenda 21:

> Environmentally sound technologies protect the environment, are less polluting, use all resources in a more sustainable manner, recycle more of their wastes and products, and handle residual wastes in a more acceptable manner than the technologies for which they were substitutes.

In this thesis I adopt a fairly broad definition of what constitutes a climate mitigation technology: a technology that contributes to lowering the GHG emissions compared to the business as usual technologies for which it is substituted.

For climate adaptation technologies, the issue of definition is much more complicated by the link between technologies that enable adaptation and those that build capacity to adapt. In part this is because a significant element of adaptation is climate resilience of communities before they are required to respond and adapt to climate change, a concept which has broader economy-wide implications. In Chapter 2, I embrace this broad approach as the only way to effectively ensure that technology transfer addresses the actual problem and not just the symptoms. In this I adopt a purposive approach to the definition of the technologies by asking which technologies would achieve the goals required instead of seeking an internal characteristic shared by all the technologies implicated. In doing so, I return to a theme which will recur throughout this book: it is important not to underestimate the scale of the problem that climate change presents if we are to design solutions that actually work and are not simply business as usual.

III. THE APPROACH OF THIS THESIS

The definition of a barrier as outlined above then requires us to provide information to establish a framework based on three specific targets: there is a *scope target,* of which technologies need to be developed and deployed; there is a *geographic target* relating to which countries specific technologies need to be deployed; there is a *timing target* determining the date by which such technologies will need to be developed and deployed. In Chapter 2, I rely on several studies and scenarios within the IPCC, as well as the UNFCCC (such as Technology Needs Assessments (TNA), Nationally Appropriate Mitigation Actions (NAMAs) and national communications) to build a picture of three crucial elements:

1. What is the scope of technologies implicated by the emissions reduction and adaptation requirements of the climate challenge?
2. What are the dates by which these technologies will need to be deployed and diffused?
3. To which countries will such technologies most likely to be required to be deployed and diffused?

This framing is crucial to the analysis of whether international intellectual property rules pose a barrier to technology transfer, by establishing what the scale of the need is. In my analysis a barrier would exist where the provision or set of standards impedes the ability to act with respect to the full scope of technology needs; retards the ability or capacity to act to ensure technology transfer by the target dates required; and limits the ability to transfer technology into the countries where it is most necessary to do so. The issue of geography is particularly important. In chapter 2 and 3 I identify the countries and discuss why it may be particularly vital to ensure that the emerging economies (China, India and to some extent Brazil and South Africa) are able to address IP related problems, particularly as they relate to export markets in other developing countries. The basis of this is findings in Chapter 2 regarding the scale and growth of emissions in emerging economies, as well as the existing and increasing trade links between emerging economies and other developing countries. There may be a need for these countries to be major intermediaries for production and distribution of technological goods appropriate to developing countries.

In Chapter 3, I evaluate the data and evidence so far on the role that intellectual property has played in technology transfer to address climate change mitigation and adaptation. This will involve a critical examination of what the available patent and other data suggest is the case with respect to the existence and distribution of patenting, the exercise of licensing, and the rate of uptake. While these results will not be dispositive with respect to the main question in this thesis, this provides important context in the discussion as it allows us to identify trends, and lacunae that can feed into an assessment, at the global level, of the necessity for the UNFCCC to act. This assessment will work in conjunction with that in Chapter 6, to determine the scope of action that the UNFCCC should take, if at all, with respect to intellectual property.

Chapter 4 will be an evaluation of the existing provisions and mechanisms for technology transfer in the UNFCCC, and whether they have been, or will be sufficient to meet the scope, scale and timing of technology transfer identified as necessary in Chapters 2 and 3. In particular, the role of financial support and its relation to technology transfer and intellectual property will be examined. The Chapter will focus particularly on the role of the Global Environmental Facility, the Clean Development Mechanism, the Technology Executive Committee, and the Climate Technology Centre and Network for delivering on the obligations under the UNFCCC.

Chapter 5 will identify a set of IP interventions that have historically been used by countries to try to ensure that technology transfer takes place. It will provide the baseline for the analysis of whether TRIPS poses a barrier in Chapter 6. In order to characterize the kinds of IP interventions that may be required, we need to assess the theoretical and empirical frameworks for: how technology transfer and intellectual property interact and relate; what evidence there is for the role that intellectual property plays in technology transfer; what data there is for the role it plays in the transfer of environmentally sound technologies and specifically for climate change. This will help us to identify and characterize the IP interventions that have historically been, and may at present be, in use and the kinds of problems at which they have been targeted.

Chapter 6 and 7, which examine the availability of specific IP-related policies, form the pivot point of this thesis. Based on the assessment in these chapters I will discuss in Chapter 9, the nature and scope of actions that the UNFCCC can and should take to address the scale, scope and timing of the challenge. In this sense, it is important to note that a negative result i.e. a finding that TRIPS does not pose a barrier to the availability of many of these measures will be almost as useful as its opposite. A key dispute between developed and developing countries is the nature and extent to which the UNFCCC should take action to address intellectual property issues. A comprehensively analysed finding that action by the UNFCCC is **not** necessary would be crucial to reframing the negotiating structure of the UNFCCC on technology financing and support. However, this is only possible if the debate can be moved beyond a static argument pointing to individual examples of failure or success at transferring a technology and instead, conducting a proper systemic analysis based on the acknowledged targets for scope, scale and timing within the UNFCCC itself.

Thus, in chapter 6, rather than take a compliance approach, which can tend to bias analyses towards a purely legalistic approach, I propose an 'availability' approach which incorporates a legal assessment but also assesses a measure of practical implementability along the criteria as developed in Chapters 2 and 3. In this discussion on TRIPS, availability has several components. A legal component consisting of whether, as a matter of WTO law:
1) the TRIPS Agreement encompasses room for the triggers for necessity discussed above. Affordability, Adoptability and Adaptability, and;
2) whether the TRIPS Agreement present a legal bar or limit to the kinds of interventions meant to address the triggering conditions.

The practical component examines whether the TRIPS Agreement allows the legally available measures to operate within the appropriate time frame, at the right scope of technologies, with the appropriate geographical impact.

The assessment of the 'availability' of particular IP interventions focuses on the TRIPS Agreement because that is the primary bone of contention between developed and developing countries.[76] While many developing countries have agreed to higher intellectual property standards in bilateral and regional free trade agreements, these obligations do not have the same almost irrevocable character that obligations in the TRIPS Agreement have. The TRIPS Agreement was negotiated as part of a package, and as such, it is not possible to withdraw from the TRIPS Agreement without losing market access in goods, services, and losing resort to rules on sanitary and phyto-sanitary measures, technical barriers to trade, trade-related investment measures, as well as dispute settlement.[77] Such a withdrawal would apply to all WTO member states. This is in contrast to bilateral and regional free trade agreements which largely affect bilateral relationships and the withdrawal from which are of a much less irrevocable nature. The effect of such a withdrawal would only be with respect to one country, or just a few countries, even though that country may represent a significant part of the export market. In general, the intellectual property sections of such agreements are not severable from the rest of the agreement,[78] but any such withdrawal would still leave the existing relationship and obligations under the WTO in place and the losses would not be absolute, as in the case of WTO withdrawal. Withdrawal would have far less consequences and the threat of withdrawal would provide stronger leverage for renegotiations where necessary. Where there is sufficient policy justification there is less of a barrier to countries withdrawing from bilateral and regional arrangements. With respect to the TRIPS Agreement, there can be no credible threat of withdrawal by any member that would force renegotiation of the terms of the TRIPS Agreement. The impetus for renegotiation will have to be on a different basis, justified by other concerns as has been the case in the public health arena.

Much the same can be said of bilateral investment treaties (BITs) that countries sign. Where these are seen as a barrier to development, countries are far freer to denounce and withdraw than they are with respect to the TRIPS Agreement.

The assessment of the availability of an IP intervention in Chapter 6 will be primarily against the legal 'availability' of an intervention i.e. does the TRIPS Agreement forbid or significantly limit, the use of such an IP intervention? This is first discussed at the level of the general principles and objectives of the agreement before discussing the specific provisions on flexibility in the rest of the agreement. This analysis will be based on the interpretation of TRIPS provisions using traditional interpretive rules under the

---

[76] See UNFCCC "Negotiating Text" FCCC /AWGLCA/2010/14, 13 August 2010 ; p34, UNFCCC "In-session draft texts and notes by the facilitators prepared at the twelfth session of the Ad Hoc Working Group on Long-term Cooperative Action under the Convention" FCCC/AWGLCA/2010/INF.1, 29 October 2010.
[77] Article XV.1, Marrakesh Agreement establishing the World Trade Organization (WTO Agreement), Marrakesh, 15 April 1994, *in force* 1 January 1995, 1867 United Nations Treaty Series (1995) 4.
[78] See Article 23.4 of the United States-Chile Trade Promotion Agreement.

WTO and general international law, with reference to direct WTO case law and decisions, relevant case law and decisions of other international bodies and national case law where pertinent. In particular, I base my analysis on the rules in the Dispute Settlement Understanding and subsequent case law applying them in WTO disputes on the determination of jurisdiction, applicable law and the application of Section 3 (Interpretation of Treaties) of the Vienna Convention on the Law of Treaties (VCLT).[79] In particular, Article 31 of the VCLT will be the basis for justifying interpretations of TRIPS provisions where I argue that the panels or the appellate body may have been mistaken or in error and that a provision may be broader or narrower than WTO case law provides for. In this sense, Chapter 6 is not purely descriptive of the law as it has been interpreted but seeks to establish a sense of the law *as it is*, so that policymakers are not unduly limited in their understandings of what the actual scope of a provision may be. It aims to provide them with a proper basis for risk assessment of whether a dispute may be brought against them for the use of a particular intervention.

Understanding that significant weight is given to the assessment of legal availability, the other criteria nevertheless provide a novel filter and framework which differs from existing analyses of TRIPS that have focused on TRIPS flexibilities with respect to health, for example.[80] However it is also important to note that there have been few comprehensive legal assessments of the TRIPS Agreement with respect to technology transfer of climate technologies[81] and none at a the level of detail and comprehensiveness of this thesis. A very useful exegesis of the nature and kind of problems in the relationship between intellectual property and innovation for climate technology was done by Matthew Rimmer[82] but he did not focus on the technology transfer dynamic specifically within TRIPS and on the legal relationship between the TRIPS and the UNFCCC. To the extent that this thesis succeeds in its aims it may be able to provide a more definitive answer to the legal question of the availability of IP interventions, while also providing a uniquely climate focused assessment of TRIPS. This may provide better guidance on what specific kinds of changes are required, if any, and what the scope of such changes should be. The hope is that it will allow other researchers to go beyond the question of whether TRIPS poses a barrier and focus their

---

[79] Vienna Convention on the Law of Treaties (VCLT), Vienna, 23 May 1969 *in force* 27 January 1980, 1155 United Nations Treaty Series (1987) 331.
[80] See e.g. Correa, C., *Integrating Public Health Concerns into Patent Legislation in Developing Countries* (South Centre: Geneva, 2000)
[81] See e.g. Hutchison, C J 'Does TRIPS Facilitate or Impede Climate Change Technology Transfer Into Developing Countries?' 3 University of Ottawa Law & Technology Journal 517 (2006). Also Consilvio, M "The Role of Patents in the International Framework of Clean Technology Transfer: A Discussion of Barriers and Solutions" 3 Intell. Prop. Brief 10 (2011); Derclaye, E. "Intellectual Property Rights and Global Warming", 12 J. MARSHALL REV. INTELL. PROP. L. 263 (2008). Derclaye, E "Not Only Innovation but also Collaboration, Funding, Goodwill and Commitment: Which Role for Patent Laws in Post-Copenhagen Climate Change Action", 9 J. MARSHALL REV. INTELL. PROP. L. 657 (2010). Sarnoff, J "The Patent System and Climate Change" 16 Virginia Journal of Law & Technology (2011)
[82] Rimmer, M *Intellectual Property and Climate Change: Inventing Clean Technologies* (London: Edward Elgar, 2011)

energies on researching the practical feasibility and design of IP interventions at the national level for a post-TRIPS world.

Particularly because this thesis looks at the relationship between two legal regimes the issue of whether and how the WTO and the TRIPS regime may incorporate or conflict with the climate regime is crucial. The question is, if TRIPS presents a barrier to the use of particular IP interventions to address technology transfer for climate change, are there broader interpretive mechanisms in the UNFCCC and the WTO that may nevertheless enable and provide legal cover for unilateral IP interventions that may not be 'available' under the TRIPS Agreement, or that lie at the margins of 'availability'? Chapter 7 explores whether the rules of the UNFCCC can be used to expand the availability of an intervention, and whether there might be a role for other connecting regimes, such as the human rights regime, in expanding that availability. My approach to Chapter 7 remains primarily descriptive, explaining how the interaction of these regimes with the WTO may play out in the specific case of technology transfer to address climate change. Only in Chapter 8 do I make a normative proposal for how the UNFCCC can and should take action to address intellectual property issues. In doing so, I will be drawing on the excellent work by the International Law Commission (ILC) on *the* fragmentation of international law.[83] Chapter 8 will be a specific application of the ILCs' systemic integration framework for managing interactions between different international regimes. I work from the position that the WTO is situated within the broader corpus of international law and is a special application of international law rather than a self-contained regime into which no outside regimes can play a part and which itself plays no part in other regimes.[84] Chapter 8 focuses specifically on the ways that the UNFCCC can take action on intellectual property without necessarily raising a conflict with the TRIPS regime. There has been some interesting initial work on this issue by Van Asselt, Sindico and Mehling and others who pointed out the relevance of the systemic integration concept of the ILC to the UNFCCC.[85] In particular, they expand the locus of interaction to include decision-making bodies of the regimes and not just legal texts and dispute settlement processes. This book takes their point a step further and applies it to the specific case of technology transfer for climate change. I propose a methodology for how systemic integration may be applied in the specific situation of technology transfer for climate change.

---

[83] Koskenniemi, M et al., 'Fragmentation of International Law: Difficulties arising from the Diversification and Expansion of International Law: Report of the Study Group of the International Law Commission' (13 April 2006) para 23, UN Doc. A/CN.4/L.682; ILC, 'Fragmentation of International Law: Difficulties Arising From the Diversification and Expansion of International Law, Report of the Study Group of the International Law Commission' (18 July 2006) UN Doc. A/CN.4/L.702

[84] See p35, Pauwelyn, J *Conflict of Norms in Public International Law: How WTO Law Relates to Other Rules of International Law.* (New York: Cambridge University Press, 2003.)

[85] Van Asselt, H et al., "Global Climate Change and the Fragmentation of International Law" 30 Law and Policy 423 (2008). See also Young, M "Climate Change Law and Regime Interaction) 2011 Carbon & Climate L. Rev. 147 (2011).

Finally, in Chapter 9, I propose some actions that the UNFCCC can take that avoid conflicts of norms with the TRIPS Agreement and address the problems identified by the Chapter 6 and 7 analysis.

IV. THE AUDIENCE

This thesis is a synthetic work, bringing together different legal frameworks in international law, looking at the practices and structure of differing international regimes. As such, there is a necessity to only include and address the issues of overlap and not turn this thesis into an elaboration on the scope and boundaries of each involved international legal regime. However, there are two specific audiences to which this thesis is aimed: practitioners and researchers in intellectual property law and policy; practitioners and researchers in international environmental law, specifically climate change.

This thesis aims to provide sufficient detail on basic background elements to satisfy theoreticians on both sides but not so much that the main element of the interaction between the two regimes is lost in the details. In some areas, this has required some simplification of complex issues, and in others I have simply left out deeper explanations that may divert from the main point in the thesis. What is left should be sufficient to allow the reader to fully engage with issues at the interface of IP and environmental law, without necessarily having to be experts in both international intellectual property and international environmental law.

Chapter 2 –
The Scope, Timing and Geographical Targets for Technology Transfer of Climate Technologies

I. INTRODUCTION

The aim of this chapter is to identify and elaborate three crucial elements for establishing the scope against which options for action, including those related to intellectual property, are to be measured. First, there is a ***scope target***, of which technologies need to be developed and deployed. Second, there is a ***timing target***, by which date such technologies will need to be developed and deployed. Third, there is a ***geographic target*** relating to which countries specific technologies will need to be deployed. To build a picture of these elements, this chapter will:

1. Draw out technologies identified from several global and regional studies, scenarios and datasets, contextualized by the IPCC assessment of global and regional emissions trends and climate impacts. Understanding which technologies are likely to present the least-cost, highest impact emissions reductions and adaptations determines the scope of technologies that will need to be addressed.
2. Draw the outer boundaries of the timing for emissions reductions and adaptation, the implied dates for peaking emissions and, the implications for technology diffusion based on emission reductions and targets outlined in the IPCC and other global assessments, as well as commitments already agreed to by UNFCCC parties.
3. Draw out the specific developing geographical regions and developing countries that will need to carry out emissions reductions and adaptations and the specific technologies required to do so. This will be drawn primarily from an assessment of mitigation scenarios, Technology Needs Assessments (TNAs), Nationally Appropriate Mitigation Actions

(NAMAs), and UNFCCC national communications of the relevant countries.

For each of these elements, I will address the mitigation and the adaptation issues separately. These elements will be the basis for the analysis of the coverage and utility of existing mechanisms in Chapter 4 and, in Chapter 3 the evaluation of the existing data on the existence, distribution and transactions relating to patents on the technologies identified.

Since the IPCC Fourth Assessment Report[86] (AR4) there have been significant developments in our understanding of what is required to avoid catastrophic climate change. To the extent that this thesis relies on specific data to construct a scenario for what action is necessary might be necessary in technology transfer, I rely on the standard consensus model of projected pathways in the IPCC combined with the acknowledged and agreed consensus statements by UNFCCC parties in the 2011 Durban Platform at COP 17. However, with respect to mitigation technology I will draw on several scenarios that have built on the IPCC's work including the Energy Technology Perspectives (ETP) series from the International Energy Agency. The 2010 and 2012 iterations[87] present a relatively conservative but nevertheless significant set of data on what the baselines are and the necessary shifts in research, development, demonstration, deployment and diffusion of climate mitigation technologies that may be needed by 2050.

The political context is also important as a boundary marker. The commitments that countries have made to reduce greenhouse gas emissions and address adaptation set the baseline for the normative aim in terms of targets, as contrasted to more data driven, science based scenarios and assessments. In the Copenhagen Accord that was agreed by all countries except Bolivia at the Conference of the Parties to the UNFCCC in 2009, parties committed themselves to maintaining the temperature rise

---

[86] IPCC, *Climate Change 2007: Synthesis Report. Contribution of Working Groups I, II and III to the Fourth Assessment Report of the Intergovernmental Panel on Climate Change* [Core Writing Team, Pachauri, R.K and Reisinger, A. (eds.)] (Geneva: IPCC, 2007). The relevant portions of the Fifth Assessment Report (in particular the report of Working Group III on Mitigation of Climate Change) are being finalized in late 2014 after the publication of this thesis, but the final drafts appear to build on and support the conclusions of the AR4. This thesis will refer only to the AR4 in keeping with its reliance on relatively conservative evaluations of future trends. The Fifth Assessment Report remains under considerations and its implications continue to be assessed and thus may not present a strong consensus view as yet, unlike the AR4.
[87] IEA, *Energy Technology Perspectives 2010: Scenarios and Strategies to 2050*, (Paris: IEA/OECD, 2010); IEA, *Energy Technology Perspectives 2012: Pathways to a Clean Energy System* (Paris: IEA/OECD 2012).

below 2 degrees Celsius relative to pre-industrial levels.[88] Annex 1 countries committed to 2020 targets for quantified economy wide emissions and non-Annex 1 parties committed to take actions to 2020 reduce emissions, consistent with provision of financial support and technology transfer.[89] In the Cancun Agreements reached at the 16th Conference of the Parties, UNFCCC parties agreed on the need to reduce GHG emissions in line with maintaining global average temperature increase below 2 degrees Celsius, and to move towards a lower goal of 1.5 degrees Celsius.[90]

In addition to these mitigation commitments, there is the ongoing commitment that all UN member states have made to reducing poverty[91], which will require access to energy products and services. Developing countries must increase their energy consumption by a significant factor if this is to be achieved. At present, access to electricity is limited to 20% of the global population and approximately 15% have only intermittent access.[92] Without a transformation in electricity production, almost all of that increase in developing countries is likely to come from coal-powered electricity generation. In 2008, developing countries produced over 70% of electricity from fossil fuels, with coal at 46%.[93] The same issues arise in the core areas of industrial and residential heat and heavy and light duty transport. In transport, emerging economy use of motorized vehicles will match that of the OECD within 10 to 20 years.[94] The question for developing countries is not whether they will decrease their consumption of electricity, heat or transport related energy, but whether it will be from cheap, GHG emissions intensive sources or from more costly and technologically intensive, renewable and efficient sources. The core of the debate on technology transfer is therefore not whether technology will be transferred to developing countries but who should bear the cost. The next sections will try to determine the timing, scope and specific geographical targets for that transfer.

II. THE TIMING TARGET

II.1 Mitigation

---

[88] p5, Report of the Conference of the Parties on its fifteenth session, held in Copenhagen from 7 to 19 December 2009 – Addendum Part Two: Action taken by the Conference of the Parties at its fifteenth session, FCCC/CP/2009/11/Add.1 (2010).
[89] p6, Id.
[90] Para 4, Decision 1/CP.16, The Cancun Agreements: Outcome of the work of the Ad Hoc Working Group on Long-term Cooperative Action under the Convention, FCCC/CP/2010/7/Add.1 (2010).
[91] *United Nations Millennium Declaration* GA. Res. 55/2, 8 September 2002; Millennium Development Goals available at: http://www.un.org/millenniumgoals/
[92] p27, Elzinga, D et al. "Advantage Energy: Emerging Economies, Developing Countries and the Private-Public Sector Interface" International Energy Agency Information Paper, September 2011.
[93] p33, Id.
[94] p40, Id.

The IPCC AR4 assessed that to avoid the significant likelihood of irreversible climate change that would occur with a mean global temperature increase above 2 – 2.4 degrees Celsius, a reduction of 50 – 85 % below 2000 levels of greenhouse gas (GHG) emissions is required by 2050.[95] Even at the time that the IPCC 4AR came out there was reliable data suggesting that GHG emissions were not being reduced at the required rate and that the acceleration in climate change suggested that the needed emissions reductions were most likely to be at closer to the top of that range at 80% below 2007 levels.[96]

To keep warming well below 2 degrees, and to maintain the possibility of stabilizing at the safe level of 1.5 degrees within reach, it may be necessary for global emissions to peak by 2015.[97] Projections from almost all models from 2007 suggested that the Earth was already locked into at least a 1 degree Celsius increase by 2100, based on past emissions.[98] None of the associated costs of climate change between now and 2050 are likely to be avoided because of this lock in.[99] Based on emissions trends in 2007, temperatures of between 2 and 5 degrees are likely to be reached by 2060.[100] At the least, the available projections of necessary reductions suggest that a peak of emissions will have to take place between 2015 and 2018, depending on the extent of cuts later in the lead up to 2050.[101] The harsher the cuts in the lead up to 2050, the less the need for an earlier peaking date. The lower the planned cuts, the earlier the required peaking date will be. It is not clear whether there is a separate peaking date for developing countries, but any such division would imply an even earlier peaking date for developed countries. Given that much of the growth in emissions is expected to come from developing countries, it makes sense to treat the peaking date as applying to them as well, leaving out the political differentiation between Annex 1 and non-Annex 1

---

[95] See p67, IPCC, *Climate Change 2007: Synthesis Report. Contribution of Working Groups I, II and III to the Fourth Assessment Report of the Intergovernmental Panel on Climate Change* [Core Writing Team, Pachauri, R.K and Reisinger, A. (eds.)] (Geneva: IPCC, 2007). The Fifth Assessment Reports Final Draft of the Summary for Policymakers of the Working Group III reports suggests a 40 – 70% reduction from a 2010, rather than a 2000 baseline. See p13, IPCC "Summary for Policymakers" in *Climate Change 2014, Mitigation of Climate Change. Contribution of Working Group III to the Fifth Assessment Report of the Intergovernmental Panel on Climate Change* [Edenhofer, O., R. Pichs-Madruga, Y. Sokona, E. Farahani, S. Kadner, K. Seyboth, A. Adler, I. Baum, S. Brunner, P. Eickemeier, B. Kriemann, J. Savolainen, S. Schlömer, C. von Stechow, T. Zwickel and J.C. Minx (eds.).] (Cambridge University Press, Cambridge, United Kingdom and New York, NY, USA, 2014)
[96] See p61, IEA, *Energy Technology Perspectives 2010: Scenarios and Strategies to 2050*, (Paris: IEA/OECD, 2010)
[97] See p67, IPCC, *Climate Change 2007: Synthesis Report. Contribution of Working Groups I, II and III to the Fourth Assessment Report of the Intergovernmental Panel on Climate Change* [Core Writing Team, Pachauri, R.K and Reisinger, A. (eds.)] (Geneva: IPCC, 2007). See also p15, Baer, et al. *The Right to Development in a Climate Constrained World* (Heinrich Böll Foundation, 2007).
[98] p12, Stern, N. et al. *The Economics of Climate Change: The Stern Review* (Cambridge: Cambridge University Press, 2007).
[99] p156, Id.
[100] p12, Id.
[101] p67, IPCC, *Climate Change 2007: Synthesis Report*

countries, when determining the technology need. This implies immediate action to reduce emissions in these countries[102], to meet 2020 targets and this will require making sure implementation of best available technologies and measures in the technologies identified below in the next section.

II.2 Adaptation

The challenge of adaptation is also quite clear, from sea-level rise to changes in the hydrological cycle leading to increased dryness is some areas, and increased wetness in others. There is also a significant chance of shifts in geographical bands in which specific diseases and disease vectors proliferate.[103] The AR4 notes several areas of impact relating to climate change that will require some form of adaptive response if warming is not kept below 2 degrees above pre-industrial levels.[104]

- Ecosystems[105]
    - A likely 20-30% of plant and animal species at increased risk of extinction.
    - For higher temperature increases the majority of plant and animal species are likely to face permanent geographical, and climate variability shifts in the conditions necessary for survival.
    - Underlying and accompanying these will be increased variability and extremes of precipitation, (drought and floods)[106], pests, wildfires, and ocean acidification.
    - Extremes of precipitation variability are likely to result in droughts in lower to mid-latitudes (sub-Saharan Africa), and floods in higher latitudes.[107]

---

[102] See p124, Fekete, H. et al "Emerging economies – potentials, pledges and fair shares of greenhouse gas reduction" ENVIRONMENTAL RESEARCH OF THE GERMAN FEDERAL MINISTRY OF THE ENVIRONMENT, NATURE CONSERVATION AND NUCLEAR SAFETY Project-no. (FKZ) 3711 41 120, (Umweltbundesamt, Bonn, April 2013).
[103] See p48, IPCC
[104] The impacts here are only those that can be expected within the small ranges above 2 degrees, with an emphasis on those that are likely to take place at the locked 1 degree increase by 2050. Where relevant, impacts projected for temperature increases significantly above that are also included. The aim is to give a sense of the impacts likely to take effect in the period leading to a 2 degree gain by 2100. Above the 2 degree temperature range, impacts become even more extreme.
[105] p48, IPCC, *Climate Change 2007: Synthesis Report. Contribution of Working Groups I, II and III to the Fourth Assessment Report of the Intergovernmental Panel on Climate Change* [Core Writing Team, Pachauri, R.K and Reisinger, A. (eds.)]. (Geneva: IPCC, 2007).
[106] p176, Kundzewicz, Z.W. et al. "Freshwater resources and their Management" in M.L. Parry et al. (Eds.) *Climate Change 2007: Impacts, Adaptation and Vulnerability. Contribution of Working Group II to the Fourth Assessment Report of the Intergovernmental Panel on Climate Change*, (Cambridge: Cambridge University Press, 2007). Available at http://www.ipcc.ch/ipccreports/ar4-wg2.htm (last visited August 15, 2014).
[107] p187, Id.

- o Water quality is likely to suffer, leading to stresses on capture, treatment and distribution infrastructure. [108] This is particularly concerning as much of the present infrastructure in both developed and developing countries has been built on the assumption of stable hydrological conditions and does not take into account the increasing variability and likely increasing or decreasing trends in volumes, depending on the region.[109] Even at temperature increases as low as 1 degree Celsius, water availability will be reduced (affecting almost 50 million people) for some populations such as those that rely on melt-water from Andean glaciers which will have largely disappeared.[110]
- Food[111]
  - o At lower latitudes, food productivity is projected to decline even at temperature increases as low as 1 degree, while demand is set to soar.[112] Above 2 degrees, significant and sharp declines of between 5-10% in yields are likely, especially in sub-Saharan Africa.[113] This is important as this covers the land mass of the majority of developing countries. At higher latitudes, there may be some expected increases in productivity for increases between 1 – 3 degrees, with projected declines for high temperatures.[114] Over 70% of the population in developing countries lives in areas dependent on agriculture for livelihoods.[115] This suggests an increase in the gap between developed and developing countries with developing countries becoming increasingly less able to feed themselves while developed countries increase their capacity, leading to a net increase in imports by developing countries.[116]
  - o A shift in crop types, plant and harvest dates is also likely, requiring new methods and shifts to new crops to adjust the new conditions.[117]

---

[108] p196, Id.
[109] p196, Id.
[110] p57, Stern, N. et al. *The Economics of Climate Change: The Stern Review* (Cambridge: Cambridge University Press, 2007)
[111] p48, IPCC,
[112] See p4, UNEP, *Towards a Green Economy: Pathways to Sustainable Development and Poverty Eradication*, (Nairobi: UNEP, 2011).
[113] p57, Stern, N. et al. *The Economics of Climate Change: The Stern Review* (Cambridge: Cambridge University Press, 2007). See also, p127, UNEP, *Towards a Green Economy*
[114] p285, Easterling, W.E. *et al.*, "Food, fibre and forest products" in M.L. Parry et al. (Eds.) *Climate Change 2007: Impacts, Adaptation and Vulnerability. Contribution of Working Group II to the Fourth Assessment Report of the Intergovernmental Panel on Climate Change*, (Cambridge: Cambridge University Press, 2007). Available at http://www.ipcc.ch/ipccreports/ar4-wg2.htm (last visited August 15, 2014).
[115] p276, Id.
[116] p297, Id.
[117] p190, Kundzewicz, Z.W. et al. "Freshwater resources and their Management" in M.L. Parry et al. (Eds.) *Climate Change 2007: Impacts, Adaptation and Vulnerability. Contribution of Working Group II to the*

- These impacts will occur even as, due to projected population growth and shifts in demand type, most models suggest that an 80% growth (compared to 1999-2001) in crop production will be needed by 2050. The same models project a need for 55% growth by 2020.[118] These imply a 19% increase in rain fed crop-land and a 30% increase in irrigated crop-land over those same periods.[119]
  - There is likely to be a shift in disease and pest bands for crops and livestock, increasing potential losses in areas that have little or no infrastructure to deal with such outbreaks.[120]
  - By 2020 in mid to low latitudes, largely in developing countries, and especially in sub-Saharan Africa, we are likely to see increases in livestock mortality, decreases in maize productivity, and more crop failures more generally.[121]
- Coasts[122]
  - A combination of coastal erosion and projected sea level rise is likely to put significant pressure on coastal human populations.
  - Many populations in low-lying deltas in Africa and Asia and small island states are projected to be subject to increased and more intensive flooding.
  - Water quality may decline due to increased salinity of coastal sources.
- Human health[123]
  - Health outcomes are due to be affected by increases in:
    - extreme weather events;
    - diarrheal diseases from unsafe water (both due to increase in precipitation in some areas and drought in others);[124] The Stern report projects, at 1 degree increases, 300 000 people annually affected by diarrheal diseases, malnutrition and malaria.[125]
  - Shifts in the geographical distribution of several diseases will stress health systems and expose new populations to diseases to which

---

Fourth Assessment Report of the Intergovernmental Panel on Climate Change, (Cambridge: Cambridge University Press, 2007).
[118] p280, Easterling, W.E. *et al.*, "Food, fibre and forest products"
[119] Id.
[120] p283, Id.
[121] Table 5.8, Id.
[122] p48, IPCC, *Climate Change 2007: Synthesis Report. Contribution of Working Groups I, II and III to the Fourth Assessment Report of the Intergovernmental Panel on Climate Change* [Core Writing Team, Pachauri, R.K and Reisinger, A. (eds.)]. (Geneva: IPCC, 2007).
[123] Id.
[124] p395, Confalonieri, U. et al., "Human Health", in M.L. Parry et al. (Eds.) *Climate Change 2007: Impacts, Adaptation and Vulnerability. Contribution of Working Group II to the Fourth Assessment Report of the Intergovernmental Panel on Climate Change*, (Cambridge: Cambridge University Press, 2007).
[125] p57, Stern, N. et al. *The Economics of Climate Change: The Stern Review* (Cambridge: Cambridge University Press, 2007)

immunities or resistances have not been developed. This includes malaria, dengue fever, tick-borne encephalitis, Lyme disease, meningococcal meningitis.[126] The Stern report projects that at 2 degree increases, up to 60 million more people will be exposed to malaria in Africa.[127]

o Climate change related health outcomes are exacerbated by existing lack of health infrastructure and resources.[128]

What does this imply about the timing of adaptation actions? The first thing to note is the lock-in effect of one degree warming by 2100 based on past emissions. These will have to be adapted to and the slower the reduction in emissions the quicker the one degree threshold will be reached. The faster and more extensive GHG mitigation action takes place, the lower the likely cost of action to address adaptation will be.[129] Of course, the lower and slower the mitigation, the more adaptation that will be needed.[130] However, due to the delay inherent in mitigating GHGs, temperatures are still likely to increase well into the middle of the 21st century even if all appropriate mitigation action is taken. The impacts that are already taking place and are projected to take place in the period to 2050 will still need to be adapted to.[131] This entails increasing adaptive capacity in the near term by providing a means of sustainable development to a minimum level of per capita GDP to cope with existing climate variability and development challenges and then a focus on specific systems and tools to address specific climate impacts relevant to a region for the period after that. The IPCC analysis of timing of impacts and mitigation peaking dates suggests that much of the initial work for addressing vulnerability and resilience, even under the most optimistic scenarios will have to be carried out almost immediately in order to be prepared to respond to impacts caused by the inevitable increase of temperatures between 1 and 2 degrees that will occur after 2050.[132]

---

[126] p400, Confalonieri, U. et al., "Human Health", in M.L. Parry et al. (Eds.) *Climate Change 2007: Impacts, Adaptation and Vulnerability. Contribution of Working Group II to the Fourth Assessment Report of the Intergovernmental Panel on Climate Change*, (Cambridge: Cambridge University Press, 2007).
[127] p57, Stern, N. et al. *The Economics of Climate Change: The Stern Review* (Cambridge: Cambridge University Press, 2007).
[128] p398, Confalonieri, U. et al., "Human Health" in M.L. Parry et al. (Eds.) *Climate Change 2007: Impacts, Adaptation and Vulnerability. Contribution of Working Group II to the Fourth Assessment Report of the Intergovernmental Panel on Climate Change*, (Cambridge: Cambridge University Press, 2007).
[129] p61, IPCC, *Climate Change 2007: Synthesis Report. Contribution of Working Groups I, II and III to the Fourth Assessment Report of the Intergovernmental Panel on Climate Change* [Core Writing Team, Pachauri, R.K and Reisinger, A. (eds.)]. (Geneva: IPCC, 2007).
[130] p66, IPCC, Id.
[131] p284, Stern, N. et al. *The Economics of Climate Change: The Stern Review* (Cambridge: Cambridge University Press, 2007).
[132] p67, IPCC, *Climate Change 2007*

There is also a complex relationship between the impacts of climate change and development, in that more severe and frequent weather events can negatively affect the very economic growth and development that would make countries less susceptible to such climate shocks. The Stern Report notes that natural disasters are a higher proportion of GDP losses in developing countries than in developed,[133] and have a more severe impact on future GDP growth in those countries. There is an opportunity cost when money that could have been spent (by both government and private sector) on investment in productive capacity and infrastructure, is instead spent on recovery efforts. It may even need to be set aside for future disasters, locking away even more funds. The speed at which the frequency of such events will increase is therefore a key determinant of how much and how quickly it is necessary to act to get as much GDP growth in place as possible in the near term. The IPCC[134] and the AR4 suggests that some impacts of climate are already being felt and that by 2025 developing countries will begin to feel more severe impacts. Several of these impacts are locked in as a function of previous GHG emissions. This suggests that much of the GDP growth necessary to reduce vulnerability and ensure adaptive capacity needs to take place in the period leading to 2020 at the latest.

III. THE SCOPE OF TECHNOLOGIES

III.1 Mitigation

There remains some debate about whether the technology mix needed to address the scale of the climate challenge can be met with already existing, deployed and demonstration-ready technologies or whether new breakthrough technologies will be required. This is a key issue as it will determine the extent to which the balance of resources is directed toward research and development versus demonstration, deployment and diffusion. The IPCC Third Assessment Report (2001) argued that existing and demonstration-ready technology would be sufficient, however, and the Fourth Assessment report confirmed that conclusion with high confidence, from an overview of the range of scenarios for stabilization.[135] The Stern report suggested that it was possible to meet the climate change challenge using existing technologies [136],

---

[133] p100, Stern, N. et al. *The Economics of Climate Change*
[134] IPCC, *Managing the Risks of Extreme Events and Disasters to Advance Climate Change Adaptation. A Special Report of Working Groups I and II of the Intergovernmental Panel on Climate Change* [Field, C.B., V. Barros, T.F. Stocker, D. Qin, D.J. Dokken, K.L. Ebi, M.D. Mastrandrea, K.J. Mach, G.-K. Plattner, S.K. Allen, M. Tignor, and P.M. Midgley (eds.)]. (Cambridge University Press, Cambridge, UK and New York, NY, USA, 2012)
[135] p65, IPCC, *Climate Change 2007: Synthesis Report. Contribution of Working Groups I, II and III to the Fourth Assessment Report of the Intergovernmental Panel on Climate Change* [Core Writing Team, Pachauri, R.K and Reisinger, A. (eds.)]. (Geneva: IPCC, 2007).
[136] p193, Stern, N. et al. *The Economics of Climate Change: The Stern Review* (Cambridge: Cambridge University Press, 2007)

although the report does state that achieving stabilization at 450 ppm, which is consistent with a 1.5 – 2 degree Celsius goal, is not likely to be achievable with current and foreseeable technologies.[137] The report foresaw that this would require a peak in 2010, which has clearly not been met. At the time the report argued that such a scenario would require[138]:

- Complete decarbonization of the transport sector;
- Increased and more effective implementation of carbon capture and sequestration;
- A total halt to deforestation.[139]

Pacala and Sokolow have argued with more confidence that, generally speaking, existing technologies would be sufficient.[140] Arguing the contrary, Hoffert et al. suggested in 2002 that existing technologies would be insufficient and that new breakthroughs would be required.[141] As the assessments suggest that faster and greater reduction will be needed to meet the challenge of reducing GHG emissions by 80% by 2050, the arguments of those suggesting that new breakthroughs will be necessary begin to seem increasingly persuasive. Taking into account that the necessary reductions suggest that a peak of emissions will have to take place between 2015 and 2018[142] the rapid deployment of existing technologies will be a prerequisite for longer term action.[143] In the longer term, technological breakthroughs may be required. The next sections outline the technologies that may be implicated and try to give a sense of their existing development and deployment, where data is available.

The IEA Energy Technology Perspectives 2010 and 2012 ('ETP 2010' and 'ETP 2012') provide some more concrete sense of what may be required in terms of technology related to energy and to mitigation. While they do not cover technology for adaptation, and exclude significant sectors such as agriculture, they nevertheless capture and elaborate the necessary scope of action for energy-related emissions, which comprise over 84% of global GHG emissions. The ETPs construct a baseline from existing emissions reductions extrapolated to 2050 and then outline scenarios for a

---

[137] p201, Id.
[138] p201, Id.
[139] p193, Id.
[140] Pacala, S and, R Socolow, "Stabilization Wedges: Solving the Climate Problem for the Next Fifty Years with Current Technologies". 305 Science 968, (2004). See also p339, De Coninck, H et al. "International technology-oriented agreements to address climate change" 36 Energy Policy 335 (2008)
[141] Hoffert, M I et al., "Advanced Technology Paths to Global Climate Stability: Energy for a Greenhouse Planet", 298 Science 981 (2002). See also p1, Egenhofer, C et al. "Low-Carbon Technologies in the Post-Bali Period: Accelerating their Development and Deployment" European Climate Platform, report No. 4, December 2007.
[142] p67, IPCC, *Climate Change 2007: Synthesis Report. Contribution of Working Groups I, II and III to the Fourth Assessment Report of the Intergovernmental Panel on Climate Change* [Core Writing Team, Pachauri, R.K and Reisinger, A. (eds.)]. (Geneva: IPCC, 2007).
[143] See p21, Baer, P et al. *The Right to Development in a Climate Constrained World* (Heinrich Böll Foundation, 2007).

technology research, and development pathway to the necessary 80% reductions by 2050. While the scenarios they construct (the Blue Map Scenario and the 2 degrees scenario(2DS)) rely significantly on controversial technologies such as Carbon Capture and Storage, as well as nuclear energy, they provide a useful, if somewhat conservative, perspective in helping to understand the scope of technologies to be developed and deployed. The scenarios are built on the use of existing or near commercial technology available within the scenario period to 2050.[144]

The Blue Map baseline scenario presumes that no new climate or technology policies are put in place in the period leading to 2050. Thus, under the Baseline scenario, energy related emissions are double those of 2007, and almost all of that increase comes from outside the OECD.[145] The growth is driven in large part by the growth in demand for oil and gas from developing countries.[146] While long terms projections can be uncertain, the ETP 2010 baseline scenario lies within the range of scenario outcomes for 2050 outlined by the IPCC AR4, although it remains somewhat on the conservative side.

The Blue Map scenario is based on a mean temperature increase of 2-2.4 degrees aiming for a 50% reduction in energy related GHG emissions by 2050 compared to 2005 levels.[147] Under the Blue Map scenario energy-related emissions must peak by 2020 and then decline steadily to 2050, if emissions reductions are to be achieved with reasonable costs.[148] This is in line with a 2-3 degrees Celsius global pathway, but only if other non-energy sectors, such as agriculture, also undertake similar if not greater reductions. If not, the burden of reductions will fall more severely on energy-related reductions. The Baseline and Blue Map scenarios share the same assumptions and references related to projections for economic growth and population growth. Under the Blue Map scenario, OECD countries must reduce their energy related emissions by 30% compared to the Baseline, meaning a 77% reduction compared to 2005 levels. Non-OECD countries must reduce their emissions by 24% compared to 2005 levels. In 2050, China will have a 30% reduction compared to 2007 levels, India a 10% increase, as compared to 81% reduction for the US and 74% reduction for OECD Europe.[149]

Generally, the Blue Map scenario is optimistic about technology research, development, demonstration, deployment and diffusion. It is especially optimistic about the rapid commercialization, uptake and diffusion of technology.[150] However, such

---

[144] p634, IEA, *Energy Technology Perspectives 2012: Pathways to a Clean Energy System* (Paris: IEA/OECD 2012).
[145] p72, IEA, *Energy Technology Perspectives 2010: Scenarios and Strategies to 2050*, (Paris: IEA/OECD, 2010).
[146] p73, Id.
[147] p68, Id.
[148] Id.
[149] p85, Id.
[150] p70, Id.

optimistic assumptions are necessary to achieving the emissions reductions required to reach 50% below 2005 levels by 2050 on which the Blue Map scenario is based.

One clear outcome of the ETP scenarios is that action will be required across a broad range of technology sectors, requiring the rapid diffusion and adoption of existing technologies, rapid commercialization of demonstrated technologies, rapid and broad demonstration of technologies in prototype or feasibility stage and significant creation of new technologies through increased research and development. Looking at the sectors implicated, the Blue Map scenario outlines the percentage contribution of technology shifts and changes in the following sectors[151]:

- End-use fuel efficiency – 24%
- End-use electricity efficiency – 14%
- Carbon Capture and Storage (CCS) in Power generation – 10%
- Carbon Capture and Storage (CCS) in Industrial Activity – 9%
- Renewables – 17%
- Nuclear – 6%
- Power generation efficiency and fuel switching – 5%
- Electric vehicles – 7%
- Fuel cell vehicles – 4%
- Other end use fuel switching – 3%

The bulk of the contributions in the Blue Map scenario come from:
- efficiency;[152]
- use of renewables; and
- the application of CCS to power generation and industrial activity.

Emphasizing the sheer scope of technologies involved, the ETP 2010 breaks the sectors further down. Including more recent data from ETP 2012, we can see that deployment has not kept up with the optimistic assumptions under the Blue Map scenarios. For example[153]:

- Electricity generation (almost entirely de-carbonised by 2050)
    - CCS – 31% contribution
        - In 2010, no projects had been fully demonstrated and applied to power generation.[154] Insufficient investment in demonstration projects; for power generation, zero in operation in 2010, compared to the 38 projected by ETP

---

[151] p76, IEA, *Energy Technology Perspectives 2010: Scenarios and Strategies to 2050*, (Paris: IEA/OECD, 2010).
[152] The Stern report also emphasizes the key role of energy efficiency. See p218, Stern, N. et al. *The Economics of Climate Change: The Stern Review* (Cambridge: Cambridge University Press, 2007)
[153] p108, IEA, *Energy Technology Perspectives 2010*
[154] p120, Id.

2010;[155] 4 as compared to 52 projected by ETP 2010 in CCS in industry;[156]

- Nuclear – 19%
    - A well developed and mature technology with low market penetration due to policy problems such as waste management and disaster risk. Existing plans to build more capacity remain well below the levels needed to meet the 2 degrees scenario.[157]
- Wind – 11%
    - A relatively mature technology with increasing market penetration. However, to meet the Blue Map scenarios, efficiencies would need to be increased as will management of connections to the grid. In developing countries, many are not yet using wind technologies, although in 2009, China was the largest wind market. Existing technology diffusion and development is on track to meet that required by the Blue Map scenario.[158]
    - Off-shore wind remains an immature technology, with low market penetration, requiring further R&D and demonstration.[159]
- Solar – Concentrated Solar Power (CSP) – 9%
    - There are three main types: troughs, towers and dishes. Trough are the most mature technology; towers are more efficient and need further development with many promising projects now defunct, and parabolic dishes , which are well-suited to decentralized power grids, need more R&D. [160] For example, in trough technologies, approaches that have been explored since 2004 include: Integrated solar combined cycle systems, combining CSP with gas turbine plants; direct steam generation in the trough itself;[161]

---

[155] p63, IEA, *Energy Technology Perspectives 2012: Pathways to a Clean Energy System* (Paris: IEA/OECD 2012).
[156] Id.
[157] p22, IEA, "Tracking Clean Energy Progress: Energy Technology Perspectives 2012 excerpt as IEA input to the Clean Energy Ministerial" IEA 2012.
[158] p26, Id.
[159] p74, IEA, *Energy Technology Perspectives 2012:* See also p212, UNEP, *Towards a Green Economy: Pathways to Sustainable Development and Poverty Eradication*, (Nairobi: UNEP, 2011).
[160] p8, Philibert, C "International Technology Collaboration and Climate Change Mitigation - Case Study 1: Concentrating Solar Power Technologies" COM/ENV/EPOC/IEA/SLT(2004)8, IEA, Paris, 2004.
[161] p11, Philibert, C "International Technology Collaboration and Climate Change Mitigation - Case Study 1: Concentrating Solar Power Technologies" COM/ENV/EPOC/IEA/SLT(2004)8, IEA, Paris, 2004.

- This is still a developing technology that needs significant investment to move from demonstration to the deployment phase. Market penetration is too low and slow; this is despite it being selected by the GEF in 2004 for its program to support rapid commercialization of near term technologies;[162] In addition further research is needed on issues such as power storage.[163] Nevertheless, because it uses largely existing materials such as glass, steel and concrete, CSP capacity is more easily installed and ramped up within existing industrial frameworks.[164]
  - Solar – Photovoltaic (PV) – 7%
    - In the 2000-10 period, PV increased by 40% per year, although from a relatively low base. This was driven by decreasing costs, especially from cheaper Chinese manufacturers. This a relatively mature technology with significant global market penetration, although policies will need to be put in place to ensure more rapid adoption, especially in regions with significant access to direct sunlight such as Africa.[165]
  - Fuel switching coal to gas – 7%
  - Integrated gasification combined cycle combustion – 4 %
    - In 2010, there were only 2 operating plants, with increasing interest in expanding in countries such as China. However, existing efficiencies remain below those necessary to achieve the Blue Map scenarios, requiring technological improvements and advances to ensure further deployment.[166]
  - Super-critical (SC) and ultra-supercritical coal (USC) – 3%
    - This technology is being increasingly used and applied but efficiencies remain below those required to meet the Blue Map scenarios. Projected advances in materials will enable greater efficiencies in the period leading up to 2030, under the Blue Map scenarios.[167] Existing diffusion of SC and USC technologies is increasing, but a significant proportion of new plant build, especially in China and India, used older,

---

[162] p7, Id.
[163] p130, IEA, *Energy Technology Perspectives 2010: Scenarios and Strategies to 2050*, (Paris: IEA/OECD, 2010).
[164] p13, Philibert
[165] p129, IEA, *Energy Technology Perspectives 2010. See also* p26, IEA, "Tracking Clean Energy Progress: Energy Technology Perspectives 2012 excerpt as IEA input to the Clean Energy Ministerial" IEA 2012.
[166] p117, IEA, *Energy Technology Perspectives 2010*
[167] p115, IEA, *Energy Technology Perspectives 2010: Scenarios and Strategies to 2050*, (Paris: IEA/OECD, 2010).

inefficient technologies.[168] Approximately 50% of coal-fired plants are being built with sub-critical technologies;[169] much of this is occurring in China, although in 2011 more new plants are being built with high efficiency technologies than non-efficient.[170] India also contributed to the increase in inefficient coal-fired plants with all plants built in 2010 using sub-critical technologies.
- Geothermal – 3%
  - In the early stages of development with significant research to be carried out before widespread deployment outside of areas such as Iceland. Present development and diffusion is falling behind that required by the Blue Map scenarios.[171]
- Hydro – 2%
  - Hydrokinetic turbines remain in the early demonstration phase;[172]
  - an otherwise mature, commercialized technology, even for micro-hydro applications.
- Biomass and Waste – 2%
  - Development and diffusion, broadly on track to meet the Blue Map scenarios.[173]
- Gas efficiency – 2%
- Biofuels
  - The agricultural-based fuels remain quite mature and are part of global value chains and trade;
  - Second generation biofuels remain at the research, development and demonstration phase, except for cellulose and lignin-based technologies which face a commercialization challenge,[174]

- Electricity grids and networks
  - Ensuring that all electricity generation can access the grid and contribute to emissions reductions is crucial. The Blue Map scenarios rely on a smarter grid infrastructure managed by software, maintained

---

[168] p16, IEA, "Tracking Clean Energy Progress: Energy Technology Perspectives 2012 excerpt as IEA input to the Clean Energy Ministerial" IEA 2012.
[169] p63, IEA, *Energy Technology Perspectives 2012: Pathways to a Clean Energy System* (Paris: IEA/OECD 2012).
[170] Id.
[171] p27, IEA, "Tracking Clean Energy Progress: Energy Technology Perspectives 2012 excerpt as IEA input to the Clean Energy Ministerial" IEA 2012.
[172] See p212, UNEP, *Towards a Green Economy: Pathways to Sustainable Development and Poverty Eradication*, (Nairobi: UNEP, 2011).
[173] p27, IEA, "Tracking Clean Energy Progress"
[174] See p212, UNEP, *Towards a Green Economy: Pathways to Sustainable Development and Poverty Eradication*, (Nairobi: UNEP, 2011).

and developed by skilled expertise to ensure the electricity generation outcomes. This is a newly developing technological field that has to deal with both legacy infrastructure as well as designing new systems, heavily reliant on computer software management systems. Much of the work leading up to 2020 will be on research, development and demonstration.[175]
- There is also a role for micro-grids, connected to community solar installations.

This complexity of sectors and technology areas that are covered by energy production is also reflected in the ETP 2012, and other IEA analyses of industry, buildings (heating, cooling, and appliances) and transport. These are listed below, without their planned contributions to GHG emissions reductions, but as an illustration of the scope of technologies that may need to be addressed to achieve the IEA scenarios.

1. Industry

Industrial energy use is largely going to play a role in reductions through increased fuel switching (fossil fuel burning to electricity), energy efficiency and application of CCS to capture incidental emissions. Progress on energy efficiency is still too slow; the diffusion of best available technologies (BATs) has proven difficult due to failure to apply energy efficiency and management standards, as well as BATs for pumps, electric motors, and boilers, and processes for managing efficiency. The deployment and diffusion need covers technologies such as:

- Iron and Steel production[176]
    - Smelting reduction technologies;
    - Top gas recycling furnaces;
    - Highly reactive material additives to lower reducing agents;
    - Molten oxide electrolysis for iron production;
    - Hydrogen smelting;
    - Use of charcoal and waste plastic;
- Cement[177]
    - Substitutes for clinker additives;
    - Fuel switching for heat processes;
- Chemicals and Petrochemicals;[178]
    - New olefin production methods;
    - Improved catalytic processes;

---

[175] p153, IEA, *Energy Technology Perspectives 2010: Scenarios and Strategies to 2050*, (Paris: IEA/OECD, 2010).
[176] p403, IEA, *Energy Technology Perspectives 2012: Pathways to a Clean Energy System* (Paris: IEA/OECD 2012).
[177] p406, Id.
[178] p411, Id.

- o   Novel membrane technologies for separation processes;
- o   Bio-based polymers to create new plastics
- Paper[179]
    - o   Advanced water removal systems
- Aluminium[180]
    - o   New inert and wetted cathode technologies;
    - o   New methods for chemical reduction of kaolin;

2. Buildings

Heating and cooling – much of the technology described below is already deployed and commercialized but at an insufficient level.[181] The areas that need greater market penetration include:

- Modern heat access[182]
    - o   Liquefied petroleum gas (LPG)
    - o   Biogas
    - o   Natural gas appliances
    - o   Improved cook stoves (especially for biomass)
- Renewables for heat[183]
    - o   Solar thermal collectors, water heaters and distributors
        - ▪ China is the largest market for such heaters, but with only 3% share of the water heating market.[184]
    - o   Advanced biomass cook stoves
    - o   Biogas digesters, and distribution pipes
    - o   Geothermal heat
- Thermal heat efficiency
    - o   Combined heat and power
    - o   Advanced building envelope seals and insulation
    - o   Coke oven gas recovery
    - o   Power generation from blast furnace gas

3. Appliances

Appliances are a significant portion of global electricity end-use. A significant portion of end-use is in electric motors (found in most large appliances, compressors, fans, mechanical systems) at about 40% of all global electricity end-use.[185] Increased efficiency and use of best available technologies have a large GHG emissions reduction

---

[179] p415, Id.
[180] p420, Id.
[181] p23, David E, *et al.* "Advantage Energy: Emerging Economies, Developing Countries and the Private-Public Sector Interface" International Energy Agency Information Paper, September 2011.
[182] p18, Id.
[183] p20, Id.
[184] p21, Id.
[185] p34, Id. See also: p43, IEA, *Energy Technology Perspectives 2012: Pathways to a Clean Energy System* (Paris: IEA/OECD 2012).

potential.[186] Other end-use sectors may also provide significant savings. The technologies implicated include:
- pumps, including for agricultural use;
- compressors, heat exchangers, insulation (foam and vacuum), heat bridge designs and fans for refrigeration and air conditioners;
- Dishwashers, clothes washers, and clothes dryers;
- lighting, including solar powered LED lighting operating off-grid;
- software and hardware, especially for managing active and standby power in portable appliances, as well as home televisions, audio, and other information, communication and entertainment devices for both residential and office use.

4. Transport

Transport is likely to be the hardest area to achieve emissions reductions because of the expense of the alternative technologies.[187] It represents over 27% of world-wide emissions.[188] That share is expected to increase as personal transport use increases in emerging economies and middle-income countries. The technologies that will need to be addressed include:
- Hydrogen Fuel cells;
- Plug-in Hybrids and electric vehicles (PHEVs);
  - A key barrier to distribution of these technologies is the price of these vehicles, slowing their adoption in developing countries and emerging economies.[189] The Blue Map scenarios project the majority of sales to 2030 to be in OECD and China.[190]
- Batteries
  - The efficiency and cost of these pose a significant bottleneck for the deployment of PHEVs.[191]
- Biodiesel and biofuels;
  - The IEA projects that advanced biofuels are unlikely to be widespread before 2020, and are unlikely to contribute to peaking in the near term, although they will play an important role in the longer term substitution of fossil fuels for transport.[192]

---

[186] See p343, UNEP, *Towards a Green Economy: Pathways to Sustainable Development and Poverty Eradication* (Nairobi: UNEP, 2011).
[187] Annex 7c, Stern, N. et al. *The Economics of Climate Change: The Stern Review* (Cambridge: Cambridge University Press, 2007)
[188] p40, Elzinga D, et al. "Advantage Energy: Emerging Economies, Developing Countries and the Private-Public Sector Interface" International Energy Agency Information Paper, September 2011.
[189] p45, Id.
[190] p46, Id.
[191] p95, IEA, *Energy Technology Perspectives 2012: Pathways to a Clean Energy System* (Paris: IEA/OECD 2012).
[192] p46, Elzinga D, et al.

- o Flex-fuel vehicles are crucial to a transition to non-fossil fuel consumption.[193]
- Fuel efficiency of petrol or diesel vehicles;
  - o The Blue Map Scenario requires at least a 50% increase in fuel efficiency by 2030, implying a 3%/year increase on average per country. The IEA argues that this is achievable with existing technologies but will require strong policy action.[194] This presumes no significant action to reduce the price of such vehicles. In terms of deployment, this technology is improving but at too slow a rate (1.7% as compared to 2.7%) projected to achieve the 2 degree scenario in the ETP 2012;

The sheer scale of technologies involved is significant, across multiple sectors, even when limited to the energy sector and not including agriculture and land use change, and not even including the full range of areas that are covered by adaptation needs.

The ETPs provide little or no information on the existing relative regional distribution of technologies and any regional variations regarding proprietary technologies. Nevertheless, in discussing the scope of action and technologies needed for the 2 degree scenarios, the ETP 2012 and 2010 agree on the same principle: that no single technology or small subset of technologies will be sufficient. Policy will have to be brought to bear on all the identified technology sectors to achieve the goals.[195] Given the longer term challenge, the ETP 2012 is clear that existing technologies will be insufficient to meet its targets and that R&D will be required to reach an 80% reduction target by 2050. This will require immediate and large scale investments in R&D.[196] The ETP 2012 scenario places an emphasis on providing funding and incentives for the generation of new technologies as necessary to achieve its goals, suggesting that dynamic efficiency will have to be a crucial part of any policy response in intellectual property regulation. The ETP 2012 also places much more emphasis on decentralized power generation managed by sophisticated software and hardware interactions.[197] This increases significantly the projected role that industries providing controllers, environmentally robust switching and control systems, as well as software control and management systems will have.

---

[193] See p404, UNEP, *Towards a Green Economy: Pathways to Sustainable Development and Poverty Eradication*, (Nairobi: UNEP, 2011).
[194] p44, Elzinga D, et al.
[195] p39, IEA, *Energy Technology Perspectives 2012: Pathways to a Clean Energy System* (Paris: IEA/OECD 2012).
[196] p56, Id.
[197] p40, id.

Like the ETP, the Stern report argues that the technology mix will require a broad portfolio, and proposes, much the same set of technologies as the IEA:

- Decarbonization of the electricity sector by 2050, including the use of the following technologies[198]:
    - Wind energy
    - Wave and tidal energy (not included in ETPs);
    - Solar PV energy;
    - CCS for electricity generation
    - Nuclear power;
    - Hydroelectric power;
    - Bioenergy in other sectors besides transport;
    - Micro-generation (Micro-hydro, micro-solar) (not included in ETPs);
    - Fuel cells for transport;
    - Fuel cells for other electric power uses;
    - Hybrid and electric vehicles.

Since no one technology is capable of providing the reductions needed the Stern report points out that the development, deployment, diffusion of a broad portfolio of technologies is required.[199]

A valuable addition that the Stern report made is the addition of agriculture to the mitigation picture, noting that the contribution of agriculture to emissions was 14% in 2000 and 38% of that came from fertilizers.[200] Livestock production, which is projected to increase significantly as countries such as China and India consume more meat, is the second largest contributor in agriculture due to methane production during digestion.[201] Technologies needed to address agricultural emissions then include:

- Less GHG intensive fertilizers;
- Plant varieties that are less reliant on GHG intensive fertilizers, either because they produce higher yields or are more efficient at soil nutrient uptake;
- Animal variants and breeds less likely to produce methane during digestion;
- Better management of animal waste, including recycling into biogas and other biomass for energy generation;
- Animal feed less likely to produce methane;

III.2 Adaptation

---

[198] p221, Stern, N. et al. *The Economics of Climate Change: The Stern Review* (Cambridge: Cambridge University Press, 2007).
[199] p211, Id.
[200] Annex 7g, Id.
[201] Id.

Most of the literature relating to technology transfer to address climate change focuses primarily on mitigation. In part this is due to the salience of the issue with respect to the major players (emerging economies and developed countries) but also in part because mitigation seems much more susceptible to traditional boundary setting. In many cases, technology transfer for adaptation is either viewed as inapplicable because of how broad the adaptation challenge is, or there is an intuition that technology does not really play a part in adaptation responses.[202] The AR4 projections are based on the assumptions related to increases in climate change and no changes in adaptive capacity. In that sense they present baseline scenarios or business as usual trajectories. Changes in adaptive capacity may mitigate some of the impacts, and may also make it possible to more usefully adapt to others that are unavoidable even under a 2 degree scenario.[203] In the near term, dealing with adaptation is an economy wide challenge involving all the policy levers required for poverty reduction and sustainable development but especially focused on increasing the adaptive capacity of the most vulnerable. As the AR4 notes, societies have a long history of adapting to ongoing changes in climate and socio-political environments[204], but additional effort will be needed to enable adaptation for climate change. The AR4 notes that adaptation capacity is unevenly distributed, both across and within societies and that this is co-extensive with uneven distributions of capacity to produce food, provide for health, and to create economic surpluses that can be reinvested in hard and soft infrastructure.[205] The majority of people in developing countries live in climate vulnerable environments and ecosystems.[206] Technology and innovative capacity are clearly co-extensive with adaptive capacity.[207] Increased technological capacity can decrease vulnerability by enabling deployment and use of relevant technologies and enable the development of new technologies to address the specific challenges of adapting to climate change impacts.[208]

---

[202] See e.g. Staley, B Childs et al."Tick Tech Tick Tech: Coming to Agreement on Technology in the Countdown to Copenhagen". WRI Working Paper, World Resources Institute, Washington DC, June 2009. Available at http://www.wri.org/climate/cop-15 (last visited August 15, 2014)
[203] p65, IPCC, *Climate Change 2007: Synthesis Report. Contribution of Working Groups I, II and III to the Fourth Assessment Report of the Intergovernmental Panel on Climate Change* [Core Writing Team, Pachauri, R.K and Reisinger, A. (eds.)]. (Geneva: IPCC, 2007). *See also* p284, Stern, N. et al. *The Economics of Climate Change: The Stern Review* (Cambridge: Cambridge University Press, 2007).
[204] p56, Id.
[205] Id.
[206] See p19, See UNEP, *Towards a Green Economy: Pathways to Sustainable Development and Poverty Eradication*, (Nairobi: UNEP, 2011). Also Agrawala, S (ed.) *Bridge Over Troubled Waters: Linking Climate Change and Development* OECD Environment Directorate, 2005; McGranahan, G. et al. "The rising tide: assessing the risks of climate change and human settlements in low elevation coastal zones." 19(1) Environment and Urbanization 17 (2007).
[207] p728, Adger, W.N. et al, "Assessment of adaptation practices, options, constraints and capacity" in in M.L. Parry et al. (Eds.) *Climate Change 2007: Impacts, Adaptation and Vulnerability. Contribution of Working Group II to the Fourth Assessment Report of the Intergovernmental Panel on Climate Change*, (Cambridge: Cambridge University Press, 2007).
[208] Agrawala, S and S Fankhauser, *Economic Aspects of Adaptation to Climate Change: Costs, Benefits and Policy Instruments* (Paris: OECD, 2008).

There are several issues that can be a barrier to effective adaptation. To the extent that access to resources, financial and otherwise, is a key determinant of whether a specific adaptation response is adopted [209], price-determining mechanisms like intellectual property may play a significant role as a barrier. This largely applies in the context of existing and available products which are protected by intellectual property and for which the producer charges a price significantly above marginal cost of production so as to recoup investments over the lifetime of the IP right. Public policy interventions at the national level may therefore be required to address the price issue, where such prices create a barrier to adoption of necessary and effective technologies.

Climate impacts can clearly impede the development path for developing countries. Their vulnerability and lack of adaptive capacity make this clear as is their reliance on unsustainable energy production, distribution and consumption technologies. Under a business as usual trajectory, likely development impacts include:

- Falling farm incomes;[210]
- Increasing urbanization and energy demand that is unlikely to be met;
- Decreased health and capacity[211] leading to lower productivity.[212]
- Opportunity costs[213] as much needed investment in growth is diverted to dealing with emergencies and short term structural problems caused by climate change.
- External migration[214], leading to loss of possibly the most capable and productive portions of society, especially in agricultural production from loss of land and capital built up by individuals.
- Internal migration leading to increased societal conflict and, in already precarious societies, outbreaks of violence as groups compete for scarce resources.

These possible impacts outline the urgency of action on climate change, especially in ensuring the technologies necessary to mitigate emissions and adapt to climate change as part of broader development policy.

---

[209] p734, Adger, W.N. et al, citing surveys of farmers pointing to price as a barrier to adoption of new cultivars, irrigation methods and crop management techniques. See also Agrawala, S and S Fankhauser, *Economic Aspects of Adaptation to Climate Change: Costs, Benefits and Policy Instruments* (Paris: OECD, 2008.)
[210] p92, Stern, N. et al. *The Economics of Climate Change: The Stern Review* (Cambridge: Cambridge University Press, 2007).
[211] Id.
[212] See p124, UNEP, *Towards a Green Economy: Pathways to Sustainable Development and Poverty Eradication*, (Nairobi: UNEP, 2011).
[213] p92, Stern, N. et al.
[214] Id.

However, one of the most important interventions that can be made in these developing countries to reduce vulnerability, while laying the groundwork for increasing adaptive capacity are ones that increase economic growth as quickly as possible in as sustainable and equitable a manner as possible.[215] The most basic and most important input into economic growth is energy, thus keeping the cost of energy production, distribution and consumption as low as possible is crucial to enable such growth in developing countries.[216] The natural path would be to allow these countries to use the cheapest and most available sources of energy to achieve these goals i.e. coal and other fossil fuels whose production and consumption is subsidized. However, that will clearly lead to more emissions, which will lead to more climate impacts and an even greater need for adaptation; a negative feedback loop. The use of renewable and sustainable energy is a fundamental element of addressing adaptation and development in developing countries.[217] It may however, entail in many least developed and lower middle income countries, off-grid and micro applications of many of these technologies.

As a focus for the areas necessary to reduce such vulnerability, the Stern report suggests that the key areas are[218]:

- Economic wealth
- Infrastructure and technology
- Information knowledge and skills
- Equity
- Social capital

Infrastructure, technology, information, knowledge and skills are precisely those areas that can be best addressed by ensuring technology transfer. Developing countries are also significantly dependent (up to 64% participation in South Asia and sub-Saharan Africa) on agriculture for economic growth and are more sensitive to climate variability.[219] A stable and sustainably growing framework for agricultural production and distribution is a necessity for reducing vulnerability and enabling

---

[215] See p12, World Bank *World Development Report 2010: Development and Climate Change* (Washington D.C.: World Bank, 2010). See also UNEP, *Towards a Green Econom*. See also p12, Stern, N. et al. See p26, Baer, et al. *The Right to Development in a Climate Constrained World* (Heinrich Böll Foundation, 2007).
[216] See p208, UNEP, *Towards a Green Economy*. Also Agrawala, S (ed.) *Bridge Over Troubled Waters: Linking Climate Change and Development* OECD Environment Directorate, 2005 and Agrawala, S and S Fankhauser *Economic Aspects of Adaptation to Climate Change: Costs, Benefits and Policy Instruments* (Paris: OECD, 2008).
[217] GNESD *Reaching the Millennium Development Goals and beyond – access to modern forms of energy as a prerequisite*. (Roskilde: Global Network on Energy for Sustainable Development,2007);
[218] p94, Stern, N. et al. *The Economics of Climate Change: The Stern Review* (Cambridge: Cambridge University Press, 2007)
[219] See p38, UNEP, *Towards a Green Economy: Pathways to Sustainable Development and Poverty Eradication*, (Nairobi: UNEP, 2011). See also p95, Stern, N. et al.

adaptive capacity in developing countries.[220] Health interventions to deal with chronic diseases (both communicable and non-communicable) in developing countries are also a necessity to reduce vulnerability and adaptive capacity.[221] This implicates general health infrastructure, and health management systems, but also the opportunity costs associated with prices of medical products, devices and services. Water also remains a significant input for a significant portion of economic activity in developing countries, for agricultural and industrial production as well as for household consumption.[222] Business as usual projections suggest that access to water in 2015 will be extremely limited with almost 650 million lacking access to potable water and over 2.5 billion lacking water for sanitation.[223] Sustainable access to water has a network effect, creating a platform on which other interventions can build and can succeed. Increasing the efficiency and the capacity of water management systems is a crucial element of the economic development framework for developing countries in ensuring adaptive capacity.[224]

In addition to these challenges there may also be insufficient legal and commercial frameworks for stable contracting, financial transactions (banking, insurance, cross-border transfers), as well as predictable environments for investment. There are basic problems of governance endemic in many developing countries, related to lack of capacity as well as corruption and insufficient regulatory oversight.[225] While many of these problems may be susceptible to policy changes in the short term, others, such as lack of governance capacity are going to have to be addressed in the longer term. This suggests that urgent near term action should focus on simple interventions that provide clear rules and signals to private sector actors to carry out their activities rather than on developing country governments to act and intervene.

These failures create barriers to the kind of financial transactions, such as licensing, that private sector actors need in order to feel confident, on both sides of a transaction. Clearly access to technology-related products, information, knowledge and skills are not a sufficient condition for the achievement of the economic growth that will reduce vulnerability and enable adaptive capacity, but it is a necessary condition without which such development cannot be achieved.

---

[220] See p38-40, UNEP, *Towards a Green Economy*
[221] See p208-209, Id.
[222] See p122, id. See also p97, Stern, N. et al.
[223] See p7, WHO *UN-Water Global Annual Assessment of Sanitation and Drinking-Water (GLAAS) 2012: Targeting Resources for Better Results.* (Geneva:WHO, 2012). Available at http://www.who.int/water_sanitation_health/glaas/en/ (last visited August 15, 2014)
[224] See p130, UNEP, *Towards a Green Economy: Pathways to Sustainable Development and Poverty Eradication*, (Nairobi: UNEP, 2011).
[225] p438, Stern, N. et al. *The Economics of Climate Change: The Stern Review* (Cambridge: Cambridge University Press, 2007).

Adaptation presents a complex challenge involving a network of existing capacity and vulnerability, with impacts and adaptations to impacts taking place within a network of co-factors such as poverty, population shifts and migration patterns, land use and land use changes.[226] This means that identifying specific technologies that are only relevant to adaptation is even harder than for mitigation. In essence, adaptation really addresses two core issues: reduction of vulnerability; and increasing capacity to adapt. The overlap with poverty reduction strategies and other core development frameworks is significant. The adaptation challenge is essentially a development challenge[227] and covers **all** sectors of technology relevant to ensuring rapid, non-fossil fuel dependent economic development. This means not only a continuation of existing best practices[228] on ensuring transfer of technology but also ramping up and introducing policies to speed up the process of development focused on technological transformation in an unprecedented manner.

The implications of the framework for adaptation, especially to ensure adaptive capacity suggest a far broader range of technologies and economy wide action in developing countries that goes beyond simply energy. In addition, the timeframes suggest actions must take place almost immediately to have an effect in the period leading to 2020 - 25. Any solutions to reduce vulnerability and address adaptive capacity for developing countries must ensure access to the best environmentally sustainable technologies for:

- energy production, distribution and consumption;
- agricultural inputs, including seeds (including flood and drought resilient varieties), low emissions fertilizers, and methods and processes;
- health infrastructure, including medicines, diagnostic and treatment tools,;
- water infrastructure for capture, treatment, distribution, and recycling.

A useful framework for creating resilience and reducing vulnerability in the climate change context was provided by UNEP in its Green Economy report.[229] The report lays out a set of pathways and scenarios for development of a green economy that focus on sustainable, non-fossil fuel economic development, within the 2020-2030 timeframe and identifies key sectors that would require transformation to enable a green economy. The green economy approach focuses on investing in efficiency, preservation, and green exploitation of natural resources (Agriculture, Fisheries, Water, Forestry) and a

---

[226] Agrawala, S (ed.) *Bridge Over Troubled Waters: Linking Climate Change and Development* OECD Environment Directorate, 2005
[227] See in support, p430, Stern, N. et al. *The Economics of Climate Change: The Stern Review* (Cambridge: Cambridge University Press, 2007). Also Agrawala, S (ed.) *Bridge Over Troubled Waters: Linking Climate Change and Development* OECD Environment Directorate, 2005.
[228] p432, Stern, N. et al. *The Economics of Climate Change: The Stern Review* (Cambridge: Cambridge University Press, 2007).
[229] UNEP, *Towards a Green Economy: Pathways to Sustainable Development and Poverty Eradication*, (Nairobi: UNEP, 2011).

fundamental investment in efficiency, alternative production processes, technological innovation and diffusion in the following key sectors: renewable energy, manufacturing, waste, buildings, transport, tourism, and cities. This implicates an extremely broad set of sectors, practices, technologies and policies but provides a strategic focus, and implementation pathways for economy wide action in the context of addressing the adaptation challenge in developing countries.

Some areas are, however, more clearly susceptible to technological interventions and the scope of these can be cabined by an understanding of the additional effects and impacts of climate change and variability outlined in the AR4. In the following areas we can already begin to see the necessity for the application of technological products, processes and know-how, for specific climate-related responses.

- Renewable Energy
    - Sustainable biomass use – efficient wood burning stoves,
    - Micro-solar, solar household systems (with solar batteries)
    - Micro-hydro
    - Micro-wind
- Water
    - To address challenges to water quality, changes to treatment infrastructure may be needed to deal with higher levels of toxicity and microbial and plant growth than systems have initially been planned for.[230]
    - Water desalination technologies, especially for coastal areas with significant tidal, estuary and island water systems.[231]
    - Smart and/or active water metering systems, managed by software to providing the ability to shift pricing based on peak demand and peak usage periods during the day and the year.
    - Water capture and storage products and processes
        - Rainwater harvesting from roofs into hardened storage tanks
        - Direct spring access and protection from contamination
        - sub-surface dams to capture underground streams and run-off
        - covered, lined and sealed hand-dug wells, to prevent wall collapse and contamination
        - tubewells and boreholes
    - Water distribution products and processes

---

[230] p196, Kundzewicz, Z.W. et al. "Freshwater resources and their Management" in M.L. Parry et al. (Eds.) *Climate Change 2007: Impacts, Adaptation and Vulnerability. Contribution of Working Group II to the Fourth Assessment Report of the Intergovernmental Panel on Climate Change*, (Cambridge: Cambridge University Press, 2007).
[231] Table 3.5, p196, Id.

- - - gravity fed schemes to distribute water from higher altitude catchment areas
    - disbursement systems such as faucet design, low flow toilets
  - Water treatment and sanitation products and processes
    - filtration processes
    - chemical treatment
    - sewerage systems
    - latrine systems
  - Efficient water use and reclamation technologies
    - Industrial recycling and re-use – iron and steel; paper; cement;
- Food
  - New varieties or adaptations and wider use of existing plant and animal varieties may be required in areas where hydrological and seasonal variations go beyond those under which existing seed and animal germplasm input strategies were developed. Needed characteristics include drought resistance, flood resistance, salt-water resistance; short harvest cycles, longer harvest cycles; ease of fertilizer use[232]; pest and plant disease resistance;[233]
  - Agricultural Information and communication technologies – including telemetry, soil monitoring – access to local weather forecasting on short and long-term cycles, satellite imagery;[234]
  - Biotechnology and animal and plant breeding will play significant roles in adaptation responses, especially where shifts in management practices and behaviour are insufficient to achieve the full scale of adaptation needed.[235] Genetic markers and alterations related to tolerance for lack of water, pest and disease resistance have already been identified demonstrated in some crops.[236]
  - Water storage and efficiency technologies specific to agricultural water use;[237]
- Human health

---

[232] See p61, UNEP, *Towards a Green Economy: Pathways to Sustainable Development and Poverty Eradication*, (Nairobi: UNEP, 2011).
[233] p294, Easterling, W.E. et al., "Food, fibre and forest products" in M.L. Parry et al. (Eds.) *Climate Change 2007: Impacts, Adaptation and Vulnerability. Contribution of Working Group II to the Fourth Assessment Report of the Intergovernmental Panel on Climate Change*, (Cambridge: Cambridge University Press, 2007).
[234] See p67, UNEP, *Towards a Green Economy*
[235] Box 5.6, p296, Easterling, W.E. et al.
[236] Box 5.6, p296, Easterling, W.E. *et al.*, "Food, fibre and forest products" in M.L. Parry et al. (Eds.) *Climate Change 2007: Impacts, Adaptation and Vulnerability. Contribution of Working Group II to the Fourth Assessment Report of the Intergovernmental Panel on Climate Change*, (Cambridge: Cambridge University Press, 2007).
[237] p294, Id.

- o One conclusion from the AR4 is that in the human health arena, adaptation needs to begin immediately to address vulnerability and increase capacity to adapt later to increasing impacts. Climate change may already be responsible for an additional 150,000 deaths each year due to increased incidence of diarrhoea, malaria and malnutrition.[238]
- o The aim must be to enable the immediate uptake of existing health interventions in those areas of ongoing high need, largely in developing countries.[239]
- o For climate change specific technologies this includes:
  - Medical products, processes and services related to managing health needs during extreme weather events; and
  - Medical products, processes and services related to managing health needs during periods of extreme heat (heat waves) and extreme cold, especially for vulnerable populations such as the elderly and young children.
- o For adaptive capacity more generally this includes:
  - Medical products, processes and services related to increasing resistance to vector borne and temperature sensitive diseases;
  - Medical products, processes and services related to increasing general immune-capacity, e.g. vaccines;
  - Products, processes and services designed to create hygienic and sanitary living and working conditions, such as access to potable water and sanitary facilities.

Other technologies for adaptation include:
- early warning systems for disasters (including communications);
- systems for stockpiling and distributing food, water, and medicines;
- systems for storing and managing water resources;
- alternative disaster-appropriate transport systems (e.g., boats);
- systems for strengthening waste disposal sites against leakage during disasters;
- disaster mitigation systems, such as flood and sea walls, flood channels; and
- extreme weather event resistant building materials.

---

[238] p75, Stern, N. et al. *The Economics of Climate Change: The Stern Review* (Cambridge: Cambridge University Press, 2007) *citing* McMichael, A., D. Campbell-Lendrum, S Kovats, et al. (2004) "Global climate change", in M.J. Ezzati, et al. (eds.), *Comparative quantification of health risks: global and regional burden of disease due to selected major risk factors*, (Geneva: World Health Organisation, 2004)

[239] p417, Confalonieri, U. et al., "Human Health", in M.L. Parry et al. (Eds.) *Climate Change 2007: Impacts, Adaptation and Vulnerability. Contribution of Working Group II to the Fourth Assessment Report of the Intergovernmental Panel on Climate Change*, (Cambridge: Cambridge University Press, 2007).

It is important to reiterate that technologies for adaptation have significant overlap with the general framework of technologies for development. Attempts to limit and cabin the scope of technologies relevant to adaptation therefore generally fail because they are based on false premises. Transformation of the entire energy systems of developing countries is a key element of adaptation, as is increasing capacity to adapt. This requires a broad approach to technology rather than a narrow one. While not necessarily implicating intellectual property, except in perhaps agriculture and health, the role of intellectual property as a tool for enabling development through investment and innovation comes much more to the fore. Adaptation brings the issue into the familiar territory of the debate over what role intellectual property plays in the broader development of a country, something which is more extensively discussed in Chapter 5.

IV. THE GEOGRAPHIC TARGET

The geographic structure of the technology need is somewhat difficult to draw from the data in the scenarios studied in this chapter. Some of this information can clearly be drawn from the Technology Needs Assessments (TNAs) conducted by many developing countries as well as NAMAs and national communications. In the discussion below, I begin with those developing countries identified and implicated by their mitigation potential, as defined in the various scenarios studies. This is then overlaid with identification of their technology needs from TNAs, NAMAs and national communications.

IV.1 Mitigation

In terms of the share of GHG emissions, IEA Projections from 2004 suggested that developing countries would account for 70% of emissions in the period 2002-2030 and surpass OECD emissions by the early 2020s, with the majority of those emissions from China, followed by India.[240] A key point is that even if by 2050 OECD countries were to reduce their emissions to zero, non-OECD countries would still have to significantly reduce their emissions below their 2007 levels.[241] This represents an immense challenge in the face of the simultaneous challenge these countries will have in meeting growing demand for energy as they lift greater portions of their population out of extreme or absolute poverty. It identifies China and India as key countries that will need to use technology to transform their economies and to reduce emissions.

From a global welfare perspective, deployment and diffusion of technology to developing countries may be the cheapest and most effective way of ensuring GHG emissions reductions, especially in the 2015 – 2020 period. Some forecasting models

---

[240] IEA, *World Energy Outlook 2004*, IEA/OECD, Paris (2004)
[241] p62, IEA, *Energy Technology Perspectives 2010: Scenarios and Strategies to 2050*, (Paris: IEA/OECD, 2010)

conclude that the learning process and speed of adoption and deployment would be faster and cheaper in developing countries than in OECD countries, suggesting that developing countries should be preferred targets for OECD investments in clean energy deployment and diffusion.[242] The 2010 World Development Report projects a least cost mitigation pathway which would have 65% of mitigation action by 2030 take place in developing countries.[243]

For developing countries, the IEA Blue Map scenario lays out the technology sector shifts that will enable reductions commensurate with the projected contributions especially for India and China.[244] They also identify the following countries for their mitigation potential: Brazil, Mexico, and South Africa. In terms of regions, ASEAN as a unit is a major contributor in terms of mitigation potentials. In both China and India, end-use fuel and electricity efficiency is a large portion of the contribution (38% and 36% respectively). CCS forms a significant part of the technology shift for China, whereas, for India, renewables play a larger part. For both countries action is needed across all sectors including transport.

A look at the IEA and other scenario models for key selected regions and countries (as well as their individual TNAs, National Communications, NAMAs) also may help to illustrate the scope of the challenge in those countries where technologies may be most needed.

- ASEAN (not including China)
    - Power generation – in 2050 Renewables form over 50% of power generation (demand grows from just above 500 TWh to almost 2200TWh), especially hydro and wind. This is compared to less than 20 percent in 2009.[245]
    - Industrial energy use – In 2009, less than a third of energy use comes from renewables, electricity and other heat sources besides coal, oil and gas. By 2050, the model suggests that this will shift to over two thirds.[246]
    - Transport – while LDV transport share triples compared to 2010 levels (with a more diverse fuel use with over 50% from FCEVs,

---

[242] See p24, Lefevre, N "Deploying Climate –friendly Technologies through Collaboration with Developing Countries" International Energy Agency, Information Paper, November 2005. This is especially true for solar PV.
[243] World Bank *World Development Report 2010: Development and Climate Change* (Washington D.C.: World Bank, 2010).
[244] p86, IEA, *Energy Technology Perspectives 2010*
[245] p540, IEA, *Energy Technology Perspectives 2012: Pathways to a Clean Energy System* (Paris: IEA/OECD 2012).
[246] p542, Id.

PHEVs and BEVs)[247], mass transit contributes the bulk of the transport share by 2050, much as in 2010.[248]

- Brazil[249]
    - Power generation - Brazil has over 45% of renewables in its total energy supply mix in 2010, with hydropower being the most significant.[250] By 2050, the proportion of wind, solar and biomass will have increased to match the increase in demand, along with natural gas. Hydropower remains the largest single portion of the mix but will hit limits.[251] From Brazil's second National Communication to the UNFCCC the needs it identified were:[252]
        - Efficient coal and gas – SC/USC - IGCC - large and small gas turbines;
        - Advanced nuclear;
        - Solar PV; Solar thermal; Concentrated solar power
        - Wind - Control technologies, turbines;
        - Gasification of biomass;
        - Hydrogen fuel cell and hydrogen storage;
        - Gas to liquid, coal to liquid.
    - Transport - Brazil has significant experience with the relevant technologies for decarbonization of transport including in biofuels for transport.[253] In 2010 Bus Rapid Transit is over 50% of transport share and will remain close to that in 2050 with a significant increase in LDVs which will consist largely of flex fuel cars, biofuels, and small shares of electric (PHEVs, BEVs).
        - In its Pledge NAMA[254], Brazil aims to increase the use of biofuels, in which it is already a major market actor.[255] The

---

[247] p544, Id.
[248] p543, id.
[249] No TNA or registered NAMA available, only a 2020 pledge NAMA.
[250] p547, IEA, *Energy Technology Perspectives 2012*
[251] p552, Id. See also See p8, UNFCCC "Compilation of information on nationally appropriate mitigation actions to be implemented by Parties not included in Annex I to the Convention" FCCC/AWGLCA/2011/INF.1, 18 March 2011.
[252] See p433, Brazil Ministry of Science and Technology *Second National Communication of Brazil to the United Nations Framework Convention on Climate Change* (Brasilia: Ministry of Science and Technology, Brazil, 2010).
[253] p547, IEA, *Energy Technology Perspectives 2012: Pathways to a Clean Energy System* (Paris: IEA/OECD 2012).
[254] National submissions of goals for emission reductions/sustainable development that are submitted to the UNFCCC Secretariat in the context of a new climate agreement to be agreed by 2015. This is in contrast to specific mitigation actions that countries either may seek recognition for, or seek support for, or simply carry out unilaterally. These represent more a means of implementing the pledge NAMA and are sometimes called "individual NAMAs".

national communication identifies R&D and demonstration of second generation biofuels as a need.[256]
- It also identified battery technology for transport but also for power storage in general.
- Industry[257]
  - CCS for industry
- Grid
  - Smart grids
- Buildings
  - Energy efficiency for small residential – implying appliances
  - Clean cooking fuels, and stoves
  - Solar heating
  - New environmentally sound design
- In Agriculture, it plans on new crop and livestock management systems.[258]
  - genetic improvements for animals and plants to deal with new climate conditions and the increase in pest and disease incidence.[259]

Brazil main mitigation potential lies in reducing deforestation, which implicates agriculture and agricultural land-use. Reducing demand for land will require better and more efficient use of existing agricultural land, increasing its productivity and reducing impact.

- China[260]
  - Power generation – by 2050, China reduces it energy related emissions by 80% compared with 2009.[261] A significant portion of that (26%) will be from nuclear, with a similar proportion for

---

[255] See p8, UNFCCC "Compilation of information on nationally appropriate mitigation actions to be implemented by Parties not included in Annex I to the Convention" FCCC /AWGLCA/2011/INF.1, 18 March 2011.

[256] See p433-434, *Second National Communication of Brazil to the United Nations Framework Convention on Climate Change*

[257] See p433-434, Brazil Ministry of Science and Technology *Second National Communication of Brazil to the United Nations Framework Convention on Climate Change* (Brasilia: Ministry of Science and Technology, Brazil, 2010).

[258] See p8, UNFCCC "Compilation of information on nationally appropriate mitigation actions to be implemented by Parties not included in Annex I to the Convention" FCCC /AWGLCA/2011/INF.1, 18 March 2011.

[259] See p436, *Second National Communication of Brazil to the United Nations Framework Convention on Climate Change*

[260] No registered NAMA available. Insufficient detail in its pledged NAMA. The TNA from 1998 is too far removed to provide reliable or accurate sense of needs articulated by China, given how quickly things have developed. The details here are drawn from p155-160, Chinese Chinese National Development and Reform Commission *Second National Communication on Climate Change of The People's Republic of China* (National Development and Reform Commission, 2012)

[261] p562, IEA, *Energy Technology Perspectives 2012: Pathways to a Clean Energy System* (Paris: IEA/OECD 2012).

renewables, some space for natural gas but with coal plus CCS providing a fifth of the portion of the energy mix.
- IGCC power generation; multi-generation; converting liquid fuels from coal; coal gasification;
- New-generation fast breeder reactors; nuclear fusion;
- Large scale offshore wind power generation;
- Core technology for solar thermal power generation; solar photovoltaic power generation;
- Advanced geothermal power generation;
- Nitrogen energy and fuel cells;
- Advanced ocean-energy power generation;
- Biomass energy;
- Smart grid and energy storage;
- Carbon Capture and Storage.
o Industry – China is the world's largest producer of cement, crude steel, aluminium, paper and board.[262] Adoption of best available technologies (BATs) will account for 40% of the reductions in 2050, compared to a 4 degree scenario.[263]
o Transport – rapid growth of LDVs is envisioned by 2050 but accompanied with significant increase in mass transit by 2050. In the LDV market, the majority of transport share is in hybrids, PHEVs, BEVs and FCEVs, with only a very small proportion of gasoline and diesel.[264] A very rapid penetration and adoption of advanced new vehicle technologies is foreseen under the IEA models.
- Improved fuel-efficient engines, transmission systems; lightweight vehicle construction materials;
- Advanced low-emission diesel engines;
- Hybrid power vehicles; high-efficiency electric vehicles.
o Buildings
- Lighting, especially LED technology;
- New building seal materials; advanced ventilation and air conditioning systems;
- District co-generation; geothermal heat pumps
- Appliances
  - High efficiency electronic devices, especially power-semiconductor components;
  - Direct current permanent–magnet brushless motors.

---

[262] p563, IEA, *Energy Technology Perspectives 2012: Pathways to a Clean Energy System* (Paris: IEA/OECD 2012).
[263] Id.
[264] p566, Id.

China's national communication is quite specific about a basic list of technologies it needs in terms of domestic action and industry. The barriers to acquiring such technology are not articulated in the communication.

- India[265]
  - Power generation – This is the largest contributor to India's emissions reduction in the IEA scenarios.[266] As of 2010, India has the fifth largest wind capacity globally. Total wind energy will increase to 6% of the 2050 energy mix from a very low share at present.[267] Solar power contributes a significant part of emissions saving by 2050 (over one fifth of the energy mix).[268]
    - Coal beneficiation and its impact on efficiency improvement/abatement of GHG emission in thermal power stations;
    - Validation of the multi stage hydrogenation (MSH) technology for converting coal to oil;
    - Abatement of GHG via in situ infusion of fly ash with CO_2 in thermal power plants;
    - CCS- CO_2 sequestration in geologic formations with enhanced coal bed methane (CBM) recovery;
    - CCS - Geological storage of CO_2 in exploration/recovery of petroleum gas;
    - developing soft coke technology as the source of rural/semi urban domestic energy;
    - CO_2 - decomposition through plasma technology;
    - Improvement in solar cell efficiency;
    - All renewables.
  - Industry
    - Steel
      - vertical retort direct reduction (VRDR)– submerged arc furnace (SAF), electroslag refining (ESR) route
      - electric arc furnaces

---

[265] No TNA, no registered NAMA, insufficient detail in pledged NAMA. Details drawn from Indian Indian Ministry of Environment and Forestry *Second National Communication of India to the United Nations Framework Convention on Climate Change* (Ministry of Environment and Forests, Government of India, 2012). India's national communication provides specific technology needs in the form of proposed projects and activities.
[266] p577, IEA, *Energy Technology Perspectives 2012: Pathways to a Clean Energy System* (Paris: IEA/OECD 2012).
[267] p580, Id.
[268] Id.

- o Buildings
    - Lighting
- o Waste
    - Recovery of methane from landfills and paddy fields
- o Transport – India is expected to have an extremely large increase in LDV usage by 2050. The majority of these will be Hybrid, PHEV, BEV and FCEV with gasoline only a small percentage. Similarly to China, the IEA scenarios envisage rapid market penetration and adoption in the post-2020 period.[269]
    - Fuel switching
- o Agriculture
    - Research, development, and demonstration of low-methane emitting feeds; feed additives in mitigating methane emission from livestock:
- o India's emissions need to peak by 2030, (under a 2% scenario), largely through rapid deployment of renewables, nuclear and biofuels. Also crucial will be deployment of best available technologies to enable greater energy use efficiency in industry.[270] As with China, the IEA ETP 2010 scenario notes that peaking in 2030 is not achievable without widespread adoption of CCS in power generation and industry.[271]

- South Africa[272]
    - o Power generation - At present South Africa's energy mix consists of 94% coal, without CCS, barely keeping up with growth in demand.[273] At the same time it exports electricity providing more than two-thirds of Africa's electricity needs.[274] In 2050, the proportion of power from nuclear, solar and coal with CCS will be 75% of the power generation mix.
        - Solar power
        - Clean coal – IGCC, SC/USC
        - Wind power
        - CCS

---

[269] p582, IEA, *Energy Technology Perspectives 2012: Pathways to a Clean Energy System* (Paris: IEA/OECD 2012).
[270] p427, Id.
[271] Id.
[272] No registered NAMA. Insufficient detail in pledge NAMA. TNA too old (from 2007). Details are from South African Department of Environmental Affairs *South Africa's Second National Communication under the United Nations Framework Convention on Climate Change* (Pretoria: Department of Environmental Affairs Republic of South Africa, 2011).
[273] p613, IEA, *Energy Technology Perspectives 2012: Pathways to a Clean Energy System* (Paris: IEA/OECD 2012).
[274] p614, Id.

- Transport – In 2010, over 50% of road share in South Africa was in buses, although these are largely inefficient minibuses.[275] Buses are expected to maintain that share in 2050 while LDV use doubles.[276] Biofuels and electricity are expected to be almost 50% of the fuel mix for transport with fossil fuels providing much of the rest.[277]
    - Improvement of urban mass-transport systems
    - Fuel-efficiency improvement
- Industry
    - Boiler improvement
    - Source reduction, recycle, and reuse.

In addition agriculture will play a significant part in the emissions of developing countries and their contribution to mitigation. Simply as a function of population, developing countries account for almost 75% of agriculture-related emissions.[278] For example, Brazil is a lead emitter amongst developing countries in the fields of meat and milk production.[279] This suggests that agricultural technologies are a crucial component of the mitigation technology portfolio for developing countries, as urgent as those related to energy and industry-related emissions.

A 2013 study for the German Environment Ministry examines the pledges and mitigation potential for emerging economies in the period up to 2020.[280] The main aim is to examine whether their 2020 pledges may be met, and focuses on cheapest available emissions reductions, using existing technologies. As such it measures emissions reductions that are significantly lower than those identified in the Scenarios above. This excludes technologies not considered available or implementable after that date (such as CCS, hydrogen fuel cells), but it provides significant agreement with the ETPs, the Stern Report, and IPCC scenarios for mitigation technology needs in emerging economies. It identifies the following technology needs (with different emphases and details) for the 6 countries reviewed (Brazil, India, China, Mexico, South Africa, South Korea[281]).

---

[275] p621, Id.
[276] Id.
[277] p622, Id.
[278] Annex 7g, Stern, N. et al. *The Economics of Climate Change: The Stern Review* (Cambridge: Cambridge University Press, 2007).
[279] p44 Fekete, H. et al "Emerging economies – potentials, pledges and fair shares of greenhouse gas reduction" ENVIRONMENTAL RESEARCH OF THE GERMAN FEDERAL MINISTRY OF THE ENVIRONMENT, NATURE CONSERVATION AND NUCLEAR SAFETY Project-no. (FKZ) 3711 41 120, (Umweltbundesamt, Bonn, April 2013).
[280] Fekete, H. et al "Emerging economies – potentials, pledges and fair shares of greenhouse gas reduction" ENVIRONMENTAL RESEARCH OF THE GERMAN FEDERAL MINISTRY OF THE ENVIRONMENT, NATURE CONSERVATION AND NUCLEAR SAFETY Project-no. (FKZ) 3711 41 120, (Umweltbundesamt, Bonn, April 2013).
[281] There was a lack of data on Korea, making it difficult to identify measures that would have mitigation potential in South Korea's 2020 pledge. See p111, Fekete, H. et al.

- Energy Supply (Not a significant measure for Brazil)
    - Efficiency of power plants - IGCC, Pressurized Fluidized bed compression, circulating fluidized bed combustion (Not considered implementable by India before 2020.)
    - Combined heat and power
    - Fuel switch to other fossils - coal to gas (Particularly important to India.)
    - Increase of nuclear energy
    - Non-bio renewables – Hydro, Wind, Solar PV,
- Industry
    - End use efficiency in: iron and steel; other mining; food production (Especially for Brazil.)
    - Heat and steam recovery
    - Cement – clinker (The primary area of potential for China)
    - Paper – recycling
    - Use of sustainable biofuels
    - Fuel switch to natural gas and other fossil fuels – non-coal waste burning
- Waste
    - Reduction of emissions from waste (landfill) (Relevant only for Mexico and Brazil.)
- Transport[282]
    - Modal shifts - Bus Rapid Transport; road freight to rail
    - Efficiency improvements – vehicle and engine design. (Not relevant for Brazil.)
    - Fuel switch - Biofuels for transport including flex-fuel motors; PHEVs, hydrogen
- Agriculture, Land use (Not relevant to India, China.)
    - Livestock breeding and management
    - Fertilizer, manure use and management
- Buildings (Not as relevant for Brazil leading up to 2020.)
    - Appliance efficiency – lighting, end use electronics and white goods
    - Refrigeration and air conditioning (pumps, bridge designs, etc.)
    - Building envelope efficiency – seals
    - Solar thermal water heating

---

[282] p42, Fekete, H. et al "Emerging economies – potentials, pledges and fair shares of greenhouse gas reduction" ENVIRONMENTAL RESEARCH OF THE GERMAN FEDERAL MINISTRY OF THE ENVIRONMENT, NATURE CONSERVATION AND NUCLEAR SAFETY Project-no. (FKZ) 3711 41 120, (Umweltbundesamt, Bonn, April 2013).

Further evidence of the scope of technologies required by developing countries can be gleaned from Technology Needs Assessments, National Communications and NAMAs provided by developing countries. This next section relies on the 2009 Synthesis of TNAs provided by the UNFCCC secretariat as well as my own examination of specific country TNA, National Communications, and NAMAs. From this data we can see that there is considerable overlap with the set of scenarios, and considerable breadth beyond renewable technologies. [283] From the review of 70 TNAs and 21 national communications in the synthesis paper we find the following mitigation sectors and technologies commonly identified[284]:

- Efficient fossil fuel power generation (major emphasis for Africa, Asia and Pacific, Latin America and the Caribbean, LDCs, SIDS)[285]
    - IGCC
    - Efficient combustion technology for traditional coal fired stations
    - Combined heat and Power
- Renewable Energy (major emphasis for Africa, Asia and Pacific, Latin America and the Caribbean, LDCs, SIDS)[286]
    - Solar PV including micro, off-grid
    - Wind
        - Wind water pumping
    - Biomass
    - Traditional Hydropower; Small and micro-hydro
    - Solar thermal
    - Geothermal
- Agriculture and Land-use (major emphasis for Africa, Asia and Pacific, Latin America and the Caribbean, LDCs, SIDS)[287]
    - New plant varieties
    - Crop management
    - Forestry management
    - Manure conversion to methane fuel
    - Less GHG intensive animal feed
- Buildings ,
    - Efficient cook stoves (major emphasis for LDCs)[288] – solar cook stoves
    - Energy efficient appliances
    - Demand side management software

---

[283] See p4, UNFCCC "Second synthesis report on technology needs identified by Parties not included in Annex I to the Convention" FCCC/SBSTA/2009/INF.1, 29 May 2009.
[284] Id.
[285] See p14-15, Id.
[286] Id.
[287] See p14-15, Id.
[288] See p14-15, p21 Id.

- Building design and materials
            - District heating
            - Efficient Ventilation and heating
            - Lighting
    - Industry – cement, iron and Steel, Aluminium, Chemicals (major emphasis for Africa, Asia and Pacific, LDCs, SIDS)[289]
        - Fuel switching
        - Alternative production processes
            - Dry cement production
        - Energy use efficiency
    - Waste (major emphasis for Africa, Asia and Pacific, LDCs, SIDS)[290]
        - Waste management technologies – recycling
        - landfill with gas recovery and waste incineration with energy utilization
        - processing of solid organic waste
        - solid waste and wastewater recovery and reuse
        - urban sewerage facilities
    - Transport (major emphasis for Asia and Pacific, Latin America and the Caribbean, SIDS)[291]
        - Energy efficient traditional fuel vehicles
        - Modal switch
        - Biofuels
        - PHEVs

One major element of this analysis is that, as a whole, the needs of LDCs and SIDS do not differ in kind from those of other developing countries but only in degree. For example, the diffusion need for renewable energy technologies is not only limited to the major emerging economies, but is highlighted by LDCs as well. Getting products, as well as increasing domestic capacity in LDCs, is crucial to the long term climate goal, despite the relatively low contribution they make to emissions in the present. More interestingly they present a ready export market for mitigation technologies which might be appropriately segmented from the developed country market so as to make it worthwhile for major developing country firms to provide hardware, and training.

A major shared emphasis is agriculture, even in major economies, something which is also reflected in the adaptation analysis. This is an area that has seen much less attention in mitigation than renewable energy but may be of most importance to developing countries. To the extent that the land-use portion refers to forestry and

---

[289] See p14-15, p21 – 30, UNFCCC "Second synthesis report on technology needs identified by Parties not included in Annex I to the Convention" FCCC/SBSTA/2009/INF.1, 29 May 2009.
[290] Id.
[291] Id.

avoided deforestation, this constitutes a major part of the mitigation potential and support need from developing countries. However, addressing deforestation will entail reducing the need for agricultural land, and increasing productivity while reducing the footprint.

IV.2 Adaptation

The geographic regions that are negatively impacted by climate change and thus are in need of technologies and development to meet the vulnerability and capacity challenge have significant overlap with the majority of developing countries i.e. tropical or sub-tropical regions with a significant population in marginal ecological niches. In terms of regions, the AR4 notes that for:

- Africa[292], by 2020 up to 250 million people are projected to be exposed to water stress and its concomitant effects. Crop yields from rain fed agriculture could reduce by up to 50%. Some crops could become entirely unsuited for production in some areas[293]; and livestock could suffer from reduced quality of rangeland feedstock grasses and scrubland;[294]
- Asia[295], heavily populated mega-deltas in South East Asia, such as Bangladesh, are projected to undergo severe and more frequent flooding.[296] This is likely to result in an increase in diarrheal and enteric diseases due to decreased water quality. Droughts in some areas will also contribute to the disease burden by increasing reliance on unsafe water resources.[297]
- Latin America[298] is projected to lose significant productivity in crucial crops, as well as in livestock productivity. Changes in precipitation are likely, and water stress will increase due to reduction in glacier size and durability.

---

[292] p50, IPCC, *Climate Change 2007: Synthesis Report. Contribution of Working Groups I, II and III to the Fourth Assessment Report of the Intergovernmental Panel on Climate Change* [Core Writing Team, Pachauri, R.K and Reisinger, A. (eds.)]. (Geneva: IPCC, 2007).

[293] p105, Stern, N. et al. *The Economics of Climate Change: The Stern Review* (Cambridge: Cambridge University Press, 2007).

[294] p297, Easterling, W.E. *et al.*, "Food, fibre and forest products" in M.L. Parry et al. (Eds.) *Climate Change 2007: Impacts, Adaptation and Vulnerability. Contribution of Working Group II to the Fourth Assessment Report of the Intergovernmental Panel on Climate Change*, (Cambridge: Cambridge University Press, 2007).

[295] p50, IPCC, *Climate Change 2007: Synthesis Report.*

[296] p187, Kundzewicz, Z.W. et al. "Freshwater resources and their Management" in M.L. Parry et al. (Eds.) *Climate Change 2007: Impacts, Adaptation and Vulnerability. Contribution of Working Group II to the Fourth Assessment Report of the Intergovernmental Panel on Climate Change*, (Cambridge: Cambridge University Press, 2007). See also p77, Stern, N. et al.

[297] p189, Kundzewicz, Z.W. et al. "Freshwater resources and their Management" in M.L. Parry et al. (Eds.) *Climate Change 2007: Impacts, Adaptation and Vulnerability. Contribution of Working Group II to the Fourth Assessment Report of the Intergovernmental Panel on Climate Change*, (Cambridge: Cambridge University Press, 2007).

[298] p50, IPCC, *Climate Change 2007: Synthesis Report. Contribution of Working Groups I, II and III to the Fourth Assessment Report of the Intergovernmental Panel on Climate Change* [Core Writing Team, Pachauri, R.K and Reisinger, A. (eds.)]. (Geneva: IPCC, 2007).

Key vulnerabilities identified by the AR4 include:
- Increased risk of extreme weather events, such as droughts, heat waves and floods;[299]
- Greater risks of climate appear to exist for the low lying latitudes in which the majority of the landmass of developing countries is located;

Even if warming were to be kept at the lower range of projections of 2 degrees Celsius, the majority of impacts would fall on developing countries.[300]

Some evidence of the scope of technologies required by developing countries can be gleaned from Technology Needs Assessments, National Communications and NAMAs provided by developing countries. This next section relies on the 2009 Synthesis of TNAs provided by the UNFCCC secretariat as well as my own examination of specific country TNAs, and National Communications. From this data we can see that there is considerable overlap with the selected scenarios, and considerable breadth beyond renewable technologies.[301] From the review of 70 TNAs and 21 national communications in the synthesis paper we find the following sectors and technologies commonly identified[302]:

- Agriculture (major emphasis for Africa, Asia and Pacific, Latin America and Caribbean, LDCs, SIDS)[303],
    - Crop management and Crop breeding, including use of molecular techniques for large-scale seed quality innovations and breeding new seed varieties;
    - Improved irrigation systems - extension and rehabilitation of existing irrigation facilities
    - integrated pest management
    - use of green manure and low GHG fertilizers
    - Livestock breeding – heat and drought tolerance
    - improving the nutritional value of animal feed

---

[299] p65, Id.
[300] p148, Stern, N. et al. *The Economics of Climate Change: The Stern Review* (Cambridge: Cambridge University Press, 2007).
[301] See p4, UNFCCC "Second synthesis report on technology needs identified by Parties not included in Annex I to the Convention" FCCC/SBSTA/2009/INF.1, 29 May 2009.
[302] See p4, Id. The analysis is insufficiently fine grained to do country specific assessment for adaptation.
[303] See p16, p21 – 30, Id. See also Brazilian Ministry of Science and Technology *Second National Communication of Brazil to the United Nations Framework Convention on Climate Change* (Brasilia: Ministry of Science and Technology, Brazil, 2010). also Indian Ministry of Environment and Forestry *Second National Communication of India to the United Nations Framework Convention on Climate Change* (Ministry of Environment and Forests, Government of India, 2012); p155-160, Chinese National Development and Reform Commission *Second National Communication on Climate Change of The People's Republic of China* (National Development and Reform Commission, 2012)

- - developing gene research and technology
  - Food processing
  - development of fast-growing forest species to adapt to new conditions
  - establishing early warning systems for forest fires
- Water (major emphasis for Africa, Latin America and Caribbean, LDCs)[304],
  - Efficient water use – recycling
  - Water harvesting
  - Sanitation
  - desalination plants
  - GIS and satellite remote-sensing
- Health (major emphasis for Africa, Latin America and Caribbean, LDCs)[305]
  - Water and food borne diseases
  - Heat stress
  - Pest borne diseases – Malaria
  - health alert information systems and disease

- Climate risk and Disaster management (major emphasis for Asia and Pacific, Latin America and Caribbean, SIDS[306])
  - Early warning systems for floods and tidal waves
  - Seawall and coastal protection technologies
    - Dykes and levees
    - Floodgates, tidal walls
    - Storm surge barriers
    - Water Pumping and drainage technologies
  - Systematic observation, monitoring and analysis
    - Conventional observations, including use of wind profilers, and application of GPS in upper-air meteorological observations.

---

[304] Id.
[305] See p16, UNFCCC "Second synthesis report on technology needs identified by Parties not included in Annex I to the Convention" FCCC/SBSTA/2009/INF.1, 29 May 2009. See also *Second National Communication of Brazil to the United Nations Framework Convention on Climate Change; Second national Communication of India to the United Nations Framework Convention on Climate Change; Second National Communication on Climate Change of The People's Republic of China*
[306] See p16, UNFCCC "Second synthesis report on technology needs identified by Parties not included in Annex I to the Convention" FCCC/SBSTA/2009/INF.1, 29 May 2009. See also Brazilian Ministry of Science and Technology *Second National Communication of Brazil to the United Nations Framework Convention on Climate Change* (Brasilia: Ministry of Science and Technology, Brazil, 2010). See also Indian Ministry of Environment and Forestry *Second National Communication of India to the United Nations Framework Convention on Climate Change* Ministry of Environment and Forests, Government of India, 2012. p155-160, Chinese National Development and Reform Commission "Second National Communication on Climate Change of The People's Republic of China" National Development and Reform Commission, 2012)

- Non-conventional observations, including development of satellite remote-sensing instruments and ground-based remote sensing technologies.
- Data analysis and assimilation, including setup of 4D-VAR [307] data assimilation systems, direct assimilation & application of massive satellite data, quick assimilation & application of near surface intensive measurements, parallel high-efficiency computation of global high-resolution 4D-VAR data assimilation systems.[308]
- Numerical prediction models, including optimized physic-process parameterization schemes and coordination with dynamic models and data assimilation systems.[309]

The TNAs are somewhat narrower in scope than the scope identified by the Green Economy report, or even the broader identification of specific adaptation needs in section III.2 above. Part of this may be the structural bias of the TNAs which have a narrower conception of technologies for adaption than is used in this thesis. For example, the UNDP TNA handbook sets as a starting point, an assessment of existing climate vulnerability rather than addressing resilience.[310] While useful this excludes climate resilience and the platform and network technologies necessary to enable appropriate responses to climate impacts. Nevertheless, it appears that at least the LDCs used poverty alleviation as major criteria for technology selection. One major problem for the TNAs is that they rarely provided time horizons, beyond the general framework of near term, medium term and longer term technology needs. While such a determination is suggested by the TNA handbook, very few countries engaged in such a characterisation of their technology priorities. In terms of adaptation it is also clear from the TNAs that the major emerging economies share many of the same needs as the SIDS, LDCs and other developing countries, again this being a matter of degree than kind.

V. Chapter Conclusion

---

[307] Systems such as this allow for data management to enable weather forecasting. 4D systems add a further dimension of data allowing for dynamic forecasting of progressions kin weather rather than snapshots of specific moments in time.
[308] p155-160, Chinese National Development and Reform Commission "Second National Communication on Climate Change of The People's Republic of China" National Development and Reform Commission, 2012)
[309] Id.
[310] See p32, UNDP "*Handbook for Carrying Out Technology Needs Assessment for Climate Change* (New York: UNDP 2010)

The purpose of this chapter was to elaborate the key criteria against which necessity for action would be measured. It identified the portfolio of technologies that were broadly implicated (including any data on state of deployment and diffusion), the timing of when they would need to be deployed and diffused and most importantly, the developing countries and regions to which such technologies are likely to need to be deployed and diffused. The next section below restates the key findings in this chapter on these three issues. In the next chapter, we proceed to evaluate what data and trends exist on the patent status of these technologies, especially those that developing countries will need to be transferred.

V.1. Timescale

The key date is the 2015 – 2018 timeframe for peaking GHG emissions and the 2025 date for increasing adaptive capacity. The scenarios examined suggest that this can largely be done with existing technologies, but has to be accomplished within the next 3 – 13 years, earlier in that time frame in the case of clean coal technologies. It may be that a significant portion of existing technologies may be in the public domain, but regardless of that fact, there is an urgent need to shift the price point to turn these technological products and processes more into commodities, at mass market prices. This will be the key short term challenge. In such a scheme, it may be inappropriate to rely on the relatively slow-moving process of existing trade and licensing patterns to encourage transactions and technology diffusion. It will require deliberate policies to encourage diffusion.[311] The ETP 2012 also argues that to achieve its 2 degree scenario, no breakthrough technologies are needed and that existing commercialized or near commercial technologies are sufficient to achieve the goal, provided the right policy mix is in place at both national and global levels.[312]

In the climate area, it is also important to take into account the lock-in effect of not deploying low GHG emissions infrastructure as soon as possible. To ensure that the right technologies are in place by 2050, technology deployment may need to start immediately, decades ahead of time.[313] There are some suggestions however that leading up to the 2050 horizon and beyond, existing technologies will be insufficient to meet the challenge of reducing GHG emissions and adaptation. It will be crucial to provide incentives for innovation in a broad portfolio of technologies, especially those with significant network and public goods characteristics. While a significant chunk of incremental innovation can come from the private sector, the risk premium and investment analysis for breakthrough innovation may require significant and

---

[311] See p3, Egenhofer, C et al. "Low-Carbon Technologies in the Post-Bali Period: Accelerating their Development and Deployment" European Climate Platform, report No. 4, December 2007
[312] p634, IEA, *Energy Technology Perspectives 2012: Pathways to a Clean Energy System* (Paris: IEA/OECD 2012).
[313] p124, Id.

coordinated public funding to create many Manhattan project-like research paths in multiple sectors.[314] Such technologies will include such things as:

- Nuclear fusion
- Hydrogen fuel cells
- Off-grid solar batteries
- Vehicle Battery storage life in general

The IEA argues that these are the kinds of technologies that will require significant public R&D support, precisely because the benefits for individual private actors to invest are too diffuse, while the initial costs are high.[315] Intellectual property protection will be crucial to ensuring private sector investment in incremental innovations, but in breakthrough innovations, which may be significantly public sector funded, the risk premium protection that IP provides may not be as necessary. There may be no need to go beyond the existing intellectual property system to enable private sector innovation for the long term. Nevertheless, there may be a need to differentiate in terms of IP action and time frames between existing technologies, and those to be developed in the post-2020 period.

V.2. Scope of technologies

The analysis on mitigation and adaptation suggests that the scope of technologies implicated may be economy wide. The need to address action across a wide portfolio of technologies also argues against attempts to limit the scope of action to enable technology transfer only to a few technology sectors. The core finding of this chapter is that a broad portfolio of technologies needs to be addressed in each sector[316], not just best available technologies and not just those that are not IP protected.

V.3. Geographical Scope

From a mitigation perspective, the cheapest and most effective action on mitigation can be achieved in developing countries. This argues for focusing energy, finance and technology on transforming the high growth economies of Brazil, India, China, South Africa into low or zero GHG emissions economies, with at least a peak of emissions by 2018. Developing countries are also the most vulnerable to the earliest

---

[314] See p233, UNEP, *Towards a Green Economy: Pathways to Sustainable Development and Poverty Eradication*, (Nairobi: UNEP, 2011).
[315] p129, IEA, *Energy Technology Perspectives 2012: Pathways to a Clean Energy System* (Paris: IEA/OECD 2012). See also p2, Egenhofer, C. et al. "Low-Carbon Technologies in the Post-Bali Period: Accelerating their Development and Deployment" European Climate Platform, report No. 4, December 2007; Jaffe, A B et al. "A Tale of Two Market Failures – Technology and Environmental Policy", 54 Ecological Economics 164 (2005).
[316] p355, Stern, N. et al. *The Economics of Climate Change: The Stern Review* (Cambridge: Cambridge University Press, 2007).

impacts of climate change and increasingly so in the period to 2050, suggesting a need for rapid technological development in the near term.

The table on the following pages lists the mitigation and adaptation technologies identified as necessary to transfer along with the key developing countries and regions identified as geographical targets for technology transfer. What is clear is that while countries may have different needs, they differ only in degree of need rather than kind of need (except at the margins e.g. small islands states and coastal sea level rise). Clearly some element of the necessity for action at the national level will be predicated on the structure of international technology markets, and determined to a significant extent by the existence, distribution and exploitation patterns of intellectual property. The next chapter looks at the available evidence regarding the technologies identified in this chapter and the implications for the necessity for intellectual property action by the UNFCCC.

Table 1: Illustrative Table of Technology Needs in Developing Countries

Data in the table is taken from the analysis in this chapter. There is some differentiation in the grain of the analysis as some scenarios aggregate climate effects and thus technology needs at the level of the region. This is especially true for adaptation. The technology need was defined as whether the technology was specifically identified within a TNA, a Technology Action Plan, a Nationally Appropriate Mitigation Action (NAMA) plan, or within a relevant scenario exercise, based on existing pledges and mitigation pathways reflecting analyses of mitigation potentials for these countries.

Specific Mitigation Technologies	Developing Countries and Regions Implicated (in terms of mitigation potentials and Technology needs articulated)
Industrial process efficiency (best available production technologies in the following sectors)	Africa, Asia and Pacific, LDCs, SIDS
- Iron and Steel	ASEAN, Brazil, China, India, South Africa
- Cement	ASEAN, Brazil, China, India, South Africa
- Chemicals and Petrochemicals	ASEAN, Brazil, China, India, South Africa
- Paper	ASEAN, Brazil, China, India, South Africa
- Aluminium	ASEAN, Brazil, China, India, South Africa
- (CCS) in Industrial Processes	Brazil, China, India, South Africa
Renewables	Africa, Asia and Pacific, Latin America and the Caribbean, LDCs, SIDS; ASEAN, , Brazil, China, India, South Africa
- Hydro	ASEAN, Brazil, China, India, South Africa
- Wind (Offshore and/or Onshore) and Large wind power generation units, turbines, controllers	ASEAN, Brazil, China, India, South Africa,
- Solar PV	ASEAN, Brazil, China, India, South Africa,
- CSP Solar	Brazil, China, India, Mexico, South Africa
- Tidal	China, India
- Geothermal	China, India
- Biomass and waste (including landfill)	Brazil, China, India,
- Hydrogen Fuel cells, Storage	Brazil, China, India,
Nuclear	ASEAN, Brazil, China, India, South Africa
- Pressurized water reactors with capacity above 1 000 MW	China
Power generation efficiency and fuel switching	Africa, Asia and Pacific, Latin America and the Caribbean, LDCs, SIDS

- (CCS) in Power generation	Brazil, China, India, South Africa
- coal to natural gas	ASEAN, Brazil, China, India,
- Coal to oil	India
- Integrated gasification combined cycle combustion	Brazil, China, India, South Africa
- Pressurized Fluidized bed compression, circulating fluidized bed combustion	Brazil, China, India, South Africa
- Super-critical and ultra-supercritical coal	Brazil, China, India, South Africa
- Coal washing and depressing technology	China, India
Transport	Asia and Pacific, Latin America and the Caribbean, SIDS;
- Plug in Hybrids and Electric vehicles, Battery electric vehicles, fuel cell vehicles	ASEAN, Brazil, China, India, South Africa
- Flex – Fuel Vehicles	Brazil, China
- Bus rapid transport	ASEAN, Brazil, China, India, South Africa
- Hydrogen Fuel cells	Brazil, India,
- Batteries	Brazil,
- Biodiesel and biofuels (including 2nd generation biofuels)	Brazil, India, South Africa
- Fuel Efficiency of petrol or diesel vehicles	ASEAN, China, India, South Africa
Electricity grid – smart and micro infrastructure and management	ASEAN, Brazil, China, India,
- Flexible AC transmission systems; High-voltage transmission systems	China,
- Monitoring and controlling electricity quality, grid interconnection and dispatching - Electricity dispatching automation technology	ASEAN, China, India
Buildings	
End-use efficiency and Appliances	ASEAN, Brazil, China, India,
- electric motors	Brazil, South Africa
- pumps, including for agricultural use	ASEAN, Brazil, China, India,
- lighting including solar powered LED lighting operating off-grid;	Brazil, China, India, South Africa
- Dishwashers, clothes washers, and clothes dryers	China
- compressors, heat exchangers, insulation (foam and vacuum), heat bridge designs and fans for refrigeration and air conditioners;	ASEAN, China, India,
- software and hardware, especially for managing active and standby power in portable appliances	ASEAN, Brazil, China, India

	- Modern heat access (cook stoves, heating appliances)	ASEAN, Brazil, China, India, Mexico, South Africa LDCs
	- Advanced building envelope seals and insulation	ASEAN, Brazil, China, India, South Africa
	- Renewables for heat (solar thermal)	Brazil, China, India, South Africa
	- Combined heat and power	ASEAN, Brazil, China, India, South Africa
Agriculture		Africa, Asia and Pacific, Latin America and the Caribbean, LDCs, SIDS; ASEAN, Brazil, China, India, South Africa
	- Less GHG intensive fertilizer	Brazil, India
	- Plant varieties that are less reliant on GHG intensive fertilizers, either because they produce higher yields or are more efficient at soil nutrient uptake;	Brazil, India
	- Animal variants and breeds less likely to produce methane during digestion;	Brazil
	- Better management of animal waste, including recycling into biogas and other biomass for energy generation;	Brazil
	- Animal feed less likely to produce methane	Brazil, India
Waste		Africa, Asia and Pacific, LDCs, SIDS
	- Landfill methane capture	Brazil, India
	- Waste management technologies –recycling	
	- processing of solid organic waste	
	- solid waste and wastewater recovery and reuse	
	- urban sewerage facilities	
	Specific Adaptation Technologies	**Developing Countries Implicated**
Agriculture		Africa, Asia and Pacific, Latin America and Caribbean, LDCs, SIDS
	- All agricultural inputs, including seeds (including flood and drought resilient varieties), low emissions fertilizers, and methods and processes;	
	- New varieties or adaptations of existing plant and animal varieties.	
	- Genetically modified seeds and animals	
	- integrated pest management	
	- Food processing and storage	
Energy		

	- All products for energy production, distribution and consumption;	
Health		Africa, Latin America and Caribbean, LDCs
	- All health infrastructure, including medicines, diagnostic and treatment tools, methods, personnel;	
	- Medical products, processes and services related to increasing resistance to vector borne and temperature sensitive diseases	
	- Medical products, processes and services related to managing health needs during periods of extreme heat (heat waves) and extreme cold,	
	- Medical products, processes and services related to increasing general immune-capacity, e.g. vaccines;	
	- Products, processes and services designed to create hygienic and sanitary living and working conditions, such as access to potable water and sanitary facilities	
Water		Africa, Latin America and Caribbean, LDCs
	- All water infrastructure for capture, treatment, distribution, and recycling	
	- Water treatment and sanitation products and processes to deal with higher levels of toxicity and microbial and plant growth	
	- Water desalination technologies for coastal areas	
	- Smart and/or active water metering systems	
	- Water capture and storage products and processes	
	- Efficient water use and reclamation technologies	
Disaster response		Asia and Pacific, Latin America and Caribbean, SIDS
	- early warning systems for disasters (including communications);	
	- Systematic observation, monitoring and analysis - Conventional observations, including use of wind profilers, and application of GPS in	

- upper-air meteorological observations. - Non-conventional observations, including development of satellite remote-sensing instruments and ground-based remote sensing technologies. - Data analysis and assimilation	
- systems for stockpiling and distributing food, water, and medicines;	
- systems for storing and managing water resources;	
- alternative disaster-appropriate transport systems (e.g., boats);	
- systems for strengthening waste disposal sites against leakage during disasters;	
- disaster mitigation systems, such as flood and sea walls, flood channels;	
- extreme weather event resistant building materials.	

Chapter 3
Evaluating the existing evidence in intellectual property on climate technologies

I. INTRODUCTION

After determining the scope of climate and adaptation technologies to be transferred and to which developing countries in chapter 2, this chapter aims to examine the data that we have on the extent to which:

- The relevant technologies are patented, and by whom;
- The relevant technologies that are patented are being licensed and on what terms;
- The existing trends in patenting and licensing of the relevant technologies.

This information is important in identifying the targets for action in terms of the economic actors to be addressed. However, while this is an important step towards examining the role of intellectual property in technology transfer of these technologies, it is important to note what studies of this kind do not do: provide a way to answer the question of whether, in a situation where the behaviour of specific intellectual property holders prevents, or unduly limits, the adoption and use of a specific climate technology by all the relevant economic actors in a specific domestic sector, a UNFCCC member state has the legal and regulatory tools necessary to address such behaviour, at sufficient scale and speed.

Nevertheless, such information is useful in providing one part of the basis for determining whether and how the UNFCCC should take action to address intellectual property. In particular, does the empirical data tell us anything about the pattern of ownership, distribution and transactions of climate technology products and knowledge that suggests that there may be problems related to: the rate of diffusion of technologies; the scope of technologies being transferred; the countries to which technologies need to be transferred? Alone this is not enough to come to direct conclusions about what action is necessary by the UNFCCC. However, in combination with the answer to the question of what interventions developing countries may take to address such problems when they arise (as we do in Chapter 6 and 7), we may be better able to determine the nature and scope of action that the UNFCCC should take.

This chapter conducts a critical literature review that looks at whether we have an answer or indications of an answer to the empirical question and Chapter 6 looks at the answer to the legal question. The necessary timing, geography and scope of technologies identified in Chapter 2 form the basic framework for analysis in this chapter.

This chapter will analyse and evaluate the methodology of the existing available studies, reports and data and the conclusions that they draw along these three vectors:

1. Do they address the full scope of relevant mitigation and adaptation technologies, and do they allow us to draw conclusions about the full scope of technologies?

2. Do they address the issue of the speed at which the relevant technologies will need to be deployed and diffused, in particular the 2015-2018 peaking date for mitigation and the 2025 date for adaptation?

3. Do they address the geographic targets, especially the role of the emerging economies (including export of technological products and know-how to other developing countries)?

Each study will be assessed on the extent to which it does this, the strength and utility of the findings that it makes, and what if any conclusions can be drawn. This chapter will present one of the first in-depth critical analyses of these studies on an individual and a comparative basis, against the key baselines defined by the climate challenge at the UNFCCC.

It needs to be noted that, to date, there have been no broad systematic surveys of actors in developing countries of the IP-related barriers that they face with respect to licensing of technologies, let alone of climate technologies.

There have been very few studies of licensing behaviour of rightholders in the climate arena. The majority of studies have focused on static patent landscapes in a limited set of technologies. There have been no studies of the pricing of technological goods in particular markets as they relate to purchasing power, which may implicate access problems relating to embedded IP costs in products, and there have been few surveys or studies of pricing and terms of licenses which would also more accurately indicate the full extent, if any, of barriers to licensing. There have also been few studies of the FDI effects on technology transfer in this arena. The importance of licensing as a form of technology transfer can be overstated and it important to put it in the context of other vectors of technology transfer. An understanding of how licensing interacts with intellectual property and how and when it can be an alternative to other forms of technology transfer is covered in this first section before moving on to analysis of the literature.

II. VECTORS FOR TECHNOLOGY TRANSFER

There are three main vehicles for formal cross-border technology transfer: licensing, foreign direct investment (FDI) and trade in goods and services. There are other vehicles such as cross-border movement of personnel.[317] There exists a tension between policies aimed at encouraging foreign companies to export, or establish themselves in your market so that needed goods and services can be produced and sold, and those aimed at ensuring sufficient spillovers in terms of skills, know-how, information and technology to enable domestic producers to move up the value chain themselves and perhaps even compete in the same market. There are various channels through which spillovers can occur such as: uncompensated imitation; departure of employees to competitors; access to patent data. There are also spillovers that are best described as efficiency savings arising from the effect that FDI can have on the behaviour of local suppliers and competitors.[318] These include the demonstration effect of use of new technologies in providing a competitive advantage, especially those that are relatively easily observable; the efficiency (cost or otherwise) of new inputs from the FDI actor for downstream producers; the efficiency and learning for suppliers of inputs to the FDI actor, provided that the actor uses local suppliers; departure and exchange of employees across firms.[319]

While these ideas make sense from an economic analysis perspective, it is important that we do not take these effects as a given for most forms of FDI. Where FDI operates in an enclave and is primarily in export oriented businesses, there is a low likelihood of natural spillovers.[320] The proliferation of bilateral investment treaties aimed especially at restricting requirements for local content[321], or technology transfer[322]

---

[317] p10, Maskus, K E "Encouraging International Technology Transfer" ICTSD Issue Paper No. 7, May 2004. Available at: www.iprsonline.org/unctadictsd/docs/CS_Maskus.pdf (last visited August 15, 2014).
[318] See n14, Saggi, K "International technology transfer to developing countries" Economic Paper 64, Commonwealth Secretariat (2004). See also p14, Maskus, K E "Encouraging International Technology Transfer" ICTSD Issue Paper No. 7, May 2004.
[319] See p14, Saggi
[320] p68, Maskus, K "The Role of Intellectual Property Rights in Encouraging Foreign Direct Investment and Technology Transfer" in Maskus, K & C Fink (eds.) *Intellectual Property and Development: Lessons from Recent Economic Research* (Washington D.C.: World Bank, 2005).
[321] See e.g. Article V.2.c, Agreement between the Government of Canada and the Government of the Republic of South Africa on the Promotion and Protection of Investments, (signed 27 November 1995, not yet entered into force).

for example, have made it much more difficult for learning by local suppliers to take place. This also includes measures that limit regulation of strict non-disclosure and non-compete agreements with employees, to prevent them taking information, especially trade secrets, with them to other employers. This makes it much more difficult to view FDI as a vehicle for these kinds of 'natural' non-market channels for FDI. As this thesis argues, it is precisely the regulatory structures around FDI and intellectual property that may be determinative of whether, how, and how much international technology transfer takes place. It cautions against treating FDI as synonymous with technology transfer[323], where the natural effects of FDI are blocked by specifically designed regulatory mechanisms or the deliberate behaviour of the investing firm. In addition, there may be a natural bias against such spillovers, given that some economic models find that the most profitable or successful affiliates are those that are most effective at preventing spillovers of proprietary and non-proprietary knowledge.[324] While the work by Maskus and others on the role that intellectual property plays in enabling FDI has been crucial in identifying channels and levers for the role of intellectual property, it has not been particularly useful in disentangling whether the kinds of spillovers from that FDI actually occur in the presence of limitations imposed by intellectual property and bilateral investment treaties.

We should also take on board the warning by Barton that the dynamics of international technology transfer have shifted significantly since the days of the New International Economic Order.[325] In particular, whereas the concerns in that period involved deeply asymmetric relationships between developed and developing countries (both in political power and technical capacity) and between multinational firms and developing country firms, the post-WTO landscape is very different. Barton points to a much larger role in the economy for FDI that is export based and is not simply focused on access to domestic markets and to a much more dispersed supply chain for many products that are internationally traded.[326] This shifts the incentives for multinational enterprises in terms of how and to whom they provide their technologies. The technical and scientific knowledge base in most developing countries has also been transformed, reflecting greater capacity for absorption and adaptation, while also providing a possible platform for R&D and production for foreign firms seeking competitive advantage for

---

[322] See e.g. Article V.2.e, Agreement between the Government of Canada and the Government of the Republic of South Africa on the Promotion and Protection of Investments
[323] As do Driffield et al "The multinational enterprise as a source of international knowledge flows: Direct evidence from Italy" 41 Journal of International Business Studies 350 (2010), noting that firms actively work to internalize and prevent spillovers from the activities of their affiliates, especially where these are wholly owned.
[324] See e.g. p357, Driffield et al "The multinational enterprise as a source of international knowledge flows: Direct evidence from Italy" 41 Journal of International Business Studies 350 (2010).
[325] See p1, Barton, J "New Trends in Technology Transfer: Implications for National and International Policy", Issue Paper No. 18, ICTSD February 2007.
[326] See p1, Barton, J "New Trends in Technology Transfer: Implications for National and International Policy", Issue Paper No. 18, ICTSD February 2007.

exports to other markets.[327] In addition, the distance between developed and developing countries, in terms of commercial information and capacity to take part in transactions has shrunk, increasing the ability for even small firms to engage in international trade and transactions. Domestic firms in developing countries also have a greater integration into the global market, and are significantly focused on export markets, meaning that the intellectual property standards and rules for market access to developed country markets have much more impact on policy decisions to imitate foreign technologies. Finally, public institutions and universities have become greater players on the commercial side of technological transactions. This means that an increasingly significant amount of technology may be held by so-called non-practicing entities that have no interest in production and do not face the same concerns as firms seeking to carry out FDI or prevent market entry by other firms. These 'public' non-practising entities may be more interested in licensing and in doing so broadly.

At the very least, this new landscape implies a greater willingness and incentive for developed country multinationals to site facilities and use their best technologies in developing countries. It also suggests a disincentive for developing country firms to circumvent or imitate foreign technologies without authorization because they may be shut out of international markets and, in particular, developed country markets. The increase in domestic technical capacity in developing countries, however, also suggests that technological catch up may be sped up, given a sufficient technological base and access to technologies at a reasonable price.

Outside of FDI, the key market based channels are those that relate to joint ventures and licensing.[328] Joint ventures require sharing of technological products, processes and know how, simply to allow the venture to succeed. They work best when both partners bring know-how and capital to the table, although these can also include specialized access to contracting (in the case of preferential procurement policies) or goodwill. To the extent that the venture is time limited, that there is an exchange of information, technology and personnel, the ability of the partners to move on after the joint venture is completed and having learned from each other is extremely useful. Joint ventures can be some of the most efficient tools for enabling learning by the domestic partners. To the extent that joint ventures between competitors are not the natural outcome of market behaviour, some countries have seen fit to condition foreign investment or market access in strategic economic sectors on the establishment of joint ventures. China has historically had such requirements, although there remains some disagreement as to whether these were successful in terms of enabling technology transfer.[329] The use of such measures however, may be restricted by the existence of

---

[327] Id.
[328] Maskus, K E "Encouraging International Technology Transfer" ICTSD Issue Paper No. 7, May 2004.
[329] See e.g. Buckley, P J. et al. "Inward FDI and host country productivity: evidence from China's electronics industry" 15(1) Transnational Corporations (2006) arguing in favor of JVs and Kinoshita, Y "Technology Spillovers through Foreign Direct Investment" CERGE-EI Working Paper No. 39 (December

provisions in bilateral investment treaties that specifically prohibit requiring that investments take place in the form of joint ventures by requiring national treatment in the establishment of investments.[330] This means that it is not possible to require that foreign investment in a particular sector take place only through joint ventures, without also applying that same standard to domestic firms.

Licensing is the primary mechanism for horizontal and vertical market based technology transfer. It can be an efficient way for rightholders to receive return for their investment in researching and developing a technology while ensuring diffusion to those who demand it. However, the technology licensing market suffers from one major structural problem that implicates technology transfer. Licensing, even horizontal licensing, tends to be exclusive to one other primary market player. Where the technology confers a competitive advantage, e.g. energy efficiency where this is a consumer differentiator, the licensee will act to ensure it has exclusive access to the detriment of other domestic firms. This runs counter to what is aimed to be achieved in the climate context which is the diffusion of relevant technologies to *all* the primary actors in the relevant market. Thus our assessment of licensing and the extent to which it takes place must look beyond whether a single license is negotiated, and whether or not it is horizontal, but also the extent to which such a license provides for spillovers of knowledge to the broader market.

Having provided some background on these mechanisms, the discussion below will now examine the existing literature and studies on IP and technology transfer in environmental law and climate change. Clearly, to the extent that there is evidence that patent distribution and trends, and licensing costs and terms pose no structural limitations to addressing the scope, timing and geographical targets above and are not likely to do so, there may be less need for urgent action by the UNFCCC on intellectual property. However, where problems are found to exist, it may become even more important to ensure that countries have the capacity to act.

In the realm of technology transfer to address climate change existing studies of patents seem to suggest that in the selected technology areas (primarily renewable energy for GHG mitigation) there are few patents in developing countries, and if there are, they do not pose a barrier because of competitive alternatives.[331] Where there has

---

1998). Available at SSRN: http://ssrn.com/abstract=157614 arguing that FDI and JVs were not a significant factor in productivity growth from technology.
[330] See e.g. e.g. Article II.3, Agreement between the Government of Canada and the Government of the Republic of South Africa on the Promotion and Protection of Investments, (signed 27 November 1995, not yet entered into force).
[331] Barton, J "Intellectual Property and Access to Clean Energy Technologies in Developing Countries: An Analysis of Solar Photovoltaic, Biofuel and Wind Technologies" Trade and Sustainable Energy Series, Issue Paper No. 2, ICTSD December 2007. See also Copenhagen Economics and the IPR Company "Are IPRs a Barrier to the Transfer of Climate Change Technology?" Study Commissioned by European Commission DG Trade, January 2009. Available at:

been an increase in patenting, almost all of that can be attributed to increased patenting in the small group of emerging economies, of which China is the most affected.[332] The next section goes further in depth to assess the existing work in this area, but it is important to note a very important caveat - while the distribution of patents worldwide in a particular sector is useful to know, it tells us very little about how those patents are exercised. The existence of a patent in a country can be indicative of several things: from a willingness to offer for sale and license to a defensive blocking patent aimed at excluding competition. This is a weakness long acknowledged in the literature on cross-country comparisons on innovative activity.[333] In combination with data on residence of the inventor or applicant, as well as counting patent families rather than individual patents, patent counts can tell us when an inventor who resides in one patent jurisdiction seeks to patent an invention in another country. To the extent that the data can be considered predictive of whether the patent will actually be granted (which is largely true for registration systems but much less so for examination systems which may have varying standards for inventive step e.g. the triadic patent families of the United States Patent and Trademark Office, the European Patent Office and the Japanese Patent Office) then that tells us something about the rate of diffusion of the patented technology.

However, in terms of technology transfer, defined as transferring, hardware, skills, know-how necessary to enable domestic actors to reproduce and adapt the technology, such data tells us very little. The existence of a patent in a country does not tell us whether the right to exercise the patent has been assigned or made available to one or more domestic actors, whether it has allowed that actor to produce for domestic and or export, and whether the technology has diffused into the market. That information can really only be gained from looking at granted patents and information regarding assignation or licensing of such patents.

In addition, the lack of a patent in a country is not necessarily an indicator of freedom to use or import the technology. For example, if all the countries where the patented product is manufactured all have patent protection then firms from the country that does not have patent protection will have to pay the IP premium included in the price of the good in the other markets or the global market, regardless of the fact that it is not patented in their domestic market. Obversely, domestic firms that produce the technology will be shut out of the markets of those countries where the technology is protected, and will not be able to benefit from the economies of scale that allow for providing products to both the national and international market. The key indicator that may best determine the nature and scale of IP issues is whether and to what extent

---

http://trade.ec.europa.eu/doclib/docs/2009/february/tradoc_142371.pdf (last visited August 15, 2014).
[332] Copenhagen Economics and the IPR Company "Are IPRs a Barrier to the Transfer of Climate Change Technology?" Study Commissioned by European Commission DG Trade, January 2009.
[333] See Dernis, H et al. "Using Patent Counts for Cross-Country Comparisons of Technology Output" 27 STI Review 129 (2001)

licensing takes place and what the terms of such licenses are, including licensing that did not take place due to proposed restrictive terms.

Finally, patent landscaping exercises suffer from a critical problem regarding the baseline for comparison. Where the landscape can tell us about the absolute number of patents in a sector, it does not tell us about what the percentage of patents are in relation to the technological field as a whole. This is compounded by the ways in which technologies are defined in patent landscapes i.e. by looking at the patent classifications which may be biased specifically towards patentable subject matter in each field. Even where such a baseline might be established, patents are not of equal value, and while there are ways of examining the data to establish the value of a patent by seeing whether it has been patented in multiple jurisdictions, that does not really let us know the technological role of the patented invention i.e. is it a central technology which is sine qua non for participating in the technological market, or are their alternatives, patented or otherwise. Thus patent landscapes can allow us to compare absolute number of patents between fields, but cannot really provide us a way of measuring patent density as compared to non-patented technology in the same field.

Keeping these issues in mind, I now carry out a critical survey of the empirical literature on patents and climate change.

III. THE EPO/UNEP/ICTSD STUDY[334]

The study that comes the closest to providing the kind of data needed (as discussed above) was carried out by the European Patent Office (EPO) in collaboration with UNEP and the International Center for Trade and Sustainable Development (ICTSD).[335] It consists of a patent landscape (based on a newly constructed set of patent classifications for Clean Energy Technologies (CETs), encompassing a much wider and deeper data set than the traditional International Patent Classification scheme) and a licensing survey.

III.1 Scope, Timing and Geography

Its main weakness is that it covers a very small pool of technologies: power generation limited to wind, biofuels, solar PV and thermal, CCS, ocean marine power, and Integrated Gasification Combined Cycle.[336] Nevertheless, the patent classification is a true advance in the state of the art, likely to enable better assessments of the full scale of patenting of environmentally sustainable technologies. It finally provides both a tool for objectively classifying technologies in patent applications, after an initial self-

---

[334] Karachalios, K et al. (eds.) "Patents and Clean Energy: Bridging the Gap between Evidence and Policy: Final report" UNEP/ EPO / ICTSD 2010.
[335] Id.
[336] See p15, id.

selection by the applicant. Most impressively however is the fact that the classification has worked retroactively to classify older patents in the EPO database, creating an unusually rich dataset for future analysis.

In terms of geography, the licensing survey only surveyed licensors, largely based in the OECD. The only developing country respondents were from Brazil and South Africa, constituting 4% of the sample.[337] The study did not address rates of diffusion of the technologies studied and so provided no information on timing.

III.2 Findings and analysis

Several things become clear from the landscape: the vast majority of patenting takes place in OECD countries with an increasing share in emerging economies.[338] However, there is comparatively little direct ownership of patents by domestic firms in China, India and Brazil in the selected sectors.[339] On the other hand, the study confirms earlier findings by John Barton[340] that the selected sectors do not have highly concentrated claimed patent ownership, although ownership is concentrated in OECD firms.[341]

This would seem to suggest that even where patents existed, there was sufficient competition such that licenses would be made available, prices would not be too high and terms not overly onerous. The limitations of the patent landscape make it difficult to draw broad conclusions, but one can note that the ability to access foreign technology will be a key need even for countries with internal manufacturing and learning capacity. Increasing the speed and scale of market transactions relating to those technologies will therefore be crucial to address the climate challenge. Information about the nature and scale of the cross-border licensing of relevant technologies is crucial and it is here that the licensing survey provides some tantalizing if preliminary data.

The licensing survey looked first at the importance of patents in the firm's activities and secondly at how these related to the firm's activities, if any, in developing countries. Methodologically, the survey suffers from not being able to get information on the terms of licenses as well as specific pricing information for specific markets. This points to a serious hurdle for empirical studies in this area in the absence of formal procedures for surveillance of licensing and/or joint venture contracts. Precisely

---

[337] See p53, Karachalios, K et al. (eds.) "Patents and Clean Energy: Bridging the Gap between Evidence and Policy: Final report" UNEP/ EPO / ICTSD 2010.
[338] See p30, Id.
[339] See p33, Id.
[340] Barton, J "Intellectual Property and Access to Clean Energy Technologies in Developing Countries: An Analysis of Solar Photovoltaic, Biofuel and Wind Technologies" Trade and Sustainable Energy Series, Issue Paper No. 2, ICTSD December 2007.
[341] See p43, Karachalios, et al. (eds.)

because of the post-contract confidentiality of most transactions, it may be necessary for countries concerned with addressing technology transfer to not rely on post-transaction measures such as competition law but to actively collect and mine the data on terms and prices beforehand so as to catch patterns and enforce rules against unacceptable terms.

The questions used to determine the importance of IP protection also present a concern.[342] There is little overlap with the criteria and measures used in indexes such as those by Park[343], making comparability somewhat difficult. However, as this is an assessment of perceptions rather than an assessment of objective strength, it may be workable even if it does make comparability to other measures of IP strength difficult. The three questions relate to 1) membership in an international protection treaty 2) ability to enforce, especially civil and criminal penalties 3) ability to gain access to know-how owned by the other third party. While the first two are quite general, the third question is actually quite specific, addressing itself to the permissible terms of the licensing contract (such as grant-back conditions). The critique is that for the first question, it is not clear that there is any awareness of membership of international treaties of these countries in many firms and in fact, whether such membership exists may pale in signaling power compared to the simple question of whether there are clear transparent rules on IP. The concern is that respondents may rate this element low when what is really relevant is whether IP protection covers their technology (product and patent) for the requisite 20 year term, and provides them with specific rights. If that is the case, then it is possible that respondents may actually have responded by placing more importance on this issue if asked these specific sub-questions. In particular, a useful approach would have focused on protective terms that go beyond the TRIPS Agreement, given that this is now the baseline and the main policy question is whether providing stronger IP than is required by TRIPS protection will induce changes in behaviour and perceptions of industry participants. It would have been useful to ask questions related to extension of patent protection to software; restrictions on research exceptions and reverse engineering. The findings may have ended up being the same but would have been more informative for the climate policy discussion.

The second question poses the same concerns. At the level of generality, this does not really provide key information. What would be good to know would be perceptions of what is necessary for enforcement such as; the ability to get injunctions and provisional measures in disputes; or speed and access to specialized IP courts. Having basic access to civil and criminal courts, may indeed be a basic condition, but perhaps because that is a basic condition of doing business in any sector. Somewhat narrower questions related to specific IP concerns may have been useful. The anomaly here is the third question which actually does address itself to a specific business

---

[342] See p85, Karachalios, K et al. (eds.) "Patents and Clean Energy: Bridging the Gap between Evidence and Policy: Final report" UNEP/ EPO / ICTSD 2010.
[343] Park, W G, "International patent protection: 1960–2005," Research Policy 37: 761–766 (2008).

concern of licensors or JV participants. This seems much better designed to extract information related to business decisions and levels of IP protection and restrictions. An additional question might also have related to enforceability of restrictions on the protection of know-how through non-compete clauses for departing employees. The overall concern related to these questions suggests that the survey would have been best served by carrying out a preliminary study on what issues in IP protection were of most concern to licensors and investors who participate in technology sectors generally, so as to test the relevance of these factors to decisions to license into developing countries.

The first important result from the licensing survey is that, for organizations involved in significant patenting in the selected sectors of the study, out-licensing was of greater significance for the majority of firms (84%) compared to the group as a whole (73%).[344] The importance of out-licensing was especially significant for academic institutions and public bodies. In part this reflects the structure of the business model for such entities who carry out fundamental research, usually with public money, and are mandated as part of their mission to transfer such technology into the domestic business sector. They rarely have production capacity themselves and are not significant actors in the manufacture and trade of goods related to the technology they license.

The study did also ask about other mechanisms such as collaborative R&D and joint ventures.[345] In terms of licensing and collaborative ventures, almost 60% noted no activity in the previous 3 years,[346] while 17% stated that they frequently did so.[347] This data is particularly useful because the question regarding whether licensing or collaborative activities took place focused on activities relating to non-majority owned subsidiaries[348], thus filtering out vertical technology transfers. The majority of that activity took place in China (25%), India (17%), Brazil (12%) and Russia (10%), again in line with where the major developing country markets are. As a rule, renewable energy intensive companies in the selected sectors were more likely to use licensing and collaborative mechanisms than the sample group as a whole, although there is no indication of the extent to which that willingness included licensing to firms in developing countries.[349] As the report notes, there may be a gap between the willingness to license and collaborate and the difficulty of finding and negotiating agreements with partners in developing countries.[350] In part, this may be because many participants in the renewable energy field are not mature businesses with significant international experience and the technology market in developing countries tends to be even less

---

[344] See p53, Karachalios, K et al. (eds.) "Patents and Clean Energy: Bridging the Gap between Evidence and Policy: Final report" UNEP/ EPO / ICTSD 2010.
[345] See p56, Id.
[346] See p58, Id.
[347] Id.
[348] See Licensing Survey Part B. Question, p84, Id.
[349] See p56, Karachalios, K et al. (eds.) "Patents and Clean Energy: Bridging the Gap between Evidence and Policy: Final report" UNEP/ EPO / ICTSD 2010.
[350] See p58, Id.

mature than traditional manufacturing and industrial sectors, all of which is complicated by linguistic, legal process, and other factors, including perceptions regarding the reliability of intellectual property protection. Indeed, the survey finds that of the concerns that firms had in engaging in licensing and other collaborative activities, protection of IP was a basic but not compelling reason to engage. More weight was placed on investment climate and market attractiveness. It would have been useful to find out how much importance was attached to IP protection by those companies that did *not* engage in any licensing to developing countries in the previous 3 years in comparison to the general sample, and in comparison to those that did engage in such licensing. This would have given some insight into how much of a barrier perceived lack of IP protection was to engaging in licensing at all. Instead, the report does the opposite, and compares the importance of IP for those that have licensed to developing countries in the previous 3 years, to the general sample.[351] The report notes that the group saw IP protection as more important by 7% over the sample group (89% to 82%).[352] This is a significant variation in the context of the numbers in the study, suggesting that something related to the experience of licensing into developing countries raises awareness of a need for greater intellectual property protection. This is something that may need to be confirmed with further empirical work, but if true, means that the IP related experiences of such licensors have not been entirely positive. However, the survey also shows that the group would be more willing than the general sample to offer easier monetary terms to firms in developing countries (78% to 70%).[353] The willingness to offer substantially more accommodating pricing was however, limited to 5% of the general sample[354] suggesting that grant or concessional terms were not an option unless the difference is made up by other measures. In addition, the question limited itself to monetary terms[355] and so provides little guidance as to whether they would also provide flexible terms on grant back conditions, geographical scope, sub-licensing etc. Finally, the group most likely to consider more flexible licensing was dominated by academic and public institutions, with multinational enterprises being the least willing to do so. Overall, the study concludes that the rate and scale of licensing to developing countries in the selected technologies is not significantly different from licensing for all technologies into developing countries.[356] This may present a real problem in that what is actually needed is for such technologies to be licensed or made available at a far higher rate than is the case at present and in comparison to other technology sectors.

III.3 Conclusions to draw from the study

---

[351] See p59, Id.
[352] Id.
[353] See p59, Karachalios, K et al. (eds.) "Patents and Clean Energy: Bridging the Gap between Evidence and Policy: Final report" UNEP/ EPO / ICTSD 2010.
[354] See p60, Id.
[355] See p86, Id.
[356] See p64, Id.

One possible conclusion to draw from this study is that academic and public institutions are best suited to be channels of flexible licensing to developing countries. In addition, if given the opportunity, SMEs who do not at present have any commercial relationships in developing countries would be happy to license, even at flexible rates, if they could be assured of predictability, transparency and a minimum level of IP protection (especially in their home markets). The only group that may be less amenable to doing so are the multinational enterprises who may already participate in developing country markets and have interests beyond simple licensing and actually engage in production and competition in these markets.

IV. THE COPENHAGEN ECONOMICS/IPR COMPANY STUDY

This study by Copenhagen Economics was commissioned by the European Union.[357] It carries out a patent landscape but without the advantage of the more accurate and well developed classification for patent applications and grants developed for the ICTSD/UNEP/EPO study. It also poses some methodological problems, ones that it has in common with other such patent landscape exercises. It presumes that the non-existence of a patent therefore indicates that there are no IP-related problems.[358] As noted above, the fact that no patent exists in the domestic market does not mean that the firms in that country that need to purchase technological products and do not produce them domestically would not have to pay the IP premium as included in products made in countries where the patent was in force.

IV.1 Scope, Timing, Geography

The core of the study is limited to a narrow set of technologies in power generation (waste, biomass, wind, solar, geothermal, fuel cell, ocean power).[359] However, the analysis of the abatement cost curve that they use covers about 50 technologies.[360] A closer examination of the data show that for the vast majority of mitigation technologies that they identify (using the McKinsey & Co abatement curve[361]), there is no information on whether they are patented in LDCs.[362] In fact for all but one of the technologies on the negative cost side of the abatement curve, and for a significant section of those on the other, the study has no data on the levels of patenting in developing countries. For the area of the curve with positive abatement costs, in the selected technology areas, they have coverage of the bare majority of technologies. This

---

[357] Copenhagen Economics and the IPR Company "Are IPRs a Barrier to the Transfer of Climate Change Technology?" Study Commissioned by European Commission DG Trade, January 2009.
[358] See p15, Id.
[359] Id.
[360] See p1, Id.
[361] Enqvist, P A et al. "A Cost Curve for Greenhouse Gas Reduction" McKinsey Quarterly 2007:1
[362] See Fig 2.2, p15, Copenhagen Economics and the IPR Company "Are IPRs a Barrier to the Transfer of Climate Change Technology?" Study Commissioned by European Commission DG Trade, January 2009.

means they have no data on: [363] Industry (efficiency); Agriculture/waste; Power generation related to CCS, coal-firing, Nuclear; transport related to power trains, hybrids, plug-ins, transit; buildings. It is on this basis that they argue that the majority of technologies are not patented in LDCs and developing countries, at least as determined by those that would be used under their extraction of an abatement curve for developing countries from the McKinsey global abatement curve. On this basis, that claim may be too large to be supported by the nature and quality of the data that they were able to gather. On the basis of the technologies that this thesis has identified in Chapter 2 as needed by developing countries, it may be especially insufficient as it only covers mitigation technologies and only a small fraction of the mitigation technology need. As noted, in Chapter 2, a significant portion of the need in developing countries will be in agriculture, industry, and buildings

The study does indeed address itself to the issue of geography and where the patents are distributed. It does not necessarily consider the role that countries such as China, India and Brazil play in providing technology to other developing countries. In terms of timing, it does not provide any data or analysis on the rate of diffusion of technologies.

IV.2 Findings and Analysis

The study looks at the distribution of the patents and finds that, especially for renewables, but also other sectors, the vast majority of patenting in developing countries takes place in China, followed far behind by other emerging economies.[364] They argue that even where a significant portion of abatement technologies are patented in China, the cost of accessing IP should not be a barrier because, in the aggregate, the relevant technologies (in efficiency and fuels switching in industry, transport, and buildings) will have a negative abatement cost.[365] While true in the aggregate, this still does little to address what occurs at the level of individual firm decisions that may not be able to entirely capture these efficiency gains all to themselves. More importantly, while cost may indeed not be a factor, firms in China and other emerging countries may have problems relating to issues such as refusals to license, restrictive licensing terms and reach through provisions that deter firms from licensing technologies. Finally, China and other emerging economies may play a role in providing technological products to other developing countries and if they are blocked from producing these for export to these other countries, it may be impossible to address climate change mitigation and adaptation within the necessary time frames.

The study also finds that while most patented technologies in the sectors studied are concentrated in OECD countries, emerging economies, in particular China,

---

[363] See Table 5.1, p49, See p15, Id.
[364] See p17, Copenhagen Economics and the IPR Company "Are IPRs a Barrier to the Transfer of Climate Change Technology?" Study Commissioned by European Commission DG Trade, January 2009.
[365] Id.

accounted for much of the recent growth. In particular, the study notes that an increasing share of patents are owned by domestic firms in emerging economies (approximately 33%).[366] The study does not tell us whether they determine ownership by name of inventor or assignee, and whether they analyzed whether the assignee is a wholly owned or majority owned subsidiary of a foreign firm. This disaggregation may be important as it could prevent erroneous conclusions regarding the actual level of control over these patents.

The largest number of patents is concentrated in the Solar PV area, and over 92% of technologies in developing countries in the 7 sectors covered by the study are owned by Chinese applicants. This means that in all other emerging economies, foreign owners may be heavily dominant in patent ownership and that far from being the rule, China may present an exception. The study also notes that, in the sectors covered, there appears to be relatively dispersed patent ownership.[367] The authors conclude that there is less likelihood of high rent extraction due to competing possibilities for access to the same or similar technologies. This indeed may be true, in the absence of anti-competitive collusive behaviour amongst patent holders. However, given the concentration of patents in the hands of foreign rightholders, there may be broader structural problems in the market. While concentrated foreign ownership may not correlate directly with firm concentration, it does imply that we should not be too sanguine about the competitive pressure on rightholders even in sectors that do not have high firm concentration. In particular, licensing costs and licensing terms are not subject to normal competitive structural influences. This is because the price of a license is not usually disclosed [368] and so other players in the market have no transparency as to what was offered by other players in similar transactions, internationally or domestically. This makes assessing whether a particular offer is market-based or not difficult and complicates how other offerors may compete on price. This makes each negotiation for a license, not a negotiation that takes place in a transparent competitive market, but one that takes place somewhat isolated from information about the nature and scope of other similar transactions in the market. This may make each offeror more likely to seek higher rents than they might otherwise seek, and create pressure on potential offerees to take the transaction in front of them rather than move on to another offeror and ask for a better deal.

IV.3 What conclusions may be drawn

Overall, while providing some insight, the study's larger conclusions may not be sustainable. However, its conclusions on concentrated OECD ownership dovetail

---

[366] See p22, Copenhagen Economics and the IPR Company "Are IPRs a Barrier to the Transfer of Climate Change Technology?" Study Commissioned by European Commission DG Trade, January 2009.
[367] See p23, Id.
[368] See p46, Lee, B et al. "Who owns our Low Carbon Future: Intellectual Property and Energy Technologies" Chatham House, September 2009.

with those of other studies. In addition, the finding that China presents the largest emerging economy share of patents in the selected sectors is also consistent with other findings, as is the finding that the majority of technologies are not patented in LDCs. A newer finding may be the relatively dispersed ownership of patents even amongst OECD rightholders. In the absence of data on licensing distribution and terms, it is difficult to draw conclusions, but multiple vendors or offerors of similar technologies may indeed be likely to increase the tendency to out-license, even for large enterprises who are themselves engaged in production in the technology sector.[369] This may not necessarily mean that restrictive licensing terms may not still be imposed. The data on this in the climate technology arena, however, seem to suggest that this tendency to license may still be limited to non-producing entities.[370]

V. Dechezleprêtre et. al. Study[371]

A comprehensive patent landscaping study was carried out by Dechezleprêtre and colleagues[372] (LSE, MINES Paris and the OECD). The study also uses a global database developed by the EPO. The authors study the process of innovation and technology transfer by looking at patent counts, weighted for propensity to patent and patent breadth.[373] The methodology, however, presents some problems, especially for the purposes of measuring technology transfer. While not uncommon in the field, their assumption that a patent is a reliable indicator of intention to 'use' the patent is difficult to reconcile with much of actual business practice regarding patenting. Patents can be sought for reasons ranging from intent to manufacture products oneself in the market, to blocking market entry.[374] In either case, little technology transfer occurs if local domestic capacity is not enabled. In this case, they presume that a patent is transferred from one country to another when it is patented in a country by an inventor who is resident in another.[375] They presume intent to 'use' to mean to either manufacture or license the patent into the market.[376] However, in the case of technology transfer, where the problems that arise are exactly those such as refusals to license, refusals to work, refusals to provide knowledge flows to other actors in the market, such an assumption is untenable. Even if it were a valid measure of market intention by a patent

---

[369] See Arora, A and A Fosfuri, "Licensing in the presence of competing technologies" 52 Journal of Economic Behavior and Organization 277 (2003).
[370] See Karachalios, K et al. (eds.) "Patents and Clean Energy: Bridging the Gap between Evidence and Policy: Final report" UNEP/ EPO / ICTSD 2010.; Lee, B et al. "Who owns our Low Carbon Future: Intellectual Property and Energy Technologies" Chatham House, September 2009.
[371] Dechezleprêtre, A et al. "Invention and Transfer of Climate Change–Mitigation Technologies: A Global Analysis" 5 Rev Environ Econ Policy 109 (2011).
[372] Id.
[373] See p110, Id.
[374] Veer, T and F Jell "Contributing to markets for technology? A comparison of patent filing motives of individual inventors, small companies and universities", 32 Technovation 513 (2012).
[375] See p121, Dechezleprêtre, A et al. "Invention and Transfer of Climate Change–Mitigation Technologies: A Global Analysis" 5 Rev Environ Econ Policy 109 (2011).
[376] See p111, Id.

holder, the failure to operationalize a proper definition of technology transfer makes it difficult to draw anything but the most indicative conclusions on the nature and scale of technology transfer from their data.

The study also uses patent levels as a proxy for the level of 'innovative activity' again, failing to account for both the strategic business reasons for patenting, but even more crucially, for significant differences not just in patent scope, for which the authors control, but in the standards for such things as inventive step. In some countries, patents which are captured by the patent system may actually end up in the utility patent or design patent system in others. The EPO data only capture the 'patent' data per se, and not these others. However, if controlled for with a measure of the extent to which a patent functions as part of a broader patent family, which the authors do, a measure of the quality of invention is introduced which shifts the measure of innovation level somewhat. The key issue here is again of proper operational definitions of what constitutes innovation. To the extent that the term innovation has a qualitative element i.e. a technology that has not been created or used in a particular way before, a patent captures only some of that and the range between countries of what constitutes an acceptable level of inventive step to qualify for a patent is so large that it may not be the most reliable indicator.

Another problem that the study has is in its use of the residence of the inventor on the patent to determine the locus of innovation.[377] While they acknowledge problems related to collection of data, the greater problem is that the question with respect to technology transfer is not necessarily *where* the innovation is taking place but whether the innovation is actually being carried out by a local firm. The study does not measure the extent to which the assignees of the patent are local companies. For the purposes of technology transfer measures, it is crucial to know who the actual owners of the technology are, something which the authors subsume and do not fully address in their measures.

V.1 Scope, Timing, Geography

The study covers 13 mitigation technologies: wind, solar, geothermal, marine energy, hydropower, biomass, and waste to energy, methane destruction, climate-friendly cement, thermal insulation in buildings, heating, electric and hybrid vehicles, and energy-efficient lighting.[378] This presents a broad sub-sample of the technologies covered by developing country needs in mitigation. It remains a narrow slice of the broader technology needs, and does not address adaptation.

---

[377] See p114, Id.
[378] See p113, Dechezleprêtre, A et al. "Invention and Transfer of Climate Change–Mitigation Technologies: A Global Analysis" 5 Rev Environ Econ Policy 109 (2011).

Again, this study is a relatively static landscaping exercise, providing little information about future trends in patenting or the rate of diffusion and licensing. In terms of geography, the patent landscape covers the major developing countries, but does not analyze LDC participation.

V. 2 Findings and analysis

The study finds that emerging economies are an increasing centre for "innovation" with China coming 4th and Brazil 12th, but after controlling for membership in patent families, China drops out of the top 10.[379] This may drop even more if controlling ownership of patent assignees were measured.

Nevertheless, the data on concentration of patenting is consistent with that found by others; that, in the fields selected, it is almost exclusively concentrated in the OECD countries, except for China.[380] By the measure of 'technology transfer' that is used, they find that the majority (77%) of transfers occur between OECD countries, with 22% occurring from OECD to non-OECD.[381] Seventy-five percent of the OECD to non-OECD transfers are to China.[382] Non-OECD to non-OECD transfers are negligible.[383] The extent of 'transfers' to China would be indicative of the lower importance of IP protection to intent to transfer, but, it may also be the case that a significant amount of this patenting is defensive in nature, to prevent market entry and production by Chinese firms, which may leak back out to other markets. The lack of 'transfer' to other developing countries would also signify that little technology transfer is taking place into those economies.

V.3 What conclusions may be drawn

The findings on the rate of patenting into China present some concern. Without further data on the reasons why such patenting is taking place, perhaps indicated by ownership and control of the patents as well as use, it seems as if there may be significant efforts to engage in blocking behaviour in China. The findings also indicate how marginal developing countries are in participating in patenting into other countries. The measure of innovation, while methodologically problematic, suggests that at the very least, developing country firms do not have the volume, or even quality of patents to engage in equal bargaining with firms from developed countries to engage in patent-based research cooperation.

---

[379] See p116, Id.
[380] See p115, Id.
[381] See p122, Dechezleprêtre, A et al. "Invention and Transfer of Climate Change–Mitigation Technologies: A Global Analysis" 5 Rev Environ Econ Policy 109 (2011).
[382] Id.
[383] Id.

VI. John Barton ICTSD study[384]

This study by John Barton has been one of the earliest and most cited pieces on the topic. In terms of methodology, Barton does not carry out a patent landscape and has no direct information relating to patenting or ownership of patents in each sector studied. He examines information on the concentration of the industry and uses that to deduce whether or not based on that concentration, if patents did exist, they would pose a problem. Barton presumes that the existence of multiple firms with dispersed ownership of patents will make access to licensing easier.[385] As also noted, I am less sanguine about the existence of competitive licensing markets in the absence of transparent information about the prices and terms of previous and ongoing licensing contracts. This is especially true where licensing would be desired from actual producing entities and not just non-practising entities such as universities and public bodies.

VI.1 Scope, Timing, and Geography

The study is limited to three sectors in power generation: Solar PV, Biomass and Wind. Therefore it can only provide an indication of the kinds of patterns that may exist but cannot bear the weight of broader conclusions regarding the actual distribution of patents in broader power generation sectors, which the author acknowledges.[386]

As with others, this study does not address itself to timing or pace of technology transfer. In terms of geography, it primarily focuses on Brazil, India and China.

VI.2 Findings and analysis

The case studies on industry structure and the role of IP are nevertheless very useful. In Solar PV, Barton notes only a moderate amount of industry concentration, largely in developed countries with some firms from developing countries.[387] He notes that the upstream firms in the solar inverter sector are somewhat more concentrated but not to the extent that significant rents could be extracted. Nevertheless he concludes that because of the large number of firms, some of whom are located in developing

---

[384] Barton, J "Intellectual Property and Access to Clean Energy Technologies in Developing Countries: An Analysis of Solar Photovoltaic, Biofuel and Wind Technologies" Trade and Sustainable Energy Series, Issue Paper No. 2, ICTSD December 2007.
[385] See p11, Barton, J "Intellectual Property and Access to Clean Energy Technologies in Developing Countries: An Analysis of Solar Photovoltaic, Biofuel and Wind Technologies" Trade and Sustainable Energy Series, Issue Paper No. 2, ICTSD December 2007.
[386] See p1, Id.
[387] See p10, Id.

countries, there is little likelihood of unreasonable royalties being demanded.[388] What is more difficult to assess is what the role of restrictive terms might be in the industry.

In Biomass (largely ethanol), the study shows a much greater degree of concentration, dominated by two companies (Monsanto and Archer Daniels Midland).[389] He notes however that there are many entrants from developing countries in the market and points especially to Brazil as having a dynamic and thriving competitive capacity. He suggests that since the basic technologies are in the public domain, participation is not likely to be blocked by intellectual property except perhaps for more recent advanced second generation biofuels (generated from cellulosic materials).[390] Even where there are such concerns, there may be fungibility between different kinds of biofuels such that despite different production processes being patented, overall participation in one of the market niches will not be blocked.[391] In addition, the need for decentralized production and local delivery of biofuels also provides an incentive to license more broadly.[392] He concludes that the likelihood of unreasonable royalties is small, albeit somewhat higher than for Solar PV.

For Wind, the study finds a higher level of concentration in the global market than for the other two sectors examined.[393] Barton argues that while the number of suppliers ensures access to technological products, entry into the market for production of wind technologies will be far more difficult. He notes that there is some evidence of a reluctance to license due to fear of creating competitors in developing countries.[394] However, there are significant players from developing countries such as Goldwind Science & Technology Co., Ltd (Goldwind) in China, and Suzlon Energy Ltd. (Suzlon) in India.[395]

VI.3 What conclusions can be drawn?

Overall, Barton is relatively sanguine about access to technology in all three sectors, both for products and for knowledge. He is less optimistic about access to technologies for use in developing country firms seeking to participate in international

---

[388] See p11, Id.
[389] See p13, Barton, J "Intellectual Property and Access to Clean Energy Technologies in Developing Countries: An Analysis of Solar Photovoltaic, Biofuel and Wind Technologies" Trade and Sustainable Energy Series, Issue Paper No. 2, ICTSD December 2007.
[390] Id.
[391] Id.
[392] See p14, Id.
[393] See p16, Id.
[394] See p16, Id. *citing* Lewis, J and R Wiser "A Review of International Experience with Policies to Promote Wind Power Industry Development", Presentation at the Energy Foundation China Sustainable Energy Program, 10 March 2005.
[395] See p17, Id.

markets and access to developed country markets.[396] The case studies presented by Barton are suggestive, especially in how they pinpoint significant developing country, (specifically India, Brazil and China) participation in all three sectors studied. The existence of capable developing country firms in each sector suggests a real opportunity for enabling and transferring technology transfer and development into these economies and enabling production for export to other developing countries. As Barton notes, there may be real entry points but concerns about competition in home markets exist for many developed country firms. This suggests that some certainty about geographical segmentation of markets may be necessary to encourage further licensing in these sectors.

VII. THE CHATHAM HOUSE STUDY[397]

A report by Chatham House[398] on patenting in selected fields confirms some of the findings of the Barton study and carries out an initial patent landscaping that comes to similar conclusions to the EPO/UNEP/ICTSD study. The authors use the landscaping exercise to try to determine the nature and scope of patent concentration in these sectors, going one step beyond the Barton study to actually demonstrate rather than infer a relationship between industry concentration and patent concentration.

VII.1 Scope, Timing and Geography

The study covers wind, solar PV, concentrated solar power (CSP), biomass-to-electricity, carbon capture and storage and cleaner coal and it attempts to go beyond the traditional IPC classification to capture a finer grained picture of the subsectors and links to other technological fields.[399]

In timing, the study is one of the few to try to assess the rates of diffusion in the sectors. Based on the 2050 timeline, the study assesses the age of the most cited patents in patent applications.[400]

On geography, the study covers all the important developing country markets but suffers because, as they acknowledge, the research methodology's reliance only on electronically accessible patent data meant that access to Indian data was limited.[401]

---

[396] See p18, Barton, J "Intellectual Property and Access to Clean Energy Technologies in Developing Countries: An Analysis of Solar Photovoltaic, Biofuel and Wind Technologies" Trade and Sustainable Energy Series, Issue Paper No. 2, ICTSD December 2007.
[397] Lee, B et al. "Who owns our Low Carbon Future: Intellectual Property and Energy Technologies" Chatham House, September 2009.
[398] Id.
[399] See p1, Id.
[400] See p48, Lee, B et al. "Who owns our Low Carbon Future: Intellectual Property and Energy Technologies" Chatham House, September 2009.

VII.2 Findings and analysis

The study finds, as did others, that patenting rates remained sluggish in all six fields studied until the 1990s when they began a rapid rise.[402] Again, the key patenting countries are the OECD (US, Japan, Germany, Denmark and South Korea) with China as a major patenting destination larger than Denmark and South Korea. A key insight from the study is that an undetermined amount of patenting in some of these countries, but especially China and the US because of their size as investment and market destinations, may be carried out by subsidiaries of firms from other countries. In such cases, data about the nationality of the inventor is not necessarily helpful and what may provide better data is the identity and ownership structure of the assignee of the patent. Even those studies, such as the Copenhagen Economics study that find significant inventorship by Chinese nationals may not really indicate the extent to which the patent is actually under the control of a firm from another country. The Chatham House analysis shows that a significant portion of Chinese patents are owned by firms whose parent companies are based outside the country.[403]

The study finds that all six sectors have relatively concentrated patent ownership[404] although it does not appear to be significantly correlated with the number of patents in the field. The study authors suggest that there does not seem to be a link between such concentration and the level of innovation (if number of patents filed per sector is used as a proxy). However, the number of patents is not and should not be used as a reliable proxy for 'level of innovation' in a sector given the number of intervening causes that exist to explain that number. More reliably, their examination of the extent of patent families[405] in the sectors studied shows that between 60% – 85% of the patents belonged to a patent family, suggesting a high concentration of high-commercial value, key patents likely to be in the hands of large commercial actors.[406]

The study also finds that much of the patent ownership in the sectors studied is concentrated (above 50% share) in multinational firms who actually produce in the market sector.[407] Combined with the concentration of patent families, this suggests a stronger likelihood of strategic behaviour aimed at maintaining market share and preventing market entry of new competitors and lowers the likelihood of horizontal

---

[401] See p2, Id.
[402] See p12, Id.
[403] See p16, Id.
[404] See p18, Id.
[405] A patent family is the set of all patent applications flowing from an initial patent, comprising those covering the same subject matter but subsequently filed abroad based on the date of filing of the initial patent. For further definition see http://www.epo.org/searching/essentials/patent-families/definitions.html
[406] See p18, Lee, B et al. "Who owns our Low Carbon Future: Intellectual Property and Energy Technologies" Chatham House, September 2009.
[407] See p17, Id.

licensing. On the other hand, it may make FDI directly into markets more likely with the attendant possibility of downstream and upstream effects on suppliers and those who use the firm's products as inputs. To the extent that these firms are export oriented, they may be more likely to ensure that subsidiaries and/or local partners have the best technology available. The analysis by Chatham House emphasizes the importance of sectoral analyses for deciding what kinds of interventions may be appropriate to increase knowledge spillovers. However, in the case where the majority of patents are owned by national corporations (second highest share overall),[408] as in the wind sector,[409] then even the likelihood of FDI is reduced, as such firms are more likely to want to protect existing markets by: preventing the possibility of production overseas leaking back into their home markets; competitors competing with them in export markets into which they have sales; and they are less likely to engage in FDI. In such cases, incentives may have to be created for these firms to either license for local production or be required to 'work' the patent rather than simply use it as a blocking mechanism. The share of patents owned by universities and public institutions is quite small suggesting that these may not be the great hope for licensing despite their business model and need to license out. In part, some of the issues with their low share of ownership of patenting may be related to transfers of patent ownership from the public sector into private hands as has been encouraged by policies in developed countries over the past two decades.

The Chatham House study also finds that diffusion of technologies in the selected sectors has been worryingly slow (e.g. 20 years for the wind sector) at least based on a methodology of assessing the age of the most cited patents in patent applications.[410] The use of the age of a patent and number of citations in a single jurisdiction (the US) leaves a lot to be desired, but it does reflect a broader intuition that existing rates of diffusion are insufficient to address climate change, even in the OECD. There is some support in other studies for the contention that environmentally sound technologies tend to diffuse more slowly, due in part to uncertainty about commercial viability in host countries, lack of information about technologies held by providers, and lack of information about level and type of technologies needed in host countries.[411] The Chatham House study points to the need for policy interventions in the near term to ensure wider dissemination of patent information especially to domestic firms. However, the effectiveness of such exercises relies on a proper and full disclosure in the patent itself, something which may not always be the case. Patent applicants have a strong incentive to disclose only the minimum necessary to be granted a patent, which

---

[408] In the study these are defined as "national firms with more than 250 employees"
[409] See p17, Lee, B et al.
[410] See p48, Lee, B et al. "Who owns our Low Carbon Future: Intellectual Property and Energy Technologies" Chatham House, September 2009.
[411] See p2932, Schneider, M et al. "Understanding the CDM's contribution to technology transfer" 36 Energy Policy 2930 (2008).

means much of the information needed to show how the technology actually works may not be available.

VII.3 What can be concluded?

This study makes clear that ownership firm type matters as it has an impact on the kind of activity firms will engage in with respect to the intellectual property they own. In particular, the six sectors studied show a high concentration of ownership by multinational corporations and a high concentration of high value patents, which is a situation that creates incentives for market share maintenance and entry-blocking behaviour, although with a significant propensity for export oriented FDI. It suggests that actions taken by developing countries in these sectors may need to focus less on licensing and more on encouraging FDI and spillovers from upstream and downstream linkages, as well as joint ventures. The in-depth sectoral analyses of the study point to significant variation in ownership structures, concentration and vertical integration, all of which implicate different policy tools for countries concerned with technology innovation and diffusion in their domestic markets. This requires countries to make sector by sector national market based analyses as to what tools will be appropriate. It implies that different sectors will require different tools e.g. those that focus on licensing versus those that focus on FDI and joint ventures. Access to a broad portfolio of regulatory tools may therefore be a prerequisite for countries to take action, even within the narrow field of these six selected technologies.

VIII. Hascic et al OECD Study (2010)[412]

A 2010 OECD review and study also attempted to provide some initial data on distribution of patents for clean technologies. It used much the same methodology as the Dechezleprêtre et al. Study[413], and looked at the rate and location of innovation, as well as the rate of diffusion of climate mitigation technologies. It looked at EPO patent data over a period of 30 years, (1977- 2007) triggering many of the same concerns and limitations addressed above regarding methodologies using patent data. It differs by focusing on claimed priorities (those with patent applications in more than one country) rather than focusing on triadic patent families, which the authors consider too restrictive and likely to miss relevant technologies and actors.[414] They also argue that claimed priorities address the issue of strategic patenting and allow them to focus on high value patents.[415]

---

[412] Haščič, I et al. "Climate Policy and Technological Innovation and Transfer: An Overview of Trends and Recent Empirical Results", OECD Environment Working Papers, No. 30, OECD Publishing (2010).
[413] Dechezleprêtre, A et al. "Invention and Transfer of Climate Change–Mitigation Technologies: A Global Analysis" 5 Rev Environ Econ Policy 109 (2011).
[414] See p11, Haščič, I et al.
[415] Id.

VIII.1 Scope, Timing and Geography

The study covers 7 technology sectors in power generation: Solar (PV and Thermal), Wind (on and off-shore), Geothermal, hydropower, marine energy, biofuels, fossil fuel (IGCC, CCS).[416] The analysis is global, but encompassing the major developing countries and it looks at trends over the past 30 years.

VIII.2 Findings and Analysis

One interesting finding that is relatively independent of their methodology but that implicates patenting more generally, is that they find that the majority of patents in the sectors studied (60%) were only claimed in a single office.[417] Either the majority of patents in the field are low value patents (as their methodology indicates), or there is an attributable difference between the types of firms that engage in multijurisdictional patenting versus those that patent in only one. One hypothesis might be that a lot of patents are held by small and medium enterprises, or national corporations (as in the Chatham House study above) and these are mostly engaged in production of the technologies themselves, primarily for the domestic market. Another could be that this reflects the patent quality difference between the offices.[418] This could be confirmed by looking at the location of the offices where the majority of the single patents applied. Appendix B of the study presents some of this information. The proportion of single patents is highest at the Japanese Patent Office followed by the Chinese Patent Office. While there is some suggestion that low patent value or quality might be explain the Chinese office data, it is much harder to reconcile this with the JPO data, given the JPO's reputation for seeking high patent quality (thus value).[419] In comparison, the EPO had the lowest percentage of single patents than the US, although both were significantly lower than the JPO and the EPO. This difference is difficult to explain, but some comparative caution might be needed as these are percentage measures, and it may be that the absolute numbers differ significantly. For example, the EPO has an extremely high proportion of duplicate patent applications probably due to the ease with which it was possible prior to 2010 to file divisional applications.

---

[416] See p10, Id.
[417] See p12, Haščič, I et al. "Climate Policy and Technological Innovation and Transfer: An Overview of Trends and Recent Empirical Results", OECD Environment Working Papers, No. 30, OECD Publishing (2010).
[418] See Baron J & H Delcamp "Patent quality and value in discrete and cumulative innovation" Working Paper 2010-07, CERNA Working Paper Series, November 2010). But this would only be true, where applicants were taking this into account in considering whether or not to apply to a particular office. See also, Guellec, D and B van Pottelsberghe de la Potterie "Applications, Grants and the Value of a Patent", 69 Economics Letters 109 (2000).
[419] Id.

A key finding is that the rate of patenting in the sectors studied increased substantially in the 2000-2010 period, at an annual rate of 20%.[420] This is much faster than the rate of patenting in general. Whether this is due to an actual increase in the rate of inventions is difficult to conclude from this data, but there is a clear policy effect.[421] In individual sectors, solar PV has seen the fastest growth, whereas fossil fuels have seen the slowest. Among the renewable energy technologies, solar thermal has had the slowest increase. The policy effect on patenting appears to differ significantly, but R&D seems to have a variable effect depending on the technology sector. What appears to have had the most effect is the network of polices, including R&D that have come into place in the period from 1990 onwards, but with one major intervening factor: initial general innovative capacity (measured by patent count for all fields of activity) seems to have the most predictive effect on whether patenting of mitigation technologies would increase over time.[422]

Looking at market structure, and using patent assignee data, the study finds that the highest concentration is in CCS-storage (36% attributable to top 10 firms), with solar thermal having the lowest (5% attributable to top 10 firms). Solar PV is at about 15%, wind at 20% and IGCC at just over 30%.[423] Biofuels is relatively low at just under 10%. The study does not provide a geographic breakdown of the assignees, but a firm level examination of CCS and IGCC shows all the top 10 assignees are from the OECD. The study does not provide data on the number of assignees in developing countries and whether those assignees are wholly owned subsidiaries or whether they are joint ventures and downstream or upstream partners.

Using patent counts to indicate inventive activity, the study finds that activity is concentrated in the OECD (Japan, US, Germany and Korea)[424] In terms of technology fields, the study does some useful disaggregation: in none of the fields do any developing countries feature as top five inventor countries.[425]

In terms of technology transfer and diffusion the study finds (looking at patents applied for in more than one country, other than that of the inventor's residence) that the majority of 'transfers' are between developed countries.[426] Only one developing country (non-OECD), China, features in terms of size of transfers. Broken down by technology area, major recipients of patenting transfers in Solar PV are China,

---

[420] See p12, Haščič, I et al. "Climate Policy and Technological Innovation and Transfer: An Overview of Trends and Recent Empirical Results", OECD Environment Working Papers, No. 30, OECD Publishing (2010).
[421] See p27, Id.
[422] See p29, Id.
[423] See p21, Id.
[424] See p16, Id.
[425] Id.
[426] See p34, Id.

Korea and Taiwan, as well as Israel, Brazil, Mexico, South Africa and Morocco.[427] China far outstrips the others, beating out Korea and Taiwan by significant margins. There is clearly a correlation to size of market, but more significantly, is there a correlation to imitative capacity? The study does not address this issue and it is difficult to draw from the data that they use, but there is at least some research that shows a strong link between propensity to patent in a country that is not the inventors first resident and the imitative capacity in that country.[428]

In terms of participation in research collaboration (measured as co-inventors from more than one country), only China features among developing countries and that only ranked 5th in Solar PV and 4th in Geothermal.[429] It is not clear from the data whether the Chinese co-inventors are from Chinese firms or wholly-owned subsidiaries of developed country firms but this suggests some, albeit not significant, amount of developing country participation in international R&D networks in the studied sectors.

Finally, the study concludes that the rate of diffusion is insufficient to address the climate change technology need especially in developing countries.[430]

VIII.3 What can be concluded?

The data are consistent with other studies that the majority of patents are held by firms in the OECD. The levels of market concentration are not high, again in line with some of the findings in Barton, above. There is evidence of patenting by residents in the major developing economies, primarily China, but it remains quite low. In comparison, there is significant evidence of patenting by non-residents into the major developing country economies, again, primarily in China. The low participation rate in research collaboration suggests that much of this patenting is not reflective of joint leaning or joint development activities involving developing countries.

IX. RESULTS FROM TNAs, NAMAs AND NATIONAL COMMUNICATIONS

The most commonly identified barriers in TNAs related to costs, market structure and human capacity, with very few directly mentioning intellectual property.[431] However, given that TNAs do not carry out analyses of whether the technologies identified as needed are patented and whether there is licensing, this is not surprising.

---

[427] See p35, Haščič, I et al. "Climate Policy and Technological Innovation and Transfer: An Overview of Trends and Recent Empirical Results", OECD Environment Working Papers, No. 30, OECD Publishing (2010).
[428] See Cohen, W M et al. "Protecting their Intellectual Assets: Appropriability Conditions and Why U.S. Manufacturing Firms Patent (or Not)". NBER Working Paper no. 7552 (2000).
[429] See p40, Haščič, I et al.
[430] See p44, Id.
[431] See p29, UNFCCC "Second synthesis report on technology needs identified by Parties not included in Annex I to the Convention" FCCC/SBSTA/2009/INF.1, 29 May 2009.

Where a need for capacity building, or for absorption or adoption of technology was identified, no TNAs identify the cost of gaining access to such knowledge or the terms in which such knowledge would be accessed. This is partly structural in that TNAs are done at the pre-commercial and pre-project identification phase meaning that such details are not part of the assessment. In addition, the guidance on how to conduct a TNA, embodied in the UNDP *Handbook for Carrying Out Technology Needs Assessment for Climate Change* focuses on intellectual property as a broader policy element in innovation policy but does not actually suggest an assessment of the intellectual property and licensing structure of the technology sectors or specific technologies identified in the TNA. It simply suggests that intellectual property may be an important element of ensuring that investors feel secure transferring technology.[432] The TNA process for identifying barriers may not really be able to address the issue of intellectual property at the level of detail required. Nevertheless, the concerns with cost and human capacity point to a need for building basic knowledge and background on technologies, as well as reducing the costs of purchasing hardware, and the costs of learning to operate and maintain said hardware. Many countries also pointed to lack of R&D capacity and networks as a crucial barrier that needed to be addressed.[433] Included by all was a basic concern about lack of technical knowledge and know-how about all the technologies identified.[434]

A key finding from the TNAs may be that in response to the barriers identified, most countries pointed to regulatory measures first, followed closely by access to investment and funding. This emphasizes that regulatory structures are seen as key to addressing many of the problems in market structure in developing countries and that freedom to implement nationally appropriate regulations to enable technology transfer may be crucial. Paramount across all TNAs were market creation and demand-side measures as a basis for all other technology transfer action.

The national communications also present similar details and conclusions. Interestingly, Brazil's 2nd national communication does not address intellectual property as a policy priority relating to technology transfer, except to note that Brazil (or a Brazilian firm) owns patented technology in the hydrogen fuel cell sector.[435]

China's communication is the most specific and detailed regarding technology needs both in mitigation and adaptation. However, as with other national

---

[432] See p154, UNDP "*Handbook for Carrying Out Technology Needs Assessment for Climate Change* (New York: UNDP 2010)
[433] See p31, UNFCCC "Second synthesis report on technology needs identified by Parties not included in Annex I to the Convention" FCCC/SBSTA/2009/INF.1, 29 May 2009.
[434] See p42, Id.
[435] See p315, Brazilian Ministry of Science and Technology *Second National Communication of Brazil to the United Nations Framework Convention on Climate Change* (Brasilia: Ministry of Science and Technology, Brazil, 2010). Available at: http://www.mct.gov.br/index.php/content/view/326984.html (last visited August 15, 2014).

communications, nothing regarding intellectual property is mentioned in detail, but only in general terms as a barrier that developed countries should remove.[436] There is no detail on the intellectual property issues related to any specific technology or sector, except for one: related to protection of plant varieties as a way of stimulating innovation in the field.[437] India only addresses intellectual property at the general level of policy issues the UNFCCC should address.[438] South Africa identifies intellectual property as a potential cost barrier but only at a general level[439] and not an economy-wide barrier.[440] Related barriers cited refer to knowledge and human resource constraints for absorption and uptake of technologies.

X. COMPARATIVE ANALYSIS AND CONCLUSIONS

What can we conclude from this critical survey and analysis of the existing empirical data?

X.1 Scope of technologies

The existing studies cover a small proportion of the technologies for mitigation and none of those for adaptation. In particular, efficiency (particularly in appliances) and transport are a significant gap whereas this is where much of the mitigation abatement from developing countries is expected to come. There is negligible coverage of agricultural emissions mitigation technology. Adaptation technology is not covered at all by any of the studies, and this is another key area of need for developing countries for which little or no data exists. The table below illustrates all the technology areas not covered by the literature.

Specific Mitigation Technologies	Developing Countries and Regions Implicated (in terms of mitigation potentials and Technology needs articulated)
Industrial process efficiency (best available production technologies in the following sectors)	Africa, Asia and Pacific, LDCs, SIDS
- Iron and Steel	ASEAN, Brazil, China, India, South Africa
- Chemicals and Petrochemicals	ASEAN, Brazil, China, India, South Africa

---

[436] See p22, Chinese National Development and Reform Commission "Second National Communication on Climate Change of The People's Republic of China" National Development and Reform Commission, 2012)
[437] See p123, Id.
[438] Indian Ministry of Environment and Forestry *Second National Communication of India to the United Nations Framework Convention on Climate Change* Ministry of Environment and Forests, Government of India, 2012.
[439] See p199, Department of Environmental Affairs *South Africa's Second National Communication under the United Nations Framework Convention on Climate Change* (Pretoria: Department of Environmental Affairs Republic of South Africa, 2011).
[440] See p204, Id.

- Paper	ASEAN, Brazil, China, India, South Africa
- Aluminium	ASEAN, Brazil, China, India, South Africa
- (CCS) in Industrial Processes	Brazil, China, India, South Africa
Nuclear	ASEAN, Brazil, China, India, South Africa
- Pressurized water reactors with capacity above 1 000 MW	China
Power generation efficiency and fuel switching	Africa, Asia and Pacific, Latin America and the Caribbean, LDCs, SIDS
Transport	Asia and Pacific, Latin America and the Caribbean, SIDS;
- Flex – Fuel Vehicles	Brazil, China
- Bus rapid transport	ASEAN, Brazil, China, India, South Africa
- Hydrogen Fuel cells	Brazil, India,
- Batteries	Brazil,
- Fuel Efficiency of petrol or diesel vehicles	ASEAN, China, India, South Africa
Electricity grid – smart and micro infrastructure and management	ASEAN, Brazil, China, India,
- Flexible AC transmission systems; High-voltage transmission systems	China,
- Monitoring and controlling electricity quality, grid interconnection and dispatching - Electricity dispatching automation technology	ASEAN, China, India
Buildings	
End-use efficiency and Appliances	ASEAN, Brazil, China, India,
- electric motors	Brazil, South Africa
- pumps, including for agricultural use	ASEAN, Brazil, China, India,
- Dishwashers, clothes washers, and clothes dryers	China
- compressors, heat exchangers, insulation (foam and vacuum), heat bridge designs and fans for refrigeration and air conditioners;	ASEAN, China, India,
- software and hardware, especially for managing active and standby power in portable appliances	ASEAN, Brazil, China, India
- Combined heat and power	ASEAN, Brazil, China, India, South Africa
Agriculture	Africa, Asia and Pacific, Latin America and the Caribbean, LDCs, SIDS; ASEAN, Brazil, China, India, South Africa
- Less GHG intensive fertilizer	Brazil, India
- Plant varieties that are less reliant on GHG intensive fertilizers, either because they produce higher yields or are more efficient at soil nutrient uptake;	Brazil, India

	- Animal variants and breeds less likely to produce methane during digestion;	Brazil
	- Better management of animal waste, including recycling into biogas and other biomass for energy generation;	Brazil
	- Animal feed less likely to produce methane	Brazil, India

Specific Adaptation Technologies	Developing Countries Implicated
Agriculture	Africa, Asia and Pacific, Latin America and Caribbean, LDCs, SIDS
- All agricultural inputs, including seeds (including flood and drought resilient varieties), low emissions fertilizers, and methods and processes;	
- New varieties or adaptations of existing plant and animal varieties.	
- Genetically modified seeds and animals	
- integrated pest management	
- Food processing and storage	
Energy	
- All products for energy production, distribution and consumption;	
Health	Africa, Latin America and Caribbean, LDCs
- All health infrastructure, including medicines, diagnostic and treatment tools, methods, personnel;	
- Medical products, processes and services related to increasing resistance to vector borne and temperature sensitive diseases	
- Medical products, processes and services related to managing health needs during periods of extreme heat (heat waves) and extreme cold,	
- Medical products, processes and services related to increasing general immune-capacity, e.g. vaccines;	
- Products, processes and services designed to create hygienic and sanitary living and working conditions, such as access to potable water and sanitary facilities	

Water	Africa, Latin America and Caribbean, LDCs
- All water infrastructure for capture, treatment, distribution, and recycling	
- Water treatment and sanitation products and processes to deal with higher levels of toxicity and microbial and plant growth	
- Water desalination technologies for coastal areas	
- Smart and/or active water metering systems	
- Water capture and storage products and processes	
- Efficient water use and reclamation technologies	
Disaster response	Asia and Pacific, Latin America and Caribbean, SIDS
- early warning systems for disasters (including communications);	
- Systematic observation, monitoring and analysis - Conventional observations, including use of wind profilers, and application of GPS in upper-air meteorological observations. - Non-conventional observations, including development of satellite remote-sensing instruments and ground-based remote sensing technologies. - Data analysis and assimilation	
- systems for stockpiling and distributing food, water, and medicines;	
- systems for storing and managing water resources;	
- alternative disaster-appropriate transport systems (e.g., boats);	
- systems for strengthening waste disposal sites against leakage during disasters;	
- disaster mitigation systems, such as flood and sea walls, flood channels;	
- extreme weather event resistant building materials.	

X.2 Ownership and distribution of patenting

To the extent possible, existing data in the very limited set of sectors show concentrated ownership of patents in developed countries, largely OECD. Of patents that exist in developing countries, the vast majority are in China. In terms of ownership by developing countries, China may have the largest ownership but this is still relatively small in comparison to OECD rightholders.

The majority of technologies in the very limited set are likely not patented in least developed countries. They are almost certain to be patented in China, and in the main emerging economies of Brazil, India and possibly South Africa.

X.3. Licensing

Only very tentative conclusions can be made with respect to licensing but with respect to some of the sectors (especially wind and solar), there appears to be some evidence of licensing to major developing countries. However, the licensing appears to be from national or smaller companies, not necessarily in possession of best available technologies, and not from transnational enterprises with significant production capacity of their own. The vast majority of technology ownership in the limited sectors studied in international flows, especially through FDI vectors, is held by large multinational corporations who are primary producers of the products that are manufactured based on the technology. These companies are least likely to license but are most likely to engage in FDI in attractive markets and even provide best available technologies to suppliers and vertically integrated subsidiaries. The levels of ownership by academic and public institutions is relatively small and while national corporations and SMEs have a significant share, they rarely engage in FDI or licensing but are primarily interested in sales. However there does appear to be a significant opportunity to increase licensing by national corporations and SMEs provided that they can be assured of preventing leakage into their home markets. These companies also present attractive acquisition targets for companies from developing countries. Any intervention has to be able to target the correct category of rightholder to achieve its goals. For FDI channels, the tools will need to be directed at spillovers, especially from movement of personnel. With respect to licensing, any interventions will have to focus on increasing the scale and rate of licensing especially from national corporations and SMEs.

X.4 Conclusion

Other reviews of the literature have reached some of the same conclusions but perhaps differ in their emphasis. A review by Pugatch (2011), of a sub-set of the studies addressed here, concludes that, for the most part, based on his review of the studies, intellectual property is not a barrier.[441] He argues that the focus should be on what are

---

[441] Perez Pugatch, M "The Role of Intellectual Property Rights in the Transfer of Environmentally Sound Technologies" Global Challenges Report, WIPO, 2011.

the best ways to use the intellectual property system to enable technology assimilation and use by firms in developing countries.[442] He also shares the conclusion that the existing data are insufficient to come to any strong policy relevant conclusions as to the exact role of intellectual property in the transfer of climate technologies.[443] The role of IP is also obscured somewhat by lack of detail on what constitutes sufficiently effective IP protection to encourage technology transfer. Pugatch points to the fact that Brazil and China, despite perceptions of weak IPR protection remain significant destinations for FDI and licensing.[444] Most importantly, he emphasizes the increasing role that mergers and acquisitions (especially of developed country firms by developing country firms) may play in the future, even if much of the activity in developing countries remains nationally-based.[445]

Khor reviews a smaller sub-set of the studies discussed above and concludes more definitively that it shows the significance of the intellectual problem, pointing in particular to the Indian case study of LEDS, and hybrid drive trains in the Ockwell study[446], and to the experience of developing countries under the Montreal Protocol.[447]

Both make the error of treating the finding of such studies as dispositive of the question of whether a barrier exists. In the end, it is imperative that capacity to act is combined with identification of problems or blockages in the market. One without the other is pointless. In thinking about the ways in which intellectual property issues arise in climate technology markets, it may be useful to examine the experience of other MEAs.

XI. LESSONS FROM OTHER MEAs AND SUCCESSFUL CASES OF TECHNOLOGY TRANSFER

Some further lessons and data can be drawn from the experience of implementation of some Multilateral Environmental Agreements (MEAs). One finding from an UNCTAD study is that technology transfer is less problematic, and refusals to license or high licensing costs are not a problem where: 1) there is little or no domestic production industry that could compete with the company providing technology and/or

---

[442] See p21, Id.
[443] See p21, Id.
[444] See p13, Id.
[445] See p17, Id.
[446] Ockwell, D et al. "UK-India Collaboration to Identify the Barriers to the Transfer of Low Carbon Technology-Final report" (London: the Department of Environment, Food and Rural Affairs, U.K., 2007). Analyzed further below on the specific case of India.
[447] See Khor, M "Climate Change, Technology and Intellectual Property Rights: Context and Recent Negotiations" Research Paper 45, South Centre, April 2012. See also Khor, M "Climate Change, Technology and IPR" in Soni, P et al. *Technological Cooperation and Climate Change Issues and Perspectives* Working papers presented at the Ministry of Environment and Forests, Government of India - UNDP Consultation on Technology Cooperation for Addressing Climate Change, 23-24 September, 2011; New Delhi, India.

2) there is a high concentration in the relevant sector, enabling transfers to vertically integrated subsidiaries.[448] In the first case, there is no actual demand for licensing, while there may be a demand for the technological products which may be entirely imported and in the second case, production is carried out by local subsidiaries to whom technology, even the best available technologies can be transferred without fear of significant spill-overs. The experience of Thailand is in contrast with that of India and South Korea under the Montreal Protocol. Both of the latter had significant domestic industries which sought to shift into the production and use of alternative technologies and found difficulties related to refusals to license or unduly restrictive licensing terms.[449] At least one study by Watal found significant concerns and some reports from survey evidence that producers in developing countries such as India, Argentina, Brazil, China, Republic of Korea, Mexico, Romania and Venezuela encountered difficulties in accessing technologies on grant, or concessional terms (as required by the Montreal Protocol), and even on 'reasonable' commercial terms.[450] The restrictive terms Watal identified included:

- Restrictions on export;
- Requirements to hand over majority shareholding in their company or joint venture.

However, she notes that the concentrated market structure of the Refrigeration and Coolants sector may have played a role in the problematic area of the primary CFC substitute, HFC134a.[451]

Another useful finding is that the existence of efficiency or technology standards in developed country markets into which developing country producers exported products was a crucial driver of the implementation of an MEA, for a country like South Korea.[452] These standards create a situation where access to the technologies

---

[448] See p27, Natural Resource Management Programme of the Thailand Environment Institute "Case Study 1: Thailand's Experience with the Montreal Protocol" in Jha, V and U Hoffman (eds.) "Achieving Objectives of Multilateral Environmental Agreements: A Package of Trade Measures and Positive Measures Elucidated by Results of Developing Country Case Studies" UNCTAD/ITCD/TED/6, UNCTAD 2000.
[449] See p15, Jha, V and U Hoffman (eds.) "Achieving Objectives of Multilateral Environmental Agreements: A Package of Trade Measures and Positive Measures Elucidated by Results of Developing Country Case Studies" UNCTAD/ITCD/TED/6, UNCTAD 2000.
[450] See p45, Watal, J "Case Study 3: India: The Issue of Technology Transfer in the Context of the Montreal Protocol" in Jha, V and U Hoffman (eds.) "Achieving Objectives of Multilateral Environmental Agreements: A Package of Trade Measures and Positive Measures Elucidated by Results of Developing Country Case Studies" UNCTAD/ITCD/TED/6, UNCTAD 2000.
[451] Id.
[452] See p60, Korea Trade Promotion Agency "Case Study 4: Korea: The Republic of Korea and the Montreal Protocol" in Jha, V and U Hoffman (eds.) "Achieving Objectives of Multilateral Environmental

becomes a necessity if the exporter in the developing country is going to be able to participate in the market. This suggests that failures to license on fair, reasonable and non-discriminatory (FRAND) terms should implicate competition law issues in both developed and developing countries. This was the experience of companies in Korea. In addition, firms in Korea experienced demands for high prices for licensing, at a level which made it economically unviable to license the technology.[453] Korean firms also experienced restrictive licensing terms. In one year, 1994, a case study found, the agreements entered into:[454]

- Required Non-assignment or sub-licensing to a third party (8.9% of licenses from Japan, 4.8% of licenses from the US);
- Would only grant on a non-exclusive basis (7.7% of licenses from Japan, 5.4% of licenses from the US);
- Required grant back clauses on improvements (7.7% of licenses from the US, a portion of 7.7% of licenses from Japan);
- Prohibited production for export (4.2% of licenses from Japan);
- Prohibited production of competing products (1.8% of licenses from Japan).

The data do not address how many licensing contracts were not entered into because of such clauses. However, from the perspective of climate change related technology transfer and encouraging spill-overs, non-exclusive grants are preferable to exclusive, so that may be less of a problem for policy, even if it presents a problem for individual technology licensees. The Korean findings suggest that problematic terms consisted of a small but significant portion of licenses granted. Some of these terms were found in the same contract so a simple addition would not be accurate but it can clearly range from approximately 9% to 20% depending on the distribution of these terms.

The Multilateral Fund of the Montreal Protocol did aim to meet "all incremental costs" including paying for patent rights and royalties.[455] The primary implementing agency for such issues was UNIDO. However, the MF did struggle with costs related to these issues[456] which suggests that for the climate arena, which is orders of magnitude larger in terms of the scope of technologies, geographical scope, and sharper time limits, the funding needed to pay for such licensing may be prohibitively large.

Agreements: A Package of Trade Measures and Positive Measures Elucidated by Results of Developing Country Case Studies" UNCTAD/ITCD/TED/6, UNCTAD 2000.
[453] See p62, Id.
[454] See p63, Id.
[455] See p347, De Coninck, H et al. "International technology-oriented agreements to address climate change" 36 Energy Policy 335 (2008).
[456] See p66-67, Andersen, S et al. *Technology Transfer for the Ozone Layer: Lessons for Climate Change* (London: Earthscan 2007).

XII. THREE TRENDS THAT IMPLICATE THE INTELLECTUAL PROPERTY STRUCTURE OF CLIMATE TECHNOLOGY MARKETS

XII. 1 Increases in Patenting of Climate Technologies

Trends in patenting suggest that there may be an increase in problems related to patents[457] in the period leading up to 2020 and especially in the period from 2020-2050. Ownership of climate mitigation technology patents remains largely concentrated in OECD countries, primarily Japan, the US and Germany.[458] Emerging economies are growing their share, increasing, on average, 18% annually between 1998 and 2003 with the caveat that a significant amount may be by subsidiaries of foreign firms.[459] Overall, the rate of patent filing in selected clean energy sectors (power generation using renewables) appears to track the overall global increases in patenting.[460] The increase in patenting is global, suggesting an increase in interest in commercialization and licensing of climate mitigation technologies but also that even if patterns of patenting may not at present cause concern, increases in patenting, especially in China, India, and Brazil, may give rise to such problems. Climate mitigation technology patent ownership remains concentrated in the hands of OECD private and public actors and that concentration does not seem likely to change significantly given the upward trend in patenting. The EPO/UNEP/ICTSD study found that for the selected technologies, while China presented the largest number of patents claimed among emerging economies, only a small percentage of ownership was actually in Chinese hands.[461] Limited domestic ownership of IP in the selected fields was also found for India and Brazil.[462] In China, much of the patenting was domestic with a very small number of patents filed first in China and then in other countries.[463] In contrast, China was the largest destination outside the OECD for patents first filed in Japan, the US and Germany.[464] This was still far below the numbers of patents filed between OECD members, where much of the primary activity takes place.[465]

---

[457] p2, Bollyky, T "Intellectual Property Rights and Climate Change: Principles for Innovation and Access to Low-Carbon Technology" CGD Notes, Centre for Global Development, December 2009.
[458] p114, IEA, *Energy Technology Perspectives 2012: Pathways to a Clean Energy System* (Paris: IEA/OECD 2012). See also See p30, Karachalios, K et al. (eds.) "Patents and Clean Energy: Bridging the Gap between Evidence and Policy: Final report" UNEP/ EPO / ICTSD 2010.
[459] p589, IEA, *Energy Technology Perspectives 2010: Scenarios and Strategies to 2050*, (Paris: IEA/OECD, 2010).
[460] See p30, Karachalios, K et al. (eds.)
[461] See p31, Id.
[462] Id.
[463] See p49, Id.
[464] Id.
[465] Id.

Measures of technology diffusion that look at whether patents are distributed across more than one country (as a proxy for intent to use or market the technology in that market) appear to show that some technologies are widely diffused (LEDs, CFLs, wind power, electric and hybrid vehicles).[466] Within that, the diffusion seems largely between OECD countries, and increasingly emerging economies.[467] Issues of licensing costs and access to licensing are likely to become even more important as emerging economies expand their use of technologies to reduce their GHG emissions to peak between 2015 and 2018. In addition, while LDCs at present do not have the same concerns, that may change with the expiration of their transition period for the implementation of the TRIPS Agreement on July 1, 2021.[468] Once their legislation is TRIPS compliant it will become much easier to patent in those countries, especially if they already participate in the Patent Cooperation Treaty system. In that case, there may be a jump in the number of patents filed in least developing countries.

Specific policies to address climate change may also have an effect on future patterns of patenting. Some governments are beginning to fast-track patents that claim 'green benefits' creating an incentive for reclassification but also perhaps a greater number of applications for climate technologies.[469]

If governments seek to establish systems for identifying best available technologies while at the same time establishing and/or requiring energy efficiency standards and targets, energy efficiency will begin to shift from being a tool for differentiation in the market, to something that becomes a necessity for participation in the market. Where the best available technologies may be proprietary (patents, trade secrets, industrial designs) access to those technologies may become a key part of enabling greater efficiency, which may require specific regulations to manage how companies whose technologies become standards must treat other market participants. Rimmer covers this issue in significant detail[470], and examples of this issue can be found in both Europe and the US. This has become a crucial issue in markets such as mobile phones, for example.[471] The appropriate regulatory response has been an arena of

---

[466] p112, IEA, *Energy Technology Perspectives 2012*
[467] p113, IEA, *Energy Technology Perspectives 2012: Pathways to a Clean Energy System* (Paris: IEA/OECD 2012).
[468] Extension of the Transition Period under Article 66.1 for Least-Developed Country Members: Decision of the Council for TRIPS of 11 June 2013, IP/C/64, 12 June 2013.
[469] See e.g. UK Intellectual Property Office's Green Channel, available at: http://www.ipo.gov.uk/pro-types/pro-patent/p-law/p-accelerated/pro-p-green.htm (last visited August 15, 2014).
[470] Rimmer, M *Intellectual Property and Climate Change: Inventing Clean Technologies"* (London: Edward Elgar, 2011)
[471] See e.g. European Commission "Antitrust: Commission sends Statement of Objections to Samsung on potential misuse of mobile phone standard-essential patents" European Commission Press Release, Brussels, 21 December 2012. Available at: http://europa.eu/rapid/press-release_IP-12-1448_en.htm (last visited August 15, 2014); See p8, Cannady, C "Access to Climate Change Technology by Developing Countries: A Practical Strategy, ICTSD's Programme on IPRs and Sustainable Development, Issue Paper No. 25, International Centre for Trade and Sustainable Development, Geneva, Switzerland (2009).

contestation between private companies, regulators and policymakers regarding what licensing obligations can be placed on those whose technologies are designated standards or become de facto standards. The issue of fair, reasonable, and non-discriminatory (FRAND) terms has been raised in the context of the European Union's Competition Commission deliberations on the relationship between competition law and standards. The Commission has issued guidance which requires FRAND terms for standards that are based on exclusive rights, noting that:

> "Where participation in standard-setting is unrestricted and the procedure for adopting the standard in question is transparent, standardization agreements which contain no obligation to comply with the standard and provide access to the standard on fair, reasonable and non-discriminatory terms will normally not restrict competition."[472]

As formal standards proliferate as a tool for achieving climate goals, and as patenting in the technology areas increases, the importance of managing standard-setting processes and ensuring access to standards will only grow. The EU approach may provide some policy models for countries going forward, but participation by developing countries and their firms in such standard setting processes in developed countries will also be crucial. Para 281 of the Guidelines ensures that unrestricted participation means participation by all competitors in the market which may leave space for firms which sell their products into the EU. The appropriateness and scope of measures to address such issues is addressed in more detail in Chapter 6, but it is important to note that this is a problem more and more likely to arise in the near future.

Aside from problems related to technology specific standards there may also be problems related to general standards that may nevertheless exclude a market actor from the market unless they have access to a specific technology or know how. This is especially true for mandatory efficiency standards, such as those which the IEA has suggested may be especially effective for dealing with appliance –related emissions.[473] In such situations, even though technology – neutral, standards exclude from the market producers that are unable to comply with the standard. Access at a reasonable cost to efficiency technologies may need to be part of a support system. Voluntary standards do not necessarily escape this problem, as it is possible for customer preference and for the market to be defined in such a way that less-efficient producers are excluded. Where these standards are unilaterally imposed by developed countries on their domestic market, such markets can become closed off to actors in developing and emerging

---

[472] See para. 280, European Commission "Guidelines on the applicability of Article 101 of the Treaty on the Functioning of the European Union to horizontal co-operation agreements," text with EEA relevance, OJ C 11, 14.1.2011, p. 1–72
[473] p15, Gueret, T "International Energy Technology Collaboration and Climate Change Mitigation: Case Study 3: Appliance Energy Efficiency" (COM/ENV/EPOC/IEA/SLT(2005)3) OECD Environment Directorate /International Energy Agency, 2005.

economies imposing the burden of complying with such standards entirely on those actors. The best approach may be to seek out international collaboration on standard setting[474], especially for products with global or regional markets. However, this is likely to run into the dynamic of developing countries demanding access to technologies to assist their companies to comply with such standards.

XII.2 Increases in Public sector Financing of Climate technologies

As developed countries have argued in the UNFCCC, the majority of technologies in developed countries are held by the private sector. In that context, obligations placed on developed country governments to provide technology transfer appear to be dead letters, nothing more than hortatory statements. In the case of purely privately funded research and development of products it may indeed be true that governments do not have the discretion to deliver those technologies themselves. However, this does not mean that there are no policy levers available to them to encourage their private enterprises to carry out licensing and transfer of technology. For example, Article 66.2 of the TRIPS Agreement places an obligation on developing countries to:

> provide incentives to enterprises and institutions in their territories for the purpose of promoting and encouraging technology transfer to least developed country members in order to enable them to create a sound and viable technological base.

Suerie Moon, in her analysis of developed country compliance with this obligation pointed to several kinds of measures that would fall directly within the provisions of this article such as:[475]

1. Financing and loans for purchasing of patents, licenses and products by developing country government, institutions and firms; (this could be tied to purchasing from home-based firms);

2. Financing, preferential tax treatment and loan guarantees for FDI, especially R&D, in technology-oriented fields, with a preference for FDI that provided licensing, transfer of skills and know to local partners and suppliers;

---

[474] See p9, Gueret, T "International Energy Technology Collaboration and Climate Change Mitigation: Case Study 3: Appliance Energy Efficiency" (COM/ENV/EPOC/IEA/SLT(2005)3) OECD Environment Directorate /International Energy Agency, 2005.
[475] See p4, Moon, S, "Meaningful Technology Transfer to LDCs: A proposal for a monitoring mechanism for TRIPS Article 66.2" ICTSD Programme on Innovation, Technology and Intellectual Property Policy Brief 9, April 2011.

3. Providing financing (paid to developed country firms and institutions) for individuals from institutions and firms in developing countries to attend training, workshops and educational research institutions as well as participate in internship programmes in technology sector of relevance to LDCs;

4. Providing business to business platforms for firms from the developed country to conduct business with firms in LDCs;

5. Providing business risk insurance, including against intellectual property losses for firms licensing and investing into LDCs;

6. Providing preferential access to R&D funds for projects that include participation of individual and institutions from developing countries.

That many developed country WTO members have not implemented many of these kinds of incentives[476] is a function not of incapacity but of policy choice. None of these options is coercive but does require financial expenditures by the developed country. This may also be due to competitiveness concerns, although it is difficult to see how many LDCs could become competitors to these countries in the near term. The concerns with respect to competitiveness can also be seen in the pattern of public funding for R&D and the ways in which developed countries use the transfer of the ownership products of such research to subsidize their private sector and maintain competitiveness.

Many developed countries maintain significant public funding structures for R&D. In absolute numbers, total US public spending was USD 124 billion in 2009. In 2005 purchasing power parity (PPP) dollars[477], the US Federal Government spend was 114 billion, Japan was 22.4 billion, Germany was 22.1 billion, France was 16.5 billion and South Korea was 12.1 billion. In comparison, China's was 32.9 billion; Brazil was 11 billion, Mexico was 2.5 billion, Turkey was 2.4 billion, Argentina was 2.3 billion, and Singapore was 2.1 billion. Other than Pakistan at 1.5 billion no other developing country features. The data show a very large gap in public R&D spending by governments in developed countries as compared to developing. However, China is the second highest individual country spender.

---

[476] See p5, Id.
[477] Data drawn from Table 28-GERD by Source of Funds "UNESCO Science and Technology Statistics", UNESCO Institute for Statistics. Available at:
http://stats.uis.unesco.org/unesco/ReportFolders/ReportFolders.aspx (last visited August 15, 2014). The data is drawn from member states submitted reports and thus may not reflect national security related spend, and may also be missing data from countries that have no reports, a significant portion of whom may be developing countries. For the European Union, the data may not reflect central EU Commission funds as the EU is not a member of UNESCO and EU spending may not be captured in EU member state R&D spending.

Many developed countries essentially subsidize their private sector actors by allowing them to seek patents for technologies or products developed from publicly – funded research and development budgets.[478] Given the very large research budget of the US this constitutes a significant annual transfer and increases the competitiveness of US technology companies by attenuating the risks associated with doing basic and demonstration research themselves, while enabling them to focus on the commercialization of products. Simultaneously, however, developed countries have also enabled themselves to maintain significant ownership of these publicly funded technologies. For example, the National Institutes of Health (NIH) Patent Cost-Sharing agreement with Universities contains a clause that retains co-ownership of the patent with the right of the US federal government to:

> An irrevocable, royalty-free, paid-up right to practice and have practiced the Patent Rights throughout the world by or on behalf of the Government and on behalf of any foreign government or international organization pursuant to any existing or future treaty or agreement to which the Government is a signatory.[479]

A similar clause is inserted into the NIH-lead and Institution lead agreements.[480] This would enable the NIH to easily make such licenses available to firms and actors in developing countries. This would be especially useful if such licensing were made to public or academic institutions in developing countries that could cooperate in with industry to further develop and commercialize technologies.

Problematically, in the licenses that it grants, the NIH has a clause in its agreement that "products used or sold in the United States embodying Licensed Products or produced through use of Licensed Processes shall be manufactured substantially in the United States, unless a written waiver is obtained in advance from the NIH."[481] This policy choice deliberately excludes firms from developing countries from accessing licenses issued by the NIH for use in their home territories, even where the license is for a patent registered in the developing country. Nevertheless the US government still retains for itself the right to carry out such licensing on the same terms

---

[478] See e.g. the United States Bayh-Dole Act (P.L. 96-517, Patent and Trademark Act Amendments of 1980), 35 USC § 200 et seq. (2006 and Supp. V 2012). See Abbott, F M "Innovation and Technology Transfer to Address Climate Change: Lessons from the Global Debate on Intellectual Property and Public Health", ICTSD's Programme on IPRs and Sustainable Development, Issue Paper No. 24, International Centre for Trade and Sustainable Development, Geneva, Switzerland, 2009.
[479] See NIH, "NIH Cost Sharing Agreement" Available at: http://www.ott.nih.gov/forms-model-agreements (last visited 15 August 2013).
[480] See NIH "The National Institutes of Health Inter-Institutional Agreement - Institution-Lead" Available at: http://www.ott.nih.gov/forms-model-agreements (last visited 15 August 2013).
[481] See Article 5.2 NIH "National Institutes of Health Patent License Agreement – Nonexclusive", Article 5.2 NIH "The National Institutes of Health Patent License Agreement – Exclusive" Available at: http://www.ott.nih.gov/forms-model-agreements (last visited 15 August 2013).

as described above in the cost-sharing agreement.[482] This provision is required by Section 202(c)(4) of the Bayh-Dole Act.[483]

In the issuance of licenses that the government owns itself, the Bayh Dole Act authorizes the issuance of exclusive or partially exclusive licenses only to the extent required for the public interest or to ensure proper incentives for commercialization.[484] More problematically, it requires that any exclusive licenses issued by the federal government impose an obligation to manufacture the products or product from the patented process substantially in the US.[485] However, this does not extend to non-exclusive licenses. To the extent that the US follows the preference for non-exclusive licensing embodied in Section 209 of the Bayh-Dole Act then it has the capacity as it stands today to make non-exclusive licenses available to firms and actors in developing countries on grant or concessional terms.

In addition, Section 203 of the Bayh-Dole Act retains the right of the US government to 'march-in" and require licensing or sub-licensing to another actor under certain conditions. These include:

- Failure to actually work the patent within a reasonable period of time (section 203(a)(1));
- To address health and safety needs not adequately met by the assignee (section 203(a)(2));
- For public use, not adequately met by assignee (section 203(a)(3))
- Failure to agree to substantially manufacture the product in the US (section 203(a)(4))

The US has the ability to essentially issue compulsory licenses for the above conditions, although it is not clear whether the existence of those conditions is limited only to the territory of the US.

In the EU, the major research funding vehicle for 2009-13 was the 7th EU-Framework Programme for Research and Technological Development (FP7), whose general principle for funding is that all intellectual property generated through the funding belongs to the funded participants, including patents applied for as a result of

---

[482] Article 5.2 NIH "The National Institutes of Health Patent License Agreement – Exclusive" Available at: http://www.ott.nih.gov/forms-model-agreements (last visited 15 August 2013).
[483] 35 USC 204 (2006 and Supp. V 2012)
[484] 35 USC 209 (2006 and Supp. V 2012)
[485] 35 USC 209 (2006 and Supp. V 2012)

the research.[486] The Model Grant Agreement[487] between the European Commission and grantees has several clauses that elaborate the exact nature of the ownership and the obligations with respect to enabling access for third parties. While grantees are free to transfer ownership the Commission may object where such transfer to third countries would be deemed to negatively affect European competitiveness (or security interests), although there is no requirement of prior notice to the Commission for such transfers.[488] This also applies to the granting of exclusive licenses.[489] There is an obligation to 'use' or work the patented material produced from the project, which includes an obligation to seek IP protection such as patents where appropriate.[490] However, only in the case where an applicant does not seek to protect the material itself or offer it to an affiliated entity in a member state will the Commission step in and claim ownership.[491] In this, the EU is explicitly engaging in a subsidy and intellectual property transfer program. However, other than an obligation to use the work, it does not obligate licensing or address the contents of licensing except where it concerns the relationships between its grantees. Because of this deliberate contractual choice, neither the European Commission nor its member states retain any intellectual property in projects funded through these FP7 programmes. It does not appear that there is any specific barrier to the EC or its member states retaining such rights, so at least there does not appear to be a barrier to amendment of the agreement to doing so for the purposes of enabling licenses to developing countries. However, the EC seems to have the opposite attitude by ensuring that the Commission can intervene to stop transfer of intellectual property where it considers such transfers may have impacts of EU competitiveness.[492]

The pattern from the US and the EU makes clear that there remain significant amounts of publicly funded intellectual property over which these governments can exercise rights. There is a deliberate and understandable policy choice that has been made to use such funds to subsidize their private sectors. However, it also means that they have the legal capacity, and can make a choice, to take action to share that technology with firms and institutions in developing countries. While it should be acknowledged that the majority of commercialized or near commercialized technologies are wholly in the hands of private actors, the role of public funding in transferring technologies or providing a basis for commercialized technologies should not be

---

[486] See II.26.1, European Commission "Seventh Framework Programme Model grant agreement" (version 3, 14 December 2012). Available at: http://cordis.europa.eu/fp7/calls-grant-agreement_en.html (last visited 24 March 2013)
[487] Id.
[488] See II.27.4, European Commission "Seventh Framework Programme Model grant agreement" (version 3, 14 December 2012). Available at: http://ec.europa.eu/research/participants/data/ref/fp7/93135/fp7-core-ga_en.pdf (last visited 15 August 2014).
[489] See II.32.8, Id.
[490] See II.29, Id.
[491] See II.28.3, Id.
[492] See II.27.4, Id.

overlooked. The opportunities for bilateral and multilateral cooperation on access to these patents and technologies presents a real opportunity to resolve a significant element of the technology transfer debate and it is incumbent upon policymakers in both developed and developing countries to provide the right set of incentives to attract FDI and licensing and to enable spillovers at a sufficient scale and speed.

In contrast, many developing country researchers do not engage in patenting[493], although an increasing number of developing countries are beginning to implement the Bayh-Dole model from the US.[494] There has been a major increase in patenting in China, encouraged and mandated by universities and the state, which has resulted in an immense jump in the number of university related patents in China.[495]

The issue of whom to license to is wrapped up in the competitiveness concerns that drive the public subsidization of patent transfers by developed countries. However, as noted in Chapter 3, emerging economies such as China present the cheapest cost opportunities for lowering GHG emissions. Lowering their emissions is also a necessity if global emissions are to be lowered sufficiently. Given their growth rate the only ways in which climate change can be addressed is if existing technologies and near commercialization technologies, both products and processes, are diffused into firms in these countries without delay.

XII.3 The Role of Emerging Economies

The past two decades have seen increasing growth in the role that middle income countries, especially upper middle income countries such as Brazil, India, and China play in international technology flows. Data from 2001 shows that upper middle income countries presented the highest growth arena for high technology exports from the OECD.[496] Their share of high technology exports was 18.9% and skills-intensive exports was 13.5%.[497] Low income countries, especially in sub-Saharan Africa have shares that are close to 0%; and their shares of global trade in technology exports (for skill and technology intensive sectors) may have actually fallen in the period 1970 – 2001.[498]

---

[493] See n1. Cannady, C "Access to Climate Change Technology by Developing Countries: A Practical Strategy, ICTSD's Programme on IPRs and Sustainable Development, Issue Paper No. 25, International Centre for Trade and Sustainable Development, Geneva, Switzerland (2009).
[494] So, A., et al. "Is Bayh-Dole good for developing countries? Lessons from the US Experience" 6(10) PLoS Biol e262 (2008).
[495] Li, X, "Behind the recent surge of Chinese patenting: An institutional view." 41 Research Policy 236 (2012).
[496] p11, Maskus, K E "Encouraging International Technology Transfer" ICTSD Issue Paper No. 7, May 2004.
[497] Id.
[498] Id.

Emerging economies are increasingly major players in renewable energy technology investments with Brazil, India and China comprising over 90% of the 72 billion invested in developing countries (just a shade more than that invested in the OECD).[499] Moreover, a significant part of the climate puzzle relates to a major shift in manufacturing from OECD countries to the large emerging economies.[500] This means that while the majority of consumption of manufactured goods still takes place in the OECD countries, emerging economies are increasingly where the negative externalities for producing such goods take place. This has complicated the accounting and the understanding of the distribution of the costs and benefits of the most recent phase of industrialization. While the emerging economies have largely engaged in labour intensive low cost manufacturing, that is shifting to higher value activity to the extent that it is encompassing product design and development. Nevertheless, product and process design and development (and its associated intellectual property) remain largely in the OECD which implicates the extent to which manufacturing processes in developing countries can be redesigned to be more green and sustainable.[501]

There is of course some divergence in interests between the large emerging economies such as China, Brazil and India and other developing countries. The former countries are beginning to compete well on production and dissemination of clean technologies, and in some areas, such as wind turbine and solar panel production and deployment, may actually be ahead of the US and Europe.

XI.3.1 The role of emerging economies as research and development and production centers

A. Brazil

Brazil has had a longer history of addressing renewable energy than India and China. It is a market leader in the implementation of hydropower, and has been instrumental in the research, development, demonstration and full blown commercialization of biofuels, especially ethanol from sugarcane.[502] Brazil has used this to move into a significant part of the automobile market with flex-fuel light and heavy duty vehicles.[503] While its total primary energy supply maintains a large role for oil, and is likely to continue due to the discovery and exploitation of new offshore oil[504], it has a very large penetration of hydropower.[505]

---

[499] See p211, See UNEP, *Towards a Green Economy: Pathways to Sustainable Development and Poverty Eradication*, (Nairobi: UNEP, 2011).
[500] See p260, Id.
[501] See p260, See UNEP, *Towards a Green Economy: Pathways to Sustainable Development and Poverty Eradication*, (Nairobi: UNEP, 2011).
[502] See p547, IEA, *Energy Technology Perspectives 2012: Pathways to a Clean Energy System* (Paris: IEA/OECD 2012).
[503] See p551, Id.
[504] See p547, Id.
[505] Id.

Brazil's major climate change contribution lies in the deforestation of the Amazon basin, the world's largest land-based carbon sink. The loss of significant portions of the Amazon to biomass use, wood exports and agriculture, contribute significantly to GHG emissions, and reduces the capacity to address it. Avoided deforestation therefore remains a significant part of policies and negotiations relating to Brazil.

Brazil does not play a major part in the international trade in other renewable technologies and is not a major supplier or provider of such technologies, except perhaps in hydropower, and basic ethanol, to other countries.[506] Brazil remains a manufacturing powerhouse in South America and is a major regional exporter of electrical goods and appliances.[507] However, it remains primarily an agricultural exporter (basic and processed products), especially as it is the world's largest meat exporter.[508]

It has plans to turn its research program on the application of hydrogen fuel cell technology in buses into an opportunity to manufacture such buses for export, especially to other developing countries.[509]

Brazil places special emphasis on South-South cooperation with a specific interest in exporting its technologies to other developing countries.[510] This is particularly true in the case of first generation biofuels based on sugar to ethanol; and in the area of Agriculture. The potential for Brazil to play a larger part in providing technology and exporting products regionally exists but is less likely to ramp up to significant levels in the near term.

B. China

China is now one of the world's largest consumers of energy,[511] and may be the largest single emitter of GHG emissions by most measures that do not take population into account.[512] Its growth has largely been based on coal energy.[513] It is highly dependent on foreign sources for its supply of oil.[514] The demand from China

---

[506] See p229, See UNEP, *Towards a Green Economy: Pathways to Sustainable Development and Poverty Eradication*, (Nairobi: UNEP, 2011). Also See p434, Brazilian Ministry of Science and Technology *Second National Communication of Brazil to the United Nations Framework Convention on Climate Change* (Brasilia: Ministry of Science and Technology, Brazil, 2010).

[507] See p385, Brazilian Ministry of Science and Technology *Second National Communication of Brazil to the United Nations Framework Convention on Climate Change* (Brasilia: Ministry of Science and Technology, Brazil, 2010).

[508] See p11, Id.

[509] See p316, Id.

[510] See p436, Id.

[511] p374, IEA, *Energy Technology Perspectives 2010: Scenarios and Strategies to 2050*, (Paris: IEA/OECD, 2010).

[512] p48, Fekete, H. et al "Emerging economies – potentials, pledges and fair shares of greenhouse gas reduction" ENVIRONMENTAL RESEARCH OF THE GERMAN FEDERAL MINISTRY OF THE ENVIRONMENT, NATURE CONSERVATION AND NUCLEAR SAFETY Project-no. (FKZ) 3711 41 120, (Umweltbundesamt, Bonn, April 2013).

[513] p374, IEA, *Energy Technology Perspectives 2010: Scenarios and Strategies to 2050*, (Paris: IEA/OECD, 2010).

[514] p374, Id.

has increased the oil price and has had two major effects: opening up incentives for new oil production from previously unprofitable sources (e.g. tar sands); and making it easier for renewable energy to more favourably compare in terms of cost for production and consumption.[515] While China is one of the largest consumers of fossil fuel based energy, it is also increasingly becoming one of the largest producers and consumers of renewable energy especially for hydropower, wind and solar PV.[516] Basic industry remains one of the largest contributors to China's energy related emissions, (cement, iron and steel and chemicals make up 50% of emissions)[517], for which the deployment of best available technologies is crucial, if energy efficiencies needed to peak emissions by 2020 are to be realized. China has been able to take advantage of opportunities in some sectors such that it is now one of the largest exporters of wind turbine towers, solar batteries, and solar concentrators.[518] While the majority of technology access has occurred through acquisition of licenses, a significant portion has occurred through joint ventures (a form of FDI which was highly encouraged and sometimes mandated by Chinese regulations), as well as through direct acquisition of firms that held the technologies.[519] Between 2005 and 2008, Chinese exports of clean technologies rose 337% while imports rose 56%.[520]

China is increasingly becoming a regional and international hub for innovation for multinational corporations. A survey report from Booz and Co. notes that 50% of companies in China develop products in China for export to global markets.[521] It also notes that over 60% over those surveyed planned to increase such development.[522] However, many continue to see IP as a key challenge although not the most important one, as talent access and retention are seen as stronger challenges.[523] A key finding of the report is that the majority of product development taking place in China for export is aimed at Asia and developing countries rather than primarily at developed countries.[524] Another is that Chinese companies have increased their innovative capacity and aim to compete on innovation and not just input costs and price.[525] China is also

---

[515] Id.
[516] p413, Id.
[517] Id.
[518] p574, Id.
[519] p575, Id.
[520] p576, Id.
[521] p6, Veldhoen, S et al. "Innovation: China's Next Advantage – 2012 China Innovation Survey" A Benelux Chamber of Commerce, China Europe International Business School (CEIBS), Wenzhou Chamber of Commerce and Booz & Company Joint Report, 2012.
[522] p6, Veldhoen, S et al. "Innovation: China's Next Advantage – 2012 China Innovation Survey" A Benelux Chamber of Commerce, China Europe International Business School (CEIBS), Wenzhou Chamber of Commerce and Booz & Company Joint Report, 2012.
[523] p9, Id.
[524] p8, Id.
[525] p10, Id.

increasing its own investment in R&D which was up by 600% between 1998 and 2008.[526]

China has one of the most active markets for coal technologies both for domestic use and export.[527] The technology to enable such production in China was acquired through experience in joint ventures as well as licensing.[528] Most of these purchases were by large state owned or state affiliated enterprises, rather than SMEs.[529] Chinese success in this sector may be the result of significant state intervention to purchase licenses, build capacity, disseminate information, data and know how to all actors in the sector.[530] Such sector wide cooperation seems to have been a necessary condition for successful adoption, adaptation and replication of technologies, driven by deliberate government policy and intervention. Licenses were sourced from Hitachi, Mitsubishi, Toshiba, Mitsui Babcock, and Alston while joint ventures were carried out with Siemens. The Japanese licensing took place within a broader capacity building cooperation between the Japanese and Chinese government creating a collaboration and training platform aimed at enabling design and production capacity in Chinese firms.[531] Some findings suggest that patent acquisition or licensing in China faced barriers in part because buyers did not feel secure that the first mover competitive advantage of paying for a license would be preserved without sufficient patent protection.[532] While the preferred mode of absorption of clean coal technology for Chinese enterprises is FDI, that apparently conflicted with the strategy of foreign firms' strategies who focused only on product and equipment sales.[533] Chinese policy has worked to ensure greater domestic manufacturing of clean coal technologies, for domestic adoption and for export.[534] One of the most successful externally supported projects for technology transfer in China involved industrial boilers.[535] The GEF project suggested many lessons for technology transfer to China including[536]:

- Knowledge transfer to local manufacturers was key; this included intellectual property through purchases of licenses;
- Capacity building to enable absorption of the technology is key to generating local interest;

---

[526] See p2, Tan, X et al. "Scaling Up Low-Carbon Technology Deployment: Lessons from China" World Resources Institute Report, 2010.
[527] p7, Philibert, C and J Podkanski "International Energy Technology Collaboration and Climate Change Mitigation - Case Study 4: Clean Coal Technologies" COM/ENV/EPOC/IEA/SLT(2005)4, IEA, Paris, 2005.
[528] See p7, Tan, X et al.
[529] p21, Philibert, C and J Podkanski
[530] See p7, Tan, X et al.
[531] Id.
[532] p21, Philibert, C and J Podkanski "International Energy Technology Collaboration and Climate Change Mitigation - Case Study 4: Clean Coal Technologies" COM/ENV/EPOC/IEA/SLT(2005)4, IEA, Paris, 2005.
[533] Id.
[534] Id.
[535] p25, Id.
[536] p25, Id.

- Market creation measures and reduction of market barriers are necessary to ensure sustainable demand for the products;
- Technology transfer of this kind is more likely where there is little risk of creating competition that will export the product back to the home market, or other existing market of the technology supplier.

In addition, government intervention to promote sector-wide cooperation on R&D, demonstration and deployment, including knowledge and cost-sharing is crucial. The SC/USC experience also suggests that learning to operate and maintain hardware purchased and implemented is a necessary precursor to building capacity to engage in adoption, adaptation and replication.[537] It seems to also suggest that there needs to already exist a capacity to engage in forms of reverse engineering; although this would be greatly assisted by active cooperation with the technology provider firm to access hard data and information on the technology specifications.[538]

China has become the world's largest manufacturer of thermal power equipment including design of super-critical and ultra-supercritical coal technology.[539] It has begun to export such technology to other developing country markets although this still remains at an initial stage.[540] China maintains a strong advantage in exporting boilers, but lags in steam turbines, and appears to have quality problems associated with its export products that may be hindering the scale and scope of its export performance.[541] It remains a laggard in production of the advanced materials necessary for construction of SC/USC technology and has to import it from Japan.[542] Once Chinese firms can access best available technologies in both sectors, they may be able to increase their export performance and lower costs of adoption of SC/USC technologies in export markets.

The Chinese steel sector's efficiency needs have also exhibited a similar pattern to that of the SC/USC sector.[543] This is driven by a competitive need to match production efficiency in other countries using best available technologies. The challenge was one of absorption and adaptation of such technologies into production processes.

---

[537] See p8, Tan, X et al. "Scaling Up Low-Carbon Technology Deployment: Lessons from China" World Resources Institute Report, 2010.
[538] Id.
[539] World Bank *Coal Power Technology Country Studies: China and India*.(Washington D.C. World Bank, 2009.)
[540] See p4, Best, D and E Levina "Facing China's Coal Future: Prospects and Challenges for CCS" Working Paper 2012, OECD/IEA 2012. Also See p10, Tan, X et al. "Scaling Up Low-Carbon Technology Deployment: Lessons from China" World Resources Institute Report, 2010.
[541] See p18, Horbach, J et al. "Lead Markets for Clean Coal Technologies: A Case Study for China, Germany, Japan and the USA" Discussion Paper No. 12-063, Center for European Economic Research, 2012.
[542] See p7, Tan, X et al. "Scaling Up Low-Carbon Technology Deployment: Lessons from China" World Resources Institute Report, 2010.
[543] See p20, Id.

The main difference in this case was concerted cooperation with the government of Japan that also provided a cooperation platform for its private sector to train and build capacity with the sectoral platform participants in China.[544] The joint cooperation focused on demonstration and deployment, with participation of firms from both countries, and with know-how as a key component.[545] This was followed by a localization program in China, creating procurement and tax credit preferences for local manufacturing of efficiency technologies.[546] However, as Chinese firms became competitors for the domestic Chinese market, Japanese firms withdrew from the collaboration[547], foreseeing potential competition in other export markets. The joint platform for demonstration and deployment was a crucial learning tool for Chinese firms, one that would not have existed were it not for state intervention to encourage cooperation in both countries. While Japan did so through state funding and incentives and China did so through state mandates, the collaboration proved fruitful for China and helped to create a domestic efficiency industry.

China is also home to what was the most successful solar PV company in the developing world, Suntech Power Co. While its main production subsidiary has recently had to declare bankruptcy,[548] at its height, it had the largest share of the Chinese Solar PV market and also exported a significant amount of its production. It was a major contributor to the price reduction of Solar PV worldwide during the 2001-2010 period, making adoption of solar PV cheaper throughout the world. The company was founded on existing available technology with some of its own patents, but also grew by acquiring other companies such as Japan's MSK.[549] To some extent, it was a contributor to what has come to be seen as an oversupply on the global market.[550] Nevertheless, China continues to have a vibrant market in solar PV with several world class manufacturers.[551]

---

[544] See p21, Id.
[545] Id.
[546] Id.
[547] See p21, Tan, X et al. "Scaling Up Low-Carbon Technology Deployment: Lessons from China" World Resources Institute Report, 2010.
[548] Riley, C "Major Chinese solar company goes bankrupt" CNN Money, 21 March 2013. Available at: http://money.cnn.com/2013/03/21/news/suntech-solar-bankruptcy/index.html (last visited 15 August 2014).
[549] See p11, Barton, J "Intellectual Property and Access to Clean Energy Technologies in Developing Countries: An Analysis of Solar Photovoltaic, Biofuel and Wind Technologies" Trade and Sustainable Energy Series, Issue Paper No. 2, ICTSD December 2007.
[550] See Bradsher, K "Glut of Solar Panels Poses a New Threat to China" New York Times, October 4, 2012. Available at: http://www.nytimes.com/2012/10/05/business/global/glut-of-solar-panels-is-a-new-test-for-china.html?pagewanted=all&_r=0 (last visited 15 August 2014).
[551] See p7, Gehl Sampath, P "Can the Climate Technology Mechanism Deliver its Promise? Some Issues and Considerations"; in Gehl Sampath, P. et al. *Realizing the potential of the UNFCCC Technology Mechanism: Perspectives on the Way Forward* ICTSD Programme on Innovation, Technology and Intellectual Property; Issue Paper No. 35; International Centre for Trade and Sustainable Development, Geneva, Switzerland (2012)

The structure and development of the wind industry differed significantly from that of the thermal power sector in SC/USC technology, as Tan et al. note.[552] This was largely driven by competitive domestic firms seeking domestic market share. Government intervention has been aimed at demand creation, and not at encouraging a significant export orientation which would require best available technologies. The competition between firms has meant that knowledge sharing and cooperation of R&D, demonstration and deployment has not been significant in the sector.[553] Lewis notes that the Chinese market has several imperfections such as fragmented grid connections[554] that limit the role of wind and of market oriented supply of electricity.

However, national policies have created significant demand for wind, even as demand for any form of electricity generation also grows. China uses local content requirements paired with a power supply concession.[555] Lewis argues that China's policy of local content, even at 70%, did provide an incentive for foreign firms to locate in China, but largely through wholly owned or majority owned subsidiaries.[556] There appeared to be little licensing to local suppliers or partnerships with Chinese companies. On the other hand, the majority of concessions have been given to existing Chinese companies such as Goldwind[557] one of the more successful wind technology firms in the world. The company serves primarily the Chinese market. Having initially licensed some of the key technology needed from REpower, a German company[558], Goldwind may also have licensed from other European and Japanese firms for other components. Its license from REpower, a German company, forbids it from exporting products made with the technology.[559] However given Goldwind's focus on the domestic market and its natural advantages in access to power supply concessions from the government, this strategy may make sense. By focusing on Chinese market share, Goldwind may be planning to create such a dominant market position in China that it becomes an indispensable partner for any foreign investors wishing to access the Chinese market. The projected demand in growth in China is such that foreign companies may have no option but to take whatever entry points into the market that they can. Goldwind has also begun to build a network of local suppliers to which it is transferring its know-how and technology.[560] It has also developed significant in-house capacity for R&D,

---

[552] See p11, Tan, X et al. "Scaling Up Low-Carbon Technology Deployment: Lessons from China" World Resources Institute Report, 2010.
[553] Id.
[554] See p217, Lewis, J "Technology Acquisition and Innovation in the Developing World: Wind Turbine Development in China and India" 42 St Comp Int Dev 208 (2007).
[555] See p218, Id.
[556] Id.
[557] See p219, Id.
[558] See p17, Barton, J "Intellectual Property and Access to Clean Energy Technologies in Developing Countries: An Analysis of Solar Photovoltaic, Biofuel and Wind Technologies" Trade and Sustainable Energy Series, Issue Paper No. 2, ICTSD December 2007.
[559] See p222, Lewis, J
[560] See p223, Id.

bolstering its local patent position, and increasing its bargaining power.[561] It has also purchased a majority stake in Vensys (a German firm), giving it access to IP related to manufacturing of larger turbines.[562]

However, Chinese manufacturers generally do not have access to best available technologies and have difficulty with the standard of quality of their smaller turbines and do not have the know-how for producing larger turbines.[563] Costs of licensing appear to be an increasing concern for the government, as well as reluctance to make best available technologies available for licensing.[564] In part this may be due to demand from Chinese firms seeking to out-compete each other in the domestic market.[565]

One may conclude from this that, overall, the barriers for Chinese firms do not go beyond those of normal commercial entrants and that there appear to be few systematic barriers to participation in the market, although perhaps there may be issues in relation to access to developed country markets. China continues to seek to participate in greater licensing and innovation in the renewable energy sector. However, the lack of access to best available technologies suggests that even where normal commercial activity has been moderately successful, China's full potential cannot be harnessed without more intervention to create sector-wide adoption of best available technologies, requiring firms to cooperate rather than compete and to engage in significant unprecedented knowledge sharing. The importance of export markets in pushing firms to adopt best available technologies is also a key lesson from the Chinese experience. While foreign FDI into the sector does exist it has done so largely as wholly owned subsidiaries, limiting spill-overs. Such FDI has also been focused on meeting local demand rather than being export oriented.[566]

China's capacity for large scale manufacturing and its ability to rapidly scale up production makes it an indispensable partner for achieving global diffusion of technologies world-wide. China's role in lowering the costs of solar PV is a case in point, even in a situation where the Chinese companies were not holders of the best available technologies they have been able to increase production to the point of possible oversupply with current market demand.

C. India

Like China, India is heavily dependent on fossil fuels for electricity production, as well as heating and transport. Its fuel mix is dominated by oil and coal with significant

---

[561] Id.
[562] See p15, Tan, X et al. "Scaling Up Low-Carbon Technology Deployment: Lessons from China" World Resources Institute Report, 2010.
[563] See p12, Id.
[564] See p14, Id.
[565] See p15, Id.
[566] See p14, Id.

shares from natural gas and nuclear power.⁵⁶⁷ India has also seen a rapid increase in its energy demand, although not on the scale or speed of China. India's emissions need to peak by 2030, (under a 2 degree scenario), largely through rapid deployment of renewables, nuclear and biofuels. Also crucial will be deployment of best available technologies to enable greater energy use efficiency in industry.⁵⁶⁸ As with China, the IEA ETP 2010 scenario notes that peaking in 2030 is not achievable without widespread adoption of CCS in power generation and industry.⁵⁶⁹

India has also taken advantage of opportunities to become a significant player in clean technologies. One of the best-selling electric vehicle manufacturers in the world (by volume) is the Reva Electric Car Company (a Mahindra subsidiary).⁵⁷⁰ Indian companies have acquired technology through licensing, through joint ventures, as well as some direct acquisitions.⁵⁷¹ Between 2005 and 2008, Indian exports of renewable technology increased 464% while imports increased by 172%.

India is also the home base of one of the most successful global wind technology manufacturers, Suzlon Energy Ltd. Lewis notes that Suzlon has focused on acquisition of technology by strategically acquiring whole companies.⁵⁷² In part this circumvents the established firms, but relies on significant in-house absorptive capacity. Suzlon's export oriented approach also made acquisition of advanced technology and access to markets crucial. This meant that Suzlon could not follow an imitation model, as its products would have been blocked from access to developed country markets where the technologies were protected. Neither could it rely solely on a licensing model since the terms of licenses from any of the established firms would contain limitations such as geographic restrictions. This also necessitated creating significant in-house R&D capacity to further develop the technology acquired from smaller second tier firms.⁵⁷³ The firm accessed technology through licenses and then later direct acquisition.⁵⁷⁴ The firm shifted quickly into R&D and sited facilities in developed countries to ensure market access.⁵⁷⁵ However, India may not have reached its full potential in the sector. Lewis points to a paucity of proper reform in India that would

---

⁵⁶⁷ p417, IEA, *Energy Technology Perspectives 2010: Scenarios and Strategies to 2050*, (Paris: IEA/OECD, 2010).
⁵⁶⁸ p427, Id.
⁵⁶⁹ p427, Id.
⁵⁷⁰ p574, Id.
⁵⁷¹ p575, Id.
⁵⁷² See p221, Lewis, J "Technology Acquisition and Innovation in the Developing World: Wind Turbine Development in China and India" 42 St Comp Int Dev 208 (2007).
⁵⁷³ See p221, Lewis, J "Technology Acquisition and Innovation in the Developing World: Wind Turbine Development in China and India" 42 St Comp Int Dev 208 (2007).
⁵⁷⁴ See p17, Barton, J "Intellectual Property and Access to Clean Energy Technologies in Developing Countries: An Analysis of Solar Photovoltaic, Biofuel and Wind Technologies" Trade and Sustainable Energy Series, Issue Paper No. 2, ICTSD December 2007.
⁵⁷⁵ Id.

allow for independent power producers who would create demand for new technologies.[576]

A case study by Ockwell et al. (Sussex Energy Group, TERI, Institute for Development Studies)[577] looked at technology development and diffusion in India of 7 mitigation technologies: coal gasification, hybrid vehicles; solar PV, Wind, LED lighting; biomass; thermal power efficiency.

In the coal gasification sector, specifically Integrated Gasification Combined Cycle (IGCC), adaption to local conditions has been key, as Indian domestic sources of coal are higher in impurities than the coals traditionally used for gasification technologies. At the time of the study, there was one major Indian firm, Bharat Heavy Electricals Ltd. (BHEL), long established with contractual and licensing arrangements with foreign companies such as Siemens and GE.[578] Perceptions of barriers in the sector focused on high capital costs and access to financing.[579] At the time of the study only 5 demonstration projects had been set up.[580] Some of this was due to lack of information and testing on how existing technologies would work with the grade of Indian coal. Such testing remained to be done at the time of the study, but it was unclear who had the resources to carry it out. This suggests that there was little demand or market for IGCC in India and what demand there was had been amply met by BHEL. Nevertheless concerns were expressed that foreign firms in partnerships retained control and secrecy of advanced design elements.[581]

In the LED sector, there were no manufacturers in India at the time of the study, although there is an importer of components which assembled LEDs for use in the domestic market.[582] Perceptions were that there is little market for LEDs in India and what demand there is can be met by direct importation of completed products. There are few skills in the manufacturing side. The one company that assembled LEDs had few connections to foreign firms. The global market is dominated by OECD firms and is perceived to be highly patented (especially in process patents) and highly litigious.[583] There appears to be an assumption that licensing would be difficult for Indian firms underlying the perceptions study.

In Biomass, there are several Indian firms involved in manufacturing biomass briquette machines. Most of the firms are exporting these to other countries, including

---

[576] See p217, Lewis, J
[577] Ockwell, D, et al. "UK-India Collaboration to Identify the Barriers to the Transfer of Low Carbon Technology-Final report" (London: the Department of Environment, Food and Rural Affairs, U.K., 2007).
[578] See p54, Id.
[579] See p57, Id.
[580] See p58, Id.
[581] See p109, Id.
[582] See p66, Id.
[583] See p72, Id.

in Africa.[584] The basic technology is in the public domain, and Indian manufacturers do not engage in much R&D. The study finds some concerns related to Indian manufacturers' reverse-engineering of some European designs, but overall, intellectual property is perceived to play a small part in the sector.[585]

In the hybrid vehicles sector, the study found two firms working on iterations of bus chassis, or three wheeled vehicles.[586] All the technology companies owning and manufacturing hybrids were based in OECD countries. The study notes that because R&D plays such a large role, patents are a significant determinant of the ability to participate in the market, even for actors in developed countries. Ford and Nissan licensed from Toyota rather than develop their own technology and Daimler Chrysler and BMW cooperated on a research partnership to develop full hybrid technologies. All car companies are seeking to enter this technology market as it is perceived as a necessity for future participation in the automobile sector.[587] IP is clearly perceived as a concern as the sector is seen as highly patented and concentrated. The fact that the licenses are held by key manufacturers with strong market positions may mean that new entrants will find it difficult. However, if sufficient capacity is built up quickly, suppliers in developing countries may have a chance to establish themselves, if governments are willing to leverage the attractiveness of their markets. This may be the case with China's requirement that all investments in the automobile sector be carried out in JVs with majority Chinese ownership.[588]

In thermal combustion efficiency, primarily for electricity production, the study finds many government users (electricity producers) who would apply the technologies, but a limited number of producers of the technologies (e.g. BHEL.).[589] The basic technology is quite mature and used in India but more efficient designs have not been applied in India, primarily because of the capitals costs of refurbishing existing plants.[590] BHEL has significant experience and perceives no need to rely on foreign technology to compete and meet market demand. At least one foreign firm also has a presence in India e.g. Alstom (France).[591] The focus appears to be on collaborations on the development of incremental improvements rather than access to or using foreign technologies.[592]

---

[584] See p77, Id.
[585] See p82, Id.
[586] See p88, Id.
[587] See p91, Id.
[588] See p95, Id.
[589] See p101, Id.
[590] See p104, Id.
[591] See p101, Id.
[592] Id.

In Phase 2[593] of the collaboration which produced the first study, the authors expanded the subject area to include Solar PV and revisited some of the subject areas covered in the first phase. As with other studies, solar PV from silicon wafers was seen as a mature technology with few barriers to entry, and many producers in India, but new materials for thin film PV have proven more complicated. While these are held by a concentrated number of firms, there appears to be ease of licensing for Indian firms.[594] This is attributed to the existence of more than enough demand which new entrants can meet without reducing market share of incumbents, even in the home markets of the OECD firms. This illustrates the crucial importance of creating strong global markets and demand for technologies to remove some of the competitive pressure to maintain market share by private sector actors. Nevertheless, differences in firm concentration along various parts of the solar PV value chain suggest that expressed concerns about blockages for downstream producers may be realized.[595]

In hybrid vehicles, the Phase II study identified other Indian actors on hybrids such as Tata Motors and Mahindra Motors. These are engaged in in-house R&D as well as acquisition of foreign firms. Patents are concentrated in a few foreign firms but also amongst a variety of components.[596] Licensing is not occurring from the major players but work-arounds and licensing from smaller players is occurring. Concerns were expressed that the lack of licensing by major players was limiting technology diffusion[597] and the economies of scale that might result from lowering prices and increasing demand for hybrids in comparison to petrol and diesel vehicles.

The study emphasizes that access to intellectual property protection on its own is not seen as a sufficient condition for successful technology transfer of climate technologies.[598] What it does conclude is that in some sectors such as hybrid vehicles, it is a necessary condition. More specifically the need for access to intellectual property and the type of intervention needed will differ across sectors depending on industry structure, business models and industry vectors for investment in the local economy.[599] The study also emphasizes that the success stories have been ones that focused on the generation and growth of local capacity to absorb, adapt and transform technologies, and most importantly, to do so both for purposes of participation not just in domestic markets but also international markets.[600] Even for a large market such as India,

---

[593] Mallet, A et al. "UK-India Collaboration to Identify the Barriers to the Transfer of Low Carbon Technology-Phase II Final report" (London: Department of Energy and Climate Change, UK 2009).
[594] See p69, Id.
[595] Id.
[596] See p87, Id.
[597] See p88, Id.
[598] See p44, Ockwell, D, et al. "UK-India Collaboration to Identify the Barriers to the Transfer of Low Carbon Technology-Final report" (London: the Department of Environment, Food and Rural Affairs, U.K., 2007).
[599] See p34, Id.
[600] See p29, Id.

successful domestic clean technology industries need access to and participation in the international technology markets.

It is important however to take on board the argument that Ockwell et al. have made in another paper[601], that for developing countries, even advanced technologies essentially have to be market ready for them to be useful in developing a clean technology economic base. What is needed in developing countries in the period to 2020 is deployment of technologies that are 'new to the industry'; and 'new to the firm' but not necessarily new in terms of inventiveness.[602] This places a greater emphasis on deployment of existing technologies in developing countries and in pushing these already commercial or near commercial technologies down to the level of the firm as quickly as possible.

India is a major hub for pharmaceutical and agrochemicals production and has in recent years begun to move from generic industries into major originator R&D. Building on its high export performance, especially to developing countries, Indian firms have been using that capital to cooperate in R&D, acquire firms, and create joint ventures, in order to participate in the lucrative developed country markets for new chemical entities and biological medicines.[603] This role for India as a crucial supplier of affordable medicines has been a large part of the structural debate about how TRIPS might limit access to medicines by forcing Indian firms to provide domestic protection for pharmaceuticals thus limiting their capacity to produce generics for export to meet the need for products in developing countries.[604]

D. South Africa

South Africa is the main manufacturing powerhouse economy in sub-Saharan Africa. It has significant exports and investment in the rest of Africa, within the general regional constraints that much of Africa trades primarily with former colonial powers such as France and the United Kingdom.

South Africa has significant potential capacity for private sector and government research and development but is not considered a highly innovative

---

[601] Ockwell, D et al. "Enhancing Developing Country Access to Eco-Innovation: The Case of Technology Transfer and Climate Change in a Post-2012 Policy Framework", OECD Environment Working Papers, No. 12, OECD Publishing 2010
[602] See p16, Id.
[603] See p39, Kumar, N "Intellectual Property Rights, Technology and Economic Development: Experiences of Asian Countries" Study paper 1b, for Commission on Intellectual Property Rights *Integrating Intellectual Property Rights and Development Policy* (London: Commission on Intellectual Property Rights 2002).
[604] See Abbott, F M "Innovation and Technology Transfer to Address Climate Change: Lessons from the Global Debate on Intellectual Property and Public Health", ICTSD's Programme on IPRs and Sustainable Development, Issue Paper No. 24, International Centre for Trade and Sustainable Development, Geneva, Switzerland, 2009.

economy. Some measures suggest that it spends less than 1% of GDP on R&D, despite several strong research universities.[605] South Africa was a leader in the development of highly GHG intensive synthetic fuels (coal to liquid) during the apartheid period, which has been maintained.[606] South Africa also had nuclear capacity and significant expertise remains. However it has significant skills gaps in relevant technology areas, and overall in science, technology, engineering and math.[607] It does not have any significant research programme on renewable energy and domestic commercial actors are mostly implementers rather than producers of the technologies.

E. Overview

As part and parcel of their overall growth strategies and economic policies, these countries are taking advantage of the attractiveness of their large markets to foreign companies. However, they have, for the most part, also put in place strong regulatory measures to encourage the diffusion and growth of renewable technologies, especially for export markets, including:

- Ambitious renewable energy production and consumption targets;
- Renewable energy and efficiency standards and labels;
- Clean energy tax incentives;
- Feed in tariffs
- Joint venture requirements for specific economic sectors;

In China, for example, the vast majority of FDI into China was required to be in the form of joint ventures that included specific performance and technology transfer requirements or at the very least, no restrictions on the freedom of movement of employees of the JV.[608] This had a significant impact on China's ability to move quickly up the value chain and move into competing in the international market on higher value goods. Brazil, China and India have significant domestic research capacity in both the public and private sector.[609]

---

[605] See p8, Department of Environmental Affairs *South Africa's Second National Communication under the United Nations Framework Convention on Climate Change* (Pretoria: Department of Environmental Affairs Republic of South Africa, 2011).
[606] See p18, Id.
[607] See p7, Id.
[608] Chapter 23, p7, Stern, N .et al. *The Economics of Climate Change: The Stern Review* (Cambridge: Cambridge University Press, 2007).
[609] See p45 Correa, C "Mechanisms for International Cooperation in Research and Development in the Area of Climate Change" in Soni, P et al. *Technological Cooperation and Climate Change Issues and Perspectives* Working papers presented at the Ministry of Environment and Forests, Government of India - UNDP Consultation on Technology Cooperation for Addressing Climate Change, 23-24 September, 2011; New Delhi, India.

In addition, all three countries provide intellectual property protection that, for the moment, is sufficiently compliant with the TRIPS Agreement and, in comparison to the pre-TRIPS era, provides a stable and relatively predictable environment for economic transactions to take place in the context of a broader enabling environment for investment. There remain concerns about sovereign risks (policy and macro-economic)[610] related to sudden shifts in government policy or the extent to which government mandates require non-voluntary sharing of technologies, especially in China, but that risk appears to be largely mitigated by the broader attractiveness of doing business in China. Nevertheless, such risk perceptions may limit the quality and volume of technologies licensed or made available to enterprises in these countries. There is some evidence that what is made available under many licensing or joint venture agreements in these countries is not best available technology.[611]

India and China are already significant players in the global R&D chain, with many companies placing significant portions of their global R&D facilities in these countries. Already by 2006, General Motors had an R&D presence in China, as did Microsoft and BP in India.[612] China, India, Brazil and Russia remain the largest recipients of licensing activity from developed countries.[613] However, they all remain relatively small players in the technology market when measured by royalty receipts. A look at royalties in the 2009 - 2012 period shows that among developing countries China remains the largest with total charges at USD 1.044 billion compared to Brazil at USD 510 million, and India at USD 321 Million.[614] China is on a par with Israel but is small compared with USD 2.69 billion for Belgium, USD 3.7 billion for Canada, USD 3.3 billion for Finland, USD 12.4 billion for France, USD 13.8 for Germany, USD 3.4 Billion for South Korea.

---

[610] p585, IEA, *Energy Technology Perspectives 2010: Scenarios and Strategies to 2050*, (Paris: IEA/OECD, 2010).
[611] Saggi, K "Trade, Foreign Direct Investment, and International Technology Transfer: A Survey" World Bank Policy Research Working Paper 2349, May 2000. See also p273, Gechlick, M "Making Transfer of Clean Technology Work: Lessons of the Clean Development Mechanism" 11 San Diego International Law Journal 227 (2009).
[612] p517, Stern, N. et al. *The Economics of Climate Change: The Stern Review* (Cambridge: Cambridge University Press, 2007).
[613] See p64, Karachalios, K et al. (eds.) "Patents and Clean Energy: Bridging the Gap between Evidence and Policy: Final report" UNEP/ EPO / ICTSD 2010.
[614] World Bank *World Development Indicators* Available at: data.worldbank.org

Table 3: Selected Royalty receipts for developed and emerging Economies - 2012[615]

World Development Indicators	IP Charges, receipts (BoP, current US$)		
Country Name	2011	2012	2013
Arab World	$43,414,575.93	$29,373,311.77	
Belgium	$2,563,560,261.17	$2,696,785,294.31	
Brazil	$590,769,562.95	$510,711,775.88	
China	$743,301,698.00	$1,044,102,041.00	
Germany	$14,784,193,689.56	$13,870,402,170.39	
Spain	$1,065,080,142.69	$1,274,602,305.52	
European Union	$75,410,643,381.96	$70,314,059,914.76	
Finland	$3,187,717,775.03	$3,315,525,772.67	
France	$16,127,805,584.34	$12,407,943,394.83	
United Kingdom	$14,082,476,426.25	$12,462,124,293.18	
Greece	$69,048,788.65	$82,133,013.96	
India	$302,615,975.49	$321,445,173.96	
Ireland	$5,003,354,614.82	$4,996,928,985.12	
Israel	$1,099,500,000.00	$1,056,500,000.00	
Italy	$3,970,640,349.05	$4,059,555,009.68	
Japan	$28,989,252,520.81	$31,892,291,571.95	
Korea, Rep.	$4,335,600,000.00	$3,435,500,000.00	
Mexico	$96,535,890.00	$95,626,260.00	
Netherlands	$5,199,537,295.25	$4,959,690,879.46	
Norway	$321,690,939.91	$374,389,392.79	
New Zealand	$334,639,811.81	$310,379,325.95	
Poland	$268,000,000.00	$229,000,000.00	
Portugal	$60,821,239.29	$46,675,765.29	
Russian Federation	$555,800,000.00	$664,200,000.00	
Singapore	$1,637,016,607.92	$1,648,987,148.75	
Sub-Saharan Africa (developing only)	$163,843,946.80	$125,872,203.65	
United States	$120,718,000,000.00	$124,182,000,000.00	
South Africa	$65,767,203.97	$67,324,145.13	

India and China may also play a role as developers and adapters of technologies that may be better suited to demands in other developing countries. For example, in the area of modern heat access (e.g. switching from low efficiency biomass, to efficient gas and solar cookers) rural and peri-urban populations in India and China provide ideal testing grounds for development and dissemination of such technologies and Indian and Chinese companies can themselves sell and transfer these technologies to other developing countries.[616] Private sector actors in OECD countries may not be

---

[615] Id.
[616] p25-26, Elzinga, D et al. "Advantage Energy: Emerging Economies, Developing Countries and the

interested in developing such products as there may be no significant domestic demand in their own countries, and technological solutions they propose may not be suited to deployment in the difficult economic and institutional environments of many developing countries. In the electricity sector, another example is the growth in overall exports (13% – 45% from 2003 – 2009) from China's Shanghai Power Corporation of super critical technologies for coal powered electricity generation primarily due to exports to developing countries.[617]

These emerging economies are also the countries in which there may be clearest evidence of significant patenting of clean technologies.[618] However, they are also the most likely developing countries to be able to afford to pay reasonable market rates for licensing of technologies, which has been the case for a significant number of successful ventures such as Goldwind and Suzlon.[619] The problems that they face are ones of accessing licenses for existing technologies from potential competitors in developed countries. They have to deal with such issues as refusals to license, above market rates for technology or restrictive licensing practices, especially for best available technologies which present the cutting edge and may be a competitive advantage in developed country markets. They also urgently want to participate in new and innovative research on clean technology and generate leading companies that are IP holders themselves.

The means to addressing the issues they face largely lie in using existing tools in the international IP system. Compulsory licensing, or the threat of it, may be available to address anti-competitive practices such as refusals to license, unreasonable pricing or restrictive licenses. They may be assisted by easier and more transparent licensing platforms and markets. In terms of participating in new technologies, these countries would be happy to see more joint research and development projects, both co-funded and multilaterally funded. Their concerns are reflected by suggestions for: subsidies; joint R&D; insurance and loan guarantees for development, diffusion and transfer of climate technology; infrastructure for information sharing and licensing platforms, global patent pools, access to publicly funded research; as well as full use of TRIPS flexibilities.[620] In a sense, it is the creation of a transparent and equal playing field for licensing of technologies that is their most urgent need as they generally have sufficient

---

Private-Public Sector Interface" International Energy Agency Information Paper, September 2011.
[617] p38, Elzinga, D et al. "Advantage Energy: Emerging Economies, Developing Countries and the Private-Public Sector Interface" International Energy Agency Information Paper, September 2011.
[618] p18, Copenhagen Economics and the IPR Company 'Are IPR and Barrier to the transfer of Climate Change Technology?' Study Commissioned by European Commission DG Trade, January 2009.
[619] p575, IEA, *Energy Technology Perspectives 2010: Scenarios and Strategies to 2050*, (Paris: IEA/OECD, 2010).
[620] See e.g. CHINA'S VIEWS ON THE FULFILLMENT OF THE BALI ACTION PLAN AND THE COMPONENTS OF THE AGREED OUTCOME TO BE ADOPTED BY THE CONFERENCE OF THE PARTIES AT ITS 15 TH SESSION. February 19, 2009 (FCCC/AWGLCA/2009/MISC.), p5. Available at: http://unfccc.int/files/kyoto_protocol/application/pdf/china060209.pdf (last visited 15 August, 2014).

domestic production capacity. However, emerging economies are also the most likely to have to take on quantified emissions reductions obligations in some form in the new post-Kyoto framework and have a fundamental need for access to existing technologies to help them make the transition out of technologies in which they have significant sunk costs. This means that they are concerned with technology to make existing energy-use less GHG intensive such as 'clean-coal' technologies, and carbon capture and sequestration. In that sense, the issues they face bear some similarity to the needs of smaller developing countries, in terms of access to existing technologies.

XI.3.2 The role of emerging economies as export and distribution centers

The least developed countries (LDCs) and other developing countries face a calculus that has only some parallels to the access to medicines issue: there is an urgent need for access to existing products at low prices that will maintain and increase energy access. In general, these countries have little capacity for production and innovation of complex clean technology, nor do they have the funds to purchase goods in the quantities necessary. They are also the ones in least need of mitigation technologies, to the extent that they have no GHG emissions reduction obligations and they have comparatively low levels of fossil fuel energy consumption. Their mitigation technology need is largely related to access to energy provided by existing technology products, and the adaptation of low level technologies to local conditions.

The evidence suggests that most mitigation technologies are not patented or otherwise IP protected in these countries.[621] However, the countries from which LDCs and other developing countries tend to purchase low cost technology products, especially China and India, may be increasingly unable to provide these if they are unable to access licenses for technologies that allow them to export to other developing countries.

In addition to India and China, countries like Brazil increased renewable technology exports, although Brazil had a net increase overall in imports.[622] China, Brazil and India tend to be best placed to provide low cost mitigation technologies to other developing countries because their companies are better placed and more willing to establish production centres and distribution systems in economies that are less interesting, or too risky for companies from developed countries. LDCs and other developing countries generally have too little purchasing power for most companies in

---

[621] Copenhagen Economics and the IPR Company "Are IPRs a Barrier to the Transfer of Climate Change Technology?" Study Commissioned by European Commission DG Trade, January 2009; and Barton, J "Intellectual Property and Access to Clean Energy Technologies in Developing Countries: An Analysis of Solar Photovoltaic, Biofuel and Wind Technologies" Trade and Sustainable Energy Series, Issue Paper No. 2, ICTSD December 2007.
[622] p577, IEA, *Energy Technology Perspectives 2010: Scenarios and Strategies to 2050*, (Paris: IEA/OECD, 2010).

developed economies to establish production centres or distribution networks. The emerging economies can fill that gap but only if they can become production and distribution centres themselves and that will need to occur through access to licensing. LDCs and other developing countries have an interest in seeing further research and development (R&D) and access to patent licensing for emerging economies, but only to the extent that the technologies licensed are relevant to their needs. South – South flows of renewable energy technology are at a very low level, the lowest among the four south-north vectors of flows.[623] However, these have been increasing since 2002 and are likely to grow as more developing countries put in place policies that create demand for such technologies. It may be appropriate, for example at a multilateral level to consider a way for least developed and developing countries to be able to selectively lower tariffs for selected technological products coming from other developing countries without having to comply with MFN obligations under the WTO.

This need for the emerging economies to provide technological products cheaply to other developing countries is even clearer when it comes to technologies for adaptation. LDCs and most developing countries are probably the most vulnerable to the extreme weather events (droughts and floods) and shifts in disease bands that the IPCC Fourth Assessment report has found to be some of the near term effects of climate change.[624] This implicates in particular areas such as agriculture and health. To become more climate-resilient, improving health systems and access to appropriate diagnostic and treatment options for diseases such as malaria and dengue fever will be crucial. To deal with droughts and floods, appropriately engineered or hybridized plants and plant varieties will be required. Health[625] and agriculture[626] are both sectors that are heavily reliant on intellectual property as a way of organizing investment, production and distribution. These technologies are more likely to be IP protected not only in emerging economies, but also in a significant number of LDCs and developing countries. This would make it more difficult to export products from major emerging economies to LDCs and developing countries as licenses are likely only to be granted for domestic production and distribution. Where these technologies are patented in LDCs and developing countries, importing them becomes even more difficult. A significant portion of LDCs and developing countries may see that the best way to ensure access to technologies for adaptation in areas such as health and agriculture is to reduce the number of patent protected technologies in all developing countries, including emerging economies.

---

[623] p573, Figure 15.3., Id.
[624] p48, IPCC *Climate Change 2007: Synthesis Report* Intergovernmental Panel on Climate Change Fourth Assessment Report, Cambridge University Press, Cambridge, UK 2007.
[625] Abbott, F M "Innovation and Technology Transfer to Address Climate Change: Lessons from the Global Debate on Intellectual Property and Public Health", ICTSD's Programme on IPRs and Sustainable Development, Issue Paper No. 24, International Centre for Trade and Sustainable Development, Geneva, Switzerland, 2009.
[626] Barton, J. "Nutrition and Technology Transfer Policies" Issue Paper 6, UNCTAD-ICTSD Project on IPRs and Sustainable Development, International Centre for Trade and Sustainable Development, May 2004)

Given that emerging economies may be more likely to have distribution networks and are more likely to take on the risks of such investment, and given that they represent low cost supply markets in many sectors for other developing countries, the issue of how the international technology market is structured is crucial. At least one recent study has noted that for CDM projects taking place in Brazil, India, China and Mexico, a small majority of technology was sourced from non-Annex 1 countries[627] with India being the top supplier.[628] This finding that Brazil, India and Mexico have been suppliers of technology in CDM projects points to the potentially useful role of these countries in providing low-cost, well-adapted solutions to clean development projects in other developing countries, reducing the need for adaptation of developed country technology to local conditions.

In particular, there is a strong interaction between the systems of exhaustion that many countries have allowing for parallel importation for goods placed on the market in third countries and the levels of IP protection and licensing terms in such 'intermediary' third countries. The more restrictive the IP protection and licensing terms (e.g. geographical limitations) in country A, the less likely it is that parallel importation becomes an effective low cost way to purchase goods for country B. In theory, this is not necessarily a bad thing as limiting parallel importation allows a rightholder to then pursue a market segmentation approach, allowing them to charge a higher price in the country A market and a lower price in the country B market. However, where the rightholder has little or no interest in either establishing distribution to the country B markets at a volume and price sufficient to meet demand in those countries or to establish production in those countries, then forbidding parallel importation in Country B only serves to increase their static costs without a benefit in FDI or even lower prices. Nevertheless, there is a case to be made that market segmentation should be enabled where it allows for beneficial price advantages for developing countries.[629] This suggests that developed economies should largely refrain from allowing parallel importation of goods that are particularly required in developing countries. This may potentially include emerging economies such as China, India and Brazil. However, to the extent that supply and/or production is not made available at a reasonable price in developing countries, it may be appropriate for developing countries as a whole to establish or maintain the ability to parallel import goods. In any case, it is likely that one of the tools to ensure that emerging economies can supply other developing countries will require some assurances regarding parallel importation and

---

[627] See p40, Doranova, A *Technology Transfer and Learning under The Kyoto Regime: Exploring the Technological Impact of CDM Projects In Developing Countries* PhD Thesis UNU-Merit, Maastricht University.
[628] Id.
[629] p177, Fink, C "Entering the Jungle of Intellectual Property Rights Exhaustion and Parallel Importation" in Maskus, K & C Fink (eds.) *Intellectual Property and Development: Lessons from Recent Economic Research* (Washington D.C.: World Bank, 2005).

preventing leakage into developed countries.[630] Of course, this structure will work only if knowledge transfer occurs into emerging economies (for production of technological goods), which can then address the access to goods problem in most developing countries.

The actual effect of parallel importation on the ground is quite murky and the empirical evidence is quite mixed[631] but having a sense of the situation is crucial if the right role is to be found for the emerging economies to play as disseminators of climate technologies to developing country economies. Precisely because a system of national exhaustion is seen as strengthening intellectual property protection[632], most developed economies maintain systems of national (or in the case of the EU, regional) exhaustion. In their negotiations for bilateral and regional free trade agreements, the IP chapters of some of these agreements have explicitly required partners to prevent parallel importation, either generally or in specific sectors.[633] National exhaustion increases the exclusive control over the domestic market that is the aim of a territorial intellectual property right. However, national exhaustion also has cross-border effects. In a system with significant international trade in goods, essentially "like products" are treated differently at the border creating what may be considered an undue barrier to trade. Most developing economies are particularly concerned with abusive pricing practices and see parallel importation as a means to restrain such practices and maintain downward pressure on prices of technological goods. This may be crucial in the absence of a well-developed regulatory infrastructure to address anti-competitive practices.[634] As things stand, in the absence of a multilateral agreement on global or sectoral exhaustion policies, it is highly unlikely that unilateral adoption of national exhaustion will be beneficial or welfare enhancing for developing countries.

XIII. Conclusion

This chapter has discussed the theory and data on intellectual property and technology transfer generally and the application to climate technologies specifically. It is difficult to overstate the methodological difficulties in any empirical work on this issue. The myriad problems make for only partial and indicative conclusions from very well carried out studies. The vast majority of studies are limited to a few technological fields and do not take into account the broader challenge that adaptation poses,

---

[630] p180, Id.
[631] p182, Fink, C "Entering the Jungle of Intellectual Property Rights Exhaustion and Parallel Importation" in Maskus, K & C Fink (eds.) *Intellectual Property and Development: Lessons from Recent Economic Research* (Washington D.C.: World Bank, 2005).
[632] Id.
[633] Article 17.9.4 of the Australia US FTA on patents; Article 15.5.2 of the Morocco-US FTA on Copyright and Article 15.9.4 on Patents
[634] p177, Fink, C

especially to increase adaptive capacity. Nevertheless, policymakers must still make decisions on what to do, given the available evidence. On what basis can such a decision be made, and how should it be framed? What message is a policymaker in a developing country to take from the existing evidence? As discussed in Chapter 2, the need to act quickly is paramount. There is a time limit to how long policymakers can wait for more data before taking action.

Few of these studies takes into account the issue of timeframe which is crucial to determining whether and when patents pose a problem. The problem of patents is as much about the rate of diffusion as it is about the existence of technology and licensing. The rate and scale of licensing must increase by unprecedented amounts if the climate technology challenge is to be met. The evidence suggests that the existing pace of technology transfer in climate change is likely to have accelerated over the past 20 years, but remains insufficient. This acceleration seems to have largely benefited the emerging economies, but primarily China. There is historical precedent for developing countries to take certain kinds of policy actions to take the first steps up the technology value chain but changes in global trade mean that exports and access to markets may make unauthorized imitation a non-viable pathway. That may nevertheless leave a suite of policy levers available to address and enable formal market mechanisms for technology transfer. The evidence suggests that effective intellectual property protection is a necessary but insufficient condition for enabling technology transfer. The question remains and has yet to be answered as to what constitutes sufficient IP protection to encourage formal market mechanisms, but still ensures sufficient spillovers into the domestic market to enable quick diffusion and uptake of technologies. In the final analysis, policymakers need to know what suite of tools is legally available to them and if that suite of tools is sufficient to enable them to address the climate technology challenge. Intellectual property interventions are part of the suite, especially to ensure that they can manage behaviours that unduly limit spillovers that should be the outcome and are the rationale for FDI, JVs and Licensing. However, one of the clearest outcomes from an examination of the experiences of countries such as China and India is that developed country firms are unlikely to make their best available technologies available if a country makes active interventions to ensure spillovers, even where the country has a legally sufficient intellectual property regime. The concern about market share and competition appears overwhelming. This is a structural market problem that countries may not be able to address by themselves. If they are to take regulatory action at the international level, it may be necessary to build some kind of bargain on protection of intellectual property that provides for some extent of market protection for developed country firms while allowing developing country firms to engage in levels of production and distribution that can meet domestic and international demand within the 2015-2025 time frame for addressing climate change mitigation and adaptation.

However, the UNFCCC was signed at a time when countries had come to a significant awareness of the potential issues around technology transfer and intellectual property. There had been experiences in other multilateral environmental agreements that provided a background against which technology transfer provisions were created.

To a real extent, the need for unilateral measures on intellectual property at the national level should have been obviated by the success of the mechanisms for technology transfer at the UNFCCC. Chapter 4 will examine the implementing structures for technology transfer in the UNFCCC and examine how and why they may be considered to have failed to provide technology transfer, or adequately address the issue of intellectual property.

Chapter 4
Evaluating the implementation mechanisms for technology transfer in the UNFCCC

I. INTRODUCTION

The purpose of this chapter is to evaluate the existing mechanisms for technology transfer in the United Nations Framework Convention on Climate Change (UNFCCC)[635] and to assess if and how well they have met the challenge of transferring mitigation and adaptation technologies. While these mechanisms cannot be expected to bear the entire load of technology transfer required by developing countries, there is clearly a role in providing institutional structures, finance and support for policies and measures. More importantly, the UNFCCC provides the basic international framework for timing and responsibility for technology-related action.

The UNFCCC and its Kyoto Protocol[636] are an example of a pattern that has become increasingly established in international negotiations on environmental law to address commons problems. In order to persuade developing countries to forgo production and consumption pathways now considered harmful to the environment, developed countries have offered concessions such as phased in timelines and obligations, financial assistance and access to technologies to help them prepare to meet their obligations under the agreement. In the case of climate change, developed countries took the greenhouse gas (GHG) emissions intensive path to development and to convince developing countries to forgo such development had to promise significant financial support and access to technology. On one side developed countries would

---

[635] United Nations Framework Convention on Climate Change (UNFCCC), New York, 9 May 1992, *in force* 21 March 1994, 1771 *United Nations Treaty Series* 107
[636] Kyoto Protocol to the United Nations Framework Convention on Climate Change (Kyoto Protocol), Kyoto, 10 December 1997, *in force* 16 February 2005, 2303 *United Nations Treaty Series* (2004) 148.

take the first steps to reduce GHG emissions.[637] Under the Kyoto Protocol, they would move towards low-carbon or carbon-free economies, while, through flexibility mechanisms such as the Clean Development Mechanism[638], they received credits for emissions they helped to reduce in developing countries. These and other mechanisms were meant to enable technology transfer to create endogenous capacity in developing countries to mitigate and adapt to climate change.[639] Thus, carbon leakage, i.e., the shifting of polluting carbon-inefficient industries from developed to developing countries, would be avoided.

In addition, developed countries would provide financial and technical assistance to developing countries to build capacities to adapt to the negative impacts of climate change. Developed countries would demonstrate to developing countries the techniques and policies necessary to achieve GHG emissions reductions while maintaining economic growth. Demonstration of this fact, in addition to the technologies developed to enable success would ensure that developing countries were in a position to act to reduce their emissions.

A key justification for this two-phase process is the concept of historical responsibility. Historical responsibility[640] is based on the idea that impacts of climate change as they are felt in the present day and near future are due to the cumulative historic emissions created by developed countries during their industrialization processes and that, under the 'polluter pays' principle, they have the responsibility to act first and bear the burden of the cost of action.[641] As the earth moves closer to the period of time when the emissions of emerging and newly developed countries will begin to have an impact, the burden of responsibility will begin to be shared more in line with their increased contribution and their share of the impacts. Historical responsibility addresses the issue of sequencing as well as the share of the total burden of the cost of action. In both cases, the concept requires that developed countries bear the greatest share and the responsibility to act first and most. Out of this arose the principle in the UNFCCC that *all* states have a common responsibility to act but these responsibilities are differentiated in scale and timing by the historical responsibility of developed countries who should act first, as embodied by the first commitment period (2008 – 2012) for Annex 1 countries under the Kyoto Protocol.

While these principles have been expressed in the treaty language and in quantitative emissions reduction commitments, their implementation has been an arena of contestation between developed and developing countries in the UNFCCC. Much of

---

[637] Article 4 UNFCCC
[638] Article 12 Kyoto Protocol
[639] Article 10 Kyoto Protocol
[640] See Baer, et al. *The Right to Development in a Climate Constrained World* (Heinrich Böll Foundation, 2007) for an elaboration and critique of the concept.
[641] See p31, Id.

the conflict has centered on the provision of financial support and access to technology. At least one state, the United States of America, has consistently objected to this framework[642] and has refused to ratify the Kyoto Protocol.

This conflict finally spilled over during the Bali Conference of the Parties (COP) in December 2007, and lay behind the refusal of developing countries to agree to negotiations for any new commitment period or new agreement that included developing country emissions reduction commitments.[643] The compromise in Bali created two working groups, one focused on developed country commitments under the Kyoto protocol's second commitment period (the Ad hoc Working Group on the Kyoto Protocol - AWGKP, and the other to discuss further implementation of the UNFCCC, under which further action on technology, financial support and developing country mitigation action would take place (the Ad Hoc Working Group on Long Term Cooperative Action - AWGLCA).[644]

Developments at the UNFCCC since Bali are crucial to understanding why there is increasing urgency to address the issue of intellectual property (IP) and technology transfer to address climate change. The proliferation of bodies and working groups is symptomatic of the ongoing conflict over whether intellectual property should be on the agenda, in which bodies it should be addressed and how to address it. An understanding of the ways that the UNFCCC may be able to respond to IP and technology transfer requires an understanding of the structures and dynamics of the processes in place at the UNFCCC to implement technology transfer.

II. BACKGROUND: THE MULTILATERAL FRAMEWORK ON TECHNOLOGY TRANSFER

From an economic development perspective, international transfer of technologies can be a significant factor in promoting growth. In economies with significant access to private capital and significant purchasing power, technology is developed through market mechanisms, such as intellectual property (IP). Technology is owned by private actors and distributed through licensing or purchasing arrangements between private actors. However, where technology is held through IP, rightholders are

---

[642] Stern, T "Statement by Special Envoy for Climate Change Todd Stern to the House Committee on Foreign Affairs" before US House of Representatives Committee on Foreign Affairs, May 25, 2011. Available at: http://www.state.gov/s/climate/releases/168093.htm (last visited 15 August, 2014).
[643] p15, Earth Negotiations Bulletin "Summary of the Thirteenth Conference of Parties to the UN Framework Convention on Climate Change and Third Meeting of Parties to the Kyoto Protocol: 3-15 December 2007" Volume 12, Number 354, 18 December, 2007. Available at: http://www.iisd.ca/climate/cop13/ (last visited 15 August, 2014).
[644] Report of the Conference of the Parties on its thirteenth session, held in Bali from 3 to 15 December 2007. Addendum. Part Two: Action taken by the Conference of the Parties at its thirteenth session." FCCC/CP/2007/6/Add.1 (2008)

primarily interested in selling their knowledge and technology at a certain price in a market with sufficient purchasing power where their technologies are not likely to be imitated and where IP enforcements is strong. The weakness in many developing countries is threefold: they do not present sufficient markets for private actors to develop technologies to serve their needs; where technologies exist and are protected by IP, they may not present sufficient markets for rightholders to sell or license their technologies; they have, or are perceived as having, low protection and enforcement of intellectual property. In such an environment, the need for technology is not met with an appropriate market response. Therefore, other options become necessary, such as the creation of domestic mechanisms to require technology sharing and establishing legal obligations at the international level to transfer technology from developed to developing countries. The history of the debate on intellectual property and technology transfer in international policy-making is one of increasing restrictions on the ability to apply domestic mechanisms to compel technology sharing, accompanied by expansive promises from developed countries to provide technology transfer.

II.1. Evolution of the Multilateral Framework on Technology Transfer

As soon as the majority of developing countries became part of the international economic system in the 1960's and 1970s, access to technology to aid in economic development was one of their core demands. The 1970's saw the peak of the effort by developing countries to refashion the global economic order into one that was more accommodating to the needs of developing countries. As a response to the dominance of the Bretton Woods Institutions (the World Bank, the International Monetary Fund and the General Agreement on Trade and Tariffs) and the investment regimes, developing countries proposed a New International Economic Order (NIEO)[645] based on the UN General Assembly principle of "one state, one vote", and on the historical obligations of developed states (especially former colonial rulers) to assist developing countries to develop and industrialize with complete freedom in the use of regulatory and policy tools. Much of the conceptual work under this project was carried out at the United Nations Conference on Trade and Development (UNCTAD). Technology transfer was a key demand of the NIEO[646], and the UNCTAD discussions created a pattern of debate that has persisted into the present day. As John Barton notes, this was a concept of technology transfer premised on a foreign direct investment model, with a firm from a developed country investing in capital stock and locating in a developing country, under which the contract established by the firm restricted the transfer of knowledge to local partners, or engaged in restricted licensing practices.[647] The driver for developing countries was that they wished to establish local content,

---

[645] Declaration for the Establishment of a New International Economic Order: United Nations General Assembly Document A/RES/S-6/3201 of 1 May 1974.
[646] Para 4(p) Id.
[647] p1, Barton, J "New Trends in Technology Transfer: Implications for National and International Policy", Issue Paper No. 18, ICTSD February 2007.

technology transfer and/or performance requirements for these investments such that technology would be transferred and that companies would be mandated to share knowledge or to lower the cost of accessing such knowledge. In this context, technology transfer discussions became a debate about what actions developing states should take and what obligations developed states had, not just to allow developing countries to take steps to access technology, but to provide financial and other support to access such technologies. In the realm of intellectual property, developing countries sought to provide less extensive protection to technologies created in developed countries by excluding certain products from being patented (e.g. pharmaceutical and agricultural products) and using regulatory tools such as working requirements that meant that patented products actually had to be produced domestically to continue to qualify for continued patent protection.

A major indicator of the end of the NIEO was the failure to come to agreement on the UNCTAD International Code of Conduct for Transfer of Technology, which would have created common ground on definitions and mechanisms that would be acceptable to both developed and developing countries.[648] The 1985 Draft addresses IP licensing practices in Chapter 4 and special treatment for developing countries in Chapter 6. Chapter 1 contained definitions which were relatively uncontroversial.[649] Chapter 4 proved the most controversial and difficult chapter, precisely because it included language on intellectual property and remained largely bracketed and under discussion.[650] The impasse moved the main focus of discussion to other venues where the bargaining power of developed countries ensured that the framing of IP and technology transfer issues worked more in their favor.[651]

In the intellectual property arena, an increased focus on intellectual property protection from developed country producers saw the increased use of unilateral measures such as "Special 301"[652] used by the US Trade Representative to list countries and threaten them with the withdrawal of preferential trade access if the US unilaterally determined that they had not met US standards for IP protection and enforcement. The movement towards increased restrictions culminated, temporarily, in 1995 with the signing of the TRIPS Agreement as a covered agreement under the WTO and subject to

---

[648] UNCTAD Draft International Code of Conduct on the Transfer of Technology in UNCTAD "Compendium of International Arrangements on Transfer of Technology: Selected Instruments - Relevant Provisions in Selected International Arrangements Pertaining to Transfer of Technology" UNCTAD/ITE/IPC/Misc.5, UNCTAD 2001.
[649] See p26, Gehl Sampath, P and P Roffe, "Unpacking the International Technology Transfer Debate: Fifty Years and Beyond" ICTSD Programme on Innovation, Technology and Intellectual Property Working Paper; International Centre for Trade and Sustainable Development, (2012).
[650] Id.
[651] See p23, Id.
[652] Section 301 of the United States. Trade Act of 1974, as amended. The provision remains in place despite the fact that one of the reasons many developing countries signed the TRIPS Agreement was to prevent the use of such unilateral mechanisms.

the new Dispute Settlement Understanding (DSU).[653] TRIPS required the vast majority of developing countries to provide intellectual property protection for products and processes in all technological fields and to redefine working requirements to include such things as sale of products in the market.[654] Technology transfer remains an objective of the TRIPS Agreement but it only contains a single obligation, in Article 66.2, for developed country governments to promote incentives for their private actors to transfer technologies. Despite the establishment of a reporting procedure, transfer of technology under this provision is widely viewed as inadequate by most observers.[655] Developing countries, however, continued to pursue the aim of technology transfer in other fora where they perceived they would have more leverage, including Multilateral Environmental Agreements.

II.2. Technology Transfer in Multilateral Environmental Agreements

As the trade discussions shifted away from the inclusion of technology transfer provisions for developing countries in trade and other international economic arrangements, technology transfer provisions became pivotal elements of the increasing number of Multilateral Environmental Agreements (MEAs) that were concluded in the period following the 1972 UN Stockholm Conference on the Human Environment.[656]

Many of these agreements were aimed at dealing with global problems whose causes and effects crossed borders and that could not be addressed through unilateral action. In general, these new agreements required that countries either take on costs in implementing environmental standards or that that they forgo certain activities or products for the common good. The direct and indirect costs of such agreements, especially for decelerating or worsening their economic development prospects have always been at the forefront of negotiating concerns for developing countries in these fora. While the international environmental system is premised on the concept of sustainable development[657] i.e. it is both possible and desirable to have economic development that is not environmentally negative and may actually accelerate development, the costs of shifting or adjustment have been considered a barrier by developing countries to their full participation in MEAs. MEAs don't just present the

---

[653] Agreement of Trade-related Aspects of Intellectual property (TRIPS Agreement), Annex 1C to the Marrakesh Agreement establishing the World Trade Organization (WTO Agreement), Marrakesh, 15 April 1994, *in force* 1 January 1995, 1867 United Nations Treaty Series (1995) 4.
[654] Article 27 TRIPS Agreement.
[655] See e.g. Moon, S "Does TRIPS Art. 66.2 Encourage Technology Transfer to the LDCS?: An Analysis of Country Submissions to the TRIPS Council (1999-2007)" Policy Brief No.2 December 2008, ICTSD, Geneva, Switzerland.
[656] Stockholm Declaration on the Human Environment, in *Report of the United Nations Conference on the Human Environment*, UN Doc.A/CONF.48/14, at 2 and Corr.1 (1972)
[657] See p54, "Report of the World Commission on Environment and Development: Our Common Future", Annex to "Development and International Cooperation: Environment" UN Doc A/42/427, 4 August 1987.

classic collective action problem, however. An emerging pattern in MEAs was that significant global problems such as cross border pollution by power plants creating acid rain, and ozone depletion, or deforestation were intimately linked with historical and continuing production and consumption patterns by developed countries. Action to address these problems required developing countries to forgo production and consumption pathways from which developed countries had already benefited. Such patterns continuously raised issues of fairness, justice, equity and historical responsibility, issues that may have reached their apotheosis in the climate change negotiations.

One of the ways that developing countries sought to address the issue of adjustment costs and equity, was to gain assurances that they would be assisted financially with any adjustment costs, and that they would be provided with the best available technologies, at grant or concessional terms, in making the adjustments required by the MEA. For example, there is strong evidence that India joined the Montreal Protocol[658] precisely on the understanding that alternative technologies would be made available on grant or concessional terms, and the Multilateral Fund was replenished at the time with this precise aim in mind.[659]

The demand for technology transfer has remained one of the strongest bargaining chips for convincing developing countries to participate in MEAs, but it has also remained, except for the notable exception of the Montreal Protocol[660], the one that has been perceived to be the least fulfilled element of such MEAs.

Almost all MEAs include some provision on Technology Transfer. These include:
- United Nations Convention on the Law of the Sea
    - Article 144 on Technology Transfer

- Montreal Protocol on Substances that Deplete the Ozone Layer
    - Article 10A on Transfer of Technology in conjunction with the financial mechanism set up under Article 10.

- Convention on Biological Diversity
    - Article 16

- Cartagena Protocol on Biosafety to the Convention on Biological Diversity
    - Article 22 on Capacity-Building

---

[658] See p6, p35, Jha, V and U Hoffman (eds.) "Achieving Objectives of Multilateral Environmental Agreements: A Package of Trade Measures and Positive Measures Elucidated by Results of Developing Country Case Studies" UNCTAD/ITCD/TED/6, UNCTAD 2000.
[659] Id.
[660] Montreal Protocol on Substances That Deplete the Ozone Layer. Montreal, 16 September 1987, in force 1 January 1989, 1522 *United Nations Treaty Series* (1989) 3

- Convention on the Transboundary Effects of Industrial Accidents
    - Article 16 on Exchange of Technology

- United Nations Protocol to the 1979 Convention on Long Range Transboundary Air Pollution on Further Reduction of Sulphur Emissions
    - Article 3 on Exchange of Technology

The extent to which technology is available at 'reasonable' cost appears to have a strong correlation to how effectively and to what extent developing countries implement the aims of an MEA.[661] While the principle of incremental costs has become increasingly prevalent in determining the exact coverage of costs, it has not always been clear whether such a definition covered the costs of patent licensing and or purchases. Even in the context of the Montreal Protocol Multilateral Fund, such costs were not always covered under the definition, despite there being at least a nominal commitment to do so.[662] In addition, there may have been impediments related to the limitations the Fund placed on such financing by limiting the number of licenses it would pay for per technology substitute per country.[663] Finally, the Fund would not provide financing for R&D efforts to develop indigenously developed alternative technologies, as a substitute for licensing, where such licensing costs were perceived as too high.[664]

Technology transfer provisions in MEAs vary in their comprehensiveness, and it is not the aim of this chapter to analyze or discuss the relative failure and success of each agreement with respect to technology transfer. It suffices to note that, in general, developing countries have expressed significant disappointments with the nature, speed, and scale of technology transfer that has occurred under almost all of these MEAs. Developed country insistence on increased protection of intellectual property has come to be seen by many developing countries as either emblematic of this failure, or the key reason why technology transfer has not occurred to any significant level.

It is this pattern of negotiation, adoption and failure to fulfill technology transfer provisions that was essentially imported into the climate change negotiations and has contributed to the significant frustration expressed by developing countries in the UNFCCC negotiations. This has been exacerbated in the climate negotiations by

---

[661] See p14, Jha, V and U Hoffman (eds.) "Achieving Objectives of Multilateral Environmental Agreements: A Package of Trade Measures and Positive Measures Elucidated by Results of Developing Country Case Studies" UNCTAD/ITCD/TED/6, UNCTAD 2000.
[662] Id.
[663] See p41, Das, S "Case Study 2: India: Effects of Trade Measures and Positive Measures in the Montreal Protocol on Selected Indian Industries" in Jha, V and U Hoffman (eds.) "Achieving Objectives of Multilateral Environmental Agreements: A Package of Trade Measures and Positive Measures Elucidated by Results of Developing Country Case Studies" UNCTAD/ITCD/TED/6, UNCTAD 2000.
[664] Id.

the sense that, even more than in other environmental arenas, the climate crisis is one for which the historical responsibility of developed countries is clearest and most urgent.

III. THE LEGAL FRAMEWORK FOR TECHNOLOGY TRANSFER IN THE UNFCCC

Against the background of this debate and the negotiation of frameworks such as the TRIPS Agreement, the UNFCCC was concluded at the 1992 Rio Earth Summit to achieve the stabilization of greenhouse gas concentrations in the atmosphere at a low enough level to prevent dangerous anthropogenic interference with the climate system.[665] The TRIPS Agreement was concluded 3 years later in 1995. Intellectual property issues were relative latecomers in the context of the WTO Agreement and are not mentioned in any way in the UNFCCC Agreement itself. However, since the inception of the UNFCCC, technology transfer has been expected to play a significant role in achieving the treaty's objective and this has been built into the structure of the agreement.

III.1. The Legal Basis for Technology Transfer Obligations in the Climate Change Regime

Technology transfer is addressed in Article 4 of the UNFCCC. This provision covers a range of issues, including financing, transfer and commitments. Notably, Article 4.7 links the ability of developing country Parties to fulfill their commitments under the UNFCCC to the effective implementation of developed country Parties fulfilling their commitments, particularly finance and technology transfer.

> The extent to which developing country Parties will effectively implement their commitments under the Convention will depend on the effective implementation by developed country Parties of their commitments under the Convention related to **financial resources and transfer of technology** *(my emphasis)* and will take fully into account that economic and social development and poverty eradication are the first and overriding priorities of the developing country Parties.

Further, while the convention provides for the diffusion of technologies amongst all Parties, the key provision for transfer of technology from Annex II to developing countries is Article 4.5.

---

[665] United Nations Framework Convention on Climate Change: Status of Ratification" Available at: http://unfccc.int/essential_background/convention/items/6036.php (last visited 15 August, 2014).

> The developed country Parties and other developed Parties included in Annex II shall take all **practicable steps** to **promote, facilitate and finance**, as appropriate, the transfer of, or access to, environmentally sound technologies and know-how to other Parties, particularly developing country Parties, to enable them to implement the provisions of the Convention. In this process, the developed country Parties shall **support the development and enhancement of endogenous capacities and technologies of developing country Parties**. Other Parties and organizations in a position to do so may also assist in facilitating the transfer of such technologies. (my emphases)

Article 4.1 addresses the diffusion of technologies amongst all Parties:

> **All Parties**, taking into account their **common but differentiated responsibilities** and their specific national and regional development priorities, objectives and circumstances, shall:
> […]
> (c) **Promote and cooperate in the development, application and diffusion, including transfer, of technologies, practices and processes** that control, reduce or prevent anthropogenic emissions of greenhouse gases not controlled by the Montreal Protocol in all relevant sectors, including the energy, transport, industry, agriculture, forestry and waste management sectors;
> […]
> (h) **Promote and cooperate in the full, open and prompt exchange** of relevant scientific, **technological**, technical, socio-economic and legal information related to the climate system and climate change, and to the economic and social consequences of various response strategies;
> […](my emphasis)

Finally, Article 4.3 addresses the financing of technologies:

> The **developed country** Parties and other developed Parties included in Annex II **shall provide new and additional financial resources** to meet the agreed full costs incurred by developing country Parties in complying with their obligations under Article 12, paragraph 1. They shall also provide such financial resources, **including for the transfer of technology**, needed by the developing countries . . . (my emphasis)

The Kyoto Protocol directly addresses the transfer of technology in Article 10(c), which requires all Parties to:

Cooperate in the promotion of effective modalities for the development, application and diffusion of, and take all possible steps to promote, facilitate and finance, as appropriate, the transfer of, or access to, environmentally sound technologies, know-how, practices and processes pertinent to climate change, in particular to developing countries, including the formulation of policies and programmes for the effective transfer of environmentally sound technologies that are publicly owned or in the public domain and the creation of an enabling environment for the private sector, to promote and enhance the transfer of, and access to, environmentally sound technologies.

The Kyoto Protocol also established the Clean Development Mechanism (CDM).[666]

The legal framework described above appears to have very clearly chosen a specific pathway for implementing the principle of historical responsibility and common but differentiated responsibility. Historical responsibility is primarily about two issues: sequencing of GHG reduction actions; and proportion and burden of GHG reductions. On sequencing, UNFCCC Article 4.7 directly expresses the underlying principle of historical responsibility.

Article 4.5 outlines the burden sharing between developed and developing countries when it comes to technology transfer. The responsibility is on developed countries in Annex II to provide technology transfer. Article 4.3 specifies the exact nature of that commitment which is to provide financial resources to cover "the agreed full incremental costs of implementing measures that are covered by paragraph 1 of this Article and that are agreed between a developing country Party and the international entity or entities referred to in Article 11, in accordance with that Article." While clearly establishing that costs of action should be borne by developed countries, but specifically only where agreed to between developed and developing countries, the article leaves the decision of exactly what should be covered under such costs to a later date. It is less clear whether or not the funds envisioned cover such issues as the costs of accessing licenses for IP. What should be covered under the "agreed full incremental costs" remains difficult to determine. With respect to "incremental" the difficulty revolves around the concept of additionality, i.e. whether all activities should be funded or only those activities that would not have otherwise occurred without the funding. The operating definition used by the World Bank's Global Environment Facility (GEF) is one where the GEF funds "additional costs associated with transforming a project with national benefits into one with global environmental benefits.[...] GEF grants cover the difference or "increment" between a less costly, more polluting option and a costlier,

---

[666] Article 11 Kyoto Protocol

more environmentally friendly option."[667] The GEF has operated as the primary funding mechanism for technology activities, in the absence of any implementing and financing mechanism within the UNFCCC itself. Projects have historically had to conform to the GEF's application and project based approach to meeting technology needs which are established through the World Bank's processes rather than as a function of the legal obligation set up by the UNFCCC. To the extent that new UNFCCC implementing structures are in place in the post-Kyoto framework, decisions such as this may be revisited.

Nothing in the UNFCCC or the Kyoto Protocol provides an enforcement structure for delivery of technology transfer. In particular, while the Kyoto Protocol sets up an elaborate procedure for measuring, reporting and verifying when countries have met their GHG reductions commitments, with sanctions for failures to achieve targets, there is nothing close to comparable for technology transfer obligations. In fact, there are not even any mechanisms for measuring the extent of technology transfer that might take place. There has been no agreement on what indicators might be used, although, as discussed below, work on indicators by the Expert Group on Technology Transfer (EGTT) was completed, but not adopted by the Subsidiary Body on Implementation (SBI) or the Conference of the Parties (COP) into the reporting structure of national communications. The reporting structure is primarily limited to national communications, but as discussed again below, there has been no agreement on how such reporting on technology transfer should take place. There is no system for verification of any claimed transfer of technology, another issue that is endemic to all the structures within the UNFCCC framework, including the CDM, as will be discussed below.

IV. IMPLEMENTING STRUCTURES FOR TECHNOLOGY TRANSFER WITHIN THE UNFCCC[668]

While the Conference of the Parties (COP) is the "supreme body of the Convention"[669] technology transfer is specifically addressed in two subsidiary bodies:

- **the Subsidiary Body for Scientific and Technological Advice (SBSTA),** which supports the work of the COP on "matters of science, technology, and methodology, including guidelines for improving standards of national communications and emission inventories"[670] ; and

---

[667] See p3, GEF "Operational Guidelines for the Application of the Incremental Cost Principle" GEF Council, June 12 – 15, 2007, GEF/C.31/12, 14 May 2007.
[668] This section is partially based on an earlier internal CIEL working paper by by D Shabalala and C Twiss. Available from the authors on request.
[669] p16, United Nations Framework Convention on Climate Change (UNFCCC), "Uniting on Climate: A Guide to the Climate Change Convention and the Kyoto Protocol", November 2007.
[670] Id.

- **the Subsidiary Body for Implementation (SBI)**, which supports the COP in assessing and reviewing implementation, "for instance by analyzing national communications submitted by Parties. It also deals with financial and administrative matters."[671] After the Bali Decisions, it also had responsibility for monitoring the Expert Group on Technology Transfer (EGTT).

Other key bodies were also set up and played a significant role in determining the content and trajectory of the debate on technology transfer in the UNFCCC and through what structures it should be implemented. The next few sections describe these bodies and their contributions and evaluates the extent to which they have been effective mechanisms for technology transfer.

IV.1 The Expert Group on Technology Transfer

Prior to the Cancun Agreements of December 2010, the key UNFCCC body for technology transfer was the **Expert Group on Technology Transfer** (EGTT), which was established with "the objective of enhancing the implementation of Article 4, paragraph 5, of the convention, including, *inter alia,* by analyzing and identifying ways to facilitating and advance technology transfer activities and making recommendations to the Subsidiary Body on Scientific and Technological Advice."[672] It never had an implementation mandate as was made clear by ensuring that it reported to the advisory body of the SBSTA rather than the implementation body of the SBI. Thus, as a mechanism for delivering technology transfer the EGTT cannot be considered to have played much of a role beyond providing technical assessments and research.

As part of the Marrakesh Accords, the COP 7 identified five "key themes" for meaningful and effective actions to enhance the implementation of Article 4.5 of the Convention. The 5 themes were:

(i) Technology needs & needs assessments
(ii) Technology information
(iii) Enabling environments
(iv) Capacity building
(v) Mechanisms for technology transfer

This framework focused on creating conditions in developing countries to encourage technology transfer. In terms of implementation the themes were structured as below:

---

[671] Id.
[672] UNFCCC Decision 4/CP.7 ¶2,

1. Technology Needs assessment

    a. This meant that developing countries agreed to engage in exercises to produce technology needs assessments, so as to identify specific technologies that they would seek to have supported under the Article 4.1(c), 4.3 and 4.5 framework. Crucially, however, conduct or completion of the TNA was not linked in any way to provision of funding for actual delivery of the technologies identified.

2. Technology information

    a. This was aimed at providing further information on technology for both developed and developing country actors. This was primarily implemented through TT:CLEAR, an online information platform. The secretariat developed TT:CLEAR to support the Parties' efforts to focus on the adoption of environmentally friendly technologies.[673] TT:CLEAR is a technology information system that includes an inventory of environmentally-friendly technologies and projects.[674] The use of TT:CLEAR is organized under the same key themes that guided the work of the EGTT.

    b. While ambitious in scope, it is also evident that TT:CLEAR was never anywhere close to operating the way it was envisioned, let alone in achieving the goal of enabling technology transfer.

3. Enabling Environments

    a. This work programme looked at conditions, primarily in developing countries, and sought to develop best practices for encouraging technology transfer. It is within this context that many debates and discussion on intellectual property arose, primarily on whether it encouraged or posed a barrier to technology transfer. It was also here that the debate as to where action should take place, in developing countries or in developed countries, continued.

4. Capacity Building

---

[673] p21, United Nations Framework Convention on Climate Change (UNFCCC), "Uniting on Climate: A Guide to the Climate Change Convention and the Kyoto Protocol", November 2007.
[674] Id.

a. This was primarily addressed through research and policy papers discussing best practices.

5. Mechanisms for technology transfer

   a. This was again addressed primarily through research and policy work aimed at discussing best practices.

In a 2006 report, the EGTT reviewed implementation of technology transfer within this framework:

Technology needs & needs assessments – the EGTT found that many countries had not taken the opportunity to conduct TNAs. In 2006, only 23 had been conducted, despite the availability of a handbook on how to conduct TNAs. The report noted that there was financing from various sources available for conducting TNAs (the GEF, the UNDP) but that once TNAs were completed there was little information or guidance on how to turn the results of TNAs into projects that could be funded by international financial institutions or other funders.[675] By 2006, it had become clear that TNAs were a useful first step but that these remained separated from any commitments to provide finance to meet the identified needs. Project proposals would still need to be made and funds sought from various multilateral and bilateral funders, something which seemed to suggest that the effort of doing TNAs would not pay off. Funding required multiple applications to funders with different application requirements. The report did not evaluate what the success rate of projects constructed from TNAs might be, but the EGTT clearly saw a need to create another handbook on how to turn TNAs into projects that could be funded. In addition, TNAs were seen to be the responsibility of recipient countries and were unconnected to any action by developed countries. The project application process also ensured that a donor-recipient relationship was maintained despite the fact that Article 4.5 established obligations to be met by developed countries. TNAs are considered to have largely failed as vehicles for enabling technology transfer.[676]

Technology information – on Technology Information, the EGTT noted the development and implementation of the TT:CLEAR clearing house hosted by the secretariat. The EGTT positively noted the results of a user survey and also noted moves to integrate TT: CLEAR with regional clearing houses and databases. However, the EGTT noted that staffing and resources were inadequate for the database, and that developing

---

[675] p10, EGTT "Recommendations of the Expert Group on Technology Transfer for enhancing the implementation of the framework for meaningful and effective actions to enhance the implementation of Article 4, paragraph 5, of the Convention" FCCC/SBSTA/2006/INF.4, UNFCCC 2006.
[676] See p12, Staley, B Childs et al. "Tick Tech Tick Tech: Coming to Agreement on Technology in the Countdown to Copenhagen". WRI Working Paper, World Resources Institute, Washington DC, June 2009.

country users especially found it difficult to use.[677] More generally, TT: CLEAR was limited by failures of execution. It was not until 2009 that it was searchable by technologies and went beyond basic data on projects. As it stands, it is unable to function as a tool for connecting technology providers and users, nor for providing a platform for managing licensing issues or linking to funding processes.

Enabling environments– as discussed above, the EGTT noted that there was insufficient information on governments' own actions to assess their progress on the enabling environments section. However, the EGTT itself pursued some further work on this, producing several technical papers on policies and regulations that could encourage and enable technology transfer. On intellectual property rights, a technical paper[678] noted:

> Past experience with IPRs and implementing the Montreal Protocol shows that where an alternative (non-ozone-depleting substance) exists, is easily accessible, commercially viable and not covered by IPRs, the transition has been smooth. On the other hand, sectors where the technology or processes are under IPRs held by only a few technology suppliers, the experience with technology switchover has been negative.[679]

The note also pointed to limited and mixed empirical evidence on the role of IPRs in either encouraging or limiting technology transfer.[680] With respect to the debate, the note described opposing viewpoints on the part of developing and developed countries. The paper discussed the view of developed countries that there was little role for 'push' factors as technologies were held in private hands, emphasizing host country or 'pull' factors. The paper noted a reluctance on the part of developed countries to exercise any "leverage" over their private actors.[681]

Under the enabling environments theme the EGTT also worked on an informal paper, produced with funding from the US based Climate Technology Initiative (CTI) on the role of IPRs and publicly funded technologies. That paper, while a useful description of the policy choice made by many countries to subsidize and transfer ownership of publicly funded research and development into private hands, does not address what policies and measures could be put in place to ensure more public access to such technologies.[682]

---

[677] p12, EGTT 2006.
[678] "Technical paper on enabling environments for technology transfer" FCCC/TP/2003/2.
[679] Para 36, Id.
[680] Para 35, Id.
[681] Para 8, Id.
[682] EGTT "Overview of IPR Practices for Publicly-funded Technologies" Informal paper, EGTT 2005.

The EGTT also noted many significant barriers in this section of work including:[683]

- Insufficient public grants and difficulties faced by developing countries in accessing risk capital and flexible loans from international financial institutions (IFIs) to support technology transfer projects;

- Limited private sector investment due to the absence of robust risk shields caused by inadequate policy and market framework conditions for the development and transfer of technologies;

The EGTT noted that the enabling environments theme required the most work to meet its stated goals.[684]

At Bali, in Decision 3/CP.13 para. 1 the parties agreed that the 5 themes (as contained in the annex to decision 4/CP.7) "continue to provide a solid basis for enhancing the implementation of Art. 4, para. 5 of the Convention."[685]

The EGTT made recommendations to both the SBI and the SBSTA after Bali.[686] The SBI was tasked with monitoring the work of the EGTT, so as to ensure that the EGTT itself did not take up implementation.

The Bali COP made technology an important element in the discussions regarding future long-term cooperative actions to address climate change. Paragraph 1(d) of the Bali Plan of Action focused on "enhanced action in technology development and transfer". The parties agreed that the work of the Bali Plan of Action was to be carried out by the Ad Hoc Working Group on Long-Term Cooperative Action (AWGLCA) which was meant to complete its work by 2009 in Copenhagen at COP 15.

EGTT Work Programme

In the EGTT, work ostensibly progressed on the five themes, especially with respect to Technological Needs Assessments (TNAs). The EGTT was responsible for

---

[683] p14, EGTT "Recommendations of the Expert Group on Technology Transfer for enhancing the implementation of the framework for meaningful and effective actions to enhance the implementation of Article 4, paragraph 5, of the Convention" FCCC/SBSTA/2006/INF.4, UNFCCC 2006.
[684] Id.
[685] "Development and transfer of technologies under the Subsidiary Body for Scientific and Technological Advice", Decision 3/CP.13, UN FCCC, 13th Sess., U.N. Doc FCCC/CP/2007/6/Add.1
[686] Para. 1, Id.

helping to implement TNAs[687] by working with non-Annex II countries on writing proposals for financial support for technology transfer projects.[688]

There was significantly less work with respect to enabling environments, capacity-building for technology transfer, and, especially, mechanisms for technology transfer. Significant dissatisfaction with its purely advisory role led to the demand for a fully-fledged implementation mechanism within the UNFCCC itself. This led to the establishment of the Technology Executive Committee (TEC) and the Climate Technology Centre and Network (CTC&N) under the 2010 Cancun Agreements. The establishment of the TEC was accompanied by the termination of the mandate of the EGTT.[689]

IV.2 The Clean Development Mechanism

The Clean Development Mechanism (CDM) is one of three flexibility mechanisms established by the Kyoto Protocol[690] designed as a mechanism to prevent carbon leakage and enable Annex 1 countries to meet a portion of their quantitative emission reduction obligations by reducing emissions in non-Annex 1 countries. While it is not explicitly a technology transfer vehicle, it has been seen as a vector through which market-based technology transfer could occur.[691] That hope has not been borne out and this is due to both structural design factors as well as the realities of the market in emissions reduction credits.

With respect to technology transfer, the CDM does not and has never had a mandate as a mechanism for fulfilling the obligations under article 4.1(c), 4.3 and 4.5. It was meant to be additional to those. It was not a structure that was related to the implementation mandate of the SBI and had no formal relationship in terms of policy or institutional linkages to the EGTT. Structurally, the CDM's aim is not primarily aimed at assisting developing countries carry out their obligations under Article 4 of the UNFCCC; in fact it was primarily designed as a mechanism to assist developed countries meet their obligations on emissions reductions and was an alternative to

---

[687] UNFCCC "Terms of reference of the Expert Group on Technology Transfer", in "Development and transfer of technologies under the Subsidiary Body for Scientific and Technological Advice", Decision 3/CP.13, UN FCCC, 13th Sess., U.N. Doc FCCC/CP/2007/6/Add.1 at Annex II subpara. 3(b).
[688] UNFCCC "Recommendations for enhancing the implementation of the framework for meaningful and effective action to enhance the implementation of Article 4, paragraph 5, of the Convention", in "Development and transfer of technologies under the Subsidiary Body for Scientific and Technological Advice", Decision 3/CP.13, UN FCCC, 13th Sess., U.N. Doc FCCC/CP/2007/6/Add.1 at Annex 1, subpara. 17(a).
[689] Section IV.B, Part Two: Action taken by the Conference of the Parties at its sixteenth session, FCCC/CP/2010/7/Add.1.
[690] Article 12, Kyoto Protocol
[691] UNFCCC "The Contribution of the Clean Development Mechanism under the Kyoto Protocol to Technology Transfer" UNFCCC 2010.

inclusion of developing countries in the Joint Implementation mechanism.[692] While sustainable development is part of the aim of Article 12(2) of the Kyoto protocol, the actual implementation structure of the CDM emphasizes assisting Annex 1 countries in meeting their GHG emissions reduction commitments. That means that the mechanisms for selection of projects and programmes to be carried out, the decisions on when and which activities would be supported largely lie with actors in developed countries. The need for credits would be determined by the extent to which domestic reductions in Annex 1 countries were insufficient to meet their commitments under the Kyoto Protocol. In terms of design, therefore, the CDM was essentially an FDI vehicle, where firms in developed countries would engage in projects in developing countries aimed at generating emissions reduction credits, with the limits and strength relating to technology transfer that FDI normally has in relation to technology transfer.[693] Much of the literature points to the conclusion that left to its own devices, the CDM has not been an effective tool for meeting sustainable development goals of developing countries more broadly,[694] although the evidence for some technology transfer may be a little stronger. The issue is that unlike much traditional FDI which has a long term component, especially for establishment of manufacturing or service centers[695], the project selection structure in the CDM has favoured one-time joint venture type structures with specific time limits that would generate credits at the lowest cost within a short time horizon of 2 – 4 years.[696] This means that the kind of interactive learning and repeat play scenarios that theoretically have most the impact on learning by a host firm may not be as prevalent in CDM projects.[697] In fact, a finding by Doranova

---

[692] See p51, Sutter, C "Sustainability Check-Up for CDM projects" Wissenschaftlicher Verlag, Berlin (2003).
[693] See Werksman, J, K Baumert and N Dubash, *Will international investment rules obstruct climate protection policies?*, Climate Notes, World Resources Institute, Washington, April 2001; p19, Cosbey, A et al. "Realizing the Development Dividend: Making the CDM Work for Developing Countries - Phase 1 Report" Pre-Publication version, International Institute for Sustainable Development (2005). Concurring, See p6, Doranova, A *Technology Transfer and Learning under The Kyoto Regime: Exploring the Technological Impact of CDM Projects In Developing Countries* PhD Thesis UNU-Merit, Maastricht University. p20, Ellis, J et al. "CDM: Taking stock and looking forward" 35 Energy Policy 15 (2007); p9, Niederberger, A and R Saner "Exploring the relationship between FDI flows and CDM potential" 14(1) Transnational Corporations 1 (2005) but also cautioning against too simplistic an assumption the CDM flows would align with existing FDI flows and patterns.
[694] See e.g. Olsen, K H "The Clean Development Mechanism's Contribution to Sustainable development: a review of the literature" 84 Climatic Change 59 (2007); Sutter, C and J C Parreno "Does the current clean development mechanism (CDM) deliver its sustainable development claim? An analysis of officially registered CDM projects". 84 Climatic Change 75 (2007).
[695] See p10, Niederberger, A and R Saner "Exploring the relationship between FDI flows and CDM potential" 14(1) Transnational Corporations 1 (2005) *citing definition from UNCTAD World Investment Report 2003. FDI Policies for Development: National and International Perspectives* (Geneva: United Nations, 2003).
[696] See p23, Cosbey, A et al. "Realizing the Development Dividend: Making the CDM Work for Developing Countries - Phase 1 Report" Pre-Publication version, International Institute for Sustainable Development (2005).; p24, Ellis, J et al. "CDM: Taking stock and looking forward" 35 Energy Policy 15 (2007). See also p2, Niederberger, A and R Saner "Exploring the relationship between FDI flows and CDM potential" 14(1) Transnational Corporations 1 (2005).
[697] See p115, Doranova, A *Technology Transfer and Learning under The Kyoto Regime: Exploring the Technological Impact of CDM Projects in Developing Countries* PhD Thesis UNU-Merit, Maastricht

suggests that even within CDM projects, the intensity of interaction with technology providers (including training activities) does not have a significant impact on learning by host firms.[698] This may be explained by the short time frame and structure of the deals constructed under the CDM which may not provide sufficient time for learning and building a knowledge base. In fact, what had the most impact on learning was learning by doing, as host firms worked to understand, install and adapt the technology to their specific circumstances and internal technological knowledge level and culture.[699]

The issue of limited scope and time for projects has been addressed to some extent by the adoption of so-called "programmatic" CDM[700], aimed at allowing registration of sector-wide initiatives within which transformative activities can take place with ongoing periodic issuance of credits. It allows host parties to create a long-term climate for investment in a particular sector, and provide a financial structure for supporting such investment. The establishment of a second commitment period from 2013 – 2020, may have helped to address this uncertainty inherited from the first commitment period, but is only going to be effective where a sufficient number of states agree to apply the Doha Amendment[701] provisionally, while waiting for it to enter into force. To date, only 7 countries have deposited their instruments of ratification and none have agreed to provisional application.[702] The demand for credits has also decreased with the refusal of several major economies (Australia, Canada, Japan, New Zealand and the Russian Federation) to participate in the second commitment period, creating a potential structural over-supply of credit providers.

Technology transfer is not a compulsory registration, validation or verification requirement for CDM projects and there exists no clear way to measure the extent of technology transferred under the CDM. However, the new second commitment period guidelines for application of CDM projects do ask that, in Section A.3 (previously A.4.3) of the Project Design Document (PDD), which forms the basis for approval of registration and validation of the project, applicants "[d]escribe the technologies and measures to be employed and/or implemented by the project activity, including a list of

---

University, for a thorough review of the literature on learning by interaction and learning by doing. See also p2932, Schneider, M et al. "Understanding the CDM's contribution to technology transfer" 36 Energy Policy 2930 (2008).
[698] See p131-132, Doranova, A. Also potentially explained by the quality of the data collected which did not provide for information on the scope, nature and quality of the training.
[699] See p32, Id.
[700] "A voluntary coordinated action by a private or public entity which coordinates and implements any policy/measure or stated goal (i.e. incentive schemes and voluntary programmes), which leads to anthropogenic GHG emission reductions or net anthropogenic greenhouse gas removals by sinks that are additional to any that would occur in the absence of the PoA, via an unlimited number of CDM programme activities (CPAs)." CDM Glossary v.6
[701] Doha amendment to the Kyoto Protocol to the United Nations Framework Convention on Climate Change, signed Doha, 8 December 2012 (not yet in force)
[702] See http://unfccc.int/kyoto_protocol/doha_amendment/items/7362.php (last visited 15 August 2014)

the facilities, systems and equipment that will be installed and/or modified by the project activity."[703] In addition they are asked to not provide:

> "information that is not essential to understanding the purpose of the project activity and how it reduces GHG emissions. Information related to equipment, systems and measures that are auxiliary to the main scope of the project activity and do not affect directly or indirectly GHG emissions and/or mass and energy balances of the processes related to the project activity should not be included."

Applicants are asked to include a description of "how the technologies and measures and know-how to be used are transferred to the host Party(ies)" in contrast to the older formulation in previous guidelines applicable under the first commitment period of "how environmentally safe and sound technology, and know-how to be used, is transferred to the host Party(ies)." This section is now separate from section A.1 where parties are asked to "[i]nclude a brief description of how the project activity contributes to sustainable development (not more than one page)." It is not clear whether this represents a downgrading of the sustainable development objective of the CDM in the PDD or whether it aims to embed the technology transfer requirements more tightly into the additionality requirement. What can clearly be seen is that the description of the technology is primarily limited to equipment and in no way addresses knowledge transfers or know-how, unlike the previous section A.4.3. On the other hand, this requirement of a statement as to the technology used is mandatory, and is required for a comparison to a baseline of existing facilities, systems and equipment. Any verification or validation should examine the claims on technology used in the project (defined as facilities, systems and equipment). We will discuss below whether this is actually the case. There is no data on how the new guidelines and application forms are affecting the provision of information in the PDD since the issuance of these new guidelines was only effective from February 1, 2013. All the studies discussed below address the prior methodology.

As we will see below, the fact that a large number of PDDs have included some description of technology transfer is an indication that applicants believe that providing such information may make their applications more likely to succeed. This is clearly not due to the CDM validation process which is required before a CDM project can be registered/approved. The designated operational entities (DOE) (responsible for validation and verification) do not have a mandate and do not examine in any way, the claims related to technology transfer that are contained in the PDDs in Section A.3 of the new Guidelines and did not in respect of the old standards. There is no requirement that the DOE assess the sustainable development or technology transfer claims in the

---

[703] Section A.3 Project Design Document, UNFCCC "Guidelines for Completing the Project Design Document Form" Annex 8, EB 66 Report.

PDD. The only extent to which the sustainable development measures are validated requires that[704]:

- The DOE shall confirm that the [designated national authority] DNA has considered whether the proposed CDM project activity assists the host Party in achieving sustainable development.

- The DOE shall determine whether the letter of approval by the DNA of the host Party confirms the contribution of the proposed CDM project activity to the sustainable development of the host Party.

- The DOE shall state whether the host Party's DNA has confirmed the contribution of the project to the sustainable development of the host Party. This may be reported together with the DOE's assessment of the validity of the host Party's approval.

Thus even in the latest version of the CDM Standard for validation and verification, there is no real measure or assessment other than confirmation that the DNA has made their statement or consideration. With respect to the claims of technology transfer in A.3, there is no validation step but there is a verification step which only requires that the DOE:[705]

- Determine whether the project activity has been implemented and operated as per the registered PDD or any approved revised PDD, and that all physical features (technology, project equipment, and monitoring and metering equipment) of the project are in place;

Verification does NOT address the claims of technology transfer in the existing standard for validation and verification. There is some indication that technology transfer may be assessed in the additionality criteria related to technology use and automatic additionality. In the PDD, where applicants have an option of providing a barrier analysis or an investment analysis to show additionality[706], guidance from the CDM Executive Board[707] provides that certain technology elements could form part of the barrier analysis, and would be part of the validation and verification process for assessing the issuance of credits. Examples of these technological barrier elements are:

---

[704] Section 7.8 "The Clean Development Mechanism Standard for Validation and Verification" Version 03.0, CDM-EB65-A04-STAN, Available at: http://cdm.unfccc.int/Reference/Standards/accr_stan02.pdf (last visited 15 August 2014).
[705] Section 9.4 Id.
[706] Section B.5 Project Design Document, UNFCCC "Guidelines for Completing the Project Design Document Form" Annex 8, EB 66 Report.
[707] UNFCCC "Methodological Tool - Combined tool to identify the baseline scenario and demonstrate additionality (Version 04.0.0)" Annex 48, EB 66 Report. Available at:
http://cdm.unfccc.int/methodologies/PAmethodologies/tools/am-tool-02-v4.0.0.pdf/history_view (last visited 15 August 2014).

1. Skilled and/or properly trained labor to operate and maintain the technology is not available in the applicable geographical area, which leads to an unacceptably high risk of equipment disrepair, malfunctioning or other underperformance;
2. Lack of infrastructure for implementation and logistics for maintenance of the technology (e.g. natural gas cannot be used because of the lack of a gas transmission and distribution network);
3. Risk of technological failure: the process/technology failure risk in the local circumstances is significantly greater than for other technologies that provide services or outputs comparable to those of the proposed CDM project activity, as demonstrated by relevant scientific literature or technology manufacturer information;
4. The particular technology used in the proposed project activity is not available in the applicable geographical area.

While still very much considered part of the hard-headed assessment of additionality, the assessment of whether the technology itself is newly introduced to the geographic area is a possibility to be validated and verified. In terms of skills and knowledge it largely relates to skills to maintain and operate the technology, but even that would be part of the validation process, where the barrier analysis is chosen. Parties can carry out a barrier analysis or an investment analysis or both, but only in the case of the barrier analysis may it be possible for the technology transfer of equipment *per se* and the minimal amount of training conducted to be subject to validation and verification. In terms of validation, the DOE must then determine[708]:

- Whether the barriers are real
- Whether barriers prevent the conclusion of this project but not the implementation of baseline alternatives to achieving the project.

To the extent that the use of such a barrier analysis is voluntary and the use of the technology elements is voluntary, it is difficult to argue that technology transfer might be assessed through an examination of compliance with the additionality criterion. Qualifying for additionality cannot be used as a proxy for technology transfer.

An important to note here is that these requirements in the additionality standard are about utilization of technology *within* the project and require no other impact beyond the project. It is entirely focused on the hardware except where the skills and labor to maintain and operate the hardware are relevant. There is no question of capacity to replicate, adapt, use or effect beyond the confines of the project.

---

[708] Section 72.12.12, UNFCCC, "Clean development mechanism validation and verification standard" CDM-EB65-A04-STAN

The presence of frequent descriptions of technology transfer in the PDD may be due to the other gatekeeping function in the project cycle; the task that is allocated to designated national authorities (DNAs) of host countries to state that the project contributes to sustainable development of the host country.[709] However, the guidance for the DNAs provides little or no information on how they are to assess claims of technology transfer. In fact, it appears that the construction of these criteria is left entirely to the host party. To the extent that the level of technology transfer that would be required for such projects may seem to be entirely left to host parties what would then seem to be the question is whether countries have actually been doing this and if not, why not? TERI carried out a mapping of the criteria that CDM hosts have used.[710] Thirty DNAs were examined. The results suffer from a lack of access to data, especially from China, but tentatively, the report concluded that technology transfer was a consistent part of most of the criteria used by DNAs, although most requirements varied as to definitions and what was considered to contribute to technological development.[711] Some of the criteria are:

- Use of best available or not-substandard technologies (6 countries)
- Use of locally appropriate technologies (3 countries)
- Enabling development of indigenous technology (1 country)
- Up take and Replication potential (3 countries)
- Project specific capacity building and training (1 country)
- Community level capacity building and training (2 countries)
- Innovation compared to a domestic baseline (1 countries)
- Transfer of knowledge (2 countries)

Haites [712] outlines some requirements of DNAs, noting that China only recommends that a project transfer technology, but does not require it[713]; India, also is non-mandatory. Only Korea's DNA has a mandatory requirement.[714] At least one study suggests that Korea has a higher share of technology transfer in its projects than Brazil, India or China, but it is unclear whether this is due to the requirement or the fact that Korea has a significantly larger share of large-scale projects in its CDM mix, which tend to have more claims of technology transfer.[715] An update from that study suggests that

---

[709] UNFCCC "Clarification on elements of a written approval" UNFCCC-CCNUCC, EB 16, Annex 6, paragraph 1. Available at: http://cdm.unfccc.int/EB/016/eb16repan6.pdf (last visited 15 August 2014).
[710] Tewari, R "Mapping of Criteria set by DNAs to Assess Sustainable development Benefits of CDM Projects" CDM Policy Dialogue, TERI (2012)
[711] See p8, Id.
[712] Haites, E et al., "Technology Transfer by CDM Projects", 6 Climate Policy 327 (2006).
[713] Wang argues that in fact China's DNA tends to avoid assessing this requirement. Wang, B "Can CDM bring technology transfer to China?—An empirical study of technology transfer in China's CDM projects" 38 Energy Policy 2572(2010)
[714] p335, Haites, E et al., "Technology Transfer by CDM Projects", 6 Climate Policy 327 (2006).
[715] See Seres, S "Analysis of Technology Transfer in CDM Projects, prepared for UNFCCC Registration & Issuance Unit CDM/SDM", Dec. 2008.

Brazil, India and China remain below the average in terms of claimed technology transfer while a list of countries including Korea (Ecuador, Guatemala, Honduras, Indonesia, Kenya, Malaysia, Mexico, Pakistan, Sri Lanka and Uzbekistan), remain above average for technology transfer claims. The variation among countries relating to DNA requirements suggests that this may not be the primary explanatory factor for why these countries have higher claimed technology transfer. However, it may also be that project size may not be fully explanatory either given the variation amongst these countries in terms of CDM project size.

Other studies suggest that the requirements by DNAs appear to be insufficiently stringent to ensure sustainable development and there is significant variation in both attention, scope, and stringency.[716] It is difficult to avoid the sense that the generation of credits is paramount in the DNA assessment, especially where these generate income from fees or taxes imposed by the host country.[717] Structurally, the income generating element appears to dominate above the sustainable development considerations as the verification and issuance process only assesses the GHG emissions reduction of the project.[718] There is also at least some argument that there is an actual structural trade-off between the sustainable development objective of the CDM and the GHG emissions reduction, given the emphasis on lowest possible cost emissions.[719]

The studies suggest that, at the least, technology is a consideration for many DNAs, but not necessarily a requirement and it is to this that project applicants may be responding in including claims of technology transfer in their PDDs. They may be assessing that there is greater likelihood of receiving a letter of approval by including such claims, and since it is seemingly costless to do so, there is an incentive to always include these where possible. In the absence of additional pro-active policies aimed at ensuring spillovers, it is not clear that the DNA gatekeeping function is sufficiently strong on its own to encourage technology transfer.

The key explanation for the supposed lack of delivery on sustainable development objectives that has been well-documented in the literature is the supply and demand structure of the CDM: an over-supply of cheap CDM potential projects and a structurally lower demand leading to a race to the bottom. The concern is that while DNAs may emphasize sustainability criteria in the letter of approval process, they do so within an incentive structure that seeks to ensure rapid approval of such projects

---

[716] See e.g. Sutter, C "Sustainability Check-Up for CDM projects" Wissenschaftlicher Verlag, Berlin (2003) p22, Cosbey, A et al. "Realizing the Development Dividend: Making the CDM Work for Developing Countries - Phase 1 Report" Pre-Publication version, International Institute forSustainable Development (2005).
[717] As suggested by survey data in Cosbey, A et al.
[718] *Concurring* see p64, Sutter, C (2003). Also van der Gaast, W et al. "Promoting sustainable energy technology transfers to developing countries through the CDM" 86 Applied Energy 230 (2009).
[719] See p66, Sutter, C "Sustainability Check-Up for CDM projects" Wissenschaftlicher Verlag, Berlin (2003).

and issuance of certified emissions reductions rather than sustainability, and a disincentive to look closely at whether the claimed sustainable development benefits have ever materialized.[720]

On the specific issue of whether CDM projects have delivered on technology transfer, to date several quantitative analyses have been attempted.[721] All but a few of them have been unable to address the basic structural flaw at the heart of the CDM, which is that there is no internal mechanism to verify whether the claimed technology transfer in the PDD has taken place. Given the gatekeeping function played by the DNAs and some evidence that technology benefits are a consideration for receiving letters of approval, there may be a systematic bias towards overstatement of technology transfer components of PDDs, in the safe knowledge that such claims may never be verified. Unlike Dechezleprêtre et al., I do not conclude that this tendency to overstate would be randomly distributed.[722] The role of the DNAs suggests that a tendency to overstate or over-include technology transfer is more likely to be a persistent structural feature of PDDs.

The majority of existing analyses measure the technology transfer claims[723] rather than project evaluations and outcomes. This means that it is difficult to measure the contribution of the CDM to technology transfer in any reliable way. At least one study, looking at sustainable development criteria also found it difficult, even within this

---

[720] See p2822, Olsen, K and J Fenhann "Sustainable development benefits of clean development mechanism projects - A new methodology for sustainability assessment based on text analysis of the project design documents submitted for validation" 36 Energy Policy 2819 (2008). See also p19, Kolshus, H H, Vevatne, J, Torvanger, A, Aunan, K "Can the Clean Development Mechanism Attain Both Cost-effectiveness and Sustainable Development Objectives?" CICERO Working Paper 2001:8, Center for International Climate and Environmental Research (CICERO), Oslo, pp. 1–22 (2001); Sutter, C "Sustainability Check-Up for CDM projects" Wissenschaftlicher Verlag, Berlin (2003); p2, Cosbey et al. "Realizing the Development Dividend: Making the CDM Work for Developing Countries - Phase 1 Report" Pre-Publication version, International Institute for Sustainable Development (2005).
[721] See e.g. Dechezleprête, A et al., "The Clean Development Mechanism and the International Diffusion of Technologies: An Empirical Study", 36 Energy Policy 1273 (2008); Dechezleprête A et al., "Technology Transfer by CDM Projects: A Comparison of Brazil, China, India and Mexico", 37 Energy Policy 703 (2009); Haites, E et al., "Technology Transfer by CDM Projects", 6 Climate Policy 327 (2006).
[722] See p1275, Dechezleprête, A et al., "The Clean Development Mechanism and the International Diffusion of Technologies: An Empirical Study", 36 Energy Policy 1273 (2008);
[723] See e.g. Seres, S et al. "Analysis of technology transfer in CDM projects: An update." 37 Energy Policy 4919 (2009); Glachant, M et al., "The Clean Development Mechanism and the International Diffusion of Technologies: An Empirical Study" FEEM Working Paper No. 105, December 2007; Dechezleprête, A et al., The Clean Development Mechanism and the International Diffusion of Technologies: An Empirical Study, 36 Energy Policy 1273 (2008); Haites, E et al., "Technology Transfer by CDM Projects", 6 Climate Policy 327 (2006). UNFCCC "The Contribution of the Clean Development Mechanism under the Kyoto Protocol to Technology Transfer" UNFCCC 2010; Wang, B "Can CDM bring technology transfer to China?—An empirical study of technology transfer in China's CDM projects" 38 Energy Policy 2572(2010) *noting this lacunae*, p234, Gechlick, M "Making Transfer of Clean Technology Work: Lessons of the Clean Development Mechanism" 11 San Diego International Law Journal 227 (2009) *and* p304, Lema, A and R Lema "Technology transfer in the clean development mechanism: Insights from wind power" 23 Global Environmental Change 301 (2013).

framework, to provide a meaningful distinction between those claims that used existing technology already available in the domestic market or through normal market purchases, and new hardware being introduced into the market; as well as technology know-how that was already available domestically versus technological know-how being introduced into the market.[724]

Setting aside the methodological problems with relying on PDD data primarily, the studies suggest that some technology transfer does take place and that it takes place in only about third of projects sampled, a percentage that has stayed relatively stable over the group of studies.[725] The type of claimed technology transfer has also stayed relatively the same.[726] However, the frequency of claimed technology transfer in relation to emissions reduction has dropped[727], something that may be attributable to an increase in the number of smaller projects and a drop in the number of larger projects. This is consistent with previous findings that existence and level of claimed technology transfer is positively correlated with the size of the project.[728] This may be due to the fact that such large projects generally involve large capital outlays on hardware. In addition, such large projects tend to be end-of-pipe solutions[729] requiring one-time installation of equipment, and some training on operation and maintenance, including measurement. At least one study suggests that there is a significant positive correlation with the technological capacity of the country, however, that this is overshadowed by the number of similar CDM projects already having taken place.[730] While this is interpreted by the study's authors as evidence that the technologies are being diffused more widely into the economy rendering the need for further technology transfer less significant in repeated experiences in the same technology arena[731], it is important to note an equally plausible explanation, given that the majority of claimed technology transfer relates to large

---

[724] See p2823, Olsen, K and J Fenhann "Sustainable development benefits of clean development mechanism projects - A new methodology for sustainability assessment based on text analysis of the project design documents submitted for validation" 36 Energy Policy 2819 (2008).
[725] See p4923, Seres, S et al. "Analysis of technology transfer in CDM projects: An update." 37 Energy Policy 4919 (2009); See also Glachant, M et al., "The Clean Development Mechanism and the International Diffusion of Technologies: An Empirical Study" FEEM Working Paper No. 105, December 2007; Dechezleprêtre, A et al., The Clean Development Mechanism and the International Diffusion of Technologies: An Empirical Study, 36 Energy Policy 1273 (2008); p330, Haites, E et al., "Technology Transfer by CDM Projects", 6 Climate Policy 327 (2006).
[726] See p4924, Seres, S et al. "Analysis of technology transfer in CDM projects: An update." 37 Energy Policy 4919 (2009);
[727] Id.
[728] See Glachant, M et al., "'The Clean Development Mechanism and the International Diffusion of Technologies: An Empirical Study,'" FEEM Working Paper No. 105, December 2007, available at: http://ssrn.com/abstract=1077151; p330, Haites, E et al., "Technology Transfer by CDM Projects", 6 Climate Policy 327 (2006).
[729] See p1277, Dechezleprêtre, A et al. (2008)
[730] Dechezleprêtre, A et al., The Clean Development Mechanism and the International Diffusion of Technologies: An Empirical Study, 36 Energy Policy 1273 (2008);
[731] See p1282, Id.

projects; that this reflects the build-up of capital stock that remains after a project has ended. For end-of-pipe solutions, the equipment simply remains installed once the project has been concluded and can therefore be moved from one installation to another if necessary. It may also reflect the declining availability of such easy low-hanging fruit for generating emissions reductions so that other less obviously hardware reliant sectors play a greater part of the claimed technology transfer.[732] This therefore does not mean that technology transfer is not needed, it may simply implicate the quality of the transfer (greater knowledge and capacity building) rather than the existence of transfer.[733]

De Coninck et al. suggest that a significant majority of projects involving technology transfer, involve not just hardware but knowledge transfer as well, or knowledge transfer and capacity building alone.[734] Dechezleprêtre et al. and others provide support for this in their findings as well.[735] However, the relatively generous definition of technology transfer used in this and other studies does not really address learning capacity and is overly and structurally biased to hardware purchases and imports.[736] All the PDD based empirical studies reflect that the majority of the knowledge and capacity building involved training local employees how to operate the machinery[737], which does not quite reach to the definition used in this thesis: enabling the ability to adapt and replicate the technology, or key components thereof.

A very few studies have attempted to look beyond the PDD data to try and determine the nature and scope of technology transfer. Doranova et al. look at a sample of host firms in Brazil, India, China and Mexico, and use survey data to look at the effects of several independent variables on the main dependent variable - Technological Capacity Building – disaggregated into sub-components: four related to operational capabilities; three to process improvement capabilities; three to innovation

---

[732] Concurring in the case of China. See p254, Gechlick, M "Making Transfer of Clean Technology Work: Lessons of the Clean Development Mechanism" 11 San Diego International Law Journal 227 (2009).

[733] *Coming to a similar conclusion in the specific case of China* see p251, Gechlick, M "Making Transfer of Clean Technology Work: Lessons of the Clean Development Mechanism" 11 San Diego International Law Journal 227 (2009).

[734] See p454, De Coninck, H et al., "Technology transfer in the Clean Development Mechanism, 7 Climate Policy 444 (2007).

[735] See p1275, Dechezleprêtre, A et al., The Clean Development Mechanism and the International Diffusion of Technologies: An Empirical Study, 36 Energy Policy 1273 (2008); p330, Haites, E et al., "Technology Transfer by CDM Projects", 6 Climate Policy 327 (2006).

[736] See p12, Doranova, A *Technology Transfer and Learning under The Kyoto Regime: Exploring the Technological Impact of CDM Projects in Developing Countries* PhD Thesis UNU-Merit, Maastricht University. See also p2936, Schneider, M et al. "Understanding the CDM's contribution to technology transfer" 36 Energy Policy 2930 (2008); Wang, B "Can CDM bring technology transfer to China?—An empirical study of technology transfer in China's CDM projects" 38 Energy Policy 2572(2010)

[737] See p448, De Coninck, H et al., (2007), and *critiquing this approach* See p7, Doranova, A *Technology Transfer and Learning under The Kyoto Regime: Exploring the Technological Impact of CDM Projects In Developing Countries* PhD Thesis UNU-Merit, Maastricht University (2009).

capabilities.[738] Based on the survey data, the study finds that, where technology transfer takes place:

1. Prior technological capacity means that CDM projects build basic technology capacity the most, and have the least effect on increasing high technological capacity. This is in line with findings that most CDM projects primarily provide minimal training on how to operate and maintain hardware.

2. Higher representation of high skilled engineers in the host firm has a positive effect on an increase in intermediate technological capability.

3. Technological training increases high technology capacity. Lack of confidence in the other areas was explained by significant variance in what was considered 'training' in terms of content, duration etc.

An earlier study by Doranova provides some details that further support some of the conclusions above.[739] The questionnaire [740] used in that research allows for some drawing out of specific technology transfer issues with key questions such as the extent to which (on a 0 - 6 point scale) the CDM project experience improved or built the competence of the host firm in:

1. Basic technological capacity
    a. Preventive maintenance - Revealing possible defects/Maintenance of machines/equipment on a regular basis
    b. Process quality control - Systematic independent control of the quality of the technological process
    c. Debugging - Removing defects, mistakes, breakages in the equipment
    d. Equipment adjustment - Adjustment of the equipment(s) to the local conditions, or to the particular technological lines/system
2. Intermediate technological capacity
    a. Equipment stretching - Increase the scope of functions or productivity of the equipment.
    b. Efficiency - improvement and cost saving; Reducing cost, energy consumption of the equipment by keeping high production level

---

[738] See p8, Doranova A. et al. "Absorptive capacity in technological learning in clean development mechanism projects" UNU-Merit Working Papers 2011-10.
[739] Doranova, A *Technology Transfer and Learning under The Kyoto Regime: Exploring the Technological Impact of CDM Projects In Developing Countries* PhD Thesis UNU-Merit, Maastricht University.
[740] Appendix C, Doranova, A *Technology Transfer and Learning under The Kyoto Regime: Exploring the Technological Impact of CDM Projects In Developing Countries* PhD Thesis UNU-Merit, Maastricht University.

    c. Process adaptation - Adaptation of the technological process to local circumstances/ conditions/ changes
3. Advanced technological capacity
    a. Basic process design - Engineering design of the technological process /technological line, inventions, with possible patenting
    b. Equipment design - Detailed design of the single equipment/ machine, inventions, with possible patenting
    c. Development of turnkey project/facility - Detailed design of a complete technological facility/ unit/ plant

This presented an ideal survey dataset for revealing not only the extent to which host firms report technology was transferred, but establishing the quality of such transfer. It also presented an opportunity to assess the role of intellectual property generated within the project, although perhaps not the licensing structure. The study also asked some key technology questions relating to:

- The source (foreign or domestic) of the technology used in the project
- Whether the technology was already available in the domestic market
- Whether the technology was considered high technology or best available technology
- What difficulties the firm had in adjusting and applying the technology
- The type of firm providing the technology (MNE, SME, large, small, domestic or foreign)
- Whether the provider was the parent company or some other relationship to the host firm
- Whether the technology provider was the rightholder or licensor of the technology provided

The survey results showed a clear conclusion that technological capability improved with experience in CDM projects, but did so most with basic technologies and least with advanced. However, the assessment on the 7 point scale for any category never went above 3.41, and most stayed below 2.[741] To a significant extent, even where respondents reported increases in technological capacity, the response indicates that both the quality and impact was not very high.[742] The short term nature of the projects may go some way to explaining the low impact scores, or it may be explained by a variable relating to whether the technologies transferred were high or best available technologies. A significant part of the explanation, as Doranova points out, may also be related to the absorptive capacity of the host firm. Logically, low absorption capacity

---

[741] See p72, Doranova, A *Technology Transfer and Learning under The Kyoto Regime: Exploring the Technological Impact of CDM Projects in Developing Countries* PhD Thesis UNU-Merit, Maastricht University (2009).
[742] As concluded by the author at Id.

explains a significant portion of the lack of impact. In this study, she finds that there is a positive relationship between higher prior technological capacity and increased technological capacity from CDM project participation but that it is strongest for building basic technological capacity and weakest for building advanced technological capacity.[743] It is unclear what the role of other regulatory factors might be but where these are captured in the control variable "POLICY"[744], this did not include level of intellectual property protection or innovation system policy, making it difficult to tease out what effect these may have had on the final outcome.

Nevertheless, she makes some other interesting policy relevant findings. Firstly, joint ventures appear to do better on building technological capacity than wholly owned foreign subsidiaries which provided the least. Wholly owned domestic firms were in the middle between those two groups.[745] Secondly, that there was significant variation across technology sectors in terms of use of domestic or foreign technology.[746] She notes in particular that hydro energy was based almost 80% on domestic technology or a mix of domestic and foreign, whereas, wind energy had a larger proportion of foreign technology. Other sectors presented too small a sample to come to any conclusions, but some of this variation may be due to specific country characteristics in the sample. For example, Brazil has a strong hydropower sector of its own[747], whereas China and India both have strong solar sectors. Curiously, both India and China also have strong wind sectors, so the strong representation of foreign technology in wind seems to be related to either use in other countries, or use of larger turbine technologies which were not within Chinese and Indian market capabilities at the time of the projects.[748] Overall, there is a trend towards greater use of local technology in CDM projects, driven, she concludes, by prior experience and existing capacity in the specific technology area.[749] This predicts that greater experience in CDM projects should result in lower need for technology transfer.

More importantly, her finding that Brazil, India and Mexico have been suppliers of technology in CDM projects, points to the potentially useful role of these countries in providing low-cost, well-adapted solutions to clean development projects in

---

[743] See Doranova A. et al. "Absorptive capacity in technological learning in clean development mechanism projects" UNU-Merit Working Papers 2011-10.
[744] See p10, Doranova A. et al. "Absorptive capacity in technological learning in clean development mechanism projects" UNU-Merit Working Papers 2011-10.
[745] See p80, Doranova, A (2009).
[746] See p37, Id.
[747] See p47, Doranova, A *Technology Transfer and Learning under The Kyoto Regime: Exploring the Technological Impact of CDM Projects in Developing Countries* PhD Thesis UNU-Merit, Maastricht University (2009).
[748] See p1276, Dechezleprêtre, A et al., The Clean Development Mechanism and the International Diffusion of Technologies: An Empirical Study, 36 Energy Policy 1273 (2008);
[749] See p62, Doranova, A (2009)

other developing countries, reducing the need for adaptation of developed country technology to local conditions. In the sample, a small majority of technology was sourced from non-Annex 1 countries.[750] The analysis of this finding cuts in two ways: it emphasizes the role that emerging economies can play as technology providers, especially of well-adapted technology; but it also implies that the CDM focus on cost-efficiency means that cheapest technology rather than best available technologies are more likely to be diffused under the CDM. More support for this could potentially be found in the response to the questionnaire used by Doranova, where she asks about whether the technology transferred was considered high or best available technology.[751] The study does not provide any findings related to these specific questions however.

One case study that does look at some of the terms of the transfer, as well as the vectors under which it took place, was carried by Hansen in Malaysia, which has a mandatory technology transfer requirement in its DNA approval process.[752] In a qualitative study, based on interviews with host firms' project implementers in Malaysia he looked at three main modes of technology transfer:

1. Technology provider partnership arrangements;
2. Technology implementation by Annex 1 country company subsidiary
3. Non-Annex 1 country company manufacturing technology under a license, royalty or fee agreement

From a final dataset of 13 firms, primarily in the biomass sector he finds that[753]:

- There are examples of all the vectors in place, within the CDM projects
- Most of the projects were based on pre-existing commercial activities or subsidiary relationships. Only one was a purpose built joint venture in order to participate in the CDM.
- In those cases where transfer of hardware took place it was under circumstances, deliberately aimed at reducing exposure of end-users and to limit their capacity to understand and potentially disseminate knowledge about the hardware. This was true for all except the purpose built joint venture.
- Except for the joint venture, knowledge transfer was limited to maintenance and operation of the hardware.

Hansen concludes that the quality of technology transfer was low and that the DNA approval process placed little emphasis on technology transfer despite what could

---

[750] See p40, Id.
[751] Survey Questions 15 and 16, Appendix C, Id.
[752] Hansen, U "An empirical case study of the transfer of GHG mitigation technologies from Annex 1 countries to Malaysia under the Kyoto Protocol's clean development mechanism (CDM)" 10(1) Int. J. Technology Transfer and Commercialisation, 1 (2011).
[753] See p13, Hansen, U "An empirical case study of the transfer of GHG mitigation technologies from Annex 1 countries to Malaysia under the Kyoto Protocol's clean development mechanism (CDM)" 10(1) Int. J. Technology Transfer and Commercialisation, 1 (2011)

initially be construed as a stringent standard.[754] Hansen's findings that CDM tends to rely on pre-existing commercial relationships is supported by other studies as well in the case of wind power in India and China.[755] They also note that India and China are both the largest hosts and providers of technologies in CDM wind power projects, although primarily to their domestic markets.[756] Much of the activity in non-India, non-China, wind CDM technology transfer constitutes arms-length equipment purchases [757] supporting Hansen's finding that Annex 1 firms largely engage in sales and minimal training in order to enable operation and maintenance. They find joint ventures to be the least used mechanism, and there is a significant amount of activity (almost 20%) by subsidiaries.[758] Lema and Lema also support Hansen's finding that mechanisms in CDM projects encompass a variety of vectors beyond FDI and equipment import, although in their study, only China has a CDM project due to licensing.[759] This is notable as the definitions of technology transfer employed by these studies may fail to include licensing as a vector because of their focus on hardware and associated know-how. Where there is domestic capacity for production a license would allow such local production but involve no equipment transfer.[760] In addition, where such licensing involved further know-how transfer associated with the license this may not be captured within the PDDs as studied. Lema and Lema conclude that CDM does not build capacity but that it is existing technological capacity that enables CDM activity and the ability to engage in local production[761], provided that there are partners available willing to engage in other, higher quality modes of activity such as joint ventures, licensing or domestic production. This suggests that the role of direct equipment transfer may drop out precipitously with increased technological capability, meaning that the main vector of CDM transfer is no longer relevant to countries that have proven through the CDM that there is a viable domestic market for the technology.

Another approach to measuring technology transfer was taken by Haščič and Johnstone in a specific study of the role of the CDM in the wind power sector.[762] They looked at patent data as a proxy for technology transfer, in particular looking at patents where an inventor resident in one country seeks patents in the host country. As they acknowledge (and as discussed in Chapter 3), there are problems with using this as a

---

[754] See p17, Id.
[755] Lema, A and R Lema "Technology transfer in the clean development mechanism: Insights from wind power" 23 Global Environmental Change 301 (2013).
[756] See p307, Id.
[757] See p308, Id.
[758] See p308, See p302, Lema, A and R Lema "Technology transfer in the clean development mechanism: Insights from wind power" 23 Global Environmental Change 301 (2013).
[759] See p302, Id.
[760] See p304, Id.
[761] See p311, Id.
[762] Haščič, I and N Johnstone "CDM and International Technology Transfer: Empirical Evidence on Wind Power", 11 Climate Policy 1303 (2011).

proxy for technology transfer, and although they suggest that propensity to patent will be attenuated by the cost of applying for patents[763], they are not really able to examine to whom patents are transferred and the use to which they are put. At most therefore, their data can tell us something about intent to participate in the host market in some fashion, but not the manner of such participation. Nevertheless, there are some interesting outcomes relating to their hypothesis that CDM activities affect the level and rate of transfer, measured by cross-country patent counts from Annex 1 to non-Annex countries in the wind sector.[764]

Their findings suggest that the direct effect of CDM has a statistically significant, positive, but relatively small effect (compared to absorptive capacity) on technology transfer in the wind sector as measured by increased contemporaneous propensity to patent into the host state.[765] In terms of specific countries, the effect for China was consistently positive and for India, consistently negative.[766] In addition, there was a significant, negative relationship between the stock of CDM projects and technology transfer, as measured by increased patenting propensity by inventors outside the home state.[767] The results are only indicative and suggest that some effect on contemporaneous patenting may exist due to CDM participation, but it is difficult to conceive of the mechanism or vector along which such an effect would take place. Considering the determinants of propensity to patent across borders, there may be a regulatory effect in that existence of CDM creates a stronger impression that there is indeed a market for the technology and therefore a technology holder would be interested in participating in the market in some fashion. However, there is also clearly a confounding variable in that such an interest would consider the imitative capacity of the country in the decision of whether to patent. That may remain a stronger driver of whether a patent is sought in relation to the technology sector especially to prevent strong imitators from taking over the entire domestic market, or from exporting to other countries. This may explain to some extent the difference between India and China observed in the study. As noted in Chapter 3, China presents a significant danger of competition in the wind sector, as Goldwind dominates the domestic market and has little interest in export for the moment. However, India also is a strong competitor in the wind sector, but its market may be more open and present less risk of imitation due to the significant export orientation of the main wind firm, Suzlon, which while it may be capable of imitation may not be willing to engage in imitation to the same extent given the need to ensure it can export its products back to OECD countries. However, in the absence of further research and data, especially data that goes beyond the patent

---

[763] See p1305, Id.
[764] See p1305, Haščič, I and N Johnstone "CDM and International Technology Transfer: Empirical Evidence on Wind Power", 11 Climate Policy 1303 (2011).
[765] See p1311, Id.
[766] Id.
[767] See p1309, id.

count, it is very difficult to tease out the mechanism and role of different variables in this study.

A specific China study by Wang (also a PDD based study) found that technology transfer in Chinese projects involved both hardware and know-how, but only the basic level related to operation and maintenance of the hardware, in line with most findings.[768]

Overall, other than Hansen and Doranova, none of the studies provide information from the PDDs on the terms of the technology transfer (concessional, grant or otherwise in line with CBDR) that is claimed to take place.[769] Additionally, only one study (Hansen, and only tangentially) addresses itself to the issue of intellectual property in terms of: the role it may play in the CDM transfer process; the number of protected technologies involved; whether any licenses are made available in the context of the project and on what terms. This is clearly an arena for further research. In fairness, the CDM provides little purchase for making findings related to this and details of deal structure, intellectual property involved and licensing are not readily available, even in the context of survey data. This has forced authors to use proxies in many circumstances that may not be reflective of the actual underlying nature and scope of activity under the CDM.

The lack of real data on the sustainable development (including technology transfer) outcomes of the CDM[770] has led to several proposals to make the delivery of sustainable development more effective. Most have revolved around assisting DNAs in developing appropriate mechanisms[771], while others have suggested adding an additional layer of international standards to be met in addition to the DNA assessment.[772] All the studies emphasize the need for an independent validation, monitoring and verification of claimed sustainable development and technology transfer claims in PDDs.[773] To the extent that this would focus energies on actual implementation of claimed technology transfer this would be a significant step beyond the existing state of affairs. However, what this would bring to the fore would be the capacity to examine the actual determinants of technology transfer in the CDM. The role of such things as absorptive

---

[768] Wang, B "Can CDM bring technology transfer to China?—An empirical study of technology transfer in China's CDM projects" 38 Energy Policy 2572(2010).
[769] See p228, Haites, F et al "Technology Transfer by CDM Projects", 6 Climate Policy 327 (2006).
[770] In agreement see p2830, Olsen, K and J Fenhann "Sustainable development benefits of clean development mechanism projects - A new methodology for sustainability assessment based on text analysis of the project design documents submitted for validation" 36 Energy Policy 2819 (2008).
[771] See e.g. Sutter, C "Sustainability Check-Up for CDM projects" Wissenschaftlicher Verlag, Berlin (2003).
[772] See Olsen, K and J Fenhann "Sustainable development benefits of clean development mechanism projects - A new methodology for sustainability assessment based on text analysis of the project design documents submitted for validation" 36 Energy Policy 2819 (2008);
[773] De Coninck, H et al., "Technology transfer in the Clean Development Mechanism, 7 Climate Policy 444 (2007).

capacity [774] (in the case of Dechezlepretre et. al., captured by the variable TECH_CAPABILITY), or level of intellectual property protection may therefore be made more clear and used to better inform policy. In the case of China, one study applying Dechezlepretre et als. methodology argues that much of the low levels of technology transfer in the data for China can be explained by the country dummy CHINA (modified and more detailed for this case), embodying characteristics related to China's rules on joint venture and limited foreign ownership requirements, levels of intellectual property protection; local content requirements.[775] However, it is precisely on these kinds of regulatory interventions that a measurement of learning would be most useful at capturing the nature and scale of technology transfer beyond the binary measure of whether technology transfer was claimed or not in the PDD. This is not to say that the 'intent' to transfer technology that appears to exist in most PDDs should not be a valuable data point, but absent any other data it cannot be reliable evidence of actual attempts to do so, except perhaps in the very limited sense of whether hardware intended to be used was actually used.

The potential of the CDM to function as a vehicle for technology transfer remains strong but there is significant concern that it has not done so, and it is difficult to find reliable data on whether it has done so. In the end it leaves us in the same position that we were in before: given some structure for encouraging and enabling FDI, how should states act to ensure sufficient spillovers from such investment in terms of technology transfer? The CDM has been successful at addressing a major FDI problem for ESTs and that is by creating a platform on which actors can exchange and share information about existing and completed opportunities, as well as potential partners who have already succeeded.[776] It is a very useful platform for encouraging certain kinds of transactions and lowering the perceived low commercial viability of some projects[777], despite the prevalence of low cost end of pipe technology solutions in its early phases.

The CDM offers a crucial leverage point in the DNA process but it also may be susceptible to other regulatory actions, such as joint venture requirements, use of domestic technology, where a domestic substitute exists,[778] rules on mobility of personnel, or rules on intellectual property developed during the joint venture. In particular, as with the Chinese experience in SC/USC boiler technology (discussed in

---

[774] For a recent attempt to examine this at the level of the firm see Doranova, A et al. "Absorptive capacity in technological learning in clean development mechanism projects" UNU-Merit Working Papers 2011-10.
[775] Gechlick, M "Making Transfer of Clean Technology Work: Lessons of the Clean Development Mechanism" 11 San Diego International Law Journal 227 (2009)
[776] p2933, Schneider, M et al. "Understanding the CDM's contribution to technology transfer" 36 Energy Policy 2930 (2008).
[777] p2936, Id.
[778] See p2574, Wang, B "Can CDM bring technology transfer to China?—An empirical study of technology transfer in China's CDM projects" 38 Energy Policy 2572(2010)

Chapter 3), programmatic CDM may provide a knowledge-sharing and regulatory platform for localization and ensuring spillovers at a sectoral level that project based CDM has largely been incapable of doing. The availability of these actions remains both a legal question and a practical one given the market demand structure of the CDM. It may be appropriate to consider a methodology for crediting projects and programmes that even where they may not directly result in reductions may nevertheless generate credits for high quality transferring of technologies that sees the best available technologies provided to enable production, or integration into productive processes – ensuring capacity to replicate, adapt and diffuse into the broader economy.

Finally, the CDM empirical studies suggest one key factor as fundamental in enabling or encouraging technology transfer and that is pre-existing technological capacity. The studies suggest that such capacity is both an outcome and an enabler of technology transfer activities, but also that these are not the primary consideration of market driven structures such as the CDM and that in some circumstances there may be a real tension between the enablement of absorptive capacity and the achievement of low-cost efficient emissions reductions through market structures. The importance of providing a market-based structure that provides an incentive for private actors to engage in such building of absorptive capacity and to do so by engaging in repeat, intensive learning and interactive activity related to technologies is crucial.[779] Chapter 9 outlines a proposal aimed at addressing this issue with respect to technologies more generally and to intellectual property protected technologies more specifically.

In the end, it is difficult to conclude that the CDM has been an effective technology transfer mechanism. The basic structure of the mechanism suggests that, absent any other policy lever, it is unlikely to ever be able to encourage the kind of high quality technology transfer involving more than equipment and minimal training on operation and maintenance of the equipment. It also has a structural incentive in the low demand for credits and the large oversupply of potential providers which may discourage host parties from imposing any regulatory requirements, something which has put pressure on the stringency of even the basic additionality requirement. Without further reform, especially to ensure income based incentives to engage in high quality technology transfer, it is unlikely that the CDM can function as a reliable technology transfer vehicle under the UNFCCC.

IV.3 The Global Environment Facility (GEF)

---

[779] See de Sepibus, J "Reforming the Clean Development Mechanism to accelerate Technology Transfer" Working Paper No 2009/42, NCCR Trade Regulation, Swiss National Centre of Competence in Research, November 2009.

Until the establishment of the Green Climate Fund in the 2010 Cancun Agreements, the Global Environmental Facility (GEF) functioned as the primary financial mechanism for the UNFCCC. The GEF has operated as the primary funding mechanism for technology activities, in the absence of any implementing mechanism within the UNFCCC itself. It has done so through both general funds and specific funds such as: The climate change mitigation programme of the GEF Trust Fund; The Poznan strategic programme on technology transfer.[780]

The Poznan Strategic Programme provides funding for[781]:

- Technology needs assessments (TNAs);
- Implementing technology transfer pilot projects;
- Disseminating GEF experience and examples of successfully demonstrated ESTs.

For the long-term implementation of the strategic programme, the GEF also has programs for:

- Support for climate technology centers and a climate technology network;
- Piloting priority technology projects to foster innovation and investments;
- Public-private partnerships for technology transfer;
- Technology needs assessments;

The GEF was aimed at providing funds to developing countries to help them meet their obligations under Article 4 of the UNFCCC. The GEF provides only incremental cost funding in the form of grants but in most cases requires co-financing.

Major concerns about the GEF revolve around the strategic focus and the structure of project financing. While separate from the World Bank (which functions as a trustee and provides administrative services), the GEF essentially functions as a donor agency, whose mandate is delivery of financial support to project applications from developing countries that have met specific criteria. This is in contrast to the structure of the UNFCCC which views financial support for technology transfer and other action by developing countries as 'obligations' to which developing countries are entitled rather than as aid, which is at the discretion of the donor. This has meant that rather than receiving direct access to funds for described plans of actions and programs, developing countries have had to "apply" for funding which is granted at the discretion of the responsible bodies appointed by the GEF Council which is controlled by donors, due to

---

[780] Established at the COP 14 in Decision 2/CP.14)
[781] See p5, GEF "Implementing the Poznan Strategic and Long-Term Programs on Technology Transfer" Global Environment Facility, November 2012.

the weighting given to financial contributions. The GEF uses levels of co-financing as part of project approval criteria[782] which also falls short of the "full" costs principle of the UNFCCC. Primarily, this has placed the burden of change and implementation of technology transfer on developing countries, especially to put in place 'enabling environments'. Nothing in the program addresses the regulatory structures and barriers that may exist in developed countries, which is the primary complaint of developing countries about being able to access technologies that are protected by intellectual property. A look at the financing criteria of the GEF provides no information about whether payment for intellectual property licenses is covered by their definition of "agreed incremental costs". The operational guidelines for determining incremental costs[783] do not address whether such costs may or should be covered. A December 2009 note on IPR issues in GEF funding[784] also does not address whether GEF funds access to licenses as part of its "full agreed incremental costs". The note focuses primarily on those situations where GEF funding results in the creation of IPRs and what policies exist for GEF to retain access and use of such IPRs. The note by the secretariat emphasizes that IPR issues are best handled through contractual arrangements but does not elaborate.[785]

A short examination of projects under the Special Climate Change Fund show that licensing of technology is envisioned under at least one project[786], although it is unclear whether GEF funding is being used to cover licensing costs, or whether such costs are covered by co-financing. In a 2011 approved Jordan project, the co-finance for the IPR appears to be coming from the technology rightholder, DuPont.[787]

The success of the GEF in enabling technology transfer is difficult to assess. In the 2010-2014 period it raised 2.5 billion in pledged funds for its activities.[788]

Some research suggest that it has been most successful at transferring mature hardware technologies, but less so at enabling demonstration-ready technologies into

---

[782] GEF "Operational Guidelines for the Implementation of the Incremental Cost Principle" GEF/C.31/12, May 14, 2007.
[783] Id.
[784] GEF "Note on Issues related to Intellectual Property Rights" GEF/C.13/Inf.14, December 1, 2009 (first issued for GEF Council Meeting, May 5 – 7, 1999.), available at: http://www.thegef.org/gef/sites/thegef.org/files/documents/GEF.C.13.Inf_.14.pdf
[785] Para. 9, GEF "Note on Issues related to Intellectual Property Rights" GEF/C.13/Inf.14, December 1, 2009 (first issued for GEF Council Meeting, May 5 – 7, 1999.), available at: http://www.thegef.org/gef/sites/thegef.org/files/documents/GEF.C.13.Inf_.14.pdf
[786] e.g. p33 "Jordan: TT-Pilot (GEF-4) DHRS: Irrigation Technology Pilot Project to face Climate Change, available at: http://www.thegef.org/gef/sites/thegef.org/files/documents/document/6-17-2011%20%20ID4036%20%20Council%20Letter..pdf
[787] p1, Id.
[788] GEF "Implementing the Poznan Strategic and Long-Term Programs on Technology Transfer" Global Environment Facility, November 2012.

commercial activity.[789] The experience relating to the China Industrial Boiler project may be illustrative. Mallet et al. note that convincing leading technology holders to participate in building capacity and knowledge for the production of boilers was very difficult and finding a willing licensing partner took 6 years, and even then, the licensor was a second tier firm with less experience in the market.[790] Ockwell et al. note that, over time, the GEF has de-emphasized direct technology transfer as a goal and focused increasingly on market creation projects, precisely because of the difficulty of finding private sector actors willing to build capacity and knowledge related to their technology.[791]

The GEF also has the problem of scale. Its funding for climate change is relatively small in absolute terms, limiting it largely to pilot projects, rather than functioning as a full scale transfer mechanism.[792] It has had to be strategic about where and when to fund to have the most impact, but has not functioned as a major funder or enabler. There are concerns about the length of the application process especially for leveraging private sector involvement.[793] It has broad sectoral coverage, both in mitigation and adaptation but the majority of projects are in mitigation and tilted towards energy efficiency.[794] It also has good geographic focus, exclusively on developing countries with a large portion of funded projects in China.[795]

IV.4. Non-UNFCCC Multilateral and Bilateral delivery under Article 4.1(c), 4.3 and 4.5, National Communications and the Role of Nationally Appropriate Mitigation Actions (NAMAs) and National Adaptation Plans of Action (NAPAs).

In the absence of any formal UNFCCC mechanism for implementation of the technology transfer provisions in the Convention, much of the weight was left to bilateral delivery and reports by Annex 1 countries, channeling their activities through bilateral Official Development Assistance (ODA), and through supporting international financial institutions (IFIs) such as the regional development banks.

---

[789] p13, Lefevre, N "Deploying Climate –friendly Technologies through Collaboration with Developing Countries" International Energy Agency, Information Paper, November 2005.
[790] See p39, Mallet, A et al. "UK-India Collaboration to Identify the Barriers to the Transfer of Low Carbon Technology-Phase II Final report" (London: Department of Energy and Climate Change, UK 2009).
[791] See p33, Ockwell, D et al. "Enhancing Developing Country Access to Eco-Innovation: The Case of Technology Transfer and Climate Change in a Post-2012 Policy Framework", OECD Environment Working Papers, No. 12, OECD Publishing 2010.
[792] See p346, de Coninck et al. "International technology-oriented agreements to address climate change" 36 Energy Policy 335 (2008).
[793] See p13, Venugopal, S et al. "Public Financing Instruments to Leverage Private Capital for Climate-Relevant Investment: Focus on Multilateral Agencies." Working Paper World Resources Institute, Washington, DC. (2012.). Available online at http://www.wri.org/project/climate-finance-private-sector (last visited 15 August 2014).
[794] See p15, Id.
[795] Id.

IV.4.1. The Clean Technology Fund

A major venue for multilateral support came from the World Bank and associated regional banks through the donor supported Climate Investment Funds[796], the specific technology related sub-part being:

- The Clean Technology Fund – aimed at middle income countries for R&D, demonstration, deployment of technologies in renewable energy, transport and energy efficiency

- The Scaling Up Renewable Energy in low Income countries Programme – aimed at market creation and support measures for renewable energy in LDCs

The main method of the CIFs was to use co-financing to leverage private sector co-investment in large sectoral programmes. Funding comes from pledges from donors and is separate from any UNFCCC mechanism.[797] Countries report their contributions to the CIFs through their regular national communications to the UNFCCC and as part of their finance pledges under the Copenhagen Accord.[798] Planned as interim measures while a UNFCCC financing mechanism was negotiated and established, the CIFs had a specific sunset clause that they would cease operations once an effective UNFCCC mechanism was functioning.[799] The main aim of the sunset clause was to address concerns of developing countries that such funds would divert funds from the planned Green Climate Fund within the UNFCCC and that the governance structure of the CIFs, which gave prominence and weight to donor countries should not be the permanent basis for climate funding.[800]

How successful have these programmes at meeting their technology transfer aims? The first thing to note is that the mandate of the CIFs but of the CTF specifically, was to demonstrate the feasibility and success of specific methods for carrying out technology transfer, so that lessons learned could be transferred into the UNFCCC financial mechanism when it was finally agreed.[801] A fair assessment cannot be aimed at whether it provided sufficient volume of technologies or financing but whether it showcased and demonstrated what worked and what did not. They were never intended

---

[796] These began operating in 2008.
[797] See Climate Investment Fund "About the Climate Investment Funds" https://www.climateinvestmentfunds.org/cif/aboutus (last visited 15 August 2014).
[798] World Bank, "Development and Climate Change Monitoring Climate Finance and ODA" World Bank May 2010.
[799] See para.53-55, Climate Investment Funds "Governance Framework for The Clean Technology Fund" Adopted November 2008 and amended December 2011. Available at:
https://www.climateinvestmentfunds.org/cif/governance (last visited 15 August 2014).
[800] Ballesteros, A et al. "Power, Responsibility and Accountability: Re-Thinking the Legitimacy of Institutions for Climate Finance" World Resources Institute, WRI Working Paper December 2009.
[801] See para. 7, Climate Investment Funds "Governance Framework for The Clean Technology Fund"

as major avenues for achieving technology transfer. So the true measure is whether the CTF provided useful lessons going forward for achieving technology transfer, including on timing, scope of technologies, and geographical scope.

The programmes have been subject to independent evaluation and so some details can be found there. The first test is to see what kind of activities were covered by its funding, including localization of technology, allowing for adoption, adaptation and replication. The structure of the financing avoids the 'incremental cost' cost principle that has so bedeviled funding under the GEF, and simply focused on providing, in its grant financing, the "additional costs" of investment necessary to make investment viable. The co-financing, concessional loans and other instruments are not dependent on any additional cost assessment but based simply on the project or programme meeting the criteria of the funding institution. The majority of funding is through concessional loans, and may not fully reflect the full costs principle in Article 4.[802] To a significant extent, the funding remains subject to the different standards of each participating regional development bank for qualifying for such projects.[803] Nevertheless, the CTF does establish investment criteria as the basis on which participating banks and countries can access the funds. There are two sets - public sector[804], and; private sector.[805] The public sector criteria look at 5 key issues:[806]

- Potential for GHG Emissions Savings
- Cost-effectiveness
- Demonstration Potential at Scale
- Development Impact
- Implementation Potential
- Additional Costs and Risk Premium

There is a list of examples of activities to be covered in a set of technology sectors, at the level of aims to be achieved, e.g. Modal shift to low carbon transportation, but no details on the means of implementation.[807] There appears to be no limitation on the use of funds to conduct technology localization, or access to licensing and know-how. The CTF seems to have modelled an exemplary additional cost methodology that does not exclude using funds for such activities, including for knowledge development

---

[802] See p3, Ballesteros, A et al. "Power, Responsibility and Accountability: Re-Thinking the Legitimacy of Institutions for Climate Finance" World Resources Institute, WRI Working Paper December 2009.
[803] See para. 12, Climate Investment Funds "Governance Framework for The Clean Technology Fund" Adopted November 2008 and amended December 2011.
[804] Climate Investment Funds "Clean Technology Fund Investment Criteria for Public Sector Operations" February 9, 2009.
[805] Climate Investment Funds "CTF Private Sector Operations Guidelines" October 24, 2012
[806] See p3, Climate Investment Funds "Clean Technology Fund Investment Criteria for Public Sector Operations"
[807] See para. 6, Climate Investment Funds "Clean Technology Fund Investment Criteria for Public Sector Operations"

platforms. Where internal costs are higher than would make a project commercially viable, then the CTF would provide a grant to cover the additional cost or risk premium to enable the commercial viability.[808] This should therefore cover those circumstances where cost of licensing might have made adoption of a technology non-viable.

The private sector funding criteria are much the same as those for the public sector with some additions. The main aim of this kind of funding is to mitigate the risk of being first mover into a new technology, and to provide real market demonstration of the viability of a technology, taking care of the risk premium that commercial lending may not be willing to take on.[809] As these are the kinds of requests that are most likely to address the commercial cost of knowledge access, the ways in which the CTF funds knowledge access and sharing is crucial. The CTF rules on this are quite clear. They require information on and will fund projects that do the following:

> "include initiatives aimed at reducing information barriers or other non-financial barriers to market transformation. These activities may include capacity building for private sector entities, particularly small- and medium-sized enterprises, and knowledge products aimed at sharing information among private sector entities, public sector organisations and public-private sector entities, including financial intermediaries, as well as between and among the MDBs, and other relevant development partners."[810]

The CTF model seems an ideal vehicle for financing localization activities enabling adoption, adaptation and replication – where such licensing and know how is available at commercial or near commercial costs. Thus one of the tests for evaluating the CTF is the extent to which it provided funding for such activities.

By focusing on middle income countries, the CTF already at least addresses to a significant extent the geographic need. In terms of scope of technologies covered, the CTF covers all the relevant activities in relevant sectors for mitigation: Efficient fossil fuel power generation, renewable energy, Industry, buildings, transport, and agriculture. There are no *a priori* sector or technology limitations.[811] In terms of timing, the CTF is only an interim body and so its work aims to be completed by the time the 2015 agreement and the GCF are operational and so also is within the timing structure for moving technologies. Of course, it cannot be expected to operate at scale, given its mandate. In the reports provided by the MDBs to the CTF on their activities, the

---

[808] See p9, Climate Investment Funds "Clean Technology Fund Investment Criteria for Public Sector Operations" February 9, 2009.
[809] See p1, Climate Investment Funds "CTF Private Sector Operations Guidelines" October 24, 2012.
[810] See para. 10(a)(iii), Climate Investment Funds "CTF Private Sector Operations Guidelines" October 24, 2012.
[811] See para. 6, Climate Investment Funds "Clean Technology Fund Investment Criteria for Public Sector Operations" February 9, 2009.

nature of specific activities funded is difficult to ascertain. The indicators used are at too high a level to examine the issue of technology transferred per se. The monitoring and evaluation framework focuses primarily on[812]:

- Indicator 1: Tons of GHG reduced or avoided (in tons of CO_2 equivalent);
- Indicator 2: Volume of direct finance leveraged through CTF funding (in US$
- millions);
- Indicator 3: Installed capacity (MW) as a result of CTF interventions;
- Indicator 4: Number of additional passengers using low-carbon transport as a
- result of CTF; and
- Indicator 5: Annual energy savings as a result of CTF interventions (GWh).

There is no measure here of the capacity built among the local producers for adaptation, or replication of the technology. While the independent report normally should have provided some ways to evaluate the technology transfer success of the CTF it is limited to these core indicators, as well as operational matters. In terms of lessons to be learned from the CTF, the independent interim evaluation report points to several key issues:

- Replicability of projects, especially the private sector ones, is difficult to assess and may be a structural problem for the CTF given that at best, its particular funding support may be difficult to replicate in the private lending market without some fundamental shifting in actual risk profile for the investment.[813]

- Very few CTF funds are directed at the policy and regulatory environment; making the sustainability and the transformational element of the funds less sure.[814]

- The CTF has no formal technical quality review of CTF proposals, other than comments from provider countries. There is no technical expert review process.[815]

---

[812] See p3, Climate Investment Funds "Clean Technology Fund First Round of Monitoring and Reporting on Results" CTF/TFC.12/Inf.2 Meeting of the CTF Trust Fund Committees, Washington D.C., October 28, 2013. Available at: https://www.climateinvestmentfunds.org/cif/content/first-round-monitoring-and-reporting-results (last visited 15 August 2014).
[813] See p19, ICF International "Final Interim report: Independent Evaluation of the Climate Investment Funds" Evaluation Oversight Committee for the Independent Evaluation of the Climate Investment Funds, July 2013. Available at: http://www.cifevaluation.org/index.html (last visited 15 August 2014).
[814] See p19, ICF International ""Final Interim report: Independent Evaluation of the Climate Investment Funds" Evaluation Oversight Committee for the Independent Evaluation of the
Climate Investment Funds, July 2013.
[815] See p103, Id.

- There is a large gap between endorsed projects and those that have had funds disbursed. Less than 10% of CIF endorsed projects have reached disbursement stage.[816] This is a concern especially for the implementation of private sector projects.

The experience of the CTF suggests the need for long term financing mechanisms to substitute to a significant extent the lack of appetite for risk of private sector actors, beyond the initial few projects to a point where there is a critical mass. It also points to the need to carry out regulatory and policy measures to restructure the market in favor of adoption of technologies in ways that spread or amortize the costs and risks in technology adoption and purchasing, while putting in place stronger demand side measures to increase potential return on investment.

A better sense of what the CTF has accomplished regarding technology transfer could be drawn from the content of the approved project applications, but there is significant variation in the project documents and, for private sector projects, a lot of material may be inaccessible. For example, the European Bank for Reconstruction and Development does not provide details for such projects beyond project summaries.[817] The Country Investment Plans provide insufficient detail as to whether they plan to engage in localization, adaption and replication, although all clearly drive at adoption. The details of how they plan to achieve adoption are not available at the level of the country investment plans. The specific project plans under each country's investment plans are not available on the CIF or the website of the responsible MDB in any reliable manner. Comparison or even determining the extent of such activities does not seem possible at this point. This issue of transparency is something that has been remarked upon by commentators.[818] To the extent that such information is not available, it makes it difficult, other than at the macro level of CTF contributions, and the reports of the independent evaluation, to verify the contribution to technology transfer made by the CTF. In particular, the failure to include extent of capacity built, extent of ability to adapt and replicate and building up of commercial producers or implementers of the technology in the core indicators is a problem. It replicates to a significant extent the broader problem of measurable, reportable and verifiable technology transfer that has historically dogged technology support in the UNFCCC.

IV.4.2 Measuring, Reporting and Verification (MRV) of Financial and Technological Support

---

[816] See p108, Id.
[817] See p10, Ballesteros, A et al. "Power, Responsibility and Accountability: Re-Thinking the Legitimacy of Institutions for Climate Finance" World Resources Institute, WRI Working Paper December 2009.
[818] See Ballesteros, A et al. "Power, Responsibility and Accountability: Re-Thinking the Legitimacy of Institutions for Climate Finance" World Resources Institute, WRI Working Paper December 2009; Olsen, K "Sustainable Development Impacts of NAMAs: An integrated approach to assessment of co-benefits based on experience with the CDM" Low Carbon Development Working Paper No. 11, UNEP Risoe Center, November 2013;

Initially, the only ways in which financial and technological support activities could be measured was through assessing individual National Communications, the primary manner in which delivery on Article 4 obligations was measured under the Convention. Due to significant concerns about the additionality of activities and funding reported, developed and developing countries worked towards new methods for meeting these obligations, embodied in *Nationally Appropriate Mitigation Actions* (NAMAs)[819] and *National Adaptation Plans of Action* (NAPAs) to which funding and activities would be directed. This section describes some of the concerns that drive this debate and the structures that it led to, and why despite this there remains significant unhappiness with NAMAs and NAPAs as delivery mechanisms for technology transfer. As with critiques of the GEF, these revolve primarily around the sense that developing countries had that sufficient funding of any initiatives that they wished to undertake, whether it be from the GEF, through NAPAs and NAMAs, would never be forthcoming, driving them to seek out unilateral options for implementing their obligations.

A key transition in the discussions on technology transfer was the report on technology transfer by the Secretariat examining the nature and scope of technology transfer as reported in national communications of Annex II Parties.[820] In the report, it noted that because reporting guidelines were so vague, national communications varied as to detail, interpretation, format, and comprehensiveness.[821] Four out of 21 reports studied did not report on technology transfer at all.[822] The definition adopted by the secretariat was quite broad, encompassing private sector activity where reported, and any funding to a multilateral fund that may have been used for technology transfer. This included contributions to the GEF, as well a bilateral official development assistance (ODA). Of what was reported, the majority addressed hardware transfers (although on what terms is unclear). Some support for multilateral R&D was reported primarily through support to the Consultative Group on International Agricultural Research (CGIAR).

This report was the beginning of serious concerns on the part of developing countries that implementation of technology transfer obligations would not occur in a sufficient and timely manner. In particular, the concern was that parties seemed to be reporting on existing and ongoing funding and activities rather than those that were additional to regular ODA and multilateral contributions. The conclusion they drew

---

[819] Agreed to in the Bali Action Plan, see p3, UNFCCC "Bali Action Plan" Decision 1/CP.13 in "Report of the Conference of the Parties on its thirteenth session, held in Bali from 3 to 15 December 2007, Addendum - Part Two: Action taken by the Conference of the Parties at its thirteenth session", FCCC/CP/2007/6/Add.1, 14 March 2008.
[820] UNFCCC "Note by the Secretariat on transfer of technology" UN Doc. FCCC/SBI/1996/5, 1995. Available at: http://unfccc.int/resource/docs/1996/sbi/05.pdf (last visited 15 August 2014).
[821] See p4, Id.
[822] See p3, Id.

was that developed countries did not aim to provide 'additional' support to that already being provided and that instead, climate support for technology would come from diversion of other funding or relabeling of existing support. The lead countries in expressing such concerns were China and Russia.[823] The response from the US and the EU focused on overcoming some of the technical barriers to providing information and emphasized the role that the private sector played, noting the limited role that government can play in providing technology transfer when technologies are primarily held by private sector actors.[824]

It was at the 4th COP that developed countries began to emphasize the issue of the lack of enabling environments as a barrier to technology transfer. Focusing on private sector delivery, they argued that developing countries needed to ensure proper regulatory environments to create demand for technologies, and that they needed to ensure intellectual property protection and enforcement to ensure that companies felt comfortable licensing technology.[825] This was part of a broader re-framing of the issue by the main developed countries, US, Australia, Japan, Canada (and sometimes the EU) to focus on market mechanisms, mitigation technologies, and on the flexibility mechanisms such as the Clean Development Mechanism (CDM).

The establishment of the EGTT at COP 6 in 2000 only served to shift the debate from one forum to another and may actually have served to delay further action on technology transfer. The work of the SBSTA from this point on tends to focus on examining the reports of the EGTT, which met in closed session. The establishment of the EGTT, which did not report to the SBI, also meant that technology transfer fell off the agenda of the SBI (with its implementation mandate) over time, as all technology transfer issues were deferred to the 'technical' body of the EGTT. The process appeared stuck in a cycle of approval or disapproval of the EGTT work program without actually addressing the substantive issues that the EGTT's work raised.

In 2006, the EGTT produced an assessment of the progress and effectiveness in the implementation of the technology transfer framework, and identification of gaps and barriers and suggestions for ways and means to better facilitate and advance its implementation.[826] One key result of the 2006 analysis was that that there was insufficient data from governments to determine what measures and policies they had taken to fulfil their commitments on technology transfer.[827] This is despite the fact that

---

[823] Earth Negotiations Bulletin "Summary: 2nd Session SBSTA & SBI" Volume 12, Number 26, February 27 - March 04, 1996.
[824] Id.
[825] Earth Negotiations Bulletin "Summary: 4th COP FCCC" Volume 12, Number 97, November 02 - 13, 1998. Available at: http://www.iisd.ca/vol12/enb1297e.html (last visited 15 August 2014).
[826] "Recommendations of the Expert Group on Technology Transfer for enhancing the implementation of the framework for meaningful and effective actions to enhance the implementation of Article 4, paragraph 5, of the Convention" FCCC/SBSTA/2006/INF.4, UNFCCC 2006.
[827] p13, Id.

at the very first COP, the Parties were urged to include in their national communication measures taken to deliver on technology transfer commitments.[828]

Relevant work by the EGTT during the post-Bali period looked at creating a set of performance indicators to try and create a standardized methodology for countries to report on their implementation of obligations. All Parties supported the development of performance indicators so as to measure the effectiveness of technology transfer as it related to the work of the EGTT.[829] Developed countries suggested indicators measuring the degree of IP protection,[830] and developing countries emphasized technology sharing.[831] The Post-Bali review of the technology transfer provisions focused on Article 4, paragraph 1(c) and 5, of the Convention.

Approved in 2008[832], a draft report was produced in 2009.[833] Parties also continued to express their views on the areas of focus of the review.[834] The review itself was produced in 2010[835] and made several key points.

With respect to legal and regulatory frameworks the review notes that enabling environments are key to successful technology transfer. Developing countries need to do more and need financial help in designing and implementing innovative institutional and regulatory systems.[836] However, the review appeared to focus almost exclusively on regulatory measures taken by developing countries and had little to say about enabling environments and 'push' actions in developed countries. Some of this was addressed in the focus area on cooperation with the private sector. The review noted that there has historically been insufficient public funding to leverage private sector participation.

On intellectual property the review stated that "enhancing the business environment through better use of IPRs will be important for promoting the sustainable development of technologies by technology innovators in developing countries."[837] This assessment also reflects a focus on regulatory and policy environments in developing countries rather than developed.

---

[828] Decision 13/CP.1, Transfer of technology, p40 FCCC/CP/1995/7/Add.1
[829] Subpara. 22(d), UNFCCC "Synthesis of views on elements for the terms of reference for the review and assessment of the effectiveness of the implementation of Article 4, paragraphs 1(c) and 5, of the Convention: Note by the secretariat", Subsidiary Body for Implementation, 28th Sess., Bonn, 4-13 June 2008, U.N. Doc. FCCC/SBI/2008/7, 20 May 2008, at Available at:
http://unfccc.int/resource/docs/2008/sbi/eng/07.pdf (last visited 15 August 2014).
[830] Annex, Id.
[831] Id. at Para. 32.
[832] FCCC/SBI/2008/19, annex I
[833] FCCC/SBI/2009/INF.
[834] FCCC/SBI/2009/MISC.4
[835] UNFCCC "Report on the review and assessment of the effectiveness of the implementation of Article 4, paragraphs 1(c) and 5 of the Convention" SUBSIDIARY BODY FOR IMPLEMENTATION, Thirty-second session, Bonn, 31 May to 9 June, FCCC/SBI/2010/INF.4.
[836] p11, FCCC/SBI/2010/INF.4
[837] p16, Id.

Finally, on R&D cooperation the review noted the gap between perceived funding needs and actual needs ranging in the billions.[838] The review also noted that the majority of such funding was taking place in developed countries with little transfer of funds to developing countries.[839]

Once completed, the AWGLCA took note of the review but took no further action regarding the uses to which the performance indicators used in the review should be applied. Despite significant work, this set of indicators was not built into the standard for national communications by parties.

However, on the broader mitigation track, elements of technology came to be associated with the broader push to have all countries, but especially emerging economies, take on some kinds of pledge mitigation actions.[840] These were finally embodied in the NAMAs[841], which, where supported by developed countries, bilaterally or through the Green Climate Fund, would form the basis for measuring, reporting and verifying actions by countries and for provision of and verifying financial and technological support.[842] NAMAs were intended to be the basis on which support would be directed to developing countries, to try and fill the information gap between the supply side (where are funds from developed countries to flow to) and the demand side (where do developed countries, need or want such funds to flow). They would also be a mechanism for recognition of action by developing countries. The exact status and role of NAMAs continues to be the subject of negotiation but a registry was created for countries wishing for support for their specific mitigation actions under the NAMAs. However, there is at present, no mechanism for directly applying for and receiving support based on the registry, and it remains at the discretion of funders to determine which NAMAs they will fund. The registry only serves a matching function for the moment and does not function as a funding mechanism or allow direct access to funds. It provides no broader verification function, although there are plans for those supported to report emissions reductions and claimed sustainable development benefits

---

[838] p43, FCCC/SBI/2010/INF.4
[839] p43, Id.
[840] See p7, Staley, B Childs et al. "Tick Tock Tick Tock: Coming to Agreement on Technology in the Countdown to Copenhagen". WRI Working Paper, World Resources Institute, Washington DC, June 2009.
[841] Agreed to in the Bali Action Plan, see p3, UNFCCC "Bali Action Plan" Decision 1/CP.13 in "Report of the Conference of the Parties on its thirteenth session, held in Bali from 3 to 15 December 2007, Addendum - Part Two: Action taken by the Conference of the Parties at its thirteenth session", FCCC/CP/2007/6/Add.1, 14 March 2008.
[842] See p5, Seligsohn, D et al. "Key Functions for a UNFCCC Technology Institutional Structure: Identifying Convergence in Country Submissions" World Resources Institute Working Paper, November 2009. Also see p3, UNFCCC "Bali Action Plan" Decision 1/CP.13

under the NAMA, although such reporting may occur on a bilateral basis between the funder and the funded.[843]

Even where the NAMAs may end up fulfilling their general function of finally ensuring direct access to funds for mitigation actions, this thesis has previously pointed out that these may best serve to address a subset of the technology transfer problematic: access to products; access to know-how and licensing, where the costs are reasonable and commercially-based[844]; but only under existing market conditions. They would do nothing to address how to restructure the market to increase the rate of technology diffusion, the scope of technologies to be diffused, and the ability of emerging economies to serve as diffusion centers to other developing countries. NAMAs as they stand suffer from much the same limitation that the CDM and TNAs do: they rely on the same mechanism of financial support, whose failure (related to lack of measurable, reportable and verifiable action[845]) was the very impetus for developing countries to seek unilateral options in the first place.[846] As a response, NAMAs fail to address the full scope of the challenge of market restructuring and to address the needs of developing countries to deal with refusals to deal in licenses, access know-how, and increase spillovers into their markets. Nevertheless, it is clear that beyond new institutional mechanisms, developing countries have not been satisfied and will not be satisfied until, at the very least, support for NAMAs is direct, predictable, measurable, verifiable, and allows them to fund activities that localize knowledge and technology i.e. allows firms in developing countries to adopt, adapt, replicate technologies. At present, it appears that implementation of the NAMAs requires an additional application process for funding from other funding institutions at the bilateral or multilateral level such as the GEF[847], replicating the same pattern that led to the failure of TNAs as technology transfer mechanisms. The lack of minimum standards for GHG reduction and or sustainable development in NAMAs makes it unclear on what basis direct access to funding of NAMAs will occur. In the absence of guarantees that such standards will indeed meet the development needs of developing countries and will fund such things as access to licensing and know-how, it is difficult to see developing countries agreeing to some kind of minimum qualification standard for supported NAMAs.

---

[843] See Olsen, K "Sustainable Development Impacts of NAMAs: An integrated approach to assessment of co-benefits based on experience with the CDM" Low Carbon Development Working Paper No. 11, UNEP Risoe Center, November 2013
[844] It remains unclear whether such costs would be covered under the NAMA support framework.
[845] p9, Staley, B Childs et al. "Tick Tech Tick Tech: Coming to Agreement on Technology in the Countdown to Copenhagen". WRI Working Paper, World Resources Institute, Washington DC, June 2009.
[846] See Olsen, K "Sustainable Development Impacts of NAMAs: An integrated approach to assessment of co-benefits based on experience with the CDM" Low Carbon Development Working Paper No. 11, UNEP Risoe Center, November 2013, arguing that NAMAs lack any sustainable development impact measures, much as the CDM.
[847] See p12, Hänsel, G et al. "Annual Status Report on Nationally Appropriate Mitigation Actions (NAMAs)", ECN, Ecofys, GIZ, CCAP (2013).

There remains significant uncertainty as to whether the GCF will have a specific technology window for funding or whether technology funding will be covered as a cross-cutting issue under the adaptation, mitigation and capacity building windows. This would require thinking differently about how to MRV support for technology actions especially where technology actions are in-kind or non-monetary. This may still require a separate process, which may be housed within the Technology Executive Committee (TEC), although for the moment, the Technology Executive Committee does not appear to have MRV within its mandate.

The extent of public funding available however, may not be anything close to what is actually required to address the full scope of action need to develop, deploy, and diffuse technologies. Looking at the mitigation scenarios, the IEA projects that from 2010 – 2020, over USD 2.3 trillion annually will need to be invested, the majority of which will be private flows.[848] The share of developing countries is USD 1.3 trillion annually, of which China represents USD 500 billion. In contrast to the scale of the projected need, total investment flows in 2010 and 2011, were USD 247 billion and 260 billion respectively.

Within the climate negotiations, developed countries in Copenhagen at COP 15 committed to provide USD 100 billion annually by 2020 in investment (from a wide variety of sources, including public funds).[849] A significant portion is meant to flow through the Green Climate Fund (GCF), which implies direct cash or other instruments under the control of the fund, rather than financial instruments operating outside of the remit of the GCF. The IEA estimates that climate mitigation related flows from developed to developing countries amount to somewhere between USD 70 and USD 199 billion a year.[850] The majority of this is private flows (USD 37 – 72 billion), and the public funds (through bilateral and multilateral mechanisms) amount to a potential maximum of USD 43 billion. Olbrisch et al. review the range of estimates for incremental investment in the literature noting significant variations for 2030 projections for annual financing needs in developing countries: from USD 177 billion to USD 565 billion per annum.[851] They do not provide estimates of the portion that would be from private flows, but their estimate of current funding suggests that private flows are the largest proportion of funding amounting to at least USD 65 billion per year.

---

[848] See Table 4.3, p139, IEA, *Energy Technology Perspectives 2012: Pathways to a Clean Energy System* (Paris: IEA/OECD 2012).
[849] See p13, Staley, B Childs et al. "Tick Tech Tick Tech: Coming to Agreement on Technology in the Countdown to Copenhagen". WRI Working Paper, World Resources Institute, Washington DC, June 2009.
[850] p152, IEA, *Energy Technology Perspectives 2012: Pathways to a Clean Energy System* (Paris: IEA/OECD 2012).
[851] See p974, Olbrisch, S et al. "Estimates of incremental investment for and cost of mitigation measures in developing countries", 11 Climate Policy, 970 (2011).

In terms of direct support, it is unlikely that existing and future public funds will suffice to meet the need in developing countries[852] and, as the IEA notes, they will have to also mobilize a significant amount of finance domestically.[853] This is all before funding for adaptation is taken into account, which under the GCF should take up half of the planned disbursements. To some extent, the burden on the GCF is mitigated by China agreeing that it would not access Green Climate Funds.[854] In part this may be because China foresees little trouble in drawing FDI into its market. The IEA and others have difficulty finding an argument that investment flows for climate will differ in any significant way from existing patterns of investment into developing countries.[855] The prescriptions for providing a proper enabling environment replicate the same tried and true axioms of:

- reducing regulatory uncertainty;
- Enabling policies for competitive, open markets and greening infrastructure investment
- Sound investment policies; market-based and regulatory policies to "put a price on carbon" and correct for environmental externalities;
- removing barriers and disincentives and incentivize for innovation and investment
- Financial policies and instruments to attract private sector participation;

but applying these specifically to climate change sectors. Other than a broader faith that these interventions will work, there is no little analysis of how these recommendations will shift the risk and investment calculus in economies that are not already attractive investment destinations (for domestic, but primarily foreign capital) as a broader matter.

While attractive regulatory and market environments are clearly necessary conditions, they may not be sufficient to mobilize foreign investment at the scale required in markets that simply do not present a sufficient rate of return and may present, even at their best, more risk than the potential worth of returns. The policy prescription here essentially tells developing countries to transform their economies as a necessary condition for being able to transform their economies, without any of the necessary financial and technological support for doing so. These policy transformations are meant to substitute for financial support, and, hopefully, make it possible for private

---

[852] See Bowen, A "Raising climate finance to support developing country action: some economic considerations, 11 Climate Policy 1020 (2011).
[853] p152, IEA, *Energy Technology Perspectives 2012: Pathways to a Clean Energy System* (Paris: IEA/OECD 2012).
[854] p153, Id.
[855] See Niziramasanga, N "Implementing NAMAs under a new Climate Agreement that Supports development in Southern Africa" in Olsen, K et al. *Elements of a New Climate Agreement by 2015* (Roskilde, Denmark: UNEP Risoe, 2013)

sector money to flow. How that presents a different, new or additional solution to the broader development challenge is not explained. In order to develop, developing countries must therefore 'develop' and where they do so, this will obviate the need for significant public money and support.

In the end, the vast majority of financing and transfer will have to come from private sector action. Developed countries hope that the financial shortfall will somehow be made up by private sector actors, as long as markets are created and regulatory incentives are put in place. However, where there is insufficient public finance to provide support to developing country actors and firms in accessing technology hardware and knowledge, a reliance on private finance leaves the additional costs of accessing knowledge in the hands of developing country firms and institutions. The only way therefore for developing countries to respond is to take regulatory action to restructure the market in knowledge and knowledge products so that the costs of action are borne by developed country actors, which leads us back to the government interventions aimed at regulating prices of products, and regulations aimed at regulating prices for accessing knowledge. This is why intellectual property intervention continues to be a major structural issue at the core of the climate change negotiations: there is not enough money, even were there political will, to provide all the financial support that developing countries need to take action to address climate change mitigation and action.

The recommendation for how developing countries need to transform their economies to become more open to investment, have better more predictable legal structures, be more open to trade, provide more room for the private sector, reflects the long running and ongoing debate on the ways in which developing countries should best ensure their broader economic development.[856] To a significant extent, these are exactly the same policy prescriptions that have been given to developing countries by multilateral financing and development institutions for much of the past 3 decades. It is an ongoing debate about which economic model is best suited to ensure development and reflects the broader development challenge for developing countries. In that sense, it is only realistic to realize that climate change is indeed congruent with the broader development challenge. The paucity of direct public funding for climate change essentially throws developing countries back into the broader set of policy choices regarding how best to ensure economic development more broadly. In the technology arena, this therefore involves asking what are the best ways for countries to ensure that they can move up the technology value chain[857], what tools have been historically

---

[856] See e.g. Helpman, E *The Mystery of Economic Growth* (Cambridge, Mass. : Belknap Press of Harvard University Press, 2004)
[857] See Helpman, E *The Mystery of Economic Growth* (Cambridge, Mass.: Belknap Press of Harvard University Press, 2004) and Trebilcock, M and Mota Prado, M *What Makes Poor Countries Poor? Institutional Determinants of Development* (London: Edward Elgar, 2011) for institutional perspectives; Santos-Paulino, A and Guanghua, W (eds.) *Southern Engines of Global Growth* (Oxford: Oxford University Press, 2010) on the lessons from the CIBS, as well as the longer running debate embodied in various

successful for other countries, and are those tools available to developing countries today? This then is the structural reason why intellectual property became and remains such an important issue. As the primary international treaty regulating the international technology market and interventions that states may make, has TRIPS limited the tools once available to countries to enable them to move up the technological value chain and develop their economies? In Chapter 5, I address the role that intellectual property plays in economic development, the role it plays in encouraging or limiting technology transfer, and the measures that countries have historically used to move up the technological value chain.

IV.5 Conclusions

The implementing structures for technology transfer in the UNFCCC have generally been unsatisfactory for developing countries, in particular because there was no specific implementation mandate and methodology. The funding that has been made through these structures has also been generally unsatisfactory, and may continue to be so. This explains to a significant extent why part of the struggle at the UNFCCC has been about formal structures and mechanisms and has not focused on the actual content of and vectors for technology transfer. However, the persistence of the issue of intellectual property in the UNFCCC is not just a political issue but a reflection of the basic structure of institutional and financial gaps in the UNFCCC. The next section discusses the evolution of the new framework on technology transfer and the role of intellectual property in the negotiations for that framework.

V. Development of the New technology Transfer framework and the role of intellectual property in the negotiations at the UNFCCC

This section aims to describe the process by which the present structures (the Technology Executive Committee and the Climate Technology Centre & Network) on technology transfer were agreed and the role that the debate on intellectual property played in their design.

From the beginning of the UNFCCC, China has been one of the primary countries pushing for effective implementation of technology transfer commitments. In the first meeting of the SBSTA in September 1995, China identified a need for renewable energy technologies, and the need for the identification of adaptation

---

theories from e.g.: Prebisch, R "The Role of Commercial Policies in Underdeveloped Countries" 49 American Economic Review 251, (1959); Agarwala, A N and Singh, S P (eds.) *The Economics of Underdevelopment*, (Oxford: Oxford University Press, 1979); Rostow, W W *The Stages of Economic Growth: A Non-Communist Manifesto*, (Cambridge: Cambridge University Press, 1990).

technologies.[858] Access to technologies protected by intellectual property was raised almost immediately as a concern by the Alliance of Small Island States (AOSIS).[859] As noted above, discussions moved quickly to a debate on how and when implementation should take place and how the UNFCCC should take action. As the debate wore on, intellectual property became a larger and larger part of the debate as developing countries came to believe that they were going to have to take unilateral action to achieve technology transfer. The technology transfer debate became particularly acute by the time of the Bali Conference. By the time of Bali the discussion had divided into two parts: new institutions to replace the EGTT; and proposals for intellectual property.

The disagreement on the role of the EGTT continued into the next meeting of the SBSTA and into the Bali COP. Despite a significant push from the G77 plus China, no new financing or implementing mechanism was established at Bali.[860] Negotiations on technology transfer were a major stumbling block at Bali and were among the last issues to be resolved.[861]

The issue of intellectual property (IP), and the possibility that it may be a barrier to technology transfer, continued to be a significant part of the debate at Bali and in the post-Bali period.[862] Under the theme of "Enabling environments for technology transfer", the Parties at Bali recommended that all Parties "avoid trade and intellectual property rights policies, or lack thereof, restricting transfer of technology."[863] Common ground on the interpretation of this recommendation, however, was not forthcoming.

The discussions on IP as it relates to technology transfer accelerated when the AWGLCA began meeting in 2008. In Bonn, Parties put forward different views on how IP could be best addressed within the framework on technology transfer.[864] Some

---

[858] Earth Negotiations Bulletin "Summary: 1st Session SBSTA & SBI" Volume 12, Number 23, August 28 - September 01, 1995. Available at: http://www.iisd.ca/vol12/1223000e.html (last visited 15 August 2014).
[859] Id.
[860] See p5, Earth Negotiations Bulletin ""Summary of the Thirteenth Conference of the Parties to the UN Framework Convention on Climate Change and third Meeting Of The Parties To The Kyoto Protocol" Volume 12, No. 354, 3 – 15 December 2007. Available at: http://www.iisd.ca/climate/cop13/ (last visited 15 August 2014).
[861] Id.
[862] See p8, Staley, B Childs et al. "Tick Tech Tick Tech: Coming to Agreement on Technology in the Countdown to Copenhagen". WRI Working Paper, World Resources Institute, Washington DC, June 2009. Earth Negotiations Bulletin "COP13 and COP/MOP 3 Highlights" Volume 12, No. 353, 14 December 2007.
[863] UNFCCC "Recommendations for enhancing the implementation of the framework for meaningful and effective action to enhance the implementation of Article 4, paragraph 5, of the Convention", in "Development and transfer of technologies under the Subsidiary Body for Scientific and Technological Advice", Decision 3/CP.13, UN FCCC, 13th Sess., U.N. Doc FCCC/CP/2007/6/Add.1 at Annex 1, subpara. 12(b).
[864] Para. 48, UNFCCC "Summary of views expressed during the first session of the Ad Hoc Working Group on Long-term Cooperative Action under the Convention on the development of the two-year work programme that was mandated under paragraph 7 of the Bali Action Plan: Note by the Chair", Ad Hoc

Parties also suggested that a working group be established to "review the barriers in trade policies and agreements, including the lack of a special intellectual property rights (IPRs) regime for climate-friendly technologies and inappropriate use of trade-related financing policies of multilateral financial institutions, with special consideration being given to supporting positive sustainable development aims"[865] which did not occur.

In 2008 a key development was a proposal from the G77 plus China for a comprehensive technology transfer mechanism under the Convention, submitted on the last day of the August 2008 meeting in Accra, Ghana.[866] It made two key proposals: a centralized implementation body within the UNFCCC with sub-bodies responsible: for creating implementation strategies, providing technical expertise, measuring and verifying technology financing and transfer; and a Multilateral Climate Technology Fund under the UNFCCC. This was a distillation of previous proposals along with some more detail on Technology Action Plans and what activities would be covered under the fund. The proposal made no mention of intellectual property. Over the course of negotiations in 2008 and in 2009 leading up to Cancun in 2010, the G77 text was further elaborated and included into the formal negotiating text. At COP 15 in Copenhagen in 2009, states reached no agreements on draft decisions on technology transfer that were put forward by the AWGLCA.[867] That decision contained bracketed language on intellectual property in paragraph 6(f) on purchasing of licenses and other IP issues[868], paragraph 10(j), on the mandate of the technology mechanism to address IP issues; and a whole section on intellectual property based on the G77 and Bolivia proposals. The COP decided to forward the draft decision into the AWGLCA in 2010 for further negotiations resulting in the text that was put forward in August 2010 in preparation for the October 2010 Tianjin meeting, and which was further elaborated in that meeting and forwarded to the Conference of the Parties (COP) in Cancun.

Working Group on Long-term Cooperative Action under the Convention, 2nd Sess. Bonn, 2-12 June 2008, U.N. Doc. FCCC/AWHLCA/2008/6.
[865] Subpara. 22(f), UNFCCC "Synthesis of views on elements for the terms of reference for the review and assessment of the effectiveness of the implementation of Article 4, paragraphs 1(c) and 5, of the Convention: Note by the secretariat", Subsidiary Body for Implementation, 28th Sess., Bonn, 4-13 June 2008, U.N. Doc. FCCC/SBI/2008/7, 20 May 2008.
[866] Earth Negotiations Bulletin "AWG-LCA 3 AND AWG-KP 6 Highlights" Volume 12, No. 382, 27 August 2008.
[867] "Draft decision -/CP.15. Enhanced action on technology development and transfer" in Annex 1 to Report of the Ad Hoc Working Group on Long-term Cooperative Action under the Convention on its eighth session, held in Copenhagen from 7 to 15 December 2009, FCCC/AWGLCA/2009/17 (2010).
[868] para 6, Id.

The 2010 AWGLCA negotiating text [869] reflects the importance of IP to developing countries, both substantively and as a bargaining chip. The main text on IP stated two options:

> [Intellectual Property Rights
> 13.
> *Option 1:*
> No reference to Intellectual Property Rights in the text
>
> *Option 2:*
> Decides that:
> Any international agreement on intellectual property shall not be interpreted or implemented in a manner that limits or prevents any Party from taking any measures to address adaptation or mitigation of climate change, in particular the development and enhancement of endogenous capacities and technologies of developing countries and transfer of, and access to, environmentally sound technologies and know-how;
>
> Specific and urgent measures shall be taken and mechanisms developed to remove barriers to the development and transfer of technologies arising from intellectual property rights protection, in particular:
>
> (a) Creation of a Global Technology Intellectual Property Rights Pool for Climate Change that promotes and ensures access to intellectual property protected technologies and the associated know-how to developing countries on non-exclusive royalty-free terms;
>
> (b) Take steps to ensure sharing of publicly funded technologies and related know-how, including by making the technologies and know-how available in the public domain in a manner that promotes transfer of and/or access to environmentally sound technology and know-how to developing countries on royalty-free terms;
>
> Parties shall take all necessary steps in all relevant forums to exclude from Intellectual Property Rights protection, and revoke any such existing intellectual property right protection in developing countries and least developed countries on environmentally sound technologies to adapt to and mitigate climate change, including those developed through funding by

---

[869] UNFCCC "Negotiating Text" FCCC/AWGLCA/2010/14, 13 August 2010 ; p34, UNFCCC "In-session draft texts and notes by the facilitators prepared at the twelfth session of the Ad Hoc Working Group on Long-term Cooperative Action under the Convention" FCCC/AWGLCA/2010/INF.1, 29 October 2010.

governments or international agencies and those involving use of genetic resources that are used for adaptation and mitigation of climate change;

Developing countries have the right to make use of the full flexibilities contained in the Trade Related Aspects of Intellectual Property Rights agreement, including compulsory licensing;

The Technology Executive Committee shall recommend to the Conference of the Parties international actions to support the removal of barriers to technology development and transfer, including those arising from intellectual property rights.];

The text reflects a fundamental tension between the developed countries, especially the US, EU and Japan, on one hand, and developing countries, largely in the G77 plus China grouping on the other. The developed countries generally supported Option 1, that there should be no negotiation of IP issues in the UNFCCC and that there is no need to, given what they believe to be the lack of any empirical evidence that IP poses a problem for the majority of developing countries.[870] Developing countries, particularly within the G77 plus China grouping, supported Option 2 believing that to ensure transfer and access to climate technologies, the international IP system must be re-interpreted, reformed or fundamentally altered. The text in option 2 reflects that range of opinion from the mainstream elements of paragraph 2 (patent pools, access to publicly funded technologies) to the more radical proposals for patent exclusions in the third paragraph.

There is clearly some sense in which the lack of trust around IP issues between developed countries and developing countries that has been embodied in the history of discussions UNFCCC created an impasse. The sense of necessary good faith to begin having negotiations about the issue was and continues, to be, lacking. However, that good faith was more apparent on the institutional track.

The Cancun Agreements flowing from the 16th Conference of the Parties established a Green Climate Fund as an operating entity of the Convention[871] and developed countries committed to providing 100 billion US dollars per year by 2020 to meet the mitigation and adaptation needs of developing countries.[872] The Cancun Agreements also decided on the establishment of a Technology Mechanism consisting of a Technology Executive Committee (TEC) and a Climate Technology Centre and Network (CTC&N), a development with its roots in the G77 proposal from Accra in

---

[870] See e.g. Copenhagen Economics and the IPR Company "Are IPR and Barrier to the transfer of Climate Change Technology?" Study Commissioned by European Commission DG Trade, January 2009.
[871] Para 102, Decision 1/CP.16, The Cancun Agreements: Outcome of the work of the Ad Hoc Working Group on Long-term Cooperative Action under the Convention FCCC/CP/2010/7/Add.1 (2010).
[872] Para 98, Id.

2008. The TEC is mandated to recommend "actions to address the barriers to technology development and transfer in order to enable enhanced action on mitigation and adaptation" but makes no mention of intellectual property.[873] The post-Cancun negotiations saw the issue of intellectual property fall off the table and the focus of discussions move to the organization and institutional linkages for the Technology Mechanism. At the sessions of the AWGLCA held in April 2011 in Bangkok and in Bonn in June 2011, the negotiating text from Tianjin remained the official one with no alterations on the language on intellectual property.[874] However, by the end of the third and fourth part of the resumed 14th session of the AWGLCA in October 2011 in Panama, and in December in Durban, the document put forward by the Chair as a draft decision of the AWGLCA to the COP[875], on his own authority, did not contain any language relating to intellectual property and focused almost exclusively on issues relating to the Technology Executive Committee and the Climate Technology Centre and Network. This appears to have occurred due to the inability of the AWGLCA to forward an official decision to the COP, largely due to the objections of Bolivia.[876] The language on Intellectual property was relegated to an in-session conference paper[877], with language stating:

Intellectual property issues in relation to technology

66. Consistent with the principles of the Convention and to enable meaningful mitigation and adaptation actions in developing countries, the flexibilities of the international regime of intellectual property as articulated by the Agreement on Trade-Related Aspects of Intellectual Property Rights may be used to the fullest extent by developing country Parties to address adaptation or mitigation of climate change, in order to enable them to create a sound and viable technological base; accordingly, consistent with the Agreement on Trade-Related Aspects of Intellectual Property Rights, each Party retains its right to grant compulsory licences and the freedom to determine the grounds upon which such licences are granted; specific and urgent measures shall be taken by developed country Parties to enhance the development and transfer

---

[873] Para 121(e), Id.
[874] Report of the Ad Hoc Working Group on Long-term Cooperative Action under the Convention on the first and second parts of its fourteenth session, held in Bangkok from 5 to 8 April 2011, and Bonn from 7 to 17 June 2011 FCCC/AWGLCA/2011/9 (2011)
[875] Outcome of the work of the Ad Hoc Working Group on Long-term Cooperative Action under the Convention to be presented to the Conference of the Parties for adoption at its seventeenth session - Draft conclusions proposed by the Chair, FCCC/AWGLCA/2011/L.4 (2011).
[876] para. 48, Report of the Ad Hoc Working Group on Long-term Cooperative Action under the Convention on the third and fourth parts of its fourteenth session, held in Panama City from 1 to 7 October 2011, and Durban from 29 November to 10 December 2011, FCCC/AWGLCA/2011/14 (2011).
[877] p11, Work undertaken in the informal groups in the preparation of a comprehensive and balanced outcome to be presented to the Conference of the Parties for adoption at its seventeenth session - Note by the Chair, FCCC/AWGLCA/2011/CRP.39 (2011).

of technologies at different stages of the technology cycle covered by intellectual property rights to developing country Parties;

67. The removal of all obstacles, including intellectual property rights and patents on climate-related technologies to ensure the transfer of technology to developing countries.

This paper serves only as a reference for the decision made in Durban but does not appear to serve as a negotiating text for the post-Durban period.[878]

The status of the 2010 AWGLCA negotiating text which contained language on intellectual property remains unclear, especially in light of the agreements in Durban. It is still nominally on the table but when the Ad Hoc Working Group on the Durban Platform for Enhanced Action (ADP) replaced the AWGLCA at the end of 2012,[879] unfinished agenda items, such as intellectual property, did not explicitly make their way onto the agenda of the ADP.

The details of what the Technology Mechanism should do were further elaborated at COP 17 in Durban. The terms of reference for the CTC&N were outlined and a process established for selection of the CTC&N host.[880] The Green Climate Fund was launched, but nothing was mentioned in terms of whether or not it would fund direct purchase of patents or licensing thereof. However, the Fund is mandated to provide financial support for technology development and transfer (defined as technology research, development, demonstration, deployment and diffusion) including especially for carbon capture and storage.[881] This is limited to the full and agreed "incremental costs'. It remains to be seen what definition of incremental costs will be applied by the GCF in its operation and whether it will use the definitions developed under the Montreal Protocol, by the Clean Technology Fund or that used by the GEF.

---

[878] p2, Outcome of the work of the Ad Hoc Working Group on Long-term Cooperative Action under the Convention to be presented to the Conference of the Parties for adoption at its seventeenth session - Draft conclusions proposed by the Chair, FCCC/AWGLCA/2011/L.4 (2011).
[879] para. 1, Decision 1/CP.17, Establishment of an Ad Hoc Working Group on the Durban Platform for Enhanced Action, in Report of the Conference of the Parties on its seventeenth session, held in Durban from 28 November to11 December 2011 – Addendum Part Two: Action taken by the Conference of the Parties at its seventeenth session, FCCC/CP/2011/9/Add.1 (2012).
[880] paras. 133, 136, Decision 2/CP.17, Outcome of the work of the Ad Hoc Working Group on Long-term Cooperative Action under the Convention, in Report of the Conference of the Parties on its seventeenth session, held in Durban from 28 November to11 December 2011 – Addendum Part Two: Action taken by the Conference of the Parties at its seventeenth session, FCCC/CP/2011/9/Add.1 (2012).
[881] Para 135, Annex to Decision 3/CP.17, Launching the Green Climate Fund, in Report of the Conference of the Parties on its seventeenth session, held in Durban from 28 November to11 December 2011 – Addendum Part Two: Action taken by the Conference of the Parties at its seventeenth session, FCCC/CP/2011/9/Add.1 (2012).

Most importantly the modalities for the Technology Executive Committee were further elaborated at Durban. The TEC may make policy recommendations to the COP to address barriers to technology development and transfer.[882] The text and language on intellectual property has dropped off the table and no longer appears as part of any decision or negotiating text in the post-Cancun period. However, intellectual property has been taken up in the TEC as part of the enabling environment framework and included in a series of thematic dialogues.[883] In the discussion on the agenda for the ADP, several countries argued that intellectual property needs to be a part of the negotiations.[884] However, intellectual property has yet to reappear on the ADP agenda as of writing.

More activity has taken place on the TEC and CTC&N. A host for the CTC&N was chosen at COP 18: a consortium led by UNEP.[885] The Advisory Board of the TM was established and began operating although modalities for interaction with the TEC and the CTC&N remain ambiguous. The CTC&N is the main structure in the UNFCCC for assisting developing countries with technology transfer. However, it is important to note that the mandate of both institutions remains facilitative and that they have no mandate to actually take an active role in transactions or direct funding of technology transfer. The CTC&N can carry out significant advisory work on policies and measures for developing countries to adopt, as well as assist in constructing projects and programmes, and in setting up collaborations. However, funding for all these plans, policies and measures will still have to be sought from either the Green Climate Fund directly or other financial sources and it remains unclear at this stage whether the CTC&N views itself as being in a position to assist countries in constructing applications for funding of programs and projects it has helped countries design. The 3 year work programme for the CTC&N approved by the Advisory Board in September 2013[886], appears to be primarily focused on information activities and advisory services on a traditional technical assistance model. It is funded through donor funds rather than any regular, predictable source. It receives no funds from the GCF for its

---

[882] Para 6(a), Annex to Decision 4/CP.17, Technology Executive Committee – modalities and procedures, in Report of the Conference of the Parties on its seventeenth session, held in Durban from 28 November to11 December 2011 – Addendum Part Two: Action taken by the Conference of the Parties at its seventeenth session, FCCC/CP/2011/9/Add.1 (2012).
[883] UNFCCC "Thematic Dialogue on Enabling Environments" Technology Executive Committee, Bangkok, Thailand, from 6-8 September 2012.
[884] See p6, Earth Negotiations Bulletin "Summary of the Bangkok Climate Talks: 30 August – 5 September 2012" Vol. 12 No. 555, 8 September 2012.
[885] (http://www.unep.org/climatechange/CTC&N/) (last visited 15 August 2014).
[886] UNFCCC "Draft Programme of Work: Climate Technology Centre and Network" September 2013. Available at: http://www.unep.org/climatechange/CTC&N/Portals/50212/Documents/PDF/CTC&N%20Programme%20of%20Work.pdf (last visited 15 August 2014).

operations and provides no direct funds to developing countries to implement their projects and programmes. There appear to be no plans at this stage to assist developing countries in applying for funds for implementation from the GCF or other funders. It does not provide any facilitative mechanisms such as platforms for matching sellers and buyers, no platforms for licensing or exchange. In addition, to the extent that the CTC&N is providing policy advice on issues such as how to encourage innovation and transfer into climate technologies, it is unclear on what empirical or ideological basis they would be doing so. Despite the hard-won effort to establish an implementation mechanism within the UNFCCC for technology transfer, the existing programme of work of the Technology Mechanism remains mired in information and advisory activities with no direct link to funding for activities identified and planned by developing countries. What the CTC&N will deliver is knowledge and information and assistance in formulating policies and measures but none in implementing them. This is both something built into the structure of the CTC&N but also an indication of how cautiously it is approaching the boundaries of its mandate. However, the CTC&N presents a real opportunity and platform for action on technology transfer and in Chapter 9, I outline some of the ways in which it may be able to improve on prior mechanisms to address their weaknesses.

VI. CONCLUSION

It is this pattern of experiences related to three core issues: lack of financing for existing mechanisms; structural deficits in mechanisms such as the CDM, and a lack of implementation mechanisms within the UNFCCC that has prompted developing countries to pursue the option of unilateral measures. To a significant extent, were developed countries to provide all the funding necessary for developing countries to access and purchase hardware and knowledge, and be able to adopt and adapt the technologies, there would be somewhat less to discuss in the realm of intellectual property. However, it is precisely because developing countries have sought to exercise some kind of unilateral measures that the issue of whether the UNFCCC should address intellectual property has arisen. There are two main issues: claims by developed countries that they can do little to influence the behaviour of technology holders in their countries; developing country claims that intellectual property holders are unable or unwilling to transfer best available and/or appropriate technologies. This is what has raised the salience of the intellectual property to issue to such a level that it remains one of the most contentious elements in negotiations and may serve as a barrier to persuading developing countries to take on emissions reduction obligations.

While there is little likelihood that positions on intellectual property will shift significantly in the near term, contributions from empirical and legal analyses may help to clarify discussions. It is more important, now more than ever, to have a clearer sense, not just of the actual distribution and future distribution of patents and trade secrets, but perhaps more importantly, what legal room may actually exist for parties to take action, if and when they recognize that intellectual property problems arise. Where a proper legal analysis shows that there does actually exist sufficient ability and room for member states to take action to address IP-related barriers, commensurate with UNFCCC principles of historical responsibility and common but differentiated responsibilities, the need for action at the UNFCCC and other venues would be obviated. Were the opposite to be found, then there would be significant justification for some action to be taken at the UNFCCC and for a new approach to the relationship between the UNFCCCC and other IP-related regimes. In the next Chapter, I identify the intellectual property interventions that countries may wish to take as a basis for the barrier analysis in Chapter 6.

Chapter 5
Identifying the Range of Intellectual Property Policy Interventions

I. INTRODUCTION

The purpose of this chapter is to create a list of the types of interventions relating to intellectual property that countries have taken, and are taking, to ensure technology transfer. These measures will each be examined for their availability under the TRIPS Agreement in Chapter 6. As this exercise proceeds, it is important to note that the aim of the examination is to determine the policy space available to countries to address intellectual property issues if and when they arise. Chapter 3 of this thesis addressed the data on the extent to which patent and licensing problems exist and pointed to several structural reasons why there is indeed such a likelihood, even in the absence of solid empirical data one way or the other. Information on both the empirical and the capacity questions is necessary to determine the necessity and the scale of UNFCCC action to address intellectual property.

The debate on the relationship between intellectual property and technology transfer beyond the confines of climate technologies is both long-running and freighted with ideological baggage. It has also generally been conducted in the context of political fights such as the North – South struggle over proper policies to ensure economic development. This has tended to drown out the few areas of consensus and agreement as to the mechanisms and the data on the determinants of technology transfer and the role of intellectual property. However, the paucity of data and certainty on how well intellectual property works as a mechanism for generating innovation, for enabling cross-border exchange in technology, and for contributing to development has also made it difficult to build a coherent picture of the appropriate set of policies that countries should follow to ensure economic development through technology development and diffusion. This chapter will not attempt to answer that question in full, but will review the existing literature to point to areas of consensus that are relevant to technology transfer of climate technologies, areas where there is little consensus, and try to extract from the existing empirical work, the set of interventions that have been used to encourage technology transfer and move up the technology value chain.

The first part of this chapter will outline some of the discussion about the role that intellectual property plays in technology transfer. It will introduce some of the basic concepts and discuss some of the tools used to structure markets in technology products and knowledge. This will be followed by an examination of the historical experience of other economies in moving up the technology value chain. Out of this, I will identify the types of measures that have historically been used to encourage or regulate technology transfer spillovers and use as a basis for analysis in Chapter 6.

II. INTELLECTUAL PROPERTY BEYOND THE BORDER

In the case of climate change, we are primarily concerned with patents, as the primary form of IP that implicates technology transfer. At the core, patents are designed as an incentive system to encourage the production and dissemination of new knowledge and information. The primary incentive is to encourage the translation of research into technological products, and to have the methods of producing those products, and the products themselves diffused. The traditional and consensus explanation is that, to do so, it has proven necessary to provide limited periods of exclusivity to inventors so that, rather than keep their inventions secret, they are willing to produce and share them through commercial activities such as sales and licensing.[887]

Intellectual property is a solution to the problem of the production of public goods. The aim is to provide sufficient incentive for private sector actors to invest in the generation of new knowledge and products, but to ensure that there is sufficient spill-over of knowledge during the life-time of the protection provided and beyond.[888] This is the classic structure underlying the patent system which provides the strongest potential for exclusivity. Of the existing forms of intellectual property protection, they are designed to provide the least amount of knowledge spillovers during their lifetime. However, because of the strength of the exclusivity provided by patents, they may sometimes have negative effects. For example, patents can create a type of monopoly control through the exclusive rights they confer on the owners of patented technology or knowledge. In this sense they may reduce competition, maintaining high prices for a product above marginal cost of production as the patent owner has little incentive to lower the price of the technology or make it more competitive. In addition, they can impose an absolute barrier to entry into both the technology and product market by refusing to allow potential competitors access to the technology. At this basic level, intellectual property policy is a trade-off between present (static) anti-competitive costs and the generation of future technologies (dynamic cost).

---

[887] See p9, Maskus, K & J Reichman (eds.) *International Public Goods and Transfer of Technology under a Globalized Intellectual Property Regime*, (Cambridge: Cambridge University Press, 2005).
[888] See p8, Id.

Achieving a balance between static and dynamic efficiency is complex enough in a purely domestic market. The problem in a global market is that there may be very large international spill-overs.[889] In a system with low international trade in products and services, such spill-overs pose little problem as they will tend to equalize over time. If all countries provide protection for their own citizens but no protection for non-citizens, all countries will benefit from spill-overs from other countries, and innovators can simply block products from other countries at the border. However, in a system with a significant amount of international trade (both bilateral and multilateral), the ability to gain protection in multiple markets becomes increasingly important. In a system where there are asymmetries in innovative capacity and thus the number and distribution of rightholders, there is an incentive for countries that are net importers of knowledge and technologies to provide little or no protection for rightholders from other countries.[890] Countries that are net exporters have a strong incentive to seek protection in other countries and, at the very least, to be treated at the same level as nationals. This principle of national treatment is a fundamental element of international treaties on intellectual property.[891] It requires national level policies on spillovers that treat both domestic and foreign rightholders equally, but does not require that all countries have the same policies on how and when to take action to increase or reduce the level of spillovers into their domestic market. Of course, existing asymmetries in innovative capacity suggest that those countries that are net importers may have policies more focused on ensuring greater spill-overs as most of the rightholders in their economies will be foreign rightholders in many cases. This may be the strategy that was followed by so-called 'imitator' economies such as Japan and South Korea in the pre-WTO era, and now China in the post-WTO era.

Net exporter countries have an incentive to seek not just national treatment, but intellectual property protection on a par with that provided to firms in their home markets, especially with respect to policies that increase spillovers and enable faster learning by potential competitors. This dynamic between net exporter countries and net importer countries results in actions taken by some countries that reduce or negatively affect the scope and exercise of intellectual property rights, as part of a broader industrial policy framework. These actions can be targeted at specific technologies and sectors, or can sometimes be economy-wide. They can be targeted at products, or can be targeted at the knowledge itself.

---

[889] See p9, Maskus, K & J Reichman (eds.) *International Public Goods and Transfer of Technology under a Globalized Intellectual Property Regime*, (Cambridge: Cambridge University Press, 2005).
[890] See p284, Maskus, K E and J H. Reichman, "The Globalization of Private Knowledge Goods and the Privatization of Global Public Goods" 7 Journal of International Economic Law 279 (2004).
[891] See e.g. Article 2 of the Paris Convention for the Protection of Industrial Property; Article 3 of the TRIPS Agreement.

III. MARKET FAILURES IN INTERNATIONAL TECHNOLOGY TRANSFER AND TECHNOLOGY TRANSFER INTERVENTIONS

Interventions aimed at ensuring technology transfer rely on two things; a particular understanding of the ways in which markets can fail to provide technology transfer; the specific vectors through which technology transfer occurs. On the first, there is a normative element that presumes that where the market is functioning, interventions cannot be justified. There is also an empirical element in determining when such market failures occur. On the second, the vectors for technology transfer are largely defined in formal market-based ways, but in a competitive market there are also many informal ways that may not be remunerated.

Maskus points to two categories of market failures associated with international technology transfer: ones that are built into the structure of technology markets, and those that are the result of factors such as policy and differential factor endowments e.g. absorptive capacity or purchasing power. [892] He argues that interventions need only occur where there are market failures.[893] In this regard, this thesis agrees that the trigger for action is indeed market failure. Where I differ is in what constitutes a market failure. Whereas Maskus may prefer an approach that focuses on whether certain procedural frameworks exist to enable markets to operate, I argue that the focus should be on outcomes defined by supply and demand: is there sufficient supply at the level of the market in technology or knowledge, at a price that will enable the majority of participants in the market to adopt technologies to meet the demand in the product market for goods and services that are reliant on such technologies? In addition, while much of Maskus' argument addresses vertical spillovers (up and down the supply chain)[894], a key element of what is needed for the climate change challenge is an increase in horizontal spill-overs to firms that are not in wholly-owned subsidiary, supplier or purchaser relationships to the rightholder and may actually be competitors. In analysing market failures, I would focus as much on the lack of horizontal spillovers as on vertical spillovers.[895] Market failures then fall into two categories: those that are inherent in the structure of the market; those that the market is not capable of addressing (such as horizontal spillovers to more than a single firm). Problems inherent to the market in technologies that affect the scale of private transactions and spillovers include[896]:

- information asymmetries between technology licensors (who are fully cognizant of technology characteristics) and potential licensees (who may

---

[892] p15, Maskus, K E "Encouraging International Technology Transfer" ICTSD Issue Paper No. 7, May 2004.
[893] Id.
[894] Id.
[895] See p20, Saggi, K "International technology transfer to developing countries" Economic Paper 64, Commonwealth Secretariat (2004). Agreeing that the key issues is horizontal spillovers.
[896] p16, Maskus, K E "Encouraging International Technology Transfer" ICTSD Issue Paper No. 7, May 2004.

not have sufficient information to fully evaluate the usefulness of the technology);

- information asymmetries between technology licensors and licensees as to the nature and scope of the market into which the technology is being licensed making it difficult for licensors to assess the market potential, and thus market value and appropriate price of the license;

- tendencies for technology holders to try to increase the natural (rather than just regulatory) excludability of the technology by masking the full nature and scope of the technology[897]: this can occur even where strong IP protection exists, through selective disclosure in patent applications, or maintenance of key process elements as trade secrets; this impedes normal modes of reverse engineering and imitation in a competitive market

- tendencies to exercise market power to capture elements of product and technology markets upstream and downstream from the technology market in which the patent is held.

The structure of private markets can impede access to public goods in areas such as climate change, public health and food security. In such cases problems with intellectual property manifest as:

- Tendencies for technology licensees to insist on exclusive licenses;
- Tendencies for licensors to insist on transferring only to wholly-owned subsidiaries or majority controlled joint ventures;
- Anticompetitive behaviour that includes:
    o Restrictive licensing terms on geographical scope;
    o Restrictive licensing terms on exports;
    o Engaging in tied sales;
    o Attempt to capture upstream and downstream markets;
    o Requiring licensees who further develop the technology to grant ownership or, no-cost exclusive or non-exclusive licenses on those newly developed technologies. These are called grant-back provisions;
    o Engaging in collusion; e.g. certain kinds of patent pools;
    o Predatory pricing and other behaviour aimed at pushing out local market actors;
    o Refusals to license.

---

[897] p15, Id.

These market failures all require interventions from regulators to ensure access to technologies, but such interventions need to be targeted. The mechanism by which the problems are manifested is crucial. The vector for technology transfer determines the scope, applicability and effectiveness of the policy intervention that a country may wish to take. The following section will discuss the role of intellectual property and identify the set of regulatory tools that have historically been used by countries to try and encourage spillovers and technology transfer.

IV. THE ROLE OF INTELLECTUAL PROPERTY PROTECTION IN THE VECTORS FOR INTERNATIONAL TECHNOLOGY TRANSFER

The broader issue of determinants of FDI is only relevant to this discussion where we accept that FDI serves as an accurate proxy for measuring international technology transfer. This may not be a safe assumption and especially in the context of regulatory structures explicitly aimed at restricting technology spillovers related to FDI, it may actually be erroneous. Caution should be exercised in evaluating studies and data using FDI as a proxy for technology transfer. However, in the context of examining the role that intellectual property protection plays, there may nevertheless be useful elements in that broader discussion of the determinants of international technology transfer. An additional caveat, addressed in Chapter 1, is that a distinction needs to be made between transfers of technological goods and transfers of knowledge. While these both contribute to technological and economic development, for our purposes the larger and more important part is transfer of knowledge if the aim is to enable firms in all sectors to shift their production processes. This division is not always clear in the studies on determinants of technology transfer, resulting in the conflation of transfers of goods with transfer of knowledge. Nevertheless, some lessons can be drawn from the literature:

- Increased trade in technological goods can lead to spillovers in learning as well as enabling reverse engineering.[898] However, this requires a significant learning capacity in firms and existing investment in R&D.[899] There is evidence from models and some empirical work that higher IP protection on average increases trade, but there is no noticeable impact on trade in high technology goods.[900] Ivus points to a possible reversal of causation

---

[898] p17, Maskus, K E "Encouraging International Technology Transfer" ICTSD Issue Paper No. 7, May 2004.
[899] p33, Id.
[900] p35, Fink, C and C Primo Braga, "How Stronger protection of Intellectual Property Rights affects Trade" in Maskus, K & C Fink (eds.) *Intellectual Property and Development: Lessons from Recent Economic Research* (Washington D.C.: World Bank, 2005). See also Ivus, O, "Do Stronger Intellectual Property Rights Raise High-Tech Exports to the Developing World?" No 2008-27, Working Papers, Department of Economics, University of Calgary. Available at: http://EconPapers.repec.org/RePEc:clg:wpaper:2008-27 (last visited 15 August 2014).

suggesting that opening up to trade leads to higher intellectual property protection rather than the other way around.[901] This may be especially true for the pre-TRIPS period, but less likely for the post-TRIPS period. However even in the post-TRIPS period, causation may be difficult to pull out as signatories to the TRIPS Agreement simultaneously opened up their trade with other countries due to the single undertaking of the broader WTO Agreement.

- As discussed above, given the appropriate regulatory environment, FDI may also generate significant spillovers, both through formal mechanisms (licensing and actual transfer to vertically integrated subsidiaries) and informal mechanisms.[902] The evidence from literature is mixed,[903] but leans to at least a positive effect for those countries with significant learning capacity in firms and ongoing investment in R&D. This is especially true for vertical spillovers rather than horizontal for which the evidence is far more mixed.[904] However, increasing IPR protection does not seem to be linked to significant short term increases in FDI.[905]

- Licensing can be a significant channel for technology transfer, provided there is sufficient absorptive capacity and capital in the licensee and surrounding firms.[906] However, the more the licensor is concerned that proprietary knowledge may leak, the less likely they are to engage in arms-length transactions and the more likely they are to license only to wholly owned subsidiaries or to joint venture structures over which they have significant control.[907] They may either refuse to license into the market or only license older technologies. Of course, the level of intellectual property protection also plays a role in a licensor's assessment of likely leakage of proprietary technologies. Theoretically, increased patent protection should make arm's length licensing to unaffiliated firms more likely.[908]

---

[901] See p3, Ivus, O.
[902] p8, Fink, C and K Maskus "Why we study Intellectual Property Rights and what we have learned" in Maskus, K & C Fink (eds.) *Intellectual Property and Development: Lessons from Recent Economic Research* (Washington D.C.: World Bank, 2005).
[903] p18, Maskus, K E "Encouraging International Technology Transfer" ICTSD Issue Paper No. 7, May 2004.
[904] Id.
[905] p8, Fink, C and K Maskus "Why we study Intellectual Property Rights and what we have learned"
[906] p20, Maskus, K E "Encouraging International Technology Transfer"
[907] Id.
[908] p114, Yang, G and K Maskus "Intellectual Property Rights and Licensing: an Econometric Investigation" in Maskus, K & C Fink (eds.) *Intellectual Property and Development: Lessons from Recent Economic Research* (Washington D.C.: World Bank, 2005). See also Saggi, K "International technology transfer to developing countries" Economic Paper 64, Commonwealth Secretariat (2004).

- Intellectual property provides a way to reduce the uncertainty and transaction costs associated with sharing of knowledge across borders and allows both providers and recipients to have secure predictable information about the nature and costs of the technology which is the subject of the exchange.[909] Intellectual property also enables the capture of a larger proportion of the spill-overs that would otherwise occur into an economy due to licensing, FDI, or trade, allowing and encouraging a firm to engage in transactions into an economy.[910] Of course, where the aim of policies is to maximize such spill-overs, there is a conflict between the desires of the foreign firm and those of the industrial policy of the domestic government. This suggests the importance of appropriate regulatory structures to manage and encourage spillovers and to prevent anticompetitive behaviour.[911]

The evidence for whether higher intellectual property protection increases the likelihood of technology transfer remains unclear.[912] At best, what can be said is that, where intellectual property is initially low and protection and enforcement increased, there is evidence that increased FDI takes place, especially in middle-income countries.[913] These findings do not seem to be replicated for low income countries, probably in large part due to the fact that they present largely uninteresting markets for rightholders, except for perhaps in the realm of pharmaceuticals and agriculture. However, as Maskus points out, there are also studies that have found little or no correlation between levels of patent protection and inward FDI even for upper middle income countries.[914] There does however appear to be a positive link between levels of IP protection and the complexity and level of technology involved in FDI or licensing: low levels of IP protection limit the transfer of high or best available technology.[915] For countries at a low level on the technology value chain, still moving from imitation to innovation, this may not necessarily be a bad thing as the learning basis for building innovative capacity will need to be built on earlier more mature technologies before adoption of newer, more complex ones.

---

[909] p14, Maskus, K "Differentiated Intellectual Property Regimes for Environmental and Climate Technologies", OECD Environment Working Papers, No. 17, OECD Publishing 2010.
[910] Id.
[911] p60, Maskus, K "The Role of Intellectual Property Rights in Encouraging Foreign Direct Investment and Technology Transfer" in Maskus, K & C Fink (eds.) *Intellectual Property and Development: Lessons from Recent Economic Research* (Washington D.C.: World Bank, 2005).
[912] See p77, Saggi, K. "International technology transfer to developing countries" Economic Paper 64, Commonwealth Secretariat (2004).
[913] p17, Maskus, K E "Encouraging International Technology Transfer" ICTSD Issue Paper No. 7, May 2004.
[914] See p24, Id. *citing* Primo Braga, C A and C Fink, "The Relationship between Intellectual Property Rights and Foreign Direct Investment," 9 Duke Journal of Comparative and International Law 163 (1998).
[915] p65, Maskus, K "The Role of Intellectual Property Rights in Encouraging Foreign Direct Investment and Technology Transfer"

The studies and data do not tell us a significant amount about the quality of that FDI, i.e. whether it results in best available technologies being transferred, the rate and scale of spill-overs, and whether the transfers are vertical (into directly owned subsidiaries) into joint ventures or horizontal (into independent entities). The evidence suggests that it is the certainty of contract enforcement and IP enforcement rather than the strength of IP protection that seems to be determinative of decisions to engage in technology related market transactions.[916]

The data on FDI and capital goods doesn't tell us whether such transfers were to vertically integrated subsidiaries or joint ventures or to genuine third parties, and what the scope and speed of such transfers were, but the implication is clear. Reforms that, at the very least, ensure compliance with the TRIPS Agreement provide an incentive to outside companies to carry out FDI and sell capital and other technological goods, as well as license, into middle income countries. This may also encourage a shift from FDI to licensing, although it is not clear whether this increases arm's length transactions.[917] The data also shows however that there is little or no positive effect for lower income or least developing countries, suggesting, that while intellectual property is a factor, it acts in conjunction with other market factors such as: purchasing power; market size; and domestic absorptive capacity.[918] If intellectual property protection was a key driver of FDI, then those countries that increased their intellectual property protection the most between 1990 and 1995 (largely sub-Saharan Africa) would have seen the largest relative increase in FDI share, which was not the case. In fact the region saw a significant drop in the share of FDI[919], losing out especially to countries like China, India and Brazil. In addition, as Ivus points out, many developing countries, former colonies of Britain and France, already had relatively high protection of intellectual property due to their colonial legacy. She notes that, by the Ginarte-Park index[920], this group increased their level of protection by 17% between 1960 and 1990.[921] It was only in the period after 1990 that they were outpaced by developed and emerging economies in their level of protection.

The key is reliable, predictable enforcement rather than IP standards *per se*. Nevertheless, the level of intellectual property protection is a major factor in decisions

---

[916] p22, Maskus, K E "Encouraging International Technology Transfer" ICTSD Issue Paper No. 7, May 2004.
[917] p24, Id.
[918] p17, Maskus, K "Differentiated Intellectual Property Regimes for Environmental and Climate Technologies", OECD Environment Working Papers, No. 17, OECD Publishing 2010.
[919] p54, Maskus, K "The Role of Intellectual Property Rights in Encouraging Foreign Direct Investment and Technology Transfer" in Maskus, K & C Fink (eds.) *Intellectual Property and Development: Lessons from Recent Economic Research* (Washington D.C.: World Bank, 2005).
[920] Park, W G "International patent protection: 1960–2005," Research Policy 37: 761–766 (2008).
[921] Ivus, O, "Do Stronger Intellectual Property Rights Raise High-Tech Exports to the Developing World?", No 2008-27, Working Papers, Department of Economics, University of Calgary.

relating to location of R&D facilities.[922] In specific sectors with low imitation thresholds, such as chemicals and pharmaceuticals, levels of IP also influenced FDI decisions, although these determined whether the nature of the FDI was to a direct and wholly owned subsidiary or to an affiliate or joint venture, rather than deterring FDI as a whole.[923]

Looking at licensing, the empirical studies on licensing are few and far between and suffer from lack of access to licensing contracts. The empirical case for a link between patent strength and licensing is mixed at best.[924] A proxy for licensing that is often used is volumes and flows of royalties and other licensing fees. Problematically, it is difficult to determine whether increases in such fees reflect actual increases in the number of transactions or simply reflect the growth in market power, and thus pricing power, that higher intellectual property standards and enforcement provide.[925] Nevertheless, the existing studies suggest a strong positive relationship between the level of intellectual property protection and levels of royalty flows.[926] This however, appears to hold true only where the initial levels of IPR protection were already relatively strong.[927] At least one study found that the effect was strongest regarding licensing to non-affiliates.[928] Another, focusing specifically on the 1995 – 2005 post-TRIPS period found a positive relationship between outward royalty flows and levels of intellectual property protection.[929]

There is also some evidence that stronger patent rights do shift activity from FDI towards licensing, although much of that takes place towards local affiliates rather than horizontally, and is largely limited to countries with significant imitative capacity.[930] Data from a 2006 study done for the World Bank suggests that where countries do indeed strengthen patent rights, there appears to be a corresponding increase in

---

[922] p56, Maskus, K "The Role of Intellectual Property Rights in Encouraging Foreign Direct Investment and Technology Transfer" in Maskus, K & C Fink (eds.) *Intellectual Property and Development: Lessons from Recent Economic Research* (Washington D.C.: World Bank, 2005), Table 3.1 citing IMF Balance of Payments Statistics.
[923] p60, Id.
[924] See p111, Yang, G and K Maskus "Intellectual Property Rights and Licensing: an Econometric Investigation" in Maskus, K & C Fink (eds.) *Intellectual Property and Development: Lessons from Recent Economic Research* (Washington D.C.: World Bank, 2005). See also, p542, Kanwar, S "Intellectual Property Protection and Technology Licensing: The Case of Developing Countries" 55 Journal of Law and Economics 539 No. 3 (2012).
[925] p25, Maskus, K E "Encouraging International Technology Transfer" ICTSD Issue Paper No. 7, May 2004.
[926] Id.
[927] p128, Yang, G and K Maskus "Intellectual Property Rights and Licensing: an Econometric Investigation"
[928] Id.
[929] *See* p543, Kanwar, S.
[930] Smith, P J "How Do Foreign Patent Rights Affect U.S. Exports, Affiliate Sales, and Licenses?" Journal of International Economics 55: 411-440 (2001)

licensing contracts by US firms to developing country firms.[931] This is in line with evidence suggesting a negative relationship between the level of imitative capacity and the willingness to license into a country.[932] There are also findings that suggest that, at least with respect to middle-income countries, strengthening patent protection increases the likelihood of licensing from developed countries.[933] The evidence for such a role in lower middle income and poorer countries appears to be zero. However, it is important to reiterate that none of these studies are able to determine whether royalty increases are a result of the exercise of market power conferred by higher patent protection or are evidence of an actual increase in licensing contracts as such. Even where such an increase in licensing contracts is found to occur, we have no information on the terms of such contracts which may inhibit spillovers beyond the licensee.

Higher patent protection may lead to an increase in the number of patents registered in a country, and where these are published and fully disclosed they form a significant part of the learning environment. There is some evidence that such increases in patent registrations and publications lead to greater technology absorption in those countries where it takes place.[934] This suggests that the disclosure function of the patent system is a key policy lever for enabling technology transfer. However, the studies do not take account of the higher costs and reduced spillovers for imitation that result from higher patent protection making it difficult to generalize an appropriate cost-benefit analysis.[935]

These findings also do not examine the consequences of that licensing, which is how rapidly after such licensing does the technology licensed diffuse into the local economy, at what rate do spill-overs occur and other questions that are key to addressing the climate change challenge. While intellectual property protection and patent protection specifically, is well-suited to encouraging cross-border licensing to one or two firms in an economy, the more pertinent issue is that intellectual property protection simultaneously inhibits the kinds of domestic spill-overs that are required in order to properly address climate change.[936] What this suggests is that the wrong question is being asked. Rather than asking whether licensing into the local economy occurs, the more pertinent question will be whether providing greater intellectual property protection that inhibits spill-overs does anything more than enable licensing to

---

[931] Branstetter, L et al. "Do Stronger Intellectual Property Rights Increase International Technology Transfer? Empirical Evidence from U.S. Firm-Level Data," Quarterly Journal of Economics, vol. 121, 321-349 (2006).
[932] p540, Kanwar, S "Intellectual Property Protection and Technology Licensing: The Case of Developing Countries" 55 Journal of Law and Economics 539 (2012).
[933] Hoekman, B, K E Maskus, and K Saggi, "Transfer of Technology to Developing Countries: Unilateral and Multilateral Policy Options" World Bank Policy Research Working Paper No. 3332. June 1, 2004.
[934] p23, Maskus, K E "Encouraging International Technology Transfer" ICTSD Issue Paper No. 7, May 2004.
[935] p24, Id.
[936] See p77, Saggi, K "International technology transfer to developing countries" Economic Paper 64, Commonwealth Secretariat (2004).

one firm? For our purposes, the key is to find that balance point between providing sufficient IP protection to provide certainty for transactions to take place, but not so much as to inhibit spillovers that occur through imitation, reverse engineering, adaptation, and inter-firm personnel movement. What policies are capable of achieving that balance? If that balance is not possible it may be more useful for countries to seek to access technologies outside of the IP licensing and FDI model. Where firms are willing to license to multiple actors the issue may be relatively easily answered, but where licensing occurs in only a limited fashion, then the problem remains. Even where there is willingness to license, any regulatory response will need to address the issue of information asymmetries between licensors and licensees that can impede the existence and number of transactions.

More difficult to address is whether, across all these studies, a consistent concept of weak (low) or strong (high) levels of intellectual property protection is used, enabling consistent comparability. This has been somewhat addressed by the construction and use of indices of patent strength, such as that constructed by Ginarte-Park.[937] This has been the basis for much of Maskus' analytical work and has proven a useful tool. However, indices such as these can only provide operational definitions, and, from a legal perspective, may not allow us to assess whether or not actions to make compulsory licensing easier, to require greater patent disclosure, or broader exceptions to patent rights would fall into the scope of 'weaker' or a 'weakening' of intellectual property rights. The Ginarte-Park[938] index gives particular weight to membership in international agreements but perhaps a truer measure is that of whether such obligations are actually implemented in national law. For much of the pre-TRIPS era, membership in the Berne Convention or the Paris Convention was not a reliable indicator of whether a country actually had implementing legislation (where the legal system was dualist), and whether that implementing legislation was compliant with its obligations under the treaty. Such a factor can be a misleading indicator of the level of protection provided. It may also create overlapping confusion when one looks at the actual content of national legislation, double counting specific types of provisions that also are required in the international treaties themselves. This may overstate the level of patent strength. In looking at the national legislation, another problem of most indices, but the Ginarte-Park one specifically, is that it focuses on the laws as written [939] and does not characterize how they may actually work as expressed in implementing regulations and case law. A key example here is the exclusion of software from patenting that can be found in the European Patent Convention Article 52(2)(c). While this appears to be an absolute bar, Article 52(3) only excludes such subject matter to the extent that an application refers to the subject matter "as such". This is a crucial proviso because this

---

[937] Park, W G "International patent protection: 1960–2005," Research Policy 37: 761–766 (2008).
[938] Id.
[939] Fink, C "Intellectual Property Rights and US and German International Transactions in Manufacturing Industries" in Maskus, K & C Fink (eds.) *Intellectual Property and Development: Lessons from Recent Economic Research* (Washington D.C.: World Bank, 2005).

has led to the practice within the European Patent Office of patents on software being allowed provided that one can show that it has a "further technical effect." This is embodied in the Guidelines for Examination in the European Patent Office[940] which justifies this by referencing the case law of the Technical Board of Appeals in cases such as T1173/97 (Computer Program product) of 1 July 1998.[941] This case law has meant that a significant amount of software has been patented in the EPC member countries, despite what appears to be an absolute ban in Article 52((2)(c). The strength of the patent law of those countries may be understated by the index. Additionally, the Ginarte and Park index primarily focuses on TRIPS and TRIPS-plus provisions looking particularly at patent terms, subject matter coverage, and a small sample of restrictions (working requirements, compulsory licenses), and the extension of patent protection to product patents. While useful, it is clear that the level of strongest protection lies beyond the TRIPS Agreement. What would be useful would be approaches to the index that compare, not the strength of patent protection but whether there are significant differences between those countries that are TRIPS-compliant with respect to the Index and those that provide protection beyond the TRIPS Agreement. To the extent that this would provide a better assessment of the policy options in a post-TRIPS environment, no studies have addressed this.

The evidence that lower levels of IP protection reduce or impede technology transfer remains empirically weak and there remains significant debate on the issue.[942] This is in part due to the fact that, where imitative capacity exists, firms may benefit from low cost or free access to producing certain technologies, while being able to export to other markets where IP protection for the technology is also low or non-existent. This can generate and contribute to development of further innovative capacity perhaps even to the point that an internal demand for higher protection is required as domestic firms become more innovative and less imitative. The experience of other developmental economies that are now considered emerging or developed may help to shed some light on the policy mix that has historically been successful at moving countries up the value chain.

V. TECHNOLOGY TRANSFER INTERVENTIONS BY NEWLY INDUSTRIALIZING COUNTRIES: A HISTORICAL SURVEY

---

[940] Part G, Chapter II, Section 3.6, European Patent Office "Guidelines for Examination in the European Patent Office" European Patent Office, June 2012. Available at: http://documents.epo.org/projects/babylon/eponetnsf/0/6c9c0ec38c2d48dfc1257a21004930f4/$FILE/guidelines_for_examination_2012_en.pdf (last visited 15 August 2014).
[941] 10 Official Journal of the European Patent Office 609 (1999). Available at: http://archive.epo.org/epo/pubs/oj99/10_99/10_6099.pdf (last visited 15 August 2014).
[942] p22, Maskus, K E "Encouraging International Technology Transfer" ICTSD Issue Paper No. 7, May 2004.

In terms of the existence and usefulness of certain policies, some lessons may be drawn from the historical practices of some emerging and now industrial economies' industrial policies in the pre-TRIPS era such as Japan, China, South Korea, Taiwan, and Singapore. Generally, there is little evidence that many countries moved up the technology value chain with an initially high set of intellectually property standards.[943] There is little dispute that the absorption and development of technology played a crucial part in the growth of Japan and the newly industrializing economies of South-East Asia.[944]

A study by Khan for the UK Commission on Intellectual Property Rights also finds that many now developed countries also used varied mixes of low and high intellectual property protection to move up the technology value chain.[945] In Britain, product patents on chemicals were excluded until 1949 (because of competitiveness concerns regarding Germany) and a compensatory liability regime was in place until 1977 to ensure licenses for agricultural and pharmaceutical products.[946] The early French system, which had an influence on many others, had a patent of importation, allowing patenting of foreign patents already granted elsewhere. [947] It also had a working requirement, which was understood as the industrial use or production of the patented product or process in the domestic economy. Importation was not sufficient to meet the requirement.[948]. The influential German patent system also used several policy levers to ensure technology transfer, such as: product patent exclusions for food, chemicals and pharmaceuticals; pre-grant publication of patents; setting up a utility/petty patent system; and working requirements. [949] In all these countries, including the US, compulsory licenses were a key tool that countries maintained the option of using. The early US system restricted patents to citizens only, before shifting to a system of discriminatory fees and finally to one of national treatment.[950] The early Japanese system emulated the German system closely with a system of utility models, working

---

[943] See p290, Maskus, K E and J H Reichman, "The Globalization of Private Knowledge Goods and the Privatization of Global Public Goods" 7 Journal of International Economic Law 279 (2004).
[944] See p21, Kumar, N "Intellectual Property Rights, Technology and Economic Development: Experiences of Asian Countries" Study paper 1b, for Commission on Intellectual Property Rights *Integrating Intellectual Property Rights and Development Policy* (London: Commission on Intellectual Property Rights 2002), in an overview of the literature.
[945] See Khan, B. Zorina "Intellectual Property and Development: Lessons from American and European History" Study paper 1a, for Commission on Intellectual Property Rights *Integrating Intellectual Property Rights and Development Policy* (London: Commission on Intellectual Property Rights 2002).
[946] See p14, Id.
[947] See p16, Id. This patent of importation, was also found in Spain (see p27).
[948] See p11, Correa, C "Intellectual Property Rights and the Use of Compulsory Licenses: Options for Developing Countries" Working Paper 5, Trade-Related Agenda, Development And Equity (T.R.A.D.E.) Working Papers, South Centre, October 1999.
[949] See p20, Khan, B. Zorina "Intellectual Property and Development: Lessons from American and European History"
[950] See p23, Id.

requirements and exclusion of product patents on food, chemicals and pharmaceuticals (until 1975). [951]

Maskus also points to analyses of Japan's post-war industrialization that suggest, not that Japan had low levels of intellectual property protection per se, but that Japan had very specific policies in place targeted at innovation in small and medium domestic enterprises, while at the same time aimed at ensuring significant diffusion of foreign technology into the domestic market.[952] He argues that this shows that Japan had a complex but deliberate approach to regulating technology flows including:

- a strong focus on utility models for domestic innovators;
- limiting each patent to a single claim (until 1988)[953];
- requiring extensive and early pre-grant publication of patent applications;
- an active pre-grant opposition system;
- active surveillance by regulatory bodies of terms in licensing contracts;
- a working requirement with a three year latency period;[954]

Japan presents a model of strong government led programs aimed at moving up the technology value chain through deliberate market structuring innovation and diffusion strategies.[955] Ajemian notes the active scrutiny that the Ministry of Trade and Industry engaged in by setting up a system of approval and surveillance for all technology projects in Japan, including ordering revision of terms it viewed as too onerous.[956] The success of Japan, partly due to preferential access to the US market, led to a significant mistrust and caution by US technology holders. They became much more aware of the dangers of creating competitors in other countries by engaging in overly permissive out-licensing.[957]

---

[951] See p22, Kumar, N "Intellectual Property Rights, Technology and Economic Development: Experiences of Asian Countries" Study paper 1b, for Commission on Intellectual Property Rights *Integrating Intellectual Property Rights and Development Policy* (London: Commission on Intellectual Property Rights 2002).
[952] p27, Maskus, K E "Encouraging International Technology Transfer" ICTSD Issue Paper No. 7, May 2004.
[953] See p23, Kumar, N "Intellectual Property Rights, Technology and Economic Development: Experiences of Asian Countries" Study paper 1b, for Commission on Intellectual Property Rights *Integrating Intellectual Property Rights and Development Policy* (London: Commission on Intellectual Property Rights 2002).
[954] Id. See p11, Correa, C "Intellectual Property Rights and the Use of Compulsory Licenses: Options for Developing Countries" Working Paper 5, Trade-Related Agenda, Development And Equity (T.R.A.D.E.) Working Papers, South Centre, October 1999.
[955] See Ajemian, C and D Reid "Preventing Global Warming: The United States, China, and Intellectual Property" 115 Business and Society Review 417 (2010)
[956] See p423, Id. citing Johnson, C *MITI and the Japanese Miracle: The Growth of Industrial Policy* (Stanford, CA: Stanford Press, 1982)
[957] See p424, Ajemian, C and D Reid

Kumar notes that over the history of the utility model system in Japan, the majority of grants (up to over 99%, in some studies) were to Japanese applicants. [958] Maskus also notes that much of the strengthening of patent protection that took place in Japan between 1988 and 1993 appears to have largely been driven by foreign firms, pressure from the US and a small but significant group of domestic innovator firms.[959] There was no concomitant growth in Japanese R&D that could explain the shift in levels and scope of patent protection.

Maskus also points to the Korean experience as one where, because of the small market size, and lack of threatening industries, many technologies were available in the public domain in South Korea well into the 1970's and early '80s.[960] This was used by the increasingly concentrated and government assisted industries to build technological capacity first for domestic markets and then for foreign markets where possible. Korea maintained relatively low levels of protection and encouraged firms to imitate, and adapt technologies. It excluded product patent protection for food, chemicals and pharmaceuticals (until 1987)[961] and has a utility model system that has historically granted over 90% of models to nationals.[962] As Korea shifted from labour intensive production and up the value chain, the necessity to access more technology and the development of large concentrated export oriented conglomerates (the so-called 'chaebols'), Korean firms ran into difficulties exporting into US and European markets. In addition, due to their capacity to imitate and innovate, they had become competitors to many firms in developed countries, increasing the reluctance of foreign firms to partner or license without firmer assurance that proprietary knowledge would not be misappropriated or leaked. Korea also strengthened its patent and IP system between 1988 and 1993, in part due to threats of trade sanctions.[963] In the case of Korea, there was a rapid increase in investment in R&D and related productivity following the strengthening of the IP system[964], potentially related to the large export orientation of the chaebols. Kim et al. also point to the example of Korea, as well as empirical work that they carried out to argue that a utility model system is more appropriate for developing countries in contrast to developed countries where patents play a stronger role in generating economic development.[965] Thus they build basic capability before they move onto more complex research. These countries, along with Taiwan did not

---

[958] See p22, Kumar, N "Intellectual Property Rights, Technology and Economic Development: Experiences of Asian Countries"
[959] p27, Maskus, K E "Encouraging International Technology Transfer" ICTSD Issue Paper No. 7, May 2004.
[960] Id.
[961] See p24, Kumar, N "Intellectual Property Rights, Technology and Economic Development: Experiences of Asian Countries"
[962] Id.
[963] p27, Maskus, K E "Encouraging International Technology Transfer". See also p24, Kumar, N "Intellectual Property Rights, Technology and Economic Development: Experiences of Asian Countries"
[964] p28, Id.
[965] See Kim, Y K et al. "Appropriate Intellectual Property Protection and economic growth in countries at different levels of protection" 41 Research Policy 358 (2012).

increase their levels of protection until the late 1980s and early 1990s as they moved into more advanced research and development activity and into foreign export markets.

Japan and South Korea are examples of successful shifts up the value chain by countries that appear to have used lower levels of intellectual property protection, combined with deliberate and sustained use of policy levers and regulations related to patent registration and licensing to enable domestic entry into technology markets, while also expanding technology spillovers from foreign firms and rightholders.[966] That this was inevitably followed by a later period of increased levels of IP protection as a mix of the natural growth of an innovative constituency (and the need for export markets) as well as clear pressure from developed countries such as the US concerned with the competitive disadvantage such policies created for their firms. This suggests a successful strategy for moving up the innovative ladder for lower and middle income countries with imitative and absorptive capacity. Maskus also argues that this pattern can be found in countries such as China, Brazil, Mexico, Malaysia and India.[967] However, much of the activity described above took place before the TRIPS Agreement came into force. There are clearly concerns that TRIPS may pose a significant barrier to entry for countries wishing to enter or move up the technological value chain in a similar fashion.[968]

The case of India's pharmaceutical industry is also sometimes cited to provide support for the premise that lower levels of intellectual property may be necessary for the initial steps up the technological value chain. The Indian Patent Act of 1970, specifically aimed at creating and growing a domestic chemicals industry, excluded pharmaceuticals (as wells as chemicals and food products) from product patent protection.[969] They also reduced the term of process patents in crucial sectors (medicines, food) to 7 years. There is significant evidence, in terms of numbers to suggest that this was a crucial element of India's successful creation of a generic pharmaceutical industry.[970] However, it is important to note that there was an existing industry that to some extent demanded these changes.[971] Indian firms engaged in active

---

[966] See p21, Kumar, N "Intellectual Property Rights, Technology and Economic Development: Experiences of Asian Countries"
[967] See p282, 283, Maskus, K E and J H Reichman, "The Globalization of Private Knowledge Goods and the Privatization of Global Public Goods" 7 Journal of International Economic Law 279 (2004).
[968] Id. See also Saggi, K "International technology transfer to developing countries" Economic Paper 64, Commonwealth Secretariat (2004).
[969] See p27, Kumar, N "Intellectual Property Rights, Technology and Economic Development: Experiences of Asian Countries"
[970] p229, Fink, C "Patent Protection, Transnational Corporations and Market Structure: a Simulation study of the Indian Pharmaceutical industry" in Maskus, K & C Fink (eds.) *Intellectual Property and Development: Lessons from Recent Economic Research* (Washington D.C.: World Bank, 2005). See also p28, Kumar, N "Intellectual Property Rights, Technology and Economic Development: Experiences of Asian Countries
[971] See p27, Kumar, N "Intellectual Property Rights, Technology and Economic Development: Experiences of Asian Countries"

and concerted imitation of new chemical entities almost as soon as they were patented in other countries.[972] India became a major supplier of generic medicines to other developing countries. There is some evidence that a crucial element of the development of India's pharmaceutical industry was the policy that excluded product patent protection for pharmaceuticals and agricultural technologies, allowing the development of an imitator/generic industry.[973] This success was dependent on a strong skills base, low costs of production, minimal additional R&D costs, as well as strong domestic markets for cheap products.[974] The pharmaceutical experience was not translated as successfully into other parts of India's economy. Kumar argues that these other sectors suffered from not having as easy access to knowledge and information as the pharmaceutical and chemical sector did through product patent exclusions and other policies.[975]

China is sometimes treated as a special case in the legal and economic literature. The sheer and unique size of the market, combined with the rapid shift from a wholly communist driven economy to a state-oligarchic capitalist model has made it difficult to draw lessons from its experience for other developing countries. Nevertheless, in comparability, it may provide a useful historical comparison to other large newcomer states such as the United States in the 19th century. Much of the shift in economic structures and policy in China happened between 1985 and 1995. This occurred in a period during which China was not a member of the WTO and did not have any TRIPS obligations. In particular, between 1990 and 1995, China's flows of inward FDI increased ten-fold.[976] More importantly it was the largest destination for FDI to developing countries by a factor of 5.[977] China did not become a WTO member until 2001. This is not to say that China did not strengthen its intellectual property protection between 1987 and 1995, or between 1995 and its accession in 2001. Looking at the Ginarte-Park Index 2008[978], the average for China between 1960 and 1990 was 1.33, in 1995 it was 2.12 (Mean: 2.58), in 2000 it was 3.09 (Mean 3.05) and in 2006 it was 4.08 (Mean: 3.34).

In 1995, comparatively speaking, it had higher protection than Brazil (1.48), Egypt (1.73) and India (1.23). It had lower protection than Argentina (2.73), Chile (3.91),

---

[972] p230, Fink, C "Patent Protection, Transnational Corporations and Market Structure: a Simulation study of the Indian Pharmaceutical industry"
[973] See p25, Maskus, K "Differentiated Intellectual Property Regimes for Environmental and Climate Technologies", OECD Environment Working Papers, No 17, OECD Publishing 2010.
[974] Id.
[975] See p28, Kumar, N "Intellectual Property Rights, Technology and Economic Development: Experiences of Asian Countries"
[976] p43, Maskus, K "The Role of Intellectual Property Rights in Encouraging Foreign Direct Investment and Technology Transfer" in Maskus, K & C Fink (eds.) *Intellectual Property and Development: Lessons from Recent Economic Research* (Washington D.C.: World Bank, 2005), Table 3.1 citing IMF Balance of Payments Statistics.
[977] Id.
[978] Park, W G, "International patent protection: 1960–2005," Research Policy 37: 761–766 (2008).

South Korea (3.89), Mexico (3.14), Nigeria (2.86), South Africa (3.39), Taiwan (3.17), and Turkey (2.65).

By 2000, in comparison, it had stronger protection than Egypt (1.86), India (2.27), and Nigeria (2.86). It had lower protection than Argentina (3.98), Brazil (3.59), Chile (4.28), South Korea (4.13), Mexico (3.68), South Africa (4.25), Taiwan (3.29), and Turkey (4.01).

In 1995 China's levels of protection were below the mean and in 2000, despite the fact that most countries would have had to change their legislation to comply with TRIPS, China's level of protection was just above the mean. By 2006 it was well above the mean.

China's reputation as a frequent and widespread infringer of intellectual property rights arises in part due to deliberate polices that it has historically engaged in to ensure spillovers and technology transfer.[979] This reputation does not appear to have deterred market entry of FDI and trade, although there is evidence of many foreign firms being reluctant to engage in arm's length licensing and to use best available technologies in China.[980] While there was clearly some increase in the level of China's IP protection policies between 1990 and 2000 (before its accession to the WTO) this did not apparently alter the strong perceptions of foreign actors of the high risks of intellectual property misappropriation in China.[981] In particular this may be due to the perceived difficulties in enforcement, even where the law is technically sufficient.[982]

Whether and to what extent the TRIPS Agreement limits the ability to move up the value chain is both an empirical and a legal question. The first is to determine whether the policy levers that were used by these countries remain sufficiently available under the TRIPS Agreement. If not, are their nevertheless alternatives that may achieve much the same ends such as, an increase in the formal market mechanisms for technology transfer? For the moment, there are no studies that point to either a positive or negative effect on growth from being TRIPS compliant, although as noted above, there appear to be FDI effects. As Maskus points out, some of the concerns about the negative effects on access to technology may be addressed by noting that patenting

---

[979] See Ajemian, C and D Reid "Preventing Global Warming: The United States, China, and Intellectual Property" 115 Business and Society Review 417 (2010)
[980] See p314, Maskus, K et al. "Intellectual Property Rights and Development in China" in Maskus, K & C Fink (eds.) *Intellectual Property and Development: Lessons from Recent Economic Research* (Washington D.C.: World Bank, 2005).
[981] See p308, Id.
[982] Id. See also p28, Copenhagen Economics and the IPR Company "Are IPRs a Barrier to the Transfer of Climate Change Technology?" Study Commissioned by European Commission DG Trade, January 2009. (whose authors' concerns even extended to the risks presented by restrictions on anti-competitive behaviour sanctioned by the TRIPS Agreement)

tends not to occur in low-income and lower middle income countries[983], except in specific sectors such as health and agriculture, primarily due to their lack of imitative capacity and small market size. In addition, even where technologies may be patented there may be several alternatives on the market, ameliorating the pricing power that a patent holder would have. Nevertheless, it is difficult to draw any conclusions for whether the effects on welfare (or sustainable development) are positive or negative[984], except perhaps in very specific circumstances in specific sectors. Theoretically, at least, the economic literature points to significant short term static costs to the increase of intellectual property protection[985], leading to an increased outflow of royalties and fees. There are of course dynamic effects, but in an open economy, it is not clear whether those effects would be of a scale to off-set the static costs.[986] In specific sectors such as health, there is some mixed evidence that there may be an increase in the static costs, without necessarily being accompanied by a lowering of the dynamic costs of patent protection.[987] The example of India suggests that increased patent protection for pharmaceuticals did not drive increased innovation in medicines relevant to the majority of the Indian population but resulted in an increased focus on medicines and diseases with markets in developed countries.[988] This suggests few dynamic benefits from increased patent protection. On the other hand, the WHO Commission on Intellectual Property Rights, Innovation and Public Health found that, in the period to 2006, prices for anti-retroviral medicines were lowered dramatically.[989] The Commission attributed this to increased generic competition, the TRIPS transition period and pressure on pharmaceutical companies from NGO's and other actors. However, it should be noted that increased use of price differentiation and agreements preventing parallel trade may also have played a significant part in the lowering of prices. As Fink and Maskus[990] point out, until more data on the demand and price elasticities for technologies and technological products is available, modeling the impact of higher intellectual property in developing countries will be difficult, if not unreliable.

---

[983] See p28, Maskus, K E "Encouraging International Technology Transfer" ICTSD Issue Paper No. 7, May 2004.
[984] See p21, Fink, C and C Primo Braga, "How Stronger protection of Intellectual Property Rights affects Trade" in Maskus, K & C Fink (eds.) *Intellectual Property and Development: Lessons from Recent Economic Research* (Washington D.C.: World Bank, 2005).
[985] See p285, Maskus, K E and J H Reichman, "The Globalization of Private Knowledge Goods and the Privatization of Global Public Goods" 7 Journal of International Economic Law 279 (2004).
[986] p22, Fink, C and C Primo Braga, "How Stronger protection of Intellectual Property Rights affects Trade"
[987] p200, Ganslandt, M et al. "Developing and Distributing Medicines to Poor Countries: the DEFEND Proposal" in Maskus, K & C Fink (eds.) *Intellectual Property and Development: Lessons from Recent Economic Research* (Washington D.C.: World Bank, 2005).
[988] p85, Commission on Intellectual Property Rights, Innovation and Public Health "Public health, innovation and intellectual property rights: report of the Commission on Intellectual Property Rights, Innovation and Public Health" Geneva: WHO (2006).
[989] p116, Id.
[990] p12, Fink, C and K Maskus "Why we study Intellectual Property Rights and what we have learned" in Maskus, K & C Fink (eds.) *Intellectual Property and Development: Lessons from Recent Economic Research* (Washington D.C.: World Bank, 2005).

One final conceptual note relates to the way in which "higher" intellectual property is perceived. As noted earlier in this chapter, firms from high intellectual property protecting countries will always believe themselves at a disadvantage in countries that do not provide the same level of intellectual property protection as their home state. The built-in structural incentive is that they will always seek to have those other countries harmonize with the level of protection that is available in their domestic market. As such, assessment of what is an appropriate level of intellectual property or what is a high enough level of intellectual property should not be based on the perception, real or otherwise, of such firms that there is insufficient protection of intellectual property in foreign markets. A case in point is the US use of the Special 301 Report[991] which is a mechanism for the US to place countries on watch lists for failing to sufficiently protect intellectual property. It uses the lever of removal of preferential trade access as a tool for encouraging countries to meet the concerns expressed by US industry through this process. Countries that have appeared on the 2013 Report[992] include: Canada, Finland, Greece, Israel, Italy, and Mexico. In 2012, the list also included Norway. These are countries not usually considered to be failing to provide adequate intellectual property protection as a general matter. All major developing countries, (Brazil, China, India,) except South Africa, have been on the list for much of its post-TRIPS existence, although no sub-Saharan African countries have appeared on the list in the past two years. We should approach with caution statements that suggest that increasing the levels of intellectual property protection will be satisfactory to foreign firms and will make them more likely to invest. As with most regulatory incentives there is a point at which the cost of the incentive may have diminishing returns on shifting the behaviour and perception of the subject of the incentive. This is especially true when the issue of intellectual property is a proxy for concerns about competitiveness. In such cases, the goal is not merely protection of intellectual property but protection of the existing market share against new entrants with strong imitative capacity. In the climate arena, it is precisely the creation of competitors or new market entrants that we are aiming for, and thus the balance between protection of rightholders and ensuring spill-overs, formal and informal, is crucial.

In considering measures to address the role of intellectual property in technology transfer, some of the theoretical, empirical and historical evidence discussed points to several key lessons.

First, the ability to duplicate/imitate/adapt technologies has been crucial to technological learning that enables moving up the value chain, at least as an initial step. The use of policies such as product patent exclusions, utility models[993], narrow patent

---

[991] 19 USC 2241-42, Title 19 Chapter 12 – of Trade Act of 1974.
[992] Available at: http://www.ustr.gov/about-us/press-office/reports-and-publications/2013/2013-special-301-report (last visited 15 August 2014).
[993] See Kim, Y K et al. "Appropriate Intellectual Property Protection and economic growth in countries at different levels of protection" 41 Research Policy 358 (2012).

claims and pre-grant publications have clearly contributed to such learning, where such capacity existed in domestic firms. There is clearly an appropriate level of intellectual property for some countries that lies at the minimum or lower than that of TRIPS and which may be better off emphasizing alternative or lower levels of protection.

Second, given the varied situations of countries, this suggests that a one size fits all approach of harmonized intellectual property protection may not be the best approach to ensuring development.[994] The variation and ambiguity of the existing data on the role of intellectual property protection in FDI, licensing and in moving up the value chain, suggests that the best approach for developing countries (and in fact all countries) is to seek to directly fit the levels and scope of intellectual property protection with specific policy goals in specific sectors. What it also suggests is that while minimum intellectual property standards play a key role in international trade and flows of technology, even more important is ensuring sufficient policy space for countries to design intellectual property policies that will best enable them to move up the value chain. This may involve following the example of countries like Japan, Korea and Japan, in some circumstances, or that of the historical experience of the UK in others. Factors such as the size of the domestic market, the dependence on imports, and the dependence on exports will all play a key role in determining the nature and scope of these policies. The goal of addressing climate change mitigation and adaptation will therefore be determinative of many countries' policies for much of the rest of 21st century. While this has significant overlap with the broader development challenge, there may also be more urgent need for ensuring technology diffusion in many sectors that may require prioritizing static efficiency over dynamic efficiency. In other sectors, the balance may shift in the other direction. The circumstances of each country will be different even in the context of a shared global challenge, placing even more emphasis on ensuring sufficient policy space to allow countries to take measures that increase technology development and diffusion in their domestic markets.

Third, the most effective system of technology transfer is one that encourages the broadest participation in the innovation system, in particular focusing on small and medium enterprises who both may wish to gain protection but also need sufficient room to innovate around and have relatively low-cost access. This implicates the use of utility models with low fees, and the use of compensatory liability approaches rather than ones focused on the pure right to exclude.

Finally, the historical evidence implicates a broad portfolio of actions that countries appear to have used to successfully move up the technology value chain. This echoes the general consensus that a portfolio approach is **fundamental to addressing**

---

[994] p13, Fink, C and K Maskus "Why we study Intellectual Property Rights and what we have learned" in Maskus, K & C Fink (eds.) *Intellectual Property and Development: Lessons from Recent Economic Research* (Washington D.C.: World Bank, 2005).

climate change mitigation, as no single policy is likely to have the necessary impact within the given time frame and that different emphases and patterns of policies will be required for different countries due to different factor endowments and positions in international trade.

VI. CONSTRUCTING A LIST OF THE TYPES OF TECHNOLOGY TRANSFER INTERVENTIONS

The kinds of IP interventions that are sometimes proposed to address the production and access to goods problem include:

1. Compulsory licenses

   These are licenses which are normally issued by the government, without the consent of the right holder, to another economic actor to use the patent. The logic is that by doing so, the government ensures downward price pressure by creating competition at the level of the product in the consumer market, or allows more production to ensure that all the demand in the market is met, where the patent holder has insufficient production capacity themselves and either is not willing to license or to license at a reasonable price to others in the market. These can therefore be aimed at addressing short term supply concerns or price spikes, or to address longer term structural weakness in pricing and supply. However, compulsory licenses are also used to address anti-competitive behaviour or to address competition concerns relating to large mergers between competitors. In this case, the concern is not the end-consumer market per se but the potential for creating undue market power that will negatively and unduly affect market entry or market participation. In such cases, to correct such behaviour, a firm is required to license to a competitor on an ongoing basis. This fully exposes the two sides of compulsory licenses: those mechanisms aimed at ensuring that patents actually serve public welfare during the life of the patent and intervene for specific policy reasons; those that aim at ensuring the proper functioning of the technology and product market, reinforcing the patent system.

2. Patent exclusions

   These entail excluding from patentability certain technology sectors deemed to be necessary and crucial to achieving specific public policy goals such as health or food security. Under the Paris Convention, such exclusions were considered to be well within the margin of discretion that a state had to manage its industrial property policy, in sectors crucial to their development and the public interest. As noted earlier, many countries prohibited product patents in pharmaceuticals, chemicals and agricultural technologies, so as to allow the same products to be produced by novel and inventive processes, allowing for competition on the product market, ensuring the existence and development of a domestic industry and ensuring sufficient price competition to provide access to such products for their citizens. This is in addition to the subject matter exclusions that countries also provide related to certain technologies that are considered outside the appropriate subject matter such as computer programs, business methods, plants and animals. In most cases these are exclusions where the products are not considered to be "inventions' within the meaning of the domestic law.

3. Parallel imports,

This involves allowing the import of goods produced and legally placed on the market in another country, or because the technology is not patent protected. This is possible where a producer of patented goods sells them (or allows an authorized distributor to do so) at a different price in different national markets [995] and the country has a policy of international exhaustion, where a patent right to control the sale of goods is exhausted after the first sale anywhere in the world. In that case, a product can then be imported from that other country, even where the product may still be protected in the importing country with respect to all the other patents rights. In such a case, the right of importation only extends to products placed on the market in other countries without some form of authorization from the patent holder.

Addressing the access to goods problem is somewhat different from that of access to the technologies. The reason a differentiation needs to be made is a distinction between immediate action and longer term sustainable action. In an emergency, the priority is the production of more goods at a cheaper price in as short a period of time as possible. Thus access to the goods is a priority, and concerns regarding the generation of future technologies fade into the background. In the climate change arena, this is most applicable to climate change adaptation, especially to address climate vulnerabilities in food security and health.

However, if the concern is for long term sustainable action, access to the knowledge or technology also needs to be ensured. This requires a more complex policy response, one that measures the gains from enforcing, or otherwise providing better technology transfer, versus reducing the levels of exclusive rights available to

---

[995] p189, Maskus, K and Y Chen "Parallel Imports in a Vertical Model of Distribution: Theory, Evidence and Policy" in Maskus, K & C Fink (eds.) *Intellectual Property and Development: Lessons from Recent Economic Research* (Washington D.C.: World Bank, 2005).

innovators. This is most relevant to the situation of mitigation technologies, where the goal is to ensure sufficient dissemination to enable appropriate action in the near term (in many cases, significant reductions will need to take place by 2020); while ensuring sufficient incentives to create a knowledge market in climate technologies that will serve to sustain GHG emissions reductions through 2050 and beyond. This means that, for those countries with sufficient manufacturing and absorptive capacity, levels of IP protection that provide a strong enough market signal to outside companies to ensure voluntary licensing and FDI are a vital part of the policy mix.[996] However, there is a point beyond which the level of protection may provide diminishing returns and it is necessary for each country to find the optimal balance for itself and its specific market. Of note is that empirical data suggests that, in comparison to other technology sectors, patents do not play a large role in providing incentives for research and development for environmentally sustainable technologies, although they may play a greater role in determining targets for outward flows of FDI and licensing for middle income countries.[997] However, there is a point beyond which patents and other IP protection may inhibit the kinds of positive technology spillovers which are the public policy aim of measures to encourage technology transfer in the first place.

An added complication in the arena of climate technologies is that there may be significant elements of technologies that are maintained as trade secrets which fall outside the realm of patents as an incentive system and form part of a broader system of protection against unfair competition. Access to such trade secrets, or undisclosed information, may be necessary to ensure effective availability and transfer of knowledge. Tools appropriate to addressing patent failures, such as compulsory licenses, may not necessarily address accompanying trade secrets.[998]

Interventions aimed at ensuring access to knowledge and technology include those described above as well as the following:

1. Working requirements

   Under such a requirement, a right holder is required to 'work', usually meaning to produce, manufacture (and sell) the patented product, use the patented process in the domestic market in order to continue to receive patent protection. Failure to do so may result in revocation or the issuance of a compulsory license. Under Article 5(A) of the Paris Convention, working clearly did not include importation. In fact, exercising the patent purely on the basis of importation was considered grounds for action, and Article 5(A)(1)

---

[996] See p15, Maskus, K "Differentiated Intellectual Property Regimes for Environmental and Climate Technologies", OECD Environment Working Papers, No. 17, OECD Publishing 2010.
[997] See p17, Id.
[998] See p15, Maskus, K "Differentiated Intellectual Property Regimes for Environmental and Climate Technologies", OECD Environment Working Papers, No. 17, OECD Publishing 2010.

was aimed at ensuring that, at the least, forfeiture of the patent was not one of the measures used. Working requirements were regulated in Article 5(A)(4), putting a waiting period of 4 years from filing or 3 years from grant, and allowing for a patent holder to justify such failure, and limiting the terms of compulsory licenses to address non-working to non-exclusive, and non-transferable ones. This concern with importation shows that the requirement was not really addressed at ensuring access to goods but to the 'use' of the patent locally. The main aim is to encourage FDI or licensing by the patent holder, either through subsidiaries or joint ventures, out of which will come the suite of formal and informal spillovers with respect to the technology. Without such local practice, it can become much more difficult for local actors to benefit from the demonstration, downstream and upstream learning effects that can be natural outcomes of FDI. Where the FDI is not the preferred mode, then licensing to local actors so that they can manufacture the product or use the process is an alternative way of meeting the requirement. Traditionally, what has not been held to meet the requirement is simple importation of the finished patented product or of products produced by a patented process, something about which the Paris Convention was very clear in Article 5A. In terms of the patent social contract, the working requirement aims to ensure that in exchange for the patent right, which is territorial, the benefit of the use and application of that patent accrues to the state in which it is granted. Simple disclosure is the formal mechanism, but the informal spillover effect of the patent grant does not operate without the network effects of having a producer or user of the patent locally. In this sense it is not discriminatory but places foreign patent holders on the same level as national patent holders rather than privileging them with the ability to exercise their rights without the responsibility of actual participation in the national market.

2. Exceptions to patent rights

These allow third parties to engage in and use the patent for stated public policy purposes without being considered to have infringed the patent e.g. a research exception or an exception for educational institutions.

Such exceptions can be categorized into three groups: those that select out a specific kind of actor who can exercise some or all of the activities usually excluded by the patent holder; those that select out a specific act or subset of acts that can be carried out with respect to the patented product or process by anybody, under certain conditions; those that select out a specific sector or sub-sector in which third parties may carry out activities in relation to the patent that they would not be able to do in other sectors. Many exceptions tend to be a mix of these, with specific actors carrying activities in a specific sector for example. The Paris Convention does not provide any limitations on the purposes or the scope of such exceptions, nor, in fact, does it prescribe a minimum set of rights that must be provided. The exceptions that may be relevant in the technology transfer and climate change arena include:

- *Research/experimental use exception* – this may be for non-commercial or commercial purposes. It is also partly built into the patent system for disclosure in that other actors must be able to experiment with the patent to test if you have truly achieved what you claim to have achieved. This allows them to seek a license, innovate around the patent, or seek a new inventive solution of their own to the problem that the patent solves. Reverse engineering can usually take place under the cover of this exception, although in some countries it is limited to non-commercial actors or for non-commercial purposes.

- Production of use for purposes of regulatory review – the patent can be used to meet the requirement for market entry established by a regulator. In the case of pharmaceuticals, this may be to meet safety and efficacy standards. A generic producer can produce the patented product during its lifetime on order to obtain marketing approval and enter the market as soon as the patent expires. This is one of two exceptions that has been actually tested under dispute settlement at TRIPS.[999]

- Stockpiling production for market entry once the patent expires

3. Patent exclusions, especially for products;
4. Patent revocations;
5. Patent of importation;

These are no longer that common. In the early period of international patent law making, these enabled domestic rightholders to lay claim to patents that had been patented elsewhere and increased the speed at which technology was imported from other countries. The need to do this was slowly eroded by the growth of global trade, the international patenting system and more widespread publication of patent applications. Their use was also modulated by new approaches to the concept of novelty and international rules on the priority date from which a patent could be considered novel. Under the Paris Convention's Article 4, a rightholder had a patent priority date of 12 months

---

[999] Panel Report, Canada – Patent Protection of Pharmaceutical Products, WT/DS114/R, adopted 7 April 2000, DSR 2000:V, 2289 (*Canada – Pharmaceutical Patents*)

from the date of first application in any convention country. This allowed them to supersede any patent application in any country during that period. After that period, another person could indeed patent that product in the country where the patent holder had declined to patent. This required that the country operate a standard of novelty that examined whether the patent was not 'known' in the territory[1000] in contrast to the present system in most countries that the patent was not known anywhere in the world.

6. Compulsory licenses; including the licensing of know-how and trade secrets;
7. Licenses of right or compensatory liability regimes;
   – These are provisions that remove the ability of the rightholder to refuse to license but require the user or second-comer innovator to nevertheless compensate the rightholder through a negotiated price, a set price, or one set by a regulator. [1001]
8. Technology transfer and other performance requirements to qualify for establishing foreign direct investment presence;
9. The application of competition law to address,
   – Required non-assignment or sub-licensing to a third party;
   – Required grant back clauses on improvements;
   – Prohibited production for export;
   – Prohibited production of competing products;
10. Setting requirements for, or imposing, fair reasonable and non-discriminatory terms for licensing of patents that are used in standards or are considered a necessity for participation in the market;
11. Regular, consistent and detailed monitoring of licensing terms in licensing contracts to guard against anti-competitive clauses. This may require a pre-approval and registration process;
12. Limiting or reducing patent terms, as a whole or in specific sectors; at the moment the standard minimum term is at least 20 years under the TRIPS Agreement.
13. Higher fees for applications and renewals for foreign patent applicant firms; higher fees for large firms;
14. Requiring full disclosure of the patent and the best mode known at the time of patenting including all know-how required to practise it;

[1000] As China did until 2009. See p273, Gechlick, M "Making Transfer of Clean Technology Work: Lessons of the Clean Development Mechanism" 11 San Diego International Law Journal 227 (2009) citing Patent Law (promulgated by the Standing Comm. Nat'l People's Cong., Mar. 12, 1984, revised Sept. 4, 1992, Aug. 25, 2000, and Dec. 27, 2008, effective Oct. 1, 2009) LAWINFOCHINA, art. 22.

[1001] The concept of using compensatory liability regimes in the space between patents and non-patentable innovations has been pursued and popularized by Jerome Reichman, most fully in Reichman, J "Of Green Tulips and Legal Kudzu: repackaging Rights in sub-patentable Innovation" 53 Vanderbilt Law Review 1743 (2000).

15. Requiring early and significant pre-grant publication of patent application, coupled with a process for dissemination to local firms;
16. Instituting formal dissemination mechanisms, beyond publications such as quarterly sectoral meetings.
17. Setting up a patent examination rather than registration system to better control the standards and quality of patent granted; - Shifting from patent registration to examination while creating and maintaining strong utility model registration system; This may involve setting higher inventive step and novelty standards;
18. Limiting the scope and number of allowable claims per patent;
19. Strong pre-grant and post-grant opposition procedures;
20. Allowing reverse engineering, especially of software: even for commercial purposes;
21. Limiting restrictions on the movement and employment of employees once they have left the firm, such as non-compete clauses;
22. Requiring that publicly funded research, where IP rights are allowed to be held by the funded organization, be made available via non-exclusive licensing, for a flat fee or for free;
23. Providing specific loans and capital for mergers with and acquisitions (shareholdings or outright purchases) of foreign companies with significant patent portfolios of relevance to climate change with the express purpose of transferring technology, know-how to the acquiring company.

VII. CONCLUSION

In considering these unilateral IP interventions developing countries are required to comply with the existing international framework for the protection of intellectual property, the TRIPS Agreement. It is precisely the issue of whether such interventions are available and in conformity with the TRIPS Agreement that drives developing country critiques of the international system and the argument for amending or restructuring the international IP framework. The conformity of these options with the requirements of the TRIPS Agreement will be examined in Chapter 6

The discussion above points to an important framework for the chapters that follow: markets can be very efficient tools for generation and dissemination of technology, but they can also fail. The key is that they can fail in relatively predictable ways, some of which are natural outcomes of the system we have chosen to provide incentives. Actions can be taken within the system to ameliorate or mitigate such market failures or problems, relating to supply, demand or market structure. The tools and solutions discussed above and in the following chapters remain largely within the realm of the existing system of incentives and course correction for generating and disseminating technologies. In that framing, the role of government is to provide a nudge or restructure market behaviour using the intended tools of exceptions, limitations and competition law.

Chapter 6
Interpreting TRIPS and the limits on unilateral action

I. INTRODUCTION

The purpose of this chapter is to serve as a pivot point leading up to the conclusion of whether the UNFCCC should take action on intellectual property issues and if so, what kind of action should it take. In Chapter 3 we look at one portion of the empirical case, the global distribution of patents and find that there may not be sufficient data on which to make a decision but that there are indeed indications of structural problems. However, the chapter also concludes that information on the actual national market conditions is a fundamental part of the determining necessity to act. In chapter 3, we examine the effectiveness of existing mechanisms for technology transfer in the UNFCCC, and suggest why their failure indicates a need to address intellectual property at the UNFCCC. In this chapter we look at the crucial third element, the contingent question; *whether, in a situation where the behaviour of specific intellectual property holders bars or unduly limits, the adoption, adaptation and replication of a specific climate technology in a specific domestic sector do UNFCCC member states have the tools necessary to address such behaviour or are these blocked, or hindered to an undue extent by the TRIPS Agreement?*

In order to make that determination it is crucial to determine the nature and scope of the barrier that TRIPS may pose for developing countries to take unilateral action to ensure technology transfer. As noted in Chapter 4, the need for unilateral action is driven by developing countries' argument that insufficient funding and support are forthcoming from developed countries at the scale, scope and timing (outlined in Chapter 2) necessary for them to meet the climate challenge. This leaves them little option but to seek other regulatory options, a major one being making intellectual property interventions, the set of which are identified in Chapter 5. To answer the question of whether TRIPS poses a barrier, it is important to reiterate what this thesis understands as the definition of a barrier: restriction that limits developing countries from:

1. *Appropriately defining necessity as:*

a. *Affordability* - ensuring that prices of products are not set so high that it is too expensive for all the relevant economic actors to afford.
b. *Adoptability* - ensuring that prices of products and or know-how are not set so high that they make it commercially unviable for all relevant actors to adopt 'climate-friendly' technologies.
c. *Adaptability* – ensuring sufficient distribution of knowledge (information, skills, know-how) to enable a critical number of existing producers/service providers in the market to adopt, adapt and replicate climate technologies and ensure their participation in the market.

2. *Taking actions that:*
   a. *address the full scope of technologies required by them to meet the climate change mitigation and adaptation needs;*
   b. *at the rate and level of diffusion appropriate to achieving those mitigation and adaptation needs;*
   c. *in the developing countries and regions that most effectively meet the climate change need.*

To answer this question I begin with a broad examination of the key condition for application of flexibilities in the WTO Agreement: the concept of "necessity". I examine this in light of the broader WTO jurisprudence and in light of specific TRIPS-related cases. In the second part I examine the flexibilities within the TRIPS Agreement itself that address the measures identified in Chapter 5, such as working requirements, research exceptions, patent exclusions, and compulsory licenses. Each section will first describe the legal rules governing the measure, and the case law interpreting it and then it will outline the possibilities for implementing such measures for climate change under the rule. I conclude each section with an assessment of its overall availability.

The Chapter concludes by looking at the full set of measures identified in Chapter 5 and whether, under TRIPS, they are a) legally available b) whether they are practically available in terms of the scale and scope of action needed, with special reference to emerging economies.

This analysis will be based on the interpretation of TRIPS provisions using traditional interpretive rules under the WTO and general international law, with reference to direct WTO case law and decisions, relevant case law and decisions of other international bodies and national case law where pertinent. In particular, I base my analysis on the rules in the Dispute Settlement Understanding and subsequent case law applying them in WTO disputes on the determination of jurisdiction, applicable law and the application of Section 3 (Interpretation of Treaties) of the Vienna Convention on the Law of Treaties.[1002] In particular, Article 31 of the VCLT will be the basis for justifying interpretations of TRIPS provisions where I argue that the panels or the Appellate Body may have been mistaken or in error and that a provision may be broader or narrower than WTO case law provides for. In this sense, this chapter is not purely descriptive of the law as it has been interpreted but seeks to establish a sense of the law *as it is*, so that policymakers are not unduly limited in their understandings of what the actual scope of a provision may be and provide them with a proper basis for risk assessment of whether a dispute may be brought against them for the use of a particular intervention. Nevertheless, I take a conservative approach and attempt to stay largely within the existing practice and substance of the WTO Appellate Body, even where I may criticize the approach and outcomes.

II. MEETING THE STANDARD OF NECESSITY IN THE WTO AND TRIPS[1003]

An examination of whether TRIPS poses a barrier to actions to address climate change rests in large part on the approach of the WTO interpretive bodies to the broader relationship between the WTO trade regime and the environmental regime and the acts considered 'necessary' to protect the environment,

There have been no WTO disputes regarding how actions to address environmental concerns should be treated under TRIPS Agreement, although there have been significant developments such as the Doha Declaration on Public Health, as well as ongoing negotiations under the Doha Round which may provide some indicia. However, the broader WTO jurisprudence on exceptions may have a strong influence on the interpretation of the TRIPS Agreement. The General Exceptions clause under the GATS, for example, has been interpreted in ways similar to those under Article XX of the GATT 1947 and the jurisprudence on the 'necessity' test in that article may be particularly useful in this context.[1004] The necessity test can also be found in other WTO Agreements including the Agreement on Sanitary and Phytosanitary Measures[1005] (SPS Agreement), in Articles 2.1 and 5.6; the Agreement on Technical Barriers to

---

[1002] Vienna Convention on the Law of Treaties (VCLT), Vienna, 23 May 1969 *in force* 27 January 1980, 1155 United Nations Treaty Series (1987) 331.

[1003] An earlier version of this chapter was published as Shabalala, D "Challenges for Technology Transfer in the Climate Change Arena: What Interactions with the TRIPS Agreement?" in D Prevost and G van Calster Research Handbook on Environment, Health and the WTO (London: Edward Elgar 2013).

[1004] p77, Bernasconi-Osterwalder, N et al., *Environment and Trade: A Guide To WTO Jurisprudence* (London: Earthscan, 2006).

[1005] Agreement on the Application of Sanitary and Phytosanitary Measures, Annex 1A to the Marrakesh Agreement establishing the World Trade Organization (WTO Agreement), Marrakesh, 15 April 1994, *in force* 1 January 1995, 1867 United Nations Treaty Series (1995) 4.

Trade[1006] (TBT Agreement) in Article 2.2; and the General Agreement on Trade in Services[1007] (GATS) in Article 14. In TRIPS, the necessity test is found in Article 8.1 where it states:

> Members may, in formulating or amending their laws and regulations, adopt measures **necessary** to protect public health and nutrition, and to promote the public interest in sectors of vital importance to their socio-economic and technological development, provided that such measures are consistent with the provisions of this Agreement (emphasis added).

The concept of necessity governs the rules on when states may justify otherwise WTO inconsistent actions. These are usually for a specific purpose and the case law evolved and been elaborated to outline when a measure can be considered 'necessary' in light of the purpose it is claimed.

II.1. The Necessity test in the broader WTO jurisprudence

Within the GATT, the Article XX exceptions are generally the last stop in a series of analytical steps looking at like products and discrimination. It is in the context of these exceptions that the public policy aim of a measure is directly addressed. In this context, the question is whether the panel or the Appellate Body will seek to defer to the public policy principles embodied by these exceptions, or whether it will take a narrow approach that tries to limit their applicability. In the context of environmental measures there is a long history relating in particular to Article XX(b) which allows for measures "necessary to protect human, animal or plant life or health".

The 'necessity' requirement of Article XX(b), is at the core of how the WTO relates to regulations to protect human, animal and plant life and health. The exact scope of this requirement remains unclear, although it has been addressed by several WTO panels and the Appellate Body.[1008] Initial decisions suggested that a measure would qualify only if there were no other available GATT-consistent measures.[1009] Otherwise the least-inconsistent and reasonably available measure would have to be

---

[1006] Agreement on Technical Barriers to Trade, Annex 1A to the Marrakesh Agreement establishing the World Trade Organization (WTO Agreement), Marrakesh, 15 April 1994, *in force* 1 January 1995, 1867 United Nations Treaty Series (1995) 4.
[1007] General Agreement on Trade in Services, Annex 1B to the Marrakesh Agreement establishing the World Trade Organization (WTO Agreement), Marrakesh, 15 April 1994, *in force* 1 January 1995, 1867 United Nations Treaty Series (1995) 4.
[1008] p149, Bernasconi-Osterwalder, N et al., *Environment and Trade: A Guide to WTO Jurisprudence* (London: Earthscan, 2006).
[1009] Para. 5.26, GATT Panel Report, United States Section 337 of the Tariff Act of 1930, L/6439, adopted 7 November 1989, BISD 36S/345 (US – Section 337 Tariff Act)

applied.[1010] Further cases also suggested that necessity did not imply that the measure should be indispensable, but should make a contribution to achieving its policy objective. In other words, the measure does not need to be sufficient, in and of itself, to meet the policy goal.[1011] A three factor balancing test was established that took into consideration:[1012]

i. the contribution made by the (non-indispensable) measure to the legitimate objective;

ii. the importance of the common interests or values protected; and

iii. the impact of the measure on trade.

This was a balancing test and outcomes shifted depending on the weight of each element in a case. The higher the common interests or values protected, the stronger the necessity.[1013] The greater the contribution to the legitimate objective, the easier it was to meet necessity. On the other hand, the more trade restrictive the measure the less likely it was to pass the necessity test. Whether an alternative less trade restrictive measure was "reasonably available" was measured against whether it would accomplish the same goal to the same extent. The domestic costs of the alternatives could also be taken into account.[1014]

In July 2011, a panel report applied these standards, especially for Article XX(b) in *China – Raw Materials*.[1015] Brought primarily by the US and Europe, the case challenged China's export restrictions (duties and quotas) on primary products and raw materials such as bauxite, coke, fluorspar, magnesium, manganese, silicon metal and zinc, and the re-use of scraps from primary production of these raw materials.

In considering the argument relating to export duties, under which, in any case, the panel found that China could not invoke Article XX to defend measures in violation of its accession protocol, there are some significant clarifications of how the standard of necessity would be applied. I primarily address the Article XX(b) analysis of the panel with respect to China's export duties and quotas on coke and silicon carbide, and looking broadly at primary product exports (EPRs). The Chinese argument on XX(b) related to the necessity of using duties and quotas to create a preference for recycling of

---

[1010] Id.
[1011] Para. 161, Appellate Body Report, Korea – Measures Affecting Imports of Fresh, Chilled and Frozen Beef, WT/DS161/AB/R, WT/DS169/AB/R, adopted 10 January 2001, DSR 2001:I, 5 (Korea – Various Measures on Beef)
[1012] p149, Bernasconi-Osterwalder, N et al. (2006)
[1013] See e.g. Appellate Body Report, European Communities – Measures Affecting Asbestos and Asbestos-Containing Products, WT/DS135/AB/R, adopted 5 April 2001, DSR 2001:VII, 3243 (EC-Asbestos)
[1014] p149, Bernasconi-Osterwalder, N et al. (2006)
[1015] Panel Reports, *China – Measures Related to the Exportation of Various Raw Materials*, WT/DS394/R and Corr.1/WT/DS395/R and Corr.1/WT/DS398/R and Corr.1, circulated to WTO Members 5 July 2011. (*China – Raw Materials*)

scrap rather than primary extraction and production of raw materials.[1016] The panel notes China's citation of the Appellate Body interpretation in *Brazil-Retreaded Tyres*[1017] in support of its contention that a measure should '(i) bring about a material contribution to the achievement of its objective; and, (ii) be apt to produce a material contribution to the objective pursued, even if the contribution is not "immediately observable."'[1018] China argued that while the materiality of a contribution can be examined by a panel, this cannot extend to an assessment of whether the right level of protection was chosen, again citing the Appellate Body in *Brazil-Retreaded Tyres*.[1019] In general the panel did not go beyond the bounds of interpretation set up in *Brazil-Retreaded Tyres*. In its examination of the evidence the panel suggests that the measures must, in their formulation or justification, state the environmental justification. Otherwise this may be evidence of post-hoc justifications for the measures.[1020] They appear to require more than just general relationships to environmental policy but specific and internally consistent justifications such that the measure is clear as to what its policy goal is. This begins to almost suggest a 'primarily' aimed at test such as that in XX(g). We note that the panel cites the inclusion of other aims in China's supporting documents such as 'energy, transport, the economy and economic development' to suggest that the primary aim is not environmental.[1021] The panel seems to require that an explicit link must be made between the specific measure and environmental protection and that such measures cannot concurrently have other goals beyond the environmental.[1022] The panel creates a standard that requires not only a statement of environmental purpose but how the measure will achieve the goals to be explicitly stated in the legislation or the law.[1023] Such a measure must then also be carried out in the context of a specific and comprehensive framework for protecting the environment and not be deduced from an accumulation of the multiplicity of related measures and goals.[1024] The member must show how it contributes, but apparently this must be done in the legislation or rule establishing the measure itself.

In addressing the issue of least trade-restrictive measures, the panel examines the availability of alternative measures, and notes that since China argued that it had already taken the measures proposed by the complainant, it had negated any argument that they are not 'reasonably available'. The panel also finds that China's evidence of the implementation of such measures is weak, and concludes that these have not been exhausted to such an extent that they are not sufficient alternatives to export duties and

---

[1016] para 7.471, Id.
[1017] Appellate Body Report, *Brazil – Measures Affecting Imports of Retreaded Tyres*, WT/DS332/AB/R, adopted 17 December 2007, DSR 2007:IV, 1527 (*Brazil – Retreaded Tyres*).
[1018] para 7.475, Panel Reports, *China – Raw Materials*
[1019] para 7.479, Id.
[1020] para 7.501, Id.
[1021] para 7.505, Id.
[1022] Id.
[1023] para 7.507, Id.
[1024] para 7.510, Id.

quotas.[1025] In essence, the panel requires that the alternative measure be fully utilized and exhausted before it will accept that they are not reasonably available and effective in materially contributing to the desired outcome, requiring the 'necessity' of export restrictions. The panel's evaluation concludes that while these measures appear to be reasonably available, China has not actually shown that it is implementing many of these measures and that there is therefore sufficient room for action to achieve its goals by implementing such actions rather than by using export restrictions.

One cannot escape the conclusion that while the standards established by the Appellate body appear to leave some room in XX(b) for application of environmental measures that may restrict trade, the panel's evidentiary standard is so high that it is less likely that such measures would survive. Of particular concern in the argument by the panel that alternative measures that have been applied must be used to their full capacity before a trade restrictive measure will be found to be justified, rather than focusing on the ability to make a material contribution, in concert with other measures. Clearly, export restrictions are viewed by the panel as one step short of the most restrictive kind of action that could have been taken i.e. a ban on trade, but the panel's analysis also suggests that the burden for meeting the Article XX(b) standard is quite high, requiring not just specific legislation but (i) implementation of the legislation in a way that specifically address the individual measures at hand; (ii) within a broader environmental regulatory framework, that states exactly how those measure fit into the broader framework; (iii) with a clear showing that other WTO-consistent measures have been exhausted, before the claimed measure is adopted. In its appeal[1026], China did not address the issue of Article XX(b) and thus the panel's analysis stands for the moment as the most recent application of the Appellate Body's articulation of the necessity test under the GATT 1994.

The necessity test also raises its head in other WTO Agreements including the Agreement on Sanitary and Phytosanitary Measures (SPS Agreement), in Articles 2.1 and 5.6; the Agreement on Technical Barriers to Trade (TBT Agreement) in Article 2.2; and the General Agreement on Trade in Services (GATS) in Article 14. While there some differences, such as the burden of proof under the SPS Agreement, these Agreements also require, to varying extents, that the least trade restrictive option be taken, where no alternative consistent measure can be found, rather than lay down a standard that focuses on the most effective environmental outcome.

[1025] para 7.569- 7.570, Panel Reports, *China – Raw Materials*,
[1026] Appellate Body Reports, *China – Measures Related to the Exportation of Various Raw Materials*, WT/DS394/AB and Corr.1/WT/DS395/AB and Corr.1/WT/DS398/AB and Corr.1, circulated to WTO Members 30 January 2012. (*China – Raw Materials*)

In September 2011 a panel report addressed the necessity issue in the TBT Agreement in *US – Tuna II (Mexico)*.[1027] The case was the third iteration of a long-running dispute between Mexico and the US regarding its "Dolphin-Safe" tuna labelling scheme. In this case, the new issue related to the fact that a regional agreement (AIDPC) had established a dolphin-safe certification scheme for the Eastern Tropical Pacific Ocean (ETP) region, which allowed for flexibility in national implementation, but provided a specific definition of "dolphin-safe", referring to mortality and injury of dolphins, unlike the US definition which refers primarily to the mode of fishing i.e. chase and encirclement of dolphins. The regional agreement allows flexibility in implementation of the procedures under the agreement especially to address where the national law of the state may conflict with the standard established by the agreement.[1028] Mexico argued that the US standard is inconsistent with Article 2.2 because "its objective is not legitimate or, in the alternative, it is more trade-restrictive than **necessary** (emphasis added) to fulfil a legitimate objective taking account of the risks non-fulfilment would create."[1029] Article 2.2 defines legitimate objectives as those aimed at addressing "national security requirements; the prevention of deceptive practices; protection of human health or safety, animal or plant life or health, or the environment". However, unlike Article XX(b) of the GATT which is an exception to positive obligations and functions as a defence, the panel characterizes Article 2.2 of the TBT agreement as a positive obligation laying the burden on the complainant to show that the requirements of the article have not been met. This is a crucial difference in how necessity is measured because the burden of evidence and showing failure to comply lies with the complainant.

The panel adopts a two-step approach: first to determine whether the measures pursue a legitimate objective and then whether the measure is more trade-restrictive than necessary to achieve that objective.[1030] In determining 'necessity', the panel notes that some degree of trade-restrictiveness is clearly envisioned by Article 2.2 and that the necessity therefore is measured against possible alternative measures that would be less-trade restrictive.[1031] Unlike GATT Article XX(b), the panel argues that necessity in TBT Article 2.2 is measured primarily against trade restrictiveness rather than against the necessity for the achievement of the objective.[1032] The panel finds more support in footnote three to Article 5.6 of the SPS Agreement, which also focuses on measuring necessity against the availability of less-restrictive trade measures. In that case, footnote 3 requires the measure not just to be less-trade restrictive but significantly less

---

[1027] Panel Report, United States – Measures Concerning the Importation, Marketing and Sale of Tuna and Tuna Products, WT/DS381/R, adopted 13 June 2012, as modified by Appellate Body Report WT/DS381/AB/R (*US – Tuna II (Mexico)*)
[1028] para 2.41, *US – Tuna II (Mexico)*
[1029] para 4.55, Id.
[1030] para 7.388, Id.
[1031] para 7.458, Id.
[1032] para 7.460, Id.

trade restrictive, which the panel uses as dispositive.[1033] The trade-restrictiveness analysis is modified by a consideration that any less-restrictive measure must not pose a greater risk of non-fulfilment of the legitimate objective.[1034] The panel's standard therefore involves a deep examination of exactly how the measure functions, so as to determine whether it actually functions to achieve the legitimate objective in the way claimed. This then allows the panel to compare it to the complainant's proposed alternative(s). The issue was therefore whether allowing Mexico to use the regional agreement standard would accomplish the same level of protection in terms of the dolphin populations aimed at by the US measures.[1035] In assessing the comparability of the measures, regarding consumer information in achieving the actual level of protection achieved by the challenged measure, the panel found that the use in conjunction of the standards in the regional agreement with those of the US would indeed be less trade restrictive. The panel found that the use of such standards was reasonably available and that the standards are equally capable of meeting the *actual* level of protection provided by the challenged measures, at least as far as the consumer information objective is concerned.[1036] With respect to the objective of protecting animal health and the environment, the panel also finds that the US measures are only truly effective in the ETP fisheries region and cannot be considered to actually extend protection of dolphins outside of the region. The issue is therefore whether allowing Mexico to use the regional agreement standard would accomplish the same level of protection in terms of the dolphin populations aimed at by the US measures.[1037] The panel finds that it does and thus the US measure was not consistent with its obligations under the TBT Agreement.[1038]

The *US – Tuna II (Mexico)* panel takes the approach that these are positive obligations in which the burden lies with the complainant. In addition, the primary assessment lies in the trade-restrictiveness of the measure in relation to other methods. However, the panel only requires that the alternative be less trade restrictive while still enabling the achievement of the legitimate objective at the level chosen by the respondent. This is supposedly in contrast to GATT XX(b) analyses which are meant to measure necessity against the capacity to contribute materially to the aim of protecting human, animal or plant life or health. However, the 2011 *China-Raw Materials* panel report suggests that even in such cases, the trade-restrictiveness of the measure is the primary measure of necessity even where there is a showing that the challenged measure contributes or is apt to contribute to the achievement of the objective.

[1033] para 7.464, Id.
[1034] Id.
[1035] para 7.612, *US – Tuna II (Mexico)*
[1036] Id., para 7.577-578
[1037] para 7.612, *US – Tuna II (Mexico)*
[1038] *Id.*

The Appellate Body reversed the approach taken by the panel on the necessity issue and reversed its findings when applying the three factor test it established in this case.[1039] In particular, the Appellate body argued that trade-restrictiveness should not have been treated as dispositive but that there should be a balancing test between the three factors, making it possible for the other two to outweigh the trade-restrictiveness of the measures. In particular, the Appellate Body notes that the 'alternative measure' proposed must be at least as equally able to achieve the objective aimed for by the measure, and pose no greater risk of non-fulfillment of the objective, in order for the challenged measure to be found inconsistent.[1040] In this case, the Appellate Body pointed to the lack of equivalence between the alternative measures proposed by Mexico in order to achieve these aims.[1041]

The Appellate body restated and re-applied the three factor test which took into account:[1042]

(i) the degree of contribution made by the measure to the legitimate objective at issue;
(ii) the trade-restrictiveness of the measure; and
(iii) the nature of the risks at issue and the gravity of consequences that would arise from non-fulfilment of the objective(s) pursued by the Member through the measure.

The key lesson from this case is the placing of the burden of showing trade restrictiveness on the challenger; the need to show that alternative measures would achieve an equivalent outcome in pursuit of a legitimate aim under the TBT; that a balancing test does not require that ALL three factors be met but that the degree of each factor in the balance matters and that even where one or two are in the negative, that may still be balanced by a positive in the others. The broad approach in *Brazil Retreaded Tyres* remains in force in terms of how much the measure should contribute:

> We recognize that certain complex public health or environmental problems may be tackled only with a comprehensive policy comprising a multiplicity of interacting measures. In the short-term, it may prove difficult to isolate the contribution to public health or environmental objectives of one specific measure from those attributable to the other measures that are part of the same comprehensive policy. Moreover, the results obtained from certain actions--for instance, measures adopted in order to attenuate global warming

---

[1039] para 331, Appellate Body Report, United States – Measures Concerning the Importation, Marketing and Sale of Tuna and Tuna Products, WT/DS381/AB/R, adopted 13 June 2012 *(US – Tuna II (Mexico))*
[1040] para 322, Id.
[1041] para 329-330, Id.
[1042] para 322, Id.

and climate change ...--can only be evaluated with the benefit of time.[1043]

This "necessity" jurisprudence in the GATT XX(b), and TBT Article 2.2 cases points to a key conclusion : there is a consistent concern for carrying out balancing tests that look at the extent to which a measure contributes to the legitimate objective, the importance (moral and otherwise) of the value that it is seeking to address[1044], weighed against the trade restrictiveness of the measure and the availability of less restrictive measures. In addition, general articles such as Article 2.2 of the TBT have been viewed as shifting the burden of proof. To the extent that similar terms and language can be found in the TRIPS Agreement it appears that such measures should be approached in a very similar way. The broad approach regarding the extent to which a measure contributes to the goal brings us much closer to privileging environmental judgment over pure trade restrictiveness. This may be an approach applicable in considering necessity within TRIPS.

The actual application of the standard in GATT article XX to the TRIPS Agreement is fairly clear. There can be no direct applicability. As Marceau and Trachtman, have argued, it would be more than just a heroic interpretation of the terms of the agreement.[1045] However, the argument is that the Appellate Body and WTO jurisprudence has an interest in having the same term having the same meaning when used across the various WTO Agreements unless due cause can be shown as to why it should be treated differently. The next section explores the extent to which the concept of necessity in TRIPS shares the same framing, and the extent to which it might be made to do so.

II.2. The necessity test in the TRIPS Agreement

The 'necessity' requirement in Article 8.1 of the TRIPS Agreement, states that:

Members may, in formulating or amending their laws and regulations, adopt measures *necessary* to protect public health and nutrition, and to promote the public interest in sectors of vital importance to their socio-economic and technological development, provided that such measures are consistent with the provisions of this Agreement (emphasis added).

[1043] WTO "Appellate Body Report - Brazil-- Measures Affecting Imports of Retreaded Tyres (Brazil-- Retreaded Tyres), WT/DS332/AB/R, adopted 17 December 2007.
[1044] See Condon, B "Climate Change and Unresolved Issues in WTO Law" 12 J. Int'l Econ. L. 895 (2009).
[1045] Marceau G and J Trachtman "The Technical Barriers to Trade Agreement, the Sanitary and Phytosanitary Measures Agreement, and the General Agreement on Tariffs and Trade' 36 JWT 811 (2002).

There is similarity with respect to the legitimate objectives analyses conducted under the GATT, and the TBT agreements. TRIPS Article 8.1 specifically mentions 'public health and nutrition' as subject matter areas, but also the more general goal 'to promote the public interest', which is broader than the language in Article XX(b) of the GATT 1994, as well as that in Article 5.6 of the SPS Agreement and Article 2.2 of the TBT.

Crucially, the wording of Article 8.1 may also be construed as a positive obligation of the kind established in Article 5.6 of the SPS Agreement and in Article 2.2 of the TBT Agreement. The burden of proof of non-compliance with Article 8.1 could lie on the complaining party to show that such measures were not "necessary". This issue remains unaddressed in the jurisprudence described below, in part because the only panel that has addressed the issue appears to have simply treated Article 8.1 as synonymous with the limitations and exceptions enumerated in TRIPS Articles 30, 31 and 40.

The issue of the burden of proof is complicated by the fact that, unlike GATT Article XX exceptions which are premised on the idea that the measures in question are not in conformity with the other requirements of the GATT, in the case of Article 8.1 of the TRIPS Agreement, the test already states that such provisions *must* be in conformity with the TRIPS Agreement before they are tested. The key part of the provision that enables this is final element of the sentence: 'provided that such measures are consistent with the provisions of this agreement.' The task for any person seeking to create some symmetry with Article 2.2 of the TBT Agreement, Article 5.6 of the SPS Agreement and Article XX(b) of the GATT 1994, is to determine the exact effect of that last sentence of Article 8.1.

As an initial premise, we must establish that Article 8 has to be given full effect and cannot simply be left as a statement devoid of any specific content. It cannot be that Article 8 is entirely subsumed by article 30 and 31 and other limitations and exceptions.[1046] The first part of Article 8.1 must be given content separate from that of other articles on limitations and exceptions and on balancing rights and obligations. Whereas Article 30 (on exceptions) and 31 (on compulsory licenses) can be considered specific sub-sets of situations under Article 8, the article itself recognizes a broad right that in and of itself constitutes an additional scope beyond those of the 'exceptions' in the TRIPS Agreement.

In addition, Article 8 has to be seen as a reiteration of the basic principle of state sovereignty and rights to make policy in these crucial areas. As such, restrictions on

---

[1046] For a slightly contrary view, see p121, Gervais, D *The TRIPS Agreement: Drafting History and Analysis*, (London: Sweet & Maxwell, 2003) who views article 8 as primarily a statement of the policy embodied on Articles 30, 31 and 40.

that broad right must function as exceptions and should be construed narrowly, even where those rights are restricted by being submitted to regulation under an international treaty. The burden for non-compliance with Article 8 should be on those claiming that the discretion under the broad right established by Article 8.1 has been abused.

However, that burden may be shifted by the last sentence of Article 8.1. We are therefore tasked with answering the question of what is meant by "consistent with the provisions of this agreement." By definition this must of course include ALL the TRIPS articles. Thus Article 7[1047] is one of the measures of consistency with the agreement, just as much as article 27, 30, or 31. The phrase may also have the consequence of shifting the burden of proof that would normally be the case in a positive obligation such as this one. In this case, we understand that the burden of showing that a measure is not in compliance with the provisions of the TRIPS Agreement lies with the defendant. The question is whether such a finding is final and dispositive regarding the TRIPS Agreement. Is it the case that where a measure is found to be in violation of one of the rights established by Article 28[1048], that Article 8 cannot be used as an independent defence? That appears to be the case if the language is taken literally. This appears to be the same outcome even where a violation of Article 28 is found, AND it is not excused under article 30.[1049] Given the literal content of the last part of Article 8.1, it does not appear possible to access or give content to the first part of Article 8.1 where a measure is already found to be inconsistent with the any of the provisions of the TRIPS Agreement. Does that mean that the first part of article 8.1 has no content? This would clearly be an absurd outcome and requires some recourse to

---

[1047] This requires that the "protection and enforcement of intellectual property rights should contribute to the promotion of technological innovation and to the transfer and dissemination of technology, to the mutual advantage of producers and users of technological knowledge and in a manner conducive to social and economic welfare, and to a balance of rights and obligations.".

[1048] Article 28 states:
1. A patent shall confer on its owner the following exclusive rights:

(a) where the subject matter of a patent is a product, to prevent third parties not having the owner's consent from the acts of: making, using, offering for sale, selling, or importing(6) for these purposes that product;

(b) where the subject matter of a patent is a process, to prevent third parties not having the owner's consent from the act of using the process, and from the acts of: using, offering for sale, selling, or importing for these purposes at least the product obtained directly by that process.

2. Patent owners shall also have the right to assign, or transfer by succession, the patent and to conclude licensing contracts.

[1049] Article 30 states: Members may provide limited exceptions to the exclusive rights conferred by a patent, provided that such exceptions do not unreasonably conflict with a normal exploitation of the patent and do not unreasonably prejudice the legitimate interests of the patent owner, taking account of the legitimate interests of third parties.

supplementary materials under Article 32 of the Vienna Convention on the Law of Treaties.[1050]

The formulation in Article 8.1 is unique and not found in any of the other WTO covered agreements. For there to be an article that appears to allow flexibility to address key issues but conditions that flexibility on compliance is an unusual but, it appears, deliberate approach. Some sense of the meaning of the provision can be found in looking at the legislative history of the two related provisions, Article 7 and Article 8 of the TRIPS Agreement, in the Uruguay Round negotiations.

The main body of the Anell text[1051] included a draft on 'Principles':[1052]

8. Principles

8B.1 PARTIES recognize that intellectual property rights are granted not only in acknowledgement of the contributions of inventors and creators, but also to assist in the diffusion of technological knowledge and its dissemination to those who could benefit from it in a manner conducive to social and economic welfare and agree that this balance of rights and obligations inherent in all systems of intellectual property rights should be observed.

8B.2 In formulating or amending their national laws and regulations on IPRs, PARTIES have the right to adopt appropriate measures to protect public morality, national security, public health and nutrition, or to promote public interest in sectors of vital importance to their socio-economic and technological development.

8B.3 PARTIES agree that the protection and enforcement of intellectual property rights should contribute to the promotion of technological innovation and enhance the international transfer of technology to the mutual advantage of producers and users of technological knowledge.

With respect to Article 8.1, the later Brussels Draft[1053] stated:

[1050] As argued by Frankel, S "WTO Application of 'the Customary Rules,'" 46 Va. J. Int'l L. 390 (2006), noting that the WTO panels and Appellate body have spent too little time looking at the object and purpose of the agreement as required by the interpretive approach of Articles 30 and 31 of the Vienna Convention on the Law of Treaties.
[1051] This was a draft titled "Chairs Draft" produced by the Chair of the TRIPS Negotiating Group Mr Lars Anell in June 1990, on his own responsibility and then later adopted as a formal negotiating document. The text was "Chairman's report to the Group of Negotiation on Goods, document MTN.GNG/NG11/W/76, dated July 23, 199 cited by D Gervais "The TRIPS Agreement: Interpretation and Implementation" E.I.P.R. 1999, 21(3), 156-162, p157.
[1052] See p 122, ICTSD/UNCTAD *Resource Book on TRIPS and Development* UNCTAD/ICTSD Capacity Building Project on Intellectual Property Rights, June 2005, (Cambridge: Cambridge University Press, 2005)

1. Provided that PARTIES do not derogate from the obligations arising under this Agreement, they may, in formulating or amending their national laws and regulations, adopt measures necessary to protect public health and nutrition, and to promote the public interest in sectors of vital importance to their socio-economic and technological development.

The constraint in Article 8.1, as it was finally adopted, is that the measures they adopt should not violate the terms of the agreement. The UNCTAD IPRs Resource Book suggests that 'measures adopted by Members to address public health, nutrition and matters of vital socio-economic importance should be presumed to be consistent with TRIPS, and that any Member seeking to challenge the exercise of discretion should bear the burden of proving inconsistency'.[1054] In that sense, this comports with approaches from the TBT and SPS Agreements. This approach presumes that the sequence of examination begins with whether the measures are of the kind envisioned, and if they are, then it goes on to address the issue of whether they are inconsistent. Again, this comports with the approach taken under the SPS and TBT Agreements. Under such an approach, there therefore exists a difference in scope between Article 30, and Article 8. Where a measure is aimed specifically to "protect public health and nutrition, and to promote the public interest in sectors of vital importance to their socio-economic and technological development" then Article 8 would create a presumption that the measure is consistent that must be rebutted by the complainant. This would comport with the structure of Article 30 which requires no subject matter limitation on exceptions, or Article 31 which places no subject matter restriction on why compulsory licenses can be granted. Article 8 would shift the burden for public interest measures whereas all other measures would be directly addressed by Article 30 and 31. This would require that a claim be structured in the following way: the complainant would assert that a measure either does not fall under those contemplated by Article 8.1, and even if they did, the measure was not consistent with the provisions of the TRIPS Agreement. The burden of showing inconsistency would then lie with the complainant which can be crucial in the weighing of evidence. This approach however only allows Article 8.1 to have a burden shifting role in certain situations. The approach, however, does not negate the fact that compliance with Article 8.1 would remain dependent on either not violating a right granted by a provision or by coming within the boundaries of an exception or limitation enumerated elsewhere in the TRIPS Agreement. There would still be no substantive effect to the first half of Article 8.1

An alternative approach to that advocated by the authors of the TRIPS Resource Book would be to take the approach that measures *must* be consistent with

---

[1053] This draft was produced 6 months later at the Brussels Conference in December 1990. See D Gervais "The TRIPS Agreement: Interpretation and Implementation" E.I.P.R. 1999, 21(3), 156-162, p157.
[1054] See p 127, ICTSD/UNCTAD *Resource Book on TRIPS and Development* UNCTAD/ICTSD Capacity Building Project on Intellectual Property Rights, June 2005, (Cambridge: Cambridge University Press, 2005)

the TRIPS Agreement before they will be covered by the terms of Article 8.1 In that case, an examination of consistency takes place first and if the measures are found to be inconsistent, Article 8.1 plays the role of a thumb on the scale to move measures that fall under its coverage back into consistency. This would not necessarily be in literal line with the wording of the article but not doing so leaves the first part of Article 8 devoid of content. The negotiating history, as well as the broader context in which the TRIPS Agreement stands suggests that *literal* consistency with the TRIPS Agreement cannot be the limit of the effect of the provision. Why is the 'necessity' language in there if the consistency requirement has to be met? Article 8.1 cannot simply be co-terminous with the sum of the exceptions and limitations in the agreement. If that is the case why have Article 8.1 in the first place? There must already be a sense in which the measures contemplated by Article 8 go beyond the strict limits of consistency. Necessity, therefore could be seen as controlling how far outside the limits of consistency they may go and that it may not allow the provisions of the agreement to be entirely null and void. It may be possible to refer back to the broader jurisprudence on 'necessity' from the SPS and TBT Agreements and argue that the necessity test standard of 'least-inconsistent and reasonably available measure' should be applied here. At the very least, the option of how the necessity test was construed in the early years should be applied: there were no other available TRIPS-consistent measures possible and the least TRIPS-inconsistent measure was taken.[1055]

In addition, Article 8.1 is supported by Article 7, with which the states must also comply in their implementation of the TRIPS Agreement[1056]. Authors such as Derclaye[1057] and Correa[1058] argue that Article 7 establishes that intellectual property rights clearly must be in service of broader social values. Where the provision of rights contradicts or conflicts with broader public welfare goals, the Article provides a means by which IP protection can be modified, diminished or removed. Correa also argues that while Article 8.1 contains the limitations on 'consistency', Article 7 does not and thus, one of the provisions with which Article 8 must be consistent is Article 7, as well as the preambles.[1059] As an overriding principle, interpreters are bound to ensure that Article 7 is given as much effect as any other provisions of the agreement and cannot be considered only hortatory.

[1055] p149, Bernasconi-Osterwalder, N et al., *Environment and Trade: A Guide To WTO Jurisprudence* Earthscan, London (2006).
[1056] Article 7 states: The protection and enforcement of intellectual property rights should contribute to the promotion of technological innovation and to the transfer and dissemination of technology, to the mutual advantage of producers and users of technological knowledge and in a manner conducive to social and economic welfare, and to a balance of rights and obligations
[1057] p270, Derclaye, E 'Intellectual Property Rights and Global Warming', 12 J. MARSHALL REV. INTELL. PROP. L. 263 (2008).
[1058] p99-101 Correa, C M, *Trade Related Aspects of Intellectual Property Rights: A Commentary to The TRIPS Agreement,* , Oxford University Press (2007)
[1059] p107, Id.

Article 7 provides guidance for the interpreter of the TRIPS Agreement, emphasizing that it is designed to strike a balance among desirable objectives. As Article 7 makes clear, TRIPS negotiators did not mean to abandon a balanced perspective on the role of intellectual property in society. However, given the structure of Article 8.1 the approach that seems to have won out over others is that any attempt to justify measures to protect health and nutrition and to promote the public interest in sectors of vital importance to socio-economic and technological development cannot rely solely on Article 7 and 8 but must enter first through other provisions in the TRIPS Agreement and then, in the course of applying these articles use the weight of Articles 7 and 8.1 to tip the scales in favour of justifiable policy actions. This has ostensibly been the approach that has been taken in the context of the interpretation of TRIPS provisions relating to exceptions and limitations.[1060] The interpretation of Article 7 and 8 remains unclear however as the Appellate Body itself has found that Article 7 and 8 have yet to be interpreted in a way that provides guidance to their applicability in future cases.[1061]

The next section addresses the extent to which this issue has been addressed by panels with respect to patents, and whether Article 8.1 has truly been given content, such that members are actually able to take measures to protect human health and nutrition and to promote the public interest in sectors of vital importance to socio-economic and technological development. Finding a way to apply necessity within the framework of the TRIPS Agreement is crucial if measures to address technology transfer of climate technologies are to be available. Without a balancing test that looks at the necessity of action, it may be much harder to justify broad sector-wide actions to address climate change as clearly envisioned by Article 8.1. To the extent that a necessity test is not applied in the evaluation of TRIPS measures to address public health and nutrition and promote the public interest, the more difficult it may be to escape narrow interpretations of TRIPS flexibilities. The next section examines the specific flexibility measures addressed by the TRIPS Agreement, measuring their legal availability and their practical availability given the scale and scope.

III. THE AVAILABILITY OF IP MEASURES TO ADDRESS TECHNOLOGY TRANSFER FOR CLIMATE CHANGE

III.1. Exceptions to Rights

III.1.1. Legal Availability

[1060] para 7.26, Panel Report, Canada – Patent Protection of Pharmaceutical Products, WT/DS114/R, adopted 7 April 2000, DSR 2000:V, 2289 (Canada – Pharmaceutical Patents)
[1061] Para 101, Appellate Body Report, Canada – Term of Patent Protection, WT/DS170/AB/R, adopted 12 October 2000, DSR 2000:X, 5093 (Canada- Patent Term).

The TRIPS Agreement contains no General Exceptions article such as that embodied by GATT Article XX, but for each specific category of rights, it establishes a standard exception (for copyright in Article 13, for trademarks in Article 17, for patents in Article 30).

In the context of the discussion on transfer of technology, the area of most concern is patent law, as well as any technology transfer provisions. In that context we can point not just to Article 8.1, but also to Article 30.[1062]

Article 30 was interpreted in the *Canada – Pharmaceutical Patents*[1063] case. In this case, Canada defended the stockpiling of medicines prior to the expiration of a patent as well as allowing generic competitors to produce samples of the product for the purposes of regulatory approval. Canada based its entire case on the assertion that the measures fell within the Article 30 exceptions. The panel divided the Article 30 test into three, cumulative steps. The measure:[1064]

(i)   must be 'limited';
(ii) must not 'unreasonably conflict with normal exploitation of the patent'; and
(iii) must not 'unreasonably prejudice the legitimate interests of the patent owner, taking account of the legitimate interests of third parties.'

Similarly to Article 13 TRIPS, this article was adopted and somewhat modified from the language in Article 9(2) of the Berne Convention.[1065] In the context of patent law it is *sui generis*, never having appeared before in any international treaty on industrial property. Gervais cautions against the transposition of principles and approaches from Article 9(2) Berne Convention on Copyright to one that is primarily aimed at industrial property.[1066] This is in line with the core difference in rationale for the grant of the right and the difference in scope e.g. where copyright protects expressions but not ideas, patents protect ideas as well. While one cannot ignore the intent of creating some consistency of approach, this also makes the differences that much more important to note. In the case of Article 30, Gervais points to the third step on the need to balance the legitimate interests of third parties against those of the right holder as a key textual

---

[1062] Article 30 states: Members may provide limited exceptions to the exclusive rights conferred by a patent, provided that such exceptions do not unreasonably conflict with a normal exploitation of the patent and do not unreasonably prejudice the legitimate interests of the patent owner, taking account of the legitimate interests of third parties.
[1063] Panel Report, Canada – Patent Protection of Pharmaceutical Products, WT/DS114/R, adopted 7 April 2000, DSR 2000:V, 2289 (*Canada – Pharmaceutical Patents*)
[1064] para 7.20 *Canada-Pharmaceutical Patents*
[1065] See p425, Abbott, F "WTO Dispute Settlement Practice Relating to the Agreement on Trade-Related Intellectual Property Rights" in Ortino, F and E U Petersmann (eds.) *The WTO Dispute Settlement System 1995-2003* (Amsterdam: Kluwer Law International, 2004)
[1066] See p333, Gervais, D *The TRIPS Agreement: Drafting History and Analysis: Third Edition*, (London: Sweet & Maxwell, 2008)

modification which suggest that Article 30 would have to be read more broadly than Article 13 or Article 9(2) of the Berne Convention.[1067]

The examination carried out by the *Canada-Pharmaceutical Patents* panel is sequential and cumulative. *All* three steps had to be met in sequence, if the measure was to be found consistent with Article 30.[1068] It is important to note that this need not be the case at all. In the TBT Agreement three factor tests for necessity, the factors were balanced against each other. While this has been the practice of panels, the Appellate body has yet to address this issue. This outcome exists in part because the parties to the dispute agreed that this should be the sequencing and the panel did not dispute their approach.[1069] There is little precedent from the interpretation and practice under the Berne Convention that suggest that such an approach is required.

As Abbott notes, the formulation in Article 30 was only adopted after there was significant disagreement as to what would be included in an enumerated list of exceptions[1070] as well as whether such a list would be closed or only exemplary. What can at least be presumed from such a failure is that all countries believed the formulation encompassed and protected all exceptions to patent rights that they had in operation at the time of the signing of TRIPS. To conclude otherwise is to essentially adopt the position of the countries that argued for a limited enumerated list, rather than that of countries who argued for the preservation of their own existing patent exceptions and the flexibility to provide more. Gervais points out that the version of Article 30 in the Draft of July 23, 1990(W37), creates an exemplary (non-exhaustive) list while also allowing for the creation of new exceptions.[1071] What list of exceptions can we then point to under this reasoning? The first list is that included in the draft:

a. Rights based on prior use;
b. Acts done privately and for non-commercial purposes;
c. Acts done for experimental purposes;
d. Acts done by a government for purposes merely for its own use;
e. Extemporaneous preparation of medicines on an individual basis by pharmacies; ("pharmacy preparation exception")

[1067] See p380, Gervais, D *The TRIPS Agreement: Drafting History and Analysis: Third Edition*, (London: Sweet & Maxwell, 2008)
[1068] para 7.20 *Canada-Pharmaceutical Patents*
[1069] Id.
[1070] See p425, Abbott, F "WTO Dispute Settlement Practice Relating to the Agreement on Trade-Related Intellectual Property Rights" in Ortino, F and E U Petersmann (eds.) *The WTO Dispute Settlement System 1995-2003* (Amsterdam: Kluwer Law International, 2004)
[1071] See p380, Gervais, D *The TRIPS Agreement: Drafting History and Analysis: Third Edition*, (London: Sweet & Maxwell, 2008)

We should note that there is no non-commercial element to the 'experimental purposes', unlike that for private actions. Garrison also points to other exceptions widely in use and accepted at the time of the signing of the TRIPS Agreement, including:[1072]

a. Exceptions for use of patented technologies contained in foreign vessels and aircraft in in port and in use in international transport;

b. Civil Aviation Exception (contained as an obligation under Chicago Convention on International Civil Aviation of 1944) such as exemption from seizure based on patent claims.[1073]

As an initial matter, the panel had to first determine the role that Article 8.1 should play: whether it constituted an independent defence; if not, what role it had on the interpretation of Article 30 with respect to burden of proof or the interpretation of the terms in Article 30. The Panel in the *Canada-Pharmaceutical Patents* case placed the burden of proof on the party claiming justification under the exceptions. As noted above in discussing the role of Article 8.1, it is not obvious that this would be the case given the approach in the TBT Agreement. Reading Article 30 and Article 8.1 together, it is equally plausible that since Article 30 contemplates measures which are in conflict with other rights provided by the TRIPS Agreement and since the right to take such measures is acknowledged and embedded in Article 8.1, the burden for showing that the measures do not comply with TRIPS Article 30 should lie with the complainant. In contrast, the panel argued that Article 30 functioned as an exception in the same way that Article XX(b) did in the GATT 1994.[1074] The Article only applies where a measure has already been found non-compliant with other positive obligations in the TRIPS Agreement, in this case Article 28. Thus as a defence that has to be asserted, the burden lies on the respondent who asserts it and should have the burden of showing it. As noted above, this approach to the burden of proof is also in part a function of the structure of the claim. The European Communities did not claim that Canada was in violation of Article 8.1, but that it was in violation of Articles 27.1, 28.1 and 33, and was in violation until it could justify it through some other TRIPS provision. In its defence, Canada did not argue for a restructuring of the claim through Article 8.1 but asserted only that it should have interpretive weight in applying Article 30. No panel has addressed what would occur in the circumstances under which a respondent argued that a claim challenging the application of a measure to protect health and nutrition and to promote the public interest in sectors of vital importance to socio-economic and technological development is more properly made under Article 8.1.

[1072] See p9, Garrison, C "Exceptions to Patent Rights in Developing Countries" ICTSD Issue Paper No. 17 (August 2006).
[1073] Article 27, Convention on International Civil Aviation
[1074] para 7.16, *Canada-Pharmaceutical Patents*, citing *United States - Measure Affecting Imports of Woven Wool Shirts and Blouses from India* a non-intellectual property case.

Canada first asserted that Article 30 should be read in light of the objectives and purposes of the TRIPS Agreement, in particular Article 8.1. The Panel acknowledged that Article 8.1 had some interpretive force, but viewed the existence of Article 30, and the way it was narrowly constructed, as a significant indicator that Article 30 should not be read to alter the 'negotiated' balance exhibited by the TRIPS Agreement.[1075] The panel stated:

> "Obviously, the exact scope of Article 30's authority will depend on the specific meaning given to its limiting conditions. The words of those conditions must be examined with particular care on this point. Both the goals and the limitations stated in Articles 7 and 8.1 must obviously be borne in mind when doing so as well as those of other provisions of the TRIPS Agreement which indicate its object and purposes."

It appeared from this that the panel would at least consider the goals stated in Article 8.1 in interpreting the provisions of the three step test. However, when examining the actual reasoning of the panel, the influence of Article 8.1 is difficult to discern.[1076]

In examining the panel's interpretation of the first step, i.e. the 'limited' nature of the measure, there appears to be no way for the Article 7 or Article 8.1 public interest elements to enter into what may be considered "limited". In the first instance the panel adopts the position that the term 'limited' must be read in conjunction with the term 'exception', so that limited is read as narrow, rather than as "definite" or defined in scope, as argued by Canada. The panel argued that by definition, an exception is already meant to be a curtailment of rights, and the use of the term 'limited' in this context must modify that curtailment so that it becomes a narrow curtailment.

In the second instance, regarding whether a measure is indeed 'limited' the panel's reasoning means that this is assessed purely against the extent to which the patent right is affected.[1077] Therefore, the test is fundamentally one that requires that the measure have a small qualitative and quantitative effect on the rights of the patent holder. If a measure does not meet this test, its public policy purpose(s) need never be examined or taken into account. No matter how dire a need the measure is attempting to address, if the measure is not limited, then it fails the test.[1078] The stockpiling exception failed at the first hurdle because it allowed unlimited production in the 6 months prior to expiry of the patent, while the regulatory exception passed because it was limited to levels of production solely for the purposes of meeting the goal of

---

[1075] para 7.26 *Canada-Pharmaceutical Patents*, WTODS114/R (2000)
[1076] Also noted by para 7.31, Frankel, S "The Consequences of Misinterpreting TRIPS" 1 W.I.P.O.J. 35 (2009)
[1077] *Canada-Pharmaceutical Patents*, WTODS114/R (2000),
[1078] Para 7.30 – 7.38 *Canada-Pharmaceutical Patents* WTO/DS/114/R (2000)

regulatory approval. At no point in the analysis does the panel address Article 7 or Article 8.1 in determining how to address the interpretation of the term 'limited'.

One can contrast this approach to the way in which an examination of "least-restrictive trade" measure embodied in GATT Article XX(b), Article 5.6 of the SPS Agreement and Article 2.2 of the TBT Agreement might take place. In those provisions, the 'limited' nature of a measure, i.e. its effect on trade, is assessed against the reasonable availability of other measures which would achieve its goal. In the approach to Article 30, there is no way to balance the 'restrictiveness' or level of violation of the measure against other less restrictive or less violating measures that would achieve the same goal. Because the panel approaches the test cumulatively and fails to use Article 8.1 to influence the interpretation of whether a measure is limited, it is possible to never address the public interest goal of a measure in assessing Article 30. This would seem to render Article 8.1 devoid of any content with respect to Article 30. Whether such an approach would be sustained by the Appellate Body is an open question as the panel decision in this case was never appealed. While the panel's decision is therefore not required to be carried over into future panel decisions on similar issues, this approach will continue to influence the interpretation of Article 30, unless a respondent makes the point of raising an Article 8.1 argument in this context.

In examining the regulatory approval exception's conformity with the second and third steps, the panel continues to fail to apply Articles 7 and 8.1. In interpreting the second step, the Panel first defined 'normal exploitation' as 'to exclude all forms of competition that could detract significantly from the economic returns anticipated from a patent's grant of market exclusivity.'[1079] They sought support for this from a dictionary definition of 'normal', that did not address the normative aspects of the definition but focused on the elements referring to "regular, usual, typical, ordinary, conventional".[1080] However, finding that the measure in question (i.e. production for regulatory approval) did not conflict with normal exploitation, the Panel did not find it necessary to decide whether the conflict was unreasonable. What is key is that the Panel worked on the presumption that a patent holder had the right to expect income from ALL forms of exploitation. At no point is a normative element included that details certain kinds of markets from which a right-holder should not be expected to receive income or be able to exploit nor certain kinds of measures that a state has a right to take as articulated by article 8.1. Public interest justifications play no part in this portion of the analysis either. The panel made no reference to any influence that Article 8.1 or Article 7 might have on their understanding on what constituted normal exploitation which would have been modified by the assertion in Article 8.1 that states may take actions to protect human health and nutrition and to promote the public interest in sectors of vital importance to socio-economic and technological development.

[1079] para 7.55, *Canada-Pharmaceutical Patents*, WTODS114/R (2000)
[1080] para 7.54, Id. citing the New Shorter Oxford Dictionary

It is possible that the panel would have referred to article 8.1 in determining the unreasonableness of the conflict, but since that was not addressed, it remains an open question. If in fact Article 8.1 is not addressed in determining whether or not a conflict exists, the only way in which Article 8.1 can have an influence on the interpretation of the second step is through an assessment of the reasonableness of the conflict. Applying Article 8.1, - those measures that passed the first step, conflicted with the normal exploitation of the right but were of the kind covered by Article 8.1 would therefore be presumed to pass the second step. Any other outcome would, again, seem to rob Article 8.1 of any content with respect to Article 30.

The Panel then moved to the third step, describing what the 'legitimate interests' of the right holder and third parties might be. The Panel noted that '[t]o make sense of the term 'legitimate interests' in this context, that term must be defined in the way that it is often used in legal discourse - as a ***normative*** (emphasis added) claim calling for protection of interests that are "justifiable" in the sense that they are supported by relevant public policies or other social norms.'[1081] This would appear to have been an ideal place to insert the measures contemplated by Article 8.1 into the assessment, as a way of deciding the extent of the legitimate interests of the rightholder and what were the legitimate interests of third parties. However, while examining what were 'legitimate interests' of the patent holder, the Panel provided no further indication of what might be encompassed by the legitimate interests of third parties, as it found that there was no legitimate interest of the patent holder at play in the regulatory approval process. As far as patent law goes, there is no indication of how future panels or the Appellate Body might view: what would constitute prejudice to the legitimate interests of the right holder; what would constitute unreasonable prejudice; what would be defined as the legitimate interests of third parties. Again, an approach that would be consistent with Article 8.1 would take measures that fell within the scope of the Article as presumptively of the kind that lay outside the legitimate interests of the rightholder given that Article 8.1 is a clear statement of WTO members' right to balance the interests of the rightholder against others as it deems appropriate in addressing public health and nutrition and promoting the public interest in sectors of vital importance to socio-economic and technological development. For exceptions that do not fall within the scope of the measures contemplated in Article 8.1, the unreasonableness of the prejudice to the legitimate interests could still be tested, including the interests of third parties that are not covered by Article 8.1.

In looking at the entire analytical approach by the panel in the *Canada-Pharmaceutical Patents* case, there still seems to be room in the approach for the application of Article 8.1 in the second and third steps. However, if the panel's approach to the application of the first step of Article 30 continues to be the standard, and the burden of proof remains as stated by the panel, then the key hurdle that any

---

[1081] para 7.69, *Canada-Pharmaceutical Patents*, WTODS114 (2000)

measures to address climate change face may be that of being appropriately limited. As such, measures can be found invalid long before any policy justification can be considered.

It remains unclear what the effect of Article 30 should be on exceptions that existed and were known at the time of the signing of the TRIPS Agreement. There is no document or statement that would represent an" agreement relating to the treaty which was made between all the parties in connection with the conclusion of the treaty;" under Article 31(2)(a) of the VCLT regarding the status of such exceptions. The case of the obligatory exception under Article 27 of the Chicago Convention on International Civil Aviation, may be no clearer. The TRIPS Agreement contains no general savings clause relating to obligations in other existing agreements. It only has such a specific savings clause in Article 2(2) stating

> Nothing in Parts I to IV of this Agreement shall derogate from existing obligations that Members may have to each other under the Paris Convention, the Berne Convention, the Rome Convention and the Treaty on Intellectual Property in Respect of Integrated Circuits.

It explicitly does not mention other agreements existing at the time under which obligations relating to intellectual property are contained. The WTO Agreement itself has no savings clause. This would imply that such pre-existing obligations would and may have been altered by the TRIPS Agreement making the exception in the Chicago Convention subject to Article 30. In the absence of a case it is difficult to assess the compliance of Article 27 of the Chicago Convention with Article 30, but as Garrison notes, the exception in the convention is quite large.[1082] Article 27(1) establishes that there shall be no "seizure or detention of the aircraft or any claim against the owner or operator thereof or any other interference therewith by or on behalf of such State or any person therein on the ground that the construction, mechanism, parts, accessories or operation of the aircraft is an infringement of any patent, design, or model duly granted or registered in the State whose territory is entered by the aircraft." In article 27(2) this protection extends to the storage and use of spare parts, provided that these are not sold internally or exported. In part, it may be possible to explain this provision as one where the aircraft and spare parts are treated as not having been 'imported' and thus not having legally entered the territory of the state. However, where the law of the state considers that such 'importation' has taken place, the rightholder may still not have any remedies for the infringement of any rights embodied in technologies or spare parts for the aircraft. This exception applies to all aircraft and would apply to any commonly used technology in aircraft with the potential effect of limiting the effect of the patent only to aircraft that are domestically

---

[1082] See p41, Garrison, C "Exceptions to Patent Rights in Developing Countries" ICTSD Issue Paper No. 17 (August 2006).

manufactured and perhaps to domestic airline operators. Foreign airline operators are entirely insulated from patent claims. As Garrison notes, the rights of the patent holder to use and import would be entirely negated for the term of the patent, something which is likely to not be in conformity with the narrow sense of 'limited' used by the panel in the *Canada-Pharmaceutical Patents* case.[1083] This leaves us with two possibilities: either the panel was mistaken in its interpretation of Article 30, or we are presented with a case of a conflict between two provisions in two different treaties that must be resolved. The second issue is addressed in Chapter 7 on how such treaty conflicts are resolved under the WTO, but at this stage, it seems appropriate to ask whether or not the panel may have been mistaken in its approach to Article 30. Garrison argues that as an example of existing state practice at the time of the signing of the agreement, widely used exceptions that almost all states had in practice MUST be taken into account in determining the scope and meaning of terms such as 'limited".[1084] He points, for example, to the international aviation and foreign vessels exceptions noting that all member states under the Chicago Convention are required to use it and all WTO member states have voiced no objections to it. If the Chicago Convention exception is allowable, others of commensurate breadth should also be allowed. One could also point to subsequent state practice under Article 31(3)(b) that a practice has been established which is evidence of an agreement as to the meaning of the term between parties. With respect to the Chicago Convention exceptions, however, it is difficult to see how any clarifying legal controversy could apply since any country that wished to challenge such a case would itself likely be guilty of the same practice. The existence and use of the exception may be less evidence of agreement as to the meaning of Article 30, and more an acknowledgement of a common lack of compliance on the part of the majority of WTO member that all have agreed to refrain from challenging. From an interpretive standpoint, the lack of a reference to the Chicago Convention exceptions in the various drafts leading up to the adoption of the three step test suggest more a lack of knowledge as to the existence of the exception than an 'agreement' that the exception was encompassed by Article 30. This is borne out by the fact that other exceptions, including those such as the "pharmacy preparation" exception are explicitly mentioned in the non-exhaustive list in the Draft of July 23, 1990(W37).

The decision of the panel in this case prompted significant concerns from developing countries regarding the interpretation of Article 8.1 and of Article 30 and this issue was part of what was addressed by the Doha Declaration on the TRIPS Agreement and Public Health.[1085] Paragraph 4[1086] reiterates members' rights to use

---

[1083] See p41, Garrison, C "Exceptions to Patent Rights in Developing Countries" ICTSD Issue Paper No. 17 (August 2006).
[1084] Id. See also Correa, C *The TRIPs Agreement: A Guide for the South. The Uruguay Round Agreement on Trade-Related Intellectual Property Rights* (Geneva: South Centre, 1997)
[1085] Declaration on the TRIPS Agreement and Public Health, WT/MIN(01)/DEC/2 (2001)
[1086] Paragraph 4: We agree that the TRIPS Agreement does not and should not prevent members from taking measures to protect public health. Accordingly, while reiterating our commitment to the TRIPS

TRIPS flexibilities, including exceptions under Article 30, to their fullest extent and that the Agreement should be interpreted in a way supportive of members' right to protect public health.

Directly addressing the issue of how TRIPS provisions should be interpreted, especially in Article 30, the Declaration notes in Paragraph 5(a) that in "applying the customary rules of interpretation of public international law, each provision of the TRIPS Agreement shall be read in the light of the object and purpose of the Agreement as expressed, in particular, in its objectives and principles." This directly addresses the role that Article 7 and 8.1, which are under the title of "Principles' in the text of the TRIPS Agreement, should play. There is little dispute that, as a declaration by **all** WTO members, the declaration functions as a subsequent Agreement under Article 31(3)(a) of the VCLT, which requires that interpreters must take into account as part of the context of the agreement "any subsequent agreement between the parties regarding the interpretation of the treaty or the application of its provisions;" Thus it would be incumbent upon any judicial interpreter to go further than the panel in *Canada Pharmaceuticals* and actively apply Article 7 and 8.1 to the interpretation of Article 30.

The interplay between Article 8.1 and Article 30 is crucial when we consider what room Article 30 leaves for the creation of exceptions to address access to and transfer of climate technologies for adaptation and mitigation. The first question to be answered is whether the proposed measures would technically fall under Article 30 as an exception. For example, a working requirement for patents would be difficult to categorize as an exception in that it functions as an additional burden placed on the rightholder to carry out certain activities in order not to lose the patent right. This would be similar to what the patent holder has to do in paying renewal fees at intervals during the life of the patent. In contrast, an exception allows third parties to carry out certain acts that would nominally be disallowed by the existence of the patent and either justifies a specific category of activities related to the patent (e.g. non-commercial research) or allows a specific category of actors to carry out activities related to the patent (e.g. exceptions to copying for students or blind-people). Given the structure of the TRIPS Agreement, compulsory licenses are also not classified as exceptions and the standards for their application are also very different, as will be addressed below. In addition, actions to exclude certain categories of technologies from patents would also not function as exceptions, as these again, relate to the conditions for grants of patents rather than directly enabling third parties to act while a patent is still in force. In addition, the issue would also be whether the proposed measure was one of those contemplated by Article 8.1 of TRIPS.

Agreement, we affirm that the Agreement can and should be interpreted and implemented in a manner supportive of WTO members' right to protect public health and, in particular, to promote access to medicines for all. In this connection, we reaffirm the right of WTO members to use, to the full, the provisions in the TRIPS Agreement, which provide flexibility for this purpose.

An additional issue when it comes to exceptions arises in the realm of computer software. Under TRIPS Article 10.1, member states are required to protect computer programs as if they were literary and artistic works. Such protection extends not just to the human-readable programming language but also to the machine readable object code. In some countries e.g. the US, software is protected by both patents and copyright. In Europe it is ostensibly excluded from patent protection (Article 52 of the European Patent Convention), except where it has a further technical effect.[1087]

Software is a significant element of the management of smart grids, and smart grid connections as well as many energy efficiency systems in electronic appliances. In many cases, other companies and programmers may wish to see the source code of a computer program to see how it works. In the context of copyright this is well within the system as a rightholder is required to communicate his or her "work". However, in many cases, firms keep the human readable source code as a trade secret while distributing the machine-readable object code. In order to see how the computer program was written, it becomes necessary for others to translate the code back into human readable source code. Under copyright rules, and absent an exception, for copyright, such an act of translation is an infringement of the right of translation or reproduction (depending on domestic law). In many countries there are exceptions that specifically allow for such acts with respect to copyright (called decompilation), but in many countries, they are restricted and set with conditions.[1088] Where software is protected by patents then (even where the source code is made available, these decompilation activities are governed by TRIPS Article 30 with its very restrictive interpretive approach.

Where software is only protected by copyright, these are protected by the even more restrictive interpretation of Article 13 by another WTO panel in a case between the US and the European Union.[1089]

Article 13 of TRIPS on copyright exceptions states:

Members shall confine limitations or exceptions to exclusive rights to certain special cases which do not conflict with a normal exploitation of the work and do not unreasonably prejudice the legitimate interests of the right holder.

[1087] T1173/97 (Computer Program product) of 1 July 1998, 10 Official Journal of the European Patent Office 609 (1999). Available at: http://archive.epo.org/epo/pubs/oj99/10_99/10_6099.pdf (last visited 15 August 2014).
[1088] See e.g. Article 6, DIRECTIVE 2009/24/EC OF THE EUROPEAN PARLIAMENT AND OF THE COUNCIL of 23 April 2009 on the legal protection of computer programs 111 Official Journal of the European Union 16 (2009).
[1089] 'United States - Section 110(5) of US Copyright Act – Report of the Panel', WT/DS160/R, available at http://www.wto.org/english/tratop_e/dispu_e/cases_e/ds160_e.htm (last visited 15 August 2014).

Importantly, unlike Article 30, Article 13 has no requirement that the legitimate interests of third parties must be taken into account in the third step, removing any possibility that absent a means for Article 8.1 to enter in the first and second steps, there is much narrower room for public welfare interests and goals. In the *US – Section 110(5) Copyright Act* case, this is compounded by the fact that the panel in this case never considered or addressed the role or meaning of Article 7 and 8.1. In addition, the panels approach to the term 'legitimate' in the third step only looked at the right-holders interest and defined them as exploitation interests only with regard to any and all income from rights rather than contrasting them or comparing them to the interests of other actors.[1090] The panel in the *US – Section 110(5) Copyright Act* case, also established the principle that the three step test was to be read cumulatively, rather than as a balancing test[1091], ensuring that the first step would never be outweighed or balanced against the others or the public interest goals of the measure. Again, there was no precedent or justification for this under anything other than a literal reading of the text as is.[1092] The narrow approach extended to the interpretation of all elements of the three step test. Essentially, the panel ruled that other than those with de minimus effects on the economic activity of the rightholder, few exceptions would pass the test.[1093] The consequences for software exceptions are clear. Where decompilation and other activities are created as exceptions, these may not pass muster under TRIPS unless they are carefully limited to activities with limited commercial effect, which contradicts the goals of exceptions that would be applied to address climate change activity related to smart grids and energy efficiency. However, thirteen years after the complaint was first instituted, the *US – Section 110(5) Copyright Act* panel decision begins to look less like the bombshell it first seemed. As a legal matter it remains a fundamentally flawed and unreliable indicator of what may occur in future cases, or as a guide to legal interpretation at national level. However, the failure to revisit the issue at the WTO over the past ten years has allowed the standard to become the *de facto* yardstick against which proposals to further copyright protection or to restrict have been made, possibly giving it far more influence than its legal reasoning would deserve. In addition, it is clear that this case significantly influenced the approach of the panel in *Canada-Pharmaceutical Patents*, extending the influence of its poor reasoning into inappropriate territory. The *Canada-Pharmaceutical Patents* case however raised many of its own problems as well, especially relating to how to deal with subsequent state practice.

[1090] See Shabalala, D "United States- Section 110(5) of the US Copyright Act" in C M. Correa (ed.) *Research Handbook on Intellectual Property Law and the WTO Volume II,* Edward Elgar 2010.
[1091] See para 6.97 'United States - Section 110(5) of US Copyright Act – Report of the Panel', WT/DS160/R
[1092] See in support, p21 Hugenholtz, P B and R G Okediji (2008), "Conceiving an International Instrument on Exceptions and Limitations to Copyright," iVir, March 06, 2008. Available at http://www.ivir.nl/publicaties/hugenholtz/finalreport2008.pdf (last visited 15 August 2014).
[1093] See Shabalala, D "United States- Section 110(5) of the US Copyright Act" in C M. Correa (ed.) *Research Handbook on Intellectual Property Law and the WTO Volume II,* Edward Elgar 2010.

The issue of how to treat subsequent state practice is difficult in the context of Article 30. This divides into two issues: the scope and extent of exceptions in existence since the signing of the TRIPS Agreement; exceptions passed since the signing of the TRIPS Agreement. *Canada-Pharmaceutical Patents* essentially split the difference by allowing the regulatory exception, existing before the TRIPS Agreement, and disallowing the stockpiling exception, passed after the TRIPS Agreement. Garrison argues that the reason this was the case relates in part to the standard for assessing subsequent state practice proposed by Canada which was that subsequent state practice should be assessed according to the extent to which the measure in question was broadly in use by member states at the time of the signing of the agreement and was not subject to persistent objection by other members.[1094] The panel essentially dismissed the arguments related to existing state practice stating specifically that:

> "The Panel did not accord any weight to either of those arguments, however, because there was no documented evidence of the claimed negotiating understanding ... because the subsequent acts by individual countries did not constitute "practice in the application of the treaty which establishes the agreement of the parties regarding its interpretation" within the meaning of Article 31.3(b) of the Vienna Convention.".

This appears to be despite the fact that Canada very clearly points to statements and practice on the regulatory review or "Bolar" exception in the US.[1095] This was clearly evidence that needed to be weighed, which the panel simply chooses to ignore. It is unclear what 'evidence' beyond this the panel would have required to substantiate an Article 31.3(b) assertion of state practice but unprotested statements during negotiations at the time of the signing of the agreement as well as unprotested subsequent practice are clearly evidence. The problem in this case may be that none of the exhibits presented by Canada provided statements made during the negotiations or after the fact. In addition, the evidence during the case of other state practice pointed to the existence and implementation of the regulatory review exception in many other developed WTO member states[1096] but almost always accompanied by a system of patent term extension related to regulatory review delays. The panel, however, does not appear to have given any weight, in either direction, to this evidence, simply dismissing it as insufficient to meet the requirements of Article 31(.3(b). This may be a significant error as the TRIPS Council has a very specific process for evaluating countries'

[1094] See p34, Garrison, C "Exceptions to Patent Rights in Developing Countries" ICTSD Issue Paper No. 17 (August 2006).
[1095] See para 7.41, *Canada-Pharmaceutical Patents*, WTODS114 (2000) *citing* First Submission of Canada, paragraph 105 and Exhibit 41, quoting letter of US Trade Representative Michael Kantor to Alfred B. Engelberg, 1 February 1996.
[1096] See p199, *Canada-Pharmaceutical Patents*, WTODS114 (2000) (Annex 5 - Questions Posed by the Panel and Replies Received from the Parties and Third Parties on the Practice in Countries Other Than Canada as Regards Regulatory Review Exceptions and Patent Term Extension or Supplementary Protection Certificate Systems)

implementation of TRIPS obligations and failure to refer to these reviews and their treatment of regulatory review exceptions is a major evidentiary lapse. For example, in the 1997 Review of the US' implementing legislation on patents the European Communities and its member states had an opportunity to specifically question the US application of the regulatory review exception, but did not.[1097] In contrast it specifically asked the US how other provisions complied with the TRIPS Agreement's Article 30, for example, the newly legislated exception for medical practitioners for use of methods of treatment.[1098] The issue of exceptions generally was raised by other countries such as Japan and New Zealand.[1099]

There is also significant international law and practice behind the interpretation of Article 31.3(b), which the panel also ignored.[1100] The failure to apply the appropriate standard for considering subsequent state practice creates significant uncertainty for countries to create new exceptions, although there may be some comfort drawn regarding existing exceptions. The next section describes what the possibilities are for crafting exceptions to patent rights to address climate change and whether they can be of sufficient scope.

III.1.2. Types of exceptions that may be available to address climate change

Article 8.1 of TRIPS clearly envisions measures capable of addressing broad sectoral issues. It allows members to take actions to promote the public interest in sectors of vital importance to socio-economic and technological development. Applying that standard to the area of climate change it can be argued that addressing climate change mitigation and adaptation is in the public interest of countries signatory to the UNFCCC. It can also be argued that certain specifically identified sectors, (e.g. drought-resistant agriculture, or fuel-efficient motor vehicles) constitute sectors of vital importance to socio-economic and technological development. This would apparently justify exceptions that are sufficiently broad to have an effect on a whole sector. However, the framework for the creation of exceptions under TRIPS as outlined in the

---

[1097] See p4 - 17, WTO, "Review of Legislation in the Fields of Patents, Layout-Designs (Topographies) of Integrated Circuits, Protection of Undisclosed Information and Control of Anti-Competitive Practices in Contractual Licences" IP/Q3/USA/1 (1 May 1998), *reproducing* the questions put to the delegation of the United States and the responses given in the review of legislation on patents, layout-designs (topographies) of Integrated circuits, protection of undisclosed information and control of anti-competitive practices in contractual licences at the Council's meeting of 26-30 May 1997.
[1098] See p13, Id.
[1099] See p2 and 17, Id.
[1100] See e.g. p33-34 Temple of Preah Vihear, (Cambodia v. Thailand) merits I.C.J. Reports; p160 Certain Expenses of the United Nations (Article 17, paragraph 2, of the Charter), Advisory Opinion of 20 July 1962, I.C.J. Reports 1962; p22, para. 22 Legal Consequences for States of the Continued Presence of South Africa in Namibia (South West Africa) notwithstanding Security Council Resolution 276 (1970), Advisory Opinion of 21 June 1971, I.C.J. Reports 1971.

Canada-Pharmaceutical Patents case, does not include Article 8.1 in determining whether and exception is limited. Only in the second and third steps of the Article 30 analysis can the justification in Article 8.1 potentially be considered. The key design limitation may be in ensuring that an exception is sufficiently limited. Given the scope of the climate change challenge, is it possible to envision useful exceptions that would meet this standard? If the aim is to fundamentally alter the direction and use of climate technologies by producers and consumer, the exception clearly cannot exclude commercial activities. It is precisely these commercial activities that an exception would aim to address through research, development, and distribution of climate mitigation and adaptation technologies. For climate change purposes, an exception that was targeted at a limited set of actors may not be very effective as it would limit the kind of broad sectoral participation that climate change measures require. However, there may be circumstances, such as a clearly identified bottleneck, where such an exception targeted at a limited set of actors might be possible. The type of exception could relate perhaps to size of business enterprise, or to a category of actors such as students or universities. For climate change, perhaps the size of the business enterprise could be relevant, but probably only when also limited to a specific product or set of products. This may be especially appropriate in an economic sector where many of the actors are small informal actors.

The other approach to exceptions, that may be more viable for designing climate change measures, would be to look at a specific set of especially desirable activities and exempt those from liability. The classic type of patent exception in such cases is the research exception. It is often limited to non-commercial research but that can actually be seen as duplicating the function of the disclosure or enablement requirement for the grant of the patent. The disclosure or enablement requirement is meant to enable a person skilled in the art to understand and reproduce your patented product or process for the purposes of determining that the rightholder has actually accomplished what he claims to have accomplished. In that sense it is a restatement of the fundamental scientific principle of falsifiability: that any discovery needs to be tested by others to determine whether the claimant has actually discovered or created what he states he has. The research exception can, however, be made broader to include research and development that could lead or is meant to lead to a commercial product. In the case of the 'regulatory approval' exception in the *Canada-Pharmaceutical Patents* case, research and development on the patented drug is allowed to enable third parties to learn how to produce generic versions of the drug AND production is allowed to the extent that such production is used only for the purposes of showing regulators that the generic version in equivalent to the patented product. However, the product cannot be stockpiled or sold until after the expiration of the patent. For the purposes of addressing climate change and ensuring technology development, it is clear that research and development and the learning that comes from carrying out research on patented products is more likely to result in the development of new products and in increase of know-how and capacity to reproduce the patented product once the patent expires. A climate research and development exception could then be limited in several dimensions: it would be limited to research and development on patented technologies with the aim of addressing climate change mitigation and adaptation; it could be used only for the development of improved, adapted or entirely new products or processes; it would be limited to research up to the point of prototyping but disallow any activity related to marketing, licensing or sales of the new product or process. Such a research exception would be of benefit to stakeholders in emerging economies who already have such research capacity, such as Brazil, India and China, who could then produce those products in countries where the patent was not protected (many developing countries).

However, it may also provide a pathway for those countries who are seeking entry into the market for production of technologies by adapting such products to local needs and conditions. The limit on marketing, licensing and sales means that permission would still be required, usually in the form of a license for the product to be actually commercially exploited. Thus it would still be possible for the rightholder to refuse to provide such a license, but such refusals would have to comply with rules on competition, market regulation, and the public interest governing the use of patents. The section below on compulsory licenses addresses the circumstances under TRIPS in which refusals to license can be addressed, as well as other circumstances under which compulsory licenses can be granted.

Another option to consider is whether an exception might possibly exist that would allow any and all production related to the patent for export to countries where the product is not patented, or which has a system of international exhaustion. Legally, there are two ways this may happen.

The first is that the exception authorizes production of any patent (or patents in a specific sector) for sale directly to enterprises and actors in other countries where the product is not patent protected. Theoretically there doesn't appear to be any barrier to such an exception as there is no 'market' affected under the second or third step of the Article 30 test. Under the first step, the curtailment of the right to make and use is affected, but the question is to what extent? In the analysis of the regulatory review exception the panel in *Canada-Pharmaceutical Patents* decided that even though almost all the rights were affected, the market effect was negligible and for a specific limited purpose outside of the normal market.[1101] It should be possible for such an exception to pass Article 30 muster. This is in contrast to Article 31(f) which limits the majority of production under a compulsory license to the domestic market. This is the strongest argument against such an exception: that such measures were contemplated and countries chose to regulate production for export under Article 31, excluding them from Article 30 coverage. In particular, the exclusion of compulsory licenses specifically for export suggests that countries intended to limit and ensure that no such use of patented products should be allowed. However, as noted in the next section on compulsory licenses, several countries have legislation that allows for compulsory licenses

---

[1101] See para. 7.45, *Canada-Pharmaceutical Patents*, WTODS114 (2000).

specifically only for export purposes, with no domestic distribution allowed.[1102] The existence of Article 31(f) may be seen as directed primarily at licenses issued for domestic production but does not exclude licenses exclusively for export, or other such measures.

The second is where the exception allows export not just to countries where the product is patented but where the product is patented but the country has a system of international exhaustion. In those situations, the products have never been placed on the market or been sold first or placed in the market in country of production, so it would be difficult to argue that the rights have been exhausted, especially where no compensation has taken place. This would be in contrast to a compulsory license where compensation for the use would have taken place in the country of production and the right would therefore be considered to have been exhausted and would perhaps be a basis for allowing parallel importation based on international exhaustion (this is addressed in more detail in the next section on compulsory licenses). In this case, an exception that allowed such export would likely fall afoul of the Article 30 second step that the exception should not unreasonably prejudice the market of the rightholder, which to some extent includes export markets in which the rightholder may compete with other producers, where such export may interfere with domestic rights in other countries.

As much as the previous set of suggestions seems to argue for the fact that designing TRIPS-compliant exceptions is a real possibility, this is modified by two caveats. The first is that, for such exceptions to be possible, TRIPS jurisprudence must be understood to have been altered by the Doha Declaration on TRIPS and Public Health, and that a different approach to the application of Article 7 and 8.1 is included in at least the second and third steps of the Article 30, three step test. The second is that exceptions are by definition a limited tool and can never go so far as to fundamentally alter the balance of power away from the rightholder. The question that arises is how many exceptions can be created and how large can their cumulative effect be before they run afoul of the broader obligation to provide effective patent protection.

III.1.3. Practical Availability

Timing

Exceptions that are placed in regulation can begin to function almost immediately. Once in place, all actors who qualify can begin to take advantage of them with respect to specific activities or sectors. In that sense they would be ideal tools to address activities that need to take place within the 2020 mitigation horizon and the

---

[1102] See e.g. Article 84.7.a(iii), Indian Patents Act, as amended by Act No. 15 of April 4, 2005.

2025 adaptation horizon. The issue is whether they are capable of speeding up the distribution and adoption of existing technologies within the timetable. This is intimately linked to their scale effect. If they were able to operate at sufficient scale then it is likely that several bottlenecks could be addressed allowing for a possible snowball effect. However, as noted below, given the interpretation of the first step in Article 30, such a scale effect is not likely. In the context of the debate on pharmaceuticals, the ability of exceptions to actually enable sufficient production and distribution have largely been avoided. The Doha Declaration chose the path of compulsory licensing as the primary means of addressing the production and distribution elements of access problems under TRIPS. To the extent that exceptions are useful and powerful it is with two groups: end-users or consumers; and producers who can engage in research and development by other producers.

Scale

The use of exceptions as a policy tool would have to be part of a broader concerted effort that will have interactions with other patent limitations and TRIPS flexibilities. Using exceptions to manage sectoral development will require a concerted effort to identify bottlenecks where exceptions may be appropriately given to categories of actors, but will also require action across a broad set of sectors, requiring the exemption of certain categories of action. Multiple sets of individual exceptions addressed to specific issues and problems may each be limited but, taken as a whole, may have a broad effect. While not a haven, those exceptions that are based on or are extensions of exceptions historically practised by most states are less likely to be challenged. Despite the narrow reading provided by *Canada-Pharmaceutical Patents* panel, there is an understanding that certain kinds of exceptions such as private use, research, educational and experimental uses, as well as other exceptions existing at the time of the TRIPS Agreement and common in most countries' patent laws would likely fall within the scope of Article 30.[1103] These, such as the regulatory approval exception, could then be extended and designed to specifically address climate change mitigation and adaptation technologies. What is especially clear is that any exception that actually involved sale of patented products, or products produced by patented processes into the market would never be able to pass the second step as interpreted by the panel in *Canada-Pharmaceutical Patents*. The panel allows no more than a *de minimus* effect of the commercial market of the rightholder.

While exceptions are still available under TRIPS, the narrow reading by the *Canada-Pharmaceutical Patents* panel means that, as a practical matter, it may not be possible to design exceptions with significant market effect of sufficient scale to address technology transfer for climate change. To the extent that an exception involves

---

[1103] Section 2, Garrison C "Exceptions to patent Rights in Developing Countries" Issue Paper No. 17, UNCTAD-ICTSD Project on IPRs and Sustainable Development, October 2006.

commercial activity, it is likely to fail under most interpretive scenarios. The exceptions that remain are not likely to be able, individually, or in the aggregate, to operate at the scale of technology sectors and the scale and speed of effect required.

Geographic scope

The issue of geographical scope is whether exceptions would be able to operate to allow innovation, production and distribution of technologies in major emerging economies and allow them to export to other developing countries. The first thing to note is that to the extent that a developing country has a system of international exhaustion, the importation of products produced within the framework of an exception would be allowed. However as noted in the discussion above, it is precisely the sale or distribution of products that is likely to fail the TRIPS Article 30 test, unless perhaps the export was to countries that already did not have patent protection for the product or process. In such a case, there is no market in the developing country to which the patent holder can be said to have a right.

III.2. Compulsory licenses

III.2.1. Legal Availability

In addition to Article 30, public policy concerns beyond simple IP protection find their way into the TRIPS Agreement with provisions on compulsory licensing (Article 31 on 'Other Use without Authorization of the Right Holder'). States may use a compulsory license to take the patent rights held by another party and either exercise the rights themselves, or license the rights to third-parties to help the state exercise such rights. There has been no WTO dispute related to compulsory licensing under the TRIPS Agreement to date. However, the issue of compulsory licensing was at the core of the debate that led to the adoption of the Doha Declaration on the TRIPS Agreement and Public Health.[1104]

There are generally two categories of compulsory license that can be taken into account, only one category of which is limited by the TRIPS Agreement. To the extent that compulsory licenses are issued in the course of addressing anti-competitive practices and abuses of patents, countries remain free to determine when and how such licenses should be issued in terms of Article 31(k) and Article 40.[1105] There is no

---

[1104] Declaration on the TRIPS Agreement and Public Health, WT/MIN(01)/DEC/2 (2001)
[1105] Article 40.2 states "Nothing in this Agreement shall prevent Members from specifying in their legislation licensing practices or conditions that may in particular cases constitute an abuse of intellectual property rights having an adverse effect on competition in the relevant market As provided above, a Member may adopt, consistently with the other provisions of this Agreement, appropriate measures to prevent or control such practices, which may include for example exclusive grantback conditions,

requirement that there be remuneration to the right holder in such cases. In the US, such licenses are issued by judges on a frequent basis for software, merger reviews, and other anti-competition remedies.[1106] These kinds of licenses are also primarily concerned with ensuring that the system operates the way that it is meant to: ensuring enough competitive room for innovation in the near and long-term.

The kind of licences that have caused the most difficulty and have been the basis of significant controversy are compulsory licenses for reasons other than addressing competitive practices, including such examples as public health emergencies. In such cases, the behaviour of the State is regulated by TRIPS Article 31 which foresees the use of such compulsory licenses as a way to address significant shortages, distribution problems and pricing issues addressed at either meeting short term demand for goods and products or at enabling public (government) non-commercial use for any reason. It is important to note that the TRIPS Agreement actually places no limitations on the grounds for issuance of compulsory licenses but only regulates the process by which such licenses are to be granted. In all the instances of compulsory licenses for non-competition purposes, adequate remuneration based on local market conditions is required.[1107] Generally, good faith negotiation with patent holders is required, except if there is national emergency or other situation of extreme urgency, in which case government may proceed without first carrying out good faith negotiations. In the case of public non-commercial use, there is never a requirement to negotiate with the patent holder. There has been no case testing the application of such compulsory licenses.

In terms of addressing climate change, Article 31 places no restrictions on the domain and sectors in which compulsory licenses can be applied. This is also true for compulsory licenses to address anti-competitive behaviour. At the very least, Article 8.1 and article 8.2 can be seen as requiring a broad interpretation of Article 31, provided that the basic procedural requirements of Article 31 are met and the substantive elements of Article 8.2 are met.[1108] A proof of concept can be found in the US Clean Air Act codified in 42 USC § 7608. It provides the possibility of compulsory licenses for those required to meet a rule or standard set up under the Clean Air Act, where the technology to meet such a standard is held by a patent holder and lack of access may place such a stakeholder at a competitive disadvantage.[1109] As Derclaye points out, the

---

conditions preventing challenges to validity and coercive package licensing, in the light of the relevant laws and regulations of that Member.
[1106] For more examples see: http://keionline.org/content/view/41/1 (last visited 15 August 2014).
[1107] Article 31(h) TRIPS
[1108] See also p281, Derclaye, E 'Intellectual Property Rights and Global Warming', 12 J. MARSHALL REV. INTELL. PROP. L. 263 (2008).
[1109] Derclaye also points to this as an example of a compulsory license provision in the public interest. See p669, Derclaye, E 'Not Only Innovation but also Collaboration, Funding, Goodwill and Commitment: Which Role for Patent Laws in Post-Copenhagen Climate Change Action', 9 J. MARSHALL REV. INTELL. PROP. L. 657 (2010). She also notes that the system has never been used in the entire time the Clean Air Act has existed, although she points to the incentive to cooperate that it establishes.

provision has never been the subject of WTO dispute settlement[1110] but its existence and lack of objection from other states suggests that such provisions can clearly be established in the context of other countries actions to address climate change.

It is easy to conclude that compulsory licensing is legally available under the TRIPS for any purposes.

III.2.2. Practical Availability

Section 84(7) of India's Patent Act allows for issuance of compulsory licenses if the "reasonable requirements of the public are not met". This includes:

a) if, by reason of the refusal of the patentee to grant a licence or licences on reasonable terms,
   i. an existing trade or industry or the development thereof or the establishment of any new trade or industry in India or the trade or industry of any person or class of persons trading or manufacturing in India is prejudiced; or
   ii. the demand for the patented article has not been met to an adequate extent or on reasonable terms; or
   iii. a market for export of the patented article manufactured in India is not being supplied or developed; or
   iv. the establishment or development of commercial activities in India is prejudiced; or
b) if, by reason of conditions imposed by the patentee upon the grant of licences under the patent or upon the purchase, hire or use of the patented article or process, the manufacture, use or sale of materials not protected by the patent, or the establishment or development of any trade or industry in India, is prejudiced; or
c) if the patentee imposes a condition upon the grant of licences under the patent to provide exclusive grant back, prevention to challenges to the validity of patent or coercive package licensing, or
d) if the patented invention is not being worked in the territory of India on a commercial scale to an adequate extent or is not being so worked to the fullest extent that is reasonably practicable, or
e) if the working of the patented invention in the territory of India on a commercial scale is being prevented or hindered by the importation from abroad of the patented article by
   a. the patentee or persons claiming under him; or
   b. persons directly or indirectly purchasing from him; or

[1110] p270., Id.

c. other persons against whom the patentee is not taking or has not taken proceedings for infringement.

India's broad approach is reflective of the freedom to choose the basis on which compulsory licenses are issued including for industrial policy to restructure markets. Compulsory licenses are ideal tools for market restructuring where sectoral development suffers from lack of production, or further research and development, due to the existence of a patent or set of patents. However, for patents that do not address anti-competitive practices, TRIPS establishes constraints that may be so limiting as to make such licenses ineffective as tools to address production and dissemination of climate change mitigation and adaptation technologies.

The primary limitation is the one requiring that patents be addressed on a case by case basis.[1111] This limits the granting of public interest licenses to an evaluation for each and every patent that must meet the rest of the requirements of Article 31. Where the technologies to be addressed are complex technologies that constitute not just a single patent but a complex of patents, the application of compulsory licenses can become a slow and cumbersome process as each patent in the family will require a separate compulsory license. Such complex technologies include windmills, fuel cells, agricultural biotechnologies for biofuels, as well as for seeds. However, it may be possible to issue patents at the product level, covering the suite of patents related to a particular product or product category. Correa points to the termination provision in Article 31(g) as also problematic from the viewpoint of the recipient of a compulsory license. It requires termination once the conditions requiring the license have been met. He argues that this creates business uncertainty as the license may be terminated at any point.[1112] I would argue that this would depend on the framing of the purpose of the compulsory licensing. Noting that countries are free to determine the reasons for issuing compulsory licenses, I would argue that countries be careful about framing the reasons for the licenses to ensure that they provide sufficient business certainty and are sufficiently long term. In addition, providing for regulatory timelines for such assessment (e.g. at 3 and 5 years from issuance) will also create certainty. The legitimate interests of the person assigned the license have to be taken into account, meaning that the business case has to be considered in any assessment.

A second limitation is that such a license must be granted primarily for supply of the domestic market.[1113] Some interpretations have suggested that this is limited

---

[1111] TRIPS Article 31(a).
[1112] See p8, Correa, C "Intellectual Property Rights and the Use of Compulsory Licenses: Options for Developing Countries" Working Paper 5, Trade-Related Agenda, Development And Equity (T.R.A.D.E.) Working Papers, South Centre, October 1999.
[1113] TRIPS Article 31(f).

exclusively for the domestic market[1114], but at least the wording contemplates some portion being produced for export. While this clearly contemplates that some portion of the supply will be exported, the wording suggests that a significant majority of the production should still go to the domestic market. If we consider the role that countries such as China, India and Brazil must play in ensuring dissemination of climate technologies to other developing countries that do not have as much R&D and production capacity, this limitation ensures that these countries will not be able to use compulsory licensing effectively to achieve that goal. This points to the largest problem with Article 31, which is that, for those countries with limited or no production capacity, compulsory licensing is not an option, since there will be no domestic actors to whom such licenses could be granted and who could thus produce for the domestic market. Article 31 does not contemplate that a member could grant a compulsory license to an actor outside its territory for the purposes of that actor exclusively producing for supply of that country's domestic market. Patent rights are territorial and can only be exercised on the territory of the patent granting state. Thus limitations and exceptions to patents created by a state can only be exercised on the territory of the patent granting state.

In principle, if the state presents a sufficiently large market, this should encourage outside companies to locate production in these states to take advantage of the possibility of being granted a compulsory license for production to meet domestic needs. However, in the absence of a guarantee that such a license would be issued, such companies are unlikely to take the investment risk. In addition, many developing countries, assessed individually, do not present sufficiently large markets to justify establishment of production facilities on their territory primarily to supply their domestic market, regardless of the existence of patents. Even where patents exist, such small markets are of little interest to originator/rightholder companies and they present an additional barrier to investment by generic or other non-originator/imitator companies. The ability to provide compulsory licenses does not add to the attractiveness of the investment.[1115] Where patents do not exist, these markets remain too small to be of interest for investors to establish facilities.

With respect to governments themselves establishing such facilities, this requires an assessment of whether it would be more cost-effective to import the drugs from elsewhere or to expend significant amounts of money to import the expertise and, facilities to enable domestic production. Such an analysis nearly always falls in favour of directly paying for the importation of products, even from markets that are extremely

---

[1114] See p16, Adam, A "Technology Transfer to Combat Climate Change: Opportunities and Obligations under TRIPS and Kyoto" 9 J. HIGH TECH. L. 1 (2009)
[1115] One untested approach to solving this FDI problem is for these countries to issue prospective compulsory licenses and then to auction them off to the highest bidder willing to establish production facilities in the domestic market. It is unclear whether such prospectively issued compulsory licenses fall within the limitations established by the TRIPS Agreement.

expensive. This is especially true for the relatively short time frames in which shortages or other needs arise and at which Article 31 appears primarily aimed.

The Declaration on the TRIPS Agreement and Public Health sought to address this issue with respect to pharmaceuticals which were seen as particularly crucial sector for small developing countries. Paragraph 6 of the Declaration recognized that the use of compulsory licenses was a problem for those countries with insufficient or no manufacturing capacity in the pharmaceutical industry and instructs the TRIPS Council to find a solution. The solution proposed by the TRIPS Council was adopted as a General Council Decision in August 2003 (The August 2003 Waiver).[1116] This decision waived the requirements of Article 31(f) and of Article 31(h) (requiring adequate remuneration) for those countries with insufficient manufacturing capacities. It allows WTO members with production capacity to export to those members lacking such capacity, where a compulsory license has been issued for that purpose in the importing country, or if there is no patent in the importing member, where the exporting country has issued a compulsory license for that purpose in conjunction with a request from an eligible importing member. The decision also contains several other requirements related to the packaging, timing, size, and that the entirety of the production must be exported to the specific member. The requirement that adequate remuneration be paid is waived for the importing member but not for the exporting member. Of particular interest for technology transfer and intellectual property issues related to climate change is paragraph 7 of the August 2003 Waiver[1117] which notes that the system should be implemented in such a way as to increase technology transfer and capacity in eligible importing members.

Paragraph 11 of the August 2003 Waiver ensures that it remains in force until such time as an amendment to the TRIPS Agreement implementing the waiver enters into force for each member that ratifies it. This led in 2005 to the adoption of an amendment (Article 31*bis*) to the TRIPS Agreement in the form of a protocol attached to a General Council Decision.[1118] The text essentially restated the conditions outlined in the waiver, as well as the paragraph 7 provision on technology transfer. The amendment enters into force after two-thirds of WTO members have ratified it and replaces the August 2003 Waiver for those countries that have ratified it. The waiver remains in force for all others until they have also ratified the amendment.

[1116] "Decision on the Implementation of Paragraph 6 of the Doha Declaration on the TRIPS Agreement and Public Health" WT/L/540 and Corr.1 adopted August 30, 2003.
[1117] "Members recognize the desirability of promoting the transfer of technology and capacity building in the pharmaceutical sector in order to overcome the problem identified in paragraph 6 of the Declaration. To this end, eligible importing Members and exporting Members are encouraged to use the system set out in this Decision in a way which would promote this objective. Members undertake to cooperate in paying special attention to the transfer of technology and capacity building in the pharmaceutical sector in the work to be undertaken pursuant to Article 66.2 of the TRIPS Agreement, paragraph 7 of the Declaration and any other relevant work of the Council for TRIPS."
[1118] Amendment of the TRIPS Agreement WT/L/641 Adopted 6 December 2005.

The success of the Waiver system and the amendment is difficult to measure. By one measure, i.e. use of the system, the waiver system has been a failure. Since the Waiver was made effective in August 2003, only one importing member (Rwanda) has used it to access drugs from Canada. Despite the fact that the product in question was not actually patented in Rwanda, the process proved so cumbersome that the company that was granted the exporting license under Canadian law declared that the system was economically unsustainable.[1119] By the same measure, it may be considered unnecessary or superfluous as apparently only a fraction of developing countries have felt the need to utilise the system. Support for this could be found in the fact that only a relatively small number of developing countries have ratified the amendment.[1120] However, this is modified by two issues: the waiver remains in force and available so there is little incentive so far for developing countries to move over to ratifying the amendment; use of the system requires implementing legislation, especially in exporting countries as they bear the larger administrative burden under both the Waiver and the Amendment. The most recent data shows that very relatively few countries (13 plus the European Union 25) have actually notified such implementing legislation.[1121] It is difficult to escape the impression that the system may not be as effective as once thought at enabling access to compulsory licensing for small developing countries and economies with little or no manufacturing capacity.

The Waiver and the Amendment apply only to pharmaceuticals and, while it is tempting to view it as a model for access to climate technologies, the complexity of the system suggests that expanding it to a broader set of products and processes may not work. In addition, unlike the pharmaceutical industry, it is not clear that most markets for climate technologies have large generic manufacturers who can easily replicate the products at a very low cost, making reliance on generic supply a key pillar of polices on access. In the case of agriculture and health this may be the case, but in many energy production and efficiency fields, the 'generic' industry does not really exist in the same way as in the pharmaceutical industry. This suggests that compulsory licensing as restricted by TRIPS as a means of managing shortages through reliance on generic producers is probably not applicable to the climate arena for economies with little or no manufacturing capacity. Even with the application of a paragraph 6-like system, this

---

[1119] Apotex Inc. "Submission to the Standing Committee on Industry, Science and Technology Bill C-393, An Act to amend the Patent Act (drugs for international humanitarian purposes) and to make a consequential amendment to another Act" (October 26, 2010). Available at: http://www.apotex.com/global/docs/submission_order_en.pdf (last visited 15 August 2014).

[1120] As of January 5, 2012, 2010 (the last date at which official WTO data are available) only 23 developing countries had notified their acceptance of the Amendment. See Members accepting amendment of the TRIPS Agreement Available at: http://www.wto.org/english/tratop_e/trips_e/amendment_e.htm (last visited 15 August 2014).

[1121] As of February 28, 2011, the most recent date on which WTO official data is available only the European Union, Canada, Norway, India, Hong Kong, Switzerland, the Philippines, Singapore, Albania, Croatia, China, South Korea and Japan, had implementing legislation and/or regulations.,

situation seems unlikely to improve. Only if licenses are more easily available for export, as part of a broader commercial process might this become an effective option.

One option that has not been fully explored is compulsory licensing specifically and exclusively for export purposes. This was addressed in the previous section on whether such an exception would be available, but there is some state practice that suggests that this is possible. The Indian Patent Act specifically allows for issuance of compulsory licenses specifically to service an export market noting that one of the bases for issuance of a compulsory license is that "a market for export of the patented article manufactured in India is not being supplied or developed"[1122] The UK Patent Act also contains such a provision but only limited to non-WTO members.[1123] The UK approach suggests a belief that such a provision may not pass muster.

One final issue to note on licenses issued under Article 31 conditions is that they only apply to patents and not to trade secrets, otherwise known as undisclosed information, sometimes described as 'know-how'. In the context of complex technologies which may constitute a large portion of climate technologies, a significant portion of the knowledge necessary to replicate, operate and, adapt the technology may be retained by the rightholder as trade secrets.[1124] Article 31 provides no authorisation for the imposition of compulsory licenses on trade secrets, but on the other hand, it does not provide a barrier. Article 39 of TRIPS provides for obligations on the protection of undisclosed information.[1125] The obligations are rooted in the requirement

---

[1122] Article 84.7.a(iii), Indian Patents Act, as amended by Act No. 15 of April 4, 2005.
[1123] Article 48B(1)(d)(i) United Kingdom Patent Act of 1977 (as amended)
[1124] See p13, Consilvio, M "The Role of Patents in the International Framework of Clean Technology Transfer: A Discussion of Barriers and Solutions" 3 Intell. Prop. Brief 10 (2011).
[1125] 1.   In the course of ensuring effective protection against unfair competition as provided in Article 10bis of the Paris Convention (1967), Members shall protect undisclosed information in accordance with paragraph 2 and data submitted to governments or governmental agencies in accordance with paragraph 3.

2.   Natural and legal persons shall have the possibility of preventing information lawfully within their control from being disclosed to, acquired by, or used by others without their consent in a manner contrary to honest commercial practices(10) so long as such information:

(a)   is secret in the sense that it is not, as a body or in the precise configuration and assembly of its components, generally known among or readily accessible to persons within the circles that normally deal with the kind of information in question;

(b)   has commercial value because it is secret; and

(c)   has been subject to reasonable steps under the circumstances, by the person lawfully in control of the information, to keep it secret

3.   Members, when requiring, as a condition of approving the marketing of pharmaceutical or of agricultural chemical products which utilize new chemical entities, the submission of undisclosed test or other data, the origination of which involves a considerable effort, shall protect such data

to protect actors against unfair competition contained in Article 10bis of the Paris Convention (1967), and paragraph two lays out the positive obligations of members. Nothing in Article 39 of TRIPS prevents the application of a compulsory obligation to reveal trade secrets and know-how as part of the issuance of a compulsory license on a patent. Some authors argue the opposite[1126]; that a compulsory license or any other mechanism is incapable of mandating exposure of know-how or a trade secret, especially since such exposure would essentially 'destroy' the secrecy of the trade secret as required by the Paris Convention. However, the silence with respect to the issue of mandating sharing does not imply that the obligation to maintain the secrecy could not also be transferred with the compulsory license. The ability to issue such concurrent obligations makes logical sense in that a compulsory license is intended to allow the licensee to practice and reproduce the technology and participate in the market. If a portion of the information necessary to actually participate in the market is held as a trade secret, it makes sense that the obligation to reveal such trade secrets is not limited. Thus, as far as the TRIPS Agreement is concerned, there are no limitations or conditions on parties being required to reveal trade secrets in conjunction with a compulsory license on a patent, where that trade secret is required to make the compulsory license actually effective. Article 5 of the Paris Convention which is incorporated into TRIPS by reference[1127] also places no limitation on the issuance of compulsory licenses related to undisclosed information related to patents.[1128] Correa points to several examples of such information being revealed as part of judgments providing compulsory licenses in US anti-trust practice.[1129]

While the forgoing discussion suggests that there are significant limitations to compulsory licensing in ensuring or enabling production of technologies and technology transfer to developing countries with insufficient or no manufacturing capacity, it remains an effective option for those countries with significant manufacturing capacity. The complexity of the TRIPS system, however, may need to be mitigated by national procedures to make it easier to apply for one. As Cannady points out, it is in most

---

against unfair commercial use. In addition, Members shall protect such data against disclosure, except where necessary to protect the public, or unless steps are taken to ensure that the data are protected against unfair commercial use.

[1126] See p25, Maskus, K "Differentiated Intellectual Property Regimes for Environmental and Climate Technologies", OECD Environment Working Papers, No. 17, OECD Publishing 2010.
[1127] Article 2 of the TRIPS Agreement
[1128] See p57, Khan, B Zorina "Intellectual Property and Development: Lessons from American and European History" Study paper 1a, for Commission on Intellectual Property Rights *Integrating Intellectual Property Rights and Development Policy* (London: Commission on Intellectual Property Rights 2002).
[1129] See p7, Correa, C "Intellectual Property Rights and the Use of Compulsory Licenses: Options for Developing Countries" Working Paper 5, Trade-Related Agenda, Development And Equity (T.R.A.D.E.) Working Papers, South Centre, October 1999.

cases, too cumbersome to use regularly as a part of business planning and strategy.[1130] The experience of Korean companies in implementing the Montreal Protocol suggests that the complexity of the administrative process proved too much for most companies who might have sought to use compulsory licensing.[1131] The effectiveness of Article 31 compulsory licenses however, may lie not so much in their issuance and use, but in the way that the existence of such a possibility alters the negotiating balance between rightholders and potential licensees.[1132] The knowledge that a compulsory license may be made available to competitors or to the government itself in cases where the government determines there is a shortage, lack of supply, or failure to work of some kind, works as an incentive for the rightholder to seek out licensees with whom it is comfortable working and to propose reasonable and commercially sustainable licensing conditions. In using the kinds of compulsory licenses contemplated by Article 31, to address sectoral supply issues, the issue of communicating as clearly as possible the willingness of the government to step in to actively manage the market is crucial. It should be noted that frequent actual use of compulsory licensing may have a detrimental effect on the dynamic side of the IP equation, reducing incentives for innovation in the second generation.[1133]

The kinds of compulsory licenses that go beyond addressing supply issues and seek to restructure the market so that it is more competitively efficient are those that are targeted at anti-competitive practices and abuses of patents. Article 31(k) exempts such compulsory licenses from the requirements of: Article 31(b) (on the need for prior negotiations with the rightholder); Article 31(f) (limiting production primarily for supply of the domestic market). It also modifies the obligation on remuneration in Article 31(h) to allow for providing little or no remuneration. These specific kinds of compulsory licenses and their potential for addressing climate change are addressed in the next sub-section.

A final note on this section is that it clearly also falls under the kinds of measures contemplated by Article 8.1. As such, where the compulsory license is issued in particular to address issues to address health, nutrition or to promote the development of vital economic sectors, this must have an influence on the

---

[1130] See p4, Cannady, C "Access to Climate Change Technology by Developing Countries: A Practical Strategy", ICTSD's Programme on IPRs and Sustainable Development, Issue Paper No. 25, International Centre for Trade and Sustainable Development, Geneva, Switzerland (2009).
[1131] See p85, Korea Trade Promotion Agency "Case Study 4: Korea: The Republic of Korea and the Montreal Protocol" in Jha, V and U Hoffman (eds.) "Achieving Objectives of Multilateral Environmental Agreements: A Package of Trade Measures and Positive Measures Elucidated by Results of Developing Country Case Studies" UNCTAD/ITCD/TED/6, UNCTAD 2000.
[1132] See p23, Correa, C "Intellectual Property Rights and the Use of Compulsory Licenses: Options for Developing Countries" Working Paper 5, Trade-Related Agenda, Development And Equity (T.R.A.D.E.) Working Papers, South Centre, October 1999.
[1133] As argued by Mandel, G "Promoting Environmental Innovation with Intellectual Property Innovation: A New Basis for Patent Rewards," 24(1) Temple Journal of Science, Technology, and Environmental Law 51 (2005).

interpretation of provisions relating to remuneration (Article 31(h)), and level of production for domestic supply (Article 31(f)).

Compulsory licensing is generally legally available, especially for emerging economies with manufacturing capacity. It may be possible to use the system to address sectoral market problems, but blanket measures that are insufficiently specific may fall afoul of the requirement of article 31(a), that such use be considered on individual merits.

III.3. Compulsory licenses and other action to address anti-competitive practices

III.3.1. Legal Availability

Other provisions which may relate to climate policy purposes are Articles 8.2[1134] and 40 of the TRIPS Agreement, which address competition policy and abuses of patent rights. Parties can adopt any measures, including compulsory licenses to address the following issues that are explicitly laid out:

- preventing the abuse of intellectual property rights by right holders (Article 8.2);
- preventing the resort to practices which unreasonably restrain trade (Article 8.2);
- preventing the resort to practices that adversely affect the international transfer of technology (Article 8.2);

Specific examples of such practices cited in the TRIPS Agreement include:

- exclusive grant back conditions;
- conditions preventing challenges to validity;
- coercive package licensing

Article 40.1, as does Article 8.2, recognizes that some IP-related practices that restrain competition may have a negative effect on trade and technology transfer.[1135] In pursuance of measures to address this, Article 40.2 ensures that nothing in the TRIPS Agreement shall limit the freedom of states to determine the nature, kind and scope of

---

[1134] Article 8.2 states "Appropriate measures, provided that they are consistent with the provisions of this Agreement, may be needed to prevent the abuse of intellectual property rights by right holders or the resort to practices which unreasonably restrain trade or adversely affect the international transfer of technology."
[1135] Members agree that some licensing practices or conditions pertaining to intellectual property rights which restrain competition may have adverse effects on trade and may impede the transfer and dissemination of technology.

practices that constitute "an abuse of intellectual property rights having an adverse effect on competition in the relevant market." [1136] Thus, states remain free to address anti-competitive behaviour by actors in their domestic markets.

III.3.2. Practical Availability

For transfer of technologies for climate change mitigation and adaptation it is important to note that included in the ambit of restrictive practices are practices that adversely affect international transfer of technology[1137] and practices that impede the transfer and dissemination of technology.[1138] This means that, by definition, where a WTO member finds that technology transfer of climate change technologies is being adversely affected by the licensing (or lack thereof) of a patented technology, action to address this can be presumptively justified. In addition, such measures can be taken pre-emptively so as not only to address a problem once it has arisen but also to prevent a problem from arising in the first place. Thus a member can pre-emptively put legislation and regulations in place to structure the market is such a way as to enable and encourage technology transfer into the relevant markets. Crucially, Article 40 also has an international dimension in that it requires consultations and sympathetic consideration of requests for information and enforcement regarding their domestic enterprises from other members seeking to investigate and/or address anti-competitive behaviour by those enterprises in their own market.[1139] This encourages cooperation and recognizes that a significant amount of the restrictive practices that Article 8.2 and 40 cover occurs across borders and that members have a right to legislate and to seek cooperation from other members to address such cross-border behaviour.

[1136] Article 40.2 states in full: Nothing in this Agreement shall prevent Members from specifying in their legislation licensing practices or conditions that may in particular cases constitute an abuse of intellectual property rights having an adverse effect on competition in the relevant market As provided above, a Member may adopt, consistently with the other provisions of this Agreement, appropriate measures to prevent or control such practices, which may include for example exclusive grantback conditions, conditions preventing challenges to validity and coercive package licensing, in the light of the relevant laws and regulations of that Member.

[1137] TRIPS Article 8.2

[1138] TRIPS Article 40.1

[1139] TRIPS Article 40.3 "Each Member shall enter, upon request, into consultations with any other Member which has cause to believe that an intellectual property right owner that is a national or domiciliary of the Member to which the request for consultations has been addressed is undertaking practices in violation of the requesting Member's laws and regulations on the subject matter of this Section, and which wishes to secure compliance with such legislation, without prejudice to any action under the law and to the full freedom of an ultimate decision of either Member. The Member addressed shall accord full and sympathetic consideration to, and shall afford adequate opportunity for, consultations with the requesting Member, and shall cooperate through supply of publicly available non-confidential information of relevance to the matter in question and of other information available to the Member, subject to domestic law and to the conclusion of mutually satisfactory agreements concerning the safeguarding of its confidentiality by the requesting Member."

However, both Article 8.2 and Article 40.2 come with the caveat that any measures taken to address restrictive practices must be consistent with the provisions of the TRIPS Agreement. Since the most common measures to address anti-competitive practices are compulsory licenses, or other involuntary measures, this includes Article 30 and 31. Focusing first on Article 31, licenses to address anti-competitive practices must still comply with all provisions except Article 31(k), which exempts such compulsory licenses from the requirements of: Article 31(b) (on the need for prior negotiations with the rightholder); Article 31(f) (limiting production primarily for supply of the domestic market; Article 31(h), modifying the obligation on remuneration to allow for providing little or no remuneration. As noted, the use of such licenses remains a powerful market restructuring tool, especially because, outside of the Paris Convention and the TRIPS Agreement, there exist no international restrictions on the criteria, nature and scope of such licenses. However, there are two issues which any framework for widespread use of such licenses for market restructuring will have to address. The first is a conceptual issue, which is how to address 'refusals to deal'; the second (addressed in the following sub-section) is how to deal with compulsory licenses for failures of 'working' the patent in the Paris Convention and the TRIPS Agreement.

The patent right is, essentially, the right to prevent others from certain acts in relation to the patented technology. The right of refusal is fundamental to the exercise of the patent right. Thus a refusal to deal cannot *per se* constitute an anti-competitive act. The question then arises as to what *kinds* of refusals to deal fall within the scope of anti-competitive behaviour or if there must be some other conditions in conjunction with the refusal to deal. There are no internationally agreed standards on this issue but the existence of the patent right means that, at a minimum, TRIPS members must acknowledge the right of the refusal although that right cannot be a refusal to supply all market actors. One way to deal with this issue is to simply avoid it altogether and focus on the market effects of the behaviour such that where certain conditions are met (e.g. adverse effect on technology transfer) such a refusal to deal would then fall within the ambit of anti-competitive practices. Another approach is to focus on the other constituents of anti-competition regulations that are concerned with the behaviour of monopolies, focusing on whether there exists market power or dominance, whether that market power is exercised in a manner that negatively affects competition. Nevertheless, compulsory licenses for refusals to deal are available in several jurisdictions[1140] and courts and legislators continue to struggle with the boundaries.

In the context of climate change, refusals to deal have been a concern, especially given anecdotal evidence from Korea and India of refusals to license

---

[1140] See p1, Correa, C "Intellectual Property Rights and the Use of Compulsory Licenses: Options for Developing Countries" Working Paper 5, Trade-Related Agenda, Development And Equity (T.R.A.D.E.) Working Papers, South Centre, October 1999. Notably however, not in the US.

technology under the Montreal Protocol system.¹¹⁴¹ Rules put in place prior to such negotiations may go a long way to levelling the playing field between rightholders and potential licensees, increasing incentives to rightholders to actively seek out licensees rather than engaging in blanket refusals. Setting up a clear system for addressing anti-competitive behaviour may also go a long way to ensuring that restrictive licensing practices are kept at a minimum. As already noted, TRIPS Article 40.1 specifically encompasses licensing practices that have an adverse effect on international transfer of technology.

It is beyond the scope of this chapter to enter into a discussion on the full scope of approaches to the relationship between competition law and intellectual property, other than to note that the TRIPS Agreement leaves ample room for the application of competition law to patent licensing practices, in ways that allow significant market restructuring. This will require concerted action ahead of time to ensure that the right incentives are in place and where these fail, that speedy action is possible to issue and manage compulsory licenses and other measures to address anti-competitive behaviour. In addition, significant training of developing country officials in the policy and practice of competition law¹¹⁴², especially in relation to technology markets will have to take place. This may need to be supplemented by cooperative mechanisms as foreseen by TRIPS Article 40.2 to allow for cross-border cooperation.

A final note is that, expertise in competition law is sorely lacking in most developing countries and thus it is very difficult to address the imbalance inherent in providing strong property rights in intellectual property without a strong mechanism for addressing abuses.¹¹⁴³ It may be appropriate to consider an *a priori* set of regulations and mechanisms that set the stage for market actors but do not require significant ex post action by regulators to determine when competition law has been breached. Clear bright line rules may be better than case by case assessments, despite some of the inefficiencies this may create in the market.

III.4. Working Requirements

III.4.1. Legal Availability

Historically, countries were able to issue compulsory licenses for failures to produce the patented product in the country where the patent right is granted. This is a

---

[1141] p531, Hutchison, C J 'Does TRIPS Facilitate or Impede Climate Change Technology Transfer into Developing Countries?' University of Ottawa Law & Technology Journal, Vol. 3, pp. 517-537, 2006.
[1142] See p26, Maskus, K "Differentiated Intellectual Property Regimes for Environmental and Climate Technologies", OECD Environment Working Papers, No. 17, OECD Publishing 2010.
[1143] See p1, Correa, C "Intellectual Property Rights and the Use of Compulsory Licenses: Options for Developing Countries" Working Paper 5, Trade-Related Agenda, Development And Equity (T.R.A.D.E.) Working Papers, South Centre, October 1999.

right explicitly recognized in the Paris Convention on Industrial Property[1144], which allows for compulsory licenses in cases where the patent has not been worked.[1145] In fact, Article 5 allows for forfeiture of the patent in those cases where the compulsory license is not sufficient to address the relevant abuses.[1146] Notably, Article 5(A)(1) provides that forfeiture of the patent under Article 5 shall not be allowed where only importation rather than manufacture of the product takes place in the country where the patent is granted. This requirement of importation therefore did not affect the issuance of compulsory licenses for those situations where products were imported but not locally manufactured.

The TRIPS Agreement appears to contain a provision very similar to Article 5(A)(1) and the scope of that provision may have a significant impact on whether compulsory licenses to address failures to produce products locally can still be subjected to compulsory licenses. Article 27.1 of TRIPS states:

> patents shall be available and patent rights enjoyable without discrimination as to the place of invention, the field of technology and whether products are imported or locally produced.

The question is, therefore, whether this provision extends the scope of Article 5(A)(1) to prohibit compulsory licenses for failures to produce locally. Clearly, failures to supply the product market through both a failure to supply and a failure to produce locally would not be subject to the anti-discrimination provisions. In addressing this issue, the first thing to note is that Article 27.1 is an anti-discrimination provision. It states that, in determining the granting, scope and extent of rights, states may not make an unjustified distinction as to whether products are locally produced or imported. To the extent that sufficient importation takes place to meet market demand, it appears that Article 27.1 does indeed apply to compulsory licenses, despite the fact that Article 31 places no limits on the grounds for issuance of compulsory licenses. Article 32 places no such limits either. However, in interaction with Article 27.1, a plain reading suggests that, in the product market, justifying a compulsory license by pointing to a failure to produce the patented goods locally would not comply with the TRIPS Agreement.[1147] To the extent that the failure to produce locally leads to anti-competitive effects however, then Article 40 would apply and the state would be free to address that problem through a compulsory license.

[1144] Article 5, Paris Convention for the Protection of Industrial Property
[1145] Article 5(A)(2) Paris Convention for the Protection of Industrial Property
[1146] Article 5(A)(3) Paris Convention for the Protection of Industrial Property. See p3, Correa, C "Intellectual Property Rights and the Use of Compulsory Licenses: Options for Developing Countries" Working Paper 5, Trade-Related Agenda, Development And Equity (T.R.A.D.E.) Working Papers, South Centre, October 1999.
[1147] Contra p82, Correa, C *The TRIPS Agreement: A Guide for the South. The Uruguay Round Agreement on Trade-Related Intellectual Property Rights* (Geneva: South Centre, 1997)

Outside of the product market however, the issue is far less clear. The first area is that of process patents. A patented process can be used to make products. Such products are not per se patented, although it is possible for a process patent rightholder to prevent their import if they were produced outside the country using the patented process by someone without authorization. However, importation of products manufactured by a patented process does not fall within the literal scope of Article 27.1 which only applies to patented products. Thus, whether a process patent is used locally or not may indeed be grounds for a compulsory license or revocation.

The second issue is that of the market in technology as contrasted to the market in products. The failure to license is a separate issue from that of the failure to produce. Thus, in addressing access to technologies and know-how, rather than access to goods, members may remain free to issue compulsory licenses for failure to license into a market even where goods are indeed being produced locally or imported.

An interesting note on this issue is that a complaint was laid by the US against Brazil with respect to an explicit local working requirement in Brazilian law[1148] A panel was established but before matters proceeded further, the issue was settled. One of the reasons that the case was settled was the dispute brought by Brazil against the US (United States - US Patent Code WTO/DS/224) for the working requirement existing in the US patent law with respect to federally supported patented inventions. This appears to have been a case of mutually assured destruction, where because both states had crucial industrial policy aims and constituencies behind the challenged provisions, success in challenging the other's provisions would have entailed removal of the similar provision in their own law. However, the cases may also be a pointer to the fact that, in negotiating the TRIPS Agreement, states such as the United States and Brazil did not intend to invalidate the use of working requirements related to domestic production and that the concern in Article 27.1 was simply to ensure that there would be no unjustified and arbitrary discrimination in the granting and exercise of patents with respect to domestically produced and imported patented products. One can point to Section 204 of the Bayh-Dole Act which requires that licensees of publicly funded technologies must manufacture them substantially in the US.[1149]

To the extent that states wish to take measures to address shortages in accessing products, Article 31 provides a tool for doing so without having to contravene the limits that Article 27.1 may place on working requirements. At the level of the market in technology or the market in licenses Article 27.1 appears to be inapplicable and failures to license may still constitutes bases for action under article 31 and 40.

[1148] Brazil — Measures Affecting Patent Protection WTO/DS/199 (2000).
[1149] See 35 USC §204 (2006 and Supp. V 2012). As also noted by p9, Barton, J "Intellectual Property and Access to Clean Energy Technologies in Developing Countries: An Analysis of Solar Photovoltaic, Biofuel and Wind Technologies" Trade and Sustainable Energy Series, Issue Paper No. 2, ICTSD December 2007.

Finally, as discussed is the previous section, the application and scope of Article 40 must also fall within the scope of Article 8.1, meaning that there may be even more leeway to address Article 40 and 8.2 anti-competitive measures where these are "necessary to protect public health and nutrition, and to promote the public interest in sectors of vital importance to their socio-economic and technological development."

III.4.2. Practical Availability

Given the ongoing impasse between the US and Brazil on the working requirement, significant uncertainty surrounds the ability to use working requirements in the post-TRIPS period. It appears that where targeted primarily at process patents, Article 27.1 does not negate the flexibility provided by the Paris Convention. This may be crucial for climate change as a significant part of the challenge for many developing countries will be process efficiency and use of working requirements may provide leverage to push rightholders to license into the economy. The TRIPS Agreement appears to be place few restrictions on the use of compulsory licenses for failure to work in such circumstances. The potential responses may also include revocation of the patent, or other measures authorized by the Paris Conventions. I would conclude that working requirements remain available for process patents but not for product patents but that it is possible to have working requirements at the scale and scope necessary to address technology transfer for climate change.

III.5. Patent exclusions and special treatment for climate technologies

III.5.1. Legal Availability

The legal basis for exclusion of patents on products or processes or both in the TRIPS Agreement is, largely non-existent. There is little leverage for excluding patents related to climate technologies except in a very few, small areas. Article 27 of the TRIPS Agreement has some provisions allowing for patent exclusions but also requires that patents be available for all fields of technology, both products and processes. The problem, for example, with Article 27.2 is that it ostensibly allows the exclusion of patents on particular products or processes for purposes of *ordre public* or public morals, including to protect human, animal or plant life or health or to avoid serious prejudice to the environment, but that also means that the purpose of such exclusions aims to stop the commercial exploitation of such products and processes.[1150] This runs counter to the aim of technology transfer, which is to expand the commercialization and

---

[1150] Some authors see this as one of the key ways in which the patent system may actually be supportive of addressing climate change by disallowing the patenting of GHG emitting technologies. See e.g. Derclaye, E 'Intellectual Property Rights and Global Warming', 12 J. MARSHALL REV. INTELL. PROP. L. 263 (2008).

adoption of the relevant technologies. Article 27.2 therefore does not provide a viable pathway to excluding patents on relevant climate technologies so as to allow common and public access.[1151]

However, looking at Article 27.1, some have argued that there may still be a possibility to discriminate among fields of technology.[1152] The Panel in the *Canada-Pharmaceutical Patents* case argued that establishing special systems for particular product sectors was acceptable as long as these were supported by justifiable and specific policy purposes.[1153] Thus, in that case, a special regime allowing an exception for use of a patent for meeting pharmaceutical regulatory requirements was allowed. The Panel saw this as a bona fide differentiation. However, the Panel also noted that the point at which differentiation began to shade into discrimination was if a policy appeared to be deliberately targeted at a sector where foreign right holders dominated.[1154] An examination of the negotiating history suggests that the initial rule proposed in 27.1 was watered down from an absolute ban on treating different technology sectors and technologies differently to one that simply required availability of patents in all fields.[1155]

This does not however, reach so far as allowing complete exclusions of those inventions which qualify as "technological" or "inventions" within the meaning of domestic law. Patent law does of course allow for exclusions based on the fact that the claimed invention is not technological, or that it represents a discovery rather than an 'invention'. This provides for the exclusions for patentability for computer software, mathematical methods, business methods that are found in some patent laws.[1156] However, these do not extend to inventions, as such. This may also be the basis for excluding products of nature as discoveries, thus countries can exclude genes, and derivatives thereof from patentability.[1157]

[1151] See also in support, Consilvio, M. "The Role of Patents in the International Framework of Clean Technology Transfer: A Discussion of Barriers and Solutions" 3 Intell. Prop. Brief 10 (2011).
[1152] See Abbott, F M "Innovation and Technology Transfer to Address Climate Change: Lessons from the Global Debate on Intellectual Property and Public Health", ICTSD's Programme on IPRs and Sustainable Development, Issue Paper No. 24, International Centre for Trade and Sustainable Development, Geneva, Switzerland, 2009. See also, p20, Maskus, K "Differentiated Intellectual Property Regimes for Environmental and Climate Technologies", OECD Environment Working Papers, No. 17, OECD Publishing 2010.
[1153] *Canada- Pharmaceuticals Patents*, WTO Doc. WT/DS1141R, 7 April 2000.
[1154] Para 7.92, Id.
[1155] p2, Abbott, F M "Innovation and Technology Transfer to Address Climate Change: Lessons from the Global Debate on Intellectual Property and Public Health", ICTSD's Programme on IPRs and Sustainable Development, Issue Paper No. 24, International Centre for Trade and Sustainable Development, Geneva, Switzerland, 2009.
[1156] See e.g. Article 52 of the European Patent Convention
[1157] Correa, C *The TRIPs Agreement: A Guide for the South. The Uruguay Round Agreement on Trade-Related Intellectual Property Rights* (Geneva: South Centre, 1997)

Article 27.3 also allows exclusions from patentability of very specific areas of technology without the requirement that they also be excluded from commercialization. These are:

a) diagnostic and therapeutic methods for treating animals and people; and

b) plant and animals other than micro-organisms; essentially biological process for the production of animals and plants other than non-biological and microbiological processes

For addressing adaptation needs in the agricultural arena, the prohibition on patenting of plants and animals is crucial. This allows free access to new and adapted products for adaptation. However, the limitations also require protection of micro-organisms, possibly limiting access, for example, to new bacteria that can be used to create biofuels from cellulosic plants. Countries are also still required to protect non-biological and micro-biological processes. Thus processes that use bacteria to produce biofuels may also be covered for example, as well as possibly processes for genetic manipulation of plants and plant genes. Thus, as Barton points out, while end-user access may be enabled by such an exclusion, participation in research may be a greater problem given that many tools for biotechnological research are patented[1158], and are not subject to being excluded in the same way as plants and animals. Even where some countries exclude these on the basis that they are not technological inventions but discoveries, the ability to export products produced using these processes or products, may be limited by patents in export markets.

In addition, there is the additional requirement that countries provide protection to plant varieties through some *sui generis* regime. However, as the *sui generis* regime is not defined, any method that they use to provide effective protection will pass muster. The question is what would constitute an 'effective' regime and whether this would require exclusive rights. Barton argues that this would require some kind of exclusivity, at least to the extent that it would prevent farmers from carrying out traditional exchange of seeds from crops they have farmed.[1159] Correa has argued that the lack of definition leaves countries much freer.[1160] I am more inclined to argue that because such exchange was allowable under UPOV 1977, and that since UPOV 1977 was encompassed as one of the methods of implementing such a *sui generis* regime that

---

[1158] See p15, Barton, J "Nutrition and Technology Transfer Policies" Issue Paper 6, UNCTAD-ICTSD Project on IPRs and Sustainable Development, International Centre for Trade and Sustainable Development, May 2004)
[1159] See p19, Barton, J "Nutrition and Technology Transfer Policies" Issue Paper 6, UNCTAD-ICTSD Project on IPRs and Sustainable Development, International Centre for Trade and Sustainable Development, May 2004)
[1160] See p29, Correa, C *The TRIPs Agreement: A Guide for the South. The Uruguay Round Agreement on Trade-Related Intellectual Property Rights* (Geneva: South Centre, 1997)

some more flexibility was considered. In particular, the fact that some version of UPOV was not explicitly mentioned militates against requiring an exclusive rights approach.

Thus a country could conceivably choose a liability regime that ensures not only access for third parties but also remuneration for the rightholder, without requiring lengthy negotiations or permitting processes. There is no term requirement or criteria for grant so countries are free to design whatever system they feel is appropriate. What is clear, however, is that many countries have chosen to become members of the UPOV 1991 which provides very strict standards of intellectual property protection for plant varieties and restricts their ability to allow other breeders to make use of the protected variety. In particular, UPOV 1991 restricts the ability of countries to provide exceptions for their farmers to save, re-use and exchange[1161] seeds that they have planted on their own fields. Fortunately, there is much more flexibility for those countries who wish to withdraw from UPOV 1991 to do so, without the level of costs that might be associated with withdrawing from the TRIPS Agreement.[1162] However, such withdrawal still requires the preservation of rights that were in existence at the time of the notice of withdrawal and thus cannot have retroactive effect to existing protected varieties. Given that the required term of protection under UPOV 1991 is 20 years, this limits the usefulness of such a withdrawal.

I conclude that, except for the area of plants and animals, there is no legal availability for excluding from patentability climate related technologies.

In terms of timing, such an exclusion of plant and animal patents can take place almost immediately. It places the cost of losing protection on both domestic and foreign innovators. However, it also allows domestic users freer access to innovations that are protected elsewhere.

It is also not clear that such exclusion can be enacted retroactively to existing protection. In such cases, domestic case law on expropriation will have to be taken into account. Where the country is signatory to investor-state dispute arbitration in a bilateral investment treaty, there may also be the possibility of an expropriation claim.

III.6. Parallel importation

III.6.1. Legal Availability

[1161] Article 15, UPOV 1991.
[1162] Article 29, UPOV 1991.

TRIPS Article 6 on exhaustion[1163] of IP rights is very clear. Nothing in the Agreement shall be deemed to address the issue of exhaustion, so Members are free to determine when and how products that have been legitimately placed on the market in other countries can be imported without the consent of the patent holder. This is called parallel importation and it is fundamental to ensuring that access to goods is enabled. This would allow products produced legitimately in other countries to be imported.

III.6.2. Practical Availability

However, the key question here is what constitutes 'legitimately placed on the market'. The traditional test is that such products have been placed on foreign markets with the consent of the right holder. Thus goods that are infringing IP rights in those foreign markets where they are produced would not be subject to the exhaustion principle. Goods produced under a compulsory license would be another matter. It can be argued that such goods, while not produced with the consent of the right holder, have been lawfully placed on the market in the foreign country where the product has been made and can therefore lawfully be imported. Article 107A(b) of the Indian Patent Act directly addresses this issue by ensuring that rights are exhausted when the products are placed on the market by an "authorised person", whether by the rightholder or a compulsory licensee. While it could be argued that such an approach clashes with the TRIPS Article 31 requirement that compulsory licenses be issued primarily for domestic supply, at the very least some portion of products produced under a compulsory license can be expected to be sold, directly across borders, even if the license is primarily for domestic production. In addition, once products have been placed on the market, Article 31(f) would not function as a limitation on onward sales by others besides the compulsory licensee, especially where the rightholder had already received adequate compensation. Thus direct sales by the producer may be limited but those by others would not be. More importantly, with respect to the right of importation, a country that applies such a regime of exhaustion cannot be brought before a WTO panel as, according to Article 6 of the TRIPS Agreement, the issue is entirely non-justiciable under the WTO.

III.7. Setting Specific standards for patentability including disclosure

III.7.1. Legal availability

[1163] Exhaustion applies primarily to product patents and the extent to which a rightholders' right to control the 'sale' and distribution of such products ends after the first sale. The principle states that, once a patented product has been placed on the market by the rightholder through a sale or distribution, the rightholder has 'exhausted' the right of sale, having benefitted from the first sale. The rightholder cannot prevent the onward sale or expect to benefit from such follow-on sales of the exact same product. However, the rightholder retains all the other rights granted by the patent. The principle of exhaustion is most significant when it interacts with the right of importation of the patented product.

The TRIPS Agreement requires states to provide patents provided that such patent are novel, inventive and industrially applicable. The TRIPS Agreement however, does not define these terms and countries are free to place the threshold for them as high or as low as they wish. While disclosure is not mentioned in the rules it is presumed that the process of application of a patent creates a disclosure. Historically some states have made sufficient and best mode disclosure a patent requirement as well, which could be the basis for refusal or revocation of the patent. The US, in the America Invents Act in 2011 has recently removed its best mode requirement as a basis for invalidating patents in infringement suits.[1164] Nevertheless states are free to impose such best mode conditions which may be appropriate to take advantage of the teaching effect of patent disclosures. To the extent that a patent should enable a person of ordinary skill in the art to reproduce it, disclosure should be a useful learning tool. This is especially true for those readers who are not located in the country of patenting. However, there is a structural tension within the patent system, as patent applicants will work to disclose as little as they can get away with in order to receive the patent.[1165] Without an active surveillance mechanism and disincentives for applicants to engage in such gaming of the system, patents will not be able to perform this information function that is so central to the patent social bargain. States are free to require levels of disclosure that actually enable a person of skill in the art to reproduce the invention, something which can be tested after the fact by competitors and, as used to be the case in the US, be used as a basis for invalidating or narrowing the scope of the patent.

Could a state provide differentiated standards of inventive step for climate technologies, thus limiting the number of patents in the field compared to others? This could entail ensuring that patents are not granted for climate technologies specifically unless they met a very high standard of inventive step. Even if justified by a strong public policy goal, i.e. focusing patent activity in this specific sector on significant technological advances rather than smaller incremental steps, such an approach would likely still be considered a form of discrimination. In particular, where the approach had a disproportionate effect on foreign rightholders, such as seeking to ensure technology transfer, it is highly unlikely that such discrimination would be allowed, under the *Canada-Pharmaceutical Patents* analysis. To succeed such a proposal would have to apply such a standard to all fields of technology rather than just climate technologies.

III.7.2. Practical Availability

[1164] *See* 35 U.S.C.A. § 282(3)(A) (2011)
[1165] See p5, Cannady, C "Access to Climate Change Technology by Developing Countries: A Practical Strategy, ICTSD's Programme on IPRs and Sustainable Development, Issue Paper No. 25, International Centre for Trade and Sustainable Development, Geneva, Switzerland (2009).

One solution that remains within the limits of the TRIPS Agreement is to use such a high standard for novelty and inventive step[1166] and then focus on a system of utility or petty patents or a liability regime, more suited to developing country entrepreneurs and creates incentives for the kind of small scale incremental innovation that developing country entrepreneurs work on. What this would allow is local, incremental and adaptive innovation, based on free access to products patented elsewhere, but not domestically, and enable export to other countries where the improved products may not be patented. The practicality of this approach is limited by the fact that the majority of developing countries have patent registration systems that do not examine their patents prior to grant. Patents are only assessed for novelty, inventive, step and industrial applicability if a challenge is made to their validity, usually during litigation. The major emerging economies have shifted to an examination system, so China, India and Brazil have better access to such possible differentiation as a policy lever.

III.8. Limiting the number of allowable claims in a patent, potentially down to 1.

III.8.1. Legal availability

This was a technique that was used by many countries to limit the number of inventions that could be included in the same application and benefit from the same priority date and from the single fee. This raised the cost of patenting, made applicants disclose more carefully the specific invention they were claiming and limited the extent to which a whole sector or technology field might be claimed by a single applicant. This capacity was limited by the Paris Convention in Article 4G, which requires countries that object to multiple inventions in the same claim to nevertheless allow them to file a separate divisional application that retains its priority date. They may also not require a divisional application to lose its priority simply because it claims matter that was not claimed in the original patent, as long as is disclosed in some fashion in any other part of the original patent application. This requirement also significantly narrows the utility of this intervention against the amount of patenting that can be done by a single applicant relating to a single invention or set of inventions. The incorporation of the Paris Convention into the TRIPS Agreement thus makes this a requirement under the TRIPS Agreement. However, countries may still charge fees for such applications, on an increasing scale[1167] or even at the same rate as the original patent. In terms of legal availability, this intervention is no longer available.

[1166] Maskus suggests this as an option against actual exclusions on patents, see p25, Maskus, K "Differentiated Intellectual Property Regimes for Environmental and Climate Technologies", OECD Environment Working Papers, No. 17, OECD Publishing 2010.
[1167] As planned by the EPO beginning in May 2014. See Rule 36, Implementing Regulations to the Convention on the Grant of European Patents. Available at: http://www.epo.org/law-practice/legal-texts/html/epc/2010/e/r36.html (last visited 15 August 2014).

IV. CONCLUSION

Looking at the portfolio of actions gathered in Chapter 5, that countries would like to take, what does the preceding analysis tells us about their availability under the TRIPS Agreement and the WTO? For a significant portion of them TRIPS is entirely silent and does not address the issue. On others, TRIPS simply forbids them generally, such as those that seek to discriminate between foreign nationals and domestic actors in acquisition, exercise or exceptions to rights. However, as noted, this does not mean that many of these may not be subject to further restrictions by regional and bilateral free trade agreements, or by bilateral investment treaties. To the extent that these are restricted in that fashion, countries may wish to revisit the wisdom of agreeing to such provisions when they need economy wide measures to address climate change.

We can divide the measures into three categories; those that are legal and practically available; those that are legally available but practically unavailable; those that are legally unavailable. For ease of assessment we can put these into these three categories:

Legally Available, Practically Available

1. Compulsory licenses for use by emerging economies; including of trade secrets
2. Working requirements for process patents
3. Compensatory liability regimes for sub-patentable inventions
4. Product patent exclusions for plants and animals
5. Application of competition law to address anti-competitive behaviour relating to IP including standard setting
6. Parallel Importation of products produced under authorization in another country.
7. Technology transfer and other performance requirements to qualify for establishing foreign direct investment presence
8. Regular, consistent and detailed monitoring of licensing terms in licensing contracts to guard against anti-competitive clauses. This may require a pre-approval and registration process;
9. Higher fees for applications and renewals higher fees for large firms;
10. Requiring full disclosure of the patent and the best mode known at the time of patenting including all know-how required to practise it;
11. Requiring early and significant pre-grant publication of patent applications, coupled with a process for dissemination to local firms;
12. Shifting from patent registration to examination while creating and maintaining strong utility model registration system;
13. Setting higher inventive step and novelty standards;
14. Strong pre-grant and post-grant opposition procedures;
15. Requirements for Joint Venture for investment in a specific sector or sectors.

16. Limiting restrictions on the movement and employment of employees once they have left the firm, such as non-compete clauses;
17. Providing specific loans and capital for mergers with and acquisitions (shareholdings or outright purchases) of foreign companies with significant patent portfolios of relevance to climate change with the express purpose of transferring technology, know-how to the acquiring company

Legally Available, Practically Unavailable

1. Working requirements
2. Research and other exceptions to patent rights
3. Compulsory licenses for public interest purpose use by LDCs

Legally Unavailable

1. Compensatory liability regimes for patents
2. Working requirements for product patents
3. Product and process exclusions generally
4. Compulsory licensing for export to other countries
5. Limiting the patent term to less than 20 years, generally or in specific sectors
6. Using a relative standard of novelty for specific sectors
7. Higher fees for patent application and renewal for foreign patent applicant firms;
8. Limiting the number of allowable claims in a patent, potentially down to 1.

At a glance, it is possible to see that the majority of measures that countries have under consideration to address IP issues related to technology transfer remain available under the TRIPS Agreement. This seems to suggest that the TRIPS Agreement may not be the limiting factor when it comes to countries use of these policy levers to address technology transfer of IP protected products and processes into their economies. However the analysis also shows and I would argue that the most effective IP-related levers have been marginalized and reduced in scope and effectiveness by the TRIPS Agreement. The use of the working requirement, one of the more powerful historical incentives for encouraging licensing and FDI has been curtailed. The use of patent exclusions in key sectors of public interest such as pharmaceuticals and agriculture is no longer available. Most importantly, few of the remaining flexibilities allow for the emerging economies to play the role as intermediaries and export products as they need to do if technologies are to be transferred to other developing countries at the scale and speed required.

The most useful tools that are left legally and practically available by the TRIPS Agreement are the application of competition law and the use of performance and technology transfer requirements, as well as requirements to have FDI take place in the form of JVs. The rest are smaller, marginal, adjustments to domestic intellectual property systems.

What the analysis tells us is that TRIPS may not present an absolute barrier to measures taken to address technology transfer but it creates a system that slows down the pace and scope of measures that developing countries can take to address technology transfer. This within our framework, it seems difficult to avoid the conclusion that, on the whole; TRIPS does indeed limit the capacity of developing countries to:

3. *Appropriately define necessity as:*
   a. *Affordability - ensuring that prices of products are not set so high that it is too expensive for all the relevant economic actors to afford.*
   b. *Adoptability - ensuring that prices of products and or know-how are not set so high that they make it commercially unviable for all relevant actors to adopt 'climate-friendly' technologies.*
   c. *Adaptability – ensuring sufficient distribution of knowledge (information, skills, know-how) to enable a critical number of existing producers/service providers in the market to adopt, adapt and replicate climate technologies and ensure their participation in the market.*
4. *Take actions that:*
   a. *address the full scope of technologies required by them to meet the climate change mitigation and adaptation needs;*
   b. *at the rate and level of diffusion appropriate to achieving those mitigation and adaptation needs;*
   c. *in the developing countries and regions that most effectively meet the climate change need.*

However, it is also clear that the extent to which TRIPS does pose a barrier is not absolute nor is it extreme. There remains room to act at the margins and, with respect to competition law to address egregious behaviour affecting the functioning of the market. What it does not allow is for member states to use intellectual property interventions to decisively shift their domestic technology markets in favour of domestic firms seeking access to knowledge and technologies. The ability to actively use such interventions to aggressively localize technologies and enable adoption, adaptation and replication is significantly restricted. This is the case within the case law and existing interpretations of the TRIPS Agreement. However, the question arises as to whether there are approaches to interpretation that may nevertheless expand the room for measures that may not be fully in compliance with the TRIPS Agreement, by reaching out to other rules to be used as applicable law within the TRIPS Agreement and opening up some further flexibility. While the analysis in this chapter stayed within the traditional framework of how to interpret the TRIPS Agreement and the broader WTO jurisprudence, the next chapter explores whether other international rules, such as the UNFCCC and the human rights regime can be brought to bear to increase the flexibility that developing countries have under the TRIPS Agreement.

Chapter 7
The Role
of other
Multilateral Regimes

I. INTRODUCTION

While the TRIPS Agreement appears to limit the scope of unilateral action within its own legal framework, there may be a role for other multilateral obligations in expanding the limits on action imposed by the TRIPS Agreement. In the case of climate change, the argument would be that the UNFCCC imposes obligations on states that WTO panels must take into account in TRIPS-related actions that are challenged. Such an approach requires two conditions to succeed: first that there are obligations within the UNFCCC and COP decisions that impose obligations to take action that may affect rights and obligations under the TRIPS Agreement; and second, that there is a mechanism, or interpretive approach, within the WTO for taking into account the rights and obligations imposed by other multilateral treaties. This section will explore whether both elements are present, and what solutions may be proposed, if they are not.

II. THE UNFCCC AND ITS LEGAL RELATIONSHIP TO THE TRIPS AGREEMENT AND OTHER FORA

To a significant extent, in order to trigger a shift in the interpretation of the TRIPS Agreement by using another treaty or regime as applicable law, there would have to be a conflict of laws (in terms of obligations or rights) between the TRIPS and the other regimes. There would have to be obligations within the UNFCCC or other regime that developing countries cannot meet, or rights that cannot be exercised without to some extent violating their obligations under the TRIPS Agreement. Such a conflict would then trigger in international law an obligation on the part of interpretive mechanisms in both regimes to resolve the conflict in some manner. In this case, I adopt the Pauwelynian notion of 'conflict', not just encompassing a purely direct conflict where the need to meet the obligations of one treaty, necessarily require a breach of the other. As Pauwelyn does, I also embrace the notion of conflict that encompasses where a treaty provides rights the exercise of which would necessitate a breach of obligations under another treaty and of course, where in order to meet the requirements of another treaty, a party is so limited in meeting its obligations under another treaty as to render its actions practically ineffective, even if not legally in breach.[1168] If developing countries can point to such a conflict then they would trigger an obligation on the part of interpretive mechanisms at the WTO and the UNFCCC to resolve it in a mutually supportive manner.

Do we have a 'conflict' between the UNFCCC and the TRIPS Agreement in the Pauwelynian sense? There is little indication within the UNFCCC of what the relationship to the broader environmental regime and to the WTO should be. Within the Convention itself, there are few mentions of how to relate to other regimes. The preamble affirms 'that responses to climate change should be coordinated with social and economic development in an integrated manner with a view to avoiding adverse impacts on the latter, taking into full account the legitimate priority needs of developing countries for the achievement of sustained economic growth and the eradication of poverty.'

Article 3.5 on principles notes:

> The Parties should cooperate to promote a supportive and open international economic system that would lead to sustainable economic growth and development in all Parties, particularly developing country Parties, thus enabling them better to address the problems of climate change. Measures taken to combat climate change, including unilateral ones, should not constitute a means of arbitrary or unjustifiable discrimination or a disguised restriction on international trade.

This provision suggests that the UNFCCC asks Parties to act in this manner in other fora relevant to the international economic system. The test that they impose here is one that imports language from the chapeau of Article XX of the GATT which, as discussed in Chapter 6, embodies the General Exceptions clause. To the extent that measures affecting trade in goods are used to address climate change, this principle provides interpretive guidance from the UNFCCC as to how the UNFCCC views the relationship between actions aimed at achieving climate aims and those actions as they relate to rules on trade in goods. The language does not, however, translate well into the TRIPS arena. As noted before, TRIPS provisions on exceptions and limitations to patents are primarily to be viewed through the lens of Articles 7 and 8, 30 and 31. The only equivalent in the TRIPS Agreement may be language pointing to arbitrary or unjustifiable discrimination (implicating TRIPS Article 27). Within the TRIPS Agreement there is no analogous 'disguised restriction on international trade' language or principle.

[1168] Pauwelyn, J *Conflict of Norms in Public International Law: How WTO Law Relates to Other Rules of International Law.* (New York: Cambridge University Press, 2003.). In line with Condon, B "Climate Change and Unresolved Issues in WTO Law" 12 J. Int'l Econ. L. 895 (2009).

UNFCCC Article 4.5 commits Parties to:

> Take climate change considerations into account, to the extent feasible, in their relevant social, economic and environmental policies and actions, and employ appropriate methods, for example impact assessments, formulated and determined nationally, with a view to minimizing adverse effects on the economy, on public health and on the quality of the environment, of projects or measures undertaken by them to mitigate or adapt to climate change.

This provision, however, seems more aimed at not interfering with economic issues, while also suggesting some degree of balancing and consideration of climate change policies in other fora. It is not clear that this translates into a commitment also to act in pursuance of climate change mitigation objectives in other international fora. In the Kyoto Protocol there is also little, if any, direction to states on how the Protocol relates to other regimes.

There is no language in the UNFCCC specifically addressing intellectual property, although the clear language on who should bear the costs of action suggests that the costs of paying for IP licenses should be financially supported by developed countries, in the absence of other measures to ensure that technology transfer takes place. It is the issue of costs that points to a key missing element: that the technology transfer and financial support obligations of the UNFCCC fall squarely on the shoulders of developed countries. Developing countries wishing to take unilateral action to enable technology transfer cannot rely on those obligations to justify their actions under the TRIPS Agreement. This suggests that other obligations or avenues are necessary. Two possibilities emerge as the most likely: first, that developing countries point to their own obligations in Article 4 of the UNFCCC to take action both individually and jointly with other UNFCCC members to mitigate GHG emissions and address climate change adaptation; or that climate change implicates these countries' human rights obligations to deliver on areas such as the right to health and the right to shelter and requires them to take actions that may not be in conformity with the TRIPS Agreement (addressed further below).

Regarding the obligation in Article 4 of the UNFCCC, developing countries could point to Article 4.1(b) which requires *all* parties to formulate and implement measures to mitigate climate change.[1169] The counter to that would be that this is not a

---

[1169] 1. All Parties, taking into account their common but differentiated responsibilities and their specific national and regional development priorities, objectives and circumstances, shall:
[...]
(b) Formulate, implement, publish and regularly update national and, where appropriate, regional programmes containing measures to mitigate climate change by addressing anthropogenic emissions by sources and removals by sinks of all greenhouse gases not controlled by the Montreal Protocol, and measures to facilitate adequate adaptation to climate change;

true obligation in that developing country parties are not required to take action where the full incremental costs of implementing measures are not covered by developed countries.[1170] Article 4.4 addresses the same issue with respect to adaptation. To the extent that the measures taken are ones that should nominally be supported under Article 4.3 or 4.4, Article 4.1 would be interpreted as not imposing a requirement of action on developing country parties. This is borne out by the statement in UNFCCC Article 4.7 that:

> The extent to which developing country Parties will effectively implement their commitments under the Convention will depend on the effective implementation by developed country Parties of their commitments under the Convention related to financial resources and transfer of technology ....

Developing countries are not truly in the position of having obligations as yet, unless and until such obligations are embedded in a new post-2015 treaty that actually imposes a non-dependent obligation of action on developing countries.

III. THE WTO AND ITS RELATIONSHIP TO OTHER FORA

The usefulness of statements in the UNFCCC or approaches to establishing obligations in the UNFCCC relies on one other key issue: whether and how the WTO jurisprudence makes space for considering these obligations. There is an enormous literature on the relationship between trade and environment and several analytical frameworks have been developed to deal with the interaction.[1171] These frameworks are generally addressed at three potential access points: jurisdiction, in which a WTO panel decides whether the dispute or claimed violation falls within the scope of rights and obligations of the covered agreements; applicable law, which is the sources of law which determine the scope and nature of the rights and obligations over which the panel has jurisdiction; and interpretive weight, addressing the evidentiary weight to be given to various sources in determining the meaning of specific terms and provisions of a covered agreement. In practice, where environmental issues are concerned this has meant that a panel has to determine whether an environmental measure is within its

---

[1170] UNFCCC Article 4.3 "The developed country Parties and other developed Parties included in Annex II shall provide new and additional financial resources to meet the agreed full costs incurred by developing country Parties in complying with their obligations under Article 12, paragraph 1. They shall also provide such financial resources, including for the transfer of technology, needed by the developing country Parties to meet the agreed full incremental costs of implementing measures that are covered by paragraph 1 of this Article and that are agreed between a developing country Party and the international entity or entities referred to in Article 11, in accordance with that Article. The implementation of these commitments shall take into account the need for adequacy and predictability in the flow of funds and the importance of appropriate burden sharing among the developed country Parties.
[1171] See e.g. Pauwelyn, J *Conflict of Norms in Public International Law - How WTO Law Relates to Other Rules of International Law* (Cambridge: Cambridge University Press 2003).

jurisdiction to address; whether the environmental treaty or regime which governs that environmental measure should be applicable law in a WTO dispute; and failing that, whether the meaning ascribed to a term or provision in an environmental treaty/regime, should inform (either by expanding or narrowing) or have the same meaning as a similar or identical term in a WTO covered agreement.

These questions have been addressed with respect to trade in goods and in the context of the SPS Agreement and the TBT Agreement. It is not the intent of this chapter to go over discussions that are much more effectively covered by other authors but the aim is to explore how these principles would apply in the context of a TRIPS dispute that addressed unilateral measures on technology transfer. Drawing from the jurisprudence we find that:

- jurisdiction over WTO matters is compulsory and, because the Appellate body uses an 'effects' test to determine jurisdiction, this requires the WTO dispute settlement system to be involved in ALL disputes that affect the rights and obligations of members under WTO covered agreements.[1172] Thus, it is not how a measure is characterized or justified but whether it has an impact on trade that triggers the compulsory jurisdiction of the dispute settlement system.

- In applying Article 31(3)(c) of the Vienna Convention on the Law of Treaties, all sources of law can be considered as applicable law including customary law, principles of international law as well as treaties. However, as applicable law in the context of a dispute between WTO members, only those rules that are applicable between the parties to the WTO can be considered meaning that only treaties to which ALL WTO members are party can be considered applicable law in a WTO dispute.[1173]

- Other rules of international law may nevertheless play a role in providing evidence of the ordinary meaning of a term or provision in a WTO covered agreement, but a panel is not required to use such evidence where it does not consider it necessary or relevant.[1174] Whatever the outcome, decisions by the DSB cannot add to or diminish the rights and obligations of members.[1175] This

---

[1172] Article 3.2, Understanding on Rules and Procedures Governing the Settlement of Disputes (DSU), Annex 2 to the Marrakesh Agreement establishing the World Trade Organization (WTO Agreement), Marrakesh, 15 April 1994, *in force* 1 January 1995, 1867 United Nations Treaty Series (1995) 4.
[1173] See p334, Panel Reports, European Communities – Measures Affecting the Approval and Marketing of Biotech Products, WT/DS291/R / WT/DS292/R / WT/DS293/R, Add.1 to Add.9, and Corr.1, adopted 21 November 2006, DSR 2006:III-VIII, 847 (*EC – Approval and Marketing of Biotech Products*)
[1174] See p341, *EC – Approval and Marketing of Biotech Products*
[1175] Article 3.2, Understanding on Rules and Procedures Governing the Settlement of Disputes (DSU), Annex 2 to the Marrakesh Agreement establishing the World Trade Organization (WTO Agreement), Marrakesh, 15 April 1994, *in force* 1 January 1995, 1867 United Nations Treaty Series (1995) 4.

suggests that no other law can function as applicable law within the context of WTO disputes.

- The Appellate body's understanding of 'exhaustible natural resources" is an evolving definition that relies on gathering international consensus around issues of concern to sustainable development.[1176]

Significant controversy has attended the panel's approach in *EC – Approval and Marketing of Biotech Products* that the applicable law referred to by Article 31(3)(c) VCLT was limited only to those treaties to which *all* WTO members were parties at the time of the dispute.[1177] The International Law Commission's report on the Fragmentation on International Law went so far as to suggest that the panel made a fundamental error, arguing that this would make it impossible for any treaty to have the role of applicable law in a WTO dispute as none could have the exact same scope of membership as the WTO[1178], or even be one to which the membership of the WTO is a subset. In the case of the Kyoto protocol for example, only 80% of Kyoto protocol parties are also WTO members.[1179]

The effect of this approach in the technology transfer, climate change and TRIPS discussion is clear. If one presumes that the approach in *EC – Approval and Marketing of Biotech Products* remains applicable, then, absent any other statement from within the institutions of the WTO, the UNFCCC cannot be used as applicable law between the parties to a dispute at the WTO that challenges a unilateral measure that has an effect on a TRIPS-related right or obligation. However, this does not preclude the use of UNFCCC terms and provisions in informing the meaning and scope of similar or identical terms in the TRIPS Agreement. Since these could not be used to actually alter or justify a measure that is TRIPS - inconsistent, this would have to enter through the traditional interpretive route of exceptions and limitations as discussed in Chapter 6.

This pattern is evident in at least one IP-related panel decision. In the context of the *US – Section 110(5) Copyright Act*[1180] copyright case, we do have an example of a

---

[1176] WTO, *United States – Import Prohibition of Shrimp and Shrimp Products* (6 November 1998) WT/DS58/R/AB, para 129-130.
[1177] See para. 7.70 – 7.71, Panel Reports, European Communities – Measures Affecting the Approval and Marketing of Biotech Products, WT/DS291/R / WT/DS292/R / WT/DS293/R, Add.1 to Add.9, and Corr.1, adopted 21 November 2006, DSR 2006:III-VIII, 847 (*EC – Approval and Marketing of Biotech Products*)
[1178] See p227, 237, Koskenniemi, M et al. "*Fragmentation of International Law: Difficulties arising from the Diversification and Expansion of International Law:* Report of the Study Group of the International Law Commission" International Law Commission, 13 April 2006 , UN Doc. A/CN.4/L.682 p. 1-256 and 18 July 2006, UN Doc. A/CN.4/L.702
[1179] Adam, A "Technology Transfer to Combat Climate Change: Opportunities and Obligations under TRIPS and Kyoto" 9 J. High Tech. L. 1 (2009)
[1180] Panel Report, United States – Section 110(5) of the US Copyright Act, WT/DS160/R, adopted 27 July 2000, DSR 2000:VIII, 3769 (*US – Section 110(5) Copyright Act*)

panel using a provision from the WIPO Copyright Treaty to inform the meaning of the copyright exception in TRIPS Article 13.[1181] In particular, the panel in that case stated:

> In paragraph 6.66 we discussed the need to interpret the Berne Convention and the TRIPS Agreement in a way that reconciles the texts of these two treaties and avoids a conflict between them, given that they form the overall framework for multilateral copyright protection. The same principle should also apply to the relationship between the TRIPS Agreement and the WCT. The WCT is designed to be compatible with this framework, incorporating or using much of the language of the Berne Convention and the TRIPS Agreement. *(footnote omitted)* The WCT was unanimously concluded at a diplomatic conference organized under the auspices of WIPO in December 1996, one year after the WTO Agreement entered into force, in which 127 countries participated. Most of these countries were also participants in the TRIPS negotiations and are Members of the WTO. (Footnote omitted) For these reasons, it is relevant to seek contextual guidance also in the WCT when developing interpretations that avoid conflicts within this overall framework, except where these treaties explicitly contain different obligations.

The panel argued that where a treaty forms part of a general framework and has similar provisions and wording, it should be interpreted in a manner that avoids conflicts with the broader framework. The overall framework of treaties that they consider relevant are those that cover intellectual property and are developed within related institutions, and that are concluded by a significant number of WTO members even if they are not in force. While not extending to making these treaties part of the applicable laws, the panel clearly stated that similar provisions using similar wording and reflecting specific understandings should be interpreted to mean the same thing so as to avoid conflict. While this discussion was in reference to article 13 on exceptions and limitations and the similarity to the same terms in Article 10 of the WIPO Copyright Treaty and to Article 9(2) of the Berne Convention, this also opens the door to the interpretation of the terms in Article 7 and 8, as well as to the provisions on working requirements in the Paris Convention. In principle, if it could be argued that technology transfer was part of the same framework of treaties as referred to by the panel, then the necessity to avoid conflicts could be applied to the provisions of the UNFCCC. At the very least, such an approach would require that the meaning of the terms should be read to be consistent across the international framework of treaties addressing the same issue. Nevertheless, the panel in this case appeared to limit its approach to the network of intellectual property treaties negotiated at WIPO, some of which are incorporated by reference in the TRIPS Agreement. It remains unclear the extent to which the panel decision's approach will be carried forward, especially to patent related disputes.

[1181] para 6.66 – 6.70, *US – Section 110(5) Copyright Act*

As a general matter therefore, there appears to be a very limited set of ways in which WTO panels must or can take into account other international treaties. Nevertheless, some specific developments on intellectual property, subsequent to the panel decisions have provided some clarity on what the WTO access points for these other treaties may be, although not necessarily enabling those treaties to function as applicable law in a dispute. The most current and salient are the public health issue and the issue of how to relate to the Convention on Biological Diversity.

The Doha Declaration on TRIPS and Public Health[1182] serves as the most authoritative statement of the WTO rule-making process' views on how the WTO relates to public health interests. There is an explicit interpretive direction in this Declaration with regard to how to interpret the TRIPS Agreement as regards other regimes related to health. Paragraph 5(a) therefore states: 'In applying the customary rules of interpretation of public international law, each provision of the TRIPS Agreement shall be read in the light of the object and purpose of the Agreement as expressed, in particular, in its objectives and principles.' This means that, in particular, Article 7 and 8 must be given due weight in interpreting other provision of the treaty. This statement is a direct instruction to panels and the Appellate body and a rebuke to the approach taken by the panel in *Canada – Pharmaceuticals* which did not appear to actually apply article 7 and 8 to its analysis of Article 30.

In addition, and of the most relevance to the exercise of compulsory licenses for climate change technologies, paragraph 5(c) states that, '[e]ach member has the right to determine what constitutes a national emergency or other circumstances of extreme urgency, it being understood that public health crises, including those relating to HIV/AIDS, tuberculosis, malaria and other epidemics, can represent a national emergency or other circumstances of extreme urgency.' While expressly mentioning public health crises as a basis for the issuance of compulsory license, the Doha Declaration also makes clear that other situations can be declared circumstances of extreme urgency. To the extent that the climate crisis can be declared a situation of extreme urgency, member states are free to use the more flexible requirements of Article 31(b).

The legal effect of the Declaration is unclear. As an authoritative instruction by the WTO General Council, it must clearly place an obligation on WTO institutions to comply with its provisions. The Dispute Settlement Body is obliged to follow the instruction contained in the Declaration. It may also function as a subsequent agreement regarding the interpretation of the treaty, in the sense of Article 31(3)(a) of the Vienna

---

[1182] Declaration on the TRIPS Agreement and Public Health WT/MIN(01)/DEC/2 (Adopted 14 November 2001)

Convention of the Law of Treaties.[1183] Its content does not suggest that it is altering or adding to the obligations or rights of members, but it nevertheless clearly creates a preference for specific interpretive outcomes. However, the Declaration provides no clear instruction to make other treaties function as applicable law in a TRIPS dispute by interpreting VCLT Article 31(3)(c) more broadly.

The second area, in which there has been significant debate in the WTO on how to relate to other regimes, has been the discussion on whether the TRIPS Agreement and the Convention on Biological Diversity (CBD) contradict each other, thereby requiring an amendment of the TRIPS Agreement, or whether they can be implemented in a mutually supportive manner. The debate is ongoing, but has focused on a proposal (now part of the single undertaking negotiations in the Doha Round) for a new Article 29*bis* to prevent misappropriation of genetic resources and traditional knowledge, through a mandatory disclosure requirement.[1184] This debate is largely polarized between developed and developing countries and thus there is no single direction or decision from the WTO. Nevertheless, the existence of the internal debate suggests that there may be room in other fora to address the linkage. The ongoing impasse in the WTO suggests that the issue is hostage to other issues relating to market access in the WTO. It may also be the case, however, that the issue itself represents a fundamental disagreement that cannot be resolved through negotiations but only through dispute settlement.

While there exist obvious links between the CBD and the TRIPS Agreement, the inability to state something conclusive about what that relationship is and should be in the WTO suggests that there is little room for consideration of other regimes except through the narrow lens provided by dispute settlement. How much more difficult then, for the UNFCCC agreement which has no provisions on intellectual property and has a specific structure on technology transfer that makes it an obligation of developed countries rather than a right of developing countries, to find a point of entry into the WTO. As noted in the section on unilateral actions, the existing flexibilities and the existing jurisprudence in the WTO suggest that there is little room for even partially integrating the technology transfer aims and goals of the climate change regime into the TRIPS framework. Where neither the UNFCCC nor the WTO provides sufficient purchase for developing countries to justify their otherwise non-TRIPS compliant actions, one avenue where they have clear obligations that can be linked to both intellectual property and climate change in is human rights. The following section

---

[1183] See p979, Yu, P "Objectives and Principles of TRIPS" 46 Houston Law Review 4 in support of this approach.
[1184] "DRAFT DECISION TO ENHANCE MUTUAL SUPPORTIVENESS BETWEEN THE TRIPS AGREEMENT AND THE CONVENTION ON BIOLOGICAL DIVERSITY: Communication from Brazil, China, Colombia, Ecuador, India, Indonesia, Peru, Thailand, the ACP Group, and the African Group" TN/C/W/59 (19 April 2011

explores how human rights may be able to knit together developing country obligations that justify non-TRIPS compliant IP measures to address climate change

IV. HUMAN RIGHTS AND TECHNOLOGY TRANSFER FOR CLIMATE CHANGE[1185]

The difficulties associated with the approach of the WTO to the flexibilities under TRIPS has prompted some scholars to seek methods to expand the limits imposed by the TRIPS Agreement, primarily by drawing on a human rights approach to technology transfer. In part this draws on insights from Pauwelyn that even in a situation where the majority of human rights treaties do not have as broad a membership as the WTO, the differential nature of the types of obligations, (reciprocal and bargained for in the case of the WTO versus integral and fundamental to general international law in the case of human rights) direct conflicts between human rights law and WTO law would be resolved in favor of human rights law.[1186] Thus if developing countries could argue that their climate needs for technology can be framed as necessary for meeting their human rights obligations, not only would they be in a position to trigger a conflict resolution process, but, it would be one that would be resolved in favor of the human rights obligation.

Any successful approach requires establishing: what, if any, rights there may be that implicate technology transfer and how these could be implemented and applied; what the relationship is or should be between the human rights regime and the TRIPS Agreement.

To answer the first part we need to determine:

- Are there Obligations in Human Rights Law that Relate to Technology Transfer?

- How Relevant is the Issue of Intellectual Property for a Rights-Based Approach to Technology Transfer in the Climate Change Context?

- What are the Possible Avenues for Adopting a Rights-Based Approach to Technology Transfer for Climate Change?

[1185] An earlier version of some of this material can be found in Orellana, M, D Shabalala, B Tuncak "Technology Transfer in the UNFCCC and other International Legal Regimes: The Challenge of Systemic Integration" ICHRP Working Paper 2010. Available at:
http://www.ichrp.org/files/papers/181/138_technology_transfer_UNFCCC.pdf (last visited 15 August 2014).
[1186] Pauwelyn, J *Conflict of Norms in Public International Law: How WTO Law Relates to Other Rules of International Law.* (New York: Cambridge University Press, 2003.).

IV.1. Are there Obligations in Human Rights Law that Relate to Technology Transfer?

There are two aspects to the question about the existence of human rights obligations relating to technology transfer. The first relates to whether there is a right to technology transfer *per se*, broadly framed. This could include a concept of a right to access technology that has extra-territorial reach or implications. The second is whether there are human rights which require technology transfer for their fulfillment.

IV.1.1. A Right to Technology Transfer? The Right to Enjoy the Benefits of Scientific Progress and its Application (ICESCR Article 15(1)(b))

The scope and full legal meaning of Article 15(1)(b) of the International Convention on Economic, Social and Cultural Rights (ICESCR) has yet to be articulated. While conceptually attractive, there is very little literature on the relation of this article to technology transfer. In addition to analyzing its text, it must read in the context of Article 15(1) as a whole,[1187] which requires States to recognize the right of everyone:

(a) To take part in cultural life;

(b) To enjoy the benefits of scientific progress and its applications;

(c) To benefit from the protection of the moral and material interests resulting from any scientific, literary or artistic production of which he is the author.

The provision would appear to establish an individual right for persons to benefit from scientific progress. Legally, this raises two questions: what does it mean to "enjoy the benefits," and what is meant by "scientific progress and its applications." The history of the article suggests that a deliberate distinction was being made between pure science research, which is generally not done for purposes of commercialization and sale versus "the applications" of science, which are more applicable to technologies and more closely linked to patents.[1188] Both categories of knowledge are included within the scope of the provision. The definition of benefit has not been elaborated. However, Article 15(1)(c) suggests that benefit should, at the least, mean access to the use, for their benefit, of scientific knowledge and applications of which others are the creators. Some

---

[1187] The Committee on Economic, Social and Cultural Rights views the provisions as a unitary set, despite the fact that it has chosen to elaborate different General Comments to address each one.
[1188] Schabas, W A "Study of the Right to Enjoy the Benefits of Scientific and Technological Progress and Its Applications," in Donders, Y and V Volodin (eds) *Human Rights in Education, Science and Culture: Legal Developments and Challenges*, UNESCO 2007, at 275.

work has begun at UNESCO[1189] on elaborating Article 15(1)(b). The provision has been included in the Universal Declaration on Bioethics and Human Rights (Article 15),[1190] which states:

> 1. Benefits resulting from any scientific research and its applications should be shared with society as a whole and within the international community, in particular with developing countries. In giving effect to this principle, benefits may take any of the following forms:
> (a) special and sustainable assistance to, and acknowledgement of, the persons and groups that have taken part in the research;
> (b) access to quality health care;
> (c) provision of new diagnostic and therapeutic modalities or products stemming from research;
> (d) support for health services;
> (e) access to scientific and technological knowledge;
> (f) capacity-building facilities for research purposes;
> (g) other forms of benefit consistent with the principles set out in this Declaration.

Thus, at least within the realm of health and bioethics, the concept of "benefit" has been interpreted to include access to scientific and technical knowledge, as well as the provision of new scientific products and capacity building. However, this has been in the context of research and what is owed to participants in research. To extend this approach to climate change, a broader approach may be needed. An experts meeting in 2007 addressed the issue.[1191] UNESCO considers that the fulfillment of the right is necessary for the fulfillment of other rights such as: the right to health, the right to education, the right to information and the right to food.[1192] Thus, it may be that the power of the provision lies at its junction with the delivery of other rights rather than as a provision which in and of itself requires technology to be transferred.

A common refrain of the experts meeting was the sense that there was an inherent tension between IP rights and the Right to Enjoy the Benefits of Scientific Progress (REBSP).[1193] In part, this viewpoint has been informed by the experience of

---

[1189] UNESCO "Report of Experts Meeting on the Right to Enjoy the Benefits of Scientific Progress and its Applications" Amsterdam, 7-9 June 2007. Available at http://unesdoc.unesco.org/images/0015/001545/154583e.pdf (last visited 15 August 2014).
[1190] Available at http://portal.unesco.org/en/ev.php-URL_ID=31058&URL_DO=DO_TOPIC&URL_SECTION=201.html (last visited 15 August 2014).
[1191] UNESCO "Report of Experts Meeting on the Right to Enjoy the Benefits of Scientific Progress and its Applications" Amsterdam, 7-9 June 2007.
[1192] See p4, Id.
[1193] See p7, Id.

access to medicines activists in their attempts to ensure that the TRIPS Agreement was not interpreted in ways that restricted access to medicines for poor and marginalized populations. However, the direct link to the REBSP is relatively new, as the majority of actors viewed the access to medicines issue through the lens of the right to health. Nevertheless, experts at this meeting almost unanimously viewed IP rules as a major source of tension for fulfilling the REBSP and related rights, such as the right to health.

One conclusion of the meeting was key support for a General Comment addressing the REBSP, especially its relationship to other economic, social and cultural rights.[1194] In particular, the extent and nature of the relationship between the REBSP and other rights remained unclear and required elaboration. Given the complexity of the needs and the different forms of technology implicated by each right, it may be appropriate to elaborate on that relationship on a case-by-case basis. It may be that climate change is just such a case, albeit, a broad one. The issues concerning balancing and conflicts of rights with Article 15(1)(c) would also have to be addressed, in determining the scope of the right and its application to technology transfer. General Comment 17 on Article 15(1)(c) has prompted groups to consider the relevance of Article 15(1)(b) in part because many felt that it had gone too far in the direction of privileging patterns of exclusive ownership over knowledge. However, the first thing that should be noted is that the General Comment is quite clear that while there may be parallels between human rights and IP, the content of Article 15(1)(c) is not synonymous with IP, by virtue of the different characteristics and the utilitarian nature of IP protection.[1195]

The Committee on Economic, Social and Cultural Rights (CESCR) also recognized an intrinsic link between Article 15(1)(c) and Articles 15(1)(b) and (a).[1196] Of particular relevance is the concept that the right in Article 15(1)(b) is not absolute and must be limited by the need to ensure that:

4. the "moral' interests of the author are protected, i.e. the connection between the creator and the creation is maintained and that the aims and goals of the creator with respect to the creation are not unjustifiably distorted;[1197] and

5. the material interests of the author are protected, i.e. some kind of remuneration with respect to the creation is provided and is linked to some

---

[1194] p9, UNESCO "Report of Experts Meeting on the Right to Enjoy the Benefits of Scientific Progress and its Applications" Amsterdam, 7-9 June 2007.
[1195] CESCR "General Comment 17: The right of everyone to benefit from the protection of the moral and material interests resulting from any scientific, literary or artistic production of which he is the author (art. 15 (1) (c))" E/C.12/GC/17 Committee on Economic, Social and Cultural Rights 2005 at 2. Available at http://www.unhchr.ch/tbs/doc.nsf/(Symbol)/E.C.12.GC.17.En?OpenDocument
[1196] Id.
[1197] See p3, Id.

extent with the standard required for the author to make an adequate standard of living.[1198]

Thus, as long as some form of recognition of creators is established and some form of ensuring some kind of earnings from the creation is maintained, States may deliver on Article 15(1)(b) by whatever means they choose. The beneficiaries of Article 15(1)(c) protection are also limited to natural persons or groups of natural persons, not legal entities.[1199] Thus, neither transnational corporations nor States have direct claims under this article.

What has been of the most significant concern for many organizations has been the language of the General Comment on limitations outside the context of Article 15. The committee states that any such limitation must be proportional and "must pursue a legitimate aim, and must be strictly necessary for the promotion of the general welfare in a democratic society, in accordance with Article 4 of the Covenant."[1200] The Comment contains very well-articulated sets of restrictions on what States must do to respect, protect and fulfill Article 15(1)(c), in language that is virtually indistinguishable from that used in the context of IP rights. Therefore, in the absence of equally compelling language and discussion on Article 15(1)(b), States and private actors may provide greater protection to technology and knowledge holders, and focus less on providing access and benefits to scientific progress and its applications.

Nevertheless, the General Comment notes that Article 15(1)(c) should not be implemented in a way that systematically impedes the fulfillment of other rights, such as the right to health, the right to education, the right to food, as well as the REBSP. In addition, a strong statement on balancing interests can be found in the discussion of the core obligations that States must comply with immediately to give effect to Article 15(1)(c) which includes:

> To strike an adequate balance between the effective protection of the moral and material interests of authors and States Parties' obligations in relation to the rights to food, health and education, as well as the rights to take part in cultural life and to enjoy the benefits of scientific progress and its applications, or any other right recognized in the Covenant.[1201]

General Comment 17 suggests that work on the REBSP is further along than may appear at first glance. It is a right that underlies several others, although its

---

[1198] See p4, Id.
[1199] See p3, Id.
[1200] See p7, Id.
[1201] See p11, CESCR "General Comment 17: The right of everyone to benefit from the protection of the moral and material interests resulting from any scientific, literary or artistic production of which he is the author (art. 15 (1) (c))" E/C.12/GC/17 Committee on Economic, Social and Cultural Rights 2005.

relationship to them may need to be further elaborated. In addition, the statements on the requirement of balance by the General Comment provide some purchase for further elaboration of the REBSP without the need to wait for the committee to begin developing a General Comment outlining the content of the REBSP. The existence of the REBSP itself can enable the review of other more established rights for the components that require access to technological products and processes for their fulfillment, especially the fulfillment of their core obligations. In the context of climate change, the obligation to transfer technology can be harmonized with the REBSP if it is considered in combination with the need for access to technologies necessary for the fulfillment of other human rights.

IV.1.2. Are there Climate-related Human Rights Obligations which may Require Technology Transfer for their Fulfillment?

In addressing the issue of which climate-related human rights may require access to technology for their fulfillment we can look to two sources. The first is the set of rights that will be directly impacted by climate change and are directly in danger of being regressed by climate change. There are several human rights that may be implicated by climate change, including[1202] the right to health, the right to food, and the right to water.

In addressing some of these, the sections below will:

- outline the relationship of the right to climate change; and

- identify what climate-related technology and knowledge the right requires access to.

In addition to specific rights, the climate discussions could be strongly impacted by Article 2(1) of ICESCR regarding the duty to provide international assistance and cooperation in fulfilling the relevant economic, social and cultural rights. In this regard, Article 2(1) ICESCR may also add a powerful rights-based substrate to the principle of common but differentiated responsibilities and the duties established under Article 4.5 of the UNFCCC for developed countries to transfer technology.

a. The Right to Life

[1202] See Appendices, Humphreys, S "Climate Change and Human Rights: A Rough Guide" International Council for Human Rights Policy 2008.

The right to life is protected by Article 6(1) of the International Convention on Civil and Political Rights (ICCPR). It has also been protected in numerous other international and regional human rights instruments.[1203]

i. How does the right to life relate to climate change?

The occurrence of extreme weather events and the attendant effects exemplify the impact of climate change on the right to life. The IPCC Fourth Assessment Report Working Group II Report on "Impacts, Adaptation and Vulnerability" points to climate-related extreme weather events, such as "extreme river floods, intense tropical and extra-tropical cyclone windstorms (along with their associated coastal storm surges), as well as the most severe supercell thunderstorms."[1204] The IPCC points to increases in extreme river flows in some regions,[1205] increased intensity of tropical cyclones with the attendant storm surges and flooding. All these events can result in severe loss of life.

ii. What climate-related technology and knowledge does fulfillment of the right to life require access to?

The key link to the right to life would be tools and resources to prevent, prepare for, manage, and recover from extreme weather events and disasters. Thus, the technologies and resources to address the right to life will require the State to implement such measures, provided that they can be attributed to action or omissions of the State.

Tentatively speaking, the technologies would include:

a. early warning systems (including communications);
b. systems for stockpiling and distributing food, water, and medicines;.
c. systems for storing and managing water resources;
d. alternative disaster-appropriate transport systems (e.g., boats);
e. systems for strengthening waste disposal sites against leakage during disasters;
f. disaster mitigation systems, such as flood and sea walls, flood channels; and
g. extreme weather event resistant building materials.

What is key about these technologies is that they also relate to reducing vulnerability and enhancing response capacity.

[1203] Article 6 of the Convention of the Rights of the Child (recognizing an inherent right to life and ensuring to the maximum extent possible the survival and development of the child); Article 2 of the European Convention on Human Rights; Article 1 of the American Declaration of the Rights and Duties of Man; Article 4 of the American Convention on Human Rights; and Article 4 of the African (Banjul) Charter on Human and Peoples' Rights.

[1204] See p9, IPCC, *Climate Change 2007: Impacts, Adaptation and Vulnerability. Contribution of Working Group II to the Fourth Assessment Report of the Intergovernmental Panel on Climate Change*, Cambridge University Press, Cambridge, UK 2007.

[1205] Id.

b. The Right to Health

Article 12 of the ICESCR affords the right to the "highest attainable standard of physical and mental health."

i. How does the right to health relate to climate change?

The CESCR General Comment 14 defines health broadly. The key element to the link to climate change impacts, as well as climate change vulnerability and adaptive capacity, is the idea that health includes a right to a healthy environment. It extends to the underlying determinants of health, such as food and nutrition, housing, access to safe and potable water and adequate sanitation, safe and healthy working conditions, and a **healthy environment**.

There are two levels at which links can be made. They can be made at the level of direct health effects such as disease burdens, but they can also be made at the level of the underlying determinants of health, especially the right to a healthy environment.

At the level of direct health impacts, climate change will result in changes in precipitation patterns, length of rainy seasons, and length of warm seasons.[1206] The IPCC report points to significant uncertainty as to the increased frequency and intensity of diseases due in large part to lack of long term epidemiological data.[1207] They note that disease incidence may in fact actually be a result of the social changes resulting from climate change as migration and population density patterns change. Nevertheless, the IPCC points to four major categories of health impacts:[1208]

- Direct effects of heat or cold
    - there have been increases in the intensity of heat waves, which seriously affect the elderly and the very young.
- Vector borne diseases
    - there is evidence for an increase in tick and insect vectors of disease that may result in greater human incidence of diseases.
    - there is greater incidence of Lyme disease further north than previously thought.
    - ecological change may also be a contributing factor to widening malarial belts
- Pollen and Dust-related diseases

[1206] IPCC, *Climate Change 2007: Impacts, Adaptation and Vulnerability. Contribution of Working Group II to the Fourth Assessment Report of the Intergovernmental Panel on Climate Change*, Cambridge University Press, Cambridge, UK 2007 at 107.
[1207] Id.
[1208] See p108, Id.

- increase in the global incidence of dust and dust storms may lead to greater respiratory problems. Evidence suggests that this may already be occurring in the Caribbean.[1209]

In general, the IPCC notes, "there is now good evidence of changes in the northward range of some disease vectors, as well as changes in the seasonal pattern of allergenic pollen. There is not yet any clear evidence that climate change is affecting the incidence of human vector-borne diseases, in part due to the complexity of these disease systems."[1210] Nevertheless, there is some guidance from the IPCC as to the elements of health relevant to climate.

At the level of the determinants of health, climate change could be considered to threaten the right to a healthy environment. However, it remains difficult, beyond the conditions surrounding extreme weather events, to characterize major ecological changes as unhealthy if they do not entail shifts in disease burdens or increases in toxicity. However, other determinants of health such as food/nutrition and water, and related aspects that can reduce climate vulnerability and enhance adaptive capacity may indeed be considered climate-related. The other determinants will be addressed below.

ii. What climate-related technology and knowledge does fulfillment of the right to health require access to?

States must deliver public health and health-care facilities, goods and services, as well as programmes. Given the difficulty in linking specific health effects to climate, the broader link to reducing vulnerability and enhancing adaptive capacity means that the technologies required to address climate issues are those that ensure sufficient health to survive and adapt to ecological changes.

From the links that have been established we can include:

- Medical products, processes and services related to managing health needs during extreme weather events; and

- Medical products, processes and services related to managing health needs during periods of extreme heat (heat waves) and extreme cold, especially for vulnerable populations such as the elderly and young children.

In addition, to address climate change vulnerability and adaptive capacity generally:

[1209] See p109, IPCC, *Climate Change 2007: Impacts, Adaptation and Vulnerability. Contribution of Working Group II to the Fourth Assessment Report of the Intergovernmental Panel on Climate Change*, Cambridge University Press, Cambridge, UK 2007.
[1210] Id.

- Medical products, processes and services related to increasing resistance to vector borne and temperature sensitive diseases;

- Medical products, processes and services related to increasing general immune-capacity, e.g. vaccines;

- Products, processes and services designed to create hygienic and sanitary living and working conditions, such as access to potable water and sanitary facilities.

The CESCR notes in General Comment 14 para 12, that delivery on the right to health entails at least two major elements: availability and accessibility.

Availability means, therefore, that health resources and technologies must be available in **sufficient** quantity. This means sufficient to address the needs of the relevant affected population. At a minimum they must include "safe and potable drinking water and adequate sanitation facilities, hospitals, clinics and other health-related buildings, trained medical and professional personnel receiving domestically competitive salaries, and essential drugs, as defined by the World Health Organization (WHO) Action Programme on Essential Drugs."[1211]

Accessibility means that the products, processes and services must be available within a reasonable distance of where the relevant populations live or can easily access, and that the products are available at a price affordable by all.

c. Right to Water

The right to water is not explicitly mentioned in the ICESCR. However, the Committee on Economic, Social, and Cultural Rights has concluded that the right to water is implied in Article 11 as an aspect of the right to an adequate standard of living.[1212]

i. How does the right to water relate to climate change?

Climate is linked to the right to water in two ways. The first is that extreme weather events associated with climate change are likely to result in temporary but severe disruptions of water supply that deprive portions of the population of access to water. During an extreme weather or sea event, water supply can be cut off due to the malfunction of desalination plants, damage to rainwater collectors, and contamination of wells.

[1211] para 12(a), CESCR General Comment 14 (2000)
[1212] CESCR, General Comment 15, (2002)

The second linkage is the reduction in available freshwater and the incidence of drought, as surface temperatures increase and surface moisture evaporates more quickly. The reduction in access to water due to climate change can be traced to:

- increased glacial melt, as well as melting of other ice systems and the general reduction in the amount of water held in ice each winter season.[1213] Such ice systems provide freshwater for much of the Indian sub-continent, for example.

- increased intensity of droughts as well as expansion of dry areas.[1214] While there will be some changes in precipitation, the data for the scale of change is still uncertain. The evaporation of surface moisture may be a greater problem.

Hydrological effects may be some of the clearest impacts of climate change resulting in uneven regional distributions of water. Dry areas appear to be getting drier, while wet areas seem to be getting wetter. However, in areas of increased run-off, they may be experiencing only temporary increase until glacial and other mountain ice systems are depleted. Centralized systems of water supply will be strained especially in terms of ensuring physical access. For example, water will have to be transported from one area to another; water storage systems will have to become more widespread; and water use will have to become more efficient.

ii. What climate-related technology and knowledge does fulfillment of the right to water require access to?

Water is generally supplied by local water authorities in centralized systems where capable local authorities exist. The vast majority of people living in rural areas rely on groundwater wells, and access to river water. The UN Office of the High Commissioner for Human Rights (OHCHR) does not provide guidance on what technologies and knowledge are necessary, but given the direct impact on the right to water, all technologies related to fulfilling the right to water are covered. At the least, we can see several related technology categories: water capture and storage products and processes; water distribution products and processes; and efficient water use and reclamation products and processes. Some of the technologies involved would therefore include:

- Water capture and storage products and processes
    o Rainwater harvesting from roofs into hardened storage tanks
    o Direct spring access and protection from contamination
    o sub-surface dams to capture underground streams and run-off

---

[1213] See p86, IPCC, *Climate Change 2007: Impacts, Adaptation and Vulnerability. Contribution of Working Group II to the Fourth Assessment Report of the Intergovernmental Panel on Climate Change*, Cambridge University Press, Cambridge, UK 2007.
[1214] See p90, Id.

- - -
    - covered, lined and sealed hand-dug wells, to prevent wall collapse and contamination
    - tubewells and boreholes
- Water distribution products and processes
    - gravity fed schemes to distribute water from higher altitude catchment areas
- Water treatment and sanitations products and processes
    - filtration processes
    - chemical treatment
    - sewerage systems
    - latrine systems
- Efficient water use and reclamation technologies

d. The Right to Food

The right to food is addressed in a number of international human rights conventions,[1215] and has been further recognized in subsequent declarations made by the international community.[1216]

i. How does the right to food relate to climate change?

Food production, both plant and animal and usually for subsistence, is the primary source of GHG emissions in many developing countries. Thus agricultural practices that involve fertilizers, soil tilling methods and bovine farming contribute to GHG emissions through nitrous oxide and methane release.[1217] Deforestation to create more agricultural land also removes carbon sinks.

On the other hand, food production is also one of the areas affected by increased dry areas and drought, as well as flooding. The loss of productive land may result in the lowering of food production. For coastal lands, increased sea-related extreme weather events such as storm surges can also lead to loss of cultivable land due to salination of the soil.

[1215] Article 25 UDHR (right to adequate standard of living, including food); ICESCR Article 11.1 and 11.3; CEDAW Article 12 (adequate nutrition during pregnancy and lactation); Article 24 CRC (combat malnutrition and provide adequate nutritious foods)

[1216] In the Rome Declaration on World Food Security, Heads of State and Government "reaffirm[ed] the right of everyone to have access to safe and nutritious food, consistent with the right to adequate food and the fundamental right of everyone to be free from hunger." The Millennium Development Goals included the goal to halve the proportion of people in the world suffering from hunger. In 2004, FAO released the Voluntary Guidelines on the Right to Adequate Food.

[1217] See p85, Baumert, K A et al *Navigating the Numbers: Greenhouse Gas Data and International Climate Policy*, World Resources Institute 2005.

In addition, changing weather patterns are affecting the lengths of growing seasons as well as humidity levels, soil acidity and a whole host of other factors. This can make existing plant varieties that have been long in use no longer as productive.[1218] The IPCC report points to increased vulnerability to extreme drought events.[1219]

ii. What climate-related technology and knowledge does fulfillment of the right to food require access to?

The relationship of the right to access to food to patterns of food production is crucial. In particular, given the increasing urbanization of poor and marginalized communities in developing countries, food production and food distributions systems are also critical. Climate-related technology and knowledge related to the right to food will have to address:

- access to diverse plant varieties and seeds, especially resistant to drought and to salinated soil; and

- access to water for food production, including irrigation systems, water capture and storage systems

One consideration, especially for considering a rights approach to climate change is that the food sector has become increasingly privatized as public funding in agricultural research has been reduced, and private companies have been able to appropriate germplasm through plant patents, plant variety protections, and patents on plant and animal genetic resources. This means that more so than in many other industries, the technologies and knowledge for fulfilling the right to food are in private hands and may be protected by IP.

e. The Right to Development

The right to development, despite a long history, is still broadly debated. Article 1 of the Declaration on the Right to Development[1220] states that "the right to development is an inalienable human right by virtue of which every human person and all peoples are entitled to participate in, contribute to, and enjoy economic, social, cultural and political development, in which all human rights and fundamental freedoms can be fully realized."

While the right to development is framed as an individual right, it has largely developed out of a dialogue between States as a means to address policy space by

---

[1218] IPCC, *Climate Change 2007: Impacts, Adaptation and Vulnerability. Contribution of Working Group II to the Fourth Assessment Report of the Intergovernmental Panel on Climate Change*, Cambridge University Press, Cambridge, UK 2007 at 104.
[1219] See p107, Id.
[1220] General Assembly resolution 41/128 1986

developing countries and to establish responsibilities on developed countries to provide development assistance. In particular it establishes an obligation for States to promote fair development policies and effective international cooperation. The right can be invoked by both individuals and peoples, suggesting that States as representatives of people can invoke some of the provisions.

The 1986 Declaration on the Right to Development has no mention of technology transfer or access to technology. However, Article 11 of the Vienna Declaration explicitly calls on the wording of ICESCR Article 15(1)(b) stating that, "Everyone has the right to enjoy the benefits of scientific progress and its applications." In addition, developing countries have sought to have technology transfer viewed as an integral component of the right (see e.g. a 2003 Non-Aligned Movement Draft resolution on the Right to Development at the 59th Session of the Human Rights Commission).[1221]

The Independent Expert on the Right to Development has also provided some guidance on technology transfer as a component of the right to development. In his report he examines the obstacles that TRIPS poses for access to technology. In particular he notes that the development path of unilateral measures to ensure technology transfer that was used by the Asian Tiger economies may no longer be available because of the TRIPS Agreement.[1222]

i. How does the right to development relate to climate change?

Within the UNFCCC and the discussion on climate, developing countries have drawn on the right to development to establish basic principles such as common but differentiated responsibilities. They have not necessarily stated it in terms of the right to development but they have nevertheless ensured that the UNFCCC recognizes it in Article 4.7.

ii. What climate-related technology and knowledge does fulfillment of the right to development require access to?

In general, therefore, the right to development would point to all technologies required to address climate impacts as outlined in all the other rights outlined in this section. The right to development draws on other rights with the added element that it is also directed at imposing obligations on developed countries. The lack of development of the right may be an impediment, but, in conjunction with other rights, may be examined for the role it can play in making the connection between human rights, technology transfer and climate change.

[1221] E/CN.4/2003/L.14 8 April 2003.
[1222] See p11, Review of progress and obstacles in the promotion, implementation, operationalization, and enjoyment of the right to development, E/CN.4/2004/WG.18/2, 17 February 2004.

f. The Duty to Provide International Assistance and Cooperation

As this paper has focused on international technology transfer, the human rights that we have examined in this study all place obligations on States to provide access to technologies for the fulfillment of those rights. To address international transfer of technology however, each right has had to establish some kind of extra-territorial obligation for other States and actors. For the economic, social and cultural rights, the international element of technology transfer to fulfill the rights comes from the duty to cooperate and provide assistance in Article 2 of the ICESCR. For other rights, the legal basis for extraterritorial obligations remains contested.

ICESCR Article 2 requires each State Party "to take steps, individually and through international assistance and co-operation, especially economic and technical, to the maximum of its available resources, with a view to achieving progressively the full realization of the rights recognized in the present Covenant by all appropriate means..." ICESCR Article 23 elaborates on this requirement, stating that international action includes "the conclusion of conventions, the adoption of recommendations, the furnishing of technical assistance," and other methods.

The CESCR has repeatedly drawn attention to the essential role of international cooperation in achieving the full realization of particular rights under the ICESCR, stating that State Parties should "comply with their commitment to take joint and separate action" to achieve this goal.[1223] With respect to the right to health, the CESCR has more fully described the contours of the obligation for international cooperation. States must firstly respect the enjoyment of the right to health in other countries and, where possible, protect this right from violation by actions of third parties. In addition to the duty to respect and protect, the international community has an obligation to facilitate access to essential health facilities, goods, and services, and "wherever possible" to provide such aid when it is needed. Finally, the CESCR has stated, "State Parties should ensure that the right to health is given due attention in international agreements, and to that end, should consider the development of further legal instruments." [1224] The CESCR has defined a similar role for the international community with respect to the right to food and the right to water. (CESCR General Comment 12, 1999; CESCR General Comment 15, 2002.) Moreover, in its discussion of the right to water the Committee has been clear that State Parties must also refrain from actions that indirectly interfere with the enjoyment of rights in other countries.[1225] (CESCR General Comment 15, 2002). The committee is also particularly clear that

---

[1223] Id.
[1224] CESCR General Comment 14, 2000
[1225] para 31, "International cooperation requires States Parties to refrain from actions that interfere, directly or indirectly, with the enjoyment of the right to water in other countries. Any activities undertaken within the State party's jurisdiction should not deprive another country of the ability to realize the right to water for persons in its jurisdiction." (CESCR General Comment 15, 2002).

States should "depending on the availability of resources, [...] facilitate realization of the right to water in other countries, for example through provision of water resources, financial and technical assistance, and provide the necessary aid when required. [...] The economically developed States Parties have a special responsibility and interest to assist the poorer developing States in this regard."[1226] The CESCR reiterates this even more strongly in paragraph 38 of General Comment 15, noting that:

> for the avoidance of any doubt, the Committee wishes to emphasize that it is particularly incumbent on States Parties, and other actors in a position to assist, to provide international assistance and cooperation, especially economic and technical which enables developing countries to fulfill their core obligations indicated in paragraph 37 above.

The CESCR has indicated particular areas that implicate the joint and individual responsibility of State Parties and necessitate international cooperation. Notably, it has stated that it is the responsibility of all State Parties to cooperate in providing disaster relief and humanitarian assistance in times of emergency. Further, "[e]ach State should contribute to this task to the maximum of its capacities." Priority in the provision of aid and funding should be given to the most vulnerable or marginalized groups of the population.[1227] The CESCR has also indicated the international community has a "collective responsibility" to address threats to human rights that are trans-boundary in nature, such as certain diseases. In addressing these trans-boundary issues, "[t]he economically developed States Parties have a special responsibility and interest to assist the poorer developing States..."[1228]

The obligations of all the State Parties to respect and protect rights, and to facilitate or provide access to resources necessary to ensure such rights apply equally to the threats posed by climate change to rights under the ICESCR. Climate change, because of its trans-boundary nature and the acute threat it poses to economic, social, and cultural rights among vulnerable populations, is an issue that implicates the responsibility of all State Parties to cooperate.

IV.2. What are the Possible Avenues for Adopting a Rights-Based Approach to the Arguments for Technology Transfer for Climate Change?

One way to view a rights-based approach is that there would be a basis for making a direct demand for access to technology from those who are holders of technology. Such a demand would be based on a direct right to access technology or on access to technology as a necessary component for the fulfillment of other rights. The

---

[1226] para 34, CESCR, General Comment 15, 2002.
[1227] CESCR General Comment 14, 2000
[1228] Id.

other view of a rights-based approach is that, in the exercise of policy choices to require third parties to transfer technologies, the human rights obligations of the party doing so could form the basis for justifying such action, even where such action would not be in conformity with the TRIPS Agreement.

The rights that I have outlined remain largely linked to adaptation in the climate arena. There is little in the analysis that enables a rights-based approach to technology transfer for mitigation, except for perhaps Article 15(1)(b). The uses of human rights to justify otherwise non-conforming measures is strongest for adaptation although there may be some purchase for mitigation based measures.

IV.2.1. Adaptation

Climate change adaptation has a basic normative structure. Developed countries have largely caused climate change. The effects of climate change will be broad-based and cross-regional and all States will have to make adjustments and adapt to new weather patterns and weather events. Developed countries are in the privileged position of having sufficient resources to pay the costs of that adjustment. In contrast, many developing countries do not have the resources to fully adapt and will suffer from the negative effects on their development from climate change. Therefore, developed countries bear a special responsibility to assist developing countries to adapt. That principle is enshrined in the UNFCCC's Article 4.8.[1229] Technology transfer is strongly related to adaptation, as it requires new and alternative products and processes to effectively enable the necessary shifts in production and consumption patterns.

The inclusion of technology transfer within the framework of adaptation is common throughout the UNFCCC documents. The Nairobi Work Programme, established in 2005 outlines the framework for adaptation in the UNFCCC. The

---

[1229] In the implementation of the commitments in this Article, the Parties shall give full consideration to what actions are necessary under the Convention, including actions related to funding, insurance and the transfer of technology, to meet the specific needs and concerns of developing country Parties arising from the adverse effects of climate change and/or the impact of the implementation of response measures, especially on:
(a) Small island countries;
(b) Countries with low-lying coastal areas;
(c) Countries with arid and semi-arid areas, forested areas and areas liable to forest decay;
(d) Countries with areas prone to natural disasters;
(e) Countries with areas liable to drought and desertification;
(f) Countries with areas of high urban atmospheric pollution;
(g) Countries with areas with fragile ecosystems, including mountainous ecosystems;
(h) Countries whose economies are highly dependent on income generated from the production, processing and export, and/or on consumption of fossil fuels and associated energy-intensive products; and
(i) Land-locked and transit countries.
Further, the Conference of the Parties may take actions, as appropriate, with respect to this paragraph

Programme has 9 sub-themes, one of which is technologies for adaptation.[1230] The work on technologies for adaptation is however, quite preliminary within the UNFCCC. One of the issues is the underlying justification for adaptation. In the UNFCCC it is framed as an equity issue for whom the obligation lies entirely with developed countries. The question then is twofold: whether there may be a role for human rights in more clearly articulating the equity justifications for technology transfer to address climate change adaptation; and how such a role would be operationalized.

From an examination of the broader literature as well as the approach within the UNFCCC, two main roles for technology transfer can be found. These are:

- technology transfer as an overarching commitment, separate from new and additional funding for adaptation; and

- technology transfer as an integral component of adaptation.

These two approaches have significant consequences for targeting action and for how a human rights framework may find purchase. If technology transfer is viewed as a separate commitment under the UNFCCC, which has to be delivered on separately from adaptation programmes, it enables the inclusion of technology transfer for mitigation. However, it has only a small overlap with the set of rights that we have examined in above. On its own, there are few if any justice claims involved beyond those of fairness and equity related to the polluter pays principle and other distributive justice claims.

Another view sees technology transfer as an integral part of the adaptation program. In the same manner that we examined the rights above for the technologies that are necessary for their fulfillment, in this view, technology transfer is justified as a means of fulfillment of adaptation aims. The justification for technology transfer for adaptation within the UNFCCC is largely from a corrective justice viewpoint: developing countries are being harmed by climate change; developed countries are responsible for climate change; ergo they are responsible for addressing and correcting the harms that they caused. Corrective justice approaches are also inherent to human rights discourse, especially where, as we have established, climate change negatively impacts the realization of specific rights. The congruence between the climate change impacts by sector (health, food, water) and climate change impacts by human rights effect is very clear. Economic, social and cultural rights also have strong congruence with the manner in which development work is carried out and the development framework has been key to informing the way that climate impacts and adaptation have been framed. Climate impacts have been seen as undermining development.

[1230] More information available at http://unfccc.int/adaptation/sbsta_agenda_item_adaptation/items/3995.php (last visited 15 August 2014).

IV.2.2. Mitigation

While corrective justice claims for technology transfer for adaptation make it easier to establish a link to human rights, the justice claims for transfer of technologies for mitigation are different altogether. As noted in chapter 4, transfer of technologies for mitigation is part of the basic contractual bargain underlying the UNFCCC. Developing countries will only take on GHG emissions reduction commitments once they have access to technologies that enable a carbon-efficient pathway, paid for by developed countries. There remains very little purchase for a rights-based approach to technology transfer for mitigation, except perhaps invoking Article 15(1)(b) in the context of fulfilling the right to development as partly articulated in UNFCCC Article 4.7. The right to enjoy the benefits of scientific progress and its applications may provide significant theoretical purchase for arguing that each State must deliver on it to its citizens. However, the practical obstacles for a human rights justification for technology transfer mitigation remains far weaker than for adaptation.

IV.3. The relationship between Human Rights, Intellectual Property and Climate Change

Traditionally, human rights obligations function in international law as obligations *erga omnes* and thus, by definition, are applicable law for all States in all their activities. Moreover, human rights are fundamental and cannot be contracted out of. In addition, certain human rights are recognized as *jus cogens*, having formal primacy over other international norms. Outside of *jus cogens*, human rights norms generally have more force than other norms given that they concern fundamental values of the international community.

To the extent that the issue of how to relate to other regimes has been taken up, the human rights committees have consistently applied the standard that human rights are fundamental obligations of states which are not subject to 'balancing' tests. They can be mutually supportive with other regimes but only to the extent that such regimes remain compatible with human rights law. Even in the realm of the application of economic sanctions the CESCR conclusively stated in General Comment 8, that:

> the provisions of the Covenant, virtually all of which are also reflected in a range of other human rights treaties as well as the Universal Declaration of Human Rights, cannot be considered to be inoperative, or in any way inapplicable, solely because a decision has been taken that considerations of international peace and security warrant the imposition of sanctions. Just as the international community insists that any targeted State must respect the civil and political rights of its citizens, so too must that State and the

international community itself do everything possible to protect at least the core content of the economic, social and cultural rights of the affected peoples of that State.[1231]

This is, however, nuanced by several doctrinal elements, especially for economic, social and cultural rights. This includes the principle of "progressive realization" of rights, taking into account the different capacities of countries to deliver on these rights, and the different timeframes in which the realization of some rights will have to occur.

From the point of view of the regime-fora relationship, the human rights bodies clearly view human rights as having priority over other standards or objectives. It is the rhetorical and substantive power of human rights that has made human rights language attractive, both to those wishing to limit the power and role of IP rights, as well as to those wishing to expand its role and power.

More importantly human rights that function as obligations *erga omnes* may provide a way back into the WTO but only if there exists a framework through which the WTO and TRIPS Agreement can address and apply human rights within their interpretive mechanisms. To the extent that the 'necessity' requirement provides an avenue in the GATT, the TBT and the SPS Agreement, human rights as a justification for otherwise non-conforming measures is possible. There remains considerable disagreement as to the flexibility of WTO bodies to take into account human rights. While Pauwelyn would be more likely to find some room, Marceau is relatively determined that human rights could never be directly applicable or set directly against WTO law in a panel.[1232]

The TRIPS Agreement poses a particular problem because the existing interpretation of necessity cannot take into account or be balanced with the moral power and common interest of the human rights regime. In addition, the role of intellectual property as a human right muddies the water, elevating the rights of intellectual property holders towards those of intellectual property users, in ways that make it difficult to argue that intellectual property is *per se* in opposition to human rights, or technology transfer for climate change conceived in human rights terms. To successfully use human rights to address TRIPS, another additional step may need to be taken in the broader interpretive approach. The next chapter examines the International Law Commission's approach and applies it to the case of technology transfer, outlining

---

[1231] See p8, UN Economic and Social Council, 'The relationship between economic sanctions and respect for economic, social and cultural rights' (12 December 1997) para. 7, S/C.12/1997/8, CESCR General Comment
[1232] Marceau, G "WTO dispute settlement and human rights' 13 European Journal of International Law 753 (2002).

how the issue can be broadened in the WTO and outlining how the UNFCCC itself can take up the issue of intellectual property to expand the limits of the TRIPS Agreement.

V. Conclusion

The attempt to find a way to bring human rights into conflict with TRIPS in order to trigger the mechanisms for interpretive conflict resolution are not likely to succeed. Such attempts fail because of the structure of the climate change obligations for developing countries in the UNFCCC; and the acknowledgement of intellectual – property like rights in the human rights framework itself. Thus rather than being external to the human rights framework the basic debate about the proper balance between rightholders and users is built into the structure of Article 15 of the ICESCR. This leaves one final option for developing countries to expand the room that they have under the TRIPS Agreement: the appeal to the rules of general international law as an overarching set of obligations and principles common to all the involved regimes that creates a framework for how they should be interpreted together, even in the absence of direct conflicts.

Chapter 8
Systemic Integration and Action on Norm setting at the WTO and the UNFCCC

I. INTRODUCTION

In the absence of internal mechanisms at the WTO for integrating other regimes such as the UNFCCC and human rights as applicable law, allowing for justification of TRIPS non-conforming measures, two options remain – creating a framework to re-enter the WTO; creating a framework for other fora to take up the issue of increasing flexibility for non-conforming measures. This requires a framework for integration of international law rather than the fragmentation that has been the consequence of WTO jurisprudence.

The most significant and authoritative attempt to address the question of fragmentation and expansion of international law has been undertaken by the International Law Commission (ILC).[1233] This chapter describes the basic principles put forward by the ILC and the basic solution to conflicts that it prescribes. It then outlines some of the potential solutions to addressing the tensions between the various international regimes bearing on technology transfer and climate change, studied above.

The ILC's report on the fragmentation of international law is actually titled: "Fragmentation of International Law: Difficulties Arising from the Diversification and Expansion of International Law". This reflects one of its key conclusions: that there is not necessarily a danger in the increasing complexity and diversity of international law.[1234] This follows from the ILC's belief that there are no conflicts between existing treaties that cannot be addressed within the framework of existing legal methodologies, including customary law and the Vienna Convention on the Law of Treaties (VCLT).

[1233] Koskenniemi, M et al. *"Fragmentation of International Law: Difficulties arising from the Diversification and Expansion of International Law:* Report of the Study Group of the International Law Commission" International Law Commission, 13 April 2006, UN Doc. A/CN.4/L.682 p. 1-256 and 18 July 2006, UN Doc. A/CN.4/L.702 p. 1-25.
[1234] para 222, Id.

The ILC's approach relies on the existence of the VCLT as a common frame for considering the issue of conflicts of rules and rule-making. The ILC analyzes concepts such as *lex specialis* and *lex posteriori*, but cautions against overly literal application of these principles. In particular, the ILC cautions that using such tools to invalidate a prior or more general law may be a fundamental error, unless a broader understanding of both treaties as operating within a system that maintains the existence, at least as an interpretive fact, of the prior or more general law.[1235] In addition, in seeking to apply such principles, the ILC grapples with the issue of "same subject matter" outlined in VCLT Article 30 on prior and subsequent treaties. The report notes that categories such as trade law, environmental law and human rights law are professional designations not based on any fundamental, natural partitioning of international law.[1236]

The ILC divides the kinds of conflicts into four categories[1237]:

(a) Relations between special and general law;

(b) Relations between prior and subsequent law;

(c) Relations between laws at different hierarchical levels; and

(d) Relations of law to its "normative environment" more generally.

The difficulty, of course, is in defining the type of relations at issue. For example, which law can be understood to be special and which one general? There can be reasonable disagreement, especially with respect to international environmental law and international economic law, as well as the increasing linkage between international environmental law and international human rights law. The issue of prior law is simpler, but surrounded by complications regarding whether the laws cover the same subject matter. For instance, the ILC categorizes the debate over trade and environment as a dispute between two special regimes under category (a), above.

II. DESCRIBING THE BOUNDARIES OF CONFLICTS & INTER-REGIME TENSIONS

The ILC defines conflicts as "a situation where two rules or principles suggest different ways of dealing with a problem."[1238] In addition to conflicts, this paper

---

[1235] para 32, Koskenniemi, M et al. *"Fragmentation of International Law: Difficulties arising from the Diversification and Expansion of International Law:* Report of the Study Group of the International Law Commission" International Law Commission, 13 April 2006, UN Doc. A/CN.4/L.682 p. 1-256 and 18 July 2006, UN Doc. A/CN.4/L.702 p. 1-25.
[1236] para 254, Id.
[1237] para 18, id.

addresses the question of inter-regime tensions, which, in addition to the interplay between rules or principles, involves governance and other structures set up within each regime that have a bearing on the attainment on other regimes' objectives. The ILC proposes to resolve conflicts in international law by emphasizing systemic integration anchored in VCLT Article 31(3)(c). This provision and the role of systemic integration are well known elements of customary law on treaty interpretation. VCLT Article 31(3)(c) states:

> 3.There shall be taken into account, together with the context:
>
> (*c*) any relevant rules of international law applicable in the relations between the parties.

Thus, general international law as well as the treaties in force between parties to the dispute must form part of the applicable law for interpreting provisions in each of the agreements. Given its emphasis on dispute settlement in its work on systemic integration, the ILC also makes a useful distinction between jurisdiction and applicable law. While jurisdiction arises from a given instrument and is therefore limited, there need not be any limit to the scope of applicable law, unless the instrument also explicitly defines one. The issue of applicable law is crucial because a party must be presumed to have intended to situate itself within a broader corpus or system of law, which includes prior and/or related treaties existing at the time of signature.[1239] Thus it takes the panel to task in *EC – Approval and Marketing of Biotech Products* for an overly restrictive reading of Article 31(3)(c), that would not allow for interpretive weight to be given to a treaty unless all WTO members were also parties to the treaty.[1240]

The ILC also spent significant effort analyzing the literature on "self-contained regimes" and whether they could truly exist in isolation from other elements of international law. The report concluded that the concept of "self-contained regimes" was an artificial construct that was not accurately descriptive of existing relationships between subject matters in international law.[1241] Except in rare cases it was not possible to contract out of general international law, and create an entirely sui generis regime that had no contact with others. In particular, it is impossible to characterize the WTO as a

---

[1238] para 25, Koskenniemi, M et al. "*Fragmentation of International Law: Difficulties arising from the Diversification and Expansion of International Law:* Report of the Study Group of the International Law Commission" International Law Commission, 13 April 2006, UN Doc. A/CN.4/L.602 p. 1-256 and 10 July 2006, UN Doc. A/CN.4/L.702 p. 1-25.
[1239] para 45, Id.
[1240] See para. 7.70 – 7.71, Panel Reports, European Communities – Measures Affecting the Approval and Marketing of Biotech Products, WT/DS291/R / WT/DS292/R / WT/DS293/R, Add.1 to Add.9, and Corr.1, adopted 21 November 2006, DSR 2006:III-VIII, 847 (*EC – Approval and Marketing of Biotech Products*)
[1241] Para 193, Koskenniemi, M et al. "*Fragmentation of International Law: Difficulties arising from the Diversification and Expansion of International Law:* Report of the Study Group of the International Law Commission" International Law Commission, 13 April 2006, UN Doc. A/CN.4/L.682 p. 1-256 and 18 July 2006, UN Doc. A/CN.4/L.702 p. 1-25.

self-contained regime precisely because in Article 3.2 of the DSU it explicitly relies on general international law to interpret its own terms, and in GATT Article XX it explicitly refers to prison labor[1242], and protecting human, animal and plant life or health. To the extent that the mechanisms for providing such protections are international treaties they fall fully within the WTO regime as applicable law. Even where they do not do so, they may by virtue of Article 31(3)(c) be applicable law as between parties to the dispute, to the extent that this does not unduly affect the rights and obligations of other WTO members not party to the dispute.

In addition to the concept of "self-contained regimes", the literature has also discussed the idea of "specialized regimes"[1243] to describe the nature of the relationships operating in international law and policy. In this regard, decisions in one specialized regime can act to limit or prevent action in another. In the face of that reality, e.g. between trade and environment and the way that the trade regime has limited particular kinds of environmental actions, there is a real substantive and legal effect. This gives rise to the issue of inter-regime tensions, where the objectives of the regimes may be undermined by decisions adopted in another forum, even where there is no formal conflict. The ILC Report, while also noting that specialized regimes may benefit from the *lex specialis* priority, nevertheless establishes that they may not derogate from *jus cogens*. Moreover, the following situations arise:[1244]

> (1) The regime may not deviate from the law benefiting third parties, including individuals and non-State entities;
>
> (2) The regime may not deviate from general law if the obligations of general law are of "integral" or "interdependent" nature, have *erga omnes* character or practice has created a legitimate expectation of non-derogation;
>
> (3) The regime may not deviate from treaties that have a public law nature or which are constituent instruments of international organizations.

However, while this provides a framework for looking at specialized regimes with respect to general international law, it provides limited guidance as to the relations *between* specialized regimes. In addition, there is not much guidance as to what actually defines a specialized regime, except as instantiated in a treaty or a set of treaties forming a formal framework, *e.g.*, the WTO Agreements. The ILC also has an extensive discussion on the limitations of so-called savings clauses that purport to define a

---

[1242] Article XX(e)
[1243] Lindroos. A and M Mehling, "From Autonomy to Integration. International Law, Free Trade and the Environment" Vol. 7 Nordic Journal of International Law 253-273, 2008.
[1244] para 154, Koskenniemi, M et al. *"Fragmentation of International Law"*

particular relationship to other treaties and regimes.[1245] The report notes that most go only so far as to seek coordination and harmony with either a specific regime or all other related regimes, but do not go so far as to detail specific rules of priority with respect to other treaties or regimes.[1246]

III. THE PRINCIPLE OF SYSTEMIC INTEGRATION

The ILC report puts forward an approach it calls "systemic integration," rooted in the application of VCLT Article 31(3)(c), to address the potential conflicts that arise as a result of the diversification and expansion of international law. The approach is premised on the insight that at the core of all the legal approaches and techniques to address conflicts is the idea of relationships within a broader system. The ILC suggests that all interpretive decisions should take place against that broader systemic background with full awareness of the links, accompanied by a proactive attempt to integrate different rules with each other and that broader systemic background which consists of general international law, *jus cogens* obligations, and obligations *erga omnes*.[1247] Thus, care must be exercised not to invalidate other provisions in other treaties and regimes. Interpretation should render both provisions operational and compatible, and if that is not possible, the rule that is determined to have priority must nevertheless take the other rule into account.

Fundamentally, systemic integration is about ensuring coherence by treating each regime as if it is part of an intentional system with a particular shared direction. The ILC reiterates, and is quite adamant, that VCLT Article 31(3)(c) is explicitly meant to treat other treaties and regimes as part of the systemic background against which interpretation should take place. It is a mandatory part of the interpretation process and is not subordinate to other interpretive sources in Article 31, including any examination of the ordinary meaning of the text. In light of the ILC's conclusions regarding the ability of systemic integration to address conflicts and tensions between specialized regimes, I propose a methodology for applying this framework to the issue of technology transfer at the UNFCCC.

[1245] For example, the TRIPS Agreement states in Article 2(2) "Nothing in Parts I to IV of this Agreement shall derogate from existing obligations that Members may have to each other under the Paris Convention, the Berne Convention, the Rome Convention and the Treaty on Intellectual Property in Respect of Integrated Circuits"
[1246] para 272 – 282, Koskenniemi, M et al. "*Fragmentation of International Law: Difficulties arising from the Diversification and Expansion of International Law:* Report of the Study Group of the International Law Commission" International Law Commission, 13 April 2006 , UN Doc. A/CN.4/L.682 p. 1-256 and 18 July 2006, UN Doc. A/CN.4/L.702 p. 1-25.
[1247] paras 410 – 415, Koskenniemi, M et al. "*Fragmentation of International Law: Difficulties arising from the Diversification and Expansion of International Law:* Report of the Study Group of the International Law Commission" International Law Commission, 13 April 2006 , UN Doc. A/CN.4/L.682 p. 1-256 and 18 July 2006, UN Doc. A/CN.4/L.702 p. 1-25.

IV. SYSTEMIC INTEGRATION APPLIED TO TECHNOLOGY TRANSFER AT THE UNFCCC

An effective fight against climate change will require action across various areas that will merit a framework of systemic integration. Systemic integration should address international, regional, and national regimes, and the interaction among the various regimes. Van Asselt, Sindico and Mehling have recently pointed out the relevance of the systemic integration concept of the ILC to the UNFCCC.[1248] This paper tries to take their point a step further and apply it to the specific case of technology transfer for climate change, IP, and human rights.

Van Asselt, Sindico and Mehling critique the narrow focus on 'conflicts' that emerged after the ILC report. This narrow focus on 'conflicts' only examined treaty language, ignoring other venues of activity and decision-making that can sometimes be more relevant.[1249] Specifically, they examine the legal role and force of decisions by bodies such as the UNFCCC COP and the relationship to other treaty fora and decision making bodies. This paper is concerned in particular with the relationship between the UNFCCC COP, the WTO TRIPS Council, the WTO General Council and the two major human rights committees (the Committee on Civil and Political Rights, and the Committee on Economic, Social and Cultural Rights). This thesis will focus on how a broader view of the venues for decision-making may provide a better indication of where actual conflicts may be, and where actual opportunities for systemic integration may exist.

The first form of application of the principle of systemic integration requires the determination of a methodology that can identify which regimes and treaties merit integration. Regimes and treaties that merit integration will depend on whether a treaty deals with the same or related subject matter. In this connection, a "basic effects" test could be employed, involving an examination of whether or not one set of provisions in a treaty would essentially limit, negate or impair the effectiveness of other provisions or regimes. However, when looking at applying the basic effects test, *i.e.*, on the realization and/or effectiveness of the provisions in another treaty or regime, the first place to look for guidance is to treaties that share objectives. Once shared objectives are established, a connection can be clarified by seeking specific shared provisions that suggest that the provisions need to be read together in some fashion to give effect to all of them.

A second form of application of the systemic integration principle may be applied by looking at the competencies of particular treaty regimes and their obligations to address particular issues. Competency is a subject matter question which overlaps

---

[1248] Van Asselt, H et al, "Global Climate Change and the Fragmentation of International Law" 30 Law and Policy 423 (2008).
[1249] See p425, Id.

with jurisdiction to a certain extent. Although competency will be rooted in the constitutive instrument of the treaty or forum, a second effects test will require a fora examination of the areas of law that may determine the effectiveness of the regime and will integrate those bodies of law as applicable law within the fora. The aforementioned approach has been adopted by the WTO Panels and the Appellate Body. Arguably, this approach should be adopted by other regimes because it provides the target for action, albeit with an important variation: competency will require a minimum awareness of the applicable law and an obligation to not to impair its effectiveness. The required minimum awareness will create an obligation to act and incorporate relevant standards into norm-setting and treaty interpretation.

The second approach above provides the tools and a methodology to determine the regime that can be integrated with outside norms against the general background of international law. By following this approach, the forum's interests and goals will continue to be pursued while also integrating common provisions to ensure its effect and proper execution of measures. In addition, the approach will ensure the elimination of artificial barriers to engagement on issues of common concern.

IV.1. Objectives and Methodologies

Within the regimes of IP, international human rights, and technology transfer the shared objective is sustainable development. The preamble to the Marrakesh Agreement establishing the WTO recognizes the objective of sustainable development. The TRIPS Agreement gives effect to sustainable development in Articles 7 and 8.1. The Appellate Body has acknowledged that the concept of sustainable development must "give colour and texture" to WTO obligations under the WTO covered agreements.[1250]

The UNFCCC also has sustainable development as a key objective. The Preamble and Objectives (Article 2) of the UNFCCC recall the principle sustainable development, as well as the Declaration of the United Nations Conference on the Human Environment, adopted at Stockholm on 16 June 1972.

While the ICESCR predates some of the conceptual framework that built the concept of sustainable development, human rights are the third pillar of sustainable development, and are thus understood as core to the concept. The International Law Association, for example, in its New Delhi Declaration Of Principles of International Law Relating to Sustainable Development, has formulated the principle of integration

---

[1250] WTO, *United States – Import Prohibition of Shrimp and Shrimp Products* (6 November 1998) WT/DS58/R/AB, para 129

and interrelationship, in particular in relation to human rights and social, economic and environmental objectives".[1251]

Sustainable development has been a useful way of reconciling objectives that have sometimes been considered conflicting i.e. social equity and stability, economic growth and environmental protection. While it has been a useful rhetorical tool, it also has substantive content which can inform legal analysis. The WTO has done so, for example, in its jurisprudence on Article XX, in considering what are exhaustible natural resources.[1252]

The Brundlandt Report (*Our Common Future*, 1987)[1253] defines sustainable development as, "development that meets the needs of the present without compromising the ability of future generations to meet their own needs." In addition, the report outlines other elements including:

- efficient resource allocation to meet basic human needs;
- equitable and just allocation of resources and benefits arising from their use;
- ecological sustainability – maintaining the long-term viability of supporting ecosystems;
- social sustainability – fulfilling people's cultural, material, and spiritual needs in equitable ways;
- increased accountability in institutions of governance;
- increased and meaningful public participation;
- strengthening of local democracy;
- focus on environmental rights;
- economic viability; and finally,
- greater sensitivity to conditions in the Global South.

The dynamic nature of the definition of sustainable development lends itself well to the intellectual property framework.[1254] The primary concern in intellectual property policy making is finding a balance between static efficiency (the present interests of present populations to access products and knowledge) with dynamic efficiency (meeting the need for the generation of new technologies that address future challenges). With such a concern at the heart of intellectual property-making, the

---

[1251] International Law Association Resolution 3/2002, 'Sustainable Development, New Delhi Declaration Of Principles Of International Law Relating to Sustainable Development' (Report of the 70th Conference New Delhi 2-6 April 2002)
[1252] For an analysis of this see p79, Bernasconi-Osterwalder, N et al., *Environment and Trade: A Guide To WTO Jurisprudence* (London: Earthscan 2006).
[1253] See p54, "Report of the World Commission on Environment and Development: Our Common Future", Annex to "Development and International Cooperation: Environment" UN Doc A/42/427, 4 August 1987.
[1254] Cullet, P *Intellectual Property and Sustainable Development* (London: LexisNexis Butterworths, 2005)

concerns and framing of sustainable development have a direct translation into the legislation and interpretive tradition in intellectual property regarding the appropriate balance between the interests of rightholders in the present and the interests of competitors and end-users on the other, and the effect that allowing greater access in the present might have on incentives for generation of new technologies in the future. In many ways, this is an argument that cannot truly be solved empirically, as it depends on finding a concrete answer to the question of whether and to what extent stronger IP protection actually does result in actual innovation. That some level of protection does provide an incentive for generation of new inventions and innovations seems intuitively true and to some extent empirically true, but generation is not the only concern of the intellectual property system. In many ways, the intellectual property system can be seen as equally concerned with ensuring disclosure and dissemination of knowledge and does so by creating a market for that knowledge.[1255] Constructed in that way, the issue is not about whether or not intellectual property protection should be provided but whether the level of intellectual property protection provided distorts and prevents the efficient functioning of a market in the knowledge so that all who wish to participate in the market can do so in commercially viable ways, both from the perspective of the rightholder and the user. Normally, such markets can be left to function by themselves[1256], but as noted in Chapter 5, there exist some asymmetries in markets for knowledge (especially across borders) that create market imperfections and make it less likely that such transactions (e.g. licensing) will take place.[1257]

In addition anti-competitive behaviour on the part of market participants remains a concern in knowledge markets given the statutory grant that give significant potential for market power. Remuneration (especially as reward for investment risk) is a fundamental element of the system of intellectual property and maintaining that remuneration is key to ensuring dynamic efficiency, but both dynamic efficiency and static efficiency require a properly functioning market in the knowledge. It is along that vector that government interventions can work to ensure diffusion without reducing dynamic or static efficiency. This means that policy-makers and judicial interpreters can take actions to address market failures of dissemination to the extent that these are limited to pricing and undue barriers to market entry, to ensure that unmet demand is addressed. Framed in this way, sustainable development in the intellectual property framework requires an efficient market in knowledge and knowledge products, where intervention by government is meant to ensure that the rightholder is sufficiently remunerated to maintain incentives for future generation of technologies, but that the structure of the market in knowledge and knowledge products does not result in unmet

---

[1255] See 609, Arrow, K "Economic Welfare and the Allocation of Resources for Invention' in *The Rate and Direction of Economic Activity Economic and Social Factors* (Princeton: Princeton University Press, 1962).
[1256] See 1092, Calabresi, G and A Melamed, 'Property Rules, Liability Rules, and Inalienability: One View of the Cathedral', 85 *Harvard LR* 1089 (1972).
[1257] Merges, R "Of Property Rules, Coase, and Intellectual Property' (1994) 94 *Columbia LR* 2655

demand, especially in areas crucial to economic welfare.[1258] Such an approach emphasizes remuneration over control, somewhat contrary to the tradition that has developed of viewing intellectual property as a means for the rightholder to structure the market according to their preferences. However, regulatory authorities, primarily in the competition or anti-trust arena have, over time, been more or less willing to intervene[1259] and remove some control from the rightholder where they view such control to have been exercised in an unduly restrictive or market damaging manner. It is at this interface that sustainable development may be best integrated into the intellectual property framework – along the economic leg of the tripod. This may require sustainable development institutions that are concerned about technology transfer to more explicitly address and frame this issue in the context of norm-setting and implementation of technology transfer obligations.

The concept of sustainable development has become a core element of international norm-setting.[1260] All mainstream definitions require three things: (1) integration of social, environmental and economic objectives and methodologies; (2) integration of the interests of future generations; and (3) transparency, participation and accountability of all relevant stakeholders.[1261] The definition provides a framework for standards and norms from other institutions to integrate and apply sustainable development as applicable law, or a form of information as to the meaning of the applicable law of another regime.

However, the concept is also useful in the way that it is fundamentally tied to human rights through its social objective and thereby linking human rights to economic and environmental considerations. The link between human rights and the environment has become an accepted element of broader international law. Specifically, the right to a healthy environment has become an increasingly important element of international policy making and has lent strength to legal challenges against environmental degradation or pollution that affects the right to life, the right to health, as well as other human rights affected by particular acts of environmental degradation or pollution. The right to a healthy environment can be found in Article 12(2)(b) of the ICESCR that calls on states to "improve all aspects of industrial and environmental hygiene." It is also found as a corollary to the realization of other rights such as the right to life, health, and

---

[1258] Lemley, M A "Taking the Regulatory Nature of IP Seriously" (January 31, 2014). Stanford Law and Economics Olin Working Paper No. 455.
[1259] See U.S. DEP'T OF JUSTICE & FED. TRADE COMM'N, *TO PROMOTE INNOVATION: THE PROPER BALANCE OF COMPETITION AND PATENT LAW AND POLICY* (2003) arguing for a more hands of approach, or more recent European cases representing a more interventionist approach: European Commission Press release "Antitrust: Commission opens proceedings against Samsung" Available at: http://europa.eu/rapid/press-release_IP-12-89_en.htm?locale=en (last visited 15 August 2014).See *Orange-Book-Standard* (BGH, 5/6/2009 – KZR 39/06) [German Federal Supreme Court];
[1260] See p3, CIEL *One Species, One Planet: Environmental Justice and Sustainable Development* (Washington DC: CIEL 2002).
[1261] Id. 4

a safe working environment.[1262] However, human rights are an integral element of international law making, where they function as *erga omnes* obligations. Thus, the failure to explicitly mention human rights law as applicable law in a treaty is no obstacle to its application in that treaty.

In addition, the standards for when and how human rights may be abrogated or limited would apply, thus placing the burden on those seeking to invalidate a measure that achieves or is aimed at achieving fundamental human rights. As noted earlier, the role of human rights in the specific context of technology transfer for climate change may pose some problems given the unfortunate role that General Comment 17 has played. However, the human rights impacts of climate change on the right to health, food, and water provide a way to argue that technology transfer is required to meet human rights standards. Thus, measures pursued with the aim of ensuring the right to health, food, and water would also be subject to the same analysis.

Finally, sustainable development is crucial to the way in which the climate change problems must be solved. Addressing climate change requires a fundamental change in economic production that will address negative impacts on human rights, while ensuring development and the progressive realization of economic, social and cultural rights. Focusing on shared objectives, such as sustainable development, may also enable a way around the problem of scope of membership of different treaties.

Per VCLT Article 30(4), as between two parties who are parties to the same set of agreements, an earlier treaty only applies to the extent that its provisions are compatible with the later treaty. While addressing a relatively narrow set of circumstances, the VCLT envisions some divergence of interpretation as to obligations between specific member states. The consensual divergence of interpretation suggests that there is no blanket restriction on the application of Article 31(3)(c) only to circumstances where all member states are parties to an agreement. In particular, the examination of whether there is incompatibility will require the application of all elements of Article 31.

Article 30(2) VCLT also provides guidance on how to relate to other treaties on the same subject matter. It notes that: "When a treaty specifies that it is subject to, or that it is not to be considered as incompatible with, an earlier or later treaty, the provisions of that other treaty prevail." In this context, there is an obligation on the part of a forum to seek out those other treaties and regimes that may state such facts and may influence the applicability of the existing treaty as to the specific parties in a dispute. Arguably, where a treaty's jurisdiction and competency reaches out to matters also

---

[1262] For more detail see p11, Id.

covered by other agreements, this constitutes the "same subject matter" for the purposes of establishing an Article 30 conflict.[1263]

By focusing on a congruence of shared objectives between the treaties and the governing bodies, we can seek entry of the objectives of another agreement through VCLT Article 31(1), "[a] treaty shall be interpreted in good faith in accordance with the ordinary meaning to be given to the terms of the treaty in their context and *in the light of its object and purpose*" (my emphasis). Thus, despite the fact that a party may not be a member of another treaty, where the treaty makes reference to another agreement or shares its objectives, the party should be the subject of attempts to integrate and to select among methods of achieving those goals that that still enable the achievement in both agreements of the shared objective. In this sense, they can be mutually limiting and supportive.

Going forward, an agreement regarding the role of an agreement to which another party is not a member would still be effective regarding non-parties because it would be a commitment that they have expressly agreed to in another forum.[1264] Article 35 of the VCLT would apply, as the State's agreement would be considered to have agreed to be bound, in a specific manner, in writing. Interestingly, Article 35 does not require that this be done through accession or treaty amendment but through some form of agreed decision, thus enabling COP decisions, and perhaps decisions of other governing bodies, to have effect. Such an agreement would also apply as an agreement between the parties to a treaty under Article 31(3)(b) on the interpretation of a treaty or the application of its provisions.

Another way to look at the shared objectives is to look at specific shared provisions aimed at technology transfer. In the TRIPS Agreement (Articles 7 and 66.2), in the ICESCR (Article 15(1)(b)) and in the UNFCCC (Article 4.5) there are shared provisions that emphasize the promotion of transfer of technology to developing countries as an important aim of the agreement. Thus, in addition to shared objectives, there are shared provisions that outline a particular methodology for achieving the goals i.e. technology transfer that goes beyond the protection of IP and requires some action by developed country governments. The effect of a systemic integration approach would be to ensure that all these provisions are made operative. A UNFCCC technology transfer mechanism that may affect IP rights and might be challenged on the basis of the TRIPS Agreement may find shelter under the principle of ensuring

---

[1263] Koskenniemi, M et al., *'Fragmentation of International Law: Difficulties arising from the Diversification and Expansion of International Law:* Report of the Study Group of the International Law Commission' (13 April 2006) para 23, UN Doc. A/CN.4/L.682; ILC, 'Fragmentation of International Law: Difficulties Arising From the Diversification and Expansion of International Law, Report of the Study Group of the International Law Commission' (18 July 2006) UN Doc. A/CN.4/L.702
[1264] Van Asselt, H et al, "Global Climate Change and the Fragmentation of International Law" 30 Law and Policy 423 (2008).

effectiveness under both the UNFCCC and TRIPS Agreement. Consideration of the jointly shared objectives will have to take into account that such methods were envisaged within the TRIPS Agreement in referring to technology transfer and that UNFCCC parties were aware and knowledgeable about the scope and meaning of such provisions when constructing a mechanism under the UNFCCC.

Finally, while the foregoing discussion focuses on the way that a shared objective analysis would enable international trade fora to better identify the outside law to apply to the interpretation of WTO Agreements, it is important to note that the analysis flows in the other direction as well. To the extent that economic fora share similar objectives and shared provisions, the objectives and relevant provisions of that agreement would be treated as applicable law in the environmental and human rights regime. While this may pose some danger, given that international trade law has already had a significant chilling effect on multilateral environmental policy-making, it may be appropriate to have that occur within a predictable and equitable framework, in which both fora are recognized to have shared competencies.

IV.2. Competencies

One of the key lessons to be learned from the TRIPS Agreement and public health debate is that economic policy, especially IP policy, is not separate from other key policy areas. Economic policy is integral to the development and achievement of issues like food security, health, and, in this case, technology transfer for climate change. Patent protections and transactions form part of the set of policy tools provided within IP frameworks i.e. the broad panoply from patent pools, open source approaches, utility models, etc. No one would suggest that policies on food security, health or technology transfer be left only to WIPO or to the WTO. The competence of WIPO in IP is extensive, but it is also limited by lack of internal expertise and knowledge regarding the various subject areas that its work affects. Likewise, the same applies to member state participation and rule-making at the WTO. Therefore, the argument that separate organizations should limit themselves to the areas of work where they have mandate and competence is no longer viable when faced by challenges of broad scope, such as climate change. Thus, one of the ways in which systemic integration is to be operationalized, in this context, is for organizations to integrate their programmes and work together. This can be referred to as the "competencies approach."

A first step in ensuring systemic integration under the competencies approach is to identify linkages between fora that require that they be linked and address the same issues. Recognition of that linkage is crucial. There may in fact be gradations of linkages, for example, the link between IP policy and child labor may be more tenuous than the link between IP and public health. In the broader context of IP, other fora who should be involved and who have competence related to IP and its relationship to other issues include: the UN Economic and Social Council and the Commission on Science and Technology for Development; the International Labour Organization (through Convention No. 169 Concerning Indigenous and Tribal Peoples in Independent States); the Food and Agricultural Organization and the International Treaty on Plant Genetic Resources for Food and Agriculture; United Nations Educational, Scientific and Cultural Organization; the Convention on Biological Diversity; the World Health Organization; the United Nations Industrial Development Organization; United Nations Conference on Trade and Development; the WTO and TRIPS; the Human Rights Council; the Committee on Economic, Social and Cultural Rights; and finally, the UNFCCC.[1265]

The argument for the institutional competencies approach is also supported by the role that the WTO has played in IP policy-making. IP is not a natural fit with a system intended to remove barriers to trade and the movement of goods. IP is specifically aimed at restricting the movement of knowledge. The WTO was able to make an argument for including IP by arguing that there are crucial 'trade-related' aspects of IP that it had to deal with. That same argument can therefore be applied by other fora, such as the UNFCCC, with far more justification.[1266]

The competencies approach also has another strong argument in its favor. The issue of how IP can ensure global welfare cannot be addressed in a single forum because no one organization has the mandate to ensure global welfare. However, some organizations may have a broader mandate that approaches ensuring global welfare, such as the UNFCCC, in addressing climate change. These types of organizations would be obligated to take on these issues and to engage other institutions in norm-setting processes to ensure that there is systemic integration. The increasing tension in this regard is due to the fact that such large issues have been left to organizations with limited mandates.[1267]

Unfortunately, this may encourage institutions to engage in fields where they have little experience or perhaps even an active antipathy. For example, institutions such as the World Bank, the WTO and others have not refrained from becoming involved with subject matter tangentially related to their regimes, with which they have little or no competence. In that sense, such institutions are already addressing human rights and environmental standards and rules within their systems. The danger that exists is that they have not recognized the need for also applying the international law related to that subject matter or their own lack of knowledge in that field. It has to be recognized that there is a need to apply other international law and that there is a lack of in-house knowledge within a particular fora. The recognition reasonably suggests the

---

[1265] For a review of the specific competencies with respect to intellectual property issues of each of these organizations see Musungu, S F 'Rethinking Innovation, Development and Intellectual Property in the UN: WIPO and Beyond" TRIPS Issues Paper 5 (Quaker International Affairs Programme, Ottawa 2005).
[1266] See p22, Id.
[1267] *See e.g.*, p6, Id.

need to interact with the decision makers who have more expertise in the relevant applicable law.

The competencies approach to systemic integration is also attractive because, before decisions are made to codify one particular approach over another, the approach allows for ongoing dialogue and innovation[1268], in multiple fora. Therefore, this suggests that each venue should fully engage in the attempt to integrate with other venues, while simultaneously bringing each actor's skills and viewpoint to the problem. This may be another way for the regular balancing to still take on some force after the fact.

In sum, fora should be far more conscious about how they intend to relate to other regimes and fora. The relationships to other regimes and fora should be based on the principles of integration, coherence, and the achievement of shared objectives like sustainable development. In many ways, the fragmentation of international law arises from the mistaken assumption of many regimes that their silence on how they should relate to other regimes will protect them from interference from other regimes. The increasing interlinkages created by the expansion and diversification of international law have put that illusion to rest. The only option available is active engagement. It is the terms of that engagement that this chapter has tried to elucidate for technology transfer to address climate change. The first lesson of the ILC report is that regimes and fora need to be far more aware of the areas of subject matter which impact their mandates, and upon which their mandates impact. This chapter has tried to provide some methodologies for accomplishing that in this specific case.

The second lesson is that regimes and fora need to be as clear as possible, without necessarily detailing every aspect, on the nature of the relationship between their norms and other relevant norms. This author believes that the systemic integration concept put forward by the ILC presents the best chance for doing so in a manner that maintains the integrity of each regime while engaging in respectful and innovative dialogue with other regimes that have shared objectives. The freedom that the climate change regime has to fashion its relationship with other fora is important because it is a rare opportunity due to the scope and scale of the challenge that is to be faced within the next few decades.

V. Conclusion

While the discussion above provides a way for the UNFCCC to take up action to address technology transfer for climate change and to take on IP issues specifically

---

[1268] For a discussion of this view see p426, H Van Asselt et al. 'Global Climate Change and the Fragmentation of International Law' 30 Law and Policy 423 (2008)

with the systemic integration framework, there still remain significant difficulties where TRIPS cannot find a way to justify otherwise non-conforming measures in the public interest, especially for an important norms such as climate mitigation and adaptation. However, part of the problem arises from the internal structure of the UNFCCC itself. The fact that developing country obligations are conditional mean that they have no justification in the UNFCCC text for taking actions to unilaterally ensure technology transfer. In order to create a conflict and the need for systemic integration and to justify non-conforming measures, it may be necessary for developing countries to take on measurable, reportable and verifiable quantified emissions reduction obligations commensurate with their historical responsibility and capacity. They should not, however, give up the conditionality. In this case, developing countries would agree to such obligations and build in countermeasures if developed countries fail to deliver on technology transfer. They would reserve the right to take unilateral measures to enforce technology transfer, where the developed countries failed to meet certain negotiated benchmarks for technology transfer and financial support. This would create a more powerful dynamic for developing countries whose obligations to reduce emissions would then either be fulfilled through provision of support or through unilateral measures; either way they would be fulfilled. Such an approach requires a small but significant shift in developing country tactics at the UNFCCC but may lead to more productive outcomes for them and for climate change more generally. Innovative solutions are needed now in the climate negotiations, ones that are focused on circumventing old patterns of debate on technology transfer and seek to harness the market power of intellectual property to enhance technology transfer in combination with the institutional strength and convening power of the UNFCCC. Chapter 9 proposes a portfolio of solutions that as a whole may go some way to increasing opportunities for technology transfer to developing countries overall.

Chapter 9
Proposals for Action at the UNFCCC

I. INTRODUCTION

As discussed in Chapter 1, the aim of this thesis was to determine the necessity for the UNFCCC to act to address intellectual property. That necessity was to be determined by two main issues:

1. The extent to which there is evidence that intellectual property standards create structural impediments in the international global market for climate technologies that prevent them from being generated and disseminated at the rate (timing), scope (volume and scope of technologies) required and to the countries required (major developed countries, as intermediaries ton other developing countries);

2. The extent to which the TRIPS Agreement bars or limits the use and effectiveness of unilateral intellectual property interventions by developing countries to enable adoption, adaptation and replication of climate mitigation and adaptation technologies.

What does the analysis in the previous chapters allow us to conclude? I argue that in many ways, developing countries are left with little but recourse to international institutions and their processes for norm-setting and decision-making. As noted, Chapter 6 finds that to a significant extent the TRIPS Agreement does act as a barrier. The answer to the first question is more complex and less certain. In Chapter 2, I identify several parameters for measuring the necessity for the UNFCCC to act on intellectual property. Thus I identify the timing by which technologies need to be generated and diffused into developing countries (between 2015 and 2025); the scope of technologies (almost all sectors but especially agriculture, energy efficiency, industry, buildings, transport, power generation); the most important countries (the major emerging economies of Brazil, China, India, South Africa). In Chapter 3, I critically assess the existing literature on intellectual property and the role patterns of ownership and distribution play in enabling or retarding the ability to distribute technologies within the appropriate time frame, address the full scope of technologies and to the appropriate countries. In general, the data on the distribution and existence of patent protection was sparse and limited and did not address the key issue of the ways in which intellectual property was being used or licensed. However some basic patterns, based on the limited information, could be discerned:

- The mitigation technology areas studied appear to have significant variation in how highly patented they are, but the trend is for increasing numbers of patents in almost all sectors (except for fossil fuels).

- The ownership of patents in climate change mitigation and adaptation is almost exclusively in the hands of OECD firms. However, there may not be high levels of firm concentration in terms of ownership of existing patents in the mitigation fields studied suggesting that licenses may be available at reasonable costs

- From the patent license patterns that have been made available, there exist pricing concerns and concerns about geographical and other restrictions on licenses. Where licensing has been seen to occur, it has largely been from national firms or non-producing entities rather than multinational firms.

- The majority of patenting of climate mitigation technologies occurs in developed countries and the emerging economies, especially China. There are few if any in other lower middle income and least developed countries. However, this means that major developing countries are not likely to be able to act as major exporters of technology and know-how to these countries, in those sectors that are highly patented.

- The rate at which climate mitigation technologies are diffusing is very slow and vast majority of technology exchanges are happening between developed countries. Developing countries remain a small percentage on international technology flows, both in terms of hardware and know-how.

More generally, we know that some sectors, agriculture and health have significant amounts of patenting.

It is important to note that much of this data is preliminary and limited to a relatively narrow group of technologies. A policy decision can clearly not be based on these data alone. More will be required to establish any necessity for the UNFCCC to act to address intellectual property norm-setting. Clearly national data as to licensing practices and experience on the ground would be the best possible evidence, especially when aggregated across countries, as well as data relating to FDI and trade spillovers. Such assessments would need to assess the pattern and existence of patents in core areas; the actual level of licensing and any problems related to licensing and knowledge sharing. The research would assess whether the behaviour in the national market by an intellectual property holder of any relevant technologies limits:

a. **Affordability** - ensuring that prices of products are not set so high that it is too expensive for all the relevant economic actors to afford.
b. **Adoptability** - ensuring that prices of products and or know-how are not set so high that they make it commercially unviable for all relevant actors to adopt 'climate-friendly' technologies.
c. **Adaptability** – ensuring sufficient distribution of knowledge (information, skills, know-how) to enable a critical number of existing producers/service providers in the market to adopt, adapt and replicate climate technologies and ensure their participation in the market.

While such data is valuable, it is clear that where a country finds such problems, it would not be in a position to address the issue in as broad and effective manner as it could have in the pre-TRIPS era and as would be necessary to meet the climate change challenge. In addition, the process of ascertaining such data does not take into account the interventions that countries might wish to take to prevent such problems from arising in their market in the first place and to pro-actively restructure their market. In addition, it is also clear that the existing mechanisms for delivery of technology transfer in the UNFCCC have been insufficient but present real potential to exert influence on international technology markets.

Thus I return to the basic framing that drove this thesis: the important question is the contingent one. What options remain for developing countries to intervene in technology markets where the behaviour of intellectual property rightholder bars or limits the adoptability, adaptability and replicability of technologies in the domestic market? The answer of this thesis is that few such effective options remain. This is not to say that developing countries cannot take significant steps to increase their basic absorptive capacity and to create appropriate enabling environments for demand and for technology transactions. It is simply that paths taken by countries prior to the advent of the TRIPS Agreement are no longer available and there exist no examples of how to move up the technology value chain with an initially high protection of intellectual property.

What then should the UNFCCC do to address the intellectual property issue? The key issue is how the UNFCCC can help to move the technologies that are in the hands of developed country actors into the hands of developing country actors as fast as possible in order to enable peaking between 2015 and 2025 and building adaptive capacity by 2025-30. This is fundamentally a market restructuring question. What can the UNFCCC do to shift the incentives of the actors in global technology markets to engage in far greater amounts of technology transactions into developing countries?

As noted in Chapter 4, provision of sufficient financial support is fundamental. However, as also noted in chapter 4, there is no realistic prospect of any significant portion of this money being public sector funds. Instead the framework will depend on private sector financing and investment, requiring policy changes in developing countries to attract investment, primarily as FDI, but also as licensing. That private sector actors will seek to limit spillovers is axiomatic, and in direct tension to the policy aim of encouraging such investment, which is to increase and expand technology spillovers. That increasing intellectual protection (thus limiting potential imitative behaviour) will attract investment and exports and encourage licensing is also considered axiomatic but is again, in tension with the goal of increasing spillovers directly into the broader economy as quickly as possible, not just to one firm or to one wholly owned subsidiary. As long as developing countries are acting individually to try to create attractive investment destinations, there will always be better, lower risk countries in which to invest or, as is the case with China, where the return on investment is so great that certain risks are worthwhile. This tension between attracting investment with the goal of ensuring significant spillovers into the economy at a pace necessary to meet the climate challenge in most developing countries that do not have the 'China premium'. Thus one of the considerations for action by the UNFCCC in this area, given that public funds may not be forthcoming, is to use its institutional and financial power to address:

- The risk issue related to engaging in transactions in developing countries, identified in chapter 3 as concerns for developed country firms;

- The aggregation problem of insufficient market power to attract investment, identified in chapter 3 and 4;

- The lack of structural incentives for firms to allow and enable spillovers of technological know-how into the relevant economies, identified in chapter 3 and 5;

- The lack of absorptive capacity, skills and know in developing countries in the relevant technology sectors identified as an issue in chapter 3 and 4.

These actions are very clearly non-norm setting solutions that do not address the issue of regulatory flexibility for developing countries to address intellectual property individually. However, this is not to say that the UNFCCC cannot play a significant part in making the remaining interventions available to developing countries more effective through international cooperation. Thus, while not engaging in norm-setting the UNFCCC can act to increase the power of such measures by enabling joint action, especially between major emerging economies and other developing countries. This is not to say that norm-setting is not desirable. There is clearly a policy need to increase the regulatory flexibility of developing countries to address intellectual property problems when they arise in the domestic sphere. However, the structural nature of the intellectual property problem as it relates to investment and the reliance on private sector investment for climate action means that enabling such unilateral actions by member states may be the least effective way for the UNFCCC to act, unless it also does a whole suite of other things. Any effective action to increase the regulatory freedom of developing countries on intellectual property will have to be on a much larger scale, in order to avoid this structural problem.

This chapter will provide some proposals for ways in which the UNFCCC can act to address intellectual property within the systemic integration framework. Before doing so, I discuss the key drivers and principles that frame the timing and scope of action by the UNFCCC. Following that, I propose a set of UNFCCC actions to facilitate investment and market access for technology and know-how in developing countries, placing them in the context of other proposals.

II. DRIVERS AND PRINCIPLES FOR FRAMING UNFCCC ACTION – UNCERTAINTY AND PEAKING DATES

One of the limiting factors when it comes to technology policy and especially to intellectual property policy with respect to climate change is that there remains significant uncertainty surrounding long-term projections of climate change and climate impacts. The farther out in time, the greater the uncertainty. Even in the near term, however, some uncertainty remains, especially on the peaking dates that may be required. In the face of such uncertainty, caution appears to be required before making major changes, some argue.[1269]

However, there is greater certainty on some of the projected changes and impacts and thus the necessary action in the near term leading up to about 2030. Climate change embodies a clear asymmetry between the relatively low cost of action in the present versus the potentially catastrophic cost of delaying action in the long term. The Stern report also points out to the inertia built into climate change: negative changes become increasingly difficult to reverse the longer action is delayed.[1270]

Much of the decision on what interventions need to take place and on what scale depends on an assessment of the timing for peaking and necessity for radical innovations and inventions in the post-peaking period. As discussed in Chapter 2, there is no consensus on whether staying below 2 degrees Celsius is achievable with existing technologies. However, there is more certainty regarding the conclusion that existing technologies are sufficient to address GHG emissions reductions to peak in 2015-2018, reduce by 80% by 2050, and to adapt by 2025-2030[1271] provided that there is sufficient

---

[1269] See p12, Maskus, K "Differentiated Intellectual Property Regimes for Environmental and Climate Technologies", OECD Environment Working Papers, No. 17, OECD Publishing 2010.
[1270] p292, Stern, N et al. *The Economics of Climate Change: The Stern Review* (Cambridge: Cambridge University Press, 2007).
[1271] See p65, IPCC, *Climate Change 2007: Synthesis Report. Contribution of Working Groups I, II and III to the Fourth Assessment Report of the Intergovernmental Panel on Climate Change* [Core Writing Team, Pachauri, R.K and Reisinger, A. (eds.)]. (Geneva: IPCC, 2007).

distribution and diffusion of existing technologies, and the pushing of near term and foreseeable technologies through deployment into diffusion.

There appears, therefore, less of a need to be concerned about the dynamic efficiency elements of the IP balance: there is no crucial need for a breakthrough technology to be created in the period to 2050 that can address mitigation. With respect to adaptation, there is little question that this can be accomplished with existing or foreseeable technologies even in the area of neglected medicines such as dengue fever. In the power sector where technology choices may last the 20 – 30 year lifetime of a specific power plant, there is an inertia to technology selections that are not GHG emission-reducing. Some nevertheless argue for focusing on technology development in the near term due to the uncertainty of the innovation process itself[1272] as well as the need to ensure a sufficient portfolio of technologies to be developed for the long term.

However, in the post-peak period, and in the period to 2050, there may be an increasing need for some breakthrough innovation and in that case, the question will arise of how to provide the most effective incentives for rapid, breakthrough research and development of technologies and whether the patent system or some other mechanism may be best suited to achieve that. In any case, this will require a strengthening of incentives for post-2050 technology research and development.

Reasonable risk assessments suggest that present costs, both in terms of price, regulatory changes, and behavioural shifts may all be less severe if carried out more immediately rather than only once greater certainty about impacts is achieved. It would be a case of too little too late. In an otherwise stable economic world there is a strong argument for largely maintaining the status quo. However, given the situation in which climate change places us i.e. a need for an unprecedented shift in the way technologies are generated and distributed in the near and long term, this may be precisely the time to review the ways in which the patent system in particular can be prodded to emphasize speed and scale of distribution, as well as generation of new technologies. The Stern Report's analyses on when action should be taken[1273] imply that changes to the international IP system that might be made in the near term would therefore be less drastic than would need to be the case if action were delayed.

All things being equal, a carbon price should be sufficient to generate the technology required and push the adoption of such technologies to the necessary levels. This would be a strong argument for leaving the global innovation system as it is and simply pushing for a sufficiently high carbon price. However, all things are not equal and in fact, climate change poses some unique problems that require an intervention in the global innovation system, regardless of the carbon price.

[1272] p360, Stern, N et al. *The Economics of Climate Change* (2007).
[1273] p297, Id.

- patent protection does not seem to play as large a part in providing incentives for R&D of environmentally sound technologies;[1274]
- the long-term challenge requires not just breakthroughs in the first generation but extremely rapid learning and follow-on innovation;
- the near-term challenge requires diffusion of technologies that requires a huge leap in the number of transactions related to technologies both in terms of product sales as well as licenses.
- Lock-in into existing technologies in key sectors such as power generation creates a significant problem for technology diffusion;[1275] the learning curves are, at present quite extended and thus limit the rate and necessity for technology development and adoption for most market actors.
- Many sectors, e.g. electricity generation and distribution, are not true markets in the sense of multiple generators and distributors of electricity, and the end product (electricity) cannot really be differentiated according to quality. In that sense, research, development and diffusion in some sectors is not likely to occur without some other form of intervention.
- In some sectors, infrastructure presents a significant barrier to entry for new technologies. For example, in transport (hybrids, plug in electrical vehicles) and in energy (electricity), the only customer for infrastructure innovations is largely the government, as existing incumbents that depend on existing infrastructure are unlikely to invest in R&D which can only serve to assist their competitors.[1276] Technologies that have network effects, those that would be best able to enable sector-wide changes are precisely those in which under-investment is likely by private sector actors unless they can capture the value of those network effects for themselves.

Nevertheless, there may be some division of labour that can be envisioned. Government policy can focus on research and development while deployment and diffusion is carried out by the private sector. Basic technologies could either be disseminated into the public domain and then picked up and turned into innovations by the private sector, or such innovations could be developed with government funding and then transferred to private sector holders to engage in transactions. Whether governments retain any ownership in the intellectual property so generated is one of the policy options open to governments in managing the challenge of diffusion.

One of the things to note in considering the scale of action is that, while IP systems, and the patent system in particular are useful for generating inventive, largely

---

[1274] p17, Maskus, K "Differentiated Intellectual Property Regimes for Environmental and Climate Technologies", OECD Environment Working Papers, No. 17, OECD Publishing 2010.
[1275] p352, Stern, N et al. *The Economics of Climate Change: The Stern Review* (Cambridge: Cambridge University Press, 2007).
[1276] p355, Id.

incremental products and processes, the system is not necessarily ideal for generating the kinds of broad and radical innovations that can impact on several branches of the economy, or even have economy-wide restructuring effects e.g. the internet.[1277] Patents, for example, are particularly useful for enabling market actors to differentiate themselves by products, rather than along quality alone. In that sense, innovation is a by-product of the competitive process in a competitive market. This shifts the focus from radical innovations to largely incremental innovations that either confer a competitive advantage due to process and production efficiency or a competitive advantage due to greater product effectiveness for end-consumers. In this view, innovation is an iterative process with firms continuously innovating to achieve product differentiation and taking advantage of the lead time provided by market exclusivity, until other firms have learned and caught up and are able to exploit the technology once the term of protection has expired. In some cases, the innovation can be sufficiently large and market defining that the innovator achieves windfall advantages for the period of protection by being able to define a whole new product category over which they have exclusive control. While not entirely desirable, such a possibility is the natural outcome of a system that provides the possibility of such extensive exclusivity.

Only in rare cases is innovative activity the primary market activity of a firm and the primary method of product differentiation available. In mature markets, with multiple actors, and in which learning and production capacity is evenly distributed and costs of absorbing and implementing new innovations are fairly low, the ability to fully capture the benefits of exclusivity arising from an innovation become increasingly important. In newer markets, with high barriers to entry, exclusivity is less important than lead-time and the ability to define the product market.

Radical economy wide restructuring innovations are more likely to arise from research and development carried out at the level of basic science which is not directly linked to a specific production processes. Most private sector market actors cannot justify the levels of investment in research required to achieve such breakthroughs.[1278] Governments step in to provide funding for such basic research. In the US, the government funded 31% of national R&D in 2009 and 53% of basic research.[1279] Over 14% of R&D was performed by academic institutions.[1280]

Public funding de-links the production of radical innovations from the need to ensure return on investment for private sector actors that exclusivity provides. This means that price may no longer need to be the basis for recouping R&D costs in some

---

[1277] Also suggested by p348, Id.
[1278] See p4, Lee, B et al. "Who owns our Low Carbon Future: Intellectual Property and Energy Technologies" Chatham House, September 2009.
[1279] See p4.4, National Science Board *Science and Engineering Indicators 2012* (Arlington VA: National Science Foundation 2012).
[1280] Id.

sectors. Intellectual property protection may not be the overriding factor in encouraging the kind of breakthrough innovations necessary to address climate change in the post-2050 period meaning that limiting the exclusivity available may be less of a concern. This suggests that interventions and policies to enable those interventions should be weighed more toward diffusion in developing countries rather than using market mechanisms to encourage R&D by developing country firms. Public R&D may be more suitable for developing countries and this can enable partnerships with developing country public and academic institutions that also carry out R&D. The developing country institutions could be allowed licenses for the purposes of carrying out proof of concept and demonstration of adapted technologies, including those that are new and inventive but largely those that are new to the industry and new to the firm. Immediate involvement in early basic R&D even for the most advanced emerging economies may not be appropriate, except in proof of concept and demonstration.

In the absence of proactive policies, insufficient technology transfer will take place under existing international market conditions. Fear of losing control over intellectual property rights by private actors, as well as the fact that IP rights can lead to prices above the socially optimal (competitive) level, means that technology development and diffusion to address climate change, at the required pace and at the required scale, is unlikely to happen without significant interventions.[1281] While many of the policies that developing countries wish to pursue are available as a legal matter, they are not available at sufficient scale and scope to achieve the kind of sector-wide effect required to address climate change, even when operating in the aggregate.[1282] This limiting effect is a deliberate rather than accidental outcome of the TRIPS Agreement which aimed to reduce state interventions against rightholders to a relatively small set of cases on the margins and to limit the use of tools best suited to enabling industrial policy level measures.

There are basic problems of governance endemic in many developing countries, related to lack of capacity as well as corruption and insufficient regulatory oversight.[1283] While many of these problems may be susceptible to policy changes in the short term, others, such as lack of governance capacity and investment climate are going to have to be addressed in the longer term. This suggests that urgent near term action should focus on simple interventions that provide clear rules and signals to private sector actors to carry out their activities rather than on developing country governments to act and intervene by themselves. This is especially crucial for opening up and

---

[1281] See p16, Hoekman, B, K E Maskus, and K Saggi, "Transfer of Technology to Developing Countries: Unilateral and Multilateral Policy Options" World Bank Policy Research Working Paper No. 3332. June 1, 2004.
[1282] See Chapter 6.
[1283] p438, Stern, N. et al. *The Economics of Climate Change: The Stern Review* (Cambridge: Cambridge University Press, 2007).

increasing access to existing technologies in the 2015 – 2018 timeframe for mitigation, and for adaptation, by 2025.[1284]

Chapter 2 and 3 showed that while the emerging economies are best placed to participate in and benefit from knowledge transfer, and may even have the capacity to pay market prices, there is a significant concern related to anti-competitive activities, including refusals to license and restrictive terms. Smaller developing countries and LDCs suffer from not being served by technology product or knowledge distribution channels. They present neither interesting nor capable markets for technology development and deployment under present market conditions, despite having almost uniformly increased their levels of IP protection since the TRIPS Agreement was signed. Cooperation between major emerging economies and other developing countries, especially LDCs must be a cornerstone of IP –related action at the UNFCCC. In parallel to this, UNFCCC action has to address the competitiveness concerns of firms and actors in developed countries, at least in the near term. In the long term it is inevitable that there will develop new market entrants and competitors in developing countries who will compete with firms in developed countries. They will have entered the market by benefiting from the knowledge and information created to a significant extent by firms in developed countries. It may be appropriate to consider ways in which market segmentation may be employed in order to address some of the competitiveness concerns. However, it should be noted that, within the climate framework such competitiveness concerns can never be fully addressed, as the final outcome of the climate change process is precisely aimed at creating competitive market actors in mitigation and adaptation technologies in developing countries.

Any proposed solutions by the UNFCCC must address the issue of the scale and scope of existing market measures; and the need for enabling industrial policy measures related to intellectual property. The first part requires the UNFCCC to take a significant role in facilitating transactions, reducing transaction costs and expanding markets. Such policy interventions should be addressed at:

- decreasing transaction costs of developing country buyers in accessing the international knowledge market;
- decreasing the transaction costs of international rightholders when making their knowledge and technologies available to developing country actors, especially in emerging economies;
- reducing the cost of acquiring technological knowledge;
- reducing the cost of absorbing existing technologies;
- increasing capacity and incentives for domestic innovation;[1285]

[1284] p67, IPCC, *Climate Change 2007: Synthesis Report. Contribution of Working Groups I, II and III to the Fourth Assessment Report of the Intergovernmental Panel on Climate Change* [Core Writing Team, Pachauri, R.K and Reisinger, A. (eds.)]. (Geneva: IPCC, 2007).

- encouraging and enabling trade in products and knowledge between emerging economies and other developing countries, especially LDCs;
- focusing on the needs of the most vulnerable countries.

Proposals to address intellectual property issues at the UNFCCC also need to take into account the existing framework of institutions. As discussed in Chapter 4, the UNFCCC has several institutional bodies with the potential to be useful vehicles for ramping up the scale of technology transfer to developing countries. These include the Green Climate Fund, the CDM and other new market mechanisms that will come out of the planned 2015 agreement; the Technology Mechanism, comprising the Technology Executive Committee, the Climate Technology Center & Network. However, the ways in which each of these operate will clearly have to take into account and address several key weaknesses identified in chapter 4:

- the need for measurable, reportable and verifiable indicators of technology transfer;
- clarity on the kinds of activities that are eligible for financial support;
- acting at the scope and rate required to move existing technologies into developing countries to enable peaking in time.

It is difficult to determine the exact scope of action required at the UNFCCC. As discussed in Chapter 2 and 3, it will have to embody a portfolio approach, sufficiently broad to address all relevant technology sectors, with a broad range of measures. It will have to avoid being overly prescriptive in order to give enough room to private sector actors to exercise their own economic judgment. At the same time it has to work at a large enough scale that it can shift the structure of market incentives so that private sector actors are sufficiently comfortable providing technology and allowing sufficient scale of spillovers, formal and informal, to firms in developing countries. It will also have to enable a shift towards relatively frictionless transactions for technology. That complexity means that a multistakeholder process is likely to be needed in order to fully elaborate the framework for action at the UNFCCC. However, it may be appropriate to provide an illustration of what such a suite of actions should look like, encompassing a response to each of the issues identified in chapters 2, 3, 4 and 6 of this thesis. With that in mind the next section provides an illustrative suite of proposals for action by the UNFCCC.

III. AN ILLUSTRATIVE PORTFOLIO OF PROPOSALS FOR ACTION AT THE UNFCCC[1286]

[1285] See p16, Hoekman, B, K E Maskus, and K Saggi, "Transfer of Technology to Developing Countries: Unilateral and Multilateral Policy Options" World Bank Policy Research Working Paper No. 3332. June 1, 2004.

[1286] Many of these proposals have been included in a submission to the Technology Executive Committee by the Climate Action Network's Working Group on Technology available at: https://unfccc.int/ttclear/pdf/Call%20for%20Inputs/EE/CAN_EE.pdf

As discussed in chapter 8, a key step to enable the UNFCCC to address technology transfer and intellectual property will be to rely on proactively avoiding recognized conflict conditions. This means solutions that do not require establishing new IP norms or UNFCCC norms. In particular, many can be seen as detailing and implementing already ongoing commitments under the UNFCCC and other international agreements. These actions by the UNFCCC, if implemented as a whole, are aimed at using the financial and institutional power of the UNFCCC mechanisms, and the platform provided by the Technology Executive Committee (TEC), Technology Advisory Board and Climate Technology Centre and Network (CTC&N).

III.1. Market access, Encouraging FDI and Licensing

A key set of recommendations relate to investment and licensing in terms of enabling distribution of products as well as for products produced by specific processes. This can be envisioned as a two way flow: moving technological products into LDCs and other countries with little or no manufacturing capacity; and encouraging location of manufacturing and other activities such as R&D in LDCs to encourage skills training and transfer of know-how to institutions and firms in developing countries. The aim would be to use the leverage of financing by the UNFCCC, largely through the Green Climate Fund and with the assistance of the CTC&N, to provide an incentive for developing country and developed country firms to participate.

As discussed in Chapter 3, emerging economies are the countries in which there may be clearest evidence of significant patenting of clean technologies.[1287] However, they are also the most likely developing countries to be able to afford to pay reasonable market rates for licensing of technologies. The problems that they face are ones of accessing licenses for existing technologies from potential competitors in developed countries thus dealing with such issues as refusals to license, above market rates for technology or restrictive licensing practices, especially for best available technologies which present the cutting edge and may be a competitive advantage in developed country markets. They also urgently want to participate in new and innovative research on climate technology and generate leading companies that are IP holders themselves.

The means to addressing the issues they face largely lie in using existing tools in the international IP system. They may be assisted by easier and more transparent licensing platforms and markets. In terms of participating in new technologies, these countries would be happy to see more joint research and development projects, both

---

[1287] p18, Copenhagen Economics and the IPR Company 'Are IPR and Barrier to the transfer of Climate Change Technology?' Study Commissioned by European Commission DG Trade, January 2009.

co-funded and multilaterally funded. In a sense, it is the creation of a transparent and equal playing field for licensing of technologies that is their most urgent need as they generally have sufficient domestic production capacity.

However, they are the countries from which LDCs and other developing countries tend to purchase low cost technology products, especially China and India, and these may be increasingly unable to provide such products if they are unable to access licenses for technologies that allow them to export to other developing countries. China, Brazil and India tend to be best placed to provide low cost mitigation and adaptation technologies to other developing countries because their companies are better placed and more willing to establish production centres and distribution systems in economies that are less interesting, or too risky for companies from developed countries. The analysis from chapter 3 shows that:

- The potential for South-South technology flows is large but there is a danger of replicating the lack of capacity building, training and know-how transfer between major emerging economies and other developing countries;

- Building sufficient domestic absorptive capacity is a necessary condition for enabling adoption, adaptation and replication of technologies;

- access to export markets is a crucial driver for the adoption of best available technologies by domestic producers in emerging economies;

- developed country firms are less inclined to make best available technologies available in emerging economies due to market share and competition concerns in their home markets and in emerging economy markets;

- with respect to products, parallel importation and market segmentation may be useful ways to address some of the competitiveness concerns of developed country firms;

The approach to licensing would seek terms on licenses to firms in developing countries that would allow export to other developing countries but limit them to developed countries. Proposals for doing this in the case of pharmaceuticals have been made[1288] and even implemented within the compulsory license for export system set up the by the Article 31bis amendment to the TRIPS Agreement. That system allows countries to issue compulsory licenses for production of patented medicines for export to LDCs and other countries without domestic manufacturing capacity. Other variations come under the umbrella of voluntary 'humanitarian' licensing, where

---

[1288] See e.g. Moon et al. "A win-win solution?: A critical analysis of tiered pricing to improve access to medicines in developing countries" 7 Globalization and Health 39 (2011).

developed country actors provide free access to their IP for actors in developing countries, with conditions. These approaches were pioneered in the realm of health where ease of manufacture by generics made such segmentation easy and have been implemented in projects such as the Drugs for Neglected Diseases Initiative.[1289]

The approach I propose would not be based on a compulsory license system but on an incentive system that would encourage the use of model licenses with market segmentation provisions in return for access to financing. The licenses would also address the knowledge transfer into other developing countries by firms in emerging economies. This would be primarily aimed at encouraging knowledge based FDI in least developed and developing countries by firms from any other UNFCCC party. The incentive in the license would be that export of products to developed country markets would be possible.

The model licenses are targeted at two groups. The first is at emerging economy firms who may need incentives to take on licenses with such restrictions and to encourage them to focus on LDCs and other developing countries as prime markets and launch pads for their products. It also removes the LDCs and smaller developing countries from the arena of competition between emerging economy firms and developed country firms. To the extent that emerging economy firms wish to have access to developed country markets they can compete on the international global field directly, or they can go through LDCs. This allows for LDCs to benefit both from the employment and technology transfer from emerging economies but to also benefit from the market access into developed economies. While many already enjoy significant tariff free access for their goods into developed economies under various preferential regimes (e.g. the Everything But Arms initiative of the European Union)[1290] these do not extend to IP protected goods or goods produced by an IP protected process, and many are bound by restrictive standards on rules of origin that limit the ability of firms from other countries to use their location in LDCs to also benefit from such access. This proposed system piggy-backs on this existing framework but requires some more flexibility in terms of rules of origin but strict standards in terms of technology transfer and benefit to the LDC.

Another key issue is the risk premium that exists in terms of licensing into developing countries. There is evidence that a significant barrier to IP related transactions is uncertainty of contract enforcement and IP enforcement rather than the

---

[1289] See p18, Abbott, F M "Innovation and Technology Transfer to Address Climate Change: Lessons from the Global Debate on Intellectual Property and Public Health", ICTSD's Programme on IPRs and Sustainable Development, Issue Paper No. 24, International Centre for Trade and Sustainable Development, Geneva, Switzerland, 2009.
[1290] REGULATION (EU) No 978/2012 OF THE EUROPEAN PARLIAMENT AND OF THE COUNCIL of 25 October 2012

strength of IP protection per se.[1291] There is a lack of predictable, stable and transparent environments for financial transactions, contracting, licensing, and dispute settlement in many developing countries, even in emerging countries. This is a problem for domestic as much as foreign firms. Both would benefit from taking some of these issues off the table. In the general investment environment, many countries have signed bilateral investment treaties (BITs) that subject disputes related to the treaty to international arbitration and commit themselves to recognizing and enforcing such judgments. In BITs, it is investor state dispute settlement that has raised much of the concerns but it is a common practice in international business transactions between private sector actors and something that would already be a familiar business practice, but now embedded in the model licenses at the UNFCCC. Such an approach will be necessary to address some of the risk premium that would attach to participation in such licensing, and an arbitration clause, subject to a particular kind of body with expertise in settling technology and IP-related contractual disputes would be necessary.

Of course some limiting principle in terms of scope of technology might be needed but not so limited as to be ineffective. It remains important to maintain the flexibility of developing countries to determine their own need, individually and in the aggregate but the concerns of developed countries of sheer technology grabbing will need to be addressed. I would propose focusing directly on technologies identified as needs in NAMAs, technology needs assessments and NAPAs, as discussed in Chapter 2. This universe of technologies, while still broad, requires states to have provided well thought out, justified climate reasons for including the technologies in their needs. For each country or license or production, the production would be limited to its expressed technology needs.

Developed countries can use the proposed mechanism as a lever to enable and encourage technological development in developing and least developed countries. They could specifically and unilaterally open their markets, by lowering their tariffs on environmentally sound technologies produced by developing countries, especially by low and middle income countries.[1292] While this could be done unilaterally, the aim would be to leverage the funding capacity of the UNFCCC to encourage and model the behaviour. The proposal is to have a COP decision or set of decisions that would mandate the Technology Executive Committee to do the following and embed in the rules of the Green Climate Fund, the following:

1. Create a ***standard model license*** to be used by firms and institutions in developing country UNFCCC parties to ***produce technologies primarily for***

[1291] p22, Maskus, K E "Encouraging International Technology Transfer" ICTSD Issue Paper No. 7, May 2004.
[1292] See p16, Hoekman, B, K E Maskus, and K Saggi, "Transfer of Technology to Developing Countries: Unilateral and Multilateral Policy Options" World Bank Policy Research Working Paper No. 3332. June 1, 2004.

*their domestic markets and for export to **LDC*** (or other countries with insufficient technological and manufacturing capacity) markets. The license would explicitly exclude the export of patented products or products produced by a patented process into other non-LDC or non-developing country markets. Recipients of funds from any UNFCCC financial mechanism who used such a license would be prioritized for receipt of funds and would be guaranteed 100% support of licensing costs, even at full commercial rates.

- o Funds for licensing of technologies covered by such a license would have to meet following criteria:
    - The technology/ies were identified in the TNAs or NAMAs of the recipient LDC markets;
- o Disputes under such a license would be subject to binding arbitration under a UNFCCC mechanism either established or designated by the TEC.[1293]

2. Create a **standard model license** to allow enterprises from any UNFCCC party **to export technological goods produced in any LDC** (or other country with insufficient technological and manufacturing capacity) **into any other UNFCCC party** (including other developing countries) where the products or process producing such products is IP protected; provided that:
    - o The technology/ies were identified in the TNAs or NAMAs of the host LDC markets;
    - o Production of the technology and/or application of the process for production is carried out in facilities located within the territory of an LDC and is committed to do so for at least 10 years;
    - o At least 30% of personnel involved each year in production are local citizens;
    - o Production involves capacity building, education, information transfer, training of local personnel, and use of local content.
    - o At least one sub-license is granted (at grant or concessional rates) for use of the technology for production and/or adaptation primarily for the domestic market of the LDC (or other country with insufficient technological and manufacturing capacity);
    - o Recipients of any UNFCCC Financial mechanism who used such a license would be prioritized for receipt of funds and would be guaranteed 100% support of licensing costs, even at full commercial rates.
    - o Disputes under such a license would be subject to binding arbitration under a UNFCCC mechanism either established or designated by the TEC.

[1293] For more detail on the binding arbitration mechanism see Section B.3

- o The same conditions shall be required to be used for any technologies further developed and patented under such a license.

3. For those LDCs (or other country with insufficient technological and manufacturing capacity) where a specific technology product or process is not IP protected, **UNFCCC parties should commit to allow import into other UNFCCC countries of that technological product** (or products produced by that process) **made in LDCs** (or other countries with insufficient technological and manufacturing capacity), provided that:
    - o The technology/ies were identified in the TNAs or NAMAs of the recipient LDC markets;
    - o Production of the technology and/or application of the process for production is carried out in facilities located within the territory of an LDC (or other country with insufficient technological and manufacturing capacity), and is committed to do so for at least 5 years;
    - o At least 30% of personnel involved each year in production are local citizens;
    - o Production involves capacity building, education, information transfer, training of local personnel,
    - o Local content (by value added) provided by domestic firms makes up 4% in the first year, 8% in the second, 12, in the third, 16% in the fourth and 20% in the final year.
    - o Recipients of any UNFCCC Financial mechanism (including multilateral and bilateral funds) who carried out such production would be prioritized for receipt of funds.
    - o Determination of compliance with these conditions would be subject to binding arbitration (between the complaining importing state and the firm concerned) under a UNFCCC mechanism either established or designated by the TEC.

It is important when considering investment issues that the CDM is essentially an investment regime, with very specific structures for rewarding FDI that successfully meets certain performance standards. It embodies the very concept of performance requirements that has largely been anathema in the broader international investment framework. As noted in chapter 4, bilateral investment treaties have generally prohibited performance, technology transfer and local content requirements. In addition, as discussed in chapter 4, the CDM has not been a very successful vehicle at meeting even its main performance requirement i.e. truly additional GHG emissions reductions, and has not been successful at meeting the implied sustainable development and technology transfer requirements. Most of the proposals around reforming the CDM and its relationship to technology transfer relate to both the issue of embedding technology transfer more tightly into the assessment of the DNA and the certification process.[1294] In part this has been to avoid stepping on the freedom that developing countries have insisted upon in defining for themselves what they would consider the sustainable development criteria that they would use for approving CDM projects through their designated national authority. I would argue that if they are seriously concerned about technology transfer, developing countries should be willing to have at least a technology transfer requirement in the registration and validation of CDM projects. This would address the ways in which countries have historically used FDI to encourage spillovers within the context of a system that also created a strong incentive for firms from developed countries to participate by rewarding them with emissions reduction credits. This would of course be premised on there being a strong incentive under the CDM or other future market mechanism for developed country firms to participate due to a high price for credits in developed country markets.

With respect to the CDM or reformed CDM, this would be a specialized investment regime governing how performance requirements for technology transfer and local content would apply within the framework of sustainable development and technology transfer. It may have to be explicitly excepted from the restrictions of the Agreement on Trade-related Aspects of Investment Measures (TRIMS Agreement)[1295] which prohibits, under Article 2 on national treatment, the following:

- Requirements for local purchase or content of goods;

- Discriminatory export performance or requirements.

Even without such an agreement excepting such measures, such actions may nevertheless be justified under GATT Article XX exceptions (see Article 3 TRIMS), and for developing countries under GATT Article XVIII (see Article 4 TRIMS). GATT Article XVIII governs in particular the process for withdrawal of concessions for the purposes of ensuring the development of domestic industries as well as addressing balance of payment issues, which is particularly well-suited as a justification for investment-related measures such as these in the specific arena of technology transfer for climate change.

[1294] Teng, F et al., "Possible development of a technology clean development mechanism in a post-2012 regime" Discussion paper 08-24, Harvard Projection International Climate Agreements, Cambridge, MA, November 2008.
[1295] Agreement on Trade-related Aspects of Investment measures ("TRIMS Agreement") Annex 1A to the Marrakesh Agreement establishing the World Trade Organization (WTO Agreement), Marrakesh, 15 April 1994, *in force* 1 January 1995, 1867 United Nations Treaty Series (1995) 4.

To the extent that many countries have signed bilateral investment treaties, it may be appropriate to consider suspending or withdrawing from obligations on performance, local content, technology transfer and other requirements. In order for the CDM to enable the best technology transfer and spillovers while not being overly prescriptive, a Kyoto protocol MOP decision should state that in the context of emissions trading and the CDM, **CDM project host countries are free to establish the performance and other requirements, as a condition for approving CDM projects**. In a sense the requirements of additionality for CDM project approval already constitute such a requirement. This would ensure that the DNA can refuse to provide domestic certification unless certain minimum requirements have been met such as, for example;

- Local participation of domestic firms in supply chains;

- Joint venture or local equity in the investment itself;

- Technology transfer relating to products, skills and know-how, data and information, including licenses,

- R&D requirements.

In addition to using the CDM to truly impose performance requirements on technology related investments, thus encouraging spillovers into the host market, a further incentive could be provided through a system that would issue some kind of emissions reduction credit bonus for projects that carried out high quality technology transfer. Thus basic hardware technology transfer would be built into the basic issuance of credits but on top of that, some percentage would be received for training in operation and maintenance, even more in exchange for transfer that resulted in the ability or capacity to adapt the technology; and the most for training and providing capacity to replicate the technology. That last could be embodied in a production license that also provided know-how. Such proposals seek to create an added incentive to transfer technology by providing emission credits for certain technology transfer outcomes such as enabling localization, adaptation and replication. There remain details to be worked out especially those that present some accounting difficulties in terms of not over-producing certified emissions reduction credits.[1296]

[1296] See p16, de Sepibus, J "Reforming the Clean Development Mechanism to accelerate Technology Transfer" Working Paper No 2009/42, NCCR Trade Regulation, Swiss National Centre of Competence in Research, November 2009.

Ghana proposed such a technology crediting mechanism within the CDM in a 2009 submission to the AWGLCA.[1297] It put forward a mechanism whereby a separate system of Environmentally Sound Technology Rewards (ESTRs) would be created, which would be tradable and which could be used for off-setting, and for meeting MRV and emissions obligations. The extent of the rewards would be linked to how much the project contributed to meeting technology needs, expressed in a country's Technology Needs Assessment. My proposal keeps the crediting within the CDM acknowledging that technology transfer normally takes place within a broader business project rather than a separate technology transaction.

Thus I would propose:

1. Regarding the CDM and its successor mechanism, the **TEC should recommend technology requirements in the CDM or future market mechanism** specifically transfer of know-how, skills, information and licenses, for:

    - Validation/Verification of projects for the CDM or whatever future CDM-like market mechanism exists in the post-Kyoto framework;
    - Registration/Issuance of credits under the CDM or whatever future CDM-like market mechanism exists in the post-Kyoto framework, requiring best available technologies.

In this scenario, an operational definition of technology transfer would be used that required more than delivery of hardware but at a minimum training in operation and maintenance of the technology. A capped but fixed percentage of credits issued per project could be benchmarked to the extent that the following criteria were addressed:

- **Transfer of Physical Capital and Goods ((outside of the firm or wholly owned subsidiary)** including, but not limited to: specialized equipment; goods embodying or incorporating the relevant technology or idea. This largely entails financing for purchase of such goods.
- **Transfer of Skills and Know How (outside of the firm or wholly owned subsidiary)** including, but not limited to: licensing or assistance with the purchase of proprietary knowledge, provision of technical and manual skills training; scientific and academic training; training and technical advice and assistance, necessary to maintain, operate, adapt and reproduce a viable system or technology. This would include scientific and educational exchanges, workshops, field education, funding, training and capacity building all along the

---

[1297] See p97, UNFCCC "Ideas and proposals on the elements contained in paragraph 1 of the Bali Action Plan: Submissions from Parties-Part 1" Ad Hoc Working Group on Long-Term Cooperative Action under the Convention, Sixth session, Bonn, 12 June 2009.

research chain: - research, development, demonstration, deployment, and commercialization. This is largely aimed at ensuring learning – acquisition and application of know how leading to an understanding of the principles of why the technology works and building the capacity to adapt and replicate it.

- **Transfer of Information and Data ((outside of the firm or wholly owned subsidiary)**, including but not limited to: manuals; designs; blueprints; operating instructions; scientific and technical publications and reports. This would include greater access to scientific and technical information, patent office publications and data. This is embodied in the formal documents and detail of patent information, licenses, as well as information to learn how to operate, adapt and replicate the technology. This is meant to provide a durable basis for building on and being able to adapt the technology.
- **Transfer of ability to adapt and improve the technology** including, but not limited to: no limitations on production and export under licenses for domestic use or export to other developing countries; no restrictions on improvement and ownership of improvement of the technology; establishment of R&D facilities in the country in which the project is placed; creation of joint R&D project or projects.

In terms of dispute settlement, the creation of a mechanism for binding arbitration will be necessary and possibly made applicable for all transactions relating to IP and contracting using funds from the UNFCCC and for issuance of credits.

1. The TEC should authorize, designate or create an ***Arbitration Mechanism*** to address contractual or intellectual property licensing problems that arise in the context of any legal dispute related to projects or programmes funded by any UNFCCC Financial Mechanism. Receipt of funds from any UNFCCC financial mechanism and use of such in any contract using, accepting or in any way transferring intellectual property, should be contingent on acceptance of a mandatory, binding arbitration clause in the funding contract and in the contract between the funding recipient and the technology provider (subject to the participants' choice of law in each contract and the designated countries' systems for recognition of mandatory arbitration terms). All UNFCCC countries would agree to implement such decisions, subject only to the constitutional requirements of domestic law. Decisions of the Arbitration mechanism would be appealable to the Advisory Board of the Technology Mechanism, which would review and only reverse such decisions by a two thirds majority of the voting members.

- It may be appropriate to designate existing mechanisms with sufficient expertise such as the WIPO Arbitration and Mediation Center[1298], provided that specific criteria are met such as:
    - Exclusion of arbitrators with conflicts of interest;
    - Inclusion of arbitrators with specific experience in environmental technologies;
    - Procedural transparency, acceptance of interventions by third party stakeholders and publication of arbitration decisions in all cases involving public bodies, governments, and quasi-public bodies such as state-owned enterprises, research institutes, and sovereign wealth funds;
    - A flat fee rate for any UNFCCC-related cases.

III.2. Reducing barriers to transactions

A significant part of the problem for technology transfer for climate change relates to the nature and scale of transactions for both products and knowledge. In Chapter 3, several of the studies pointed out that rates of diffusion were too slow for the technology sectors studied. One of the contributions that the UNFCCC can make is to provide standardized, centralized and trustworthy mechanisms for negotiating and carrying out such transactions. A crucial part of this will be providing transparency, certainty, predictability, and conflict resolution. The basic aim is to deal with the issue of lack of information that limits the ability of commercial actors to properly evaluate available technologies, available partners and available projects. While the CDM provides a venue for some of this, the structure does not lend itself to encouraging a volume of arms-length transactions related to technologies. Enabling such a resource and platform is crucial to scaling up market based activity related to technology transactions.[1299] What also needs to be taken into account however is the need for addressing the deficit related to directly operating in developing country markets relating to:

- Enforcement of intellectual property
- Enforcement of contracts
- Reliability as to financial and managerial capacity of partners
- Information as to each countries rules on technology export and import
- Advisory services for such transactions related to contract structure
- Contracting and dispute settlement

[1298] See http://www.wipo.int/amc/en/
[1299] See p10, Egenhofer, C et al. "Low-Carbon Technologies in the Post-Bali Period: Accelerating their Development and Deployment" European Climate Platform, report No. 4, December 2007

This is particularly crucial for the SMEs who are the vast majority of individual economic actors that have to be reached in developing countries and in whom a significant portion of technology is held in developed countries.[1300] The aim is to provide a way to speed up transactions and provide a one-stop shop that works to address several concerns at once and create a market that may not be subject to the vagaries of domestic variations in contracting and legal protection while providing standard licensing terms. This means creating platforms for conducting business that provide services beyond basic matchmaking and provide methodologies for assessing trustworthiness, reputation, and capacity. In particular, such a platform could be a useful advisory service for identifying and advising on import-export rules on products and sales for different countries.

Cannady is sceptical of what she calls "grand" plans although she acknowledges the usefulness of coordinating and facilitating transactions in some fashion.[1301] She notes precedents for providing access to packages of technology involving patents, know-how and training, such as the Public Intellectual Property Resource for Agriculture (PIPRA). This approach is also reflected in suggestion for standard licensing of Green Technology Packages [1302] and suggestions that the administration and handling of these could be carried out through the CTC&N.[1303] More generally, as many such licensing platforms and online licensing aggregation mechanisms have folded in the past decade, there are clearly limitations to what such platforms can and cannot do. Cannady suggests that more than standard terms and contracts what is needed are advisory services to help developing country firms negotiate licensing contracts or training and capacity building in carrying out such negotiations.[1304] Given the mandate of the CTC&N, such advisory services may be well within its capacity and mission even in the first few years of operation. Cannady focuses on mechanisms for increasing the bargaining power of developing countries and developing country firms in licensing negotiations and technology transactions as key to succeeding in technology transfer.[1305] Again, there seems to be no reason that these tasks could not be embedded in a platform.

Such exchanges make the process of identifying licensees, technologies on offer and carrying out negotiations and pricing much easier and simpler, including

---

[1300] See p2932, Schneider, M et al. "Understanding the CDM's contribution to technology transfer" 36 Energy Policy 2930 (2008).
[1301] See p12, Cannady, C "Access to Climate Change Technology by Developing Countries: A Practical Strategy, ICTSD's Programme on IPRs and Sustainable Development, Issue Paper No. 25, International Centre for Trade and Sustainable Development, Geneva, Switzerland (2009).
[1302] See p13, Id.
[1303] See p14, Consilvio, M "The Role of Patents in the International Framework of Clean Technology Transfer: A Discussion of Barriers and Solutions" 3 Intell. Prop. Brief 10 (2011).
[1304] See p13, Cannady, C "Access to Climate Change Technology by Developing Countries"
[1305] See p23, Id.

standard licensing. They are particularly useful for those institutions and firms that are primarily engaged in manufacturing and for whom licensing is not a central activity. The opportunity costs related to negotiating, and licensing out are much reduced in such an exchange for such actors who may not be willing to put significant resources into licensing activity. The exchanges may also be very useful for weakly resourced institutions and actors, such as university technology transfer offices.

A pilot version of such an exchange for environmentally sound technologies was Green Xchange, established in 2009 as a collaboration of Creative commons and several firms. (http://www.greenxchange.cc/), which implemented a patent commons approach first pioneered by Creative commons in the copyright arena and extended now to the field of patents. Green Xchange offered four kinds of standard licenses: *Intellectual capital* which provided free and open access to all for any purposes; *Research Non-exempt*, which is limited to free access for non-profits for non-commercial research purposes only[1306]; *Standard* which provided a royalty free license for exploitation for commercial purposes; and Standard PLUS which required some payments and could contain other restrictions. Assessment of the project suggests that it never expanded much beyond the primary provider of the initial patents, Nike, and that the business model was never able to overcome issues related to existing IP management practices in firms who primarily viewed IP as a strategic blocking tool.[1307] The Xchange was never able to build up a critical mass of patents and also found that users were primarily interested not just in the patent but in the associated know-how requiring further building up of relationships and value-added service that the exchange was not in a position to provide.[1308] In addition, while the focus on open innovation was laudable, it made it difficult to make a business case to firms that they should place their patents into the Xchange. This may have made the Xchange more of a CSR exercise for many companies rather than a new business opportunity. In this case of this proposal, the presence of the CTC&N, in combination with the exchange, as well as access to financing and a critical mass due to the worldwide scale of the exchange would go a long way to addressing some of the challenges encountered by the Green Xchange approach.

The importance of putting together technology packages and having sufficient internal financial support and funding to hire people with sufficient expertise to do so is crucial. Patent holders would also have to be willing to have their patents included in such packages rather than licensed separately. Such an approach requires an active technology transfer manager both in the providing institution and in the platform, who would actively identify market opportunities, work with rightholders to create agreements to pool their technologies and to make them available as packages on the

---

[1306] Patenting for non-commercial purposes is also allowed.
[1307] See p5, Ghafele, R and R D O'Brien "Open innovation for Sustainability: Lessons from the GreenXchange Experience" Policy Brief No. 13, International Centre for Trade and Sustainable Development, Geneva, Switzerland, June 2012.
[1308] Id.

platform. This is why, to a significant extent, there is overlap between this proposal and proposals for pooling of patents. In the case of the platform, such pooling would have to take place voluntarily, potentially increasing the transaction costs for the platform itself, but perhaps increasing the likelihood of remuneration for licenses by provider firms.

The way to address the creation of technology packages may be the establishment of global voluntary patent pools although these have generally been proposed as a tool for providing cheaper, easier or free access to technologies for developing country firms.[1309] Global voluntary patent pools consist of rightholders placing technologies in exchange pools where rightholders are able to access each other's technologies, the know-how, and the capacity building to make the most effective use these other technologies. There are several weaknesses to traditional global patent pools and I am more sceptical of these than authors such as Maskus.[1310] Pools are only as effective as their memberships, their content, and the licensing structure that they create.[1311] The first concern would be to ensure that the pool was open to all relevant actors and did not unduly exclude firms from developing countries. Where the establishment of these is voluntary, it may be possible to rely on market forces to best identify the stakeholders. Where these are government structured or mandated, the difficulty lies in designing a system that would be seen as fair by both insiders and outsiders. In both cases, significant concerns arise about anti-competitive effects. A patent pool is most efficient where it brings together sets of different, complementary technologies that in the aggregate provide a package which allows the manufacture of a product. One example could be the smartphone market.[1312] Many patents from many different partners on different aspects of the technology are necessary for the product to be created and it is more efficient to allow all participants to pool their patents, allowing easy or cheap access for all participants to the package. However, where the pool charges higher prices to outsiders for accessing the technology than to its own members, this creates a barrier to entry in the product market. Thus incumbents may be unduly protected. Where the pool consists not just of

---

[1309] See p59, Lee, B et al. "Who owns our Low Carbon Future: Intellectual Property and Energy Technologies" Chatham House, September 2009. See also Abbott, F M "Innovation and Technology Transfer to Address Climate Change: Lessons from the Global Debate on Intellectual Property and Public Health", ICTSD's Programme on IPRs and Sustainable Development, Issue Paper No. 24, International Centre for Trade and Sustainable Development, Geneva, Switzerland, 2009.
[1310] See p27, Maskus, K "Differentiated Intellectual Property Regimes for Environmental and Climate Technologies", OECD Environment Working Papers, No. 17, OECD Publishing 2010. As is Cannady, C "Access to Climate Change Technology by Developing Countries: A Practical Strategy, ICTSD's Programme on IPRs and Sustainable Development, Issue Paper No. 25, International Centre for Trade and Sustainable Development, Geneva, Switzerland (2009).
[1311] Cannady, C "Access to Climate Change Technology by Developing Countries: A Practical Strategy, ICTSD's Programme on IPRs and Sustainable Development, Issue Paper No. 25, International Centre for Trade and Sustainable Development, Geneva, Switzerland (2009).
[1312] See e.g. the Sisvel LTE Patent Pool, available at: http://www.sisvel.com/index.php/lte. (last visited 15 August 2014).

complementary technologies which may be linked in some network, but of companies with similar technologies and patents, the anti-competitive concerns are that much larger as this allows the firms to not just prevent market entry into the product market but allows them to collude to charge a joint higher price in the licensing market. Thus where these licensors might have competed on price and terms they can now present the same, likely higher costs and terms to non-pool members.

What is problematic is that much of what people envision pools achieving in the realm of climate technology is the pooling of similar technologies allowing firms to more efficiently research and improve each other's technologies.[1313] Such patent pools seem to be viewed as tools for accessing technologies for firms in developing countries but where these firms are not able to provide sufficiently valuable patents to the pool, there will be no market incentive to include them in the pool.[1314] In either case, voluntary pools outside of an exchange pose too much of a danger in competitive terms in that they are likely to exclude developing country firms, and they are unlikely to allow competitors to share technologies. Where the package of patents offered by the pool contains non-essential patents but the pool uses the leverage to require purchase of these as part of the package, this also creates significant problems for the market.

One iteration of the pool idea is the Marshall Plan-type, country level pool proposed by Ajemian and Reid.[1315] Based on the successful support to Japan and Europe in the post-World War II period, they argue that climate change presents just as large a security issue and that such a pool would be an appropriate model of organization between four main countries: the US, Japan, China and the European Union. All the countries would pool and not compete on climate technology. The pool would pay or insure against losses, the IP owned by their private sectors for the material that they placed in the pool and these would be licensed at similar low costs or freely, among the members of the pool. Primarily as a China directed mechanism, this approach asks the involved countries to reframe their competitive relationship around clean technology and cooperate on a scale unprecedented since the Marshall Plan. The basis is that even where China may not be an equal partner, it still would have IP to contribute to the pool, something which may become increasingly true but may not be entirely the case at the moment. It is not clear whether standard licenses are envisaged, whether some kind of market segmentation is considered or what would be done about subsequent innovations based on technology licensed from the pool. It is also not clear

---

[1313] See e.g. p59, Lee, B et al. "Who owns our Low Carbon Future: Intellectual Property and Energy Technologies" Chatham House, September 2009.
[1314] See p10, Cannady, C "Access to Climate Change Technology by Developing Countries: A Practical Strategy, ICTSD's Programme on IPRs and Sustainable Development, Issue Paper No. 25, International Centre for Trade and Sustainable Development, Geneva, Switzerland (2009).
[1315] Ajemian, C and D Reid "Preventing Global Warming: The United States, China, and Intellectual Property" 115 Business and Society Review 417 (2010)

how they would envision outside countries' role in accessing or using the technology in the pool, or whether they contemplate some mechanism for participation.

It is important to consider the kind of problems that pools are meant to solve. If the issue is one where production of a technological good is blocked because of patent thickets and high transaction costs, voluntary or even publicly backed pools can be useful tools. They can provide a one stop shop for all participants in the product market. If the issue is to try to solve the issue of such things as refusals to license, or reluctance to share technology and knowledge, voluntary pools are not likely to change the behaviour of those firms who see the patent primarily as a tool for creating room to operate and prevent market entry, unless they can use the pool to exclude new market entrants. As noted, given the gaps in ownership in patenting between firms in developed and developing countries, cross-licensing within a pool creates little incentive for the inclusion of firms in developing countries without valuable IP. They would most likely end up as outsiders to the pool. In designing around this, what is actually being created is the concept of a repository, from which stakeholders can pick and choose which technologies they wish to license, at a flat rate. Given the variation in the utility and value of different patents, such a repository is unlikely to be able to provide a flat rate and each patent will have to be priced differently. This effectively then becomes a publicly run IP licensing platform rather than a pool per se. The idea of aggregation is correct but the label of a "patent pool" and the understanding of the limits of what it can accomplish are sometimes missing from recommendations to pool patents, enable cross-licensing and provide low cost access. Thus an IP Platform or exchange would have to build in an incentive for participants to first place their patents on the exchange and then allow them to be placed in packages. Pricing is also a serious challenge and firms that placed their technologies would have to indicate a priori what prices they would like to charge (either in absolute numbers or as percentages of gross income) when licensed individually or as part of a package. In order to be licensed within a package rightholder may have to lower their price in order to ensure that the package does not become prohibitively expensive. A significant amount of control may have to be relinquished to the platform manager in such cases, which may also present a problem.

Approaches such as these are aimed at providing a way to speed up transactions and provide a one-stop shop that works to address several concerns at once and create a market that may not be subject to the vagaries of domestic variations in contracting and legal protection while providing standard licensing terms. As such it may be better for any proposal to focus purely on facilitation, including allowing a space for rightholders to self-select if they want to combine and create packages. What would then be required is transparency about all the technologies, the firms, the goods, the prices all in a trusted venue. The main task of the platform would be a venue for enabling transactions rather than managing transactions. It would ensure processes for registration for firms that would entail background checks and creditworthiness checks among other things.

As such I propose that:

1. The TEC should authorize/designate/create an *intellectual property exchange/licensing platform* specifically for climate change mitigation and adaptation technologies. Such an exchange/platform would enable secure, efficient and transparent arms-length transactions for intellectual property licensing at a one-stop shop, with the weight and authority of the UNFCCC behind it. It may be appropriate for the TEC and/or CTC&N to select one or more existing exchanges in an open and competitive process provided that the exchange that is finally selected meets basic criteria such as:

    - Providing a low flat nominal fee for those posting assets or seeking to access licenses;
    - Providing security and reliability for financial transactions;
    - Providing secure, speedy and predictable dispute settlement;
    - Enabling special licensing arrangements for LDCs.

2. In parallel, The TEC should authorize/designate/ create a *B2B platform for commercial transactions related to climate change mitigation and adaptation goods and services* specifically targeted at projects and programmes funded by UNFCCC financial mechanisms that leverages the information and categorization achieved by TT:CLEAR and its affiliated databases to allow easy access to publicly available technologies in particular. Such a platform would enable global, transparent offers for sale and offers for purchasing of technological goods and services on a web-based platform and enable secure, efficient arms-length transactions without long protracted negotiation processes. Registration requirements and placing of financial bonds for participation could reduce transaction risks for sellers and buyers, as would processes for reputational ranking. Such a platform should:
    - Enable optimal searching; input window self-selection and reliable and secure financial transactions, especially suited to government procurement departments in developing countries;
    - Enable standard simple contracting terms, billing, purchase orders, sales and delivery tracking, and expedited dispute resolution through a mandatory arbitration process provided by the platform.

It may be appropriate for the TEC to select, through an open tender process for the development, implementation and running of such a platform that would be funded by a basic fee for participation charged to private stakeholders. The CTC&N may be an appropriate host for the B2B platform.

III.3 Enabling Joint Research & Development, Demonstration and Deployment

Collaborative research and development (R&D) is seen by many as a way to circumvent IP-related issues by engaging in joint research in structures that provide for sharing of IP.[1316] Thus joint cross-border R&D will ensure that all involved parties have ownership. Studies have shown that investment in R&D has a significant impact on technology productivity and capacity building and can be a powerful tool in enabling not just deployment but capacity to adopt and adapt technologies to local needs.[1317]

One of the key advantages of these forms of collaborative R&D structures is that they address two key market failures that have the potential to bedevil climate technologies. The first is the difficulty in getting private sector investment into innovation where the benefits of such innovation are imperfectly captured by the innovator.[1318] In fact, such imperfect capture is a desirable outcome in the climate arena, given the need for rapid dissemination. This makes resource pooling measures, supported by public financing much more likely to be effective in moving private sector actors to carry out research that they otherwise would not. The second is the costs of adopting technology for first movers, especially where such technologies have network externalities[1319] as in power generation, water, transport, agriculture and buildings.

In looking for models, several scholars have looked at the CGIAR model of sector-specific directed research groups. Milford made a proposal for a Consultative Group on Climate Innovation in 2007 based on the CGIAR model.[1320] This model allows pooling of resources by governments rather than creating competing research programs. Joint R&D and Demonstration platforms have been suggested by others as a way to address especially problems related to the commercialization, and uptake of climate technologies. [1321] Correa presents the most thorough analysis of the opportunities and limits of the CGIAR. The argument from supporters is that the model presents a collaborative R&D model for generating and disseminating public goods.[1322] The CGIAR was the successful driver behind the Green Revolution that saw

---

[1316] See p59, Lee, B et al. "Who owns our Low Carbon Future: Intellectual Property and Energy Technologies" Chatham House, September 2009. See also p110, Ockwell, D et al. "UK-India Collaboration to Identify the Barriers to the Transfer of Low Carbon Technology-Final report" (London: the Department of Environment, Food and Rural Affairs, U.K., 2007).
[1317] See p8, Hoekman, B, K E Maskus, and K Saggi, "Transfer of Technology to Developing Countries: Unilateral and Multilateral Policy Options" World Bank Policy Research Working Paper No. 3332. June 1, 2004.
[1318] See p338, De Coninck et al. "International technology-oriented agreements to address climate change" 36 Energy Policy 335 (2008).
[1319] Id.
[1320] Milford, L "Consultative Group on Climate Innovation: A Proposed Complementary Technology Track for the Post-2012 Period" Clean Energy Group, paper presented at Road to Copenhagen 2009- Conference on Leadership, Sustainable Development and Climate Change, 23 November 2007, Brussels, Belgium.
[1321] See p61, Lee, B et al. "Who owns our Low Carbon Future: Intellectual Property and Energy Technologies" Chatham House, September 2009.
[1322] See Correa, C "Fostering the Development and Diffusion of Technologies for Climate Change: Lessons from the CGIAR Model" Policy Brief 6, ICTSD Programme on IPRs and Sustainable Development,

introduction of high yield varieties in South East Asia and Africa. The CGIAR is an association of thematically or sectorally specific research centers, that cooperate, share information, cooperate on joint projects and each one presents a research platform for coordinating research on a specific set of issues (maize, rice, wheat). The centres purposefully did not assert intellectual property rights to products so as to ensure the greatest dissemination and uptake of products. In addition, given that the funding for the research was public, the need for addressing the risk premium associated with frontier research was non-existent. In addition, the end-use community of farmers could access the products directly for the most part without an additional intermediary to turn the research into products.

The structure of the model remains appealing but it remains to be seen whether the type of research and relationship to end user communities is replicated in other technology areas related to climate. Within the UNFCCC structure, the CGIAR may play a role as the platform for agricultural research and development, demonstration and deployment of mitigation and adaptation technologies. As Correa points out, the farther away from basic scientific research, the more difficulties in establishing sustainable collaboration structures, especially if private sector actors wish to have a significant ownership role of research products for commercialization.[1323] A key lesson that Correa points to is the diffusion oriented structure of the CGIAR platform, including the use of social science research to ensure acceptability and affordability of its research products, and using that to guide the kind of products they researched.[1324]

The structure and success of R&D approaches to dealing with the technology transfer and IP issue of course depends on the kind of R&D required. Again, where this concerns new technologies and related basic research, IP issues tend to be much more easily managed, and in any case, tend to have a more public character. However, where difficulties arise is in the demonstration and deployment phase, the so-called

---

December 2009 and p66, Correa, C "Mechanisms for International Cooperation in Research and Development in the Area of Climate Change" in Soni, P et al. *Technological Cooperation and Climate Change Issues and Perspectives* Working papers presented at the Ministry of Environment and Forests, Government of India - UNDP Consultation on Technology Cooperation for Addressing Climate Change, 23-24 September, 2011; New Delhi, India.

[1323] See p66, Correa, C "Mechanisms for International Cooperation in Research and Development in the Area of Climate Change" in Soni, P. et al. *Technological Cooperation and Climate Change Issues and Perspectives* Working papers presented at the Ministry of Environment and Forests, Government of India - UNDP Consultation on Technology Cooperation for Addressing Climate Change, 23-24 September, 2011; New Delhi, India.

[1324] Correa, C "Fostering the Development and Diffusion of Technologies for Climate Change: Lessons from the CGIAR Model" Policy Brief 6, ICTSD Programme on IPRs and Sustainable Development, December 2009.

"valley of death" prevalent even in developed countries.[1325] Most of the technologies needed in developing countries relate to commercial or near commercial technologies. This requires cooperation in learning and adapting technologies to local needs. As such, adaptation of technologies may form an ideal platform for collaboration[1326] provided that the resultant solution is available to all participants equally and does not provide an unfair competitive advantage to any particular participant. It may even present a real opportunity for cross-border sectoral cooperation between developing countries. The key issue is what structure could there be for carrying out such cooperation that did not rely on establishing new multilateral or bilateral mechanisms. Looking sectorally and using existing institutions may be the right approach, but at least within the UNFCCC, this is a role that the CTC&N seems to have within its mandate, with the potential to provide funding for those smaller countries that cannot afford to participate. There would also be a way to re-direct existing research funds to those areas of more interest to developing countries e.g. adaptation, mitigation in agriculture and energy efficiency in industry and buildings.

Providing equal access to R&D subsidies and fund to firms from developing countries is a crucial way to encourage technology transfer. Since the expiration of the provisions in the Agreement on Subsidies and Countervailing Measures (SCM Agreement)[1327] on non-actionable subsidies on 31 December 1999[1328], research and development subsidies fall within the category of 'actionable' subsidies, as do environmental subsidies more generally. Thus, discriminatory R&D subsidy regimes by developed countries may be subject to WTO dispute settlement if they do not meet the standards in Articles, 1, 2 and 5 of the SCM Agreement. However, it may be better to address such issues with prior commitments to provide access negotiated at the UNFCCC. This could include specific access to such subsidies for developing countries as part of meeting obligations under TRIPS Article 66.2 and more generally TRIPS Article 7. The use of tax benefits for R&D could be extended to R&D carried out in developing countries, especially for LDCs.

The IEA Technology Implementing Agreements (TIAs) may be an appropriate way in which to address the need for increasing international R&D collaboration in energy related mitigation. These TIAs serve as vehicles for directed collaboration, with defined roadmaps and research and development goals in which countries participate

---

[1325] CAP "Breaking Through on Technology: Overcoming the barriers to the development and wide deployment of low-carbon technology" Center for American Progress and Global Climate Network, July 2009.
[1326] See p52 Correa, C "Mechanisms for International Cooperation in Research and Development in the Area of Climate Change"
[1327] Agreement on Subsidies and Countervailing Measures (SCM) Annex 1A to the Marrakesh Agreement establishing the World Trade Organization (WTO Agreement), Marrakesh, 15 April 1994, *in force* 1 January 1995, 1867 United Nations Treaty Series (1995) 4.
[1328] See http://www.wto.org/english/tratop_e/scm_e/subs_e.htm

voluntarily, and which may include both IEA member and non-member countries as well as associated parties from industry and academia.[1329]

A key component of many of these TIAs is that they envision either a cost-sharing framework, with a contribution from each participating party or a task sharing framework, in which each party takes on a task and pays the costs of that itself within its own national framework.[1330] It is not clear whether this is the main cause for the limited participation of developing country parties or private sector actors from developing countries in these TIAs, but a survey of the membership of all forty current TIAs shows a very low participation of developing countries. In addition, the issue of intellectual property is structured in such as fashion as to assure rightholders that any IP that they make available as part of the project will not be disclosed or transferred to others.[1331] What is done with the information and possibly patentable improvements that may occur as a result of the collaborations is also unclear. A major problem is that the TIAs focus almost exclusively on information sharing arrangements such as workshops and platforms or collecting and describing best practices but rarely involve carrying out proof of concept or demonstration projects.[1332] They also do not seem to involve additional funding for their activities as they rely largely on existing national budgets.[1333]

If the IEA aims to become a useful venue for enhancing R&D collaboration it will need to:

- Find a financing structure that appeals to participation of developing countries, by perhaps applying for GCF funds to enable participation;

- Have clarity on the IP sharing of technologies brought in and those developed under the TIAs;

- Focus on tangible cooperation regarding proof of concept, demonstration and adaptation of technologies to specific conditions and markets.

If we take to heart the argument that the primary need in developing countries is for technologies that are either new to the domestic industry or new to the domestic

---

[1329] p3, IEA, "IEA Implementing Agreements: Background and Framework as of 2003" IEA Paris, 2003.
[1330] p5, p11, Id.
[1331] p6, IEA, Id.
[1332] See p113, Ockwell, D et al. "UK-India Collaboration to Identify the Barriers to the Transfer of Low Carbon Technology-Final report" (London: the Department of Environment, Food and Rural Affairs, U.K., 2007).
[1333] See p343, De Coninck et al. "International technology-oriented agreements to address climate change" 36 Energy Policy 335 (2008).

firm, but not necessarily inventive[1334], then the focus should be on dissemination of existing technologies in the near term. Collaborative frontier R&D will be useful for avoiding IP problems once developing countries have built up sufficient domestic capacity to compete on the global market in these sectors and this may already be true in some sectors such as wind and solar PV. Thus joint R&D *per se* is best suited for the post-2030 technological landscape and not a panacea for the short term problems of access to advanced technological but already commercialized products and processes. As discussed in Chapter 3, what is needed is demonstration and adaptation of commercialized or near commercialization technologies to market and environmental factors in developing countries. The TIAs may be better suited to creating the breakthrough technologies of the future post-2030, but less well-suited to enabling work directed at near-term demonstration and deployment of already commercialized or near commercialized technologies.

There is also a need in both developed and developing countries for a clear policy focus on ensuring that publicly funded technologies are made available at grant or concessional rates on a non-exclusive basis to firms and institutions in developing countries. As discussed in chapter 3, the choice to engage in large scale transfer of IP to the private sector may lead to increased patenting of climate technologies, as R&D funding increases. In the absence of concerted action and policy to retain and work collaboratively with developing countries this has the potential to increase the technology gap rather than close it. Developed countries do have the legislative and policy capacity to retain rights in such publicly funded technologies precisely for the purposes envisioned for technology transfer, as can be seen for example, in the US licenses provided National Institutes of Health.[1335] Such a policy change would require that funding agencies maintain ownership or retain non-exclusive licenses, with the option of sub-licensing on a non-exclusive basis and geographically limited to developing countries, on a grant or concessional basis.

Looking at the experience of the Montreal Protocol's Multilateral Fund with public technologies, Andersen et al. also point out that a significant number of technologies had been cooperatively developed and delivered to the public without restriction.[1336] This suggest that collaborative R&D can be effective in disseminating technology where the result are made freely available rather than turned into proprietary information. As long as there is sufficient demand for mitigation and climate solutions there will be competition to turn the research into products and processes in the market.

[1334] See p16, Ockwell, D et al. "Enhancing Developing Country Access to Eco-Innovation: The Case of Technology Transfer and Climate Change in a Post-2012 Policy Framework", OECD Environment Working Papers, No. 12, OECD Publishing 2010

[1335] See NIH "Model Non-profit License Agreement for NTDs, HIV, TB and Malaria Technologies" Available at: http://www.ott.nih.gov/non-profit-license-agreement-summary (last visited 15 August 2014)

[1336] See p66-67, Andersen, S et al. *Technology Transfer for the Ozone Layer: Lessons for Climate Change* (London: Earthscan 2007)

One weakness of the Multilateral Fund was the decision to refuse to fund what was considered experimental research and development of indigenous technology. To the extent that it created a disincentive for countries to engage in research and development to enable domestic production in the face of refusals to license, this caused a serious barrier for some countries (India and Korea).[1337] The UNFCCC will need to adopt a different policy as the need to create domestic producers of these technologies is crucial to the success of the technology transfer to address climate change. Understanding that this will not always be the case, joint R&D will nevertheless need to focus on developing countries engaging in R&D of already commercialized or near commercialization technologies. However, the calculus is different for the major emerging economies who may have both the capacity and the interest to engage in frontier R&D.

As discussed in chapter 3, the R&D capacity for the majority of developing countries remains very low. Joint R&D collaborations cannot just focus on research outcomes but also on providing deliberate and structured training, education and capacity building. The UNFCCC also needs to leverage its institutional and financial power to retain some power of how and what it licenses and focus its work on demonstration and deployment, allowing the bulk of breakthrough research to take place in the IEA and other fora.

With these issues in mind, I propose that:

1. The TEC should require that all **R&D projects funded by any UNFCCC financial mechanism (or that wishes to be credited under MRV rules) establishes joint intellectual property rights for the UNFCCC**, through the TEC and/or CTC&N as its authorized representative, and that the TEC and/or CTC&N shall not require permission from other joint rightholders to sub-license the technology (at grant or concessional rates and terms, with proceeds shared jointly with other rightholders) to enterprises and institutions located in LDCs (or other countries with insufficient technological and manufacturing capacity) provided that:

    o the enterprise or institution is located within the territory of an LDC (or other country with insufficient technological and manufacturing capacity), and is committed to carry out activities related to adaptation, demonstration and deployment of commercialized, or near commercialization technologies in the country for at least 5 years;

[1337] See p262, Id.

- the enterprise or institution carries out capacity building, education, information transfer, training of local personnel relating to the licensed technology.

2. As a condition of receiving funds, all R&D, demonstration and deployment projects with a funding component from any UNFCCC Financial Mechanism, must involve at least one public research institution from an LDC and, at the very least, intellectual property rights in technologies and knowledge developed under the research project or programme so funded must be vested jointly in that public institution.

3. Developed country parties should commit to giving preference for any publicly funded research collaborations on climate technology to those that include participation by public and/or academic institutions from developing countries. This would, for example, require that the EU Horizon 2020 research funding framework program give preference to projects in the climate mitigation and adaptation sector, to those that include public institutions from developing countries.

4. UNFCCC developed country parties should commit to retaining the IP right or full non-exclusive licensing rights to publicly funded technologies and commit to license or sub-license technologies developed using public funds to firms and institutions in developing countries (or to the CTC&N and related joint R&D platforms) on non-exclusive grant or concessional terms. It may be appropriate to limit these licenses to domestic use and for export of products (or products produced by protected processes) only to other developing countries.

III.4. Increasing the effectiveness of existing UNFCCC mechanisms

There are some key existing issues that the UNFCCC can clarify that can go a long way to providing further certainty for member states and firms in those states. Most important is the issue of funding and the measuring, reporting and verifying of support for technology transfer. To the extent that it is unclear what kinds of activities the UNFCCC would fund, this creates significant uncertainty, as in the case of whether or not the Green Climate Fund will fund purchases of licenses and acquisition of patents.

I argue that the following should be priorities in the near term.

1. The TEC should make clear in its rules and regulations, including for those that establish the relationship between the TEC and the CTC&N, and the TEC and the Green Climate Fund, that the effect of the provisions of Article

4.1c, 4.3, 4.5, and 4.7 requires the UNFCCC to provide *support for, and include within the definition of 'incremental costs',:*

- Purchases of products embodying the best available technologies in the context of projects and programmes funded by all recognized financial mechanisms of the UNFCCC;
- Purchases of licenses (at full cost, or concessional rates) for best available technologies in the context of projects and programmes funded by all recognized financial mechanisms of the UNFCCC, especially in the context of activities undertaken by the CTC&N.

This recommendation would need to be implemented in the finalization of the rules for operationalization of the CTC&N and the Green Climate Fund, and included as an implementation mandate for the GEF, in its role as a financial mechanism of the Convention.

2. In terms of addressing the information gap regarding the status of technologies identified in TNAs and NAMAs, the TEC needs to revisit the guidelines for conducting TNAs and constructing NAMAs and ensure that countries doing so engage in the following, and are provided funding, for that purpose:

   a. A domestic patent landscaping of the technologies identified as priority needs in their technology needs assessment or NAMAs – including identification of the rightholders, or assignees;

   b. A survey of domestic firms of licensing practices (costs and terms) related to the technologies identified in the TNAs and NAMAs.

In order to also address a key missing element of MRV, which, as discussed in chapter 4, has been a major bone of contention between UNFCCC parties, it is important for developed countries to provide accurate and comparable information of the delivery of their obligations under the UNFCCC.

The TEC should set standards for measuring, reporting and verification (MRV) of technology transfer by Annex 1 and emerging economies.[1338] These should be used to elaborate the reporting requirements for technology support in the tabular template format of Table 8 in the National Communications of Annex 1 parties.[1339]

[1338] For example the performance indicators developed for use in UNFCCC "Report on the review and assessment of the effectiveness of the implementation of Article 4, paragraphs 1(c) and 5 of the Convention" SUBSIDIARY BODY FOR IMPLEMENTATION, Thirty-second session, Bonn, 31 May to 9 June, FCCC/SBI/2010/INF.4.

[1339] Decision 19/CP.18 "Common tabular format for "UNFCCC biennial reporting guidelines for developed country Parties" in UNFCCC "Report of the Conference of the Parties on its eighteenth session, held in

III.5 Increasing the effectiveness of existing flexibilities available under TRIPS

As discussed in Chapter 5, the main remaining tool of significant effectiveness available to developing countries is the application of competition law to address market structure problems related to distribution of climate technological products and know-how. However, as I also noted in Chapter 5, there is a significant lack of capacity in developing countries on competition law. There is however an opening for multilateral cooperation that can be used as both a capacity building platform as well as a platform for cooperating to address anti-competitive behaviour related to patents. Especially in the major developing economies, the capacity for using competition law is much greater but would be made much more effective by cooperating with developed country competition authorities to carry out surveillance and monitoring and to assess remedies that may have cross-border effects. To that end I would propose that:

1. The TEC should establish *a Competition and Standards Multi-Stakeholder Platform* which will operate as a TRIPS Article 40.3 consultative mechanism on information sharing and enforcement of anti-competitive practices and standard setting. This platform will work to bring relevant stakeholders (primarily member state competition and standards authorities) together to voluntarily work out, agree and implement market-based and sector-wide solutions to competition problems identified under TRIPS Article 40 and propose solutions, especially related to standard-setting in climate technologies.

The competition authorities of developed countries should commit under this framework to investigate anti-competitive behaviour of their companies in developing countries with little or no capacity to pursue competition policy, including adequate remedies.[1340] As discussed in Chapter 8, the importance of a clear and consciously chosen strategy for interacting with other regimes cannot be overstated with respect to the climate change regime. Given the broad range of areas affected by climate change, conflicts regarding both objectives and methodologies are inevitable.

The new UNFCCC Agreement, or the COP decisions relating to any such Agreement(s), will need to elaborate general interaction and savings clauses that account for the broad shared objectives and the specific shared provisions among the UNFCCC and other regimes. These "interaction clauses" will enable the agreement to more comprehensively address the relationship to other regimes, and put forward a pro-active

---

Doha from 26 November to 8 December 2012 - Addendum Part Two: Action taken by the Conference of the Parties at its eighteenth session" FCCC /CP/2012/8/Add.3, 28 February 2013.
[1340] As suggested at p36, Maskus, K E "Encouraging International Technology Transfer" ICTSD Issue Paper No. 7, May 2004.

mode of cooperation rather than one of avoidance.[1341] In the specific case of technology transfer, an option may be the use of an International Declaration on Climate Change and Intellectual Property Rights (DCCIPR). First mooted in the UNFCCC context by the Brazilian Trade Minister Celso Amorin at the Bali COP[1342], this has been revisited several times by member states and civil society organizations, although the details of what it would contain remain unclear, in the climate context. As with the Doha Declaration on TRIPS and Public Health, it would be a soft law, interpretive statement regarding flexibilities and the way the use of such flexibilities should be treated by the interpretive organs of the WTO and other bodies. There are differing opinions on the usefulness of such an approach, although Khor sees it as providing a useful signalling function to developing and developed countries as to the exact boundaries of available action and flexibility.[1343] Abbott expresses concerns that it may involve significant trade-offs for not much substantive gain for developing countries.[1344] He does note that if such a measure is pursued it should address all multilateral regimes concerned, not just the WTO.

The South Centre, in 2009, provided some suggestions for what such a declaration might contain:[1345]

- It should be a ministerial Declaration at the WTO;
- It should address the scope of TRIPS Article 8.2 to address anti-competitive behaviour, in particular interpreting the 'consistency' element;
- It should ensure a differential standard for ESTs including exceptions to the term of patentability;
- It should require a broader interpretation of article 30 to allow for export to other developing countries;
- Interpret TRIPS article 39, to ensure that know-how necessary for public interest uses is allowed to be exposed;
- Clarify the freedom to set standards to revoke patents;
- Refrain from bringing dispute settlement for actions understood to be in pursuit of UNFCCC aims.

[1341] See p431 Van Asselt, H et al, "Global Climate Change and the Fragmentation of International Law" 30 Law and Policy 423 (2008).
[1342] Celso Amorin "Trade Ministers' Informal Dialogue on Climate Change - Intervention by Minister Celso Amorim" Bali, December 8 - 9, 2007. Available at: http://www.itamaraty.gov.br/sala-de-imprensa/notas-a-imprensa/2007/09/trade-ministers-informal-dialogue-on-climate (last visited 15 August 2014)
[1343] See Khor, M "Climate Change, Technology and Intellectual Property Rights: Context and Recent Negotiations" Research Paper 45, South Centre, April 2012.
[1344] See Abbott, F M "Innovation and Technology Transfer to Address Climate Change: Lessons from the Global Debate on Intellectual Property and Public Health", ICTSD's Programme on IPRs and Sustainable Development, Issue Paper No. 24, International Centre for Trade and Sustainable Development, Geneva, Switzerland, 2009.
[1345] See p25, South Centre "Accelerating Climate-Relevant Technology Innovation and Transfer to Developing Countries: Using Trips Flexibilities under The UNFCCC" Analytical Note, SC/IAKP/AN/ENV/1, SC/GGDP/AN/ENV/8, August 2009.

While a useful outline I believe that at least one of the provisions goes beyond the existing standards and actually alters the substantive content of a TRIPS standard, by changing the potential term. There is no precedent for understanding that the rules on exceptions could be applied to the term of the patent. This also applies to the proposal to set absolute freedom to revoke patents. The TRIPS Agreement is not actually silent on this; it establishes a right to a patent except under specific circumstances outlined in the TRIPS Agreement and the Paris Convention.

Generally, there is a clear need for a statement that existing international flexibilities on patents, plant varieties, and copyright especially relating to competition law, compulsory licensing, exceptions and limitations must be interpreted in ways conducive to enabling rapid and efficient uptake of technologies to address mitigation and adaptation.

There are some lessons that can be learned from the experience of the Doha Declaration on TRIPS and Public Health. One key lesson is that a discussion on the proposed declaration should not and is not, required to take place in the context of the WTO. Abbott has argued that the economic and political power imbalance may be less pronounced against developing countries in the UNFCCC than in the WTO.[1346] It may be more appropriate to seek such a declaration in the context of the broader mandate of the UNFCCC rather than the relatively narrow focus of the WTO's TRIPS Agreement.[1347] There is of course the problem that negotiating such a declaration may absorb a significant amount of energy without achieving a significant amount beyond an interpretive statement. However, where the Doha Declaration focused on the freedom to operate of developing countries, the DCCIPR that I propose commits developed countries to refraining from taking certain kinds of actions, to committing to specific interpretations and applying to a much broader set of international treaties.

The proposed DCCIPR would outline the urgency of climate change, the urgency of the human rights challenge, the key obligations of states to fulfil and protect those human rights, and the necessity for technology transfer to achieve those rights. A discussed in Chapter 7, this may pose a slight problem for states that are not a party to the ICESCR, but language that is not explicitly based on the ICESCR may also be found. The proposed declaration could provide interpretive force, but only if adopted through a COP decision and directed to be shared with the Human Rights Council, the WIPO General Assembly, and the WTO General Council as well as UPOV. Unlike Abbott, I do not believe that a joint sitting of the decision-making bodies of all the relevant bodies

---

[1346] See p40, Abbott, F M "Innovation and Technology Transfer to Address Climate Change: Lessons from the Global Debate on Intellectual Property and Public Health", ICTSD's Programme on IPRs and Sustainable Development, Issue Paper No. 24, International Centre for Trade and Sustainable Development, Geneva, Switzerland, 2009.
[1347] Id.

would be appropriate, or manageable[1348], but I do recognize his point that an explicit relationship must be established between the DCCIPR and other venues. As a matter of international law, this would require first negotiating multiple mandates in each forum. It may be more appropriate to first discuss and negotiate and then propose the declaration or similar language be adopted within each organization according to its own rules and competences.

The ***Declaration on Climate Change and Intellectual Property*** should, at a minimum, state that:

- Given a peaking date of 2015-2025, All UNFCCC parties recognize that climate change is recognized as global public emergency condition to which all countries must respond, and must be treated as such in the context of the interpretation of all obligations in international law, including, but not limited to the TRIPS Agreement (Articles 7, 8, 30 and 31). The parties agree that measures to address adaptation shall be especially treated as emergencies.
- All possible policy avenues to accelerate research, development, demonstration and diffusion of climate-friendly technology, should be explored, including the use of all flexibilities, exceptions and limitations in international and national patent and related intellectual property rules, as well as innovative uses of intellectual property mechanisms, licensing practices, and alternative modes of innovation and diffusion.
- UNFCCC parties agree that the TRIPS Agreement, the International Convention for the Protection of New Varieties of Plants, the International Treaty on Plant Genetic Resources for Agriculture, and the WIPO Copyright Treaty ("the international IP treaties') do not and should not prevent UNFCCC parties from taking measures to address climate change mitigation and adaptation. Accordingly, while reiterating their commitment to the international IP treaties, they should affirm that these agreements can and should be interpreted and implemented in a manner supportive of UNFCCC members obligations to adopt measures necessary to address climate change mitigation under Article 4 of the Convention, to enable their citizens to adapt to the effects of climate change and to promote the public interest in sectors of vital importance to their socio-economic and technological development. They should reaffirm the right of UNFCCC parties to use, to the full, the provisions in these international treaties, which provide flexibility for this purpose.
- In disputes relating to the application and interpretation of measures under this declaration, parties agree that they shall submit to prior binding

---

[1348] Id.

arbitration under the TEC (under rules to be negotiated by the TEC and Advisory Board) for a determination of whether the measure in dispute was carried out in pursuit of meeting the obligation of the defending party under the UNFCCC, its protocols and COP decisions. Parties agree to be bound by such a determination in any dispute settlement complaints that they bring before any other body. This is meant to address the balancing requirement for necessity required by the panel approaches to GATT and TRIPS exceptions, and the 'necessity' requirement.

- Parties also agree that they shall refrain from unilateral measures to address disputes related to actions taken under this declaration, specifically threats or unilateral measures such as withdrawal of trade preferential treatment or market access.

IV. Chapter Conclusion

The proposals that conclude this chapter draw from the findings in the earlier chapters. They are extensions in many cases of existing practices in the UNFCCC or from other regimes. They address directly identified gaps in the UNFCCC mechanisms themselves, based directly on the scale of the problem in terms of timing, scope and geography. Crucially, they are not norm-setting proposals and cannot be characterized as such. Nothing about them requires a change in the existing norms and standards for intellectual property protection. The contingent question that this thesis asked has been answered in the affirmative: TRIPS does bar or limit the effectiveness of interventions that countries can take to address behaviour by an intellectual property rightholder that limits the adoption, adaptation and replication of climate technologies. However, when it comes to norm setting, the hurdle for necessity may not have been reached. What makes it difficult to answer whether norm-setting is really required is the paucity of real data regarding the existence and use of patent in the relevant technology sectors in the relevant national situations. We need more information, but as discussed in the early part of this chapter, waiting is not costless and waiting for certainty may result in higher costs and necessitate more extreme action in the future. What is clear is that any norm setting proposal cannot just tinker around the edges of the existing system if it is to address the full scale of the climate challenge. It seems appropriate to close this chapter with a reminder of what is at stake:

First, the timing issue – it is difficult to avoid the evidence that peaking will have to take place between 2015 and 2018. The data and scenarios tend to agree that peaking somewhere between 2015 and 2018 will be required if we are to stand a reasonable chance of reducing emissions by 80% by 2050 (relative to 2007 levels) and to stabilize at an increase of only 1.5-2 degrees Celsius.[1349] There is significant evidence and consensus that peaking can be achieved with existing or near commercialization technologies.[1350]

Second, there is also the issue of scope of technologies. Peaking can only be achieved with rapid uptake of existing technology at a rate unprecedented in human history. The need for rapid distribution of technological products is clearly paramount and economies of scale have to be achieved in a very short period of time. The immediate availability of more efficient and low emission processes in all fields is crucial to shifting industries away from GHG-reliant paths and to preventing lock-in. In Chapter 2, and Chapter 3, the evidence on existing rates of market diffusion, even between developed country partners suggests that existing rates of licensing and transactions related to deployment and diffusion of climate technology are likely to be insufficient.[1351] The process of licensing negotiations or other bilateral exchanges between rightholders and users of their technologies are too slow. While the facilitative mechanisms outlined above present serious attempts to reduce the costs of transactions, what is needed is an almost frictionless system. However, we may also need to address the issue of uncertainty by not making unduly permanent changes in the innovation system, especially if we wish to maintain the dynamic efficiencies and production of new technologies in the post-2025 period after peaking. As noted in Chapter 3, adaptive capacity must also be built up as quickly as possible in the near term to ensure increased resilience and survivability in the post-peak period, when changes of at least 1 degree Celsius appear to be already locked-in.[1352]

It is also important in a world in which complex technologies consist of multiple patents that the focus is on increasing the capacity to access, use and adapt products rather than specific patented components. The solutions proposed must operate at the level of the product, not just at the one or more technological inventions contained within a product. With respect to processes, the need is to address products produced by such processes and to the specific technologies that enable process change or efficiency, which are more likely embedded in the single patent or technology. What this means is that actions aimed at these technologies are not likely to have 100% congruence with specific patent classifications. The scope and effect of action will therefore be limited only to those situations wherein a patent (product or process) is being used for a particular designated climate technological purpose. A norm-setting solution would also have to address not just patents but the full panoply of intellectual

---

[1349] See p67, IPCC, *Climate Change 2007: Synthesis Report. Contribution of Working Groups I, II and III to the Fourth Assessment Report of the Intergovernmental Panel on Climate Change* [Core Writing Team, Pachauri, R.K and Reisinger, A. (eds.)] (Geneva: IPCC, 2007).
[1350] p68, Id.
[1351] See e.g. p48, Lee, B et al. "Who owns our Low Carbon Future: Intellectual Property and Energy Technologies" Chatham House, September 2009.
[1352] p12, Stern, N et al. *The Economics of Climate Change: The Stern Review* (Cambridge: Cambridge University Press, 2007).

property rights including: plant breeders' rights, copyright and trade secrets rights embedded, contained in, or consisting of technological products and processes for climate change mitigation and adaptation.

The elements above outline one simple proposition: that norm-setting measures to address intellectual property to address climate change cannot consist of half-measures. TRIPS has become the primary regulatory tool for managing the global generation and diffusion of technologies. A response to the challenge of climate change will have to operate at that global level. It may be too early as it stands to specify exactly what the response should be. Further research may indicate further structural problems in global technology markets related to intellectual property and the trend lines continue in the direction in which they appear to be heading. Without data on licensing and the kinds of costs and terms being imposed, any concrete proposal will be flying somewhat blind in terms of hitting its target.

Climate change presents a radical challenge to existing structures of production and consumption, and in particular to our existing modes of decision-making and legal implementation. The uncertainty does not just lie in the extent to which we must act to mitigate and adapt to climate change but also in whether or not existing regulations pose a barrier or create too much friction to enable action to address climate change. In implementing solutions, there is always the fear of doing more damage and creating new problems while trying to solve another problem. There is also, however, the sense that delayed action may make effective action at a later date extremely costly or not possible at all. These uncertainties are complicated by deep divisions between developed and developing countries on burden sharing, on the scale and sources of financing, on the scale and sources of technology transfer. Pragmatism requires that any workable solution must balance between all of the competing demands and uncertainties. The scale of the climate change problem however, may require radical solutions that have broad impact. There is clearly much more work to be done to provide better information on which to base solutions, especially in the arena of empirical evidence relating to the scale and scope of technology transfer and the role of intellectual property. However, I believe that this book has provided at least one key to the puzzle: an assessment of the existing limits of the international IP system and the ways in which it is insufficient as things stand to enable technology transfer at the scale and scope necessary. What I have tried to show is that the response to this need not be to rip the system up root and branch, but to target very specific mechanisms which can be adjusted and made to work *for* rather than *against* technology transfer through facilitation of transactions, and elaboration of existing obligations. Most importantly, this book has demonstrated not only that the UNFCCC can act to address these issues as a matter of international law and its own competence and mandate, and, hopefully, it has shown that it *should* act.

Chapter 10
Summary

This thesis faced the challenge of answering a question that may have seemed to many to already have been asked and answered. However, it was that very assumption that this thesis proposed to challenge and doing so required looking at the manner in which the question was framed and the context in which it was asked. The question had been asked in order to address the question of whether it was necessary for the UNFCCC or any other international body to address intellectual property regarding climate change. The way in which it was answered, was to ask empirical questions about the existence and distribution of patents, and whether this was a barrier to technology transfer. The error in focusing on the empirical issues was two-fold: it did not address the actual problem which was not the existence of patents, but the uses to which they were put, especially licensing; and it did not address the actual issue of regulatory freedom to address intellectual problems if they were to arise.

Understandably wishing to avoid having to revisit the entire intellectual property system, empirical studies aimed to design around the issue by showing that there are no empirical concerns regarding intellectual property protection in developing countries. If there are few patents in the industries studied, if there are few patents in the countries studied, if the patents that exist are not in the hands of concentrated ownership, then the necessity for developing countries to take unilateral actions beyond the existing intellectual property framework does not exist, and there is no need to renegotiate international intellectual property norms. The Copenhagen Economics/IPR Company Study,[1353] the Chatham House Study[1354], the EPO/UNEP/ICTSD Study[1355], the Dechezleprêtre et. al. Study[1356] and the John Barton ICTSD study[1357] all work within this framework. They all seek to answer the question of whether intellectual property

---

[1353] Copenhagen Economics and the IPR Company "Are IPRs a Barrier to the Transfer of Climate Change Technology?" Study Commissioned by European Commission DG Trade, January 2009.
[1354] Lee, B et al. "Who owns our Low Carbon Future: Intellectual Property and Energy Technologies" Chatham House, September 2009.
[1355] Karachalios, K et al. (eds.) "Patents and Clean Energy: Bridging the Gap between Evidence and Policy: Final report" UNEP/ EPO / ICTSD 2010.
[1356] Dechezleprêtre, A et al. "Invention and Transfer of Climate Change–Mitigation Technologies: A Global Analysis" 5 Rev Environ Econ Policy 109 (2011).
[1357] Barton, J "Intellectual Property and Access to Clean Energy Technologies in Developing Countries: An Analysis of Solar Photovoltaic, Biofuel and Wind Technologies" Trade and Sustainable Energy Series, Issue Paper No. 2, ICTSD December 2007.

poses a barrier to action empirically. However, I argued that the barrier question has always been a contingent one rather than one that is susceptible solely through empirical determination. Thus, in this thesis, I divided the broader question into two elements: the necessity to act; and where there is necessity to act, is there capacity to act? The first is an empirical question but the second is a legal question. The issue of whether the UNFCCC, or any other international regime, should act to address intellectual property lies, primarily in the answer to the second question rather than the first. This is because necessity to act (of the country, not the UNFCCC) is actually an issue that is primarily legal rather empirical. The room and the ability to act is determined by how necessity is framed in the international rules as much by the conditions in the national market, the behaviour of rightholders in that market, framed within the policy goal of addressing climate change. To the extent that global assessments of the distribution of patents, ownership of patents, can tell us where problems are likely to arise, if at all, they provide useful information. To the extent that such global assessments tell us something about the nature and scope of licensing and other uses of intellectual property protected technologies, they provide useful information as to the kinds of interventions that may be needed. However, given the variety of different countries, with different markets, with varying technology needs, and varying distributions of patent protection use, *a priori* determinations that a country or set of countries they will not need to take particular kinds of action to address intellectual property issues can never truly be made.

However, I do not aim to dismiss such global empirical approaches. I believe they can provide crucial information to policymakers regarding potential opportunities and blockages in international technology markets. It is on this basis that I have made several proposals in Chapter 9 for the ways in which the UNFCCC should address technology transfer and especially investment, market access and licensing related to intellectual property protected technologies. After all, based on the existing studies examine in Chapter 4, it was possible to tentatively conclude that:

- existing data in the very limited set of sectors studied show concentrated ownership of patents in developed countries, largely OECD. Of patents that exist in developing countries, the vast majority are in China. In terms of ownership by developing countries, China may have the largest ownership but this is still relatively small in comparison to OECD rightholders;

- The majority of technologies in the very limited set are likely not patented in least developed countries. They are almost certain to be patented in China, and in the main emerging economies of Brazil, India and China;

- with respect to licensing in some of the sectors (especially wind and solar), there appears to be some evidence of licensing to major developing countries, but with some suggestion of geographical and other restrictions;

- What licensing there is appears to be from national or smaller companies, not necessarily in possession of best available technologies, and not from transnational enterprises with significant production capacity of their own.

The lesson from these studies lies in the insight they provide regarding the dearth of technology transactions, and the pace of diffusion of intellectual property protected technologies. What data we have from Chapter 3 also points to trends in patenting; increasing overall patenting in climate technologies, and a significant jump in R&D accompanied by significant transfers of IP into private sector hands.

I also argue that, for the most part, the studies on the distribution of patenting fail by their own measures. The studies tell us very little about how patents in the sectors studied are exercised. In addition, there are basic methodological differences regarding the use of patent data that limit the scope of conclusions that they can make. This critical analysis of the relatively small pool of studies so far has not really been carried out before, especially within the framework that has been used here by looking at the scope of technologies, the timing of distribution of technologies, and the geographic focus. This critique provides a way of properly assessing the claims made as to nature and scale of the intellectual property problem for technology transfer; and this thesis concludes that while a useful start they do not provide sufficient purchase for a policy decision based purely on their findings.

The problem of course is that the default of taking no action is entirely congruent with the untenable recommendations [1358] that no action is necessary to address intellectual property at this time. The mistake is to conflate taking action regarding intellectual property with taking action to address intellectual property norm-setting. It seems entirely appropriate to conclude from their findings that some action regarding intellectual property needs to take place, especially regarding licensing and transaction, without necessarily concluding that norms on intellectual property need to be changed.

The primary sin is one of scope: the landscapes and studies cover only a small sector of relevant technologies, mostly focused on mitigation, and within that power generation. The discussion in chapter 2 constructed a set of technologies of particular relevance to developing countries based on TNAs, NAMAs, National Communications and several scenarios based on mitigation potentials. That extensive discussion was necessary to drive the point home that the scope of technologies is necessarily wide and that studies and recommendations for action must be commensurate with that.

[1358] See e.g. Copenhagen Economics and the IPR Company "Are IPRs a Barrier to the Transfer of Climate Change Technology?" Study Commissioned by European Commission DG Trade, January 2009.

The importance of timing is also crucial. Almost all studies looking at intellectual property and climate change ignore the issue of timing and the role of timing in influencing the assessment of how a barrier operates. Intellectual property creates a friction in the number and scope of technology transactions that take place. We have to be concerned not just about the static volume of patenting but also the effect of patenting on the rate of diffusion. That means that we must ask about the extent to which patenting may delay adoption and diffusion of technologies by relevant peaking dates, in the case of mitigation, 2015-2018, in terms of adaptation, 2025-2030. Where the existence and exercise of patent rights creates frictions that delay the adoption adaptation and replication of climate technologies in developing countries, we have to consider that this may indeed pose a barrier, even if it is not an absolute bar. This thesis concludes that while there is insufficient data to address this in the existing studies, there is some small indication (e.g. the Chatham House study) that diffusion is not happening fast enough due to the limited number of transactions into developing countries.

Finally, the studies generally have committed the sin of not taking geography and the potential of major emerging economies seriously enough. While all focus on the nature and scale of patenting into major developing countries, especially in relation to developed countries, there is rarely enough in depth study of the intellectual property structure of relevant technology sectors at the national level and the role of exports of technology and goods to other developing countries. Some of the best data could have been obtained by focusing on the key developing country markets of Brazil, China, India and South Africa, and, in those jurisdictions and asking:

- Based on the technology needs identified for that country, what is the portion of patenting in those technologies and technology sectors;

- Based on the patented sectors, what is the nature (cost and terms) and scale of licensing of those technologies to domestic firms;

- Looking at technological capacity; what is the trend in the capacity of domestic firms to adopt, adapt and replicate the technologies in the sectors identified in the technology needs.

This kind of research program will still allow some comparative sectoral based work, but will be rooted in the actual technology needs of developing countries and provide sufficient depth to provide useful information about the necessity to act on norm-setting at the international level if the data show that developing countries are unable to take action to address key issues that arise in multiple jurisdictions at a significant scale. Only such findings may provide sufficient impetus for a multilateral solution of sufficient scale in intellectual property norm-setting. Without such information, this thesis finds it difficult to recommend with confidence a course of action at the UNFCCC or any other international body aimed at norm-setting, despite the finding that where the behaviour by an intellectual property right holder bars or limits or TRIPS does indeed bar or limit the capacity of developing countries to make interventions to address:

> a. *Affordability - ensuring that prices of products are not set so high that it is too expensive for all the relevant economic actors to afford.*
>
> b. *Adoptability - ensuring that prices of products and or know-how are not set so high that they make it commercially unviable for all relevant actors to adopt 'climate-friendly' technologies.*
>
> c. *Adaptability – ensuring sufficient distribution of knowledge (information, skills, know-how) to enable a critical number of existing producers/service providers in the market to adopt, adapt and replicate climate technologies and ensure their participation in the market.*

The findings in Chapter 6 depended on identifying the kinds of interventions that developing countries would ostensibly use and examining them in the light of existing WTO and TRIPS jurisprudence. This framework brings something new to the literature which has traditionally looked simply at the agreement itself and the flexibilities it contains. This thesis adds to the literature by first identifying a universe of interventions that have historically been used to encourage technology transfer and that are relevant to technology transfer for climate change; examining whether or not TRIPS addresses them; and finally, discussing the scope of activity available under TRIPS as a legal matter. The novel approach that this thesis takes is to situate the legal analysis directly within the framework of the policy goal that such interventions are meant to achieve. Thus, availability was defined not just in legal terms but in terms of whether it enabled action at the right speed, at the right scope, and in the right countries. Where a purely legal analysis might indeed have found that the TRIPS Agreement does not pose a significant limitation on the universe of potential actions, this allows me to examine the scope and nature of the actions that are legally available and note the ways in which the TRIPS Agreement limits their potential impact, and to conclude that their ability to make changes to market structures and behaviour is severely curtailed. The IP-related interventions that would be most effective as levers have been marginalized and reduced in scope and effectiveness by the TRIPS Agreement. The use of working requirements, one of the more powerful historical incentives for encouraging licensing and FDI has been curtailed. The use of patent exclusions in key sectors of public interest such as pharmaceuticals and agriculture is no longer available. Most importantly, few of the remaining flexibilities allow for the emerging economies to play the role as intermediaries and export products and know-how as they need to do if technologies are to be transferred to other developing countries at the scale and speed required.

The most useful tools that are left legally and practically available by the TRIPS Agreement are the application of competition law and the use of performance and technology transfer requirements, as well as requirements to have FDI take place in the form of JVs. The rest are smaller, marginal adjustments to domestic intellectual property systems.

This is not to say that there do not remain significant interventions available to developing countries. The list of activities in Chapter 6 that the TRIPS Agreement does not address or limit remains quite extensive. Further research should examine the extent to which these options are actually being exercised by developing countries, looking at their effectiveness in timing, scale and scope. It may be that developing countries have indeed not taken up and used to the fullest the available measures to encourage technology transfer. It may be that some have even signed on to other international regimes, such as bilateral investment treaties, that place additional limits on the measures that TRIPS does not address. In addition, many may have signed on to bilateral and regional free trade agreements that further restrict their ability to use measures identified as legally available in this thesis. It will be important to assess for each country the extent to which this has occurred and the extent to which they are free to take action to remove such restrictions.

Finally, developing countries find themselves placed in a peculiar position in the relationship between TRIPS and the climate change regime. In the event that a country finds that there are actions that it wishes to undertake in order to benefit from rights or implement obligations from one treaty that are prevented by their obligations under another treaty, they can appeal to conflict resolution mechanisms in international law that provide a framework for interpreters to either give priority to one set of obligations or to find a way to make the obligations mutually supportive and implementable.[1359] This thesis concludes that the UNFCCC does not present such an obligation to developing countries because their obligations under the treaty to reduce emissions are conditional. Article 4.7 of the UNFCCC makes the implementation of their obligations under the UNFCCC dependent on being provided sufficient technology and financial support. Chapter 7 shows that they cannot use their obligations under the UNFCCC as a justification for taking actions that are not compliant with the TRIPS Agreement. This limitation is also exacerbated by the fact that WTO law remains hostile to the intrusion of non-WTO law in its dispute settlement process providing very little purchase for entry of UNFCCC treaty language in any case, even if it applied. As long as the approach in the WTO panel case *EC – Approval and Marketing of Biotech Products*[1360] remains applicable, then, absent any other statement from within the institutions of the WTO, the UNFCCC cannot be used as applicable law between the

---

[1359] Pauwelyn, J *Conflict of Norms in Public International Law: How WTO Law Relates to Other Rules of International Law*. (New York: Cambridge University Press, 2003.). In line with Condon, B "Climate Change and Unresolved Issues in WTO Law" 12 J. Int'l Econ. L. 895 (2009).
[1360] See para. 7.70 – 7.71, Panel Reports, European Communities – Measures Affecting the Approval and Marketing of Biotech Products, WT/DS291/R / WT/DS292/R / WT/DS293/R, Add.1 to Add.9, and Corr.1, adopted 21 November 2006, DSR 2006:III-VIII, 847 (*EC – Approval and Marketing of Biotech Products*)

parties to a dispute at the WTO that challenges a unilateral measure that has an effect on a TRIPS-related right or obligation.

I also conclude, in Chapter 7, that the hope that framing technology transfer as a human rights matter and thus part of the general international law that the WTO must consider remains an untested assertion at best. There is no indication that the rights most relevant in this framework of economic, social and cultural rights are of such universality and integral nature as to trigger the obligation of other regimes to integrate them as applicable law. In addition, intellectual property law has a special place in human rights law where intellectual property-like rights are part of the human rights framework rather than external to it. Thus one cannot reach to the human rights framework to try and use it to impose other considerations when the human rights framework itself contains an obligation of a sort to protect rights in intangible creative property. In the end, in Chapter 8, I suggest that recourse to broader structures of international law may be the only option, with developing countries working in the UNFCCC and other international fora to take a far more active role in integrating the values of regimes such as the UNFCCC into the WTO by using 'interaction' clauses that explicitly state the intention to construct a particular relationship to the other regime. The limits of this are clearly political: to the extent that countries are unable to negotiate relaxations of norms in the WTO itself, they may not be able to agree to do so in the UNFCCC or other fora. I provide some framing that developing countries can use to make an effective case for the jurisdiction and competence of one venue over another on issues such as sustainable development and technology transfer, and to take advantage of the differing constitutional frameworks of the UNFCCC regime compared to that of the WTO.

The scale of the climate challenge can be daunting. The combination of the language of catastrophe, with the long time frame for action, and the initially slow growth of climate impacts creates an environment where caution and incrementalism prevail. Nobody wants to spend all their time staring into the sun. And yet, in the case of climate change, it seems the incrementalists may not be the true realists. In addressing climate change true realism may require that we all become radicals, an uncomfortable thought, especially for traditional intellectual property scholars and lawyers. It is a habit of thought to which environmental lawyers and scholars have had more time to become accustomed. It is my hope that this thesis, by working to bridge the frameworks of both areas of law goes some way to providing a proper basis for a fruitful conversation between the intellectual property and climate change regimes.

Bibliography

Books

Abbott, F M *International Intellectual Property in an Integrated World Economy*, (New York, NY: Aspen Publishers/Wolters Kluwer, 2007).

Agrawala, S (ed.) *Bridge Over Troubled Waters: Linking Climate Change and Development* OECD Environment Directorate, 2005.

Agrawala, S and S Fankhauser *Economic Aspects of Adaptation to Climate Change: Costs, Benefits and Policy Instruments* (Paris: OECD, 2008.)

Andreassen, B A and S P Marks (eds.) *Development as a Human Right: Legal, Political, and Economic Dimensions* (Cambridge: Harvard University Press, 2006.)

Baumert, K A.et al *Navigating the Numbers: Greenhouse Gas Data and International Climate Policy*, World Resources Institute 2005. Available at: http://archive.wri.org/publication_detail.cfm?pubid=4093

Bellman, C *Trading in Knowledge: Development Perspectives on TRIPS, Trade and Sustainability*, (London: Earthscan Publications, 2003).

Bernasconi-Osterwalder, N et al., *Environment and Trade: A Guide to WTO Jurisprudence* (London: Earthscan, 2006).

Correa, C *Integrating Public Health Concerns into Patent Legislation in Developing Countries* (Geneva: South Centre, 2000)

Correa, C M *Trade Related Aspects of Intellectual Property Rights: A Commentary on the TRIPS Agreement*, (Oxford: Oxford Univ. Press, 2007).

Cullet, P *Intellectual Property and Sustainable Development* (London: LexisNexis Butterworths, 2005)

Deere, C *The Implementation Game: The TRIPS Agreement and the Global Politics of Intellectual Property Reform in Developing Countries* (Oxford: Oxford University Press, 2008)

Doranova, A *Technology Transfer and Learning under The Kyoto Regime: Exploring the Technological Impact of CDM Projects In Developing Countries* PhD Thesis UNU-Merit, Maastricht University (2009). Available at: http://arno.unimaas.nl.ezproxy.ub.unimaas.nl/show.cgi?fid=20141

Drahos, P *Global Intellectual Property Rights: Knowledge, Access and Development*, (New York: Palgrave Macmillan, 2002)

Gad, M O *Representational Fairness in WTO Rule Making: Negotiating, Implementing, and Disputing the TRIPS Pharmaceutical-related Provisions*, (London: British Institute of International and Comparative Law, 2006).

Gervais, D *The TRIPS Agreement: Drafting History and Analysis*, (London: Sweet & Maxwell, 2003)

Gervais, D *Intellectual Property, Trade and Development: Strategies to Optimize Economic Development in a TRIPS-Plus Era*, (Oxford: Oxford University Press, 2007).

GNESD *Reaching the Millennium Development Goals and beyond – access to modern forms of energy as a prerequisite*. (Roskilde: Global Network on Energy for Sustainable Development, 2007);

Helpman, E *The Mystery of Economic Growth* (Cambridge, Mass.: Belknap Press of Harvard University Press, 2004)

Hoekman, B *Global Integration and Technology Transfer*, (Basingstoke, UK; New York: Palgrave Macmillan; Washington, D.C.: World Bank, 2006)

IEA, *Energy Technology Perspectives 2010: Scenarios and Strategies to 2050*, (Paris: IEA/OECD, 2010).

IEA, *Energy Technology Perspectives 2012: Pathways to a Clean Energy System* (Paris: IEA/OECD 2012). Available at: www.iea.org/etp

IPCC, *Climate Change 2007: Synthesis Report. Contribution of Working Groups I, II and III to the Fourth Assessment Report of the Intergovernmental Panel on Climate Change* [Core Writing Team, Pachauri, R.K and Reisinger, A. (eds.)]. (Geneva: IPCC, 2007)

Malthus T R *An essay on the principle of population*, (London: J. Johnson, in St. Paul's Church-yard, 1798.)

Maskus, K & J Reichman (eds.) *International Public Goods and Transfer of Technology under a Globalized Intellectual Property Regime*, (Cambridge: Cambridge University Press, 2005).

Maskus, K & C Fink (eds.) *Intellectual Property and Development: Lessons from Recent Economic Research* (Washington D.C.: World Bank, 2005).

May, C and S Sell *Intellectual Property Rights: A Critical History* (Lynne Rienner Publishers, 2005).

National Science Board *Science and Engineering Indicators 2012* (Arlington VA: National Science Foundation, 2012). Available at: http://www.nsf.gov/statistics/seind12/start.htm (last visited 15 August 2014)

OECD *Invention and Transfer of Environmental Technologies*, OECD Studies on Environmental Innovation, OECD Publishing. (2011)

Ostergard, R L *The development dilemma: the political economy of intellectual property rights in the international system*, (New York: LFB Scholarly Pub., 2003).

Patel, S. et al. (eds.), *International Technology Transfer: The Origins and Aftermath of the United Nations Negotiations on a Draft Code of Conduct*, (Amsterdam: Kluwer, 2001). A 1985 version of the Draft International Code of Conduct on the Transfer of Technology is available at http://stdev.unctad.org/compendium/documents/totcode%20.html (last visited 15 August 2014)

Pauwelyn, J *Conflict of Norms in Public International Law - How WTO Law Relates to Other Rules of International Law* (Cambridge: Cambridge University Press 2003).

Penrose, E T *The Economics of the International Patent System*, (Baltimore: Johns Hopkins Press, 1951).

Rao, M B *Understanding TRIPS: Managing Knowledge in Developing Countries*, (New Delhi: Response Books; Thousand Oaks, CA: Sage Publications, 2003)

Rimmer, M *Intellectual Property and Climate Change: Inventing Clean Technologies* (London: Edward Elgar, 2011)

Roffe, P *Negotiating Health: Intellectual Property and Access to Medicines*, (London; Sterling, VA: Earthscan, 2006).

Santos-Paulino, A and W Guanghua, (eds.) *Southern Engines of Global Growth* (Oxford: Oxford University Press, 2010)

Sinjela, M *Human Rights and Intellectual Property Rights: Tensions and Convergences*, (Leiden & Boston: Martinus Nijhoff Publishers, 2007).

Smith, D *Just One Planet: Poverty, Justice, and Climate Change* Practical Action Publishing, 2006.

Stern, N et al. *The Economics of Climate Change: The Stern Review* (Cambridge: Cambridge University Press, 2007)

Trebilcock, M and M Mota Prado *What Makes Poor Countries Poor? Institutional Determinants of Development* (London: Edward Elgar, 2011)

UNDP *Handbook for Carrying Out Technology Needs Assessment for Climate Change* (New York: UNDP 2010)

UNEP, *Towards a Green Economy: Pathways to Sustainable Development and Poverty Eradication*, (Nairobi: UNEP, 2011). Available at: www.unep.org/greeneconomy, (last visited March 9, 2014).

Weeramantry, C G (ed.) *Human Rights and Scientific and Technological Development* (The United Nations University Press, 1990). Available at: http://www.unu.edu/unupress/unupbooks/uu06he/uu06he00.htm (last visited 15 August 2014)

WHO UN-*Water Global Annual Assessment of Sanitation and Drinking-Water (GLAAS) 2012: Targeting Resources for Better Results*. (Geneva:WHO, 2012). Available at http://www.who.int/water_sanitation_health/glaas/en/ (last visited 15 August 2014)

Wilkins, G *Technology transfer for renewable energy: overcoming barriers in developing countries* (London: Earthscan, 2002).

World Resources 1998-1999: *Environmental Change and Human Health – 1998: A Guide to the Global Environment*, A joint publication of the World Resources Institute (WRI), the United Nations Environment Programme (UNEP), the United Nations Development Programme (UNDP) and the World Bank (New York and Oxford: Oxford University Press, 1998).

Reports, Chapters and Articles

Abbott, F M "Innovation and Technology Transfer to Address Climate Change: Lessons from the Global Debate on Intellectual Property and Public Health", ICTSD's Programme on IPRs and Sustainable Development, Issue Paper No. 24, International Centre for Trade and Sustainable Development, Geneva, Switzerland, 2009.

Adger, W N, J Paavola, and S Huq, S. "Towards Justice in Adaptation to Climate Change" In Adger, W N, J Paavola, S Huq and J Mace (eds) Fairness in Adaptation to Climate Change MIT Press, 2006.

Adger, W N et. al, "Assessment of adaptation practices, options, constraints and capacity" in in M.L. Parry et. al. (Eds.) Climate Change 2007: Impacts, Adaptation and Vulnerability. Contribution of Working Group II to the Fourth Assessment Report of the Intergovernmental Panel on Climate Change, (Cambridge: Cambridge University Press, 2007). Available at http://www.ipcc.ch/ipccreports/ar4-wg2.htm (last visited 15 August 2014)

Ajemian, C and D Reid "Preventing Global Warming: The United States, China, and Intellectual Property" 115 Business and Society Review 417 (2010)

Akers, D Y and S Ecer "The TRIPS Agreement and its Effects on R&D Spending of US-Owned Multinational Enterprises in Developing Countries" Journal of World Trade Vol. 43, No. 6 (2009).

Alam, S "Trade Restrictions to Multilateral Environmental Agreements: Developmental Implications for Developing Countries" Journal of World Trade Vol. 45, No. 1 (2007).

Arora, A and A Fosfuri, "Licensing in the presence of competing technologies" 52 Journal of Economic Behavior and Organization 277 (2003).

Arrow, K "Economic Welfare and the Allocation of Resources for Invention' in The Rate and Direction of Economic Activity Economic and Social Factors (Princeton: Princeton University Press, 1962).

Arrow, K J et.al. , "Are We Consuming Too Much?" 18 Journal of Economic Perspectives 147 (2004).

Avato, P and J d'Entremont Coony "Accelerating Clean Energy Technology Research, Development, and Deployment: Lessons from Non-energy Sectors" World Bank Working Paper No. 138, World Bank, 2008.

Baer, P, T Athanasiou, and S Kartha, The Right to Development in a Climate Constrained World Heinrich Böll Foundation, 2007.

Baer, P, T Athanasiou, and S Kartha, "Revised Executive Summary" to The Right to Development in a Climate Constrained World, Heinrich Böll Foundation, June 2008.

Ballesteros, A et al. "Power, Responsibility and Accountability: Re-Thinking the Legitimacy of Institutions for Climate Finance" World Resources Institute, WRI Working Paper December 2009.

Baron, J & H Delcamp "Patent quality and value in discrete and cumulative innovation" Working Paper 2010-07, CERNA Working Paper Series, November 2010).

Barton, J "New Trends in Technology Transfer: Implications for National and International Policy", Issue Paper No. 18, ICTSD February 2007. Available at http://www.iprsonline.org/resources/docs/Barton%20-%20New%20Trends%20Technology%20Transfer%200207.pdf (last visited 15 August 2014)

Barton, J "Intellectual Property and Access to Clean Energy Technologies in Developing Countries An Analysis of Solar Photovoltaic, Biofuel and Wind

Technologies" Trade and Sustainable Energy Series, Issue Paper No. 2, ICTSD December 2007.

Bazilian, M et al. "Measuring Energy Access: Supporting a Global Target" Columbia University Earth Institute, 2010.

Best, D and E Levina "Facing China's Coal Future: Prospects and Challenges for CCS" Working Paper 2012, OECD/IEA 2012.

Boldrin, M and D Levine "The Case against Patents", 27 The Journal of Economic Perspectives, 3 (2013)

Bollyky, T "Intellectual Property Rights and Climate Change: Principles for Innovation and Access to Low-Carbon Technology" CGD Notes, Centre for Global Development, December 2009.

Bowen, A "Raising climate finance to support developing country action: some economic considerations, 11 Climate Policy 1020 (2011).

Bradbrook, A J and J G Gardam, "Placing Access to Energy Services within a Human Rights Framework" 28 Human Rights Quarterly 389 – (2006)

Branstetter, L et al. "Do Stronger Intellectual Property Rights Increase International Technology Transfer? Empirical Evidence from U.S. Firm-Level Data," Quarterly Journal of Economics, vol. 121, 321-349 (2006).

Brazil Ministry of Science and Technology Second National Communication of Brazil to the United Nations Framework Convention on Climate Change (Brasilia: Ministry of Science and Technology, Brazil, 2010). Available at: http://www.mct.gov.br/index.php/content/view/326984.html (last visited 15 August 2014)

Buckley, P J et al. "Inward FDI and host country productivity: evidence from China's electronics industry" 15(1) Transnational Corporations (2006)

Burleson, E "Energy Policy, Intellectual Property and Technology Transfer to Address Climate Change" 18 (1) Transnational Law and Contemporary Problems (2008).

Burleson, E "The Bali Climate Change Conference" 12(4) American Society of International Law Insights, (2008). Available at: http://ssrn.com/abstract=1107667 (last visited 15 August 2014)

Burleson, E "A Climate of Extremes: Transboundary Conflict Resolution" 32 Vermont Law Review, 477 (2008). Available at: http://ssrn.com/abstract=1017003 (last visited 15 August 2014)

Burleson, E "Multilateral Climate Change Mitigation" 41 University of San Francisco Law Review 373 (2007). Available at: http://ssrn.com/abstract=982763 (last visited 15 August 2014)

Carroll, M "One Size Does Not Fit All: A Framework for Tailoring Intellectual Property Rights" 70 Ohio St. L.J. 1361 (2009).

Chandra, V (ed.) "Technology, Adaptation, and Exports: How Some Developing Countries Got It Right" World Bank 2006.

Chapman, A "Development of Indicators for Economic, Social and Cultural Rights: The Rights to Education, Participation in Cultural Life and Access to the Benefits of Science," in Donders Y. and Volodin V. (eds) Human Rights in Education, Science and Culture: Legal Developments and Challenges, UNESCO 2007.

Chapman, A R "Approaching Intellectual Property as a Human Right: Obligations Related to Article 15(1)(c)" UN Doc. E/C.12/2000/12, 3 October 2000.

Chapman, A R "A Human Rights Perspective on Intellectual Property, Scientific Progress and Access to the Benefits of Science," in WIPO Intellectual Property and Human Rights World Intellectual Property Organization, 1999 pp. 127-68.

Chinese National Development and Reform Commission Second National Communication on Climate Change of The People's Republic of China (National Development and Reform Commission, 2012).

Chowdhury, A K et al. "The Impact of Climate Change on Least Developed Countries and Small Island Developing States" Report, United Nations Office of the High Representative for the Least Developed Countries, Landlocked Developing Countries And Small Island Developing States, June 2007.

CIEL "ICHRP Feasibility Study: Climate Change, Technology Transfer and Human Rights" Center for International Environmental Law, 2009. Available from CIEL on request.

Cohen, W M et al. "Protecting their Intellectual Assets: Appropriability Conditions and Why U.S. Manufacturing Firms Patent (or Not)". NBER Working Paper no. 7552 (2000).

Commission on Intellectual Property Rights, Innovation and Public Health "Public health, innovation and intellectual property rights: report of the Commission on Intellectual Property Rights, Innovation and Public Health" Geneva: WHO (2006). Available at:

http://www.who.int/intellectualproperty/documents/thereport/ENPublicHealthReport.pdf (last visited 15 August 2014)

Condon, B "Climate Change and Unresolved Issues in WTO Law" 12 J. Int'l Econ. L. 895 (2009).

Confalonieri, U et al., "Human Health", in M L Parry et al. (Eds.) Climate Change 2007: Impacts, Adaptation and Vulnerability. Contribution of Working Group II to the Fourth Assessment Report of the Intergovernmental Panel on Climate Change, (Cambridge: Cambridge University Press, 2007). Available at http://www.ipcc.ch/ipccreports/ar4-wg2.htm (last visited 15 August 2014)

Consilvio, M "The Role of Patents in the International Framework of Clean Technology Transfer: A Discussion of Barriers and Solutions" 3 Intell. Prop. Brief 10 (2011)

Copenhagen Economics and the IPR Company "Are IPR a Barrier to the transfer of Climate Change Technology?" Study Commissioned by European Commission DG Trade, January 2009. Available at:
http://trade.ec.europa.eu/doclib/docs/2009/february/tradoc_142371.pdf (last visited 15 August 2014)

Cordes-Holland, O "The Sinking of the Strait: The Implications of Climate Change for Torres Strait Islanders' Human Rights Protected by the ICCPR" ANU College of Law Research Paper No. 08-06 October 31, 2007
Available at: http://ssrn.com/abstract=1129087 (last visited 15 August 2014)

Correa, C M "The TRIPS Agreement: How Much Room for Maneuver?" (2001) 2 Journal of Human Development 79.

Correa, C "Intellectual Property and Competition Law: Exploration of Some Issues of Relevance to Developing Countries, ICTSD IPRs and Sustainable Development Programme Issue Paper No. 21, International Centre for Trade and Sustainable Development, Geneva, Switzerland. 2007.

Cosbey, A et al., "Which Way Forward? Issues in Developing an Effective Climate Regime after 2012" International Institute on Sustainable Development, 2005. Available at
http://www.iisd.org/pdf/2005/climate_which_way_forward.pdf (last visited 15 August 2014)

Craig, R K "A Public Health Perspective on Sea-Level Rise: Starting Points for Climate Change Adaptation" 15(2) Widener Law Review, 521 (2010).
Available at: http://ssrn.com/abstract=1119563 (last visited 15 August 2014)

Crespi, R S and J Straus "Intellectual Property, Technology Transfer and Genetic Resources: An OECD Survey of Current Practices and Policies" OECD 1996). Available at: http://www.oecd.org/dataoecd/60/11/1947170.pdf (last visited 15 August 2014)

Daily, G and P Erlich "Population, Sustainability and Earth's Carrying Capacity" 42 BioScience, 761 (1992).

Dasgupta, S et al. "The Impact of Sea Level Rise on Developing Countries: A Comparative Analysis" World Bank Policy Research Working Paper No. 4136, February 1, 2007. Available at SSRN: http://ssrn.com/abstract=962790 (last visited 15 August 2014)

Davis, K E "Regulation of Technology Transfer to Developing Countries: The Relevance of Institutional Capacity" 27 Law & Policy 6 (2005). Available at: http://ssrn.com/abstract=639770 (last visited 15 August 2014)

Dechezleprête, A et al. "The Clean Development Mechanism and the International Diffusion of Technologies: An Empirical Study", 36 Energy Policy 1273 (2008)

Dechezleprête A et al. "Technology Transfer by CDM Projects: A Comparison of Brazil, China, India and Mexico", 37 Energy Policy 703 (2009)

Dechezleprêtre, A et al. "Invention and Transfer of Climate Change–Mitigation Technologies: A Global Analysis" 5 Rev Environ Econ Policy 109 (2011).

De Coninck, H et al "Technology Transfer in the Clean Development Mechanism" 7 Climate Policy 444 (2007).

De Coninck, H et al. "International technology-oriented agreements to address climate change" 36 Energy Policy 335 (2008)

de Sepibus, J "Reforming the Clean Development Mechanism to accelerate Technology Transfer" Working Paper No 2009/42, NCCR Trade Regulation, Swiss National Centre of Competence in Research, November 2009.

den Uijl, S. et al. "Managing Intellectual Property Using Patent Pools: Lessons from Three Generations of Pools in the Optical Disc Industry" 55 California Management Review 31 (2013).

Derclaye, E "Intellectual Property Rights and Global Warming", 12 J. MARSHALL REV. INTELL. PROP. L. 263 (2008).

Derclaye, E "Not Only Innovation but also Collaboration, Funding, Goodwill and Commitment: Which Role for Patent Laws in Post-Copenhagen Climate Change Action", 9 J. MARSHALL REV. INTELL. PROP. L. 657 (2010).

Dernbach, J "Sustainable Development: Now More than Ever" 32 ELR 10004 (2002)

Dernis, H et al. "Using Patent Counts for Cross-Country Comparisons of Technology Output" 27 STI Review 129 (2001)

Domingos, N de Paula "The Interface between Climate Change and Trade Regimes through the Eyes of Brazil" 6 Fla. A & M U. L. Rev. 239 (2010-2011).

Driffield et al "The multinational enterprise as a source of international knowledge flows: Direct evidence from Italy" 41 Journal of International Business Studies 350 (2010).

Dernbach, J C "Energy Efficiency and Conservation as Ethical Responsibilities: Suggestions for IPCC Working Group III" Paper presented at Side-Event, Ethical Dimensions of Climate Change: Looking at the Work of the IPCC, at the Conference of the Parties to the U.N. Conference on Climate Change in Bali, Indonesia, December 14, 2007. Available at: http://ssrn.com/abstract=1089423 (last visited 15 August 2014)

Drumbl, M "Poverty, Wealth, and Obligation in International Environmental Law" Washington & Lee Public Law and Legal Theory Research Paper Series, Working Paper No. 01-19, September 2001. 76 Tulane Law Review, Winter 2002) Available at: http://ssrn.com/abstract=283204 (last visited 15 August 2014)

Easterling, W E et al., "Food, fibre and forest products" in M.L. Parry et al. (Eds.) Climate Change 2007: Impacts, Adaptation and Vulnerability. Contribution of Working Group II to the Fourth Assessment Report of the Intergovernmental Panel on Climate Change, (Cambridge: Cambridge University Press, 2007). Available at http://www.ipcc.ch/ipccreports/ar4-wg2.htm (last visited 15 August 2014)

Egenhofer, C et al. "Low-Carbon Technologies in the Post-Bali Period: Accelerating their Development and Deployment" European Climate Platform, report No. 4, December 2007.

EGTT "Overview of IPR Practices for Publicly-funded Technologies" Informal paper, EGTT 2005.

Ellis, J et al. "CDM: Taking stock and looking forward" 35 Energy Policy 15 (2007)

Elzinga, D et al. "Advantage Energy: Emerging Economies, Developing Countries and the Private-Public Sector Interface" International Energy Agency Information Paper, September 2011.

Enqvist, P A et al. "A Cost Curve for Greenhouse Gas Reduction" McKinsey Quarterly 2007:1

Farber, D A "Basic Compensation for the Victims of Climate Change" University of California, Berkeley Public Law Research Paper No. 954357, December 1, 2006. Available at: http://ssrn.com/abstract=954357 (last visited 15 August 2014)

Fekete, H. et al "Emerging economies – potentials, pledges and fair shares of greenhouse gas reduction" ENVIRONMENTAL RESEARCH OF THE GERMAN FEDERAL MINISTRY OF THE ENVIRONMENT, NATURE CONSERVATION AND NUCLEAR SAFETY Project-no. (FKZ) 3711 41 120, (Umweltbundesamt, Bonn, April 2013). Available at: http://www.umweltbundesamt.de/publikationen/emerging-economies-potentials-pledges-fair-shares (last visited 15 August 2014)

Foray, D "Technology Transfer in the TRIPS Age: the Need for New Types of Partnerships between the Least Developed and Most Advanced Economies" ICTSD Programme on IPRs and Sustainable Development, Issue Paper No. 23, International Centre for Trade and Sustainable Development, Geneva, Switzerland (2009).

Garrison, C "Exceptions to Patent Rights in Developing Countries" ICTSD Issue Paper No. 17 (August 2006).

Gechlick, M "Making Transfer of Clean Technology Work: Lessons of the Clean Development Mechanism" 11 San Diego International Law Journal 227 (2009)

GEF "Operational Guidelines for the Implementation of the Incremental Cost Principle" GEF/C.31/12, May 14, 2007, available at: http://www.thegef.org/gef/sites/thegef.org/files/documents/C.31.12%20Operational%20Guidelines%20for%20Incremental%20Costs.pdf (last visited 15 August 2014).

GEF "Note on Issues related to Intellectual Property Rights" GEF/C.13/Inf.14, December 1, 2009 (first issued for GEF Council Meeting, May 5 – 7, 1999.). Available at: http://www.thegef.org/gef/sites/thegef.org/files/documents/GEF.C.13.Inf .14.pdf (last visited 15 August 2014)

GEF "Implementing the Poznan Strategic and Long-Term Programs on Technology Transfer" Global Environment Facility, November 2012.

Gehl Sampath, P and P Roffe, "Unpacking the International Technology Transfer Debate: Fifty Years and Beyond" ICTSD Programme on Innovation, Technology and Intellectual Property Working Paper; International Centre for Trade and Sustainable Development, (2012).

Gehl Sampath, P et al. "Realizing the potential of the UNFCCC Technology Mechanism: Perspectives on the Way Forward" ICTSD Programme on Innovation, Technology and Intellectual Property; Issue Paper No. 35; International Centre for Trade and Sustainable Development, Geneva, Switzerland (2012)

Ghafele, R and R D O'Brien "Open innovation for Sustainability: Lessons from the GreenXchange Experience" Policy Brief No. 13, International Centre for Trade and Sustainable Development, Geneva, Switzerland, June 2012.

Glachant, M et al. "The Clean Development Mechanism and the International Diffusion of Technologies: An Empirical Study" FEEM Working Paper No. 105, December 2007. Available at: http://ssrn.com/abstract=1077151 (last visited 15 August 2014)

Goklany, I M "Applying the Precautionary Principle to Global Warming" Weidenbaum Center Working Paper No. PS 158 November 2000. Available at: http://ssrn.com/abstract=250380 (last visited 15 August 2014)

Guadamuz, A L "The Future of Technology Transfer in the Global Village" 3 Journal of World Intellectual Property 589 (2000) Available at: http://ssrn.com/abstract=569108 (last visited 15 August 2014)

Guellec, D and B van Pottelsberghe de la Potterie "Applications, Grants and the Value of a Patent", 69 Economics Letters 109 (2000).

Gueret, T "International Energy Technology Collaboration and Climate Change Mitigation: Case Study 3: Appliance Energy Efficiency" (COM/ENV/EPOC/IEA/SLT(2005)3) OECD Environment Directorate /International Energy Agency, 2005.

Hall, B H and C Helmers "The Role of Patent Protection in (Clean/Green) Technology Transfer" 26 Santa Clara Computer & High Tech. L.J. 487 (2009-2010).

Haites, E et al. "Technology Transfer by CDM Projects", 6 Climate Policy 327 (2006).

Hänsel, G et al. "Annual Status Report on Nationally Appropriate Mitigation Actions (NAMAs)", ECN, Ecofys, GIZ, CCAP (2013).

Hansen, U "An empirical case study of the transfer of GHG mitigation technologies from Annex 1 countries to Malaysia under the Kyoto Protocol's clean development mechanism (CDM)" 10(1) Int. J. Technology Transfer and Commercialisation, 1 (2011)

Haščič, I et al. "Climate Policy and Technological Innovation and Transfer: An Overview of Trends and Recent Empirical Results", OECD Environment Working Papers, No. 30, OECD Publishing (2010).

Haščič, I and N Johnstone "CDM and International Technology Transfer: Empirical Evidence on Wind Power", 11 Climate Policy 1303 (2011).

Helfer, L "Toward a Human Rights Framework for Intellectual Property" 40 University of California Davis Law Review Volume 971 (2007).

Heinzerling, L "Climate Change, Human Health, and the Post-Cautionary Principle" Georgetown Public Law Research Paper No. 1008923, September 2007. Available at: http://ssrn.com/abstract=1008923 (last visited 15 August 2014)

Hoekman, B, K E Maskus, and K Saggi, "Transfer of Technology to Developing Countries: Unilateral and Multilateral Policy Options" World Bank Policy Research Working Paper No. 3332. June 1, 2004. Available at: http://ssrn.com/abstract=610377 (last visited 15 August 2014)

Hodas, D and A Mumma "Designing a Global Post-Kyoto Climate Change Protocol that Advances Human Development" 20 Georgetown International Environmental Law Review 619 (2008). Available at: http://ssrn.com/abstract=1162770 (last visited 15 August 2014).

Hoffert, M I et al. "Advanced Technology Paths to Global Climate Stability: Energy for a Greenhouse Planet", 298 Science 981 (2002).

Horbach, J et al. "Lead Markets for Clean Coal Technologies: A Case Study for China, Germany, Japan and the USA" Discussion Paper No. 12-063, Center for European Economic Research, 2012.

Hugenholtz, P B and R G Okediji (2008), "Conceiving an International Instrument on Exceptions and Limitations to Copyright," iVir, March 06, 2008.

Humphreys, S "Climate Change and Human Rights: A Rough Guide" International Council for Human Rights Policy 2008. Available at: http://www.ichrp.org/en/projects/136 (last visited 15 August 2014).

Hutchison, C J "Does TRIPS Facilitate or Impede Climate Change Technology Transfer into Developing Countries?" 3 University of Ottawa Law & Technology Journal, 517 (2006). Available at: http://ssrn.com/abstract=1019365 (last visited 15 August 2014).

Imperial College Centre for Energy Policy and Technology "Assessment of technological options to address climate change: A report for the prime minister's strategy unit" Centre for Energy Policy and Technology, Imperial College London, 2002. Available at: http://www3.imperial.ac.uk/portal/pls/portallive/docs/1/7294718.PDF (last visited 15 August 2014).

International Climate Change Task Force "Meeting the Climate Challenge: Recommendations of the International Climate Change Task Force" Center for American Progress, January 2005.

ICHRP "Duties sans Frontières: Human Rights and Global Social Justice" International Council on Human Rights Policy, 2003.

IEA, "Tracking Clean Energy Progress: Energy Technology Perspectives 2012 excerpt as IEA input to the Clean Energy Ministerial" IEA 2012.

IEA, "IEA Implementing Agreements: Background and Framework as of 2003" IEA Paris, 2003.

ILC, 'Fragmentation of International Law: Difficulties Arising From the Diversification and Expansion of International Law, Report of the Study Group of the International Law Commission' (18 July 2006) UN Doc. A/CN.4/L.702

Indian Ministry of Environment and Forestry Second National Communication of India to the United Nations Framework Convention on Climate Change (Ministry of Environment and Forests, Government of India, 2012). Available at: https://unfccc.int/essential_background/library/items/3599.php?rec=j&priref=7626#beg (last visited 15 August 2014).

Intermediate Technology Development Group "Powering Poverty Reduction" Intermediate Technology Development Group Position Paper for Renewables 2004 Bonn, 1-4 June 2004. Available at: http://practicalaction.org/docs/advocacy/powering_poverty_reduction%20.pdf (last visited 15 August 2014).

Intermediate Technology Development Group "Power to the People" Intermediate Technology Development Group Briefing Paper 2002. Available at: http://practicalaction.org/docs/advocacy/powering_poverty_reduction%20.pdf (last visited 15 August 2014).

Intermediate Technology Development Group "Sustainable Energy for Poverty Reduction: An Action Plan" Intermediate Technology Development Group 2002. Available at: http://practicalaction.org/?id=energy_action_plan (last visited 15 August 2014).

IPCC, "Special Report on Renewable Energy Sources and Climate Change Mitigation. Prepared by Working Group III of the Intergovernmental Panel on Climate Change" [O. Edenhofer, R. Pichs-Madruga, Y. Sokona, K. Seyboth, P. Matschoss, S. Kadner, T. Zwickel, P. Eickemeier, G. Hansen, S. Schlömer, C. von Stechow (eds)]. (Cambridge University Press, Cambridge, United Kingdom and New York, NY, USA, 2011)

IPCC, "Managing the Risks of Extreme Events and Disasters to Advance Climate Change Adaptation. A Special Report of Working Groups I and II of the Intergovernmental Panel on Climate Change" [Field, C.B., V. Barros, T.F. Stocker, D. Qin, D.J. Dokken, K.L. Ebi, M.D. Mastrandrea, K.J. Mach, G.-K. Plattner, S.K. Allen, M. Tignor, and P.M. Midgley (eds.)]. (Cambridge University Press, Cambridge, UK, and New York, NY, USA, 2012)

IPCC "Summary for Policymakers" in Climate Change 2014, Mitigation of Climate Change. Contribution of Working Group III to the Fifth Assessment Report of the Intergovernmental Panel on Climate Change [Edenhofer, O., R. Pichs-Madruga, Y. Sokona, E. Farahani, S. Kadner, K. Seyboth, A. Adler, I. Baum, S. Brunner, P. Eickemeier, B. Kriemann, J. Savolainen, S. Schlömer, C. von Stechow, T. Zwickel and J.C. Minx (eds.).] (Cambridge University Press, Cambridge, United Kingdom and New York, NY, USA, 2014)

Ivus, O "Do Stronger Intellectual Property Rights Raise High-Tech Exports to the Developing World?" No 2008-27, Working Papers, Department of Economics, University of Calgary. Available at: http://EconPapers.repec.org/RePEc:clg:wpaper:2008-27 (last visited 15 August 2014).

Jha, V and U Hoffman (eds.) "Achieving Objectives of Multilateral Environmental Agreements: A Package of Trade Measures and Positive Measures Elucidated by Results of Developing Country Case Studies" UNCTAD/ITCD/TED/6, UNCTAD 2000. Available at: http://unctad.org/en/Docs/itcdted6_en.pdf (last visited 15 August 2014).

Johnson, D Gale, "Population, Food and Knowledge" 90 The American Economic Review 1 (2000).

Kallmorgen, J "Towards a Global Green Recovery – Supporting Green Technology Markets - Atlantic Task Force recommendations to the Policy Planning Staff of the German Federal Foreign Office" Atlantic Initiative, Berlin, 2009.

Kanwar, S "Intellectual Property Protection and Technology Transfer: Evidence from US Multinationals" University of California San Diego Department of Economics Discussion Paper No. 2007-05, July 1, 2007. Available at: http://ssrn.com/abstract=1001128 (last visited 15 August 2014).

Karachalios, K et al. (eds.) "Patents and Clean Energy: Bridging the Gap between Evidence and Policy: Final report" UNEP/ EPO / ICTSD 2010.

Kaswan, A "Environmental Justice and Domestic Climate Change Policy" Environmental Law Reporter, May 2008. Available at: http://ssrn.com/abstract=1077675 (last visited 15 August 2014).

Khan, B. Zorina "Intellectual Property and Development: Lessons from American and European History" Study paper 1a, for Commission on Intellectual Property Rights Integrating Intellectual Property Rights and Development Policy (London: Commission on Intellectual Property Rights 2002). Available at: http://www.iprcommission.org/graphic/documents.htm (last visited 15 August 2014).

Khor, M "Climate Change, Technology and Intellectual Property Rights: Context and Recent Negotiations" Research Paper 45, South Centre, April 2012.

Kim, Y K et al. "Appropriate Intellectual Property Protection and economic growth in countries at different levels of protection" 41 Research Policy 358 (2012).

Klein, R J T et al. "Application of Environmentally Sound Technologies for Adaptation to Climate Change" FCCC/TP2006/2, UNFCCC Technical Paper May 2006. Available at: http://unfccc.int/resource/docs/2006/tp/tp02.pdf (last visited 15 August 2014).

Kolshus, H H, J Vevatne, A Torvanger, K Aunan, "Can the Clean Development Mechanism Attain Both Cost-effectiveness and Sustainable Development Objectives?" CICERO Working Paper 2001:8, Center for International Climate and Environmental Research (CICERO), Oslo, pp. 1–22 (2001)

Koskenniemi, M et al. 'Fragmentation of International Law: Difficulties arising from the Diversification and Expansion of International Law: Report of the Study Group of the International Law Commission' (13 April 2006)

Kumar, N "Intellectual Property Rights, Technology and Economic Development: Experiences of Asian Countries" Study paper 1b, for Commission on Intellectual Property Rights Integrating Intellectual Property Rights and Development Policy (London: Commission on Intellectual Property Rights 2002). Available at: http://www.iprcommission.org/graphic/documents.htm (last visited 15 August 2014).

Kundzewicz, Z W et al. "Freshwater resources and their Management" in M.L. Parry et al. (Eds.) Climate Change 2007: Impacts, Adaptation and Vulnerability. Contribution of Working Group II to the Fourth Assessment Report of the Intergovernmental Panel on Climate Change, (Cambridge: Cambridge University Press, 2007). Available at http://www.ipcc.ch/ipccreports/ar4-wg2.htm (last visited 15 August 2014).

Kurukulasuriya, P and R O Mendelsohn "Crop Selection: Adapting to Climate Change in Africa" World Bank Policy Research Working Paper No. 4307, August 2007. Available at: http://ssrn.com/abstract=1005546 (last visited 15 August 2014).

Lee, B et al. "Who owns our Low Carbon Future: Intellectual Property and Energy Technologies" Chatham House, September 2009.

Lefevre, N "Deploying Climate –friendly Technologies through Collaboration with Developing Countries" International Energy Agency, Information Paper, November 2005.

Lema, A and R Lema "Technology transfer in the clean development mechanism: Insights from wind power" 23 Global Environmental Change 301 (2013).

Lemley, M A "Taking the Regulatory Nature of IP Seriously" (January 31, 2014). Stanford Law and Economics Olin Working Paper No. 455. Available at SSRN: http://ssrn.com/abstract=2388850 (last visited 15 August 2014).

Lewis, J "Technology Acquisition and Innovation in the Developing World: Wind Turbine Development in China and India" 42 St Comp Int Dev 208 (2007).

Li, X, "Behind the recent surge of Chinese patenting: An institutional view." 41 Research Policy 236 (2012).

Lindroos, A and M Mehling, "From Autonomy to Integration. International Law, Free Trade and the Environment" Vol. 7 Nordic Journal of International Law 253-273, 2008.

Lybbert, T "Technology Transfer for Humanitarian Use: Economic Issues and Market Segmentation Approaches" IP Strategy Today, No. 5, 2002, 17 – 25.

Mallet, A et al. "UK-India Collaboration to Identify the Barriers to the Transfer of Low Carbon Technology-Phase II Final report" (London: Department of Energy and Climate Change, UK, 2009).

Mandel, G "Promoting Environmental Innovation with Intellectual Property Innovation: A New Basis for Patent Rewards," 24(1) Temple Journal of Science, Technology, and Environmental Law 51 (2005).

Maskus, K E "Encouraging International Technology Transfer" ICTSD Issue Paper No. 7, May 2004. Available at: www.iprsonline.org/unctadictsd/docs/CS_Maskus.pdf (last visited 15 August 2014).

Maskus, K E "The Role of Intellectual Property Rights in Encouraging Foreign Direct Investment and Technology Transfer." 9 Duke J. of Comp. & Int'l L. 109 (1998). Available at: http://www.law.duke.edu/shell/cite.pl?9+Duke+J.+Comp.+&+Int%27l+L.+109 (last visited 15 August 2014).

Maskus, K E and J H Reichman, "The Globalization of Private Knowledge Goods and the Privatization of Global Public Goods" 7 Journal of International Economic Law 279 (2004). Available at: http://ssrn.com/abstract=692902 (last visited 15 August 2014).

Maskus, K "Differentiated Intellectual Property Regimes for Environmental and Climate Technologies", OECD Environment Working Papers, No. 17, OECD Publishing 2010.

McGranahan, G et al. "The rising tide: assessing the risks of climate change and human settlements in low elevation coastal zones." 19(1) Environment and Urbanization 17 (2007).

McGray, H et al. Weathering the Storm: Options for Framing Adaptation and Development World Resources Institute, 2007. Available at: http://www.wri.org/publication/weathering-the-storm (last visited 15 August 2014).

Metz, B et al., "Methodological and Technological Issues in Technology Transfer" A Special Report of the Intergovernmental Panel on Climate Change, July 2000. Available at: http://www.ipcc.ch/ipccreports/sres/tectran/index.htm (last visited 15 August 2014).

Misati, E and K Adachi, "The Research and Experimentation Exceptions in Patent Law: Jurisdictional Variations and the WIPO Development Agenda" UNCTAD- ICTSD Project on IPRs and Sustainable Development, Policy Brief Number 7, March 2010.

Moon, S "Does TRIPS Art. 66.2 Encourage Technology Transfer to the LDCS?: An Analysis of Country Submissions to the TRIPS Council (1999-2007)" Presentation at Workshop on "Encouraging Technology Transfer to LDCs: Towards a more effective implementation of TRIPS Article 66.2" Organized by ICTSD and UNCTAD, 16 June 2008, Palais des Nations, Geneva, Switzerland. Available at: http://www.iprsonline.org/ictsd/Dialogues/2008-06-16/2008-06-16_doc.htm (last visited 15 August 2014).

Multilateral Fund Secretariat "Indicative List of Categories of Incremental Costs" Annex IX.3 to "Multilateral Fund for the Implementation of the Montreal Protocol: Policies, Procedures, Guidelines and Criteria" April 2011, UNEP, available at: http://www.multilateralfund.org/Our%20Work/policy/default.aspx (last visited 15 August 2014).

Mytelka, L "Technology Transfer Issues in Environmental Goods and Services" ICTSD Trade and Environment Issue Paper No. 6, April 2007.

Nicholson, M W "Intellectual Property Rights, Internalization, and Technology Transfer" Federal Trade Commission Bureau of Economics Working Paper No. 250, July 2002. Available at: http://ssrn.com/abstract=393661 (last visited 15 August 2014).

Niederberger, A and R Saner "Exploring the relationship between FDI flows and CDM potential" 14(1) Transnational Corporations 1 (2005)

Niziramasanga, N "Implementing NAMAs under a new Climate Agreement that Supports development in Southern Africa" in Olsen, K et al. Elements of a New Climate Agreement by 2015 (Roskilde, Denmark: UNEP Risoe, 2013)

Ockwell, D et al. "UK-India Collaboration to Identify the Barriers to the Transfer of Low Carbon Technology-Final report" (London: the Department of Environment, Food and Rural Affairs, U.K., 2007)

Ockwell, D et al. "Enhancing Developing Country Access to Eco-Innovation: The Case of Technology Transfer and Climate Change in a Post-2012 Policy Framework", OECD Environment Working Papers, No. 12, OECD Publishing 2010.

OECD "Transfer of environmental technologies", in *Measuring Globalisation: OECD Economic Globalisation Indicators 2010*, (Paris: OECD Publishing, 2010).

OHCHR "Report of the United Nations High Commissioner for Human Rights on the scope and content of the relevant human rights obligations related to equitable access to safe drinking water and sanitation under international human rights instruments" A/HRC/6/3, August 2007. Available at: http://www2.ohchr.org/english/issues/water/index.htm (last visited 15 August 2014).

Olbrisch, S et al. "Estimates of incremental investment for and cost of mitigation measures in developing countries", 11 Climate Policy, 970 (2011).

Olsen, K H "The Clean Development Mechanism's Contribution to Sustainable development: a review of the literature" 84 Climatic Change 59 (2007)

Oxfam "Adapting to Climate Change: What's Needed in Poor Countries, and Who Should Pay" Oxfam Briefing Paper 104, May 29, 2007.

Pacala, S and R Socolow, "Stabilization Wedges: Solving the Climate Problem for the Next Fifty Years with Current Technologies". 305 Science 968, (2004).

Park, W G "International patent protection: 1960–2005," Research Policy 37: 761–766 (2008).

Park, W G and D Lippoldt "Technology Transfer and the Economic Implications of the Strengthening of Intellectual Property Rights in Developing Countries", OECD Trade Policy Papers, No. 62, OECD Publishing, 2008.

Perez Pugatch, M "The Role of Intellectual Property Rights in the Transfer of Environmentally Sound Technologies" Global Challenges Report, WIPO, 2011.

Philibert, C and J Podkanski "International Energy Technology Collaboration and Climate Change Mitigation - Case Study 4: Clean Coal Technologies" COM/ENV/EPOC/IEA/SLT(2005)4, IEA, Paris, 2005.

Philibert, C "International Technology Collaboration and Climate Change Mitigation - Case Study 1: Concentrating Solar Power Technologies" COM/ENV/EPOC/IEA/SLT(2004)8, IEA, Paris, 2004.

Pogge, T "Poverty and Human Rights" Paper Presentation at Independent Expert on Human Rights and Extreme Poverty - Expert Seminar: Extreme Poverty and Human Rights, United Nations, Geneva 23-24 February 2007. Available at: http://www2.ohchr.org/english/issues/poverty/expert/docs/Thomas_Pogge_Summary.pdf (last visited 15 August 2014).

Posner, E A and C R Sunstein "Climate Change Justice" University of Chicago Law & Economics, Olin Working Paper No. 354, August 2007. Available at: http://ssrn.com/abstract=1008958 (last visited 15 August 2014).

Practical Action "Climate Change and the Challenge of Energy Poverty" Practical Action Policy Briefing. Available at: http://practicalaction.org/docs/advocacy/Climate%20change%20briefing%202%20-%20energy.pdf (last visited 15 August 2014).

Practical Action "Poverty, Justice and Climate Change" Practical Action Policy Briefing. Available at: http://practicalaction.org/docs/advocacy/Climate%20change%20briefing%201%20-%20poverty,%20justice%20and%20climate%20change.pdf (last visited 15 August 2014).

Primo Braga, C A and C Fink "International Transactions in Intellectual Property and Developing Countries" International Journal of Technology Management Volume 19, Number 1: pp35-56, (2000).

Qiu, L D "Multilateral Environmental Agreements and Environmental Technology Transfer" Hong Kong Univ. Science & Technology Working Paper, December 2001. Available at: http://ssrn.com/abstract=298303 (last visited 15 August 2014).

Rübbelke, D T G and V Mukherjee "Global Climate Change, Technology Transfer and Trade with Complete Specialization" FEEM Working Paper No. 114.06, September 2006. Available at: http://ssrn.com/abstract=929058 (last visited 15 August 2014).

Saggi, K "Trade, Foreign Direct Investment, and International Technology Transfer: A Survey" World Bank Policy Research Working Paper 2349, May 2000.

Sarma, K. Madhava "Montreal Protocol as Model for Technology Transfer Mechanism for Climate" Institute for Global Sustainable Development, March 2008. Available at: http://www.igsd.org/docs/SarmaTT%2024Mar08.pdf (last visited 15 August 2014).

Schabas, W A "Study of the Right to Enjoy the Benefits of Scientific and Technological Progress and Its Applications," in Donders, Y. and V Volodin (eds) Human Rights in Education, Science and Culture: Legal Developments and Challenges UNESCO, 2007.

Schneider, M et al. "Understanding the CDM's contribution to technology transfer" 36 Energy Policy 2930 (2008).

Schneider, S H et al., "Assessing key vulnerabilities and the risk from climate change", in M.L. Parry et al. (Eds.) Climate Change 2007: Impacts, Adaptation and Vulnerability. Contribution of Working Group II to the Fourth Assessment Report of the Intergovernmental Panel on Climate Change, (Cambridge: Cambridge University Press, 2007). Available at http://www.ipcc.ch/ipccreports/ar4-wg2.htm (last visited 15 August 2014).

Seligsohn, D et al. "Key Functions for a UNFCCC Technology Institutional Structure: Identifying Convergence in Country Submissions" World Resources Institute Working Paper, November 2009.

Seres, S et al. "Analysis of technology transfer in CDM projects: An update." 37 Energy Policy 4919 (2009)

Simms, A et al. "Up In Smoke: Threats from, and Responses to, the Impact of Global Warming on Human Development" The Working Group on Climate Change and Development 2004. Available at http://www.iied.org/pubs/display.php?o=9512IIED (last visited 15 August 2014).

Sinden, A "Climate Change and Human Rights" 27 J. LAND RES. & ENVTL. L. 255 (2007) Available at: http://ssrn.com/abstract=984266 (last visited 15 August 2014).

Sinden, A "The Power of Rights: Imposing Human Rights Duties on Transnational Corporations for Environmental Harms" Temple University Legal Studies Research Paper No. 2006-22, November 2007. Available at: http://ssrn.com/abstract=925679 (last visited 15 August 2014).

Smith, P J "How Do Foreign Patent Rights Affect U.S. Exports, Affiliate Sales, and Licenses?" Journal of International Economics 55: 411-440 (2001)

So, A., et al. "Is Bayh-Dole good for developing countries? Lessons from the US Experience" 6(10) PLoS Biol e262 (2008).

South African Department of Environmental Affairs South Africa's Second National Communication under the United Nations Framework Convention on Climate Change (Pretoria: Department of Environmental Affairs Republic of South Africa, 2011).

South Centre "Submission by the South Centre to the Technology Executive Committee (TEC) on ways to Promote Enabling Environments and Address Barriers to Technology Development and Transfer and the Role of the TEC" South Centre, 2012.

Staley, B Childs et al."Tick Tech Tick Tech: Coming to Agreement on Technology in the Countdown to Copenhagen". WRI Working Paper, World Resources Institute, Washington DC, June 2009.

Stern, D and C Cleveland, "Energy and Economic Growth" Rensselaer Working Papers in Economics 0410, March 2004.

Strong, A et al. "Climate Science 2009–2010: Major New Discoveries" WRI Issue Brief, World Resources Institute (2011).

Sunstein, C R "Of Montreal and Kyoto: A Tale of Two Protocols" 31(1) Harvard Environmental Law Review (2007).

Sutter, C "Sustainability Check-Up for CDM projects" Wissenschaftlicher Verlag, Berlin (2003).

Sutter, C and J C Parreno "Does the current clean development mechanism (CDM) deliver its sustainable development claim? An analysis of officially registered CDM projects". 84 Climatic Change 75 (2007).

Tan, X et al. "Scaling Up Low-Carbon Technology Deployment: Lessons from China" World Resources Institute Report, 2010.

Teske, S et al. "Energy [r]evolution: A Sustainable World Outlook", Greenpeace International and European Renewable Energy Council 2007.

Tewari, R "Mapping of Criteria set by DNAs to Assess Sustainable development Benefits of CDM Projects" CDM Policy Dialogue, TERI (2012).

Tol, R S J, L Wietze and B van der Zwaan "Technology Diffusion and the Stability of Climate Coalitions" (February 2000). FEEM Working Paper No. 20.2000. Available at: http://ssrn.com/abstract=229260 (last visited 15 August 2014).

UNCTAD "Transfer of Technology for Successful Integration into the Global Economy" UNCTAD/ITE/IPC/2003/6, UNCTAD 2003. Available at: http://www.unctad.org/en/docs//iteipc20036_en.pdf (last visited 15 August 2014).

UNCTAD "Compendium of International Arrangements on Transfer of Technology: Selected Instruments - Relevant Provisions in Selected International Arrangements Pertaining to Transfer of Technology" UNCTAD/ITE/IPC/Misc.5, UNCTAD 2001. Available at http://www.unctad.org/en/docs//psiteipcm5.en.pdf (last visited 15 August 2014).

UNFCCC "Development and Transfer of Technologies: Technology and Technology Information Needs arising from the Survey of Developing Country Parties" UN Doc. FCCC/SBSTA/1998/INF.5, UNFCCC, May 1998.

UNFCCC "Uniting on Climate: A Guide to the Climate Change Convention and the Kyoto Protocol" UNFCCC November 2007.

UNFCCC "The Contribution of the Clean Development Mechanism under the Kyoto Protocol to Technology Transfer" UNFCCC 2010.

UNFCCC "Synthesis Report on Technology Needs Identified by Parties not included in Annex I to the Convention: Note by the Secretariat" U.N. Doc. FCCC/SBSTA/2006/INF.1, 21 April 2006.

UNFCCC "Second synthesis report on technology needs identified by Parties not included in Annex I to the Convention" FCCC/SBSTA/2009/INF.1, 29 May 2009.

UNFCCC "Report on the review and assessment of the effectiveness of the implementation of Article 4, paragraphs 1(c) and 5 of the Convention" SUBSIDIARY BODY FOR IMPLEMENTATION, Thirty-second session, Bonn, 31 May to 9 June, FCCC/SBI/2010/INF.4.

UNFCCC "Compilation of information on nationally appropriate mitigation actions to be implemented by Parties not included in Annex I to the Convention" FCCC/AWGLCA/2011/INF.1, 18 March 2011.

UN Sub-Commission on the Promotion and Protection of Human Rights "U.N. Norms on the Responsibilities of Transnational Corporations and Other Business Enterprises with Regard to Human Rights" U.N. Doc. E/CN.4/Sub.2/2003/12/Rev.2, 2003.

Van Asselt, H et al., "Global Climate Change and the Fragmentation of International Law" Law & Policy, Vol. 30, No. 4, October 2008.

van der Gaast, W et al. "Promoting sustainable energy technology transfers to developing countries through the CDM" 86 Applied Energy 230 (2009).

Veer, T and F Jell "Contributing to markets for technology? A comparison of patent filing motives of individual inventors, small companies and universities", 32 Technovation 513 (2012).

Veldhoen, S et al. "Innovation: China's Next Advantage – 2012 China Innovation Survey" A Benelux Chamber of Commerce, China Europe International Business School (CEIBS), Wenzhou Chamber of Commerce and Booz & Company Joint Report, 2012.

Venugopal, S et al. "Public Financing Instruments to Leverage Private Capital for Climate-Relevant Investment: Focus on Multilateral Agencies." Working Paper World Resources Institute, Washington, DC. (2012.).

Wang, B "Can CDM bring technology transfer to China?—An empirical study of technology transfer in China's CDM projects" 38 Energy Policy 2572(2010)

Wara, M "Measuring the CDM's Performance and Potential" Stanford University Program on Energy and Sustainable Development Working Paper #56, July 2006. Available at: http://iis-db.stanford.edu/pubs/21211/Wara_CDM.pdf

Wellington, Fred et al. "Scaling Up: Global Technology Deployment to Stabilize Emissions" World Resources Institute, April 2007. Available at http://www.wri.org/publication/scaling-up

Werksman, J, K Baumert and N Dubash, "Will international investment rules obstruct climate protection policies?" Climate Notes, World Resources Institute, Washington, April 2001.

Wheeler, D and K Ummel "Another Inconvenient Truth: A Carbon-Intensive South Faces Environmental Disaster, No Matter What the North Does" Center for Global Development Working Paper 134, December 3, 2007. Available at SSRN: http://ssrn.com/abstract=1101471 (last visited 15 August 2014).

World Bank "Warming up to Trade? Harnessing International Trade to Support Climate Change Objectives" World Bank, June 2007. Available at: http://www-wds.worldbank.org/external/default/WDSContentServer/WDSP/IB/2007/07/05/000310607_20070705152626/Rendered/PDF/402170REVISED01and1Climate01PUBLIC1.pdf (last visited 15 August 2014).

World Wildlife Fund "Technology and Climate Change" World Wildlife Fund Background Briefing Paper June 2006. Available at http://assets.panda.org/downloads/g8technologybrief_final_2006_1.pdf

WTO, A Taxonomy on Country Experiences on International Technology Transfers: Note by the Secretariat, WT/WGTTT/W/3, 11 November 2002.

WTO, Report of the Working Group on Trade and Transfer of Technology to the General Council, WT/WGTTT/5, 14 July 2003.

Young, M "Climate Change Law and Regime Interaction) 2011 Carbon & Climate L. Rev. 147 (2011).

Yu, P K, "Reconceptualizing Intellectual Property Interests in a Human Rights Framework," 40(3) University of California Davis Law Review Volume 1039 (2007).

Yu, P K "The Objectives and the Principles of the TRIPS Agreement" 46 HOUS. L. REV. 979 (2009).

Decisions of International Treaty Bodies

UNFCCC

"Development and Transfer of technologies" Decision 4/CP.7 in "Report Of The Conference Of the Parties on its Seventh Session, held At Marrakesh from 29 October to 10 November 2001: Addendum - Part Two: Action Taken By The Conference Of The Parties" FCCC/CP/2001/13/Add.1, 21 January 2002.

Report of the Conference of the Parties on its Ninth Session, held at Milan from 1 to 12 December 2003, FCCC/CP/2003/6/Add.1 (2004)

Report of the Conference of the Parties on its thirteenth session, held in Bali from 3 to 15 December 2007. Addendum. Part Two: Action taken by the Conference of the Parties at its thirteenth session." FCCC/CP/2007/6/Add.1 (2008)

Report of the Conference of the Parties on its fourteenth session, held in Poznan from 1 to 12 December 2008 – Addendum, FCCC/CP/2008/7/Add.1 (2009).

Report of the Ad Hoc Working Group on Long-term Cooperative Action under the Convention on its eighth session, held in Copenhagen from 7 to 15 December 2009, FCCC/AWGLCA/2009/17 (2010).

Report of the Conference of the Parties on its fifteenth session, held in Copenhagen from 7 to 19 December 2009 – Addendum Part Two: Action taken by the Conference of the Parties at its fifteenth session, FCCC/CP/2009/11/Add.1 (2010).

Ad Hoc Working Group on Long-term Cooperative Action under the Convention - Twelfth session, Tianjin, 4–9 October 2010, Item X of the provisional agenda - Negotiating text, FCCC/AWGLCA/2010/14 (2010).

Decision 1/CP.16, The Cancun Agreements: Outcome of the work of the Ad Hoc Working Group on Long-term Cooperative Action under the Convention FCCC/CP/2010/7/Add.1 (2011).

Report of the Ad Hoc Working Group on Long-term Cooperative Action under the Convention on the first and second parts of its fourteenth session, held in Bangkok from 5 to 8 April 2011, and Bonn from 7 to 17 June 2011 FCCC/AWGLCA/2011/9 (2011).

Report of the Ad Hoc Working Group on Long-term Cooperative Action under the Convention on the third and fourth parts of its fourteenth session, held in Panama City from 1 to 7 October 2011, and Durban from 29 November to 10 December 2011, FCCC/AWGLCA/2011/14 (2011).

Outcome of the work of the Ad Hoc Working Group on Long-term Cooperative Action under the Convention to be presented to the Conference of the Parties for adoption at its seventeenth session - Draft conclusions proposed by the Chair, FCCC/AWGLCA/2011/L.4 (2011).

Work undertaken in the informal groups in the preparation of a comprehensive and balanced outcome to be presented to the Conference of the Parties for adoption at its seventeenth session - Note by the Chair, FCCC/AWGLCA/2011/CRP.39 (2011).

Decision 1/CP.17, Establishment of an Ad Hoc Working Group on the Durban Platform for Enhanced Action, in Report of the Conference of the Parties on its seventeenth session, held in Durban from 28 November to11 December 2011 – Addendum Part Two: Action taken by the Conference of the Parties at its seventeenth session, FCCC/CP/2011/9/Add.1 (2012).

Decision 2/CP.17, Outcome of the work of the Ad Hoc Working Group on Long-term Cooperative Action under the Convention, in Report of the Conference of the Parties on its seventeenth session, held in Durban from 28 November to11 December 2011 – Addendum Part Two: Action taken by the Conference of the Parties at its seventeenth session, FCCC/CP/2011/9/Add.1 (2012).

Decision 3/CP.17, Launching the Green Climate Fund, in Report of the Conference of the Parties on its seventeenth session, held in Durban from 28 November to11 December 2011 – Addendum Part Two: Action taken by the Conference of the Parties at its seventeenth session, FCCC/CP/2011/9/Add.1 (2012).

Decision 4/CP.17, Technology Executive Committee – modalities and procedures, in Report of the Conference of the Parties on its seventeenth session, held in Durban from 28 November to11 December 2011 – Addendum Part Two: Action taken by the Conference of the Parties at its seventeenth session, FCCC/CP/2011/9/Add.1 (2012).

Decision 5/CP.17, National adaptation plans, in Report of the Conference of the Parties on its seventeenth session, held in Durban from 28 November to11 December 2011 –

Addendum Part Two: Action taken by the Conference of the Parties at its seventeenth session, FCCC/CP/2011/9/Add.1 (2012).

WTO

Declaration on the TRIPS Agreement and Public Health, adopted on 14 November 2001 by the Fourth WTO Ministerial Conference, Doha, Qatar (WT/MIN(01)/DEC/2). Available at http://www.wto.org/english/thewto_e/minist_e/min01_e/mindecl_trips_e.htm (last visited 15 August 2014).

Ministerial Declaration, Ministerial Conference, Fourth Session Doha, 9 - 14 November 2001, WT/MIN(01)/DEC/1, 20 November 2001.

Extension of the Transition Period under Article 66.1 for Least-Developed Country Members: Decision of the Council for TRIPS of 29 November 2005, IP/C/40, November 2005.

Extension of the Transition Period under Article 66.1 of The TRIPS Agreement for Least-Developed Country Members for Certain Obligations with respect to Pharmaceutical Products: Decision of the Council for TRIPS of 27 June 2002, IP/C/25, June 2005.

Implementation of article 66.2 of the TRIPS Agreement - Decision of the Council for TRIPS of 19 February 2003, IP/C/28.

Ministerial Declaration, Ministerial Conference, Fourth Session Doha, 9 - 14 November 2001, WT/MIN(01)/DEC/1, 20 November 2001.

Legislative texts and treaties

UNFCCC

Kyoto Protocol to the United Nations Framework Convention on Climate Change (Kyoto Protocol), Kyoto, 10 December 1997, in force 16 February 2005, 2303 United Nations Treaty Series (2004) 148.

United Nations Framework Convention on Climate Change (UNFCCC), New York, 9 May 1992, in force 21 March 1994, 1771 United Nations Treaty Series 107

WTO

Marrakesh Agreement establishing the World Trade Organization (WTO Agreement), Marrakesh, 15 April 1994, in force 1 January 1995, 1867 United Nations Treaty Series (1995) 4.

Agreement of Trade-related Aspects of Intellectual property (TRIPS Agreement), Annex 1C to the Marrakesh Agreement establishing the World Trade Organization (WTO Agreement), Marrakesh, 15 April 1994, in force 1 January 1995, 1867 United Nations Treaty Series (1995) 4.

Other

Agenda 21 of the Rio Declaration on Environment and Development adopted at United Nations Conference on Environment and Development (UNCED), Rio de Janeiro, 3-14 June 1992. Available at: http://sustainabledevelopment.un.org/index.php?page=view&nr=23&type=400&menu=35

Convention on Biological Diversity, 5 June 1992, United Nations Treaty Series, vol. 1760, p. 79.

Rio Declaration on Environment and Development, in Report of the United Nations Conference on Environment and Development, UN Doc. A/CONF.151/26 (Vol. I), 12 August 1992, Annex I.

Stockholm Declaration on the Human Environment, in Report of the United Nations Conference on the Human Environment, UN Doc.A/CONF.48/14, at 2 and Corr.1 (1972)

United Nations Millennium Declaration GA. Res. 55/2, 8 September 2002

Vienna Convention on the Law of Treaties (VCLT), Vienna, 23 May 1969 in force 27 January 1980,
1155 United Nations Treaty Series (1987) 331.

Cases

WTO

Brazil – Measures Affecting Imports of Retreaded Tyres, WT/DS332/AB/R, adopted 17 December 2007, DSR 2007:IV, 1527 (Brazil – Retreaded Tyres).

Brazil — Measures Affecting Patent Protection WTO/DS/199 (2000).

Canada – Patent Protection of Pharmaceutical Products, WT/DS114/R, adopted 7 April 2000, DSR 2000:V, 2289 (Canada – Pharmaceutical Patents)

Canada – Term of Patent Protection, WT/DS170/AB/R, adopted 12 October 2000, DSR 2000:X, 5093 (Canada- Patent Term).

China – Measures Related to the Exportation of Various Raw Materials, WT/DS394/R and Corr.1/WT/DS395/R and Corr.1/WT/DS398/R and Corr.1, circulated to WTO Members 5 July 2011. (China – Raw Materials)

European Communities – Measures Affecting Asbestos and Asbestos-Containing Products, WT/DS135/AB/R, adopted 5 April 2001, DSR 2001:VII, 3243 (EC-Asbestos)

European Communities – Measures Affecting the Approval and Marketing of Biotech Products, WT/DS291/R / WT/DS292/R / WT/DS293/R, Add.1 to Add.9, and Corr.1, adopted 21 November 2006, DSR 2006:III-VIII, 847 (EC – Approval and Marketing of Biotech Products)

Korea – Measures Affecting Imports of Fresh, Chilled and Frozen Beef, WT/DS161/AB/R, WT/DS169/AB/R, adopted 10 January 2001, DSR 2001:I, 5 (Korea – Various Measures on Beef)

United States – Measures Concerning the Importation, Marketing and Sale of Tuna and Tuna Products, WT/DS381/R, adopted 13 June 2012, as modified by Appellate Body Report WT/DS381/AB/R (US – Tuna II (Mexico))

United States – Measures Concerning the Importation, Marketing and Sale of Tuna and Tuna Products, WT/DS381/AB/R, adopted 13 June 2012 (US – Tuna II (Mexico))

United States – Section 110(5) of the US Copyright Act, WT/DS160/R, adopted 27 July 2000, DSR 2000:VIII, 3769 (US – Section 110(5) Copyright Act)

GATT

United States Section 337 of the Tariff Act of 1930, L/6439, adopted 7 November 1989, BISD 36S/345 (US – Section 337 Tariff Act)

Index

absorptive capacity, 135, 179, 185, 186, 219, 221, 237
access to medicines, 11, 139, 144, 316
adaptation, 52, 55, 145, 236
   climate impacts, 35
   definition of adaptation technology, 24
   human rights, 329, 330
   technology need, 51, 58, 73, 110, 145
   timing of action, 38
Agricultural
   Brazil, 128
   patents, 230
   technology need, 55, 57
Annex II, 158, 159, 160, 195
AWGLCA, 152, 166, 198, 204, 205, 206, 208, 209, 369
Bali COP, 166, 204, 387
Bali Plan of Action, 166
Barton, 85, 90, 100, 153, 295
Bayh-Dole, 124, 126, 292
Berne Convention, 224
   Exceptions, 261
   TRIPS, 260, 266, 310
Bharat Heavy Electricals Ltd. (BHEL),, 136
Bilateral free trade agreements, 300
Bilateral investment treaties, 27, 84, 85, 87, 364, 366, 368, 398
Biofuels, 45, 48, 61, 65, 66, 69

Biomass, 47, 56, 61, 63, 68 136
Brazil
   CDM, 146, 173
   patenting of climate technology, 92, 101, 109, 118
   R&D, 122, 126
   technology exports, 128
   technology need, 61
   working requirement, 292
Brazil-Retreaded Tyres, 248
Brundlandt Report, 341
Canada-Pharmaceutical Patents, 261, 265, 267, 271, 276, 298
Carbon Capture and Storage, 41, 42, 63, 102, 209
Carbon leakage, 5, 151, 167
Carrying capacity, 3
CDM, 167
CESCR General Comment, 320, 327
CGIAR, 195, 378, 379
China, 6, 134
   CDM, 173, 174, 182, 183, 185
   emissions, 41, 59
   FDI, 140, 230
   intellectual property protection, 230
   patenting of climate technology, 88, 90, 92, 95, 96, 99, 103, 107, 118
   R&D, 122, 129
   technology need, 43, 44, 47, 50, 62
   UNFCCC negotiations, 203
China – Raw Materials, 247
Clean Development Mechanism, 151, 167

climate resilience, 24, 73
Committee on Economic, Social and Cultural Rights, 316
Common but differentiated responsibilities, 159, 212, 318
Competition law, 11, 91, 117, 120, 240, 290, 300, 302, 386, 397
Compulsory license, 235, 274, 275, 277, 278, 279, 281, 282, 285, 286
    competition law, 287, 289
    historical use, 226
    use in US, 124
    working requirement, 237, 290, 291
Concentrated solar power, 43, 61
Concessional terms, 93, 116, 124, 156, 384
Convention on Biological Diversity, 156, 311, 312
Copyright, 260, 269, 310
Creative commons, 373
CTC&N, 167, 207, 209, 210, 372, 377, 380, 384
Doha Amendment, 169
Doha Declaration on TRIPS and Public Health, 275, 311, 387, 388
EC – Approval and Marketing of Biotech Products, 309, 336, 398
EGTT, 22, 161, 162, 164, 166, 196, 204
Enabling environments, 19, 22, 163, 165, 166, 167, 188, 196, 204
European Patent Office, 88, 89, 225
Exceptions to patent rights, 224, 238, 272

Fair, reasonable and non-discriminatory, 117
FDI, 84, 85, 86, 153, 363
    CDM, 168, 182
    intellectual property protection, 220, 222
    Joint Venture, 86
Ginarte-Park, 221, 224, 230
Global Environment Facility, 160, 186
Goldwind, 101, 133, 143, 183
Green Climate Fund, 190, 198, 200, 207, 209, 210, 361, 384
Green Xchange, 373
Hydropower, 61, 68
ICESCR, 314, 318, 320, 340, 345
IEA, 40, 46, 75
    peaking projections, 59
    standards, 120
    technology implementing agreements, 380
IGCC, 10, 61, 63, 65, 67, 68, 106, 107, 136
ILC, 29, 334, 335, 337, 339
incremental costs, 117, 157, 160, 188, 209, 307, 385
India
    CDM, 146, 173, 182
    emissions, 41, 59
    Montreal Protocol, 156
    Patent Act, 279
    patenting of climate technology, 92, 114, 118, 136, 137, 138
    pharmaceutical industry, 229
    R&D, 135, 141

technology need, 44, 64, 65
International Energy Agency, 32
IPCC, 21, 22, 32, 320, 325
    AR4, 41, 145
    third assessment report, 39
Japanese Patent Office, 88
Kyoto Protocol, 5, 152, 159, 161, 309
Licensing, 9, 16, 92, 114, 143, 240
    Bayh-Dole, 124
    CDM, 182
    exclusivity, 87
    Montreal Protocol, 117
    studies, 83
    vector for technology transfer, 84
Mahindra Motors, 138
Malthus, Thomas 1, 2
McKinsey, 94
Montreal Protocol, 115, 116, 157, 165, 286, 382
Multilateral Environmental Agreement, 21, 148, 155
NAMAs, 59, 71, 108, 195, 198, 385
National Communications, 59, 68, 195, 198
Necessity test, 245, 246, 247, 249, 253, 258
NIEO, 153, 154
Nuclear, 41, 42, 43, 50, 62, 75
Paris Convention, 224
    compulsory license, 291
    exceptions, 238
    patent exclusions, 235
    priority, 239
    trade secret, 285

TRIPS, 266
    working requirement, 237
Patent counts, 88, 97, 107, 183
Patent exclusions, 11, 235, 293, 397
Patent families, 88, 99, 103, 105
Patent landscape, 83, 89, 90, 94
Patent pool, 10, 143, 207, 346, 374, 375
Pauwelyn, 304, 305, 313, 332
Peaking
    emissions, 34, 352, 390
Performance requirements, 154, 367, 368
    CDM, 366
R&D
    Joint, 378
    publicly funded, 122
    spending, 6
Refusal to deal, 289
REpower, 133
Research exception, 10, 91, 273
Reverse engineering, 91, 131, 217, 218, 239
SBI, 161, 162, 166
SBSTA, 166, 203, 204
Software, 45, 49, 68, 91, 224, 269, 270
Solar PV, 61, 67, 68, 134
SPS, 245, 249, 254, 258, 264, 308
State practice, 267, 270, 271, 272
Stern report, 37, 39, 50, 53, 354
Stern Report, 39
Suntech, 132
Suzlon, 101, 135, 143
Tata, 138
TBT, 246, 250, 254, 257, 261, 308

Technology Executive Committee, 167, 203, 210, 360
Technology Needs Assessments, 59, 68, 163, 187
Trade secret, 16, 85
   compulsory license, 237, 285
   source code, 269

United States - US Patent Code, 292
UPOV, 295, 388
US – Section 110(5) Copyright Act, 270
US – Tuna II (Mexico), 250, 251
Wind, 43, 50, 60, 61, 68, 133, 135
WIPO Copyright Treaty, 310, 389

Biography

Dalindyebo Shabalala

Dalindyebo Shabalala is Assistant Professor, International Economic Law (Intellectual Property) at Maastricht University Faculty of Law and Visiting Assistant Professor at case Western Reserve Law School in Cleveland, USA. His research focuses on Climate Change and Intellectual Property issues on one hand and on IP and Development issues on the other. He focuses in particular on the role of Brazil, India and China in the regulation of international technology transfer and intellectual property. Previously, Dalindyebo was the managing attorney of CIEL's Geneva office, and Director of CIEL's Intellectual Property and Sustainable Development Project. He focused on issues at the intersection of Intellectual Property and Climate Change, Human Health, Biodiversity and Food Security, as well as addressing systemic reform of the international intellectual property system. Dalindyebo was a Research Fellow in the Innovation, Access to Knowledge, and Intellectual Property Programme at the South Centre (2005–2006), an intergovernmental organization of developing countries in Geneva, Switzerland.

Dalindyebo received his B.A. degree in Political Science and Cognitive Science, from Vassar College in 1998. At Vassar he was a Ford Foundation Scholar in the Political Science Department and an Undergraduate Research Science Institute Scholar in the Cognitive Science Department. Dalindyebo received his Juris Doctor, cum laude, from the University of Minnesota Law School in 2004, where he worked with Prof. David Weissbrodt on researching the Human Rights Responsibilities of Transnational Corporations.
Dalindyebo was born in Johannesburg, South Africa in 1972 and he received his International Baccalaureate from Waterford Kamhlaba UWCSA in 1992.

www.ingramcontent.com/pod-product-compliance
Lightning Source LLC
Chambersburg PA
CBHW071353170526
45165CB00001B/21